Michael Drabble
2000

A HISTORY OF THE ARAB PEOPLES

A HISTORY OF
THE ARAB PEOPLES

Albert Hourani

faber and faber

First published in 1991
by Faber and Faber Limited
3 Queen Square London WCIN 3AU
Reprinted (twice)
Reprinted with corrections 1991

Photoypeset in Input Typesetting Ltd, London
Printed in England by Clays Ltd, St Ives plv

Maps © John Flower, 1991

A CIP record for this book
is available from the British Library

ISBN 0-571-13378-9

2 4 6 8 10 9 7 5 3

To my colleagues and students at
St Antony's College, Oxford

Contents

CONTENTS

CONTENTS

ix

CONTENTS

CONTENTS

List of Maps

Preface

The subject of this book is the history of the Arabic-speaking parts of the Islamic world, from the rise of Islam until the present day. During some periods, however, I have had to go beyond the subject: for example, when I consider the early history of the caliphate, the Ottoman Empire, and the expansion of European trade and empire. It would be possible to argue that the subject is too large or too small: that the history of the Maghrib is different from that of the Middle East, or that the history of the countries where Arabic is the main language cannot be seen in isolation from that of other Muslim countries. A line has to be drawn somewhere, however, and this is where I have chosen to draw it, partly because of the limits of my own knowledge. I hope the book will show that there is sufficient unity of historical experience between the different regions it covers to make it possible to think and write about them in a single framework.

The book is intended for students who are beginning to study the subject and for general readers who wish to learn something about it. It will be clear to specialists that, in a book with so large a scope, much of what I say is based upon the research of others. I have tried to give the essential facts and to interpret them in the light of what others have written. Some of my debts to their work are indicated in the bibliography.

Writing a book which covers such a long period, I have had to make decisions about names. I have used the names of modern countries to indicate geographical regions, even when those names were not used in the past; it seemed simpler to use the same names throughout the book, rather than change them from period to period. Thus 'Algeria' is used for a certain region in North Africa, even though the name came into use only in modern centuries. In general, I have used names which will be familiar to those who read mainly in English; the word 'Maghrib' is probably familiar enough to be used rather than 'North-west Africa', but 'Mashriq' is not and so I have used 'Middle East' instead. I have called the Muslim parts of the Iberian peninsula Andalus, because it is simpler to use one word than a phrase. When I use a name which is now that of a sovereign state in writing about a period before that state came into existence, I employ it to refer to a certain region roughly defined; it is only when I write of the modern period that I intend it to refer to the area included within the frontiers of the state. For example, throughout most of the book 'Syria' refers to a certain region which has common features, both physical and social, and on the whole has had a single historical experience, but I use it only to refer to the state of Syria once it has come into existence after the First World War. I need scarcely say that such uses do not imply any political judgement about which states should exist and where their frontiers lie.

The main geographical names used are shown in Map 1.

Acknowledgements

I should like to thank Patrick Seale, who encouraged me to write this book and arranged for it to be published, and the friends who gave many hours to reading it, correcting mistakes and suggesting how it could be improved: Patricia Crone, Paul Dresch, Leila Fawaz, Cornell Fleischer, the late and much lamented Martin Hinds, Charles Issawi, Tarif Khalidi, Philip Khoury, Ira Lapidus, Wilferd Madelung, Basim Musallam, Robin Ostle, Roger Owen, Michael Rogers and Mary Wilson. Among them I owe a special debt to Paul Dresch, who followed my line of thought with remarkable insight as well as wide knowledge.

Other friends and colleagues provided me with information I needed, among them Julian Baldick, Karl Barbir, Tourkhan Gandjei, Israel Gershoni and Venetia Porter.

I am most grateful to Elizabeth Bullock, who typed successive drafts with devotion and skill, to my editors at Faber and Faber, Will Sulkin and John Bodley, to John Flower who drew the maps, Brenda Thomson who copy-edited a difficult manuscript in a sensitive and intelligent way, Bryan Abraham who corrected the proofs with scrupulous care, and Hilary Bird who made the index.

Some of the translations from Arabic are my own, some are made by other translators, others again have been adapted by me from translations already existing. I must thank the following publishers for giving me permission to use translations or extracts from books:
Cambridge University Press for translations from A. J. Arberry, *Arabic Poetry* (1965) and *Poems of al-Mutanabbi* (1967), and from John A. Williams, *Al-Tabari: the Early Abbasid Empire*, Vol. 1 (1988).
Columbia University Press for lines from a poem by Badr Shakir al-Sayyab, translated by Christopher Middleton and Lena Jayyusi in Salma Khadra

Jayyusi, ed. *Modern Arabic Poetry*, copyright © Columbia University Press, New York (1987).

Edinburgh University Press for a passage from George Makdisi, *The Rise of Colleges* (1981).

Quartet Books for a passage from Alifa Rifaat, *Distant View of a Minaret*, translated by Denys Johnston-Davies (1983).

State University of New York Press for a passage from *The History of al-Tabari*, general editor E. Yar-Shater: Vol. 27, *The 'Abbasid Revolution*, translated by J. A. Williams, copyright © State University of New York (1985).

Unwin Hyman Limited for quotations from A. J. Arberry, *The Koran Interpreted*, copyright © George Allen and Unwin Limited (1955).

Wayne State University Press for a translation from J. Lassner, *The Topography of Baghdad in the Early Middle Ages* (1970).

Note on Spelling

Words or names which have a familiar English form are used in that form. For transliteration of other Arabic words or names I have used a simple system based upon that of the *International Journal of Middle East Studies*:

no diacritical marks are used;

the letter *'ayn* is indicated by ', and *hamza* is indicated by ', but only when it comes in the middle of a word (in pronouncing words, those who are not concerned with their Arabic form can ignore both these signs);

for plurals of words I have added an *s*, except for the plural of *'alim*, which is given as *'ulama*;

doubled vowels in the middle of a word are indicated by *-iyya* or *-uwwa*;

diphthongs are indicated by *-aw* or *-ay*;

al- is prefixed the first time an Arabic name is used, but omitted later (e.g. al-Ghazali, Ghazali);

Turkish names and words are normally spelled in their modern Turkish form.

Note on Dates

From early Islamic times, Muslims have dated events from the day of Muhammad's emigration from Mecca to Madina in AD 622: this emigration is known in Arabic as the *hijra*, and the usual way of referring to Muslim years in European languages is by the use of the initials AH.

A year according to the Muslim calendar is not of the same length as a year according to the Christian calendar. The latter is measured by a complete revolution of the earth around the sun, which takes approximately 365 days, but the former consists of twelve months each of which corresponds to a complete revolution of the moon around the earth; the length of a year measured in these terms is approximately 11 days less than that of a solar year.

Information about ways of converting Muslim into Christian dates, or vice versa, can be found in G. S. P. Freeman-Grenville, *The Muslim and Christian Calendars* (London, 1977).

Christian era dates are used, except when the context makes it important to indicate the Muslim date or century.

For rulers, dates of accession and death (or deposition) are given; for other persons, dates of death and birth. When the date of birth is not known, that of death alone is given (e.g. d. 1456); when the person is still alive, only the date of birth is given (e.g. b. 1905). When the date is known only approximately, *c.* is used (e.g. *c.* 1307–58).

Prologue

In the year 1382 an Arab Muslim scholar who served the ruler of Tunis asked his permission to make the pilgrimage to Mecca, and having received it took ship for Alexandria in Egypt. In his fiftieth year he was leaving, as it turned out for ever, the countries of the Maghrib in which he and his ancestors had played an important and varied part.

'Abd al-Rahman ibn Khaldun (1332–1406) belonged to a family which had gone from southern Arabia to Spain after it was conquered by the Arabs, and settled in Seville. When the Christian kingdoms of northern Spain expanded southwards the family left for Tunis. Many families with a tradition of culture and state service did the same, and they formed in the cities of the Maghrib (the western part of the world of Islam) a patriciate whose services were used by local rulers. Ibn Khaldun's great-grandfather played a part in the court politics of Tunis, fell from favour and was killed; his grandfather was also an official, but his father abandoned politics and service for the retired life of a scholar. He himself received a careful education in the manner of the time, from his father and from scholars teaching in the mosques and schools of Tunis or visiting the city, and he continued his studies when in early manhood he lived in other cities, for it was part of the tradition he inherited that a man should seek knowledge from all who could impart it. In his autobiography he gives the names of those whose lectures he heard and the subjects they taught: the Qur'an, regarded by Muslims as the Word of God revealed in the Arabic language through the Prophet Muhammad; the Hadith, or traditions of what the Prophet had said and done; jurisprudence, the science of law and social morality formally based upon Qur'an and Hadith; the Arabic language without which the sciences of religion could not be understood; and also the rational sciences, mathematics, logic and philosophy. He gives details of the personalities and lives of his teachers, and tells us that most of them, as well as his parents, died in the Black Death, the great plague which swept the world in the middle of the fourteenth century.

At an early age Ibn Khaldun's mastery of language and knowledge of jurisprudence drew him into the service of the ruler of Tunis, first as a secretary and later in more responsible and therefore insecure posts. There followed twenty years of varying fortune. He left Tunis and took service with other rulers in the Maghrib; he went to Granada, capital of the last surviving kingdom of Muslim Spain, won favour there, was sent on a mission to the Christian ruler of Seville, his ancestral city, but fell under suspicion and departed hurriedly for Algeria. Once more he held office, transacting government business in the morning and then teaching in the mosque. He played a part in drawing Arab or Berber chiefs of the steppes and mountains into political allegiance to the rulers he served, and the influence he gained with them was useful when, as happened again and again in his life, he fell out of favour with his master. At one such time he spent four years (1375–9) living in a castle in the Algerian countryside under the protection of an Arab chieftain. They were years when he was free from the world's business and spent his time writing a history of the dynasties of the Maghrib, set within a broad framework.

The first part of this history, the *Muqaddima* (*Prolegomena*), has continued to attract attention until today. In it Ibn Khaldun tried to explain the rise and fall of dynasties in a way which would serve as a touchstone by which the credibility of historical narratives might be judged. The simplest and earliest form of human society, he believed, was that of the people of the steppes and mountains, growing crops or rearing livestock, and following leaders who had no organized power of coercion. Such people had a certain natural goodness and energy, but could not by themselves create stable governments, cities or high culture. For that to be possible, there had to be a ruler with exclusive authority, and such a one could establish himself only if he was able to create and dominate a group of followers possessing *'asabiyya*, that is to say, a corporate spirit oriented towards obtaining and keeping power. This group could best be drawn from the energetic men of the steppe or mountain; it could be held together by the sense of common ancestry, whether real or fictitious, or by ties of dependence, and reinforced by common acceptance of a religion. A ruler with a strong and coherent group of followers could found a dynasty; when its rule was stable populous cities would grow up and in them there would be specialized crafts, luxurious ways of living and high culture.

Every dynasty, however, bore in itself the seeds of its decline: it could be weakened by tyranny, extravagance and the loss of the qualities of command. Effective power might pass from the ruler to members of his own group, but sooner or later the dynasty might be replaced by another formed in a similar way. When this happened, not only the ruler but the whole people on whom his power had rested, and the life they had created, might disappear; as Ibn Khaldun said in another context, 'when there is a general change of conditions, it is as if the entire creation had changed and the whole world been altered'.[1] The Greeks and Persians, 'the greatest powers of their time in the world',[2] had been replaced by the Arabs, whose strength and cohesion had created a dynasty of which the power stretched from Arabia to Spain; but they in their turn had been replaced by Berbers in Spain and the Maghrib, and by Turks further east.

The turning fortunes of rulers carried with them those of their servants. When he left for Alexandria, Ibn Khaldun was starting on a new career. He did not make the pilgrimage at this time, although he was to do so later, but went to Cairo, which struck him as a city on a different scale from those he had known: 'metropolis of the world, garden of the universe, meeting-place of nations, ant-hill of peoples, high place of Islam, seat of power'.[3] Cairo was the capital of the Mamluk sultanate, one of the greatest Muslim states of the time, covering Syria as well as Egypt. He was presented to the ruler, won his favour, and received first a pension and then a position as teacher in one and then another of the royal schools. He sent for his family to come to him from Tunis, but they were all drowned on the sea-journey.

Ibn Khaldun lived in Cairo until his death. Much of his time was spent in reading and writing, but the pattern of his earlier life repeated itself in those alternations of influence and disfavour which he blamed on his enemies but which may have had causes in his own personality. Several times the ruler appointed him as judge in one of the principal courts, but each time he lost or left the position. He went with the sultan to Syria and visited the holy places of Jerusalem and Hebron; he went there a second time when Damascus was besieged by Timur (Tamerlane), one of the great Asian conquerors, who had created an empire which stretched from northern India to Syria and Anatolia. He had conversations with Timur, in whom he saw an example of that power of command, securely based on the strength of his army and people, which could found a new dynasty. He was not able to save Damascus from pillage, but secured a safe passage for himself back to Egypt; on the way, however, he was held up and robbed in the hills of Palestine.

Ibn Khaldun's life, as he described it, tells us something about the world to which he belonged. It was a world full of reminders of the frailty of human endeavour. His own career showed how unstable were the alliances of interests on which dynasties relied to maintain their power; the meeting with Timur before Damascus made clear how the rise of a new power could affect the life of cities and peoples. Outside the city, order was precarious: a rulers' emissary could be despoiled, a courtier fallen out of favour could seek refuge beyond the range of urban control. The death of parents by plague and children by shipwreck taught the lesson of man's impotence in the hands of fate. Something was stable, however, or seemed to be. A world where a family from southern Arabia could move to Spain, and after six centuries return nearer to its place of origin and still find itself in familiar surroundings, had a unity which transcended divisions of time and space; the Arabic language could open the door to office and influence throughout that world; a body of knowledge, transmitted over the centuries by a known chain of teachers, preserved a moral community even when rulers changed; places of pilgrimage, Mecca and Jerusalem, were unchanging poles of the human world even if power shifted from one city to another; and belief in a God who created and sustained the world could give meaning to the blows of fate.

PART I

THE MAKING OF A WORLD

(Seventh–Tenth Century)

In the early seventh century a religious movement appeared on the margins of the great empires, those of the Byzantines and Sasanians, which domi-nated the western half of the world. In Mecca, a town in western Arabia, Muhammad began to call men and women to moral reform and submission to the will of God as expressed in what he and his adherents accepted as divine messages revealed to him and later embodied in a book, the Qur'an. In the name of the new religion, Islam, armies drawn from inhabitants of Arabia conquered the surrounding countries and founded a new empire, the caliphate, which included much of the territory of the Byzantine Empire and all that of the Sasanian, and extended from central Asia to Spain. The centre of power moved from Arabia to Damascus in Syria under the Umayyad caliphs, and then to Baghdad in Iraq under the 'Abbasids.

By the tenth century the caliphate was breaking up, and rival caliphates appeared in Egypt and Spain, but the social and cultural unity which had developed within it continued. A large part of the population had become Muslims (that is to say, adherents of the religion of Islam), although Jewish, Christian and other communities remained; the Arabic language had spread and became the medium of a culture which incorporated elements from the traditions of peoples absorbed into the Muslim world, and expressed itself in literature and in systems of law, theology, and spirituality. Within different physical environments, Muslim societies developed distinctive institutions and forms; the links established between countries in the Mediterranean basin and in that of the Indian Ocean created a single trading system and brought about changes in agriculture and crafts, provid-ing the basis for the growth of great cities with an urban civilization expressed in buildings of a distinctive Islamic style.

CHAPTER I

A New Power in an Old World

THE WORLD INTO WHICH THE ARABS CAME

The world of Ibn Khaldun must have seemed everlasting to most of those who belonged to it, but he himself knew that it had replaced an earlier one. Seven hundred years before his time, the countries he knew had had a different face, beneath the sway of 'the two greatest powers of their time'.

For many centuries the countries of the Mediterranean basin had been part of the Roman Empire. A settled countryside produced grain, fruits, wine and oil, and trade was carried along peaceful sea-routes; in the great cities, a wealthy class of many origins shared in the Greek and Latin culture of the empire. From the fourth century of the Christian era, the centre of imperial power had moved eastwards. Constantinople replaced Rome as the capital city; there the emperor was the focus of loyalty and the symbol of cohesion. Later there appeared what has been called a 'horizontal division' which was to remain in other forms until our own time. In Germany, England, France, Spain and northern Italy, barbarian kings ruled, although the sense of belonging to the Roman Empire still existed; southern Italy, Sicily, the north African coast, Egypt, Syria, Anatolia and Greece remained under direct imperial rule from Constantinople. In this shrunken form, the empire was more Greek than Roman. (In its later phases it is more commonly called 'Byzantine' than Roman, after the former name of Constantinople, Byzantium.) The emperor ruled through Greek-speaking civil servants; the great cities of the eastern Mediterranean, Antioch in Syria and Alexandria in Egypt, were centres of Greek culture and sent members of local élites into the imperial service.

Another and a deeper change had taken place. The empire had become Christian, not just by formal decree of the ruler but by conversion at different levels. The majority of the population was Christian, although pagan philosophers taught in the school of Athens until the sixth century, Jewish communities lived in the cities, and memories of the pagan gods still haunted the temples turned into churches. Christianity gave a new

7

dimension to the loyalty felt towards the emperor and a new framework of unity for the local cultures of those he ruled. Christian ideas and images were expressed in the literary languages of the various regions of the empire as well as in the Greek of the cities: Armenian in eastern Anatolia, Syriac in Syria, Coptic in Egypt. Tombs of saints and other places of pilgrimage might preserve, in a Christian form, the immemorial beliefs and practices of a region.

The self-governing institutions of the Greek cities had disappeared with the expansion of the imperial bureaucracy, but bishops could provide local leadership. When the emperor left Rome, the bishop of the city, the Pope, could exercise authority in a way impossible for the patriarchs and bishops in the eastern Roman cities; they were closely linked with the imperial government, but they could still express local feelings and defend local interests. The hermit or miracle-working saint, too, living on the edge of the city or settled land in Anatolia or Syria, could act as arbiter of disputes or spokesman of the local population, and the monk in the Egyptian desert gave an example of a society differing from that of the secular urban world. Beside the official Orthodox Church, there grew up others which differed from it in doctrine and practice and which gave expression to the loyalties and opposition to central authority of those whose language was other than Greek.

The main doctrinal differences concerned the nature of Christ. The Council of Chalcedon in 451 had defined the second person of the Trinity as possessing two natures, divine and human. This was the formulation accepted by the main body of the Church, whether in the east or west, and supported by the imperial government. It was only later and gradually, and mainly over the question of authority, that there took place a division between the Church in the Byzantine territories, the Eastern Orthodox Church with its Patriarchs as heads of its priesthood, and those in western Europe who accepted the supreme authority of the Pope in Rome. There were some communities, however, which held that Christ had only a single nature, composed of two natures. This, the Monophysite doctrine, was held by the Armenian Church in Anatolia, by most Egyptian Christians (known as 'Copts' from the ancient name for Egypt), and by many of the indigenous, Syriac-speaking Christians of Syria (known as Syrian Orthodox, or 'Jacobites' from the name of their most prominent theologian). Others again made a sharper division between the two natures, in order to maintain the full humanity of Jesus, and thought of the Word of God as dwelling in the man Jesus from his conception; this was the doctrine of those commonly known as Nestorians, from the name of a thinker identified with the doctrine; their Church was most important among the Christians in Iraq, beyond the eastern frontier of the Byzantine Empire. In the seventh century, a further group appeared, as a result of an attempt at compromise between the Orthodox and Monophysite positions: the Monotheletes, who held that Christ had two natures but one will.

To the east of the Byzantine Empire, across the Euphrates river, lay another great empire, that of the Sasanians, whose rule extended over what are now Iran and Iraq, and stretched into central Asia. The land now called Iran or Persia contained a number of regions of high culture and ancient cities inhabited by different ethnic groups, divided from each other by steppes or deserts, with no great rivers to give them easy communications. From time to time they had been united by strong and lasting dynasties; the latest was that of the Sasanians, whose original power lay among the Persian-speaking peoples of southern Iran. Theirs was a family state ruled through a hierarchy of officials, and they tried to provide a solid basis of unity and loyalty by reviving the ancient religion of Iran, traditionally associated with the teacher Zoroaster. For this religion, the universe was a battle-ground, beneath the supreme God, between good and evil spirits; the good would win, but men and women of virtue and ritual purity could hasten the victory.

After Alexander the Great conquered Iran in 334–33 BC and drew it into closer ties with the eastern Mediterranean world, ideas from the Greek world moved eastwards, while those of a teacher from Iraq, Mani, who tried to incorporate all prophets and teachers into a single religious system (known as Manichaeism) moved westwards. Under the Sasanians the teaching associated with Zoroaster was revived in a philosophical form, with more emphasis on the dualism of good and evil, and with a priesthood and formal worship; this is known as Mazdaism or Zoroastrianism. As a state Church, Mazdaism supported the power of the ruler, regarded as a just king who preserved harmony between the different classes of society.

The Sasanian capital lay not in the plateaux of Iran but at Ctesiphon in the fertile and populous area of central Iraq, watered by the Tigris and Euphrates rivers. Besides Zoroastrians and followers of Mani, Iraq had Christians of the Nestorian Church, who were important in the service of the state. This area was also the main centre of Jewish religious learning, and a refuge for pagan philosophers and medical scientists from the Greek cities of the Mediterranean world. Various forms of the Persian language were widespread; the written form used at the time is known as Pahlavi.

Widespread too was Aramaic, a Semitic language related to Hebrew and Arabic and current throughout the Middle East at the time; one of its forms is known as Syriac.

The two empires included the main regions of settled life and high culture in the western half of the world, but further south, on either side of the Red Sea, lay two other societies with traditions of organized power and culture maintained by agriculture and by trade between the Indian Ocean and the Mediterranean. One was Ethiopia, an ancient kingdom with Christianity in its Coptic form as the official religion. The other was Yemen in south-western Arabia, a land of fertile mountain valleys and a point of transit for long-distance trade. At a certain stage its small local states had been incorporated in a larger kingdom, which had grown weak when trade declined in the early Christian era but revived later. Yemen had its own language, different from Arabic which was spoken elsewhere in Arabia, and its own religion: a multiplicity of gods were served by priests in temples which were places of pilgrimage, votive offerings and private, but not communal, prayer, and also centres of great estates. In later centuries Christian and Jewish influences had come down from Syria on the trade-routes or across the sea from Ethiopia. In the sixth century, a centre of Christianity had been destroyed by a king attracted to Judaism, but invasions from Ethiopia had restored some Christian influence; both the Byzantines and the Sasanians had been involved in these events.

Between the great empires of the north and the kingdoms of the Red Sea lay lands of a different kind. The greater part of the Arabian peninsula was steppe or desert, with isolated oases having enough water for regular cultivation. The inhabitants spoke various dialects of Arabic and followed different ways of life. Some of them were nomads who pastured camels, sheep or goats by using the scanty water resources of the desert; these have traditionally been known as 'beduin'. Some were settled cultivators tending their grain or palm trees in the oases, or traders and craftsmen in small market towns; some combined more than one way of life. The balance between nomadic and sedentary peoples was precarious. Although they were a minority of the population, it was the camel-nomads, mobile and carrying arms, who, together with merchant groups in the towns, dominated the cultivators and craftsmen. Their ethos of courage, hospitality, loyalty to family and pride of ancestry was also dominant. They were not controlled by a stable power of coercion, but were led by chiefs belonging to families around which there gathered more or less lasting groups of supporters, expressing their cohesion and loyalty in the idiom of common ancestry; such groups are usually called tribes.

The power of tribal leaders was exercised from oases, where they had close links with merchants who organized trade through the territory controlled by the tribe. In the oases, however, other families were able to establish a different kind of power through the force of religion. The religion of pastoralists and cultivators seems to have had no clear shape. Local gods, identified with objects in the sky, were thought to be embodied in stones, trees and other natural things; good and evil spirits were believed to roam the world in the shape of animals; soothsayers claimed to speak with the tongue of some supernatural wisdom. It has been suggested, on the basis of modern practice in southern Arabia, that gods were thought of as dwelling in a sanctuary, a *haram*, a place or town set apart from tribal conflict, serving as a centre of pilgrimage, sacrifice, meeting and arbitration, and watched over by a family under the protection of a neighbouring tribe.[1] Such a family could obtain power or influence by making skilful use of its religious prestige, its role as arbiter of tribal disputes, and its opportunities for trade.

Throughout this Near Eastern world, much was changing in the sixth and early seventh centuries. The Byzantine and Sasanian Empires were engaged in long wars, which lasted with intervals from 540 to 629. They were mainly fought in Syria and Iraq; for a moment the Sasanian armies came as far as the Mediterranean, occupying the great cities of Antioch and Alexandria as well as the holy city of Jerusalem, but in the 620s they were driven back by the Emperor Heraclius. For a time too Sasanian rule extended to south-western Arabia, where the kingdom of Yemen had lost much of its former power because of invasions from Ethiopia and a decline in agriculture. The settled societies ruled by the empires were full of questionings about the meaning of life and the way it should be lived, expressed in the idioms of the great religions.

The power and influence of the empires touched parts of the Arabian peninsula, and for many centuries Arab pastoral nomads from the north and centre of the peninsula had been moving into the countryside of the area now often called the Fertile Crescent: the interior of Syria, the land lying west of the Euphrates in lower Iraq, and the region between Euphrates and Tigris in upper Iraq (the Jazira) were largely Arab in population. They brought with them their ethos and forms of social organization. Some of their tribal chiefs exercised leadership from oasis towns and were used by the imperial governments to keep other nomads away from the settled lands and to collect taxes. They were able therefore to create more stable political units, like that of the Lakhmids with its capital at Hira, in a region where the Sasanians did not exercise direct control, and that of the Ghassanids in a similar region of the Byzantine Empire. The people of these states acquired political and military knowledge, and were open to ideas and beliefs coming from the imperial lands; Hira was a Christian centre. From these states, from Yemen, and also by the passage of traders along the trade-routes, there came into Arabia some knowledge of the outside world and its culture, and some settlers from it. There were Jewish craftsmen, merchants and cultivators in the oases of Hijaz in western Arabia, and Christian monks and converts in central Arabia.

THE LANGUAGE OF POETRY

There appears also to have been a growing sense of cultural identity among the pastoral tribesmen, shown in the emergence of a common poetic language out of the dialects of Arabic. This was a formal language, with refinements of grammar and vocabulary, which evolved gradually, perhaps by the elaboration of one particular dialect, or perhaps by a conflation of several. It was used by poets from different tribal groups or oasis towns. Their poetry may have developed out of the use of rhythmic, elevated and rhymed language for incantations or magical spells, but that which has come down to us is in no sense primitive. It is the product of a long cumulative tradition, in which not only tribal gatherings and market towns, but the courts of Arab dynasties on the fringes of the great empires played a part, in particular that of Hira on the Euphrates, open as it was to Christian and Mazdaean influences.

The poetic conventions which emerged from this tradition were elaborate. The poetic form most highly valued was the ode or *qasida*, a poem of up to 100 lines, written in one of a number of accepted metres and with a single rhyme running through it. Each line consisted of two hemistiches: the rhyme was carried in both of them in the first line, but only in the second in the rest. In general, each line was a unit of meaning and total enjambment was rare; but this did not prevent continuity of thought or feeling from one line to another, and throughout the poem.

Poetry was not written down, although it could have been, because writing was known in the peninsula: inscriptions in the languages of southern Arabia go back for centuries. The earliest Arabic inscriptions, in Aramaic script, can be dated to the fourth century, and later an Arabic script was evolved; apart from inscriptions, writing may well have been used in long-distance trade. Poems, however, were composed to be recited in public, either by the poet himself or by a *rawi* or reciter. This had certain implications: the sense had to be conveyed in a line, a single unit of words of which the meaning could be grasped by listeners, and every performance was unique and different from others. The poet or *rawi* had scope for improvisation, within a framework of commonly accepted verbal forms and patterns, the use of certain words or combinations of them in order to express certain ideas or feelings. There may therefore have been no single authentic version of a poem. As they have come down to us, the versions were produced later by philologists or literary critics in the light of the linguistic or poetic norms of their own time. In the process of doing so, they may have introduced new elements into the poems, changing the language to suit their ideas of what was correct and even forming *qasidas* by combining shorter pieces. In the 1920s two scholars, one British and one Egyptian, built upon these undoubted facts a theory that the poems were themselves the products of a later period, but most of those who have studied the subject would now agree that in substance the poems do come from the time to which they have traditionally been ascribed.

Among scholars and critics of a later period, it was common to refer to certain poems, among the mass of those which have survived, as supreme examples of the ancient Arabian poetry. These came to be called the *Mu'allaqat* or 'suspended poems', a name of which the origin and meaning are obscure; the poets who wrote them – Labid, Zuhayr, Imru'l-Qays and some half-dozen others – were regarded as the great masters of the art. It was customary to call the poetry of this time the *diwan* of the Arabs, the register of what they had done, or the expression of their collective memory, but the strong imprint of the personality of the individual poet was also there.

Later critics and scholars were accustomed to distinguish three elements in the *qasida*, but this was to formalize a practice which was loose and varied. The poem tended to begin with the evocation of a place where the poet had once been, which could also be an evocation of a lost love; the mood was not erotic, so much as the commemoration of the transience of human life:

The abodes are deserted, the places where we halted and those where we camped, in Mina; Ghawl and Rijan are both abandoned. In the flood-courses of Rayyan the riverbeds are naked and worn smooth, as writing is preserved on stone. The blackened dung lies undisturbed since those who stayed there departed: long years have passed over it, years of holy and ordinary months. Springs which the stars have caused to flow have fed them, and they have been nourished by the waters of thunder-clouds: heavy downpours and light showers, the clouds of night, those that cover the sky at morning, and the evening clouds whose voices answer each other.[2]

After this, there may come a journey on camel-back, in which the poet speaks of the camel, the countryside and the hunting of animals, and, by implication, of the recovery of his strength and confidence when tested against the forces of nature. The poem may culminate in praise of the poet's tribe:

A house with a high roof has been built for us, and young and old alike try to reach its height . . . They are those who fight when the tribe is in distress, its knights and its arbiters. They are like the spring for those who seek their help, or for widows whose year of mourning is long. They are such a tribe, envy cannot harm them and none of their people are so unworthy as to go with the enemy.[3]

Beneath the praise and boasting, however, can sometimes be heard another note, that of the limits of human strength in the face of all-powerful nature:

I am tired of the burdens of life; make no mistake, whoever lives to fourscore years grows tired. I know what is happening today and what happened yesterday, but I cannot tell what tomorrow will bring. I have seen the Fates stamp like a camel in the dark; those they touch they kill, and those they miss live on to grow old.[4]

MUHAMMAD AND THE APPEARANCE OF ISLAM

By the early seventh century there existed a combination of a settled world which had lost something of its strength and assurance, and another world on its frontiers which was in closer contact with its northern neighbours and opening itself to their cultures. The decisive meeting between them took place in the middle years of that century. A new political order was created which included the whole of the Arabian peninsula, the whole of the Sasanian lands, and the Syrian and Egyptian provinces of the Byzantine Empire; old frontiers were erased and new ones created. In this new order, the ruling group was formed not by the peoples of the empires but by Arabs from western Arabia, and to a great extent from Mecca.

Before the end of the seventh century, this Arab ruling group was identifying its new order with a revelation given by God to Muhammad, a citizen of Mecca, in the form of a holy book, the Qur'an: a revelation which completed those given to earlier prophets or messengers of God and created a new religion, Islam, separate from Judaism and Christianity. There is room for scholarly discussion about the way in which these beliefs developed. The Arabic sources which narrate the life of Muhammad and the formation of a community around him are later in date; the first biographer whose work we know did not write until more than a century after Muhammad's death. Sources written in other languages fully attest to the conquest of an empire by the Arabs, but what they say about the mission of Muhammad is different from what the Muslim tradition says, and still needs to be studied and discussed. On the other hand, there seems little reason to doubt that the Qur'an is substantially a document of seventh-century Arabia, although it may have taken some time to assume its definitive literary form. Moreover, there seem to be elements in the traditional biographies and histories which are not likely to have been invented. Undoubtedly such writings reflect later attempts to fit Muhammad into the Near Eastern pattern of a holy man, and the Arabian pattern of a man of noble descent; they reflect also the doctrinal controversies of the time and place where they were composed – Iraq in the eighth century. Nevertheless, they contain facts about Muhammad's life, his family and friends which could scarcely have been invented. It seems best therefore to follow the traditional account of the origins of Islam, although with caution. To do so has an advantage: since that account, and the text of the Qur'an, have remained living without substantial change in the minds and imaginations of believers in the religion of Islam, to follow it makes it possible to understand their view of history and of what human life should be.

The most obscure part of the life of Muhammad, as the biographers narrate it, is the early one. They tell us that he was born in Mecca, a town in western Arabia, perhaps in or near the year 570. His family belonged to the tribe of Quraysh, although not to its most powerful part. Members of the tribe were traders, who had agreements with pastoral tribes around Mecca and also relations with Syria as well as south-western Arabia. They are also said to have had a connection with the sanctuary of the town, the Ka'ba, where the images of local gods were kept. Muhammad married Khadija, a widow engaged in trade, and looked after her business for her. Various anecdotes recorded by those who later wrote his life portray a world waiting for a guide and a man searching for a vocation. A seeker after God expresses his wish to be taught: 'O God, if I knew how you

wished to be worshipped I would so worship you, but I do not know'.
Jewish rabbis, Christian monks and Arab soothsayers predict the coming
of a prophet: a monk, met by Muhammad on a trading journey to southern
Syria, 'looked at his back and saw the seal of prophethood between his
shoulders'. Natural objects saluted him: 'Not a stone or tree that he passed
but would say, "Peace unto you, O apostle of God!" '⁵

He became a solitary wanderer among the rocks, and then one day,
perhaps when he was about forty years old, something happened: some
contact with the supernatural, known to later generations as the Night of
Power or Destiny. In one version, an angel, seen in the form of a man on
the horizon, called to him to become the messenger of God; in another, he
heard the angel's voice summoning him to recite. He asked, 'What shall I
recite?' and the voice said:

> Recite: in the name of thy Lord who created,
> created man of a blood-clot.
> Recite: and thy Lord is the most bountiful,
> who taught by the pen,
> taught man what he knew not.
> No, indeed: surely man waxes insolent,
> for he thinks himself self-sufficient.
> Surely unto thy Lord is the returning.⁶

At this point there occurred an event known in the lives of other claimants
to supernatural power: the claim is accepted by some to whom it is told,
and this recognition confirms it in the mind of him who has made it. Those
who responded were few in number, and included his wife Khadija:
'Rejoice, O son of my uncle, and be of good heart. By Him in whose hand
is Khadija's soul, I hope that thou wilt be the prophet of His people'.

From this time Muhammad began communicating to those who adhered
to him a succession of messages which he believed to have been revealed
by an angel of God. The world would end; God the all-powerful, who had
created human beings, would judge them all; the delights of Heaven and
the pains of Hell were depicted in vivid colours. If in their lives they
submitted to God's Will, they could rely on His mercy when they came to
judgement; and it was God's Will that they should show their gratitude by
regular prayer and other observances, and by benevolence and sexual
restraint. The name used for God was 'Allah', which was already in use for
one of the local gods (it is now also used by Arabic-speaking Jews and
Christians as the name of God). Those who submitted to His Will came

eventually to be known as Muslims; the name for their religion, Islam, is derived from the same linguistic root.

Gradually there gathered around Muhammad a small group of believers: a few young members of the influential families of Quraysh, some members of minor families, clients of other tribes who had placed themselves under the protection of Quraysh, and some craftsmen and slaves. As support for Muhammad grew, his relations with the leading families of Quraysh became worse. They did not accept his claim to be a messenger of God, and they saw him as one who attacked their way of life. 'O Abu Talib,' they said to his uncle, who was his protector among them, 'your nephew has cursed our gods, insulted our religion, mocked our way of life, and accused our forefathers of error.' His situation grew worse when his wife Khadija and Abu Talib died in the same year.

As his teaching developed, its differences from accepted beliefs became clearer. The idols of the gods and ceremonies connected with them were attacked; new forms of worship were enjoined, in particular regular communal prayer, and new kinds of good works. He placed himself more explicitly in the line of prophets of the Jewish and Christian tradition.

Finally his position became so difficult that in 622 he left Mecca for an oasis settlement 200 miles to the north, Yathrib, to be known in future as Madina. The way had been prepared by men from Yathrib who had come to Mecca for trade. They belonged to two tribes and needed an arbiter in tribal disputes; having lived side by side with Jewish inhabitants of the oasis, they were prepared to accept a teaching expressed in terms of a prophet and a holy book. This move to Madina, from which later generations were to date the beginning of the Muslim era, is known as the *hijra*: the word has not simply the negative meaning of a flight from Mecca, but the positive one of seeking protection by settling in a place other than one's own. In later Islamic centuries, it would be used to mean the abandonment of a pagan or wicked community for one living in accordance with the moral teaching of Islam. The early biographers have preserved the texts of agreements said to have been made between Muhammad and his adherents on the one side and the two main tribes, together with some Jewish groups, on the other. It was an agreement not unlike those made in modern south Arabia when a *haram* is set up: each party was to keep its own laws and customs, but the whole area of the *haram* was to be one of peace, disputes were not to be settled by force but judged by 'God and Muhammad', and the alliance would act together against those who broke the peace.

From Madina, Muhammad began to gather a power which radiated throughout the oasis and the surrounding desert. He was soon drawn into an armed struggle with Quraysh, perhaps for control of the trade-routes, and in the course of the struggle the nature of the community was shaped. They came to believe that it was necessary to fight for what was right: 'when Quraysh became insolent towards God and rejected His gracious purpose . . . He gave permission to His apostle to fight and protect himself'. They acquired the conviction that God and the angels were fighting on their side, and accepted calamity when it came as a trial by which God tested believers.

It was in this period of expanding power and struggle that the Prophet's teaching took its final form. In the parts of the Qur'an which are thought to have been revealed then, there is a greater concern with defining the ritual observances of religion and with social morality, the rules of social peace, property, marriage and inheritance. In some regards specific injunctions are given, in others general principles. At the same time the teaching becomes more universal, directed to the whole of pagan Arabia and by implication to the whole world, and it separates itself more clearly from that of the Jews and Christians.

The development of the Prophet's teaching may have been connected with changes in his relations with the Jews of Madina. Although they had formed part of the original alliance, their position became more difficult as Muhammad's claim for his mission expanded. They could not accept him as a genuine messenger of God within their own tradition, and he in turn is said to have accused them of perverting the revelation given to them: 'you have concealed what you were ordered to make plain'. Finally some of the Jewish clans were expelled and others killed.

It may have been a sign of the breach with the Jews that the direction which the community faced in prayer was changed from Jerusalem to Mecca (qibla), and a new emphasis was placed on the line of spiritual descent which bound Muhammad to Abraham. The idea that Abraham was the founder of a high monotheistic faith and of the sanctuary at Mecca already existed; now he was seen as neither a Jew nor a Christian, but the common ancestor of both, and of Muslims too. This change was also connected with a change in Muhammad's relations with Quraysh and Mecca. A kind of reconciliation of interests took place. The merchants of Mecca were in danger of losing their alliances with tribal chiefs and their control of trade, and in the city itself there was a growing number of adherents to Islam; an agreement with the new power would remove certain dangers, while the community of Muhammad for its part could not feel safe so long as Mecca was hostile, and it needed the skills of the Meccan patricians. Since the *haram* at Mecca was thought to have been founded by Abraham, it could be accepted as a place to which pilgrimage was allowed, although with a changed meaning.

By 629 relations had become close enough for the community to be permitted to go to Mecca on pilgrimage, and next year the leaders of the city surrendered it to Muhammad, who occupied it virtually without resistance and announced the principles of a new order: 'every claim of privilege or blood or property is abolished by me except the custody of the temple and the watering of the pilgrims'.

Madina still remained his capital, however. There he exercised authority over his followers less by regular government than by political manipulation and personal ascendancy; of the several marriages he made after Khadija's death, some, although not all, were contracted for political reasons. There was no elaborate administration or army, simply Muhammad as supreme arbiter with a number of deputies, a military levy of believers, and a public treasury filled by voluntary gifts and by levies on tribes which submitted. Beyond the towns, Muhammad's peace stretched over a wide area. Tribal chiefs needed agreements with him because he controlled the oases and markets. The nature of the agreements varied; in some cases there was alliance and renunciation of conflict, in others acceptance of the prophet-hood of Muhammad, the obligation of prayer and the regular giving of financial contributions.

In 632 Muhammad made his last visit to Mecca, and his speech there has been recorded in the traditional writings as the final statement of his message: 'know that every Muslim is a Muslim's brother, and that the Muslims are brethren'; fighting between them should be avoided, and the blood shed in pagan times should not be avenged; Muslims should fight all men until they say, 'There is no god but God'.

Later that year he died. He left more than one legacy. First was that of his personality as seen through the eyes of his close companions. Their testimony, handed down mainly by oral transmission, did not assume its definite shape until much later, and by that time it was certainly swollen by accretions, but it seems plausible to suggest that from an early time those who had known and followed Muhammad would have tried to model their behaviour upon his. In the course of time there evolved a type of human personality which may well be to some extent a reflection of his. Mirrored in the eyes of his followers, he appears as a man searching for truth in early life, then bemused by the sense of some power falling upon him from on high, eager to communicate what had been revealed to him, acquiring confidence in his mission and a sense of authority as followers gathered around him, an arbiter concerned to make peace and reconcile disputes in the light of principles of justice believed to be of divine origin, a skilful manipulator of political forces, a man not turning his back on habitual modes of human action but trying to confine them within limits which he believed to have been ordained by the Will of God.

If an image of Muhammad was gradually elaborated and transmitted from one generation to another, so was that of the community he founded. As pictured by later ages, it was a community which revered the Prophet and held his memory dear, trying to follow his path and strive in the way of Islam for the service of God. It was held together by the basic rituals of devotion, all of which had a communal aspect: Muslims went on pilgrimage at the same time, fasted throughout the same month and united in regular prayer, the activity which marked them off most clearly from the rest of the world.

Above all, there was the legacy of the Qur'an, a book which depicts in language of great force and beauty the incursion of a transcendent God, source of all power and goodness, into the human world He has created; the revelation of His Will through a line of prophets sent to warn men and bring them back to their true selves as grateful and obedient creatures; God's judgement of men at the end of time, and the rewards and punishments to follow from it.

Orthodox Muslims have always believed that the Qur'an is the Word of God, revealed in the Arabic language through an angel to Muhammad, at various times and in ways appropriate to the needs of the community. Few non-Muslims would entirely accept this belief. At most, some of them would think it possible that in a sense Muhammad received inspiration from outside the human world, but would maintain that it was mediated through his personality and expressed in his words. There is no purely rational way in which this difference of belief can be resolved, but those who are divided by it can agree on certain questions which might legitimately be asked about the Qur'an.

First is the question of when and how it took its final form. Muhammad communicated the revelations to his followers at various times, and they recorded them in writing or kept them in their memories. Most scholars would agree that the process by which different versions were collected and a generally accepted text and arrangement established did not end until after Muhammad's death. The traditional account is that this happened during the time of his third successor as head of the community, 'Uthman (644–56), but later dates have been suggested, and some Muslim sects have accused others of inserting into the text material not derived by transmission from the Prophet.

A more important question is that of the originality of the Qur'an. Scholars have tried to place it in the context of ideas current in its time and place. Undoubtedly there are echoes in it of the teaching of earlier religions: Jewish ideas in its doctrines; some reflections of eastern Christian monastic piety in the brooding on the terrors of judgement and the descriptions of Heaven and Hell (but few references to Christian doctrine or liturgy); Biblical stories in forms different from those of the Old and New Testaments; an echo of the Manichaean idea of a succession of revelations given to different peoples. There are also traces of an indigenous tradition: the moral ideas in some ways continue those prevalent in Arabia, although in others they break with them; in the early revelations the tone is that of the Arabian soothsayer, stammering out his sense of an encounter with the supernatural.

Such traces of the past need cause no anxiety to a Muslim, who can regard them as signs that Muhammad came at the end of a line of prophets who all taught the same truth; to be effective, the final revelation might use words and images already known and understood, and if ideas or stories took a different form in the Qur'an, that might be because adherents of earlier prophets had distorted the message received through them. Some non-Muslim scholars, however, have drawn a different conclusion: that the Qur'an contains little more than borrowings from what was already available to Muhammad in that time and place. To say this, however, is to misunderstand what it is to be original: whatever was taken over from the religious culture of the age was so rearranged and transmuted that, for those who accepted the message, the familiar world was made anew.

CHAPTER 2

The Formation of an Empire

THE SUCCESSION TO MUHAMMAD:
THE CONQUEST OF AN EMPIRE

When Muhammad died, there was a moment of confusion among his followers. One of their leaders, Abu Bakr, proclaimed to the community: 'O men, if you worship Muhammad, Muhammad is dead; if you worship God, God is alive.' Beneath God there was still a role to be filled: that of arbiter of disputes and maker of decisions within the community. There were three main groups among the followers of Muhammad: the early companions who had made the *hijra* with him, a group linked by intermarriage; the prominent men of Madina who had made the compact with him there; and the members of the leading Meccan families, mainly of recent conversion. At a meeting of close associates and leaders, it was one of the first group who was chosen as the Prophet's successor (*khalifa*, hence the word 'caliph'): Abu Bakr, a follower of the first hour, whose daughter 'A'isha was wife to the Prophet.

The caliph was not a prophet. Leader of the community, but not in any sense a messenger of God, he could not claim to be the spokesman of continuing revelations; but an aura of holiness and divine choice still lingered around the person and office of the early caliphs, and they did claim to have some kind of religious authority. Abu Bakr and his successors soon found themselves called upon to exercise leadership over a wider range than the Prophet. There was a universalism implicit in Muhammad's teaching and actions: he claimed universal authority, the *haram* which he established had no natural limits; in his last years military expeditions had been sent against the Byzantine frontier lands, and he is supposed to have sent emissaries to the rulers of the great states, calling on them to acknowledge his message. When he died, the alliances he had made with tribal chiefs threatened to dissolve; some of them now rejected his prophetic claims, or at least the political control of Madina. Faced with this challenge, the community under Abu Bakr affirmed its authority by military action (the 'wars of the *ridda*'); in the process an army was created, and the momentum of action carried it into the frontier regions of the great empires and then, as resistance proved weak, into their hearts. By the end of the reign of the second caliph, 'Umar ibn 'Abd al-Khattab (634–44), the whole of Arabia, part of the Sasanian Empire, and the Syrian and Egyptian provinces of the Byzantine Empire had been conquered; the rest of the Sasanian lands were occupied soon afterwards.

In the space of a few years, then, the political frontiers of the Near East had been changed and the centre of political life had moved from the rich and populous lands of the Fertile Crescent to a small town lying on the edge of the world of high culture and wealth. The change was so sudden and unexpected that it needs explanation. Evidence uncovered by archaeologists indicates that the prosperity and strength of the Mediterranean world were in decline because of barbarian invasions, failure to maintain terraces and other agricultural works, and the shrinking of the urban market. Both Byzantine and Sasanian Empires had been weakened by epidemics of plague and long wars; the hold of the Byzantines over Syria had been restored only after the defeat of the Sasanians in 629, and was still tenuous. The Arabs who invaded the two empires were not a tribal horde but an organized force, some of whose members had acquired military skill and experience in the service of the empires or in the fighting after the death of the Prophet. The use of camel transport gave them an advantage in campaigns fought over wide areas; the prospect of land and wealth created a coalition of interests among them; and the fervour of conviction gave some of them a different kind of strength.

Perhaps, however, another kind of explanation can be given for the acceptance of Arab rule by the population of the conquered countries. To most of them it did not much matter whether they were ruled by Iranians, Greeks or Arabs. Government impinged for the most part on the life of cities and their immediate hinterlands; apart from officials and classes whose interests were linked with theirs, and apart from the hierarchies of some religious communities, city-dwellers might not care much who ruled them, provided they were secure, at peace and reasonably taxed. The people of the countryside and steppes lived under their own chiefs and in accordance with their own customs, and it made little difference to them who ruled the cities. For some, the replacement of Greeks and Iranians by Arabs even offered advantages. Those whose opposition to Byzantine rule was expressed in terms of religious dissidence might find it easier to live under a ruler who was impartial towards various Christian groups, particularly as the new faith, which had as yet no fully developed system of doctrine or law, may not have appeared alien to them. In those parts of Syria and Iraq already occupied by people of Arabian origin and language, it was easy for their leaders to transfer their loyalties from the emperors to the new Arab alliance, all the more so because the control over them previously held by the Lakhmids and Ghassanids, the Arab client-states of the two great empires, had disappeared.

As the conquered area expanded, the way in which it was ruled had to change. The conquerors exercised their authority from armed camps where the Arabian soldiers were placed. In Syria, these for the most part lay in the cities which already existed, but elsewhere new settlements were made: Basra and Kufa in Iraq, Fustat in Egypt (from which Cairo was later to grow), others on the north-eastern frontier in Khurasan. Being centres of power, these camps were poles of attraction for immigrants from Arabia and the conquered lands, and they grew into cities, with the governor's palace and the place of public assembly, the mosque, at the centre.

In Madina and the new camp-cities linked to it by inland routes, power was in the hands of a new ruling group. Some of its members were Companions of the Prophet, early and devoted followers, but a large element came from the Meccan families with their military and political skills, and from similar families in the nearby town of Ta'if. As the conquests continued others came from the leading families of pastoral tribes, even those who had tried to throw off the rule of Madina after the Prophet's death. To some extent the different groups tended to mingle with each other. The Caliph 'Umar created a system of stipends for those who had fought in the cause of Islam, regulated according to priority of conversion and service, and this reinforced the cohesion of the ruling élite, or at least their separation from those they ruled; between the newly wealthy members of the élite and the poorer people there were signs of tension from early times.

In spite of its ultimate cohesion, the group was split by personal and factional differences. The early Companions of the Prophet looked askance at later converts who had obtained power; claims of early conversion and close links with Muhammad might clash with claims to the nobility of ancient and honourable ancestry. The people of Madina saw power being drawn northwards towards the richer and more populous lands of Syria and Iraq, where governors tried to make their power more independent.

Such tensions came to the surface in the reign of the third caliph, 'Uthman ibn 'Affan (644–56). He was chosen by a small group of members of Quraysh, after 'Umar had been assassinated for private vengeance. He seemed to offer the hope of reconciling factions, for he belonged to the inner core of Quraysh but had been an early convert. In the event, however, his policy was one of appointing members of his own clan as provincial governors, and this aroused opposition, both in Madina from the sons of Companions and from the Prophet's wife 'A'isha, and in Kufa and Fustat; some of the tribes resented the domination of men from Mecca. A movement of unrest in Madina, supported by soldiers from Egypt, led to 'Uthman's murder in 656.

This opened the first period of civil war in the community. The claimant to the succession, 'Ali ibn Abi Talib (656–61), was of Quraysh, an early convert, a cousin of Muhammad and married to his daughter Fatima. He found himself faced with a double opposition. The kin of 'Uthman were against him, but so were others who disputed the validity of his election. The struggle for power in Madina was carried into the camp-cities. 'Ali established himself as caliph in Kufa, the dissidents in Basra; he defeated them, but was now faced with a new challenge from Syria, where the governor, Mu'awiya ibn Abi Sufyan, was a close kinsman of 'Uthman. The two forces met at Siffin on the upper Euphrates, but after fighting for a time they agreed on arbitration by delegates chosen from the two sides. When 'Ali agreed to this, some of his supporters abandoned him, for they were not willing to accept compromise and submit the Will of God, as they saw it, to human judgement; the honour due to early conversion to Islam was at stake. In the months of discussion between the arbiters, 'Ali's alliance grew weaker, and finally he was assassinated in his own city of Kufa. Mu'awiya proclaimed himself caliph and 'Ali's elder son, Hasan, acquiesced in it.

THE CALIPHATE OF DAMASCUS

The coming to power by Mu'awiya (661–80) has always been regarded as marking the end of one phase and the beginning of another. The first four caliphs, from Abu Bakr to 'Ali, are known to the majority of Muslims as the *Rashidun* or 'Rightly Guided'. Later caliphs were seen in a rather different light. First of all, from now on the position was virtually hereditary. Although some idea of choice, or at least formal recognition, by the leaders of the community remained, in fact from this time power was in the hands of a family, known from an ancestor, Umayya, as that of the Umayyads. When Mu'awiya died, he was succeeded by his son, who was followed briefly by his own son; after that there was a second period of civil war and the throne passed to another branch of the family.

The change was more than one of rulers. The capital of the empire moved to Damascus, a city lying in a countryside able to provide the surplus needed to maintain a court, government and army, and in a region from which the eastern Mediterranean coastlands and the land to the east of them could be controlled more easily than from Madina. This was the more important because the caliph's rule was still expanding. Muslim forces advanced across the Maghrib. They established their first important base at Qayrawan in the former Roman province of Africa (Ifriqiya, the present day Tunisia); from there they moved westwards, reached the Atlantic coast of Morocco by the end of the seventh century and crossed into Spain soon afterwards; at the other extreme, the land beyond Khurasan reaching as far as the Oxus valley was conquered and the first Muslim advances were made into north-western India.

Such an empire demanded a new style of government. An opinion widespread in later generations, when the Umayyads had been replaced by a dynasty hostile to them, held that they had introduced a government directed towards worldly ends determined by self-interest in place of that of the earlier caliphs who had been devoted to the well-being of religion. It would be fairer to say that the Umayyads found themselves faced with the problems of governing a great empire and therefore became involved in the compromises of power. Gradually, from being Arab chieftains, they formed a way of life patterned on that traditional among rulers of the Near East, receiving their guests or subjects in accordance with the ceremonial usages of Byzantine emperor or Iranian king. The first Arabian armies were replaced by regular paid forces. A new ruling group was formed largely from army leaders or tribal chiefs; the leading families in Mecca and Madina ceased to be important because they were distant from the seat of power, and they tried more than once to revolt. The cities of Iraq too were of doubtful loyalty and had to be controlled by strong governors loyal to the caliph. The rulers were townspeople, committed to settled life and hostile to claims to power and leadership based upon tribal solidarity; 'you are putting relationship before religion', warned the first Umayyad governor of Iraq, and a successor, Hajjaj, dealt even more firmly with the tribal nobility and their followers.

Although armed power was in new hands, the financial administration continued as before, with secretaries drawn from the groups which had served previous rulers, using Greek in the west and Pahlavi in the east. From the 690s the language of administration was altered to Arabic, but this may not have marked a large change in personnel or methods; members of secretarial families who knew Arabic continued to work, and many became Muslims, particularly in Syria.

The new rulers established themselves firmly not only in the cities but in the Syrian countryside, on crown lands and land from which the owners had fled, particularly in the interior regions which lay open to the north Arabian steppe. They seem carefully to have maintained the systems of irrigation and cultivation which they found there, and the palaces and houses they built to serve as centres of economic control as well as hospitality were arranged and decorated in the style of the rulers they had replaced, with audience-halls and baths, mosaic floors, sculptured doorways and ceilings.

In this and other ways the Umayyads may seem to have resembled the barbarian kings of the western Roman Empire, uneasy settlers in an alien world whose life continued beneath the protection of their power. There was a difference, however. The rulers in the west had brought little of their own which could stand against the force of the Latin Christian civilization into which they were drawn. The Arab ruling group brought something with them which they were to retain amidst the high culture of the Near East, and which, modified and developed by that culture, would provide an idiom through which it could henceforth express itself: belief in a revelation sent by God to the Prophet Muhammad in the Arabic language.

The first clear assertion of the permanence and distinctiveness of the new order came in the 690s, in the reign of the Caliph 'Abd al-Malik (685–705). At the same time as Arabic was introduced for purposes of administration, a new style of coinage was brought in, and this was significant, since coins are symbols of power and identity. In place of the coins showing human figures, which had been taken over from the Sasanians or struck by the Umayyads in Damascus, new ones were minted carrying words alone, proclaiming in Arabic the oneness of God and the truth of the religion brought by His messenger.

More important still was the creation of great monumental buildings, themselves a public statement that the revelation given through Muhammad to mankind was the final and most complete one, and that its kingdom would last for ever.

The first places for communal prayer (*masjid*, hence the English word 'mosque', perhaps through Spanish *mezquita*) were also used for assemblies of the whole community to transact public business. They had no marks to distinguish them clearly from other kinds of building: some were in fact older buildings taken over for the purpose, while others were new ones in the centres of Muslim settlement. The holy places of the Jews and Christians still had a hold over the imagination of the new rulers: 'Umar had visited Jerusalem after it was captured, and Mu'awiya was proclaimed caliph there. Then in the 690s there was erected the first great building which clearly asserted that Islam was distinct and would endure. This was the Dome of the Rock, built on the site of the Jewish Temple in Jerusalem, now turned into a Muslim *haram*; it was to be an ambulatory for pilgrims around the rock where, according to Rabbinic tradition, God had called upon Abraham to sacrifice Isaac. The building of the Dome in this place has been convincingly interpreted as a symbolic act placing Islam in the lineage of Abraham and dissociating it from Judaism and Christianity. The inscriptions around the interior, the earliest known physical embodiment of texts from the Qur'an, proclaim the greatness of God, 'the Mighty, the Wise', declare that 'God and His angels bless the Prophet', and call upon Christians to recognize Jesus as an apostle of God, His word and spirit, but not His son.[1]

A little later there began to be built a series of great mosques designed to meet the needs of ritual prayer: in Damascus and Aleppo, Madina and Jerusalem, and later in Qayrawan, the first Arab centre in the Maghrib, and in Cordoba, the Arab capital in Spain. All show the same basic design. An open courtyard leads to a covered space so shaped that long lines of worshippers led by a prayer-leader (*imam*) can face in the direction of Mecca. A niche (*mihrab*) marks the wall to which they face, and near it is a pulpit (*minbar*) where a sermon is preached during the noon prayer on Friday. Attached to the building or lying close to it is the minaret from which the muezzin (*mu'adhdhin*) calls the faithful to prayer at the appointed times.

Such buildings were signs not only of a new power but of the growth of a new and distinct community. From being the faith of a ruling group, acceptance of the revelation given to Muhammad gradually spread. We know little of the process, and can only speculate on the course it took. Arabs already living in the Syrian and Iraqi countryside could easily make the act of acceptance out of solidarity with the new rulers (although part of one tribe, that of Ghassan, did not). Officials working for the new rulers might accept their faith out of self-interest or a natural attraction towards power; so too might prisoners captured in the wars of conquest, or Sasanian soldiers who had joined the Arabs. Immigrants into the new cities might convert in order to avoid the special taxes paid by non-Muslims. Zoroastrians, adherents of the ancient Persian religion, may have found it easier to become Muslims than did Christians, because their organized Church had been weakened when Sasanian rule came to an end. Some Christians, however, touched by controversies about the nature of God and revelation, might be attracted by the simplicity of the early Muslim response to such questions, within what was broadly the same universe of thought. The absence of a Muslim Church or an elaborate ritual of conversion, the need only to use a few simple words, made acceptance an easy process. However simple it was, the act carried with it an implication: the acceptance of Arabic as the language in which revelation had been given, and this, together with the need to deal with Arab rulers, soldiers and landowners, could lead to its acceptance as the language of everyday life. Where Islam came, the Arabic language spread. This process, however, was still young; outside Arabia itself, the Umayyads ruled lands where most of the population were neither Muslims nor speakers of Arabic.

The growing size and strength of the Muslim community did not work in favour of the Umayyads. Their central region, Syria, was a weak link in the chain of countries being drawn into the empire. Unlike the new cities in Iran, Iraq and Africa, its cities had existed before Islam and had a life independent of their rulers. Its trade had been disrupted by its separation from Anatolia, which remained in Byzantine hands, across a new frontier often disturbed by war between Arabs and Byzantines.

The main strength of the Muslim community lay further east. The cities of Iraq were growing in size, as immigrants came in from Iran as well as the Arabian peninsula. They could draw on the wealth of the rich irrigated lands of southern Iraq, where some Arabs had installed themselves as landowners. The new cities were more fully Arab than those of Syria, and their life was enriched as members of the former Iranian ruling class were drawn in as officials and tax-collectors.

A similar process was taking place in Khurasan, in the far north-east of the empire. Lying as it did on the frontier of Islam's expansion into central Asia, it had large garrisons. Its cultivable land and pastures also attracted Arab settlers. From an early time there was therefore a considerable Arab population, living side by side with the Iranians, whose old landed and ruling class kept their position. A kind of symbiosis was gradually taking place: as they ceased to be active fighters and settled in the countryside or in the towns – Nishapur, Balkh and Marv – Arabs were being drawn into Iranian society; Iranians were entering the ruling group.

The growth of the Muslim communities in the eastern cities and provinces created tensions. Personal ambitions, local grievances and party conflicts expressed themselves in more than one idiom, ethnic, tribal and religious, and from this distance it is hard to say how the lines of division were drawn.

There was, first of all, among converts to Islam, and the Iranians in particular, resentment against the fiscal and other privileges given to those of Arab origin, and this grew as the memory of the first conquests became weaker. Some of the converts attached themselves to Arab tribal leaders as 'clients' (*mawali*), but this did not erase the line between them and the Arabs.

Tensions also expressed themselves in terms of tribal difference and opposition. The armies coming from Arabia brought tribal loyalties with them, and in the new circumstances these could grow stronger. In the cities and other places of migration, groups claiming a common ancestor came together in closer quarters than in the Arabian steppe; powerful leaders claiming nobility of descent could attract more followers. The existence of a unified political structure enabled leaders and tribes to link up with each other over wide areas and at times gave them common interests. The struggle for control of the central government could make use of tribal names and the loyalties they expressed. One branch of the Umayyads was linked by marriage with the Banu Kalb, who had already settled in Syria before the conquest; in the struggle for the succession after the death of Mu'awiya's son, a non-Umayyad claimant was supported by another group of tribes. At moments some common interest could give substance to the idea of an origin shared by all tribes claiming to come from central Arabia or from the south. (Their names, Qays and Yemen, were to linger as symbols of local conflict in some parts of Syria until the present century.)

Of more lasting importance were the disputes about the succession to the caliphate and the nature of authority in the Muslim community. Against the claims of Mu'awiya and his family there stood two groups, although each was so amorphous that it would be better to describe them as tendencies. First were the various groups called Kharijis. The earliest had been those who had withdrawn their support from 'Ali when he had agreed to arbitration on the day of Siffin. They had been crushed, but later movements used the same name, particularly in regions under the control of Basra. In opposition to the claims of tribal leaders, they maintained that there was no precedence in Islam except that of virtue. Only the virtuous Muslim should rule as *imam*, and if he went astray obedience should be withdrawn from him; 'Uthman, who had given priority to the claims of family, and 'Ali, who had agreed to compromise on a question of principle, had both been at fault. Not all of them drew the same conclusions from this: some acquiesced for the time in Umayyad rule, some revolted against it, and some held that true believers should try to create a virtuous society by a new *hijra* in a distant place.

The other group was that which supported the claims of the family of the Prophet to rule. This was an idea which could take many different forms. The most important in the long run was that which regarded 'Ali and a line of his descendants as legitimate heads of the community or *imams*. Around this idea there clustered others, some of them brought in from the religious cultures of the conquered countries. 'Ali and his heirs were thought of as having received by transmission from Muhammad some special quality of soul and knowledge of the inner meaning of the Qur'an, even as being in some sense more than human; one of them would arise to inaugurate the rule of justice. This expectation of the coming of a *mahdi*, 'him who is guided', arose early in the history of Islam. In 680 the second son of 'Ali, Husayn, moved into Iraq with a small party of kinsmen and retainers, hoping to find support in and around Kufa. He was killed in a fight at Karbala in Iraq, and his death was to give the strength of remembered martyrdom to the partisans of 'Ali (the *shi'at 'Ali* or Shi'is). A few years later there was another revolt in favour of Muhammad ibn al-Hanafiyya, who was also 'Ali's son, although not by Fatima.

During the first decades of the eighth century, Umayyad rulers made a series of attempts to deal with movements of opposition expressed in these various ways, and with the inherent difficulties of ruling an empire so vast and heterogeneous. They were able to strengthen the fiscal and military bases of their rule, and for a time had to face few major revolts. Then in the 740s their power suddenly collapsed in the face of yet another civil war and a coalition of movements with different aims but united by a common opposition to them. These movements were stronger in the eastern than the western parts of the empire, and particularly strong in Khurasan, among some of the Arab settler groups who were on the way to being assimilated into local Iranian society, as well as among the Iranian 'clients'. There as elsewhere there was a Shi'i sentiment widely diffused but having no organization.

More effective leadership came from another branch of the family of the

Prophet, the descendants of his uncle 'Abbas. Claiming that the son of Muhammad ibn al-Hanafiyya had passed on to them his right of succession, from their residences on the edge of the Syrian desert they created an organization with its centre at Kufa. As their emissary to Khurasan they sent a man of obscure origin, probably of an Iranian family, Abu Muslim. He was able to form an army and a coalition from dissident elements, Arab and other, and to come out in revolt under the black banner which was to be the symbol of the movement, and in the name of a member of the Prophet's family; no member was specifically mentioned, thus widening support for the movement. From Khurasan the army moved westwards, the Umayyads were defeated in a number of battles in 749–50, and the last caliph of the house, Marwan II, was pursued to Egypt and killed. In the meantime, the unnamed leader was proclaimed in Kufa; he was Abu'l-'Abbas, a descendant not of 'Ali but of 'Abbas.

The historian al-Tabari (839–923) has described how the announcement was made. Abu'l-'Abbas's brother Dawud stood on the pulpit steps of the mosque in Kufa and addressed the faithful:

Praise be to God, with gratitude, gratitude, and yet more gratitude! Praise to him who has caused our enemies to perish and brought to us our inheritance from Muhammad our Prophet, God's blessing and peace be upon him! O ye people, now are the dark nights of the world put to flight, its covering lifted, now light breaks in the earth and the heavens, and the sun rises from the springs of day while the moon ascends from its appointed place. He who fashioned the bow takes it up, and the arrow returns to him who shot it. Right has come back to where it originated, among the people of the house of your Prophet, people of compassion and mercy for you and sympathy toward you ... God has let you behold what you were awaiting and looking forward to. He has made manifest among you a caliph of the clan of Hashim, brightening thereby your faces and making you to prevail over the army of Syria, and transferring the sovereignty and the glory of Islam to you ... Has any successor to God's messenger ascended this your *minbar* save the Commander of the Faithful 'Ali ibn Abi Talib and the Commander of the Faithful 'Abd Allah ibn Muhammad? – and he gestured with his hand toward Abu'l-'Abbas.[2]

THE CALIPHATE OF BAGHDAD

One ruling family succeeded another, and Syria was replaced as centre of the Muslim caliphate by Iraq. The power of Abu'l-'Abbas (749–54) and his successors, known from their ancestor as 'Abbasids, lay less in the eastern Mediterranean countries, or in Hijaz which was an extension of them, than in the former Sasanian territories: southern Iraq and the oases and plateaux of Iran, Khurasan and the land stretching beyond it into central Asia. It was more difficult for the caliph to rule the Maghrib, but it was also less important.

In some ways 'Abbasid rule did not differ much from that of the later Umayyads. From the beginning they found themselves involved in the inescapable problem of a new dynasty: how to turn the limited power derived from an uneasy coalition of separate interests into something more stable and lasting. They had won their throne through a combination of forces united only in opposition to the Umayyads, and the relationships of strength within the coalition now had to be defined. First of all the new caliph rid himself of those through whom he had come to power; Abu Muslim and others were killed. There were conflicts too within the family itself; at first members were appointed as governors, but some of them grew too powerful, and within a generation a new ruling élite of high officials had been created. Some were drawn from Iranian families with a tradition of service to the state and newly converted to Islam, others from members of the ruler's household, some of them freed slaves.

This concentration of power in the hands of the ruler took place in the time of Abu'l-'Abbas's successors, particularly al-Mansur (754–75) and Harun al-Rashid (786–809), and it was expressed in the creation of a new capital, Baghdad. Al-Tabari records a story about Mansur's visit to the site of the future city:

he came to the area of the bridge and crossed at the present site of Qasr al-Salam. He then prayed the afternoon prayer. It was in summer, and at the site of the palace there was then a priest's church. He spent the night there, and awoke next morning having passed the sweetest and gentlest night on earth. He stayed, and everything he saw pleased him. Then he said, 'This is the site on which I shall build. Things can arrive here by way of the Euphrates, Tigris, and a network of canals. Only a place like this will support the army and the general populace.' So he laid it out and assigned monies for its construction, and laid the first brick with his own hand, saying, 'In the name of God, and praise to Him. The earth is God's; He causes to inherit of it whom He wills among His servants, and the result thereof is to them that fear Him.' Then he said, 'Build, and God bless you!'[3]

Baghdad was situated at a point where the Tigris and Euphrates flowed close to each other, and where a system of canals had created a rich countryside which could produce food for a large city and revenues for the government; it lay on strategic routes leading to Iran and beyond, to the

Jazira of northern Iraq where grain was produced, and to Syria and Egypt where Umayyad loyalties remained strong. Since it was a new city, the rulers could be free from the pressure exercised by the Arab Muslim inhabitants of Kufa and Basra. In accordance with a long tradition by which Near Eastern rulers kept themselves apart from those they ruled, the city was planned to express the splendour and distance of the ruler. At the centre, on the west bank of the Tigris, there lay the 'round city' of palace, barracks and offices; markets and quarters of residence lay outside it.

In his description of the reception of a Byzantine embassy by the Caliph al-Muqtadir in 917, the historian of Baghdad, al-Khatib al-Baghdadi (1002–71), evokes the splendour of the court and its ceremonial. Having been taken into the presence of the caliph, they were then by his command shown the palace: the halls, courts and parks, the soldiers, eunuchs, chamberlains and pages, the treasures in the store-chambers, elephants caparisoned in peacock-silk brocade. In the Room of the Tree, they saw

a tree, standing in the midst of a great circular tank filled with clear water. The tree has eighteen branches, every branch having numerous twigs, on which sit all sorts of gold and silver birds, both large and small. Most of the branches of this tree are of silver, but some are of gold, and they spread into the air carrying leaves of different colours. The leaves of the tree move as the wind blows, while the birds pipe and sing.

Finally they came once more into the presence of the caliph:

He was arrayed in clothes . . . embroidered in gold being seated on an ebony throne . . . To the right of the throne hung nine collars of gems . . . and to the left were the like, all of famous jewels . . . Before the caliph stood five of his sons, three to the right and two to the left.[4]

Within these secluded palaces, the caliph exercised power in accordance with forms inherited from earlier rulers and which other dynasties would imitate. An elaborate court ceremonial marked his splendour; court officials guarded access to him; the executioner stood near him to deal out summary justice. In the early reigns there emerged an office which was to become important, that of *wazir*: he was the adviser of the caliph, with varying degrees of influence, and later would become head of the administration and intermediary between it and the ruler.

The administration was divided into a number of offices or *diwans*, in a way which would appear again under other dynasties. There was a *diwan* for the affairs of the army, a chancery which drew up letters and documents in proper form and preserved them, and a treasury which supervised and kept records of revenue and expenditure. A ruler governing through a hierarchy of officials spread over a wide area had to make sure they did not become too strong or abuse the power they exercised in his name. A system of intelligence kept the caliph informed of what was happening in the provinces, and he and his governors held public sessions at which complaints could be heard and remedied.

Absolute rule mediated through a bureaucracy needed revenue and an army. It was in the 'Abbasid period that the canonical system of taxation emerged from the practices of the early Islamic times. It was linked as far as possible with Islamic norms. The main taxes were two. The first was levied on the land or its produce (*kharaj*); to begin with there had been a distinction between the rates and kind of taxes paid by Muslim and non-Muslim holders of land, but this became less important in practice, although it remained in the law books. The second was a poll tax levied on non-Muslims, graded roughly according to their wealth (*jizya*). In addition, various dues were levied on goods being imported or exported and on urban crafts, as well as occasional levies on urban wealth made according to need; these were officially condemned by those who adhered to the strict letter of Islamic law.

The soldiers of Khurasan through whom the 'Abbasids came to power were divided into groups under separate leaders. It was not easy for the caliphs to retain their loyalty, and they became less of an effective military force as they were drawn into the population of Baghdad. After the death of Harun al-Rashid there was a civil war between his sons al-Amin and al-Ma'mun. Amin was proclaimed caliph and the army of Baghdad fought for him but was defeated. In the early ninth century the need for an effective and loyal army was met by the purchase of slaves, and by recruiting soldiers from the Turkish-speaking pastoral tribes on or across the frontier in central Asia. These Turks, and other similar groups from the frontiers of settled government, were aliens who had no links with the society they helped to rule, and who stood in a relationship of personal clienthood to the caliph. The entry of Turkish soldiers in the 'Abbasid service began a process which was to give a distinctive shape to the political life of the world of Islam.

It was partly to keep the soldiers away from the population of Baghdad, who had become hostile to the caliph's rule, that al-Mu'tasim (833–42) moved his capital from Baghdad to a new city, Samarra, lying further north on the river Tigris. The seat of government remained there for half a century; but, although it was relieved of pressure from the populace, it fell under the influence of the leaders of the Turkish soldiers, who came to dominate the caliph's government. This was also a period when rulers of outlying provinces of the empire became virtually independent, and in Iraq itself the power of the caliph was threatened by a large and protracted revolt of black slaves in the sugar plantations and salt-marshes of southern Iraq: the revolt of the Zanj, 868–83. A few years later, in 892, the Caliph al-Mu'tadid returned to Baghdad.

The more remote and powerful the caliph, the more important it was for him to give his power roots in the moral sentiments of those he ruled. More systematically than the Umayyads, the 'Abbasids tried to justify their rule in Islamic terms. From the beginning they used religious symbols. The caliph claimed to rule by divine authority as a member of the Prophet's family. He claimed also to be governing in accordance with the Qur'an and the rules of right conduct, which were increasingly defined in terms of the Prophet's habitual behaviour (*sunna*). It was in line with this claim that religious specialists played some part in his rule, and the office of judge (*qadi*) was given greater importance. His functions were separated from those of the governor. He had no political or financial duties; his role was to decide conflicts and give decisions in the light of what was gradually emerging as a system of Islamic law or social norms. The chief *qadi* was a dignitary of some importance in the hierarchy of state.

In putting forward their claim to be legitimate rulers, the early 'Abbasids had to meet that of another branch of the Prophet's family, the descendants of 'Ali, and their supporters, the Shi'is. Not all the Shi'is were hostile to 'Abbasid rule; Ja'far al-Sadiq (*c.* 700–65), whom they regarded as the sixth *imam*, was a quietist who taught his followers passive resistance until the advent of the *mahdi*, the one whom God would send to restore the reign of religion and justice. In the first two generations of 'Abbasid rule, however, there were various movements of revolt using the names of members of 'Ali's family, and it was in answer to such movements that the son of Harun, Ma'mun (813–33), made two attempts to give himself a firmer title to rule. The first was to proclaim 'Ali al-Rida, regarded by many Shi'is as the eighth *imam*, as his successor; the argument used was that he was the worthiest member of the Prophet's family to succeed and this had the implication that, if succession was to go by moral worth within the family, then in principle the descendants of 'Abbas had as much right as those of 'Ali. Later, Ma'mun gave his support to the ideas of certain Mu'tazili theologians and tried to make their acceptance a condition of official service. This attempt met with opposition from those theologians, led by

Ahmad ibn Hanbal, who held that the Qur'an and the habitual behaviour of the Prophet, literally interpreted, offered sufficient guidance. After a period of persecution, the attempt to impose a single interpretation of the faith by the power of the ruler was ended, almost never to be resumed. The belief in a unity which includes differences of legal opinion, and in the importance of the Qur'an and the practice (*sunna*) of the Prophet as the bases of it, gradually created a mode of thought which came to be known generally as Sunnism, as distinct from Shi'ism.

CHAPTER 3

The Formation of a Society

THE END OF POLITICAL UNITY

Even when the 'Abbasid caliph's power was at its height, his effective rule was limited. It existed mainly in the cities and the productive areas around them; there were distant regions of mountain and steppe which were virtually unsubdued. As time went on, his authority was caught in the contradictions of centralized, bureaucratic systems of government. In order to rule his far-flung provinces, the caliph had to give his governors the power to collect taxes and use part of the proceeds to maintain local forces. He tried to keep control of them by a system of intelligence, but could not prevent some of the governors building up their own positions to the point where they were able to hand power on to their own families, while remaining – at least in principle – loyal to the major interests of their suzerain. In this way local dynasties grew up, such as those of the Saffarids in eastern Iran (867–c. 1495), the Samanids in Khurasan (819–1005), the Tulunids in Egypt (868–905), and the Aghlabids in Tunisia (800–909); from Tunisia the Aghlabids conquered Sicily, which continued to be ruled by Arab dynasties until taken by the Normans in the second half of the eleventh century. As this happened, less revenue flowed to Baghdad, at a time when there was a certain decline in the system of irrigation and agricultural production in lower Iraq itself. In order to strengthen his position in the central provinces, the caliph had to rely more upon his professional army, whose leaders in their turn acquired greater power over him. In 945 one family of military leaders, the Buyids, who came from the fringe of the Caspian Sea, having seized control of some of the provinces, took power in Baghdad itself.

The Buyids assumed various titles, including the ancient Iranian title of *shahanshah* ('King of Kings'), but not that of caliph. The 'Abbasids were to remain for three more centuries, but a new phase began in their history.

From now on, effective power in the central regions of the empire lay in the hands of other dynasties supported by military groups, but they continued to recognize the caliphate of the 'Abbasids, who at times could reassert a residual authority. That authority was exercised over a more limited area than before, however, and there were some parts of the former empire where the local rulers not only had power but did not accept even the formal authority of the 'Abbasids.

In certain regions there were movements of opposition and separation in the name of some dissident form of Islam. Such movements resulted in the creation of separate political units, but at the same time they helped the spread of Islam by giving it a form which did not disturb the social order.

Some of these were movements in the name of Kharijism, or at least of one of its offshoots, that of the Ibadis. The belief that the office of head of the community or *imam* should be held by the person most worthy, who if he showed himself unworthy should be removed, was well suited to the needs of loose collections of tribal groups living in secluded places, who might need a leader or arbitrator from time to time but did not want him to have a permanent and organized power. Thus an Ibadi *imamate* emerged in Oman ('Uman) in south-eastern Arabia from the middle of the eighth until the end of the ninth century, when it was suppressed by the 'Abbasids. In parts of the Maghrib, some of the Berber population resisted the coming of Islamic rule, and when they did become Muslims Khariji ideas spread among them. For a time there was a powerful dynasty of Ibadi *imams*, that of the Rustamids, with their capital at Tahart in western Algeria (777–909); their claims were also recognized by the Ibadis in 'Uman.

More widespread were movements of support for the claims of the descendants of 'Ali ibn Abi Talib to the *imamate*. The main body of Shi'is, in and around Iraq, accepted 'Abbasid rule, or at least acquiesced in it. The *imams* whom they recognized lived quietly under the 'Abbasids, although at times they were under confinement in the capital. The Buyids were Shi'is in some vague sense, but did not challenge the suzerainty of the caliphs; this was also true of the local dynasty of the Hamdanids in northern Syria (905–1004).

There were other Shi'i movements, however, which ended in the creation of separate dynasties. The Zaydis held that the *imam* should be the worthiest member of the Prophet's family who was willing to oppose illegitimate rulers. They did not recognize Muhammad al-Baqir (d. 731), who was acknowledged by the main body of Shi'is as the fifth *imam*, but his brother Zayd instead (hence their name). They created an *imamate* in

Yemen in the ninth century, and there was also a Zaydi *imamate* in the region of the Caspian Sea.

A more direct challenge to the 'Abbasids came from movements linked with another branch of Shi'ism, the Isma'ilis. Their origins are not clear, but they seem to have begun as a secret movement with its centre first in Iraq and Khuzistan in south-western Iran, and then in Syria. It supported the claim to the *imamate* of Isma'il, the eldest son of Ja'far al-Sadiq who is regarded by the main body of Shi'is as the sixth *imam*. Isma'il died in 760, five years before his father, and the majority of Shi'is eventually recognized his brother Musa al-Kazim (d. 799) as *imam*. The Isma'ilis, however, believed that Isma'il had been irrevocably appointed as successor to his father, and that his son Muhammad had become *imam* after him. They held that Muhammad would return sooner or later as the *mahdi*, sent to disclose the inner meaning of the Qur'anic revelation and to rule the world with justice.

The movement organized missionary activities on a large scale. One group of its adherents created a kind of republic in eastern Arabia, that of the Qaramita (Carmathians), and another established themselves in the Maghrib, enlisted Berber soldiers and occupied Qayrawan. In 910 there arrived in Tunisia 'Ubaydullah, claiming to be descended from 'Ali and Fatima. He proclaimed himself caliph, and in the next half-century his family created a stable dynasty which was given the name of Fatimids after the Prophet's daughter Fatima. Both for religious and for political reasons it moved eastwards towards the 'Abbasid lands, and in 969 occupied Egypt. From there it extended its rule into western Arabia and Syria, but it soon lost Tunisia.

The Fatimids used both the titles *imam* and caliph. As *imams* they claimed universal authority over Muslims, and their state became a centre from which missionaries were sent. Long after the Fatimid state ceased to exist, communities created by those who had connections with it continued: in Yemen, Syria, Iran and later in western India.

The Fatimids were not only *imams*, but rulers of a great state with its centre in the Nile valley. Cairo was their creation, an imperial city built to the north of Fustat, and the symbol of their power and independence. Their government followed the lines set by the caliphate in Baghdad. Power was concentrated in the hands of the caliph and expressed through magnificence and elaborate ceremonial. It was the practice of the Fatimid caliphs to show themselves to the people of Cairo in solemn processions. The great officers of state would enter the hall of the palace; the caliph would come from behind a curtain, holding his sceptre in his hands; he would mount his horse and proceed to the palace gate, where all the trumpets would sound. Preceded and followed by his entourage and soldiers, he would ride through streets adorned by the merchants with brocades and fine linen. The processions expressed both aspects of Fatimid rule. Some of them were religious, while others showed the identification of the ruler with the life of the city and the river.

The basis of Fatimid power was the revenue from the fertile lands of the Nile delta and valley, the crafts of the cities, and trade in the Mediterranean basin as well as the Red Sea. This was sufficient to maintain an army drawn from outside Egypt: Berbers, blacks from the Sudan, and Turks. The caliph made no systematic attempt to impose the Isma'ili doctrines on Egyptian Muslims, who remained for the most part Sunnis, with large Christian and Jewish populations living on the whole in peaceful symbiosis with them.

The Fatimid claim to the caliphate was a direct challenge to the 'Abbasids; another challenge, both to 'Abbasids and Fatimids, came from the far west of the Muslim world. The regions, conquered by the Arabs, Morocco and most of Spain, were difficult to control from the eastern Mediterranean, and impossible from Iraq. The Arab soldiers and officials there soon acquired interests of their own, and could easily express them in terms which revived memories of the impulse which had taken them so far from Arabia. Towards the end of the eighth century, Idris, a great-grandson of 'Ali, went to Morocco, won support there and founded a dynasty which was important in the history of Morocco, for the Idrisids built Fez and began a tradition which has lasted until today, of independent dynasties ruling Morocco and justifying their rule by claims to descent from the Prophet.

More important for the history of the Muslim world as a whole was the separate path taken by Spain, or Andalus, to give it its Arabic name. The Arabs first landed in Spain in 710 and soon created there a province of the caliphate which extended as far as the north of the peninsula. The Arabs and Berbers of the first settlement were joined by a second wave of soldiers from Syria, who were to play an important part, for after the 'Abbasid revolution a member of the Umayyad family was able to take refuge in Spain and found supporters there. A new Umayyad dynasty was created and ruled for almost three hundred years, although it was not until the middle of the tenth century that the ruler took the title of caliph.

In their new kingdom the Umayyads were involved in the same process of change as took place in the east. A society where Muslims ruled over a non-Muslim majority gradually changed into one where a considerable part of the population accepted the religion and language of the rulers, and a government which ruled at first in a decentralized way, by political manipulation, became a powerful centralized one ruling by bureaucratic control.

Once more a new capital was created: Cordoba, lying on the river Guadalquivir. The river provided the waterway to bring the bulk goods needed for food and industry; in the plains around it, the grain and other produce the city needed were grown on irrigated land. Cordoba was also a meeting place of roads and a market for the exchange of produce between regions. Once more, as the dynasty became more autocratic it withdrew from the life of the city. The ruler moved from Cordoba to a royal city, Madinat al-Zahra, some way outside the capital. There he reigned in state, surrounded by a ruling group which included Arab and arabized families – for the separation of rulers from society was not so great as in Baghdad – but which also had an element drawn from slaves imported from the Black Sea region, Italy and elsewhere. The army too had a core of mercenaries from abroad, although it also included Arabs and Berbers settled on the land in return for military service.

As in Syria, the Umayyads, townspeople from their origins in Hijaz, used their power to further the interests of the towns and settled countryside. The cities grew – first Cordoba and later Seville – supported by irrigated land, from which a surplus was produced by techniques imported from the Near East. In these areas Arabs were important as landowners and cultivators, although much of the indigenous population remained. Beyond the irrigated plains, in the highlands, Berber immigrants from the mountains of the Maghrib lived by small-scale agriculture and the pasturing of sheep.

The movement of Berbers from the Maghrib into Spain continued longer than Arab immigration from the east, and was probably larger. In time, too, part of the indigenous population was converted to Islam and by the end of the tenth century possibly a majority of the people of Andalus were Muslims; but side by side with them lived those who did not convert, Christians and a considerable Jewish population of craftsmen and traders. The different groups were held together by the tolerance of the Umayyads towards Jews and Christians, and also by the spread of the Arabic language, which had become that of the majority, Jews and Christians as well as Muslims, by the eleventh century. Toleration, a common language and a long tradition of separate rule all helped to create a distinctive Andalusian consciousness and society. Its Islamic religious culture developed on rather different lines from those of the eastern countries, and its Jewish culture too became independent of that of Iraq, the main centre of Jewish religious life.

It was therefore not only the interests of the dynasty but also the separate identity of Andalus which was expressed by the assumption of the title of caliph by 'Abd al-Rahman III (912–61). His reign marks the height of the independent power of the Umayyads of Spain. Soon afterwards, in the eleventh century, their kingdom was to splinter into a number of smaller ones ruled by Arab or Berber dynasties (the 'party kings' or 'kings of factions', *muluk al-tawa'if*), by a process similar to that which was taking place in the 'Abbasid Empire.

A UNIFIED SOCIETY: THE ECONOMIC BASES

The disappearance of a unitary structure of government, in east and west, was not a sign of social or cultural weakness. By now there had been created a Muslim world held together by many links, and with many centres of power and high culture.

The absorption of such a large area into a single empire had in due course created an economic unit important not only by its size but because it linked together two great sea basins of the civilized world, those of the Mediterranean and the Indian Ocean. The movement of armies, merchants, craftsmen, scholars and pilgrims between them became easier, and also that of ideas, styles and techniques. Within this vast sphere of interaction it was possible for there to grow up strong governments, large cities, international trade and a flourishing countryside, maintaining the conditions for each other's existence.

The creation of the Muslim Empire, and then of states within its former territories, led to the growth of large cities, where palaces, governments and urban populations needed foodstuffs, raw materials for manufacture, and luxuries to display wealth and power, and where the changes and complexities of city life led to a desire for novelty and for imitation of the fashions of the powerful or the stranger. Urban demand and the relative ease of communications gave new directions and methods of organization to the long-distance trade which had always existed. Very bulky goods could not profitably be carried a very long way, and for most of its food the city had to look to its immediate hinterland; but on some goods the return was such as to justify their being carried over long distances. Pepper and other spices, precious stones, fine cloth and porcelain came from India and China, furs from the northern countries; coral, ivory and textiles were sent in return. The Middle Eastern cities were not only consumers but producers of manufactured goods for export as well as their own use. Some of the production was on a large scale – armaments of war produced in state arsenals, fine textiles for the palace, sugar refineries and paper mills – but most took place in small workshops for textiles or metalwork.

Before the coming of the railway and then the motor-car in modern times, transport by water was cheaper, quicker and safer than by land. To feed its inhabitants it was almost essential for a large city to lie near a sea or a navigable river, and the main routes of long-distance trade too were sea-routes, in this period particularly those of the Indian Ocean. Under the 'Abbasids the main organizing centres for trade on these routes were Basra in lower Iraq and Siraf on the Iranian coast of the Persian Gulf, both of them lying within 'Abbasid control and in a position to meet the demands of the capital. By the tenth century there was a certain shift of trade from the Gulf to the Red Sea, because of the rise of Cairo as a centre of trade and power and a growing demand from the trading cities of Italy, but this was only a beginning.

From Basra and Siraf, trade with the east was mainly carried on by Iranian, Arab or Jewish merchants, on Arab ships sailing to the ports of western India or even beyond; at one time they went as far as China, but after the tenth century they did not go further than ports of south-east Asia. They went southwards also, to southern and western Arabia and east Africa. From Basra goods could be carried by river to Baghdad, and then onwards by the Syrian desert routes to Syria and Egypt, or through Anatolia to Constantinople and Trebizond, or by the great route which went from Baghdad to Nishapur in north-eastern Iran and thence to central Asia and China. Over long distances goods were carried on camel-back in large, well-organized caravans, over shorter distances by mule or donkey. In the greater part of the Near East wheeled transport disappeared after the rise of the Muslim Empire, not to come back until the nineteenth century, and various reasons have been suggested for this: the Roman roads decayed, the new Arab ruling groups had an interest in the rearing of camels, and transport on camel-back was more economical than by cart.

Trade in the Mediterranean was at first more precarious and limited. Western Europe had not yet reached the point of recovery where it produced much for export or could absorb much, and the Byzantine Empire tried for a time to restrict Arab naval power and seaborne commerce. The most important trade was that which went along the southern coast, linking Spain and the Maghrib with Egypt and Syria, with Tunisia as the entrepôt. Along this route merchants, many of them Jews, organized trade in Spanish silk, gold brought from west Africa, metals and olive oil. Later, in the tenth century, trade with Venice and Amalfi began to be important.

Strong governments and large cities could not live without a productive countryside, but the countryside in its turn could not flourish unless there were a strong government and cities to invest in production. In the countries conquered by the Arabs, and particularly those where there was a large Arab immigration, a new land-holding class grew up. Land which had been taken from previous owners and formally belonged to the ruler was granted to Arabs with the obligation of paying taxes; later, in the tenth century, an arrangement began to grow up by which the collection of taxes on pieces of land was given to officials or army commanders, who by this means became virtual owners and had an interest in maintaining production. To a great extent the cultivators who had been there before continued to look after work on the land, although in some places peasants and herdsmen migrated. Such evidence as exists indicates that the relations between land-holders and cultivators were those of sharecropping, in one form or another: after payment of tax, the produce was divided in agreed proportions between those who contributed the land, seed, animals and labour. There were more complicated arrangements for irrigated land, or that on which trees were to be planted.

Land-holders who accumulated money in trade or other ways could use it for agricultural production, and with the help of their capital new techniques were brought in. There is evidence that the expansion of the Muslim Empire brought new crops, or at least led to the extension of those already known. In general the movement was westwards, from China or India by way of Iran into the Mediterranean basin: rice, sugar-cane, cotton, watermelons, aubergines, oranges and lemons were cultivated over a wide area. Some of these crops needed large investment in irrigation and the improvement of land. Old irrigation works were restored, for example those in southern Iraq, and new ones made. The westward movement can be seen in Spain, which acquired the water-wheel (na'ura, noria) from Syria and the underground canal (qanat) from Iran; new methods of crop-rotation also came into Spain.

By such improvements the agricultural surplus was enlarged and this, together with the growth of manufacture and trade, increased the importance of money in the economy of the Near East and the Mediterranean basin. An internationally recognized monetary system grew up. The flow of precious metals, and particularly of African gold, into the lands of the caliphate made possible an expansion of the coinage; the 'Abbasid gold dinar remained an instrument of exchange for centuries, and Islamic silver coins have been found in Scandinavia and in Wychwood Forest north of Oxford. Connected with the development of coinage was that of a system of credit. Large merchants would take deposits and make loans; money-lenders and tax-collectors also would use their accumulated cash for loans. Merchants who had correspondents or clients in other places would draw bills upon them or issue letters of credit.

A complex and farflung economy could not have existed without a system of shared expectations between those who had to deal with one another without personal contact or knowledge. Family ties could provide these in some instances, for example among the Jewish merchants who travelled over the Mediterranean world and beyond, crossing the frontiers between Muslim and Christian countries. If such ties did not exist, there was a need for laws or norms of social morality generally recognized. In the same way, land-holders and cultivators needed clear and accepted rules about property, the division of produce, taxation, and rights over water, trees and minerals beneath the ground.

Economic relations thus demanded a common system of behaviour, and this became possible as more and more of the population of lands ruled by Muslims became Muslims themselves, and as the implications for social life of the revelation given to Muhammad were drawn out.

UNITY OF FAITH AND LANGUAGE

It is not easy to discover much about the stages by which the subject peoples became Muslims, but a study based on the evidence of adoption of specifically Muslim names has suggested orders of magnitude which seem plausible.[1] According to this estimate, by the end of the Umayyad period (that is to say, in the middle years of the second Islamic and eighth Christian century) less than 10 per cent of the population of Iran and Iraq, Syria and Egypt, Tunisia and Spain was Muslim, although the proportion must have been much greater in the Arabian peninsula. Apart from the Arab tribes who had already been in Iraq and Syria before the Muslim conquest, most converts may have come either from the lower ranks of society – for example, soldiers captured in battle – or from officials of the Sasanian government who took service with the new rulers; there was no pressure or positive incentive for others to convert. The converts lived for the most part in or near the main urban centres of Arab population and power, where there were the beginnings of specifically Islamic institutions – the mosque, the law court – and it was these cities, those of Iraq and Iran, Qayrawan in Africa and Cordoba in Spain, which served as centres for the radiation of Islam.

By the end of the fourth Islamic century (the tenth century AD), the picture had changed. A large part of the population had become Muslim. Not only the townspeople but a considerable number of the rural people must have been converted. One reason for this may have been that Islam had become more clearly defined, and the line between Muslims and non-Muslims more sharply drawn. Muslims now lived within an elaborated system of ritual, doctrine and law clearly different from those of non-Muslims; they were more conscious of themselves as Muslims. The status of Christians, Jews and Zoroastrians was more precisely defined, and in some ways it was inferior. They were regarded as 'People of the Book', those who possessed a revealed scripture, or 'People of the Covenant', with whom compacts of protection had been made (the so-called Pact of 'Umar). In general they were not forced to convert, but they suffered from restrictions. They paid a special tax; they were not supposed to wear certain colours; they could not marry Muslim women; their evidence was not accepted against that of Muslims in the law courts; their houses or places of worship should not be ostentatious; they were excluded from positions of power (although in various places Jews and Christians worked as secretaries or financial officials for Muslim rulers). How seriously such rules were applied depended on local conditions, but even in the best circumstances the position of a minority is uneasy, and the inducement to convert existed.

The process of conversion was not complete, however. Jews had been excluded from the greater part of the Arabian peninsula in the early days of Islam, but they continued to be present in the great cities of other Muslim countries as merchants and craftsmen, and also as small traders in some country districts: northern Iraq, Yemen, Morocco. That they survived and flourished was due not only to the strength of their communal organization but to their being able to occupy certain economic positions in the interstices of a complex society, and also to their not being identified with any of the states with which Muslim rulers were at war from time to time.

The situation of Christians was not the same. Some had religious links with the Byzantine Empire, and may have incurred suspicion in times of war. They did not have the same close-knit communal organization as the Jews; in parts of the countryside they may not have been deeply Christian. In some places Christianity died out completely, although not for a long time; in others it remained as the faith of a minority. In Spain a large part of the population continued to belong to the Roman Catholic Church; elsewhere, those who survived tended to belong to dissident churches which had broken off from the main body because of the great controversies in the first centuries about the nature of the Christ: Nestorians, Monophysites, Monotheletes. Christians lived not only in the cities, but in parts of the countryside, especially upper Egypt, the Lebanese mountains and northern Iraq.

The Arabic language spread together with Islam, or even before it in some places. In inner Syria and western Iraq much of the population already spoke Arabic at the time of the Muslim conquest. The new cities, with their immigrant populations and their governments dominated by Arabs, served as centres for a wider radiation of the language. It spread both as a spoken language, in various local dialects influenced by the previous vernacular languages, and as a written one in a form of which the unity and continuity were preserved by the Qur'an, the book sent down in the Arabic language.

So far as the language of speech was concerned, Arabic came up against a frontier in Iran, where use of the Persian language continued. As a written language, however, Arabic found no frontier within the world of Islam. The religion carried the language with it. Converts of non-Arab origin, and particularly Iranians, read the Qur'an in Arabic and played a large part in articulating the system of thought and law which grew out of it. Those who were not converted continued to use their own languages for religious and literary purposes: the liturgies of some of the eastern Churches still retained Syriac and Coptic; Hebrew and Aramaic were the languages of Jewish worship and religious learning; the Zoroastrian scriptures received their final shape in Pahlavi, the form of Persian used before the conquest, after the coming of Islam. Even here, however, a change took place: Arabic became a language of worship and religious literature in some of the eastern Churches; Jews in Spain came to use Arabic for philosophy, science and poetry. The first serious check to the spread of Arabic took place in the ninth century, when Persian began to emerge in an islamized form as a literary language; but in Iran too Arabic continued to be the main language of religious and legal learning.

Thus in the writing of this period words like 'Arab' and 'Arabic' take on broader meanings which overshadowed the older ones. They may refer to those whose origin lay in the Arabian peninsula, and in particular those who could claim to belong to the nomadic tribes with a military tradition; or they may be used in connection with all those, from Morocco and Spain to the frontier of Iran, who had adopted Arabic as their vernacular language; or in a sense they may extend even further, to those for whom Arabic had become the principal medium of expression of a high literary culture.

Under the Umayyads the tradition of poetic composition continued to flourish, and the most famous poets of the early period were still of Arab beduin origin: Akhtal, Farazdaq, Jarir. There was a difference, however: the patronage of courts – that of the Umayyads themselves in Damascus, but also those of powerful tribal leaders – extended the geographical range of poetry and also tended to change its nature. Panegyrics of rulers and powerful men became more prominent, and at the same time the poetry of love, the *ghazal*, acquired a more personal note.

In the later Umayyad period, and in the early period of 'Abbasid rule, a more fundamental change took place. The coming of Islam altered the way in which people looked at the Arabic language. The Qur'an was the first book to be written in Arabic, and Muslims believed it was the language in which it had been revealed. It was expressed in the high language in which the poetry of earlier times had been composed, but which was now used for a different purpose. It was essential for those who accepted the Qur'an as the Word of God to understand its language; for them, the ancient poetry was not only the *diwan* of the Arabs, it was also the norm of correct language.

Arabic was now becoming the medium of expression not only for those who came into the various regions of the empire from the Arabian peninsula, but for those of other origins who accepted the religion of Islam, or who needed at least to use the language for purposes of work or life, and in particular for the Persian and other officials who served the new rulers. The centre of literary activity moved from the oasis towns and tribal encampments to the new cities: Basra and Kufa at first, and then the new imperial capital, Baghdad. The literary milieu changed and expanded, to include the caliphs and their courts, the high officials, and the new urban élite of mixed origins. Although the practice of oral composition and recitation of poetry may well have continued, literary works began to be written down, and from the beginning of the ninth century the circulation of written works was aided by the introduction of paper. Previously papyrus and parchment had been used, but in the later part of the eighth century the technique of making paper was brought from China. Manufactured at first in Khurasan, it spread to other parts of the empire, and by the middle of the tenth century had more or less replaced papyrus.

It was a natural effect of the spread of the Arabic language that some of those who used it should wish to understand it. The sciences of language were largely created by those for whom Arabic was an acquired tongue and who therefore had to think about it: lexicography, the collection and classification of words, was developed by scholars frequenting the market places where beduin came; grammar, the explanation of the way in which Arabic worked, was first systematically expounded by a man of non-Arab origin, Sibawayh (d. 793), from whose writings all later works were derived. The same impulse led scholars to collect and study the ancient poetry of Arabia. In the process of editing the poems they must have changed them, and at the same time formal principles of poetic composition were elaborated, and these were to have much influence upon later poets. The first important literary theorist, Ibn Qutayba (828–89), produced a description of the typical *qasida* which later poets were to take into account: the *qasida*, he suggested, should begin with the evocation of lost dwelling places and lost love, continue with the description of a journey, and culminate in the real subject, panegyric, elegy or satire.

The writings of theorists were perhaps of less importance in the development of poetry than the practice of poets of new kinds. Their poetry was more individual than that of the authors of the pre-Islamic *quasidas*. Some were of non-Arab origin, living in cities, aware of the poetic tradition which they inherited but using it with a self-conscious literary artistry. A new style grew up, the *badi'*, marked by the use of elaborate language and rhetorical figures: a rare vocabulary was used, words were set in antithesis to each other, and all was expressed within the rigid framework of metres and rhymes which had marked the earlier poetry.

The subjects of poetry were more varied than before. Poets wrote of erotic love, not simply formalized regret for the lost or forbidden beloved. Some of them took part in the religious and ethical controversies of the early Islamic centuries: a Syrian poet, Abu'l-'Ala al-Ma'arri (973–1057), wrote poems and an elaborate prose-work in which doubt was cast on generally accepted ideas about revelation and life after death.

It was natural that a special emphasis should be placed upon panegyric, the praise not so much of the poet's tribe as of the ruler or patron. In the panegyric, the first part of what Ibn Qutayba had regarded as the typical *qasida* shrank and became simply an introduction to the main subject; the ruler or patron would be praised in elaborate and formal language, through which there might sometimes appear the personality of the poet and his feelings.

Al-Mutanabbi (915–68) was acknowledged by later literary critics as the supreme master of this kind of poetry. Born in Kufa, of Arab origin, he spent some of his early years among the Arab tribe of Banu Qalb. He passed part of his youth in political activity, and his later years as court-poet to a succession of rulers, in Aleppo, Cairo, Baghdad and Shiraz. Perhaps his most fruitful years were those during which he was poet to the Hamdanid ruler of Aleppo and northern Syria, Sayf al-Dawla. The ruler is praised in terms of hyperbole. On his recovery from illness, his poet declared:

Glory and honour were healed when you were healed, and pain passed from you to your enemies . . . Light, which had left the sun, as if its loss were a sickness in the body, returned to it . . . The Arabs are unique in the world in being of his race, but foreigners share with Arabs in his beneficence . . . It is not you alone I congratulate on your recovery; when you are well all men are well.[2]

Mingled with this, however, there is a strain of self-praise, as in a poem written when, as he thought, Sayf al-Dawla had transferred his favour to another:

O most just of men, except in your treatment of me, my quarrel is with you, and you are both my adversary and my judge . . . I am he of whom even the blind can see what he has written, and who has caused even the deaf to listen to his words. I sleep with my eyelids closed to the words which wander abroad, while other men are sleepless because of them, and compete with each other . . . with what language do the riff-raff, neither Arabs nor Persians, proclaim their poetry before you? This is a reproach to you, but it is done with love; it is inlaid with pearls, but they are my words.[3]

The poets were continuing an old tradition, but the writing of Arabic prose was something new. the Qur'an was the first prose work composed in the high Arabic language (or at least the first which has survived), and the production of others was in a sense a natural consequence of it. Stories about the Prophet and the victories of the Arabs were collected and written down, and popular preachers created a rhetoric of Islamic themes. Rather later, a new kind of artistic prose emerged, exploring themes taken from other cultures; one of the earliest and most famous examples of this was

Kalila wa Dimna, a collection of moralistic fables of animal life, derived ultimately from Sanskrit by way of Pahlavi and put into Arabic prose by an 'Abbasid official of Iranian origin, Ibn al-Muqaffa' (*c.* 720–56).

He was an example of the arabized and islamized secretaries who were bringing into Arabic ideas and literary genres derived from their own inherited tradition, but side by side with them was another group of writers who drew their inspiration from the vast world which had been brought into existence by the spread of Islam and its empire: the multiplicity of peoples and countries, the new variety of human characters, the new problems of morality and behaviour. They tried to see these in the light of the norms of the new Islamic faith, and to express them in an agreeable literary form. Among the practitioners of this new kind of literature or *adab*, al-Jahiz (776/7–868/9) stands out as a writer of exceptional range and vividness of response, expressed in an exemplary language. His roots lay in one of the African families, of slave origin, who were attached to Arab tribes but had long been completely arabized. He was brought up in Basra, but later had the patronage of the Caliph al-Ma'mun. His intellectual curiosity was far-reaching, and his works are collections of rare and interesting knowledge concerning the human and natural world: countries, animals, the oddness of human beings. Beneath it there runs a vein of moral commentary: on friendship and love, envy and pride, avarice, falsity and sincerity:

A man who is noble does not pretend to be noble, any more than an eloquent man feigns eloquence. When a man exaggerates his qualities it is because of something lacking in himself; the bully gives himself airs because he is conscious of his weakness. Pride is ugly in all men . . . it is worse than cruelty, which is the worst of sins, and humility is better than clemency, which is the best of good deeds.[4]

The *adab* which developed in the early 'Abbasid period was intended to edify and to entertain. A *qadi* of Baghdad, al-Tanukhi (940–94), wrote three volumes of tales which are both a literary entertainment and a series of social documents about the world of ministers, judges and lesser dignitaries who surrounded the 'Abbasid court. In the next century Abu Hayyan al-Tawhidi (d. 1023) wrote essays and treatises on a wide range of topics which were fashionable among the scholars and writers of his age; composed in an attractive literary style, they reveal wide knowledge and a distinguished mind. Entertainment was the main purpose of the *maqamat*: a sequence of narratives written in rhymed prose (*saj'*), in which a narrator tells stories of a trickster or vagabond encountered in a variety of situations.

Brought to a high peak of development by al-Hamadhani (968–1110) and al-Hariri (1054–1122), this genre was to remain popular in Arab literary circles until the twentieth century.

The record of what has happened in the past is important in all human societies, but it has a special significance in communities founded on the belief that unique events occurred at certain times and in certain places. Before the rise of Islam, Arab tribes had their own oral records of the deeds of their ancestors, and to some extent these are embodied in the poems which have come down to us from that period. In the early centuries of Islam, history acquired a new kind of importance and began to be recorded in writing. Two different kinds of historical writings developed, closely connected with each other. On the one hand, philologists and genealogists collected and wrote down the oral history of Arab tribesmen; these were not only important for the study of the Arabic language, but might also provide important evidence relevant to practical questions about the distribution of booty from the conquests or of lands in the new settlements. On the other hand, it was even more important to record the events of the Prophet's life, the early caliphs, the first conquests and the public affairs of the Muslim community. Transmitted by responsible scholars, sometimes changed or even invented in the course of political and theological controversies, embroidered by storytellers, a mass of narratives was gradually formed, and out of this several kinds of literature emerged: collections of *hadiths*; biographies of the Prophet; collections of lives of transmitters of *hadiths*; and finally works of narrative history, recording the *gesta Dei*, God's providence for His community – these contained an element of exemplary narrative, but a solid core of truth. The invention of the Islamic calendar, providing a chronology dating from the *hijra*, gave a framework within which events could be recorded.

The tradition of history-writing came to its maturity in the ninth century, with the appearance of histories of broader scope and greater power of understanding: those of al-Baladhuri (d. 892), al-Tabari (839–923), and al-Mas'udi (d. 928). Such writers took the whole of Islamic history as their subject, and sometimes the whole of what they considered to be significant human history. Thus Mas'udi deals with the annals of the seven ancient peoples whom he regards as having had a real history: the Persians, Chaldaeans, Greeks, Egyptians, Turks, Indians and Chinese. The mass of information had to be ordered: in the case of Islamic history by years, in others by such criteria as the reigns of kings. It also had to be judged by critical standards. The most obvious criterion was that provided by the *isnad*: what was the chain of witnesses to a certain event, and how far could their testimony be trusted? There were other criteria, however: a transmitted record could be regarded as plausible or not in the light of a general understanding of how rulers acted and how human societies changed.

Another writer, al-Biruni (973–c. 1050), is unique in the range of his interests and understanding. His famous *Tahqiq ma li'l-Hind* (*History of India*) is perhaps the greatest sustained attempt by a Muslim writer to go beyond the world of Islam and appropriate what was of value in another cultural tradition. His work is not a polemic, as he himself makes clear in his foreword:

This is not a book of controversy and debate, putting forward the arguments of an opponent and distinguishing what is false in them from what is true. It is a straightforward account, giving the statements of Hindus and adding to them what the Greeks have said on similar subjects, so as to make a comparison between them.[5]

Indian religious and philosophical thought is depicted at its best:

Since we are describing what there is in India, we mention their superstitions, but we should point out that these are matters for the common people only. Those who follow the way of salvation or the path of reason and argument, and who want the truth, would avoid worshipping anyone except God alone, or any graven image of him.[6]

Ultimately, he points out, the beliefs of Hindus are similar to those of Greeks; among them too the common people worshipped idols, in the days of religious ignorance before the coming of Christianity, but the educated had views similar to those of Hindus. In one way, however, even the Hindu élite differed from Muslims:

The Indians in our time make numerous distinctions among human beings. We differ from them in this, for we regard all men as equal except in piety. This is the greatest barrier between them and Islam.[7]

THE ISLAMIC WORLD

By the third and fourth Islamic centuries (the ninth or tenth century AD) something which was recognizably an 'Islamic world' had emerged. A traveller around the world would have been able to tell, by what he saw and heard, whether a land was ruled and peopled by Muslims. These external forms had been carried by movements of peoples: by dynasties and their armies, merchants moving through the worlds of the Indian Ocean and the Mediterranean Sea, and craftsmen attracted from one city to another by the patronage of rulers or the rich. They were carried also by imported and exported objects expressing a certain style: books, metalwork, ceramics and particularly perhaps textiles, the staple of long-distance trade.

The great buildings above all were the external symbols of this 'world of Islam'. At a later period regional styles of mosque building would appear, but in the early centuries there were some common features to be found from Cordoba to Iraq and beyond. In addition to the great mosques were smaller ones for bazaars, quarters or villages, where prayer was offered but the Friday sermon was not preached; these were likely to be built of local materials and reflect local tastes and traditions.

The mosque by now could lie at the centre of a whole system of religious buildings, the house where the *qadi* gave justice, hostels for wayfarers or pilgrims, and hospitals for the sick; to found and maintain these were works of charity enjoined by the Qur'an. There was another kind of building which played a special part in binding together the Muslim community beyond the bounds of a single city or region. This was the shrine. Certain shrines marked places of pilgrimage and prayer taken over from earlier religious traditions and given an Islamic meaning: the Ka'ba in Mecca, the Dome of the Rock in Jerusalem, the tomb of Abraham at Hebron. Side by side with them there grew up new points of attraction: the tombs of those associated with the early history of Islam. Although Muslims regarded Muhammad as a man like others, the idea became accepted that he would intercede for his people on the Day of Judgement, and Muslims would visit his tomb in Madina during the pilgrimage to Mecca. The Shi'i *imams*, particularly those who had suffered, attracted pilgrims from an early time; the tomb of 'Ali at Najaf has elements dating from the ninth century. Gradually the tombs of those who were regarded as being 'friends of God' and having powers of intercession with Him multiplied throughout the Muslim world; no doubt some of them grew up in places regarded as holy by earlier religions or by the immemorial tradition of the countryside.

A second type of building was that which expressed the power of the ruler. Among them were great works of public utility, caravanserais on the trade-routes, and aqueducts or other waterworks; in the parched countries of the Middle East and the Maghrib, to bring water to the inhabitants of the cities was an act of sound policy, and irrigation of the land was a practice which spread with the expansion of the Arabs in the Mediterranean. It was the palaces, however, which best expressed imperial greatness: pleasure pavilions set amidst gardens and running water, emblems of a secluded paradise, and official palaces, centres of government and justice as well as of princely life. Something is known of the 'Abbasid palaces from descriptions by writers and the ruins which remain at Samarra. They were approached across open spaces for parades or games of horsemanship; within high walls, paths running through gardens led to a succession of inner gates, until at the centre there was seen the residence and offices of the caliph, and the domed hall where he held court. These buildings, signifying power, magnificence and enjoyment, and separation from the world outside, were imitated throughout the Muslim world and created an international style which endured for centuries.

In a sense, there was nothing particularly 'Islamic' about the palaces. Once more, the inclusion of so much of the world in a single empire brought together elements of different origin into a new unity. Rulers were in contact with one another beyond the world of Islam; presents were exchanged, embassies brought home marvellous stories, and ruling élites are particularly open to the desire for novelty. The decoration of the palaces expressed traditional themes of the life of princes everywhere, the battle and the hunt, wine and dancing.

These themes were used for wall-paintings, in which the figures of animals and human beings were prominent. In buildings with a religious purpose, however, figures of living creatures were avoided; although the depiction of living forms was not explicitly forbidden by the Qur'an, most jurists, basing themselves on Hadith, held that this was an infringement of the sole power of God to create life. In the Umayyad mosque in Damascus, the mosaics, made at an early period, portray the natural world and houses in a fairly realistic way, and one reminiscent of Roman wall-painting, but show them without living creatures. The walls of mosques and other public buildings were by no means plain, however. Surfaces were covered with decoration: forms of plants and flowers, tending to become highly stylized, and patterns of lines and circles intricately connected and endlessly repeated, and above all calligraphy. The art of fine writing may have been created largely by officials in the chanceries of rulers, but it had a special significance for Muslims, who believed that God has communicated Himself to many by His Word, in the Arabic language; the writing of that language was developed by calligraphers in ways which were suitable for architectural decoration. Words in endlessly varied forms, repeated or in sentences, were blended with vegetal or geometric forms. Thus calligraphy became one of the most important of Islamic arts, and Arabic writing adorned not only buildings, but coins, objects of brass or pottery, and textiles, particularly those woven in royal workshops and given as presents. The writing was used to proclaim the glory and eternity of God, as in the inscriptions round the Dome of the Rock, or the generosity and splendour of a benefactor, or the skill of an architect.

The houses built in this period by the Muslim population of the cities have disappeared, but enough has remained of the artefacts used in them to show that some of them contained works of art similar to those in the palaces. Books were transcribed and illustrated for merchants and scholars; glass, metalwork and pottery were made for them; textiles were especially important – floors were covered with carpets, low settee-frames had textile coverings, walls were hung with carpets or cloths. All these show, on the whole, the same kind of decoration as that of religious buildings, formalized plants and flowers, geometrical designs and Arabic words. There is a lack of specifically royal themes, but the human figure is not absent, or at least not for long; ceramics made in Egypt show human figures, and manuscripts use animals and human beings to illustrate fables or depict scenes from everyday life.

By the tenth century, then, men and women in the Near East and the Maghrib lived in a universe which was defined in terms of Islam. The world was divided into the Abode of Islam and the Abode of War, and places holy to Muslims or connected with their early history gave the Abode of Islam its distinctive feature. Time was marked by the five daily prayers, the weekly sermon in the mosque, the annual fast in the month of Ramadan and the pilgrimage to Mecca, and the Muslim calendar.

Islam also gave men an identity by which to define themselves in regard to others. Like all men, Muslims lived at different levels. They did not think of Judgement and Heaven all the time. Beyond their individual existence, they defined themselves for most daily purposes in terms of the family or broader kinship group, the herding unit or tribe, the village or rural district, the quarter or city. Beyond these, however, they were aware of belonging to something broader: the community of believers (the *umma*). The ritual acts which they performed in common, the acceptance of a shared view of man's destiny in this world and the next, linked them with each other and separated them from those of other faiths, whether living among them in the Abode of Islam or beyond its frontiers.

Within this 'world of Islam', at an intermediate level between it and the small cohesive units of everyday life, there were identities of a kind which did not, on the whole, create such strong and lasting loyalties. Service or obedience to a dynasty, particularly if it was long-lasting, could create such a loyalty. Sharing a language too must have created a sense of ease in communication, and a kind of pride. In the eleventh century, the identification of the Arabs with Islam was still strong enough for al-Biruni, himself of Iranian origin, to say:

Our religion and our empire are Arab and twins, the one protected by the power of God, the other by the Lord of Heaven. How often have the tribes of subjects congregated together in order to impart a non-Arab character to the State! But they could not succeed in their aim.[8]

The concept of modern ethnic nationalism, that those who share a common language should live together in an exclusive political society, did not of course exist, nor did that of the territorial nation, living in a piece of land clearly marked off from others by natural frontiers. There was, however, some consciousness of the special features of a city and its hinterland, which could express itself in Islamic terms. A study of Egypt has shown how the consciousness of its special nature persisted: its natural gifts and fertility, its place in Islamic history, its heroes, martyrs and saints. Behind this there still lived some memory of a past reaching back beyond Islam: the wonders left from the ancient world, the Pyramids and Sphinx, and the ancient shrines, rituals and beliefs of the countryside, to which men and women could still look for protection.[9]

CHAPTER 4

The Articulation of Islam

THE QUESTION OF AUTHORITY

The spread of the Arabic language to other peoples changed the nature of what was written in it, and this was shown not only in secular writing, but even more strikingly in a new kind of literature in which the meaning and implications of the revelation given to Muhammad were articulated. Those who accepted Islam found themselves faced with inescapable questions about it: questions which arose not only from intellectual curiosity but from criticisms made by Christians, Jews and Zoroastrians, and still more perhaps from the need to draw out the implications of the faith for life in society. They naturally tried to answer such questions in the light of their existing stock of knowledge and their own methods of thought: that which they brought with them into their new community, or found among those who were not converted, for in the early centuries Judaism, Christianity and Islam remained more open to each other than they were later to be. Naturally too the process took place most fruitfully in those places where traditions of thought and bodies of knowledge were strongest. The change of scale and transfer of the centre of gravity which took place in the body politic of Islam had its parallel in the realm of thought. Madina and Mecca did not cease to be important, but Syria was more so, and Iraq most important of all, with its rich cultural soil of Judaism, Nestorian Christianity and the religions of Iran.

The articulation of Islam into a body of religious sciences and practice took place largely in Iraq in the 'Abbasid period, and in a sense it was a continuation of movements of thought which had begun long before the appearance of Islam, although to say this is not to imply that Islam did not give new directions to it.

The materials on which scholars and thinkers could work were of more than one kind. There was, first of all, the Qur'an. Whenever it took its final

59

form, there seems no reason to doubt that its substance existed from the time of the Prophet: God the all-powerful; the prophets through whom He communicated with mankind; the faith, gratitude and works of prayer and charity which He demanded of men; the judgement of the last day, when His mercy as well as His justice would be shown. There was, secondly, a living tradition of how the community had behaved from the time of the Prophet onwards, handed on and elaborated by later generations, with, at its heart, some kind of collective memory of what the Prophet himself had been like. There was also the memory of the public acts of the community and of its leaders, the caliphs, their policies and conflicts; and in particular of the dissensions and conflicts of the reign of 'Uthman, the movements of opposition in which it ended, and that of 'Ali and the first schisms among the followers of Muhammad.

Not only the tradition of literate converts, but the essential nature of Islam itself – the revelation of words, and therefore of ideas and knowledge – made it imperative that those who wished to conform to the Will of God should seek knowledge and reflect upon it. The search for religious knowledge, *'ilm*, began early in the history of Islam, and there gradually developed a body of informed and concerned Muslim scholars (*'alim*, pl. *'ulama*).

The lines of thought and study along which Islam was articulated were numerous, but clearly connected with each other. The problem which emerged first and most urgently was that of authority. The preaching of Muhammad had given rise to a community committed to living in accordance with the norms contained or implied in the Qur'an. Who should have authority in that community, and what kind of authority should he have? This was a question raised by the dissensions and conflicts of the first half-century, and answered in the light of reflection on those troubles. Should the succession to Muhammad, the caliphate or, as it was also called, the *imamate*, be open to all Muslims, or only to the Companions of the Prophet, or only to his family? How should the caliph be chosen? What were the limits of his legitimate action? If he acted unjustly, should he be disobeyed or deposed?

Gradually there took place a crystallization of different attitudes towards such problems. The attitude of those who at a certain point came to be called Sunnis was that it was important for all Muslims to live together in peace and unity, and this implied that they should accept what had happened. They came to accept all four of the first caliphs as legitimate, and as virtuous or rightly guided (*rashidun*); later caliphs might not always have acted justly, but they should be accepted as legitimate so long as they did not go against the basic commandments of God. There is some evidence that the Umayyad caliphs put forward claims to be not only the successors of the Prophet as leaders of the community, but vice-gerents of God on earth and the ultimate interpreters of the divine law.[1] Sunnism in its developed form, however, regarded the caliph neither as a prophet nor as an infallible interpreter of the faith, but as a leader whose task it was to uphold peace and justice in the community; for this he should possess adequate virtues and a knowledge of religious law. It was widely accepted that he should be descended from the tribe of Quraysh, to which the Prophet had belonged.

Those movements which challenged the authority of the caliphs gradually developed their own theories of legitimate authority. The Ibadis held that it was not necessary for there to be an *imam* at all times, but any Muslim could become *imam*, irrespective of his family or origin. He should be chosen by the community; he should act justly in accordance with the law derived from the Qur'an and Hadith, and if he proved unjust he should be deposed. The Shi'i movements did not accept the claims of the first three caliphs, but believed that 'Ali ibn Abi Talib had been the sole legitimate and appointed successor of the Prophet as *imam*. They differed among themselves, however, about the line of succession from 'Ali, and the authority of the *imams*. The Zaydis were closest to the Sunnis in their views. They held that any descendant of 'Ali by his wife Fatima could be *imam*, provided he had the necessary knowledge and piety and had shown the strength to rise against injustice. There could therefore be a line of *imams* perpetually renewed. They did not believe that the *imam* had infallible or more than human authority.

The other two important Shi'i movements went further than this, however. Both held that the *imamate* was handed on by designation of the *imam* of the time, and that the *imam* thus designated was the sole and infallible interpreter of the revelation of God through the Prophet. The movement which was to gain most adherents held that succession had passed among the descendants of 'Ali until the twelfth in the line had disappeared from view in the ninth century (hence their popular name of 'Twelvers' or *Ithna 'ashariyya*). Since the world could not exist without an *imam*, it was believed that the twelfth one had not died but was still living in 'occlusion' (*ghayba*); at first he communicated with the Muslim people through intermediaries, but after that he was out of the view of the living world, which remained in expectation of his reappearance to bring in the reign of justice. The Isma'ilis for their part agreed that the *imam* was the infallible interpreter of the truth, but held that the line of visible *imams* had ended with the seventh, Muhammad ibn Isma'il. (Some of them modified their belief, however, when the Fatimid caliphs put forward their own claim to be *imams*.)

These different views of the caliphate or *imamate* were in due course to have varying implications for the nature of government and its place in society. Both the Ibadis and the Zaydis were communities which had withdrawn from the universal Islamic society in rejection of the rule of unjust governments; they wished to live under the religious law as they interpreted it, and were unwilling to give an *imam* or any other ruler the power which might lead him to act unjustly. On the other hand, Sunnis, 'Twelver' Shi'is and Isma'ilis each in their own way wanted an authority which could both uphold the law and maintain the order of society; once the first age was over, the consequence of this was the *de facto* separation between those who maintained the law (for Sunnis the *'ulama* and for Shi'is the hidden *imam*) and the men of the sword who had the power to enforce temporal order.

THE POWER AND JUSTICE OF GOD

The question of human authority was in a sense a reflection of more fundamental questions which sprang from the Qur'an: questions about the nature of God and His dealings with mankind, about His unity and justice.

The God of the Qur'an is transcendent and one, but the Qur'an speaks of Him as having attributes – will, knowledge, hearing, sight and speech; and in some sense the Qur'an is His Word. How can the possession of attributes be reconciled with the unity of God? How, in particular, can those attributes which are also those of human beings be described in terms which preserve the infinite distance between God and man? What is the relationship of the Qur'an to God? Can it be called the speech of God without implying that God has an attribute of speech similar to that of His creatures? These are problems of a kind inherent in any religion which believes that there is a supreme God who reveals Himself in some form to human beings. For Christians, the revelation is that of a person, and the basic theological question in the early centuries was that of the relationship of this Person with God; for Muslims, the revelation is a Book, and the problem of the status of the Book is therefore fundamental.

The question of the nature of God leads logically to that of His dealings with men. Two impressions were certain to be left on the mind of anyone who had read the Qur'an or heard it being recited: that God was all-powerful and all-knowing, but that in some way man was responsible for his actions and would be judged by God for them. How could these two statements be reconciled with each other? Once more, this is a problem inherent in a monotheistic faith: if God is all-powerful, how can He permit evil, and how can He justly condemn men for their evil deeds? To put it in broader terms: is man free to initiate his own acts, or do they all come from God? If he is not free, can it be just for God to judge him? If he is free, and can therefore be judged by God, will he be judged by some principle of justice which he can recognize? If so, is there not a principle of justice determining God's acts, and can God then be called all-powerful? How will Muslims be judged: by their faith alone, or by faith together with verbal expression of it, or also by good works?

Such questions are implicit in the Qur'an and confronted anyone who took it seriously, but systematic thought about them involved not only a text to consider but a method of doing so: a belief that knowledge could be attained by human reason working according to certain rules. This belief in reason rightly directed had formed the intellectual life of the regions into which Islam spread, including Hijaz; there are traces of dialectical reasoning in the Qur'an itself. It is not surprising therefore that, perhaps by the end of the first Islamic century or the seventh century AD, the earliest extant documents show it being applied to the elucidation of the Qur'an in Hijaz, Syria and Iran. The first groups which can be called schools of thought appeared: those who argued that man has free will and creates his own acts, and those who maintained that he has no free will, and also that God has no attributes which He shares with men and by which He can be described.

In the middle of the second Islamic century (the eighth century AD) there emerged a school in a fuller sense, of thinkers with clear and consistent views of a whole range of problems; but of course to call them a school does not imply that they all had exactly the same ideas or that their ideas did not develop from one generation to another. These were the Mu'tazilis (or 'those who keep themselves apart'). They believed that truth could be reached by using reason on what is given in the Qur'an, and in this way they reached answers to questions already posed. God is One. He has no attributes which belong to His essence. In particular, He has no human attributes; the Qur'an could not have been spoken by Him – it must have been created in another way. God is just, and so bound by a principle of justice; man must therefore be free, for to judge men for acts they are not free to commit would not be just. If human acts are free and subject to judgement, it follows that faith is not enough without good works; a Muslim who is guilty of grave faults cannot be called either an infidel or a true believer, but has a position in between the two.

At the same time, however, there was emerging another way of looking at these problems, one more cautious and more sceptical about the possibility of reaching agreed truth by reason, and more conscious too of the danger to the community of carrying rational argument and disputation too far. Those who thought in this way placed the importance of maintaining the unity of God's people above that of reaching agreement on matters of doctrine. For them, the word of the Qur'an was the only firm basis on which faith and communal peace could be placed; and the Qur'an should be interpreted, in so far as interpretation was necessary, in the light of the habitual practice of the Prophet and his Companions, the *sunna*, as transmitted to later generations. This was a mood which must have existed from an early time, but by its nature it tended to crystallize into a body of doctrines rather later than the more speculative schools. The person most responsible for formulating the mood was Ahmad ibn Hanbal (780–855), who himself was touched by the persecution. The only stand to be taken is on the Qur'an and the *sunna* of the Prophet, and these show us that God is all-powerful, and His justice is not like human justice. If the Qur'an ascribes attributes to Him, they must be accepted as divine attributes, not on the analogy of human ones, and without asking how they inhere in Him. Among these attributes is the Qur'an. It is His speech, because the Qur'an itself says so; and it is uncreated, for 'nothing of God is created, and the Qur'an is of God'. Man should respond to God's Will by acts as well as faith. This concept of a God who judges in mysterious ways may seem a harsh one, but implicit in it is a kind of assurance of some ultimate divine care for the world, even if its ways are not those of men, and that what has happened in their history is part of God's Will for them. With this body of ideas Sunnism becomes articulate.

The controversy between the rationalists and the followers of Ibn Hanbal continued for a long time, and the lines of argument changed. Later Mu'tazili thinkers were deeply influenced by Greek thought; gradually they ceased to be important within the emerging Sunni community, but their influence remained strong in the Shi'i schools of thought as they developed from the eleventh century. A thinker who broadly supported the 'traditionalist' position used the method of rational discourse (*kalam*) to defend it:

al-Ash'ari (d. 935) held to the literal interpretation of the Qur'an, but maintained that it could be justified by reason, at least up to a certain point, and beyond that point it must simply be accepted. God was One; His attributes were part of His essence; they were not God, but they were not other than God. Among them were those of hearing, sight and speech, but they were not like the hearing, sight and speech of men; they must be accepted 'without asking how' (*bila kayf*). God is the direct cause of all that happens in the universe, and is not limited by anything outside Himself. At the moment of action He gives men the power to act; He wills and creates both what is good and what is evil in the world. The proper response of man to God's revealed Word is faith; if he has faith without works he is still a believer, and the Prophet will intercede for him on the last day.

In Ash'ari's thought there is an emphasis on the importance of not quarrelling in religion, and also of accepting the rule of the *imam* or caliph and not revolting against it with the sword. There were differences of opinion which persisted, however: about the legitimacy of a metaphorical as against the literal interpretation of the Qur'an; about the precise sense in which the Qur'an is 'uncreated' – does this refer to the text itself, or only to the transmission of the text to men? – and about the necessity of works as well as faith. Such differences, however, did not usually lead to conflict within the Sunni community.

THE *SHARI'A*

Except by implication, the Qur'an does not contain within itself a system of doctrines, but it does tell men what God wishes them to do. It is above all a revelation of His Will: what men must do to please Him, and how they will be judged on the last day. It contains some specific commands, for example in regard to marriage and the division of a Muslim's property after death, but these are limited, and for the most part God's Will is expressed in terms of general principles. Commands and principles concern both the ways in which men should worship God and those in which they should act towards one another, but to some extent this is an artificial distinction, for acts of worship have a social aspect, and acts of justice and charity are also in a sense directed towards God.

Reflection upon the Qur'an and the practice of the early community soon produced general agreement upon certain basic obligations of the Muslim, the so-called 'Pillars of Islam'. These included the oral testimony that 'there is no god but God, and Muhammad is the Prophet of God'. Secondly, there was ritual prayer, with certain forms of words repeated a certain number of times with particular postures of the body; these should take place five times a day. Other 'Pillars' were the giving of a certain proportion of one's income for specified kinds of work of charity or public benefit; a strict fast, from daybreak to sunset, throughout a whole month of the year, that of Ramadan, ending in a festival; and the Hajj, the pilgrimage to Mecca, at a fixed time of the year, involving a number of ritual acts, and also ending in a festival celebrated by the whole community. To these specific acts was also added a general injunction to strive in the way of God (*jihad*), which might have a wide meaning or a more precise one: to fight in order to extend the bounds of Islam.

From the beginning, however, more was needed than an agreement about the essential acts of worship. On the one hand there were those who took the Qur'an seriously and believed that it contained by implication precepts for the whole of life, since all human acts have significance in the eyes of God and all will be taken into account on the Day of Judgement. On the other there were the ruler and his deputies, needing to make decisions on a whole range of problems, and both their own convictions and the terms in which they justified their rule would lead them to decisions which at the very least would not be in contradiction of what the Qur'an was taken to mean or imply.

In the period of the first caliphs and the Umayyads, therefore, two processes took place. The ruler, his governors and special deputies, the *qadis*, dispensed justice and decided disputes, taking into account the existing customs and laws of the various regions. At the same time, serious and concerned Muslims tried to bring all human acts under the judgement of their religion, to work out an ideal system of human conduct. In doing so they had to take into account the words of the Qur'an and to interpret them, and also the transmitted memories of the community: how the Prophet was supposed to have acted (his habitual behaviour or *sunna*, increasingly recorded in 'traditions' or *hadiths*); how the early caliphs made decisions; what the accumulated wisdom of the community believed to be the right way to act (the *sunna* of the community).

These two processes were not wholly different from each other. The caliph, governor or *qadi* no doubt would modify existing customs in the light of developing ideas of what Islam demanded; the scholars would introduce into their ideal system something taken from the inherited customs of their communities. During the early phases, however, they

66

remained broadly separate. Within each process, moreover, there were different tendencies. Given the way in which the empire was created and administered, the customs and regulations of the various regions must have differed widely. The scholars for their part were scattered over various cities, Mecca and Madina, Kufa and Basra, and cities of Syria, and each of them had its own ways of thought, reflecting its transmitted memories as well as the needs and practices of the region, and crystallized in a local consensus (*ijma‘*).

With the coming of the 'Abbasids in the middle of the second Islamic century (the eighth century AD) the situation changed. The creation of a centralized state, bureaucratically ruled, made it necessary to reach agreement on ways in which disputes should be settled and society regulated; and the claim of the 'Abbasids to a religious justification for their rule made it essential that whatever was agreed upon should be seen to be based on the teachings of Islam. Thus the two processes drew closer to each other. The *qadi* became, in theory at least, a judge independent of the executive power and making decisions in the light of the teachings of religion. The need therefore for some general agreement about the practical implications of Islam became greater. The Qur'an, the practice or *sunna* of the Prophet embodied in *hadiths*, the opinions of groups of scholars, the developing practice or *sunna* of local communities: all these were important, but so far there was no agreement about the relations between them. Scholars held varying views: Abu Hanifa (*c.* 699–767) placed more emphasis on opinions reached by individual reasoning, Malik (*c.* 715–95) on the practice of Madina, although he also admitted the validity of reasoning in the light of the interest of the community.

The decisive step in defining the relations between the different bases for legal decisions was taken by al-Shafi'i (767–820). The Qur'an, he maintained, was the literal Word of God: it expressed God's Will in the form both of general principles and of specific commandments in regard to certain matters (prayer, alms, fasting, pilgrimage, the prohibition of adultery, of drinking wine and eating pork). Equally important, however, was the practice or *sunna* of the Prophet as it was recorded in *hadiths*; this was of greater weight than the cumulative practice of communities. The *sunna* of the Prophet was a clear manifestation of God's Will, and its status was confirmed by verses of the Qur'an: 'O you who have believed, obey God and His Apostle.'[2] The deeds and words of the Prophet drew out the implications of the general provisions of the Qur'an, and also gave guidance on matters on which the Qur'an was silent. According to Shafi'i, Qur'an and *sunna* were equally infallible. The *sunna* could not abrogate the Qur'an, but equally the Qur'an could not abrogate the *sunna*. They could not contradict each other; apparent contradictions could be reconciled, or else a later verse of the Qur'an or saying of the Prophet could be regarded as abrogating an earlier one.[3]

However clear might be the expression of God's Will in Qur'an or *sunna*, there would remain questions of interpretation, or of applying principles to new situations. For the way of thought articulated by Shaf'i, the only method of avoiding error was for ordinary Muslims to leave it to those learned in religion to use their reason in order to explain what was contained in Qur'an and Hadith, and to do so within strict limits. Confronted with a new situation, those who were qualified to exercise their reason should proceed by analogy (*qiyas*): they should try to find some element in the situation which was similar, in a relevant way, to an element in a situation on which a ruling already existed. Such a disciplined exercise of reason was known as *ijtihad*, and the justification for it could be found in a *hadith*: 'The learned are the heirs of the prophets.'[3] When there was general agreement as a result of such an exercise of reason, then this consensus (*ijma'*) would be regarded as having the status of certain and unquestionable truth.

Shafi'i himself stated this principle in the broadest form: once the community as a whole had reached agreement on a matter, the question was closed for ever; according to a *hadith*, 'in the community as a whole there is no error concerning the meaning of the Qur'an, the *sunna* and analogy'. Later thinkers, however, including those who regarded Shafi'i as their master, formulated the principle rather differently: the only valid *ijma'* was that of the scholars, those competent to exercise *ijtihad*, in a particular period.

To these principles of interpretation a kind of appendage was added by Shafi'i, and generally accepted: those who interpreted Qur'an and *sunna* could not do so without an adequate knowledge of the Arabic language. Shafi'i quoted passages from the Qur'an which mentioned the fact that it had been revealed in Arabic: 'We have revealed to thee an Arabic Qur'an ... in a clear Arabic tongue'.[4] Every Muslim, in Shafi'i's view, should learn Arabic, at lest to the point at which he could make the act of testimony (*shahada*), recite the Qur'an, and invoke the name of God (*Allahu akbar*, 'God is most great'); a religious scholar needed to know more than this.

Once these principles had been stated and generally accepted, it was possible to attempt to relate the whole body of laws and moral precepts to them. This process of thought was known as *fiqh*, and the product of it came ultimately to be called *shari'a*. Gradually there grew up a number of 'schools' of law (*madhhab*), taking their names from early writers from whom they traced their descent: the Hanafis from Abu Hanifa, Malikis from Malik, Shafi'is from al-Shafi'i, Hanbalis from Ibn Hanbal, and some others which did not survive. They differed from each other on certain substantive points of law, and also on the principles of legal reasoning (*usul al-fiqh*), and in particular on the place of Hadith and the legitimacy, limits and methods of *ijtihad*.

The four schools all lay within the Sunni community. Other Muslim groups had their own systems of law and social morality. Those of the Ibadis and Zaydis did not differ greatly from the Sunni schools, but among the 'Twelver' Shi'is the bases of law were defined in different ways; the consensus of the community was only valid if the *imam* was included in it. There were also some distinctive points of Shi'i substantive law.

In spite of the partly theoretical nature of the *shari'a*, or perhaps because of it, those who taught, interpreted and administered it, the *'ulama*, were to hold an important place in Muslim states and societies. As guardians of an elaborated norm of social behaviour they could, up to a point, set limits to the actions of rulers, or at least give them advice; they could also act as spokesmen for the community, or at least the urban part of it. On the whole, however, they tried to hold themselves apart from both government and society, preserving the sense of a divinely guided community, persisting through time and not linked with the interests of rulers or the caprice of popular feeling.

THE TRADITIONS OF THE PROPHET

The political and theological controversies of the first three centuries made use of Hadith, and for the system of jurisprudence as it developed, too, Hadith was important as one of the bases of law. The relationship of theology and law with Hadith was more complex than that, however. Not only did they make use of Hadith, to a large extent they created the body of traditions as they have come down to us, and this process led to the emergence of another religious science, that of Hadith-criticism, the development and use of criteria to distinguish traditions which could be regarded as authentic from those which were more doubtful or obviously false.

From the beginning, the community which grew up around Muhammad had a system of customary behaviour, a *sunna*, in two different senses. As a community it gradually created its own pattern of righteous behaviour, developing and guaranteed by some kind of consensus. It also contained in itself people who tried to preserve the *sunna* of the Prophet, the memory of what he had done and said. His Companions would have remembered him, and have handed on what they knew to the next generation. The record of his behaviour and words, the *hadiths*, was passed on not only orally but in writing from an early time. Although some devout Muslims looked askance at the writing of *hadiths*, thinking it might detract from the unique status of the Book, others encouraged it, and by the end of the Umayyad period many of the *hadiths* which were later to be incorporated into biographies of the Prophet had assumed a written form.

The process did not end there, however. Both the *sunna* of the community and the record of that of the Prophet varied from place to place and from time to time. Memories grow dim, stories are changed in the telling, and not all who record them are truthful. At first the *sunna* of the community had been the more important of the two, but as time went on lawyers and some theologians came to lay more emphasis upon that of the Prophet. Legal specialists wished to relate the social customs and administrative regulations which had grown up to religious principles, and one way of doing this was to trace them back to the Prophet. Those engaged in the great controversies about where authority should lie, or about the nature of God and the Qur'an, tried to find support for their views in the life and sayings of Muhammad. Thus, during the second and third Islamic centuries (roughly the eighth and ninth centuries AD) the body of sayings attributed to the Prophet expanded. Up to a point this was generally accepted as a literary device, itself justified by a *hadith*: 'What is said of good speech is said by me'. From an early time, however, the dangers inherent in it were recognized, and there began a movement of criticism, with the aim of distinguishing the true from the false. The practice grew up, perhaps by the end of the first Islamic century, of specialists travelling far and wide to search for witnesses who had themselves received a tradition from a parent or teacher, and trying to trace the tradition back through a chain of witnesses to the Prophet or a Companion. In so doing, the local bodies of tradition were unified.

By this process, partly recollection and partly invention, the *hadiths* took the form they were to retain. Each of them had two parts: a text which preserved an account of something said or done by the Prophet, and in some cases containing words which he claimed to have received from God, and a record of a chain of witnesses going back to a Companion of the Prophet who had usually seen or heard them. Both these elements could be open to doubt. The text could be invented or wrongly remembered, but so could the chain; and it seems that, in many cases at least, the prolongation of the chain right back to the Prophet was also a device of lawyers or polemicists. Thus there was a need for a science of *hadith*-criticism, by which true could be distinguished from false in accordance with clear principles.

The main attention of scholars who took as their task the critical scrutiny of *hadiths* was given to the recorded chains of witnesses (*isnad*): whether the dates of birth and death and places of residence of witnesses in different generations were such as to have made it possible for them to meet, and whether they were trustworthy. This activity, to be properly carried out, involved some feeling for the authenticity or plausibility of the text itself; an experienced traditionist would develop a sense of discrimination.

By the use of these criteria the *hadith* scholars were able to classify them according to their degrees of reliability. The two great collections, those of al-Bukhari (810–70) and Muslim (c. 817–75) discarded all except those of whose truth they were sure; other collections generally regarded as having some authority were not so strict. The Shi'is had their own collections of *hadiths* of the *imams*.

Most western scholars, and some modern Muslims, would be more sceptical than Bukhari or Muslim and regard many of the *hadiths* which they took to be authentic as being products of polemics about authority and doctrine or of the development of law. To say this, however, is not to cast doubt on the very important role which they have played in the history of the Muslim community. No less important than the question of their origins is that of the way in which they have been used. At moments of political tension, when the enemy was at the gates, the ruler might ask the *'ulama* to read selections from Bukhari in the great mosque, as a kind of assurance of what God had done for His people. Later writers on law, theology or the rational sciences could support their ideas by *hadiths* drawn from the enormous store which remained even when Bukhari and Muslim had done their work.

THE PATH OF THE MYSTICS

The sciences of theology, law and tradition all began with what was given in the Qur'an, and ended by reinforcing the claims of Islam and heightening the barrier between it and the other monotheistic religions to which it was kin. There were other strands of thought, however, which, beginning in much the same way, tended to lead towards the assertion of something which Muslims might have in common with others.

One of them was that line of thought and practice which is commonly called 'mysticism'; the Arabic equivalent to this word is *tasawwuf* (from which comes the anglicized form Sufism) possibly derived from the robes of wool (*suf*) which one of the early groups was supposed to have worn. It is now generally agreed that it drew its inspiration from the Qur'an. A believer meditating on its meaning might be filled with a sense of the overwhelming transcendence of God and the total dependence of all creatures on Him: God the all-powerful, the inscrutable, guiding those who had faith in Him, for all His greatness was present and near to every human soul which relied on Him, 'nearer to you than the vein in your neck'. The Qur'an contains potent images of the nearness of God to man, and the way in which man can respond. Before the world was created, God is said to have made a covenant (*mithaq*) with human beings. He asked them, 'Am I not your Lord?' and they answered, 'Yes, we testify.'⁵ In his life Muhammad is said to have made a mysterious journey, first to Jerusalem and then to Paradise, where he was allowed to approach to a certain distance from God and have a vision of His face.

From an early time in the history of Islam, there seem to have begun two processes, closely intertwined. There was a movement of piety, of prayer aiming at purity of intention and renunciation of self-regarding motives and worldly pleasures, and one of meditation upon the meaning of the Qur'an; both movements took place in Syria and Iraq more than Hijaz, and it was natural that they should draw sustenance from the modes of thought and moral action already existing in the world in which Muslims were living. Those converts to the new religion had brought into Islam their own inherited ways; they were living in an environment which was still more Christian and Jewish than Muslim. This was the last great age of eastern Christian monasticism, and of ascetic thought and practice. In principle the Prophet had frowned upon monasticism: 'no monasticism in Islam', ran a famous *hadith*, and the Islamic equivalent was said to be *jihad*. In fact, however, the influence of Christian monks seems to have been pervasive: their idea of a secret world of virtue, beyond that of obedience to law, and the belief that abandonment of the world, mortification of the flesh and repetition of the name of God in prayer, might, with God's help, purify the heart and release it from all worldly concerns to move towards a higher intuitive knowledge of God.

The germ of such ideas, in a Muslim form, can be seen as early as the first Islamic century, in the sayings of al-Hasan al-Basri (642–728):

the believer wakens grieving and goes to bed grieving, and this is all that encompasses him, because he is between two fearful things: the sin which has passed, and he does not know what God will do with him, and the allotted term which remains, and he does not know what disasters will befall him . . . beware this dwelling place, for there is no power and no might save in God, and remember the future life.[6]

In the early mystics, the sense of the distance and nearness of God is expressed in the language of love: God is the sole adequate object of human love, to be loved for Himself alone; the life of the true believer should be a path leading to knowledge of Him, and as man draws near to God He will draw near to man and become 'his sight, his hearing, his hand and his tongue'.

In a fragment of autobiography, a writer on spiritual subjects during the third Islamic and ninth Christian century, al-Tirmidhi, has shown how a soul could be drawn towards the path. While on pilgrimage and praying in the *haram*, he had a sudden moment of repentance for his sins; searching for the right way to live, he came upon a book by al-Antaki which helped him towards self-discipline. Gradually he made progress on the path, curbing his passions and withdrawing from society. He was helped by dreams of the Prophet, and his wife also had dreams and visions. He was persecuted and slandered by those who claimed he was bringing illegitimate innovations into religion, but these afflictions helped to purify his heart. Then one evening, returning from a session of recollection of God, his heart opened and was flooded with sweetness.[7]

In the next century, both the exploration of the path by which men and women might draw near to God and speculation about the end of it were carried further. Perhaps as early as the eighth century there emerged the distinctive ritual of collective repetition of the name of God (*dhikr*), accompanied by various movements of the body, exercises in breathing, or music, not as things which would automatically induce the ecstasy of seeing God face to face, but as ways of freeing the soul from the distractions of the world. The thoughts of Sufi masters about the nature of the knowledge which would come at the end of the path were first preserved orally and later recorded in writing by those who came to them to learn the path. In this fashion there grew up a collective language in which the nature of mystical preparation and experience could be expressed, and a sense of corporate identity among those engaged on the journey.

It was in this third Islamic century (roughly, the ninth century AD) that the way to knowledge of God and the nature of that knowledge were first expressed in systematic form. In the writings of al-Muhasibi (d. 857) the way of life of the seeker after true knowledge was described, and in those of al-Junayd (d. 910) the nature of the experience which lay at the end of the way was analysed. At the end of the path, the true and sincere believer may find himself face to face with God – as all men were at the moment of the Covenant – in such a way that God's attributes replace his own, and his individual existence disappears; but only for a moment. After it he will return to his own existence and to the world, but carrying with him the memory of that moment, of the nearness of God but also His transcendence:

The love of God in its essence is the illumination of the heart by joy, because of its nearness to the Beloved; and when the heart is filled with that radiant joy, it finds its delight in being alone with the recollection of the Beloved . . . and when solitude is combined with secret intercourse with the Beloved, the joy of that intercourse overwhelms the mind, so that it is no longer concerned with this world and what is therein.[8]

Muhasibi and Junayd lived and wrote within the sober Sunni tradition; they were men who knew the *shari'a* and were concerned that, however advanced on the mystical path a Muslim might be, he should observe its commands with sincerity. Their sense of the overwhelming greatness and power of God is not so far from that of a theologian like al-Ash'ari, for whom the power to act comes from God and the believer can hope for His guidance. In both there is a sense of the incursion of the divine into human life, of an inscrutable providence shaping men's lives in its own way. The sense of being filled with the presence of God, if only for a moment, can be intoxicating, and some of the Sufis, whose ideas may not have differed much from those of Junayd, tried to express the inexpressible experience in heightened and coloured language which could arouse opposition. Abu Yazid al-Bistami (d. *c.* 875) tried to describe the moment of ecstasy, when the mystic is denuded of his own existence and filled with that of God; and yet in the end he understood that in this life it is an illusion, that human life at best is filled with the alternation of the presence and absence of God. A more famous case is that of al-Hallaj (*c.* 857–922), executed in Baghdad for blasphemous utterances. A pupil of Junayd, his doctrines may not have been very different from those of his master, but he expressed them in the tone of ecstatic and fulfilled love. His exclamation, 'I am the Truth [or God]', may have been no more than an attempt to state the mystical experience in which man's attributes are replaced by God's, but could well be taken for something more; so too his suggestion that the true pilgrimage was not that to Mecca, but the spiritual journey which the mystic could carry out in his own room, might be taken to imply that literal fulfilment of the obligations of religion was not important. There may have been something in him which welcomed such misunderstandings, for he had been influenced by a trend in Sufi thought (that of the Malamatis) which may have come from eastern Christian monasticism: the wish to abase onself by acts which incur the reproaches of the world, a kind of mortification of one's self-esteem.

THE PATH OF REASON

Later Sufi speculation about how God created man and how man could return to Him was to be much influenced by another movement of thought which began early, an attempt to assimilate into Arabic the tradition of Greek science and philosophy; or, it might be said, to continue and develop that tradition through the medium of the Arabic language.

The coming to power of an Arab dynasty did not cause an abrupt break in the intellectual life of Egypt or Syria, Iraq or Iran. The school of Alexandria continued to exist for a time, although its scholars were ultimately to move to northern Syria. The medical school at Jundishapur in southern Iran, created by Nestorian Christians under the patronage of the Sasanians, also continued to exist. In these and other places there was a living tradition of Hellenistic thought and science, although by this time its interests were more limited than before, and it was carried on through the medium of Syriac rather than Greek. There was also a high tradition of Jewish learning in Iraq, and an Iranian tradition expressed in Pahlavi and incorporating some important elements coming from India.

During the first generation of Muslim rule it was not necessary to translate from Greek to Syriac into Arabic, since most of those who carried on the tradition were still Christians, Jews or Zoroastrians, and even those who had been converted would still have retained their knowledge of the languages of thought, or at least continued to be in contact with those who did. The Arab ruling group may not have been much concerned to know what their subjects were studying, and could scarcely have done so, for the Arabic language had not yet acquired the capacity to express the concepts of science and philosophy in a precise way.

From the later part of the second to the fourth Islamic century (roughly the eighth until the tenth century AD), however, the work of translation was carried on intensively and – a rare phenomenon – with the direct encouragement of some of the 'Abbasid caliphs. For the most part the work was done by Christians whose first language of culture was Syriac, and who translated from Syriac into Arabic, but some works were translated directly from Greek into Arabic. An essential part of their work was to expand the resources of the Arabic language, its vocabulary and idiom, to make it an adequate medium for the whole intellectual life of the age. An important part in this was played by the greatest of the translators, Hunyan ibn Ishaq (808–73).

Virtually the whole of the Greek culture of the time, as it was preserved in the schools, was assimilated into this expanded language. In some ways it was a shrunken culture. Rhetoric, poetry, drama and history were no longer taught or studied much. The familiar studies included philosophy (most of Aristotle, some dialogues of Plato, some neo-Platonic works); medicine; the exact sciences, mathematics and astronomy; and the occult sciences, astrology, alchemy and magic. Philosophy, science and the occult studies were not so clearly distinguished as they are now. The frontiers of what is regarded as 'scientific' have moved from time to time, and it was quite consistent with what was known of the nature of the universe to believe that nature regulated human life, that the heavens controlled what happened in the world lying beneath the moon, and to try to understand these forces and use them.

The motives of the translators and of their patrons, the caliphs, may have been partly practical; medical skill was in demand, and control over natural forces could bring power and success. There was also, however, a wide intellectual curiosity, such as is expressed in the words of al-Kindi (c. 801–66), the thinker with whom the history of Islamic philosophy virtually begins:

We should not be ashamed to acknowledge truth from whatever source it comes to us, even if it is brought to us by former generations and foreign peoples. For him who seeks the truth there is nothing of higher value than truth itself.[9]

These words express not only the excitement which the discovery of the Greek tradition could arouse, but also the self-confidence of an imperial culture resting on worldly power and the conviction of divine support.

The translations lie at the origin of a scientific tradition expressed in Arabic. To a great extent it continued and developed the late Greek tradition. It was a sign of this continuity that the historian of Arab medicine, Ibn Abi Usaybi'a, reproduced in full the Hippocratic oath of Greek doctors: 'I swear by God, Lord of life and death . . . and I swear by Asclepius, and I swear by all the saints of God . . .'[10]

Intermingled with sciences of Greek origin, however, were elements coming from the Iranian and Indian traditions. As early as the ninth century, the mathematician al-Khwarazmi (c. 800–47) was writing about the use of Indian – the so-called Arabic – numerals in mathematical calculations. This blend of elements is significant. Just as the 'Abbasid caliphate brought the lands of the Indian Ocean and Mediterranean Sea into a single trading area, so too the Greek, Iranian and Indian traditions were brought together, and it has been said that 'for the first time in history, science became international on a large scale'.[11]

Whatever its origins, science was accepted without difficulty in the culture and society which expressed themselves in Arabic: the astronomers became time-keepers, fixing the times of prayer and often ritual observances; doctors were generally respected and could have influence over rulers. Some of the sciences, however, raised questions about the limits of human knowledge. Many of the doctors rejected the claims of astrology that the conjunction of humours in the body was ruled by the conjunction of the stars; the claims of the alchemists also were not wholly accepted. Above all, it was philosophy which posed questions, for in some ways the methods and conclusions of Greek philosophy seemed difficult to reconcile with the basic teachings of Islam, as they were being developed by theologians and lawyers.

The assumption of philosophy was that human reason rightly used could give man certain knowledge of the universe, but to be Muslim was to believe that some knowledge essential for human life had come to man only through the revelation of God's Word to the prophets. If Islam was true, what were the limitations of philosophy? If the claims of the philosophers were valid, what need was there of prophecy? The Qur'an taught that God had made the world by His creative word, 'Be'; how could this be reconciled with Aristotle's theory that matter was eternal and only the form of it had been created? Plato came to the Arabic-speaking world as interpreted by later thinkers, and even Aristotle was interpreted in the light of a neo-Platonic work wrongly called 'The Theology of Aristotle'. For these later thinkers, God had created and maintained the world through a hierarchy of intermediate intelligences emanating from Him; how could this view be reconciled with the idea of a god of total power who nevertheless intervened directly in the human world? Was the human soul immortal? How could the Platonic view that the best form of government was that of the philosopher–king be reconciled with the Muslim view that the government of the time of the Prophet and the first caliphs was that which best conformed to God's Will for men?

A famous medical writer of the ninth century, Abu Bakr al-Razi (865–925), answered such questions in an unequivocal way. Human reason alone could give certain knowledge, the path of philosophy was open to all uses, the claims of revelation were false and religions were dangerous.

Perhaps more typical of philosophers who still remained convinced Muslims was the attitude of al-Farabi (d. 950). The philosopher, he believed, could attain to truth by his reason and could live by it, but not all human beings were philosophers and able to grasp the truth directly. Most could attain to it only through symbols. There were some philosophers who had the power of understanding truth by the imagination as well as the intellect, and of stating it in the form of images as well as ideas, and these were the prophets. Thus prophetic religion was a way of stating truth by means of symbols intelligible to all men. Different systems of symbols formed the different religions, but all tried to express the same truth; this did not necessarily imply that all would express it with the same adequacy.

Philosophy and the religion of Islam do not therefore contradict each other. They express the same truth in different forms, which correspond to the different levels at which human beings can apprehend it. The enlightened man can live by philosophy; he who has grasped the truth through symbols but has reached a certain level of understanding can be guided by theology; the ordinary people should live by obedience to the *shari'a*.

Implicit in the ideas of al-Farabi was the suggestion that philosophy in its pure form was not for everyone. The distinction between the intellectual élite and the masses was to become a commonplace of Islamic thought. Philosophy continued to exist, but was carried on as a private activity, largely by medical men, pursued with discretion and often met with suspicion. Nevertheless, some of the ideas of the philosophers did penetrate the thought of the age and of later ages. The time of al-Farabi was also that of the Fatimids, and neo-Platonic ideas of the hierarchy of divine emanations can be found in the fully developed system of the Isma'ilis. At a rather later period, they were also to enter the theoretical systems by which Sufi writers were to try to explain their search and what they hoped to find at the end of it.

PART II

ARAB MUSLIM SOCIETIES

(Eleventh–Fifteenth Century)

The five centuries which form the subject of this part were a period during which the world of Islam was divided in some respects but preserved its unity in others. The frontiers of the Muslim world changed: it expanded in Anatolia and India, but lost Spain to Christian kingdoms. Within these frontiers, a division appeared between those areas where Arabic was the main language of life and culture, and those where it continued to be the principal language of religious and legal writing but the revived Persian language became the main medium of secular culture. A third ethnic and linguistic group became important, the Turks, who formed the ruling élite in much of the eastern part of the Muslim world. Within the Arabic-speaking regions, the 'Abbasid caliphate continued to exist in Baghdad until the thirteenth century, but a broad political division emerged between three areas: Iraq, which was usually linked with Iran; Egypt, which usually ruled Syria and western Arabia; and the Maghrib with its various parts.

In spite of political divisions and changes, however, the Arabic-speaking parts of the Muslim world had social and cultural forms which were relatively stable during this period, and showed similarities from one region to another. This part explores the worlds of townspeople, peasants and nomadic pastoralists and the links between them, and shows how there grew up an alliance of interests between the dominant elements of the urban population and the rulers, whose power was justified by a number of ideas of authority. At the heart of the high culture of the cities lay the tradition of religious and legal learning, transmitted in special institutions, the madrasas. *Linked with it were other traditions of secular literature, philosophical and scientific thought, and mystical speculation transmitted by Sufi brotherhoods, which played an important role in integrating the different orders of Muslim society. Jews and Christians, although dimin-*

ished in numbers, preserved their own religious traditions, but Jews in particular took part in the flowering of thought and literature, and were important in the trade of the cities.

CHAPTER 5

The Arab Muslim World

STATES AND DYNASTIES

By the end of the tenth century there had come into existence an Islamic world, united by a common religious culture expressed in the Arabic language, and by human links which trade, migration and pilgrimage had forged. This world was no longer embodied in a single political unit, however. There were three rulers claiming the title of caliph, in Baghdad, Cairo and Cordoba, and others who were in fact rulers of independent states. This is not surprising. To have kept so many countries, with differing traditions and interests, in a single empire for so long had been a remarkable achievement. It could scarcely have been done without the force of religious conviction, which had formed an effective ruling group in western Arabia, and had then created an alliance of interests between that group and an expanding section of the societies over which it ruled. Neither the military nor the administrative resources of the 'Abbasid caliphate were such that they could enable it to maintain the framework of political unity for ever, in an empire stretching from central Asia to the Atlantic coast, and from the tenth century onwards the political history of countries where the rulers, and an increasing part of the population, were Muslim was to be a series of regional histories, of the rise and fall of dynasties whose power radiated from their capital cities to frontiers which on the whole were not clearly defined.

No attempt will be made here to give in detail the history of all these dynasties, but the general pattern of events should at least be made clear. For this purpose, the Islamic world can be divided into three broad areas, each with its own centres of power. The first of them included Iran, the land beyond the Oxus, and southern Iraq; for some time after the tenth century its main centre of power continued to be Baghdad, standing as it did at the heart of a rich agricultural district and a widespread network of trade, and with the influence and the prestige accumulated during centuries of rule by the 'Abbasid caliphs. The second area included Egypt, Syria and western Arabia; its centre of power lay in Cairo, the city built by the Fatimids, in the midst of an extensive and productive countryside and at the heart of a system of trade which linked the world of the Indian Ocean with that of the Mediterranean Sea. The third included the Maghrib and the Muslim parts of Spain known as Andalus; in this area there was not one predominant centre of power but several, lying in regions of extensive cultivation and at points from which trade between Africa and different parts of the Mediterranean world could be controlled.

In a rather simplified way, the political history of all three regions can be divided into a number of periods. The first of them covers the eleventh and twelfth centuries. In this period, the eastern area was ruled by the Saljuqs, a Turkish dynasty supported by a Turkish army and adhering to Sunni Islam. They established themselves in Baghdad in 1055 as effective rulers beneath the suzerainty of the 'Abbasids, held sway over Iran, Iraq and most of Syria, and conquered parts of Anatolia from the Byzantine emperor (1038–1194). They did not claim to be caliphs. Among the terms used to describe this and later dynasties, it will be most convenient to use that of 'sultan', meaning roughly 'holder of power'.

In Egypt, the Fatimids continued to rule until 1171, but were then replaced by Salah al-Din (Saladin, 1169–93), a military leader of Kurdish origin. The change of rulers brought with it a change of religious alliance. The Fatimids had belonged to the Isma'ili branch of the Shi'is, but Salah al-Din was a Sunni, and he was able to mobilize the strength and religious fervour of Egyptian and Syrian Muslims in order to defeat the European Crusaders who had established Christian states in Palestine and on the Syrian coast at the end of the eleventh century. The dynasty founded by Salah al-Din, that of the Ayyubids, ruled Egypt from 1169 to 1252, Syria to 1260, and part of western Arabia to 1229.

In the Western area, the Umayyad caliphate of Cordoba broke up in the early years of the eleventh century into a number of small kingdoms, and this made it possible for the Christian states which had survived in the north of Spain to begin expanding southwards. Their expansion was checked for a time, however, by the successive appearance of two dynasties which drew their power from an idea of religious reform combined with the strength of the Berber peoples of the Moroccan countryside: first the Almoravids, who came from the desert fringes of southern Morocco (1056–1147), and then the Almohads, whose support came from Berbers in the Atlas mountains, and whose empire at its greatest extent included Morocco, Algeria, Tunisia and the Muslim part of Spain (1130–1269).

A second period is that which covers, very roughly, the thirteenth and fourteenth centuries. During the thirteenth, the eastern area was disturbed by the irruption into the Muslim world of a non-Muslim Mongol dynasty from eastern Asia, with an army formed of Mongolian and Turkish tribesmen from the steppes of inner Asia. They conquered Iran and Iraq, and brought to an end the 'Abbasid caliphate of Baghdad in 1258. A branch of the ruling family reigned over Iran and Iraq for almost a century (1256–1336) and was converted to Islam in the course of it. The Mongols tried to move westwards, but were stopped in Syria by an army from Egypt, formed of military slaves (*mamluks*) who had been brought into the country by the Ayyubids. The leaders of this army deposed the Ayyubids and formed a self-perpetuating military élite, drawn from the Caucasus and central Asia, which continued to rule Egypt for more than two centuries (the Mamluks, 1250–1517); it ruled Syria also from 1260, and controlled the holy cities in western Arabia. In the western area, the Almohad dynasty gave way to a number of successor-states, including that of the Marinids in Morocco (1196–1465) and that of the Hafsids, who ruled from their capital at Tunis (1228–1574).

This second period was one in which the frontiers of the Muslim world changed considerably. In some places the frontier contracted under attack from the Christian states of western Europe. Sicily was lost to the Normans from northern Europe, and most of Spain to the Christian kingdoms of the north; by the middle of the fourteenth century they held the whole country except for the kingdom of Granada in the south. Both in Sicily and Spain the Arab Muslim population continued to exist for a time, but in the end they were to be extinguished by conversion or expulsion. On the other hand, the states established by the Crusaders in Syria and Palestine were finally destroyed by the Mamluks, and the expansion into Anatolia, which had begun under the Saljuqs, was carried further by other Turkish dynasties. As this happened, the nature of the population changed, by the coming in of Turkish tribesmen and the conversion of much of the Greek population. There was also an expansion of Muslim rule and population eastwards into northern India. In Africa too Islam continued to spread along the trade-routes, into the Sahil on the southern fringes of the Sahara desert, down the valley of the Nile, and along the east African coast.

In the third period, covering roughly the fifteenth and sixteenth centuries, Muslim states were faced with a new challenge from the states of western

Europe. The production and trade of European cities grew; textiles exported by merchants from Venice and Genoa competed with those produced in the cities of the Muslim world. The Christian conquest of Spain was completed with the extinction of the kingdom of Granada in 1492; the whole peninsula was now ruled by the Christian kings of Portugal and Spain. The power of Spain threatened the Muslim hold over the Maghrib, as did that of southern European pirates in the eastern Mediterranean.

At the same time, changes in military and naval techniques, and in particular the use of gunpowder, made possible a greater concentration of power and the creation of more powerful and long-lasting states, which extended over the greater part of the Muslim world in this period. In the far west, new dynasties succeeded the Marinids and others: first the Sa'dids (1511–1628), and then the 'Alawis, who have ruled from 1631 until the present day. At the other end of the Mediterranean, a Turkish dynasty, that of the Ottomans, grew up in Anatolia, on the disputed frontier with the Byzantine Empire. It expanded from there into south-eastern Europe, and then conquered the rest of Anatolia; the Byzantine capital, Constantinople, became the Ottoman capital, now known as Istanbul (1453). In the early sixteenth century the Ottomans defeated the Mamluks and absorbed Syria, Egypt and western Arabia into their empire (1516–17). They then took up the defence of the Maghrib coast against Spain, and by so doing became the successors of the Hafsids and rulers of the Maghrib as far as the borders of Morocco. Their empire was to last, in one form or another, until 1922.

Further east the last great incursion of a ruler with an army drawn from the tribesmen of inner Asia, that of Timur (Tamerlane), left behind it a dynasty in Iran and Transoxania, but not for long (1370–1506). By the early sixteenth century it had been replaced by a new and more lasting one, that of the Safavids, who extended their rule from the north-western region of Iran to the whole country and beyond (1501–1732). The Mughals, a dynasty descended from the Mongol ruling family and from Timur, created an empire in northern India, with its capital at Delhi (1526–1858).

Beyond these four great states, those of the 'Alawis, Ottomans, Safavids and Mughals, there lay smaller ones, in the Crimea and the land beyond the Oxus, in central and eastern Arabia, and in the lands newly converted to Islam in Africa.

ARABS, PERSIANS AND TURKS

These political changes did not destroy the cultural unity of the world of Islam; it grew deeper as more and more of the population became Muslims and the faith of Islam articulated itself into systems of thought and institutions. In the course of time, however, a certain division began to appear within this broad unity of culture; in the eastern part of the Islamic world, the coming of Islam did not submerge consciousness of the past to the same extent as it did in the west.

In the western part of the Muslim world, the Arabic language gradually extinguished the vernaculars. In Iran and other eastern regions, however, Persian continued to be used. The difference between Arabs and Persians persisted from the time when the Arab conquerors engulfed the Sasanian Empire, drawing its officials into the service of the 'Abbasid caliphs and its educated class into the process of creating an Islamic culture. The sense of difference, with overtones of hostility, found expression in the *shu'ubiyya*, a literary controversy carried on in Arabic about the relative merits of the two peoples in the formation of Islam. Pahlavi continued to be used by Persians both in Zoroastrian religious writings and, for a time, in the administration of government.

In the tenth century something new began to appear: a high literature in a new kind of Persian language, not very different in grammatical structure from Pahlavi but written in Arabic script and with a vocabulary enriched by words taken from Arabic. This seems to have happened first in eastern Iran, at the courts of local rulers not familiar with Arabic. To some extent, the new literature reflected the kinds of writing in Arabic which were current at other courts: lyrical and panegyric poetry, history and to some extent works of religion. There was another form of writing, however, which was distinctively Persian. The epic poem recording the traditional history of Iran and its rulers had existed in pre-Islamic times; it was now revived and expressed in the new Persian and given its final form in the *Shah-nameh* of Firdawsi (*c.* 940–1020). Among Muslim countries, Iran was virtually unique in having a strong, conscious link with its pre-Islamic past. This did not lead, however, to a rejection of its Islamic heritage; from this time onwards, Persians continued to use Arabic for legal and religious writing and Persian for secular literature, and the influence of this double culture extended northwards into Transoxania and eastwards into northern India.

In this way the Muslim countries were divided into two parts, one where

Arabic was the exclusive language of high culture and another where both Arabic and Persian were used for different purposes. Intertwined with the linguistic division was one between centres of political power. The rise of the Fatimids in the west and then that of the Saljuqs in the east created a frontier, although a shifting one, between Syria and Iraq. In the thirteenth century, the abolition of the 'Abbasid caliphate and the destruction of the power of Baghdad by the Mongols, and then their defeat by the Mamluks in Syria, made this division permanent. From now onwards, in the east there lay regions ruled by states with their centres in Iran, Transoxania or northern India, and to the west those ruled from Cairo or cities in the Maghrib and Spain; southern Iraq, which had been the centre, became a frontier region. This division continued to exist, in another form, when the Safavids rose to power in Iran and the Ottomans absorbed most of the countries of Arabic speech into their empire; for a time the two empires fought for control of Iraq.

The political division, however, could not be called one between Arabs and Persians, because from the eleventh century onwards most ruling groups in both areas were neither Arab nor Persian in origin, language or political tradition, but Turks, descended from the nomadic pastoral peoples of inner Asia. They had begun to move across the north-eastern frontier of the domain of Islam during the 'Abbasid period. At first individuals had come, but later whole groups had moved across the frontier and become Muslims. Some had taken service in the armies of rulers, and in due course dynasties emerged among them. The Saljuqs were of Turkish origin, and as they expanded westwards into Anatolia Turks moved with them. Many of the Mamluks who ruled Egypt came from Turkish lands; the larger part of the Mongol armies was formed of Turks, and the Mongol invasion had as a permanent effect the settlement of large numbers of Turks in Iran and Anatolia. Later, the Ottoman, Safavid and Mughal dynasties all drew their strength from Turkish armies.

The dynasties established by Turks continued to use forms of the Turkish language in the army and palace, but in time they were drawn into the world of Arabic or Arabo-Persian culture, or at least acted as its patrons and guardians. In Iran, Turkish was the language of rulers and armies, Persian that of administration and secular culture, and Arabic that of religious and legal culture. To the west, whatever the language of rulers, Arabic was that of civil officials and high culture; later this changed to some extent, when the rise of the Ottoman Empire led to the formation of a distinctive Ottoman Turkish language and culture, which was that of the high officials as well as the palace and army. In the Maghrib and what was left of Muslim Spain, Arabic was the dominant language of government as well as of high culture; although Berbers from the Atlas and the fringes of the Sahara played a political role at times, to the extent to which this happened they were drawn into the Arabic culture. Even here, however, the Ottoman conquest in the sixteenth century brought something of their language and political culture to the coast of the Maghrib.

This book is concerned with the western part of the Islamic world, that in which Arabic was the dominant language both of high culture and, in one form or another, of colloquial speech. It would be wrong, of course, to think that this was a region sharply cut off from the world around it. Countries of Arabic speech still had much in common with those of Persian and Turkish; lands lying around the Indian Ocean or the Mediterranean Sea had close links with each other, whether or not their dominant religion was Islam; the whole world lived within the same constraints imposed by the limitation of human resources and of the technical knowledge of how to use them. It would also be too simple to think of this vast region as forming a single 'country'. It would be better to think of the places where Arabic was the dominant language as a group of regions, differing from each other in geographical position and nature, and inhabited by peoples who had inherited distinctive social and cultural traditions, which still survived in ways of life and perhaps also in habits of thought and feeling, even where the consciousness of what had existed before the coming of Islam had grown weak or virtually disappeared. Rather similar social processes can be seen in these regions, and a common language and the culture expressed in it gave the urban literate classes a certain ease of intercourse with one another.

GEOGRAPHICAL DIVISIONS

Within the area where Arabic was dominant, it is possible – with some simplification – to distinguish five regions. The first is the Arabian peninsula, where the Arabic-speaking Muslim community had grown up. The peninsula is a land-mass marked off from the surrounding world on three sides, by the Red Sea, the Persian Gulf and the Arabian Sea (a part of the Indian Ocean), and divided into a number of areas differing from each other in physical nature and, at most periods, in historical development. The basic line of division is one which runs roughly from north to south, parallel to the Red Sea. On the western side of the line is an area of volcanic rock. The coastal plain, the Tihama, rises into ranges of hills and plateaux, then into higher mountain ranges – Hijaz, 'Asir and Yemen – with peaks as much as 4,000 metres above sea-level in the south. The southern mountains are prolonged towards the south-east, with a large valley, the Wadi Hadramawt, cutting through them.

The mountains of Yemen lie at the extreme point of the area touched by the monsoon winds of the Indian Ocean, and this was an area where regular cultivation of fruit and grains had long been carried on. Further north, rainfall is more limited and irregular, there are no rivers of any size, but a limited supply of water comes from springs, wells and seasonal streams; the way of life which best made use of natural resources was one which combined the rearing of camels and other animals, by a more or less regular movement over the year, with the cultivation of date-palms and other trees in the oases where water was plentiful.

To the east of the mountains the land slopes eastwards towards the Gulf. In the north and south are sandy deserts (the Nafud and the 'Empty Quarter'), and between them a rocky steppe, Najd, and its extension on the shore of the Gulf, al-Hasa. Except for some highlands in the north, rainfall is small, but springs and seasonal flows made it possible to maintain a settled life based on cultivation in the oases; elsewhere, camels were pastured by seasonal migrations over long distances. In the south-eastern corner of the peninsula, there is a third area, Oman, not dissimilar to Yemen in the south-west. From the coastal plain there rises a mountain range reaching a height of more than 3,000 metres; here springs and streams give water which, distributed by an ancient system of irrigation, made settled agriculture possible. On the coast lies a chain of harbours from which fishing in the waters of the Gulf and diving for pearls have been carried on since ancient times.

In the western part of the peninsula, routes running from south to north linked the lands lying around the Indian Ocean with the countries of the Mediterranean basin. In the eastern part, the main routes were those which ran along a chain of oases into Syria and Iraq. The harbours on the coast of the Gulf and Oman were linked by sea-routes with the coasts of India and east Africa. The production of food and raw materials was too small, however, for ports and market towns to grow into large cities, centres of manufacture and power. Mecca and Madina, the holy cities, were maintained by the largess of neighbouring countries.

To the north, the Arabian peninsula joins a second area, the Fertile Crescent: the crescent-shaped land running around the rim of the Hamad or Syrian desert, which is a northern extension of the steppe and desert of Najd. This is a land of ancient and distinctive civilization, overlaid in the western half by those of Greece and Rome, and in the eastern by that of Iran; it was here, rather than in the peninsula, that the specific society and culture of Islam had developed.

The western half of the Fertile Crescent forms an area known to an earlier generation of scholars and travellers as 'Syria'. Here, as in western Arabia, the main geographical divisions run from west to east. Behind a coastal strip of plain there is a range of highlands, rising in the centre to the mountains of Lebanon and sinking in the south to the hills of Palestine. Beyond them, to the east, lies a hollow, part of the Great Rift which runs through the Dead Sea and the Red Sea into east Africa. Beyond this again is another region of highlands, the great plain or plateau of the interior which changes gradually into the steppe and desert of the Hamad. In some places, ancient systems of irrigation used the waters of the Orontes and smaller rivers to maintain fertile oases, in particular that lying around the ancient city of Damascus; for the most part, however, the possibility of cultivation depended on rainfall. On the eastward slopes of the coastal hills and mountains, rainfall is adequate to make possible regular cultivation, provided the soil is fixed by the terracing of the hillsides; elsewhere it is more precarious, varying greatly from year to year, and extremes of heat and cold also are greater. In the inner plains, therefore, the relative advantages of cultivating grain and pasturing camels or sheep varied greatly from time to time.

Syria was linked closely with the rest of the eastern Mediterranean basin, by sea-routes from its ports and by the land-route running along the coast to Egypt; inland it was linked also with western Arabia, and, by routes running across the Hamad or round its northern rim, with lands lying to the east. The combination of long-distance trade with the production of a surplus of foodstuffs and raw materials had made possible the growth of large cities, lying in the inner plains but linked with the coast – Aleppo in the north and Damascus in the centre.

The routes which ran across or around the Hamad led to the valleys of the twin rivers, Euphrates and Tigris. Rising in Anatolia, they flow roughly in a south-easterly direction, draw near each other, then separate, and finally come together to flow into the northern end of the Gulf. The land lying between and around them is divided into two areas. In the north, the Jazira, known to earlier travellers and scholars as upper Mesopotamia, the nature of the elevation made it difficult to use the river water for irrigation and the cultivation of grain, except in the immediate neighbourhood of the rivers or their tributaries; away from the rivers rainfall is uncertain and the soil thin, and the balance lay for the most part in favour of the rearing of sheep, cattle and camels. To the north-east of the rivers, however, there is land of another kind, part of the mountain ranges of Anatolia: often called Kurdistan, after the Kurds who inhabit it. Here, as in the mountain valleys of the Syrian coast, land and water could be used for the cultivation of trees in the highlands and grain lower down, but also for raising sheep and goats by regular transhumance from winter pastures in the river valleys to summer pastures in the high mountains.

Further south, in Iraq, the nature of the land is different. The snows of the Anatolian mountains melt in spring and a great volume of water comes down the rivers and overflows into the surrounding plains. The deposit of silt left by the floods over the millennia has created a vast alluvial plain, the Sawad, where grain and date-palms were cultivated on a large scale. Irrigation was easier here than in the north, because the plain was almost without relief, and from the times of ancient Babylon a great system of canals carried the water over the Sawad. The flatness of the plain and violence of the floods made it necessary to keep the canals in order. If they were not cleaned and repaired, the flood-waters could overflow the river banks, inundate the surrounding country, and form areas of permanent marsh. The absence of relief also made it easy for nomadic pastoralists from Najd to move into the river valleys and use the land for pasture instead of agriculture. The security and prosperity of the Sawad depended on the strength of governments, but they in their turn drew their food, materials, and wealth from the countryside they protected. A succession of great cities had risen in the heart of the Sawad, where Euphrates and Tigris come close together; Babylon, Ctesiphon of the Sasanids, and the 'Abbasid capital, Baghdad.

Apart from the links with Syria and Najd, routes ran from Iraq into the Iranian highlands to the east, but more easily in the south than the north. The rivers were not easily navigable for most of their length, but from the point where they joined and flowed together into the Gulf, sea-routes went to the ports of the Gulf and Indian Ocean. The main terminal of these routes, Basra, was for a time the foremost port of the 'Abbasid Empire.

To the west of the Arabian peninsula, lying across the Red Sea and a narrow land-bridge to the north of it, there is sandy desert, and beyond it a third area, the valley of the river Nile. Rising in the highlands of east Africa, the river gathers force as it moves northwards and is joined by tributaries coming down from the mountains of Ethiopia. It flows through an alluvial basin created by the silt it has deposited over the centuries, in parts a broad plain and in others a narrow strip, and in its final stage it divides into branches and runs through a fertile delta into the Mediterranean Sea. In the summer, after the snows melt in the east African highlands, the level of the water rises and the river comes down in flood. From early times, a number of devices – the screw, the waterwheel, the bucket on the end of a pole – made it possible to raise water on a small scale from the river. In places, particularly in the north, there was an ancient system of dykes, which diverted water when the Nile flooded into basins of land surrounded by banks, where it stood for a time and was then drained back into the river as the flood fell, leaving its silt behind to enrich the soil. On land irrigated in this way, grain and other crops were grown in abundance. In the desert which stretched along the western side of the river valley, there were also some oases of settled cultivation.

The northern part of the Nile valley forms the land of Egypt, a country with a tradition of high civilization and a social unity created or made permanent by a long history of political control, exercised by rulers from a city lying at the point where the river divides into branches and flows through the delta. Cairo was the latest in a succession of cities stretching back to Memphis in the third millennium BC. It stood at the centre of a network of routes running northwards to the ports on the Mediterranean, and from there by sea to Syria, Anatolia, the Maghrib and Italy, eastwards into Syria by the coastal road, eastwards also to the Red Sea and from there to the Indian Ocean, and southwards to the upper valley of the Nile and to east and west Africa.

In the upper part of the Nile valley, the social domination of the delta and the capital city was weaker. The Nile flows through a region virtually without rainfall. On its east bank, the cultivable area formed only a narrow strip, but on the west the flatness of the land made it possible to extend the cultivable strip by irrigation. South of this rainless area is one of heavy summer rainfall, which may last from May to September. Here grain could be grown and cattle raised in an area which extended westwards beyond the river valley until it reached sandy semi-desert, and southwards into broad areas of perennial vegetation. This was the Sudan, a land of agriculture and pastoralism, of villages, nomadic encampments and market towns, but not of large cities. It was linked by the Nile with Egypt, and by land-routes with Ethiopia and the Sahil, the region lying around the southern rim of the Sahara desert.

From the western desert of Egypt to the Atlantic coast there stretches a fourth region, known in Arabic as the Maghrib, the land of the west or of the setting sun; this includes the countries now known as Libya, Tunisia, Algeria and Morocco. Within this area the most obvious natural division runs from north to south. Stretching along the Mediterranean and Atlantic coasts is a strip of low land which broadens in places into plains: the Sahil of Tunisia and the plain on the Atlantic coast of Morocco. Inland from this strip rise ranges of mountains: the Jabal Akhdar in Libya, the mountains of northern Tunisia, the Tellurian Atlas, and the Rif in Morocco. Inland again there are high plains or steppes, and beyond them other ranges of mountains, the Aurès in Algeria, the Middle Atlas and High Atlas further west. To the south lies steppe, changing gradually into desert, the Sahara, in parts stony and in others sand, with oases of palm trees. To the south of the Sahara is an area of grassland watered by rainfall and the river Niger, the Sahil of western Sudan.

The Maghrib has few rivers which could be used for irrigation, and it was the volume and time of rainfall which determined the nature and extent of human settlement. In the coastal plains and on the seaward slopes of mountains, which precipitate the rainclouds coming from the Mediterranean or Atlantic, a permanent cultivation of grain, olives, fruit and vegetables was possible, and the upper slopes of the mountains were well forested. Beyond the mountains, in the high plains, however, rainfall varies from year to year and even within the year, and the land could be used in a mixed way: the cultivation of grain, and the pasturage of sheep and goats by seasonal migration. Further south, in the steppe and desert, the land was more suited to pasturage; breeders of sheep mingled with the breeders of camels, moving northwards in the summer from the desert. The Sahara indeed was the only part of the Maghrib where camels were raised; the camel had come into the area in the centuries before the rise of Islam. Its sandy regions were little inhabited, but in the other part of it breeders of livestock mingled with cultivators of date-palms and other trees in the oases.

The main routes which joined the Maghrib with the surrounding world also ran from north to south. The ports of the Mediterranean and Atlantic linked the region with the Iberian peninsula, Italy and Egypt; routes ran south from them, through the settled country and a chain of oases in the Sahara, to the Sahil and beyond. In certain places, the routes came to the sea through wide areas of cultivated land, and here large cities could grow up and maintain themselves. Two such areas were of particular importance.

One lay on the Atlantic coast of Morocco; here there had grown up in early Islamic times the city of Fez, while further south, and rather later, there grew also that of Marrakish. The other was the coastal plain of Tunisia; here the main city in early Islamic times was Qayrawan, but later its place was taken by Tunis, lying on the coast near the site of the ancient city of Carthage. These two areas, with their large cities, radiated their economic, political and cultural power over the lands around and between them. Algeria, lying between the two, did not have a large and stable enough area of settled life to give rise to a similar centre of power and tended to fall into the sphere of influence of its two neighbours. Similarly, the power of Tunis extended over western Libya (Tripolitania), while Cyrenaica in the east, separated from the rest of the Maghrib by the Libyan desert which here came to the edge of the sea, lay more within the sphere of influence of Egypt.

The fifth area is the Iberian peninsula, or Andalus, that part of it which was ruled and largely inhabited by Muslims (the greater part in the eleventh century, but gradually shrinking until it disappeared by the end of the fifteenth). In some ways similar to Syria, it consisted of small regions more or less cut off from each other. The centre of the peninsula is a vast plateau surrounded and cut across by mountain ranges. From here a number of rivers flow through lowlands to the coast: the Ebro runs into the Mediterranean in the north, the Tagus into the Atlantic by way of the Portuguese lowlands, and the Guadalquivir into the Atlantic further south. Between the mountains which surround the central plateau and the Mediterranean Sea lie the mountainous area of Catalonia in the north and plains further south. Variations in climate and rainfall create differences in the nature of the land and the ways in which it could be used. In the cold climate of the high mountains there were forests of cork, oak and pine, and among them lay pastures where grain was grown and livestock raised. The central plateau, with a climate of extremes, was suitable for a mixed regime, the cultivation of grain and olives and the pasturage of sheep and goats. In the warm climate of the river valleys and coastal plains, citrus and other fruits were grown. It was here, in areas of rich cultivation and with access to river transport, that the large cities lay – Cordoba and Seville.

Spain was part of the Mediterranean world, and the ports on its east coast linked it with the other countries of the basin: Italy, the Maghrib, Egypt and Syria. Its most significant connections were with Morocco, its southern neighbour; the narrow straits which separated the two landmasses were no barrier to trade, migration, or the movement of conquering ideas or armies.

MUSLIM ARABS AND OTHERS

By the eleventh century Islam was the religion of the rulers, the dominant groups, and a growing proportion of the population, but it is not certain that it was the religion of a majority anywhere outside the Arabian peninsula. In the same way, while Arabic was the language of high culture and much of the urban population, other languages still survived from the period before the coming of the Muslim conquerors. By the fifteenth century the flood of Arabic Islam had covered the whole region, and for the most part it was Islam in its Sunni form, although adherents of doctrines evolved in the early centuries still existed. In south-eastern Arabia and on the fringes of the Sahara there were communities of Ibadis, claiming spiritual descent from the Kharijis who had rejected the leadership of 'Ali after the battle of Siffin, and had revolted against the rule of the caliphs in Iraq and the Maghrib. In Yemen, much of the population adhered to Shi'ism in its Zaydi form. Shi'ism in its 'Twelver' and Isma'ili forms, which had dominated much of the eastern Arab world in the tenth century, had receded; the 'Twelvers' were still numerous in parts of Lebanon, southern Iraq where they had their main shrines, and the west coast of the Gulf; and Isma'ilis still clung to their faith in parts of Yemen, Iran and Syria, where they had been able to put up a local resistance to Sunni rulers, the Ayyubids in Syria and the Saljuqs further east. (News of their activities, brought back to Europe during the time of the Crusades, gave rise to the name of 'Assassins' and the story, not found in the Arabic sources, that they lived under the absolute rule of the 'Old Man of the Mountains'.) Adherents of other offshoots of Shi'ism, the Druzes and Nusayris, were also to be found in Syria. In northern Iraq there were Yazidis, followers of a religion which had elements derived from both Christianity and Islam, and in the south the Mandaeans had a faith drawn from older religious beliefs and practices.

By the twelfth century the Christian Churches of the Maghrib had virtually disappeared, but a large part of the population of the Muslim kingdoms of Andalus were Christians of the Roman Catholic Church. Coptic Christians were still an important element of the Egyptian population by the fifteenth century, although their numbers were shrinking by conversion. Further south, in the northern Sudan, Christianity had disappeared by the fifteenth or sixteenth century, as Islam spread across the Red Sea and down the Nile valley. All over Syria and in northern Iraq Christian communities remained, although in a diminished form. Some, mainly in the cities, belonged to the Eastern Orthodox Church, but others were members of those other Churches which had their origins in the controversies about the nature of Christ: the Syrian Orthodox or Monophysites, and the Nestorians. In Lebanon and other parts of Syria there was a fourth Church, that of the Maronites; they had held the Monothelete doctrine, but in the twelfth century, when the Crusaders ruled the coasts of Syria, they had accepted Roman Catholic doctrine and the supremacy of the Pope.

Jews were spread more widely throughout the world of Arabic Islam. In the Maghrib a considerable part of the peasantry had been converted to Judaism before the coming of Islam, and there were still Jewish rural communities, as there were in Yemen and parts of the Fertile Crescent. Jews were found also in most of the cities of the region, for they played an important part in trade, manufacture, finance and medicine. The greater number of them belonged to the main body of Jews who accepted the oral law and the interpretation of it contained in the Talmud and maintained by those trained in Talmudic scholarship. In Egypt, Palestine and elsewhere, however, there were also Karaites, who did not accept the Talmud and had their own laws derived by their teachers from the Scriptures.

A large part of the Jewish communities were Arabic-speaking by this time, although they used forms of Arabic which were special to them and still used Hebrew for liturgical purposes. Among the Christians, too, Arabic had spread in the Fertile Crescent, Egypt and Spain; Aramaic and Syriac were shrinking as spoken and written languages, although used in liturgies, and the Coptic language of Egypt had virtually ceased to be used for any except religious purposes by the fifteenth century; many of the Christians of Andalus had adopted Arabic as their language, although the Romance languages they had inherited survived and were beginning to revive. At the margins of the Arabic flood, in mountain and desert districts, other languages were spoken: Kurdish in the mountains of northern Iraq, Nubian in the northern Sudan and various languages in the south, Berber dialects in the mountains of the Maghrib and the Sahara. Kurds and Berbers were Muslims, however, and to the extent to which they were educated they came within the sphere of the Arabic language.

CHAPTER 6

The Countryside

LAND AND ITS USE

These countries, strung along a line from the shores of the Atlantic to those of the Indian Ocean, shared not only a dominant religion and culture but also, up to a point, certain features of climate, relief, soil and vegetation. It has sometimes been claimed that these two factors were closely connected, that the religion of Islam was particularly suitable to a certain kind of environment, or indeed had created it: that Muslim societies were dominated by the desert, or at least by a certain relationship between the desert and the city. Such theories are dangerous, however; there are countries with a different kind of climate and society, such as parts of south and south-east Asia, where Islam has spread and taken root. It is better, therefore, to look at the two factors separately.

Certain general statements can be made about the climate of most parts of the countries which by this period were mainly Muslim in faith and Arabic in speech. On the coasts, where the winds coming in from the sea are humid, the climate is damp; inland, it is a 'continental' climate, with a wide variation between temperatures by day and by night, and between summer and winter. Everywhere January is the coldest month, June, July and August are the hottest. In some regions rainfall is plentiful and regular. For the most part these are areas lying on the coast or the seaward slopes of mountains. The rainclouds coming from the sea are precipitated by the mountains: the Atlas on the Atlantic seaboard of Morocco; the Rif, the mountains of eastern Algeria and northern Tunisia, and the massif of Cyrenaica on the southern coast of the Mediterranean; and on its eastern coast the mountains of Lebanon and, far inland, those of north-eastern Iraq. In south-west Arabia the rain is brought by clouds coming from the Indian Ocean. Here the rainy season is that of the monsoon winds in the summer months; elsewhere, rain falls for the most part from September to

January. In these regions, the average annual rainfall is above 500 mm, and considerably more in some places.

On the other side of the coastal mountains, in the plains and plateaux, rainfall is less, averaging 250 mm a year. Averages may be deceptive, however; in these inner regions rainfall varies greatly from month to month and year to year. This can affect the crops; in some years rain scarcely comes at all and the harvest can fail.

Beyond this belt of considerable but irregular rainfall are others where rain is scantier or scarcely falls at all; some of these lie near the coast, as in lower Egypt where there are no mountains to precipitate the rain, and others are far inland. Rainfall here may vary between nil and 250 mm a year. Most of these areas, however, are not wholly without water. In parts even of the Arabian and Sahara deserts there are springs and wells, fed by occasional rains or by subterranean penetration of water from the foothills or mountain ranges which lie nearer to the sea. In other places land which does not itself receive rain may be watered by rivers bringing rainfall from distant mountains. Many of the rivers are no more than seasonal *wadis*, dry in summer and filling with floods in the rainy season, but others are perennial: those flowing from mountains to sea in Spain, Atlantic Morocco, Algeria and Syria, and above all the two great river-systems – that of the Nile and that of the Tigris and Euphrates.

Both these bring life to large areas of flatland through which they pass, but they are different in their rhythms. The Nile and its tributaries bring water from the rains which fall in the highlands of Ethiopia and east Africa; these come in spring and summer, causing a succession of floods, first in the White Nile, then in the Blue Nile and tributaries. The floods reach Egypt in May, then rise until they attain their height in September, after which they decline and die away in November. In the highlands of Anatolia, from which both Euphrates and Tigris come, the snows melt in the spring. The Tigris brings down its floods from March to May, the Euphrates a little later; in both the floods are violent enough to overflow the banks of the rivers and at times have changed their courses. In the south of Iraq, because of the sinking of the ground, permanent marshes had been formed in the period shortly before the coming of Islam.

Variations of relief, temperature and water supply have combined to create varieties of soil. In the coastal plains and on the seaward slopes of the mountains the soil is rich, but in the mountains it needs to be kept in place by terracing if it is not to be carried down by the water in the rainy season. In the plains of the interior it is thinner but still fertile. Where the inner plains shade into steppe and desert, the nature of the land changes. Patches of soil, in places where underground water is plentiful, are surrounded by areas of rock and gravel, volcanic massifs, and sand-dunes such as those of the 'Empty Quarter' and the Nafud in Arabia, and the Erg districts in the Sahara.

From time immemorial, wherever there was soil and water, fruit and vegetables have been grown, but favourable conditions are necessary for certain products. Three frontiers of cultivation were particularly important. The first was the olive tree, which yielded food, cooking oil and lighting fuel; this could be grown where rainfall exceeded 180 mm and the soil was sandy. Secondly, the growing of wheat and other cereals, for human consumption and animal fodder, demanded either rainfall of more than 400 mm or irrigation from rivers or springs. The third frontier was that of the date-palm, which needs a temperature of at least 16°C to produce fruit, but can flourish where water is scarce. If there was sufficient water and pasturage, land could be used for the grazing of livestock as well as cultivation. Goats and sheep needed pasture and grazing at intervals not too great for them to travel; camels could travel long distances between their pastures and needed to drink less frequently.

Because of this variety of natural conditions, the Middle East and Maghrib were divided, from before the rise of Islam, into certain broad areas of production, lying between two extremes. At one extreme stood areas where cultivation was always possible: coastal strips where olive trees could be grown, plains and river valleys where grains were cultivated, oases of palm trees. In all these areas fruits and vegetables also were produced, and one of the results of the formation of an Islamic society stretching from the Indian Ocean to the Mediterranean was to introduce new varieties. Cattle, sheep and goats found pasturage here, and in the high mountains a variety of trees produced timber, gall-nuts, gum or cork. At the other extreme were areas where water and vegetation were adequate only for the rearing of camels or other animals by seasonal migration over long distances. Two such areas were of particular importance: the Arabian desert and its northern extension the Syrian desert, where camel-breeders would spend the winter in the Nafud and move north-westwards to Syria or north-eastwards to Iraq in the summer; and the Sahara, where they would move from the desert into the high plains or the southern fringes of the Atlas mountains.

Between these two extremes, one of a more or less assured life of sedentary cultivation and the other of an enforced nomadic pastoralism, were areas where cultivation, although possible, was more precarious, and where land and water could be used equally well for pasturage. This was particularly true of those regions which lay on the margins of the desert and where rainfall was irregular: the steppe in Syria, the valley of the Euphrates, the outer fringes of the Nile delta and other irrigated areas in the Nile valley, the plains of Kordofan and Darfur in the Sudan, and the high plains and Saharan Atlas in the Maghrib. In certain circumstances almost every area of cultivated land could be taken over for pasture, unless it was protected by its relief; pastoralists from the Sahara did not, for example, penetrate the High Atlas mountains in Morocco.

It would be too simple, therefore, to think of the countryside as being divided into areas where peasants fixed on the land tended their crops and others where nomads moved with their animals. Intermediate positions were possible between a wholly sedentary and a wholly nomadic life, and it was these which were the norm. There was a wide spectrum of ways of using land. In some areas there would be settled people in firm control of their land, the only livestock being looked after for them by hirelings; in others, settled cultivators and pastors of sheep shared the use of the land; in others again, the population was transhumant, migrating with its flocks from lowland to highland pasturage, but cultivating the land in certain seasons; in yet others, it was purely nomadic, but might control some settled areas in oases or on the desert fringes, where peasants worked for the profit of the nomads.

The relations between those who tilled the land and those who moved with their animals cannot be explained in terms of some age-old and ineradicable opposition between 'the desert and the sown'. Settled cultivators and nomadic pastoralists needed each other for an exchange of the commodities which each had to sell: the pure pastoralists could not produce all the food they needed, whether cereals or dates; the settled people needed the meat, hides and wool of the animals bred by the pastoralists, and camels, donkeys or mules for transport. In areas where both kinds of group existed, they used the same water and the same land with its vegetation, and needed if possible to make acceptable and lasting arrangements with each other.

The symbiosis between cultivators and pastoralists was a fragile one, however, and liable to shift in favour of one or the other. On the one hand, the mobility and hardiness of the nomadic pastoralists tended to give them a dominant position. This was particularly true of the relationship between those who bred camels in the desert and those who lived in the oases. Some of the larger oases lying on important trade-routes might have a class of merchants who were able to maintain control over the markets and date-palms, but in others it was the pastoralists who controlled the land and cultivated it by means of peasants, or, in some places, of slaves. On the fringes of the desert too the pastoralists might be strong enough to levy a kind of tribute, *khuwwa*, on the settled villages. This unequal relationship was expressed, in the culture of the Arab pastoralists, by a certain hierarchical conception of the rural world; they regarded themselves as having a freedom, nobility and honour which were lacking to peasants, merchants and craftsmen. On the other hand, there might be forces at work which would curb the freedom and strength of the pastoralists and draw them into settled life once they came into the plain or steppe country.

When the symbiosis was strongly disturbed, therefore, it was not because of a perpetual state of warfare between the two kinds of society, but for other reasons. Changes in climate and water supply may have occurred over the centuries; the progressive desiccation of the Sahara region over a long period is well attested. There were shifts in the demand for the products of countryside and desert: a larger or smaller demand for olive oil, grain, hides, wool, meat, or camels for transport. At times there might be a crisis of over-population among the nomads, who on the whole led a healthier life than the people of the villages and might therefore expand beyond their means of subsistence. From time to time there were political changes; when rulers were strong they tended to extend the area of settled agriculture, from which they drew the food to feed cities and taxes to support armies.

The Arab conquests of the surrounding countries in the early Islamic period were not a nomadic flood which engulfed the settled world and overturned the symbiosis. The Arab armies were small, reasonably disciplined bodies of soldiers of varying origins; they were followed, at least in Iraq and Iran, by large migrations of pastoral Arabs, of a size which cannot be estimated. The interest of the new rulers, however, was to preserve the system of cultivation and therefore of taxation and revenue. Those who had formerly owned the land were largely displaced or else absorbed into the new ruling élite, but the indigenous peasantry remained, and soldiers and immigrants were settled on the land or in the new cities. The growth of cities larger than those which had formerly existed, from Khurasan and Transoxania in the east to Andalus in the west, shows that there was a settled countryside large and productive enough to supply their food. On the other hand, the growth of long-distance trade within the farflung

Islamic community, and the annual pilgrimage to Mecca, led to a demand for camels and other animals of transport.

In so far as there was a disturbance of the symbiosis, it occurred later, from the tenth or eleventh century onwards. On the fringes of the Muslim world there were incursions of nomadic groups which changed the balance of population. Turkish pastoralists moved into Iran and the newly conquered regions of Anatolia, and this movement was carried further during and after the Mongol invasions; in the far west, Berbers from the Atlas and the Saharan fringes moved northwards into Morocco and Andalus. In the central parts of the Muslim world, however, the process may have been different. A study made of one area throws light on it.[1] The area is that lying around the Diyala river, a tributary of the Tigris, in the great irrigated plain of southern Iraq which provided Baghdad with food and raw materials for its enormous population. The system of irrigation, developed from Babylonian times onwards, needed a government with the strength to maintain it. Such a government existed in the early 'Abbasid period, when the system was repaired and restored after a decline at the end of the period of the Sasanians. As the centuries passed the situation changed. The growth of Baghdad and its trade meant that more of the wealth derived from the rural surplus was used in the city rather than for the maintenance of the countryside; the growing weakness of the central government caused the control of the countryside to fall into the hands of local governors or tax-collectors who had less of a permanent interest in maintaining the irrigation works. There may also have been some ecological changes, leading to the formation of large marshes. In these circumstances, the system of irrigation gradually decayed over the centuries. The cultivators themselves did not have the resources needed to keep it in order, the flow of water into the canals diminished, areas of cultivation were abandoned or turned over to pasturage.

The spread of nomadic pastoralism may therefore have been a result of the decline of agriculture rather than the cause of it. What happened in the Maghrib, however, may have been the opposite of this. Modern historians, taking over an idea which may first have been put forward by Ibn Khaldun, have been accustomed to ascribe the decline of settled life in the Maghrib to the coming of certain Arab tribes, in particular that of Banu Hilal in the eleventh century. Their incursions and depredations are thought to have deeply affected the whole later history of the Maghrib, destroying the strong governments which were the guardians of settled life, changing the use of land from agriculture to pastoralism, and submerging the indigenous population in a sea of new Arab immigration. Modern research has shown, however, that the process was not so simple as this. Elements of the Banu Hilal did indeed enter Tunisia from Egypt in the first half of the eleventh century. They were involved in attempts by the Fatimid dynasty in Egypt to weaken the power of the Zirids, the local rulers of Qayrawan, who had been Fatimid vassals but had thrown off their allegiance. The Zirids were already losing their strength, however, because of a decline in the trade of Qayrawan, and their state was distintegrating into smaller principalities based on provincial towns. It may have been the weakening of authority and the decline of trade, and therefore of demand, which made it possible for the pastoralists to expand. No doubt their expansion caused destruction and disorder, but it does not appear that the Banu Hilal were hostile to settled life as such; they were on good terms with other dynasties. If there was a shift in the rural balance at this time, it may have resulted from other causes, and it seems to have been neither universal nor perpetual. Parts of the Tunisian countryside revived when strong government was restored by the Almohads and their successors, the Hafsids. The expansion of pastoralism, in so far as it existed, was possibly therefore an effect rather than the main cause of the breakdown in the rural symbiosis. If later it was regarded as the cause, that was a symbolic way of seeing a complicated process. It does not appear, moreover, that the Banu Hilal were so numerous as to have replaced the Berber population with Arabs. From this time onwards there was, indeed, an expansion of the Arabic language, and there came with it the idea of a link between the rural peoples of the Maghrib and those of the Arabian peninsula, but its cause was not the spread of Arab tribes so much as the assimilation of Berbers into them.[2]

TRIBAL SOCIETIES

The history of the countryside in these centuries has not been written, and can scarcely be written, because the essential sources are lacking. For the Ottoman period sources do exist, in the vast Ottoman archives which are only now beginning to be explored, and for more recent periods it is possible to supplement documents by direct observation. It is dangerous to argue back from what existed two or three centuries ago, and what exists now, to what may have existed several centuries earlier. It may help us to understand events and processes of those times, however, if we use our knowledge of later times to construct an 'ideal type' of what a rural society may have looked like in a geographical environment such as that of the Middle East and the Maghrib.

If left to themselves, economic and social processes in such rural areas tended to produce a kind of society which is often referred to as 'tribal', and it is necessary first of all to ask what is meant by a tribe.

In pastoral and village communities alike, the basic unit was the nuclear family of three generations: grandparents, parents and children living together in village houses made of stone, mud-brick or whatever material was locally available, or in the woven tents of the nomad. The men were mainly responsible for looking after land or livestock, the women for cooking and cleaning and the rearing of children, but they would also help in the fields or with the flocks. Responsibility for dealings with the outside world lay formally with the men.

It is reasonable to suppose that the values expressed in the concept of 'honour', which has been much studied by social anthropologists, have existed from time immemorial in the countryside, or at least in those parts of it not deeply touched by the formal religions of the cities. On this assumption, it is possible to say – with many variations of time and place – that women in the villages and the steppe, although not veiled or formally secluded, were subordinate to men in significant ways. By widespread custom, although not by Islamic law, landed property belonged to men and was passed by them to their male children: 'sons are the wealth of the house'. It was part of a man's honour to defend what was his and to respond to demands upon him from members of his family, or of a tribe or larger group of which he was part; honour belonged to an individual through his membership of a larger whole. The women of his family – mother and sisters, wives and daughters – were under his protection, but what they did could affect his honour: a lack of modesty, or behaviour which would arouse in men who had no claims over them strong feelings that might challenge the social order. Mingled with a man's respect for his womenfolk there might therefore be a certain suspicion or even fear of women as a danger. A study of beduin women in the western desert of Egypt has drawn attention to the poems and songs which women exchange among themselves and which, by evoking personal feelings and loves which can overshadow accepted duties or cross forbidden frontiers, cast doubt upon the social order by which they live and which they formally accept:

> he reached your arms stretched on the pillow,
> forgot his father, and then his grandfather.[3]

As a woman grew older, however, she might acquire greater authority, as mother of male children or senior wife (if there was more than one), not only over the younger women of the family but also over the men.

In most circumstances, such a nuclear family was not self-sufficient, either economically or socially. It could be incorporated in two kinds of larger unit. One of them was the kinship group, of those linked, or claiming to be linked, by descent from a common ancestor four or five generations ago. This was the group to which its members could look for help in case of need, and which would assume responsibility for vengeance if a member of it were harmed or killed.

The other kind of unit was that created by a permanent economic interest. For those who cultivated the land and did not move, the village – or the 'quarter' if the village was large, as those in plains and river valleys might be – was such a unit. In spite of differences between families, arrangements had to be made for the cultivation of the land. This was done in some places by the permanent division of the village land among families, with grazing ground being held in common; in others by a periodical division, done in such a way that each family would secure a share which it was able to cultivate (the *musha'* system). On irrigated land, arrangements also had to be made for sharing the water; this could be done in a variety of ways, for example by the division of the water in a stream or canal into a number of shares, each of them allotted, permanently or by periodical redistribution, to the owner of a particular piece of land. Arrangements might also have to be made in regard to cultivation; a cultivator whose holding was insufficient, or who had no holding of his own, might look after someone else's land in return for a fixed proportion of the produce, or might plant and tend fruit trees on someone else's land and be regarded as their owner. In pastoral groups, the herding unit – those who moved together from one pasture to another – was a unit of a similar kind, since nomadic pastoralism could not be practised without a certain degree of co-operation and social discipline. Here there was no division of land, however; grazing land and water were regarded as the common property of all those who used them.

Between these two types of unit, the one based on kinship and the other on common interest, there was a complex relationship. In illiterate societies few remember their ancestors five generations back, and to claim a common descent was a symbolic way of expressing a common interest, of giving it a strength it would not otherwise have. In some circumstances, however, there could be a conflict. A member of a kinship group called upon for help might not give it fully because it went against some other interest or personal relationship.

Beyond these more or less permanent minimal units there might be larger ones. All the villages of a district, or all the herding units of a grazing area, or even groups widely separated from each other, might think of themselves as belonging to a larger whole, a 'fraction' or 'tribe', which they would regard as differing from and standing in opposition to other similar groups. The existence and unity of the tribe were usually expressed in terms of descent from a common ancestor, but the precise way in which any fraction or family might be descended from the eponymous ancestor was not usually known, and the genealogies which were transmitted tended to be fictitious, and to be altered and manipulated from time to time in order to express changing relationships between the different units. Even if they were fictitious, however, they could acquire a force and strength by intermarriage within the group.

The tribe was first of all a name which existed in the minds of those who claimed to be linked with each other. It had a potential influence over their actions; for example, where there was a common danger from outside, or in times of large-scale migration. It could have a corporate spirit ('asabiyya) which would lead its members to help each other in time of need. Those who shared a name shared also a belief in a hierarchy of honour. In the desert, the camel-breeding nomads regarded themselves as the most honourable, because their life was the freest and the least restrained by external authority. Outside the tribal system, in their view, were the merchants of the small market towns, itinerant pedlars and craftsmen (such as the Jewish metalworkers in the Sahara, and the Solubba, also metalworkers, in the Arabian desert), and the agricultural labourers of the oases.

Such names, with the loyalties and claims which clustered around them, could continue to exist for centuries, sometimes in a single area, sometimes extending over wide regions. The Banu Hilal provide an example of the way in which a name, enshrined in popular literature, could persist and could give a kind of unity to groups of differing origins, both Arabs and Berbers. Similarly, in south-western Arabia the names of Hashid and Bakil have continued to exist in the same district at least from early Islamic times until the present, and in parts of Palestine the ancient Arabian tribal names of Qays and Yemen served until modern times as a means of identification and a rallying call for help among alliances of villages. In the Berber regions of the Maghrib, the names of Sanhaja and Zanata played a similar role.

In the herding unit and the village (or quarter) such authority as existed lay with the elders, or heads of families, who preserved the collective memory of the group, regulated urgent common concerns and reconciled differences which threatened to tear the group apart. At a higher level, in both settled and pastoral groups, there might appear a leadership of another kind. In a number of villages in the same mountain valley or district of the plains, or in a number of herding units using the same name, there could emerge a dominant family of which one member would assume the leadership of the whole group, either by choice or by his own prowess. Such families might have come in from outside and have acquired their position by military prestige, religious position or skill in arbitrating disputes, or by mediating for the group in its dealings with the city and its government. Whatever their origin, they would be regarded as part of the tribe, having the same real or fictitious origin.

The power of such leaders and families varied across a wide spectrum. At one extreme stood leaders (*shaykhs*) of nomadic pastoral tribes, who had little effective power except that which was given them by their reputation in the public opinion of the group. Unless they could establish themselves in a town and become rulers of another kind they had no power of enforcement, only that of attraction, so that nomadic tribes could grow or diminish, depending on the success or failure of the leading family; followers might join or leave them, although this process might be concealed by the fabrication of genealogies, so that those who joined the group would appear as if they had always belonged to it.

Near the other end of the spectrum were the leading families of settled agricultural communities, particularly the more or less isolated communities of mountain valleys. They might be long established there, or else intruders from outside who had won their position by military incursion or religious prestige, or had been placed there by the government of a neighbouring city. The ties of tribal solidarity linking them with the local population might have grown weak, but in their stead they might possess some degree of coercive power, based on control of strong places and possession of armed forces. To the extent to which power was concentrated in their hands, the *'asabiyya* of a tribe was replaced by a different relationship, that of lord and dependants.

CHAPTER 7

The Life of Cities

MARKETS AND CITIES

Peasants and nomads could produce much of what they needed for themselves. Peasants could build their own houses of mud-brick, their rugs and clothes could be woven by women, metalwork could be made or repaired by wandering craftsmen. They needed, however, to exchange that part of their production which was surplus to their requirements for goods of other kinds, either the produce of other parts of the countryside or goods manufactured by skilled craftsmen, the tents, furnishings, animal accoutrements, cooking utensils and arms which were necessary for their lives.

At points where different agricultural districts met, regular markets were held, at some place generally known, easily accessible and accepted as a neutral meeting-place; these might be held weekly – and so known, for example, as *suq al-arba'a* or 'Wednesday market' – or once a year, on a day connected with the shrine of some man or woman regarded as a 'friend of God'. Some of these markets, in course of time, became permanent settlements, towns where merchants and craftsmen free from the need to grow their own food or tend their own flocks carried on their specialized activities. The majority of such market towns were small, smaller indeed than some villages: a few hundred or thousand inhabitants, with a central market, and a main street with some shops and workshops. They were not clearly marked off from the countryside around them: beyond the core of permanent townspeople, the population could shift between town and country as circumstances changed. In the smaller towns distant from large cities or lying in oases, the authority of the *shaykh* of a neighbouring tribe, or of a local lord, might be dominant. Tribal or village feuds were not carried on in the market; craftsmen and small merchants might be regarded as lying outside the tribal system, not subject to the code of honour and vengeance by which tribesmen lived.

Some towns were more than local market towns, however. They were points where a number of agricultural districts of different kinds met and the exchange of produce was particularly large and complex. Aleppo in northern Syria, for example, was a meeting-place for those who sold or bought the grain from the inner Syrian plains, the produce of the fruit trees and forests of the hills lying to the north, sheep reared in the hills and camels in the expanses of the Syrian desert. If the surrounding districts produced a large surplus of foodstuffs and raw materials, which could be brought easily to the market, the town could become a centre for skilled craftsmen who produced manufactured goods on a large scale. If it lay near to sea or river or desert routes which linked it with other towns of this kind, it could also be an organizing centre or a port of shipment for long-distance trade in valuable goods, on which the profits were such that they made it worthwhile to bear the costs and risks of transportation.

When such conditions existed, and if there was a certain stability of life over decades or centuries, large cities could grow and maintain themselves. The creation of an Islamic empire, and then the development of an Islamic society linking the world of the Indian Ocean with that of the Mediterranean, provided the necessary conditions for the emergence of a chain of great cities running from one end of the world of Islam to the other: Cordoba, Seville and Granada in Andalus, Fez and Marrakish in Morocco, Qayrawan and later Tunis in Tunisia, Fustat and then Cairo in Egypt, Damascus and Aleppo in Syria, Mecca and Madina in western Arabia, Baghdad, Mosul and Basra in Iraq, and beyond them the cities of Iran, Transoxania and northern India. Some of these cities had already existed in the time before the coming of Islam, others were creations of the Islamic conquest or the power of later dynasties. Most of them lay inland, not on the coast; the Muslim hold over the coast of the Mediterranean was precarious, and ports were liable to attack by enemies from the sea.

By the tenth and eleventh centuries the great cities of the Islamic countries were the largest in the western half of the world. Figures can be no more than rough estimates, but it seems not impossible, on the basis of the area of the city and the number and size of its public buildings, that by the beginning of the fourteenth century Cairo had a quarter of a million inhabitants; during that century the population shrank because of the epidemics of plague known as the Black Death, and it was some time before it increased to its former size. The figure sometimes given for Baghdad during the period of greatest 'Abbasid power, a million or more, is almost certainly too large, but it must have been a city at least of comparable size to Cairo; by 1300 it had declined greatly, because of the decay of the irrigation system in the surrounding countryside and the conquest and sack of the city by the Mongols. Cordoba in Spain may also have been a city of such a size. Aleppo, Damascus and Tunis may have had populations of the order of 50–100,000 by the fifteenth century. In western Europe at this time there was no city of the size of Cairo: Florence, Venice, Milan and Paris may have had 100,000 inhabitants, while the cities of England, the Low Countries, Germany and central Europe were smaller.

THE CITY POPULATION

A wealthy and dominant part of the city population was composed of the large merchants, those engaged in bringing supplies of food and raw materials from the countryside, or concerned with long-distance trade in valuable goods. The staples of this trade, during this period, were textiles, glass, porcelain from China, and – perhaps the most important of all – spices; these were brought from south and south-east Asia, in earlier Islamic times to the ports of the Gulf, Siraf and Basra, and later on up the Red Sea to one of the Egyptian ports and thence to Cairo, from where they were distributed all over the Mediterranean world, by land-routes or else by sea from the ports of Damietta, Rosetta and Alexandria. Gold was brought from Ethiopia down the Nile and by caravan to Cairo, and from the regions of the river Niger across the Sahara to the Maghrib; slaves were brought from the Sudan and Ethiopia, and from the lands of the Slavs.

Not all the trade was in the hands of Muslim merchants. The Mediterranean carrying trade was controlled to a large extent by European ships and merchants, first those of Amalfi, then those of Genoa and Venice; in the fifteenth century the French and English also began to appear. Merchants in the Muslim cities controlled the great land-routes in the Maghrib and western and central Asia, and also the routes of the Indian Ocean, until the Portuguese opened the route round the Cape of Good Hope at the end of the fifteenth century. Most of these merchants were Muslims, such as the Karimi merchants who dominated the spice trade of Egypt for a time; but there were also Jews of Baghdad, Cairo and the cities of the Maghrib who had connections of family and community with the cities of Italy, northern Europe and the Byzantine Empire. In addition to merchants from the larger cities, there were close-knit groups from smaller places, who were able to control certain kinds of trade. (This tradition continued to exist until modern times; in the Maghrib at a later period, such groups came from the island of Jarba off the Tunisian coast, the Mzab oasis on the edge of the desert and the Sus district in southern Morocco.)

For merchant ventures there were two common kinds of arrangement. One was that of partnership, often between members of the same family; two or more partners would share the risks and profits in proportion to their investments. The other was the *commenda* (*mudaraba*), by which an investor entrusted goods or capital to someone who used them for trade, and then returned to the investor his capital together with an agreed share of the profits. Merchants in one city might have agents in another, and although organized banks did not exist, there were various ways in which credit could be given over long distances, for example by the drawing of bills. The basis of the trading system was mutual confidence grounded in shared values and recognized rules.

The great cities were centres also of manufacture, producing staple goods for a local market – textiles, metalwork, pottery, leather goods and processed foods – and goods of quality, in particular fine textiles, for a wider market. There is some evidence, however, that production for markets outside the Muslim world became less important from the eleventh century onwards, and transit trade of goods produced elsewhere, in China, India or western Europe, more important. This change was connected with the revival of urban life in Europe, and in particular the growth of textile industries in Italy.

In general, units of production were small. The master would have a few workers and apprentices in his workshop; larger-scale industries were those producing for a ruler or an army – arsenals, and royal workshops for textiles – and the sugar factories of Egypt and some other places. The merchants were not the only class whose roots were firmly planted in the city. Shopkeepers and skilled craftsmen formed an urban class with a continuity of its own. Skills were transmitted from father to son. Ownership or possession of a shop or workshop could be passed on for generations, and their number was limited by lack of space and sometimes by regulation of the authorities. A historian of modern Fez has pointed out that the situation and size of the main bazaars and the areas of workshops were roughly the same at the beginning of the twentieth century as they had been, according to a writer of the time, Leo Africanus (c. 1485–1554), in the sixteenth. Those in this stratum of society stood at a lower level of income than did the large merchants. The fortunes to be made from craftsmanship or retail trading were not so great as those to be derived from long-distance trade in valuable goods. Many craftsmen did not possess extensive capital resources; a study of Cairo has shown that a considerable proportion of the shops and workshops were owned by large merchants or by religious foundations. They could enjoy prestige, however, as a stable population pursuing honourable trades in accordance with generally accepted codes of honesty and decent workmanship. There was a hierarchy of respect in the crafts, ranging from work in precious metals, paper and perfume, down to such 'unclean' crafts as tanning, dyeing, and butchering.

Surrounding this stable population of craftsmen and shopkeepers with fixed and permanent places in the city, there was a larger population of those engaged in work which demanded less skill: itinerant pedlars, street-cleaners, the semi-employed proletariat of a large city. In most circumstances, this stratum must have included a large proportion of rural migrants. The line between city and countryside was not sharply drawn; surrounding the city were market gardens, such as those in the Ghuta, the vast, irrigated, fruit-growing region round Damascus, and men who cultivated the gardens might live in the city. On the outskirts of cities were districts where the long-distance trading caravans were marshalled and animals were bought and equipped, and these attracted a floating population from the countryside. Periods of drought or disorder could also bring in peasants fleeing from their villages.

LAW AND THE 'ULAMA

Life in large cities had needs different from that of the dwellers in villages and tents. The interaction of specialized workers and dealers in produce, the meeting of people of different origins and faiths, the varied chances and problems of life in the streets and the market all demanded shared expectations about how others would act in certain circumstances, and a norm of how they ought to act, a system of rules and habits generally accepted as valid and obeyed more often than not. Local custom (*'urf*), preserved and interpreted by the elders of the community, was no longer adequate by itself. From the time of the 'Abbasids onwards the *shari'a* was generally accepted by Muslim townspeople, and upheld by Muslim rulers, as giving guidance to the ways in which Muslims should deal with each other. It regulated the forms of commercial contract, the limits within which profits could be legitimately made, the relations of husbands and wives, and the division of property.

The judges who administered the *shari'a* were trained in special schools, the *madrasas*. A *qadi* sat by himself in his home or in a court house, with a secretary to record decisions. In principle, only oral testimony from reputable witnesses was acceptable, and there emerged a group of legal witnesses (*'udul*) who would vouch for, and give acceptable status to, the testimony of others. In practice, written documents could in fact be accepted, if they were authenticated by *'udul* and so converted into oral evidence. In course of time some dynasties came to accept all four *madhhabs*, or schools of law, as being equally valid: under the Mamluks, there were officially appointed *qadis* from all of them. Each *qadi* gave his judgements in accordance with the teachings of his own *madhhab*. There was no system of appeal and the ruling of a judge could not be overturned by another one except for legal mistakes.

In principle, the judge administered the only recognized law, that derived from revelation, but in practice the system was not so universal or inflexible as this might imply. The *shari'a* did not in fact cover the whole range of human activities: it was most precise on questions of personal status (marriage, divorce and inheritance), less so on commercial matters, and least of all on penal and constitutional questions. The *qadi* had a certain competence in penal matters, in regard to certain acts which were specifically prohibited by the Qur'an and to which precise penalties were attached (unlawful sexual intercourse, theft and drinking wine); he also had a more general competence to punish acts which offended against religion. (In practice, however, most criminal justice, particularly in regard to matters which touched the welfare of the state, was administered by the ruler or his officials, not the *qadi*.)

Even within the field of justice which was generally left to the *qadi*, the law he administered was not so inflexible as it might appear from the law books. He might interpret his role as that of a conciliator, attempting to preserve social harmony by reaching an agreed solution to a dispute, rather than applying the strict letter of the law. In addition to the *qadi* there was another kind of legal specialist, the jurisconsult (*mufti*), who was competent to give rulings (*fatwa*) on questions of law. *Fatwas* could be accepted by the *qadi* and incorporated in due course in the treatises of law.

The *qadi* was a central figure in the life of the city. He not only administered the law, but was also responsible for the division of a property after a person's death in accordance with the laws of inheritance, and could have other powers of supervision given him by the ruler.

Those who taught, interpreted and administered the law, together with those who exercised certain other religious functions – who led the prayers in the mosques or preached the Friday sermon – had come to form a distinct stratum in urban society: the *'ulama*, the men of religious learning, the guardians of the system of shared beliefs, values and practices. They cannot be regarded as a single class, for they were spread throughout the whole of society, performing different functions and attracting various degrees of public respect. At their summit, however, stood a group which was fully a part of the urban élite, the upper *'ulama*: judges in the main courts, teachers in the great schools, preachers in the principal mosques, guardians of shrines if they were also known for learning and piety. Some of these claimed descent from the Prophet through his daughter Fatima and her husband 'Ali ibn Abi Talib. By now the descendants of the Prophet, the *sayyids* or *sharifs*, were regarded with a special respect, and in some places could exercise leadership; in Morocco, the two dynasties which ruled from the sixteenth century onwards based their claim to legitimacy on their status as *sharifs*.

The upper *'ulama* were closely linked with the other elements in the urban élite, the merchants and masters of respected crafts. They possessed a common culture; merchants sent their sons to be educated by religious scholars in the schools, in order to acquire a knowledge of Arabic and the Qur'an, and perhaps of law. It was not uncommon for a man to work both as a teacher and scholar and in trade. Merchants needed *'ulama* as legal specialists, to write formal documents in precise language, settle disputes about property and supervise the division of their property after death. Substantial and respected merchants could act as *'udul*, men of good repute whose evidence would be accepted by a *qadi*.

There is evidence of intermarriage between families of merchants, master-craftsmen and *'ulama*, and of the intertwining of economic interests of which marriage might be the expression. Collectively they controlled much of the wealth of the city. The personal nature of the relationships on which trade depended made for a rapid rise and fall of fortunes invested in trade, but families of *'ulama* tended to last longer; fathers trained their sons to succeed them; those in high office could use their influence in favour of younger members of the family.

Whether merchants or higher *'ulama*, it was possible for those who had wealth to transmit it from generation to generation by means of the system of religious endowments authorized by the *shari'a* (*waqf* or *hubus*). A *waqf* was an assignment in perpetuity of the income from a piece of property for charitable purposes, for example, the maintenance of mosques, schools, hospitals, public fountains or hostels for travellers, the freeing of prisoners or the care of sick animals. It could also be used, however, for the benefit of the founder's family. The founder could stipulate that a member of the family would act as administrator and assign a salary to him, or else he could provide that the surplus income from the endowment should be given to his descendants as long as they survived, and be devoted to the charitable purpose only when the line died out; such provisions could give rise to abuses. *Waqfs* were placed under the care of the *qadi*, and ultimately of the ruler; they thus provided some safeguard for the transmission of wealth against the fortunes of trade, the extravagance of heirs, or the depredations of rulers.

SLAVES

The vertical division of the urban population in terms of wealth and social respect was crossed by other kinds of division: between slaves and free, Muslims and non-Muslims, and men and women.

A more or less distinct element in the working population was that of the domestic servants. They stood apart because many of them were women, since such service, or other work which could be done in the house, was almost the only kind of urban occupation which was open to women, and also because many of them were slaves. The idea of slavery did not have exactly the same associations in Muslim societies as in the countries of North and South America discovered and peopled by the nations of western Europe from the sixteenth century onwards. Slavery was a status recognized by Islamic law. According to that law, a free-born Muslim could not be enslaved: slaves were non-Muslims, captured in war or otherwise procured, or else the children of slave parents and born in slavery. They did not possess the full legal rights of free men, but the *shari'a* laid down that they should be treated with justice and kindness; it was a meritorious act to liberate them. The relationship of master and slave could be a close one, and might continue to exist after the slave was freed: he might marry his master's daughter or conduct his business for him.

The legal category of slavery included very different social groups. From a time early in the 'Abbasid period, the caliphs had recruited slaves coming from the Turkish peoples of central Asia into their armies, and this practice continued. Military slaves and freedmen, drawn mainly from central Asia and the Caucasus, and in the Maghrib and Andalus from the lands of the Slavs, were the supporters of dynasties, and could be their founders; the

Mamluks who ruled Egypt and Syria from 1250 to 1517 were a self-perpetuating group of soldiers recruited and trained as slaves, converted to Islam and freed.

These military slaves, however, formed a distinct category which can scarcely be regarded as having the same status as most of those who were enslaved. In some regions there were agricultural slaves. Those brought from east Africa had been important in southern Iraq during part of the 'Abbasid period; slaves cultivated the land in the upper valley of the Nile and the oases of the Sahara. For the most part, however, slaves were domestic servants and concubines in the cities. They were brought from black Africa, through the Indian Ocean and Red Sea, down the Nile, or by the routes across the Sahara. Most of these were women, but there were also eunuchs to guard the privacy of the household.

MUSLIMS AND NON-MUSLIMS IN THE CITY

The city was a place of meeting and separation. Outside the Arabian peninsula, almost all cities had inhabitants belonging to one or other of the various Jewish and Christian communities. They played a part in the public activities of the city, but formed a distinct portion of its society. Various factors set them apart from the Muslims. They paid a special poll tax (*jizya*) to the government. By Islamic law and custom they were required to carry signs of their difference: to wear dress of a special kind, avoid certain colours associated with the Prophet and Islam (green in particular), not to carry arms or ride horses; they should not build new places of worship, repair old ones without permission, or construct them in such a way as to overshadow those of the Muslims. Such restrictions were not always or uniformly enforced, however. More strictly observed were the laws about marriage and inheritance. A non-Muslim could not inherit from a Muslim; a non-Muslim man could not marry a Muslim woman, but a Muslim man could marry a Jewish or Christian woman. Conversion of Muslims to other religions was strictly forbidden.

It was a sign of the separate existence of Jews and Christians that they tended to occupy a position of special importance in certain economic activities, but to be virtually excluded from others. At a high level, some Jews and Christians held important positions at the court of certain rulers or in their administrations. In Egypt of the Fatimids, Ayyubids and Mamluks, Coptic officials were important in the financial service. Medicine was a profession in which Jews were prominent, and Jewish court doctors could have great influence. If a Jew or Christian was converted to Islam, he could rise even higher; some converts became chief ministers and held effective power.

Jews of the Muslim cities also played an important part in long-distance trade with the ports of Mediterranean Europe and, until Mamluk times, with those of the Indian Ocean. Among the crafts, those concerned with drugs and with gold and silver tended to be in the hands of Jews or Christians, working for themselves or for Muslims.

The relationship of Muslim and non-Muslim was only one part of the complex of social relations in which those who lived side by side in the same city were involved, and circumstances decided which part of the complex was dominant at any time or place. In the early centuries of Islamic rule there appears to have been much social and cultural intercourse between adherents of the three religions. Relations between Muslims and Jews in Umayyad Spain, and between Muslims and Nestorian Christians in 'Abbasid Baghdad, were close and easy. As time went on, however, the barriers became higher. The conversion of Christians and, perhaps to a lesser extent, of Jews to Islam turned a majority into a diminishing minority. As Islam changed from being the religion of a ruling élite to being the dominant faith of the urban population, it developed its own social institutions, within which Muslims could live without interacting with non-Muslims.

In the long centuries of Muslim rule there were some periods of sustained and deliberate persecution of non-Muslims by Muslim rulers: for example, the reign of the Fatimid Caliph al-Hakim (996–1021) in Egypt, that of the Almohads in the Maghrib, and that of some of the Mongol rulers in Iran and Iraq after they were converted to Islam. Such persecution was not instigated or justified by the spokesmen of Sunni Islam, however; the men of religious learning, the *'ulama*, were concerned to ensure that non-Muslims did not infringe the laws which regulated their status, but within those limits they upheld the protection which the *shari'a* granted them. Pressures upon Jews and Christians may have come mainly from the urban masses, particularly in times of war or economic hardship, when hostility might be directed against the non-Muslim officials of the ruler. At such moments, the ruler might respond by enforcing the laws strictly, or dismissing his non-Muslim officials, but not for long. Such crises occurred several times during the period of Mamluk rule in Egypt and Syria.

The communal organization of Jews and Christians could provide some kind of protection and maintain a certain solidarity in the face of occasional pressures and of the permanent disadvantages of being in a minority. The various Christian and Jewish communities were held together by the solidarity of the local group clustered around a church or synagogue, and by higher authorities. Among the Jews, in the period of the 'Abbasid caliphs, a primacy of honour was given to the 'Exilarch' or 'Head of the Captivity', an office which belonged to those claiming descent from King David: more effective leadership, however, was given by the heads of the main colleges or groups of men of learning, two in Iraq and one in Palestine. It was they who appointed the judges of the different congregations. Later, when the caliphate split up, local leaders appeared: judges and scholars, and 'secular' leaders, such as the *nagid* or *ra'is al-yahud* in Egypt, an office held by descendants of the great thinker Maimonides.

Similarly, in the various Christian communities the patriarchs and bishops exercised authority. Under the 'Abbasid caliphs the Nestorian patriarch in Baghdad, and under the later Egyptian dynasties the Coptic patriarch in Cairo, held a special position of influence and respect. The heads of the communities were responsible for ensuring that the terms of the *dhimma* or contract of protection between the Muslim ruler and the non-Muslim subjects were honoured: peace, obedience and order. They may have played a part in assessing the poll tax, but normally it seems to have been collected by officials of the government. They also had a function inside the community: they supervised the schools and social services, and tried to prevent deviations in doctrine or liturgical practice. They also supervised the courts in which judges administered law in civil cases involving two members of the community, or reconciled disagreements; if they wished, however, Jews and Christians could take their cases to the Muslim *qadi*, and they seem to have done so frequently.

WOMEN IN THE CITY

So far as our information goes, women played a limited part in the economic life of the city. They were domestic servants, some of them may have helped their husbands in their trades and crafts, and there were women entertainers, dancers and singers. In general, however, they did not take part in the central activities of the great cities, the production of valuable goods on a large scale for export. Those who were openly active were women of poor families. To the extent to which a family was wealthy, powerful and respected, it would seclude its women, in a special part of the home, the *harim*, and beneath the veil when they ventured from the house into the streets and public places. An Egyptian jurist of the Maliki school, Ibn al-Hajj (b. 1336), said that women should not go out to buy things in the market, because they might be led into improper acts if they sat with shopkeepers:

some of the pious elders (may God be pleased with them) have said that a woman should leave her house on three occasions only: when she is conducted to the house of her bridegroom, on the deaths of her parents, and when she goes to her own grave.[1]

To live in the seclusion of the *harim* was not to be totally excluded from life. Within the women's quarters of large households, in visits to each other, at the public bath-houses, which were reserved for women at special times, and at celebrations of marriages or the birth of children, women met each other and maintained a culture of their own. Some of them took an active part in administering their properties, through intermediaries, and cases are recorded of women appearing in the *qadi*'s court to demand their rights. As in the countryside, when a woman grew older, and if she had produced male children, she could acquire great power in the family.

Nevertheless, the social order was based upon the superior power and rights of men; the veil and the *harim* were visible signs of this. A view of the relations between men and women which was deeply rooted in the culture of the Middle East, which had existed long before the coming of Islam, and was preserved in the countryside by immemorial custom, was strengthened but also changed in the city by the development of the *shari'a*.

The Qur'an asserted in clear terms the essential equality of men and women: 'Whoso doeth right, whether male or female, and is a believer, all such will enter the Garden.'[2] It also enjoined justice and kindness in dealings between Muslims. It seems likely that its provisions in regard to marriage and inheritance gave women a better position than they had had in pre-Islamic Arabia (although not necessarily in the lands conquered by Muslims). The system of law and ideal social morality, the *shari'a*, gave formal expression to the rights of women, but it also laid down their limits.

According to the *shari'a*, every woman should have a male guardian – her father, brother or some other member of her family. A woman's marriage was a civil contract between the bridegroom and her guardian. A father as guardian could give his daughter in marriage without her consent, if she had not yet reached the age of puberty. If she had reached that age, her consent was necessary, but, if she had not previously been married, consent could be given by silence. The marriage contract provided for a dowry (*mahr*) to be given by the bridegroom to the bride; this was her property, and whatever else she owned or inherited also remained her property. The wife owed her husband obedience, but in return had a right to suitable clothes, lodging and maintenance, and to sexual intercourse with her husband. Although legal writers accepted that contraception was permitted in certain circumstances, the husband should not practise it without the consent of his wife.

There were, however, a number of ways in which the relations between husband and wife were those of unequals. While a wife could divorce her husband only for good reason (impotence, madness, denial of her rights) and only by recourse to a *qadi*, or else by mutual consent, a husband could repudiate his wife without giving any reason, and by a simple form of words in the presence of witnesses. (In Shi'i law the rules for repudiation were somewhat stricter, but on the other hand there was provision for temporary marriage, *mut'a*, for a specific period.) The marriage contract could provide some safeguard against this, if it stipulated that part of the dowry, the so-called 'postponed' part (*mu'ajjal*), should be paid by the husband only if and when he repudiated his wife. A wife could hope for the support and defence given her by her own male relations; if repudiated, she could return with her property to her family home. She would have the custody of the children of the marriage and the duty of bringing them up, until they reached a certain age, defined differently in the various legal codes; after that the father or his family would have their custody.

The *shari'a*, basing itself upon the Qur'an and the example of the Prophet, allowed a man to have more than one wife, to a limit of four, provided he could treat them all with justice and did not neglect his conjugal duty to any of them. He could also have slave concubines to any number, and without their having any rights over him. The marriage contract might, however, stipulate that he should take neither additional wives nor concubines.

The inequality was shown too in the laws of inheritance, also derived by the *shari'a* from the words of the Qur'an. A man was allowed to bequeath not more than one-third of his property as he wished, to persons or purposes who would not otherwise inherit from him. The remainder would be divided according to strict rules. His wife would receive at most one-third. If he left sons and daughters, a daughter would inherit only half the share of a son; if he left only daughters, they would receive a certain proportion of his property, but the remainder would go to his male relations. (This was the Sunni law; in Shi'i law, however, daughters would inherit everything if there were no sons.) The provision that daughters would receive only half as much as sons echoes another stipulation of the *shari'a*: in a legal case, the testimony of a woman would have only half the weight of that of a man.

THE SHAPE OF THE CITY

A city was a place where merchants and artisans worked, scholars studied and taught, rulers or governors held court guarded by their soldiers, judges administered justice, villagers and dwellers in the desert came to sell their produce and buy what they needed, merchants from afar to buy and sell, and students to read with some famous master. The structure of the city had to accommodate all their needs.

In the *madina*, at the heart of every great city (although not necessarily at its geographical centre), there lay two kinds of complexes of buildings. One of them included the main congregational mosque, which was a place of meeting and study as well as prayer, and where the collective consciousness of the Muslim population could express itself at moments of crisis. Near it would be the house or court of the chief *qadi*, schools of higher learning, and the shops of those who sold books, or candles and other objects of piety; there might also be the shrine of a saint whose life was identified in some special way with the life of the city. The other complex would include the central marketplace (the *suq*), the main point of exchange. In or near it would lie the shops of those who sold textiles, jewellery, spices and other valuable goods, the storehouses for imported wares, and the offices of the money-changers, who acted as bankers for the financing of foreign trade. These shops, storehouses and offices could be arranged in a line, a quadrilateral of streets parallel to or crossing each other, or a tight mass of buildings too closely linked for roads to intersect them. A third complex which would be found near the centre of modern cities was not prominent. The power of the government was present, in its watchmen, supervisors of the market and police force, but it did not express itself in large and ostentatious buildings.

The market area was mainly for exchange; much of it, in particular the places where valuable goods were kept, would be locked and guarded at night. The workshops and places for textiles and metalwork would lie at some distance from it, and so too would the places of residence of those who worked in it. Wealthier merchants and scholars might live near it, but most of the population lived outside the centre, in residential quarters, each of them a mass of small streets and culs-de-sac opening off a main street; at some periods, the quarters had gates which were shut and guarded at night. A quarter might contain a few hundred or a few thousand inhabitants; it would have its mosque, church or synagogue, its local subsidiary market (*suwayqa*) catering for daily needs, and perhaps its public bath (*hammam*), an important meeting-place. Some wealthy and powerful families would have their houses in the quarter, where they could maintain influence and exercise patronage, but others might have their main or subsidiary homes on the outskirts of the city, where more spacious houses could be built and surrounded by gardens. The quarter belonged to its inhabitants, and in a sense was an extension of the houses. Its privacy was protected, in case of need, by its young men, sometimes organized into groups (*zu'ar*, *'ayyarun*, *fityan*) which had a continuous existence and possessed a certain moral ideal. Such groups might have a wider sphere of operation at moments of disturbance in the city.

Further from the centre, near the walls or beyond them, there would be poorer quarters where rural immigrants lived. Here caravans were equipped, marshalled, despatched and received, animals of burden were bought and sold, and the country-dwellers would bring their fruit, vegetables and livestock for sale. Here too would lie the workshops where noisy or malodorous work, such as tanning or butchering, was carried on. Beyond these quarters and outside the city wall were the cemeteries, which were important meeting-places, and not only at times of funerals.

There was a tendency for the inhabitants of a quarter to be linked by common origin, religious, ethnic or regional, or by kinship or intermarriage; such links created a solidarity which might be strong. Jews and Christians tended to live in certain quarters rather than others, because of ties of kinship or origin, or because they wanted to be near their places of worship, or else because their different customs in regard to the seclusion of women made close propinquity with Muslim families difficult. In the Maghrib, Jews of Berber or oriental origin might live separately from those who came from Andalus. The quarters in which they lived would not be exclusively Christian or Jewish, however. The ghetto did not exist in most places. By the end of the fifteenth century, however, Morocco had become an exception: in Fez and other cities, separate Jewish quarters were established by the ruler in order to protect Jews from popular disturbances.

There were many variations of this general pattern, depending on the nature of the land, historical tradition and the acts of dynasties. Aleppo, for example, was an ancient city which had grown up long before the coming of Islam. The heart of the city continued to lie where it had been in Hellenistic and Byzantine times. The main streets were narrower than they had been; as transport by camel and donkey replaced that by wheeled vehicle, they needed only to be wide enough for two loaded animals to pass each other. The quadrilateral pattern of the main streets could still, however, be traced in the maze of stone-vaulted lanes in the *suq*. The great mosque lay at the point where the pillared central street of the Hellenistic city had broadened into the forum or main meeting-place.

Cairo, on the other hand, was a new creation. During the early centuries of Islamic rule in Egypt, the centre of power and government had moved inland from Alexandria to the point where the Nile entered the delta, and a succession of urban centres had been built to the north of the Byzantine stronghold known as Babylon: Fustat, Qata'i, and finally al-Qahira or Cairo, the centre of which was created by the Fatimids and was to remain virtually unmoved until the second half of the nineteenth century. At its heart lay the Azhar mosque, built by the Fatimids for the teaching of Islam in its Isma'ili form; it continued to exist as one of the greatest centres of Sunni religious learning and the main congregational mosque of the city. Close to it was the shrine of Husayn, son of the fourth caliph, 'Ali, and his wife Fatima, the Prophet's daughter; the popular belief was that Husayn's head had been brought there after he was killed at Karbala. Within a short distance there lay the central street which ran from the northern gate of the city (Bab al-Futuh) to the southern (Bab Zuwayla), and along both sides of it, and in alleys leading off it, were mosques, schools, and the shops and warehouses of merchants in cloth, spices, gold and silver.

Fez had been formed in a different way again, by the amalgamation of two settlements lying on either side of a small river. The centre of the city was finally fixed at that point, in one of the two towns, where lay the shrine of the supposed founder of the city, Mawlay Idris. Near it was the great teaching mosque of the Qarawiyyin, with its dependent schools, and a network of *suqs*, protected at night by gates, where were kept and sold spices, gold and silver work, imported textiles, and the leather slippers which were a characteristic product of the city.

The great mosque and central *suq* of a city were the points from which cultural and economic power radiated, but the power of the ruler had its seat elsewhere. In early Islamic times, the ruler and his local governors may have held court in the heart of a city, but by a later period a certain separation had become common between the *madina*, the centre of essential urban activities, and the royal palace or quarter. Thus the 'Abbasids had moved for a time out of the city which they had created, Baghdad, to Samarra further up the Tigris, and their example was followed by later rulers. In Cairo the Ayyubids and Mamluks held court in the Citadel, built by Salah al-Din on the Muqattam hill overlooking the city; the Umayyads of Spain built their palace at Madinat al-Zahra outside Cordoba; later Moroccan rulers made a royal city, New Fez, on the outskirts of the old. The reasons for such a separation are not difficult to find: seclusion was an expression of power and magnificence; or the ruler might wish to be insulated against the pressures of public opinion, and to keep his soldiers away from contact with urban interests, which might weaken their loyalty to his exclusive interest.

Inside the royal city or compound would lie the palace itself, with its royal treasury, mint, and offices for secretaries. In the outer courts of the palace public business would be transacted: ambassadors would be received, royal troops reviewed, the council sit to do justice and hear petitions. Those having business would be admitted to this part of the palace, and the ruler himself would appear there on certain days and for certain purposes. The inner courts were for the ruler himself: his family, his women guarded by eunuchs, and the palace slaves who formed a kind of extension of his personality. Degrees of seclusion varied, however, from one dynasty to another: the Hafsids lived in public with little seclusion, the Mamluks had more.

In the royal city there would also be barracks for the royal guards, the palaces or houses of high officials and specialized *suqs* producing goods for the needs of court and army: the arsenal, markets for horses and arms, workshops where fine textiles for the use of the palace were made. Those working in such crafts might live nearby: the quarter where Jewish gold- and silversmiths lived lay in the royal city of Fez.

HOUSES IN THE CITY

By the fifteenth century, the *suqs* of cities contained large buildings constructed around courtyards, with storerooms on the ground floor; above them there might be hostels for visiting merchants and others. Such buildings in their various forms were known as *khans* in Syria and Iraq, *wikalas* in Egypt, and *funduqs* in the Maghrib. Another kind of building, in the Maghrib at least, was the *qaysariyya*, where valuable goods were stored. Many of these buildings were constructed by rulers or great men of the city and constituted into *waqfs*, so that the income from them should be used for religious or charitable purposes.

So far as they are known, the domestic buildings of the city fell into three categories. In some cities the housing of the poor seems to have consisted largely of open courtyards with huts. In the crowded centre of Cairo the poor, as well as artisans and retail merchants who needed to be near their places of work, lived in apartment houses. A typical house might be built around a courtyard, with workshops on the ground floor and a number of staircases leading to two or three upper floors with separate apartments of several rooms opening from them.

For families in easier conditions, or living in less congested areas, other kinds of house had gradually evolved. In south-western Arabia these were of a distinctive type, built of stone, carefully and symmetrically designed, and rising several storeys; animals were kept on the ground floor, grain above them, and then there were two or three floors of living rooms, and the main reception room at the top, with the best air and views. Elsewhere, the typical form of large family house may have developed, with many variations of region and period, from a blend of the Graeco-Roman Mediterranean house with the traditions of Iran and Iraq.

The house would be approached by an alley leading off a main street. Nothing except the size of the door would expose the wealth of its owner to the envy of rulers or the curiosity of those who passed by; houses were built to be seen from within, not from outside. The door was the main external feature: made of iron or wood, with a surround of sculpted stone, and perhaps a window above it from which those who were approaching could be seen. Inside the door a corridor, turned at an angle so that nothing beyond it could be seen from the street, led to a central courtyard from which a number of rooms opened, including the main reception room (*majlis* or *qa'a*); in congested areas, the courtyard might be replaced by a covered central room. The reception room would often lie on the side of the courtyard facing the entrance, and would itself be entered by way of a door or an *iwan*, the large circular arch which had spread westwards from Iran. In some places, the main room would have an anteroom in front of it. In Mamluk Cairo, the room had developed into a kind of covered courtyard, with a sunken area and a fountain in the centre and sitting areas on either side. Separate from this reception room with its attendant rooms and offices was the family area, where the women and their children and attendants could be as secluded as they or the master of the house wished. In very large houses the division between areas for reception and those for the family was expressed by the existence of two courtyards, in smaller ones by a difference of function between ground floor and upper floor. In large houses there would be a bath-house or *hammam*.

To build in stone was expensive in most places, and houses were more often built of brick or mud-brick, with the main doors having stone surrounds. The ceilings of the main rooms on the ground floor were often brick vaults, in order to prevent humidity and to bear the weight of the upper floors; other ceilings would be made of wood. In the ceilings various devices allowed for ventilation and the circulation of air. Walls, doors and ceilings were decorated. Wood was painted in various colours (the characteristic colour of Morocco was green, that of Tunisia blue). Walls were plastered and stuccoed with floral designs. Stone was sculpted with calligraphic or floral motifs. Windows had wooden shutters; the latticed woodwork known as *mashrabiyya* was known in Egypt in the Fatimid period, and became common in that of the Mamluks.

Houses had little permanent furniture in them, apart from chests and cupboards for storage. A historian of Cairo has suggested that the role played by wooden furniture in European houses was here taken by textiles. Reception rooms had sofas with cushions on them. Stuffed mattresses and pillows, laid on the floor or on bases of wood or stone, took the place of beds. The walls were covered with hangings, floors and beds with carpets. At night, copper oil-lamps were used for light; in cold weather, copper braziers were brought in, burning charcoal or aromatic woods. Meals were served on large round trays of silver or copper, resting on wooden stools. Bowls and cups of earthenware – or, among the rich, of Chinese porcelain – were used for food; copper, glass or earthenware cups for drinking. Pieces of flat bread could be used to take food from the central dish, but spoons and knives were used among the wealthy.

Bread was of fundamental importance in the life of the poor; governments placed great emphasis on the need to guarantee the grain supply of the cities, and popular disturbances broke out when grain became scarce or dear. Made in most places of wheat, it was softened with olive oil and eaten with vegetables – onions, garlic, or those, such as aubergines, brought into the Mediterranean world by the expansion of Islam. Most people ate meat rarely, on festivals or great occasions. The diet of the well-to-do was more varied: a wider range of vegetables, fruits (according to the possibilities of growing or importing them – grapes, oranges, peaches and apricots in Mediterranean countries, dates in Iraq, on the desert fringes and in oases) and meat: lamb rather than beef, poultry, fish near the sea or rivers and lakes. Meat was cooked in olive or sesame oil and seasoned with spices. Although the Qur'an forbade the drinking of alcohol, wine and other strong drinks, made by local Christians or imported from western Europe, seem to have been widely consumed.

THE CHAIN OF CITIES

So long as urban order and control of the dependent countryside continued, protected by the alliance of interests between ruler and urban élite, wealth and power could be transmitted from generation to generation, and with them also was handed on a culture, a system of learning, values, modes of behaviour and ideal types of personality. It has been suggested that the code of acceptable conduct, the *qa'ida*, which existed in Fez in the early years of the twentieth century was much the same as that described by Leo Africanus in the sixteenth.[3] The canons of correct behaviour and thought, of learning and high skills linked the generations, but they also linked cities with each other. A network of routes ran through the world of Islam and beyond it. Along them moved not only caravans of camels or donkeys carrying silks, spices, glass and precious metals, but ideas, news, fashions, patterns of thought and behaviour. When merchants and leaders of caravans met in the marketplace, news was exchanged and its meaning assessed. Merchants from one city settled in others and kept a close and permanent link between them. From time to time more violent movements would pass down the routes, as an army carried the power of another ruler or of a challenger to the existing power; and these too might bring with them new ideas about how to live in society, and new ethnic elements to add to the population.

From the beginning of Islamic history too men moved in search of learning, in order to spread the tradition of what the Prophet had done and said from those who had received it by line of transmission from his Companions. In course of time the purposes of travel expanded: to learn the sciences of religion from a famous teacher, or to receive spiritual training from a master of the religious life. Seekers after knowledge or wisdom came from villages or small towns to a metropolis: from southern Morocco to the Qarawiyyin mosque in Fez, from eastern Algeria and Tunisia to the Zaytuna in Tunis; the Azhar in Cairo attracted students from a wider range, as the names of the student hostels show – *riwaq* or cloister of the Maghribs, Syrians and Ethiopians. The schools in the Shi'i holy cities of Iraq – Najaf, Karbala, Samarra, and Kazimayn on the outskirts of Baghdad – drew students from other Shiʻi communities, in Syria and eastern Arabia.

The life of the famous traveller Ibn Battuta (1304–c. 1377) illustrates the links between the cities and lands of Islam. His pilgrimage, undertaken when he was twenty-one years old, was only the beginning of a life of wandering. It took him from his native city of Tangier in Morocco to Mecca by way of Syria; then to Baghdad and south-western Iran; to Yemen, east Africa, Oman and the Gulf; to Asia Minor, the Caucasus, and southern Russia; to India, the Maldive Islands and China; then back to his native Maghrib, and from there to Andalus and the Sahara. Wherever he went, he visited the tombs of saints and frequented scholars, with whom he was joined by the link of a common culture expressed in the Arabic language. He was well received at the courts of princes, and by some of them appointed to the office of *qadi*; this honour, conferred on him as far from home as Delhi and the Maldive Islands, showed the prestige attached to the exponents of the religious learning in the Arabic tongue.[4]

CHAPTER 8

Cities and Their Rulers

THE FORMATION OF DYNASTIES

The maintenance of law and urban order needed a power of enforcement, a ruler whose position was different from that of the tribal *shaykh* deriving his unstable authority from custom and consent.

By what may seem to be a paradox of Islamic history (and perhaps of other histories as well), dynasties of rulers often drew their strength from the countryside and some even had their origins there, but could survive only by establishing themselves in the cities and drawing a new strength from a compact of interests with the urban population.

In order to survive, a dynasty needed to strike roots in the city: it needed the wealth to be derived from trade and industry, and the legitimacy which only the *'ulama* could confer. The process of formation of dynasties consisted in the conquest of cities. A conqueror would move up a chain of cities lying on a trade-route. The creation and growth of cities in their turn depended largely upon the power of dynasties. Some of the greatest cities in the world of Islam were virtually the creation of dynasties: Baghdad of the 'Abbasids, Cairo of the Fatimids, Fez of the Idrisids, Cordoba of the Umayyads. Within limits, a powerful ruler could divert trade-routes and attract them to his capital; a city might decline when its ruler left it or could no longer defend it, as Qayrawan declined when the Zirids virtually ceased to live there.

The first purpose of a dynasty was to maintain itself in power, and the ruler therefore lived somewhat apart from the city population, surrounded by a court which was largely of military or alien origin: his family and *harim*, his personal *mamluks* – black Africans or converted Christians in the Maghrib, Turks, Kurds or Circassians further east – and high palace officials, largely drawn from these *mamluk* groups. The professional army which replaced that with which the dynasty had obtained power was also drawn from outside the city. The Saljuq army was mainly Turkish, that of the Ayyubids more mixed: in Syria, its leadership came from a military aristocracy of varied origins, Turks, Kurds or converted Greeks, in Egypt mainly from Turkish and Kurdish newcomers. Under the Mamluks too the army was of mixed composition: the core of it consisted of a body of royal *mamluks* enlisted by the ruler or taken over from his predecessors and trained in the palace schools, but the high military officers each had his own body of military retainers trained in his household. The solidarity of a group brought up in the same household could last a lifetime or longer. The *mamluk* soldiers did not form a hereditary group, and the sons of *mamluks* could not themselves become members of the central military force. There was another force formed of free-born Muslims, however, and sons of *mamluks* could join it and rise to office. Among the Hafsids, the original army was drawn from the tribes of the countryside, but when the dynasty established itself firmly it came to rely more upon mercenary soldiers, Arabs from Andalus, European Christian converts and Turks.

To the extent to which a dynasty was able to establish itself firmly, it would try to appoint provincial governors from within the ruling group, but with varying degrees of success: the nature of the countryside and the tradition of the ruling family might both make this difficult. The Saljuqs ruled a farflung empire of fertile areas separated from each other by mountain or desert, and inherited a tradition by which authority was vested in a family rather than any individual members of it; their empire was therefore less of a centralized state than a group of semi-independent kingdoms under different members of the family. In Syria, the Ayyubids ruled in a similar fashion; theirs was a kind of confederation of states centred in different cities, each ruled by a member of the Ayyubid family, who gave formal allegiance to the head of the family but did not allow him to interfere too much. In Egypt, however, the nature of the land and the long tradition of centralized rule made it possible for the Ayyubids to maintain direct control. Under the Mamluks, too, the provincial governors in Syria, although drawn from the military élite, were less fully under the control of Cairo than those in lower Egypt; in upper Egypt, however, the Mamluks found it difficult to retain complete control, because of the growth of a powerful family of tribal *shaykhs*, the Hawara. The Hafsids also had difficulty in controlling the more distant parts of their state: some tribal *shaykhs* and distant cities were more or less autonomous; as time went on, however, the power of the central government increased.

Powerful control of a large empire needed an elaborate bureaucracy. In most states, the main divisions between officials continued to be those which had existed under the 'Abbasids. There was a chancery (*diwan al-insha*) where letters and documents were written in correct and precise language and in accordance with recognized forms and precedents, and where they were preserved; a treasury which supervised the assessment, collection and expenditure of revenues; and a special department which kept the accounts and records of the army. Under the Saljuqs the *wazir* continued to be the controlling official of the whole civil bureaucracy, as he had been under the 'Abbasids, but under some other dynasties his functions and powers were more limited. In the Mamluk state he was no more than a superintendent of the treasury; in that of the Hafsids there was a separate *wazir* for each of the three departments, and the court chamberlain (*hajib*), who controlled access to the ruler, could be more important than any of them.

The *wazir* and other high officials might be drawn from the military élite, but in general the civil administration was the sphere of government in which members of the local urban population could play a part. It was they, rather than the soldiers, who had the education and training needed for work in the chancery or treasury. To some extent officials may have been drawn from those who had had the full education of an *'alim*, but it may have been more common for aspirants to public office to enter the service at an early age, after a basic education in the sciences of language and religion, and to learn the special skills of drawing up documents or keeping accounts by a process of apprenticeship. An aspirant might attach himself to a high official and hope to benefit not only from his example but from his patronage. In these circumstances there must have been a hereditary element in the civil service, sons being trained and promoted by their fathers, and it seems likely that there was a certain continuity even when dynasties changed; officials from a previous dynasty would serve the new one, and certainly there was a continuity of chancery or treasury practice.

In this way, members of the urban society which was ruled by an alien dynasty or group could enter the dominant élite, at least at a certain level; Persian officials served the Turkish Saljuqs, Egyptians and Syrians worked for the Mamluks. Rulers could also, however, bring in officials who came from outside the urban élite and who were likely therefore to be more dependent on them. The Ayyubids in Syria brought in officials from Egypt, Iraq and western Iran, the Hafsids made use of exiles from Andalus, and under the Mamluks in Egypt there were Jewish and Coptic officials, most of them converted to Islam.

To administer justice was one of the main duties of a Muslim ruler, and here too there was a way in which educated members of the urban population could be drawn into his service. He appointed the *qadis*, from those educated in the religious schools and belonging to the legal school which he wished to promote. For the most part, *qadis* and *muftis* came from the local population, but a strong ruler might make appointments from outside; for example, the Hafsids gave high office to Andalusian scholars.

The alliance of the holders of military power and members of the urban learned élite was shown also when the ruler himself, or his provincial governor, did justice. Not all cases and disputes went to the *qadi*. The ruler could decide which to refer and which to reserve to himself: most criminal cases, those which affected public order or the interests of the state, and also those which posed difficult legal problems. It was particularly important for an autocratic ruler to hear complaints (*mazalim*) against officials to whom he had delegated power. He had to keep a line of access open to the subjects. Already in 'Abbasid times there had been regular sessions held by a special official to hear petitions of grievances. Under later dynasties, this procedure continued to exist. Some matters would be dealt with by ordinary administrative methods, but the ruler himself would hold sessions to receive petitions and issue decrees. Every week the Mamluk ruler in Cairo would sit in solemn judicial council, surrounded by his chief military and civil officials, the *qadis* of the four *madhhabs*, a special military *qadi*, and the principal *muftis*; he made decisions after consulting them, and was not strictly bound by the legal codes. In the same way, in Hafsid Tunis the ruler would meet each week with the principal *qadis* and *muftis*.

THE ALLIANCE OF INTERESTS

Between the two poles of the city, the palace and the market, relations were close but complex, based on mutual need but divergent interests. The ruler needed the economic activities of the city to provide him with arms and equipment for his army and ships, furnishings and adornments for his person, his entourage and family, and the money to pay for them, whether through regular taxation or by special levies; the merchants provided his financial reserve, to which he could turn when he needed more money than regular taxes could provide. In the same way, the learned class formed a human reserve from which he could draw civil and judicial officials, and poets and artists embellished his court and gave him a reputation for magnificence. For their part, the urban population, and in particular those who possessed wealth and standing, needed the power of the ruler in order to guarantee the supply of food and raw materials from the countryside, guard the trade-routes and conduct relations with other rulers in order to smooth the path of trade.

They needed him also to maintain order and the fabric of law, without which life in a complex and civilized community could not be carried on. The activities of the market had to be regulated, streets lighted, cleaned and protected against thieves and disturbers of the peace, garbage removed, water-pipes cleaned and maintained. For such purposes the ruler appointed a governor of the city, known by different titles in different places. He had at his disposal a police force (*shurta*), usually recruited locally, and there were also guards for the quarters and nightwatchmen for the markets and streets. In the market there was a special official, the *muhtasib*, who supervised prices, weights and measures, the quality of goods and the conduct of business; his authority was derived from a verse of the Qur'an which enjoined upon Muslims the duty of 'bidding unto good and rejecting what is disapproved', and in some circumstances he was appointed from among the religious class, but in others from the military. In some cities, for example San'a in Yemen, there was a written code which expressed the customary agreement about the way in which business should be conducted.

The maintenance of order and the raising of revenue were closely linked. A large part – perhaps the greater part – of the ruler's revenue came from taxes on the produce of the countryside, but urban taxes and dues were numerous and important. In addition to the poll tax on Jews and Christians, there were customs duties on goods coming into the city or going out of it, and dues of various kinds paid by those who owned shops or workshops.

The city could not be governed without some degree of co-operation between the ruler and the inhabitants, or at least those of them who had an interest in stable order. In addition to those who were officials in the full sense, there were also members of urban communities who were recognized by the ruler as their spokesmen or representatives, and as being responsible for maintaining order and obedience and dividing whatever taxes were due among members of the community. The most important of them, for the preservation of urban order, were the headmen of the quarters, who collected such taxes as were levied upon households or domestic buildings. There were also heads of different groups of craftsmen or merchants. All those who practised the same craft were not necessarily treated as a single group; there might be several groups divided territorially. There does not seem to be any substantial evidence that such groups were organized as 'guilds' in the medieval European sense, with an autonomous corporate existence which expressed itself in mutual aid or strict rules about entry or apprenticeship; but the fact that the ruler treated them as a single body liable to pay certain special dues or provide special services, and that they worked together in the same part of the market, must have given them a certain solidarity. A third kind of group was that composed of members of a specific Jewish or Christian community: they too had to have their spokesmen, responsible for the collection of the poll tax and for their loyalty, which might in some circumstances be open to suspicion.

At a higher level, there might be spokesmen for more general interests. Under the Hafsids, for example, there was an *amin al-umana* who spoke for the heads of all the crafts. There might be a *ra'is al-tujjar*, the representative of the large merchants engaged in the lucrative long-distance trade; he would be particularly important when the ruler needed to raise substantial sums of money in a hurry. At a still higher level, there might be those who could, in some circumstances, speak for the city as a whole; although the city might have no formal corporate institutions, it did have a kind of unity of spirit which could find expression at moments of crisis, for example when one dynasty succeeded another. The chief *qadi* might act in this way: besides being an official appointed by the ruler, he was the head of those who preserved the *shari'a*, the normative statement of what life in common should be, and he could therefore express the collective consciousness of the community. In some places there was at times also a 'headman' (*ra'is*) for the city as a whole, but it is not clear what he did.

Little is known about the ways in which the heads or spokesmen of groups were appointed, and they must have varied. It seems certain, however, that they could not have performed their functions if they had not had the confidence both of the ruler or his governor and of those for whom they spoke.

The links between ruler and city, maintained by officials and spokesmen, were precarious and shifting, moving on a spectrum between alliance and hostility. There was a basic community of interest, which could be strengthened by economic co-operation. Members of the ruling élite must have invested in joint commercial ventures. They owned a large proportion of the public buildings, baths, markets and *khans*. Rulers and high officials built public works on a large scale and endowed *waqfs*. A study of the great cities of the Mamluk state has shown that of 171 buildings for religious purposes constructed or repaired in Damascus, 10 were paid for by the sultan himself, 82 by high military officers, 11 by other officials, 25 by merchants and 43 by *'ulama*.[1] Similarly, a survey of buildings in Jerusalem during the Mamluk period has shown that, out of 86 *waqfs*, at least 31 were founded by *mamluk* officers who had settled in local society, and a smaller number by officials, *'ulama* and merchants.[2]

The alliance of interests was expressed in the great ceremonies in which the whole city took part and the ruler showed himself to the people. When a ruler assumed the throne, there was a ceremony of investiture (*bay'a*), a vestige of the early Islamic convention that the ruler was chosen by the people. In Hafsid Tunisia, for example, there were two such ceremonies: at the first, the leading officials of the government pledged their allegiance; at the second, the ruler was presented to the people of the capital. In a sense, this presentation and acceptance were repeated every Friday when the name of the legitimate ruler was mentioned in the sermon at the midday prayer. There were also great annual ceremonies, some but not all of them having a religious meaning, when the ruler appeared in public. A chronicle of Cairo in the Mamluk period, that of Ibn Iyas, mentions each year the ceremonies of the Prophet's birthday, the cutting of the dyke which allowed water from the Nile to enter the canal which ran through Cairo in the flood season, the beginning and end of Ramadan, the departure of the pilgrim caravan from Cairo for Mecca and its return. There were also special occasions: when foreign ambassadors were received, or a son was born to the ruler, the city was illuminated at the expense of the merchants and shopkeepers, and the ruler might appear in public.

The alliance of interests which expressed itself in such ways could break down, however. Within the ruling group itself, the balance of power between the ruler and those on whom he relied could be shaken. In the Mamluk state, for example, some of the main functions of the ruler's officials were taken over by the main *mamluk* military leaders and their own households. In some circumstances, the soldiers would break their obedience and disturb the peace of the city or threaten the ruler's power; this was the way in which Ayyubids succeeded Fatimids in Cairo, then Mamluks replaced Ayyubids, and then one household of *mamluks* took over from another. On the side of the urban population, the spokesmen who mediated the wishes and commands of the ruler to the people could also express the grievances and demands of the groups which they represented. When taxation was too high, soldiers were unruly, officials abused their power, or food was short, the higher *ulama* had a role to play. They tried therefore to preserve a certain independence of the ruler.

The discontent of the possessing classes in the city did not usually take the form of open disobedience. They had too much to lose by disorder. Their rare moments of free action came when the ruler was defeated by an enemy and rival, and the leading men of the city could negotiate its surrender to the new master. Among the ordinary people, however, discontent could take the form of disturbance of order. The skilled craftsmen and shopkeepers would not easily revolt except under pressure of hardship, the oppression of officials, high prices, shortage of food or materials; their normal condition was one of acquiescence, since their interest too lay in the preservation of order. The proletariat, however, the mass of rural immigrants, unskilled casual workers, beggars and habitual criminals on the outskirts of the city, was in a more permanent state of unrest.

In moments of fear or hardship, the whole population of the city might be disturbed. Moved perhaps by popular preachers denouncing oppression (*zulm*) and holding out the vision of a just Islamic order, mobs would break into the *suq*, merchants shut their shops, and some spokesman of the people would bring to the ruler complaints against his officials, or against merchants suspected of causing an artificial scarcity of bread. Faced with such a movement, the ruler might adjust his policy to satisfy some of the demands; officials would be dismissed or executed, the storehouses of the grain merchants opened. The market would open again, the coalition of forces dissolve, but the urban mass would still be there, appeased or controlled for the moment, but as far as ever from a just Islamic order.

CONTROL OF THE COUNTRYSIDE

The ruler and the urban population (or at least the dominant element in it) had a common interest in controlling the countryside and making sure that the surplus of rural production, above that which the cultivator needed for himself, should be brought into the city on terms as favourable as possible. The ruler needed the produce, in itself or transmuted into money, to maintain his court, officials and army; he needed also to control the countryside itself, in order to prevent either attacks from outside or that process by which a new dynasty might arise to challenge his hold over his capital city. The city population for its part needed the rural surplus in order to feed itself and obtain the raw materials of its crafts. Its dominant elements tended also to look on the countryside and its inhabitants as a danger, standing outside the world of urban civilization and the *shari'a*, and threatening it. Thus an Egyptian writer of the sixteenth century, al-Sha'rani (d. 1565), gives thanks to God for 'my *hijra*, with the Prophet's blessing from the countryside to Cairo . . . from the region of hardship and ignorance to the city of gentleness and knowledge'.[3]

Before the modern age, frontiers were not clearly and precisely delimited, and it would be best to think of the power of a dynasty not as operating uniformly within a fixed and generally recognized area, but rather as radiating from a number of urban centres with a force which tended to grow weaker with distance and with the existence of natural or human obstacles. Within the area of radiation there would be three kinds of region, in each of which the nature and extent of control would differ. First of all, in steppe or desert country, or mountainous areas too poor, distant or inaccessible to make the effort of conquering them worthwhile, the ruler would limit himself to keeping the main trade-routes open and preventing revolt. The local tribal chiefs could not be checked, or forced to yield their rural surplus, if it existed, on unfavourable terms. They might have an economic relationship with the city, selling their produce there in order to buy what they could not produce for themselves. In such regions the ruler could secure a certain influence only by political manipulation, setting one tribal chieftain against another or giving formal investiture to one member of a family rather than another. In some circumstances, however, he could have another kind of influence, that given him by inherited religious prestige; this was true of the Zaydi *imams* in Yemen, the Ibadi *imams* in Oman, and those rulers of Morocco, from the sixteenth century onwards, who claimed to be *sharifs*, descendants of the Prophet.

There was a second zone of mountain, oasis or steppe country where the ruler might be able to exercise more direct power, because it lay nearer to the city or great trade-routes and produced a larger surplus. In such regions the ruler would not administer directly, but by means of local chiefs whose position was rather more ambiguous than that of the chiefs of the high mountains or deserts. They would be given investiture in return for payment of an annual or periodical tribute, enforced where necessary by the sending of a military expedition or the withdrawal of recognition and its transfer to someone else.

The line of division between these two zones was not a fixed one. It depended on the power of the ruler, and the changing balance between the use of land for agriculture and its use for pasture. Settled districts were easier to control than those given up to nomadic pastoralism. There is some evidence that, from the tenth or eleventh century onwards, the first zone grew larger at the expense of the second. In upper Egypt, tribal groups which could be controlled from Cairo ('*arab al-ta'a*, 'Arabs of obedience') were replaced during the Mamluk period by the Hawara, a pastoral group of Berber origin, who were to continue to dominate much of the region until the nineteenth century. Similarly in the Maghrib, the complex economic social process which was later to be given symbolic expression in the story of the invasion of Banu Hilal led to a shrinking in the power of the rulers of the cities which was to continue for centuries.

There was a third zone, however: that of the open plains and river valleys where grain or rice or dates were grown, and of the market gardens from which fruit and vegetables were brought into the city. Here the ruler and the urban strata with which he was linked had to maintain a stronger and more direct control, particularly in places where production depended on large-scale irrigation works. Permanent military garrisons or regular military expeditions could keep this zone in order and prevent the emergence of local chieftains.

In this dependent countryside, the economic exchanges would run in favour of the city. The principal means by which the rural surplus was brought in on favourable terms was the system of taxation. In principle this was much the same throughout the Islamic countries. The ruler drew his resources from three kinds of taxation: the poll tax paid by members of recognized non-Muslim communities, various taxes on urban trades and crafts, and taxes on the produce of the land. In cultivated areas, the tax could either be levied on the land, by an assessment which in some countries was changed from time to time (for example, in Egypt, where the practice of periodical reassessment was a survival from ancient times), or it could be a fixed proportion of the produce. The tax on grain and other produce which could be stored was often paid in kind, that on perishable produce such as fruit in money. Similarly, the tax on pasture-land – in places where the government was strong enough to collect it – could be assessed either by area or by a certain proportion of the livestock.

From the time of the Buyids in the tenth century the practice grew up, in some countries, of making an assignment (*iqta'*) of the proceeds of these rural taxes. Such an assignment might be given to a member of the ruling family, or to a high official instead of a salary. The tax resources of a whole province might be given to its governor, who would undertake the expenses of administration and tax-collection and keep a certain proportion of it instead of a salary; or else the tax on a certain piece of land would be assigned to an army officer in return for service with a number of soldiers whom he would himself raise, equip and pay. This last type of assignment was to become particularly important and widespread. Developed considerably by the Saljuqs in Iran and Iraq, it was carried westwards by the Ayyubids, and further developed by the Mamluks. In the Maghrib an analogous system grew up. Control of a certain area of land was given to a tribal leader in return for military service: tribes recruited or formed in this way were known as *jaysh* or army tribes.

It could scarcely have been the intention of any ruler to alienate the tax permanently, or to give those to whom assignments were made a permanent and total control over the land. Various means were used in order to limit the *iqta's*. In Mamluk Egypt, about which our information is particularly full, only half the land was assigned as *iqta'*, the rest being kept for the ruler and his family. That part which was assigned was given either to the ruler's own *mamluks* or to high military officials, who in principle were allowed to keep a certain proportion of it for themselves and were supposed to use the rest to pay the 10, 40 or 100 mounted soldiers whom they were obliged to contribute to the army. The assignee did not normally have a personal connection with the area of his *iqta'*. If he was given more than one *iqta'*, they were not contiguous with each other; he did not collect the tax himself, but left it to the ruler's officials, at least until late Mamluk times; the *iqta'*, did not pass to his sons. In other countries at other times, however, the assignee seems to have been held under less strong and permanent control, and the right to keep the proceeds of the tax became a power to collect it, supervise production and exercise lordship over the peasants.

The collection of taxes provided one of the ways by which the direct control of the rural hinterland by the ruler turned into control by individuals living in the city, who were able to appropriate part of the rural surplus for themselves. It is easy to refer to them as landowners, but it may be misleading; what is essential is that they were able to establish claims upon the agricultural surplus, and to make the claims effective through the use of the ruler's military power. Those who were given assignments might take the lion's share, but officials who played a part in the collection of taxes, merchants who advanced money to finance cultivation or pay the taxes when they were due, and *'ulama* who controlled *waqfs* might be in a similar position.

In the absence of documents, it seems safe to believe that the forms of agricultural contract authorized and regulated by the *shari'a* were widespread. One of them in particular seems to have existed at all times: *muzara'a*, sharecropping or métayage. This was an agreement between the owner and the cultivator of a piece of land: they would share the produce, in proportions which depended on the contribution that each made. If the owner gave the seed, draft animals and equipment, he might receive four-fifths, and the cultivator who gave only his labour might receive one-fifth. In law, such an agreement could be made for a limited period only, but in practice it must often have been prolonged indefinitely. Many variations were possible, and it seems probable that the precise division of the produce depended on such factors as the supply of land and labour, and the relative strength of the two parties. At the extreme point, a cultivator could be virtually fixed on the land because he was permanently indebted to the landowner, was unable to resist his power and could not find other land to cultivate.

IDEAS OF POLITICAL AUTHORITY

Between the ruler and the remote countryside – the mountain valleys, steppe and desert – relations were too distant and indirect to need to be expressed in moral terms: the ruler's power was accepted if it did not come too close; the men of the mountains and steppes provided soldiers for his army, but might also provide them for the challenger who would overthrow him. Between the ruler and his non-Muslim subjects, too, the relationship was not strengthened by a moral bond. Even if it was a peaceful and stable relationship, there was a sense in which Christians and Jews lay outside the community; they could not give the ruler the strong and positive allegiance which would come from an identity of beliefs and purposes. The Muslim inhabitants of the cities, however, were in a different position. The ruler and his officials impinged directly and continuously upon their lives, collecting taxes, maintaining order, administering justice; they exercised the power without which industry and commerce could not flourish, nor the tradition of law and learning survive. In these circumstances, it was natural that those who created and preserved the moral universe of Islam, the *'ulama*, should ask who was the legitimate ruler and what were the limits within which he should be obeyed, and that the ruler for his part should claim obedience by right as well as by power.

There were many kinds of bond between the ruler and particular individuals or groups: pledges of loyalty expressed in oaths and vows, gratitude for benefits received, and hopes of future favour. Beyond these, however, there lay certain general concepts of legitimate authority which could be accepted by larger groups, or by the community as a whole.

The question of who had a right to rule had already been raised in an acute form during the first century of Islamic history. Who was the legitimate successor of the Prophet as head of the community, caliph or *imam*? How should he be chosen? What were the limits of his authority? Did he have an unconditional right to obedience, or was it legitimate to revolt against, or depose, a ruler who was impious or unrighteous? Ibadis and Shi'is of different kinds had given their own answers to such questions. Sunni *'ulama* had gradually moved to the belief that the caliph was head of the community but not the infallible interpreter of the faith, and the *'ulama* were guardians of the faith and therefore, in a sense, the heirs of the Prophet. They had accepted the possibility that a caliph might be unrighteous, and it might be the duty of the faithful to reject him; this had been the argument used by supporters of the 'Abbasids to justify their revolt against the Umayyads, who were depicted as having turned their authority into secular kingship.

It was not until the fourth Islamic century (the tenth century AD) that the fullest formulation was given of the theory of the caliphate. A change of circumstances, which threatened the position of the 'Abbasid caliphs, gave rise to an attempt to defend it by way of defining it. The threat came from two different quarters. The creation of the Fatimid caliphate in Cairo and the revived Umayyad caliphate in Andalus posed not only the question of who was the legitimate caliph, but also another: could there be more than one caliph, or did the unity of the *umma* imply that it should have a single head? Within the region which still acknowledged 'Abbasid sovereignty, local rulers were becoming virtually independent. Even in Baghdad, the capital, a military dynasty, that of the Buyids, established control over the caliph's chancery and was therefore able to issue decrees in his name; at times the Buyids seemed to be claiming independent authority, by reviving for their own use the ancient Iranian title of *shahanshah*.

It was in this context that the most famous theoretical exposition and defence of the caliphate was written, that of al-Mawardi (d. 1058). The existence of the caliphate, he said, was not a natural necessity; its justification lay in a statement of the Qur'an, 'O believers, obey God, and obey the Messenger and those in authority over you,'[4] and it was therefore ordained by God. Its purpose was to protect the community and administer its affairs on the basis of true religion. The caliph must possess religious knowledge, a sense of justice, and courage. He should belong to the

Quraysh tribe from which the Prophet came, and there could be only one caliph at a time. He could delegate his power, either for a limited purpose or without limit, and either in a province of his empire or in the whole of it; but the *wazir* or *amir* to whom power was delegated should recognize the authority of the caliph and exercise his power within the limits of the *shari'a*. This formulation made it possible to reconcile the existing distribution of power with the theoretical authority of the caliph, and gave the caliph the right to preserve such power as he still possessed and take back from other dynasties the power he had relinquished to them.

Until the end of the caliphate of Baghdad, such a balance between authority and power could be maintained in one form or another; the *'ulama* could accept that the sultan, the holder of military power, had a right to exercise it, provided he remained loyal to the caliph and ruled in accordance with right religion. It was not a stable balance, however. The caliph still had a residue of effective power in and around the capital, and attempted to increase it, particularly in the time of the Caliph al-Nasir (1180–1225); a strong sultan would try to expand his independent power; and there was a third authority, that of the *'ulama*, who claimed to determine what right religion was. It was in order to define the conditions in which the relationship should be stable that al-Ghazali (1058–1111) and others within the religious tradition put forward the idea that power belonged to the caliph, but the exercise of it could be divided between more than one person. The caliphate (or *imamate*, as the theorists usually called it) possessed three elements: that of legitimate succession to the Prophet, that of directing the affairs of the world and that of watching over the faith. Ghazali held that ideally these three aspects should be united in one person, but in case of necessity they could be separated, and this was the situation in his time. The caliph embodied succession from the Prophet; the sultan, the holder of military power, exercised the functions of government; and the *'ulama* watched over religious belief and practice.

In time the three-sided relationship became a two-sided one. The caliph-ate of Baghdad came to an end when the Mongols occupied Baghdad in 1258, and the 'Abbasid caliphs maintained in Cairo by the Mamluk sultans were not generally recognized. Although the memory of the caliphate remained, and was recognized by the law books as being the ideal form of Islamic authority, and although some powerful rulers, such as the Hafsids, continued to use the title, the main purpose of political thought, among those who wrote within the legal tradition, was to determine the relations between the ruler who wielded the sword and the *'ulama* who guarded true religion and claimed to speak in the name of the *umma*. There was an ancient saying, coming down from Sasanian times and often repeated, that 'religion and kingship are two brothers, and neither can dispense with the other'.[5] It was generally accepted that power was acquired by the sword, and by the general acquiescence expressed in the ceremony of *bay'a*; it could, however, become legitimate authority if it was used to maintain the *shari'a* and therefore the fabric of virtuous and civilized life. The ruler should uphold the courts of justice, respect the *'ulama* and rule in consultation with them. Within the bounds of the *shari'a*, he could exercise statecraft, making regulations and decisions and dispensing criminal justice in matters where the welfare of society and the security of the state were involved. The *'ulama* in their turn should give a just sultan that perpetual recognition which was expressed in the weekly invocation of the ruler's name in the Friday sermon.

In this, as in other matters, however, Ibn Taymiyya (1263–1328), one of the foremost religious writers of the Mamluk period, drew the logical implications of the situation in his time. For him, the unity of the *umma* – a unity of belief in God and acceptance of the Prophet's message – did not imply political unity. There must be authority in the *umma* in order to maintain justice and keep individuals within their limits, but it could be exercised by more than one ruler; how he obtained his power was less important than how he used it. The just exercise of power was a kind of religious service. He should exercise statecraft within the bounds of the *shari'a*, and should rule in co-operation with the *'ulama*. This relationship of rulers and *'ulama* carried with it the implication that the ruler should respect the interests of the Muslim urban élite. In the countries east of Maghrib, where from the tenth century onwards most rulers were of Turkish or alien origin, it had a further implication: the local, Arabic-speaking population should be consulted and given their share in the process of government.

Even if the ruler was unjust or impious, it was generally accepted that he should still be obeyed, for any kind of order was better than anarchy; as Ghazali said, 'the tyranny of a sultan for a hundred years causes less damage than one year's tyranny exercised by the subjects against one another'.[6] Revolt was justified only against a ruler who clearly went against a command of God or His prophet. This did not mean, however, that the *'ulama* should look on an unjust ruler in the way in which they looked on a just one. A powerful tradition among the *'ulama* (among Sunnis and Shi'is alike) was that they should keep their distance from the rulers of the world. Ghazali quoted a *hadith*: 'in Hell there is a valley uniquely reserved for *'ulama* who visit kings'. The virtuous *'alim* should not visit unjust princes or officials. He could visit a just ruler, but without subservience, and should reproach him if he saw him doing anything reprehensible; if he was afraid he could keep silent, but it would be better not to visit him at all. If he received a visit from a prince, he should return his salutation and exhort him to virtue. It would be better, however, to avoid him altogether. (Other *'ulama*, however, held that they should support the ruler in everything that was licit, even if he were unjust.)

Intertwined with such ideas, put forward by theologians and jurists, were others drawn from intellectual traditions which helped to form the culture of the Islamic world. In the tenth century, the philosopher al-Farabi defined the standards by which states should be judged in his book *al-Madina al-fadila* (*The Ideas of the Citizens of the Virtuous City*). The best of states is that which is ruled by one who is both a philosopher and a prophet, in contact through both his intellect and his imagination with the Active Intelligence which emanates from God. In the absence of such a ruler, the state can be virtuous if it is ruled by a combination of those who collectively possess the necessary characteristics, or by rulers who maintain and interpret laws given by the founder (such would have been the early caliphate). At the other extreme there are societies of which the ruling element do not possess the knowledge of the good; these societies have no common good, and are held together by force, or by some natural characteristic such as common descent, character or language.

Of more general influence were theories coming from another origin: the ancient Iranian idea of kingship. They were sometimes expressed in the form of an image of a circle. The world is a garden; its fence is a ruler or dynasty; the ruler is supported by soldiers; the soldiers are maintained by money; money is acquired from the subjects; the subjects are protected by justice; and justice is maintained by the ruler. To formulate it in a different way, the human world consists of different orders, each of them pursuing its own activities and interests. So that they should live together in harmony and contribute what they have to give to society, there is needed a regulative power, and it is for this that kingship exists; it is a natural human order maintained by God. 'In every age and time, God (be He exalted) chooses one member of the human race and, having endowed him with goodly and kingly virtues, entrusts him with the interests of the world and the well-being of His servants.'[7] To perform his functions he needs above all wisdom and justice. When he lacks these, or the power to uphold them, then

'corruption, confusion and disorder spread . . . kingship disappears altogether, opposing swords are drawn, and whoever has the stronger hand
does what he wishes.'[8]

To do what he is chosen by God to do, the ruler must stand outside the
different orders of society. He is not chosen by them – the general assumption of such writings is that his is an inherited position – nor is he
responsible to them, but only to his own conscience and, on the Day of
Judgement, to God, to whom he must render an account of his stewardship.
There should be a clear distinction between those who rule and those who
are ruled; the monarch and his officials should stand aloof from the
interests which they regulate.

Throughout Islamic history there was a succession of writings which
gave expression to such ideas and drew implications from them. Just as the
writings of the jurists expressed the interests and outlook of the *'ulama*,
and those classes of which they were the spokesmen, so this other kind of
writing expressed the interests of those who stood near the exercise of
power, the bureaucrats who might serve one dynasty after another, preserving their own traditions of service. The most famous of such writings was
the *Book of Government* of Nizam al-Mulk (1018–92), the chief minister
of the first Saljuq sultan to rule Baghdad. His book, and others like it,
contain not only general principles, but practical advice on statecraft for
rulers and for use in the education of princes; hence the name by which
this genre is sometimes known, that of 'Mirrors for Princes' (a term used
for a similar kind of literature in Europe). The prince is advised how to
choose officials; how to control them by obtaining intelligence about them,
how to deal with the petitions and grievances of his subjects, in order to
prevent his servants from abusing the power they exercise in his name;
how to take counsel from the old and wise, and choose the companions of
his leisure hours; how to recruit soldiers from different races and keep
them loyal to him. The advice is directed mainly against the dangers to
which the absolute ruler is exposed: that of becoming isolated from his
subjects, and that of permitting subordinates to abuse the power they
exercise in his name.

CHAPTER 9

Ways of Islam

THE PILLARS OF ISLAM

Between these varied communities, living in a wide circle of lands stretching from the Atlantic to the Gulf, separated by deserts, subject to dynasties which rose and fell and competed with each other for control of limited resources, there was nevertheless a common link: at first a dominant group, and then later a majority of their members, were Muslims, living under the authority of the Word of God, the Qur'an, revealed to the Prophet Muhammad in the Arabic language. Those who accepted Islam formed a community (*umma*). 'You are the best *umma* brought forth for mankind, bidding unto good, rejecting what is disapproved, believing in God':[1] these words of the Qur'an express something important about the adherents of Islam. By striving to understand and obey God's commandments, men and women created a right relationship with God, but also with each other. As the Prophet said in his 'pilgrimage of farewell': 'know that every Muslim is a Muslim's brother, and that the Muslims are brethren'.[2]

Certain acts or rituals played a special part in maintaining the sense of belonging to a community. These were obligatory for all Muslims capable of observing them, and they created a link not only between those who performed them together but between successive generations. The idea of a *silsila*, a chain of witnesses stretching from the Prophet to the end of the world, and handing on the truth by direct transmission from one generation to another, was of great importance in Islamic culture; in a sense this chain formed the true history of mankind, behind the rise and fall of dynasties and peoples.

These acts or rituals were commonly known as the 'Pillars of Islam'. First of them was the *shahada*, the testimony that 'there is no god but God, and Muhammad is the Prophet of God'. The making of this testimony was the formal act by which a person became a Muslim, and it was repeated daily in the ritual prayers. It contained in essence those articles of faith by which Muslims distinguished themselves from unbelievers and polytheists, and also from Jews and Christians who lay within the same tradition of monotheism: that there is only one God, that He has revealed His Will to mankind through a line of prophets, and that Muhammad is the Prophet in whom the line culminates and ends, 'the Seal of the prophets'. A regular affirmation of this basic creed should be made daily in the ritual prayer, *salat*, the second of the Pillars. At first, *salat* was performed twice a day, but it later came to be generally accepted that it should take place five times a day: at daybreak, noon, mid-afternoon, after sunset, and in the early part of the night. The times of prayer were announced by a public call (*adhan*) made by a muezzin (*mu'adhdhin*) from a high place, usually a tower or minaret attached to a mosque. Prayer had a fixed form. After a ritual washing (*wudu'*) the worshipper performed a number of motions of the body – bowing, kneeling, prostrating himself to the ground – and said a number of unchanging prayers, proclaiming the greatness of God and the lowliness of man in His presence. After these prayers had been said there might also be individual supplications or petitions (*du'a*).

These prayers could be performed anywhere except in certain places regarded as unclean, but it was thought a praiseworthy act to pray in public together with others, in an oratory or mosque (*masjid*). There was one prayer in particular which should be performed in public: the noon prayer on Friday was held in a mosque of a special kind (*jami'*) possessing a pulpit (*minbar*). After the ritual prayers, a preacher (*khatib*) would mount the pulpit and deliver a sermon (*khutba*), which also followed a more or less regular form: praise of God, blessings invoked on the Prophet, a moral homily often dealing with the public affairs of the community as a whole, and finally an invocation of God's blessing on the ruler. To be mentioned in this way in the *khutba* came to be regarded as one of the signs of sovereignty.

A third Pillar was in a sense an extension of the act of worship. This was *zakat*, the making of gifts out of one's income for certain specified purposes: for the poor, the needy, the relief of debtors, the liberation of slaves, the welfare of wayfarers. The giving of *zakat* was regarded as an obligation on those whose income exceeded a certain amount. They should give a certain proportion of their income; it was collected and distributed by the ruler or his officials, but further alms might be given to men of religion for them to distribute, or else given directly to those in need.

There were two more obligations no less binding upon Muslims, but to be fulfilled less frequently, coming as solemn reminders of the sovereignty of God and man's submission to him, at a certain time in the liturgical year. (For religious purposes the calendar used was that of the lunar year, which was approximately eleven days shorter than the solar year. Thus these ceremonies might be performed at different seasons of the solar year. The calendar used for religious purposes, and generally adopted in cities, could not be used by cultivators for whom the important events were rains, the flooding of rivers, the variations of heat and cold. For the most part they used more ancient solar calendars.)

These two Pillars were *sawm*, or fasting once a year, in the month of Ramadan, and Hajj, or pilgrimage to Mecca at least once in a lifetime. During Ramadan, the month in which the Qur'an was first revealed, all Muslims above the age of ten were obliged to abstain from eating and drinking, and from sexual intercourse, from daybreak until nightfall; an exception was made for those who were too physically weak to endure it, those of unsound mind, those engaged in heavy labour or war, and travellers. This was regarded as a solemn act of repentance for sins, and a denial of self for the sake of God; the Muslim who fasted should begin the day with a statement of intention, and the night might be filled with special prayers. In drawing nearer to God in this way, Muslims would draw nearer to each other. The experience of fasting in company with a whole village or city would strengthen the sense of a single community spread over time and space; the hours after nightfall might be spent in visits and meals taken in common; the end of Ramadan was celebrated as one of two great festivals of the liturgical year, with days of feasting, visits and presents (*'id al-fitr*).

Once in a lifetime at least, every Muslim who was able to make the pilgrimage to Mecca should do so. He could visit it at any time of the year (*'umra*), but to be a pilgrim in the full sense was to go there with other Muslims at a special time of the year, the month of Dhu'l-Hijja. Those who were not free or not of sound mind, or who did not possess the necessary financial resources, those under a certain age and (according to some authorities) women who had no husband or guardian to go with them, were not obliged to go. There are descriptions of Mecca and the Hajj made in the twelfth century which show that by that time there was agreement about the ways in which the pilgrim should behave and what he could expect to find at the end of his journey.

Most pilgrims went in large companies which gathered in one of the great cities of the Muslim world. By the Mamluk period it was the pilgrimages from Cairo and Damascus which were the most important. Those from the Maghrib would go by sea or land to Cairo, meet the Egyptian pilgrims there, and travel by land across Sinai and down through western Arabia to the holy cities, in a caravan organized, protected and led in the name of the ruler of Egypt. The journey from Cairo took between thirty and forty days, and by the end of the fifteenth century perhaps 30–40,000 pilgrims made it every year. Those from Anatolia, Iran, Iraq and Syria met in Damascus; the journey, also by caravan organized by the ruler of Damascus, also took between thirty and forty days and it has been suggested that some 20–30,000 pilgrims may have gone each year. Smaller groups went from West Africa across the Sudan and the Red Sea, and from southern Iraq and the ports of the Gulf across central Arabia.

At a certain point on the approach to Mecca, the pilgrim would purify himself by ablutions, put on a white garment made of a single cloth, the *ihram*, and proclaim his intention to make the pilgrimage by a kind of act of consecration: 'Here am I, O my God, here am I; no partner hast Thou, here am I; verily the praise and the grace are Thine, and the empire.'[3]

Once he arrived in Mecca, the pilgrim would enter the sacred area, the *haram*, where were various sites and buildings with hallowed associations. By the twelfth century at the latest these had taken the shape which they were to keep: the well of Zamzam, believed to have been opened by the Angel Gabriel to save Hagar and her son Ishmael; the stone on which Abraham's footstep was imprinted; certain places associated with the *imams* of the different legal *madhhabs*. At the heart of the *haram* stood the Ka'ba, the rectangular building which Muhammad had purged of idols and made the centre of Muslim devotion, with the Black Stone embedded in one of its walls. The pilgrims would go round the Ka'ba seven times, touching or kissing the Black Stone as they passed it. On the eighth day of the month they would go out of the city in the eastern direction to the hill of 'Arafa. There they would stand for a time, and this was the essential act of the pilgrimage. On the way back to Mecca, at Mina, two more symbolic acts would be performed: the casting of stones at a pillar signifying the Devil, and the sacrifice of an animal. This marked the end of the period of dedication which had begun with the putting on of the *ihram*; the pilgrim would take off the garment and return to the ways of ordinary life.

The pilgrimage was in many ways the central event of the year, perhaps of a whole lifetime, that in which the unity of Muslims with each other was most fully expressed. In a sense it was an epitome of all kinds of travel. Those who went to pray in Mecca might remain to study in Madina; they might bring goods with them in order to pay the expenses of the journey; merchants would travel with the caravan, with goods to sell on the way or in the holy cities. The pilgrimage was also a market for the exchange of news and ideas brought from all parts of the world of Islam.

The famous traveller Ibn Battuta expressed something of what the experience of pilgrimage meant:

Of the wondrous doings of God Most High is this, that He has created the hearts of men with an instinctive desire to seek these sublime sanctuaries, and yearning to present themselves at their illustrious sites, and has given the love of them such power over men's hearts that none alights in them but they seize his whole heart, nor quits them but with grief at separation from them.[4]

The Hajj was an act of obedience to God's command as expressed in the Qur'an: 'It is the duty of all men towards God to come to the House a pilgrim, if he is able to make his way there.'[5] It was a profession of belief in the one God, and also a visible expression of the unity of the *umma*. The many thousands of pilgrims from all over the Muslim world made the pilgrimage at the same time; together they went round the Ka'ba, stood at 'Arafa, stoned the Devil and sacrificed their animals. In doing so, they were linked with the whole world of Islam. The departure and return of pilgrims were marked by official celebrations, recorded in local chronicles, in later times at least depicted on the walls of houses. At the moment when the pilgrims sacrificed their animals at Mina, every Muslim household too would kill an animal, to usher in the other great popular festival of the year, the Feast of Sacrifice (*'id al-adha*).

The sense of belonging to a community of believers expressed itself in the idea that it was the duty of Muslims to look after each other's consciences, and to protect the community and extend its scope where possible. *Jihad*, war against those who threatened the community, whether hostile unbelievers outside it or non-Muslims within it who broke their covenant of protection, was usually regarded as an obligation practically equivalent to one of the Pillars. The duty of *jihad*, like the others, was based on a Qur'anic saying: 'O you who believe, fight the unbelievers who are near to you.'[6] The nature and extent of the obligation were carefully defined by the legal writers. It was not an individual obligation of all Muslims, but an obligation on the community to provide a sufficient number of fighters. After the great expansion of Islam in the early centuries, and with the beginnings of the counterattack from western Europe, *jihad* tended to be seen in terms of defence rather than expansion.

Of course, not all who called themselves Muslims took these obligations with equal seriousness, or gave the same meaning to the fulfilment of them. There were different levels of individual conviction, and differences in general between the Islam of the city, the countryside and the desert. There was a spectrum of observance ranging from the scholar or devout merchant of the city, performing the daily prayers and annual fast, able to pay *zakat* and make the pilgrimage, to the ordinary beduin, not praying regularly, not fasting in Ramadan because his whole life was lived on the edge of privation, not making the pilgrimage, but still professing that there is no god but God and Muhammad is His Prophet.

THE FRIENDS OF GOD

From the beginning there had been some followers of the Prophet for whom external observances were of no worth unless they expressed a sincerity of intention, a desire to obey God's commands from a sense of His greatness and the littleness of man, and unless they were regarded as the elementary forms of a moral discipline which should extend to the whole of life.

From an early date, the desire for purity of intention had given rise to ascetic practices, perhaps under the influence of eastern Christian monks. Implicit in them was the idea that there could be a relationship between God and man other than that of command and obedience: a relationship in which man obeyed God's Will out of love of Him and the desire to draw near Him, and in so doing could become aware of an answering love extended by God to man. Such ideas, and the practices to which they gave rise, were developed further during these centuries. There was a gradual articulation of the idea of a path by which the true believer could draw nearer to God; those who accepted this idea and tried to put it into practice came to be known generally as Sufis. Gradually too there emerged a consensus, although an incomplete one, about the main stages (*maqam*) on the path. The first stages were those of repentance, a turning away from the sins of past life. This would lead on to abstinence, even from things which were lawful but could distract the soul from seeking its proper object. The traveller on the path should go on to learn trust in God, reliance upon Him, and patient waiting upon His Will, and then, after a period of fear and hope, there might come a revelation of the divine Being: a spiritual awakening in which all objects vanished and only God was there. The human qualities of the traveller who had reached this point were annihilated, their place was taken by divine qualities, and man and God were united in love. This momentary experience of the divine (*ma'rifa*) would leave its mark: the soul would be transformed once it returned to the world of everyday life.

This movement towards union with God was one which affected the emotions as well as the mind and soul, and corresponding to the various stages there might be graces (*hal*, pl. *ahwal*), emotional states or vivid experiences which could be expressed only, if at all, in metaphor or image. In Arabic and the other literary languages of Islam, there gradually developed a system of poetic imagery by which poets tried to evoke the states of grace which might come along the path towards knowledge of God, and the experience of unity which was its goal: images of human love, in which the lover and beloved mirrored each other, of the intoxication of wine, of the soul as a drop of water in the divine ocean, or as a nightingale seeking the rose which is a manifestation of God. Poetic imagery is ambiguous, however, and it is not always easy to say whether the poet is trying to express human love or the love of God.

Serious and concerned Muslims were aware of the danger of the path; the traveller might lose the way, the graces might beguile him. It was generally accepted that some human souls were able to walk on it alone, suddenly rapt into ecstasy, or guided by the direct leadership of a dead teacher or the Prophet himself. For most travellers, however, it was thought to be necessary to accept the teaching and guidance of someone who had advanced further on the path, a master of the spiritual life (*shaykh*, *murshid*). According to a saying which became familiar, 'he who has no *shaykh*, the Devil is his *shaykh*'. The disciple should follow his master implicitly; he should be as passive as a corpse beneath the hands of the washer of the dead.

In the late tenth and eleventh centuries, a further development began to take place. Those who followed the same master began to identify themselves as a single spiritual family, moving along the same path (*tariqa*). Some of these families continued over a long period and claimed a lineage which went back to some great master of the spiritual life, after whom the *tariqa* was named, and through him to the Prophet, by way of 'Ali or else of Abu Bakr. Some of these 'paths' or 'orders' extended over a wide area within the world of Islam, carried by disciples to whom a master had given a 'licence' to teach his way. For the most part they were not highly organized. Disciples of a master could found their own orders, but in general they recognized an affinity with the master from whom they had learned their path. Among the most widespread and lasting of the orders were some which began in Iraq; such were the Rifa'iyya which goes back to the twelfth century, the Suhrawardiyya in the thirteenth century, and – the furthest extended of all – the Qadiriyya, named after a Baghdad saint, 'Abd al-Qadir al-Jilani (1077/8–1166), but which did not emerge clearly until the fourteenth century. Of the orders which grew up in Egypt, the Shadhiliyya was to become the most widespread, particularly in the Maghrib, where it was organized by al-Jazuli (d. *c.* 1465). In other parts of the Muslim world, other orders or groups of orders were important: for example, the Mawlawiyya in Anatolia and the Naqshbandiyya in central Asia. Some of these were later to spread in Arabic-speaking countries too.

Only a minority of adherents of such orders devoted their whole lives to the path, living in convents (*zawiya, khanqa*); some of these, particularly in cities, might be small buildings, but others might be larger, including a mosque, a place for spiritual exercises, schools, hostels for visitors, all clustered around the tomb of the master after whom the order was named. Most of the members of the order lived in the world, however; these might include women as well as men. For some of them, affiliation to an order might be little more than nominal, but for others it implied a certain initiation into doctrines and practices which could help them to move on the way towards the ecstasy of union.

The orders differed in their view of the relationship between the two ways of Islam: that of *shari'a*, obedience to the law derived from God's commands in the Qur'an, and that of *tariqa*, the search for direct experiential knowledge of Him. On one side stood the 'sober' orders, which taught that, after the self-annihilation and intoxication of the mystical vision, the believer should return to the world of everyday activities and live within the bounds of the *shari'a*, fulfilling his duties to God and his fellow men, but giving them a new meaning. On the other side stood those for whom the experience of union with God left them intoxicated with a sense of the divine presence, such that their real life was henceforth lived in solitude; they did not care whether they incurred blame by neglect of the duties laid down in the *shari'a*, and might even welcome such blame as a way of helping them to turn away from the world (Malamatis). The first tendency was associated with those who claimed to descend from Junayd, the second with those who looked to Abu Yazid al-Bistami as their master.

There was a process of initiation into an order: the taking of an oath of allegiance to the *shaykh*, the receiving from him of a special cloak, the communication by him of a secret prayer (*wird* or *hizb*). In addition to individual prayers, however, there was a ritual which was the central act of the *tariqa* and the characteristic which marked it off from others. This was the *dhikr* or repetition of the name of Allah, with the intention of turning the soul away from all the distractions of the world and freeing it for the flight towards union with God. The *dhikr* could take more than one form. In some of the orders (in particular the Naqshbandiyya) it was a silent repetition, together with certain techniques of breathing, and with concentration of the mind's attention upon certain parts of the body, upon the *shaykh*, the eponymous founder of the order, or the Prophet. In most, it was a collective ritual (*hadra*), performed regularly on certain days of the week in a *zawiya* of the order. Drawn up in lines, the participants would repeat the name of Allah; there might be an accompaniment of music and poetry; in some orders there was ritual dancing, as in the graceful circular dance of the Mawlawis; there might be demonstrations of particular graces, knives thrust into cheeks or fire into mouths. The repetition and action would go faster and faster, until the participants were caught up into a trance in which they lost awareness of the sensible world.

Surrounding these public acts was a penumbra of private devotions, praise of God, expressions of love for Him, petitions for spiritual graces. Some were brief ejaculations praising God or invoking blessings on the Prophet, others were more elaborate:

> Glory to Him the mountains praise with what is on them;
> Glory to Him whom the trees praise as they put forth their leaves;
> Glory to Him whom the date-palms praise at the maturity of their
>   fruits;
> Glory to Him whom the winds praise in the ways of the sea.[7]

Collections of them came to be attributed to great masters of the spiritual life.

The idea of a path of approach to God implied that man was not only the creature and servant of God, but could also become His friend (*wali*). Such a belief could find its justification in passages of the Qur'an: 'O Thou, Creator of the heavens and the earth, Thou art my Friend in this world and the next.'[8] Gradually a theory of sainthood (*wilaya*) emerged. The friend of God was the one who always stood near Him, whose thoughts were always on Him, and who had mastered the human passions which took a man away from Him. A woman as well as a man could be a saint. There had always been saints in the world and always would be, to keep the world on its axis. In time this idea was given formal expression: there

155

would always be a certain number of saints in the world; when one died he would be succeeded by another; and they constituted the hierarchy who were the unknown rulers of the world, with the *qutb*, the pole on which the world turned, at their head.

The 'friends of God' could intercede with Him on behalf of others, and their intercession could have visible results in this world. It could lead to cures for sickness or sterility, or relief of misfortunes, and these signs of grace (*karamat*) were also proofs of the sanctity of the friend of God. It came to be widely accepted that the supernatural power by which a saint called down graces into the world could survive his or her death, and requests for intercession could be made at his or her tomb. Visits to the tombs of saints, to touch them or pray in front of them, came to be a supplementary practice of devotion, although some Muslim thinkers regarded this as a dangerous innovation, because it interposed a human intermediary between God and each individual believer. The tomb of the saint, quadrangular, with a vaulted dome, whitewashed inside, standing by itself or in a mosque, or serving as the nucleus round which a *zawiya* had grown, was a familiar feature of the Islamic landscape and townscape.

Just as Islam did not reject the Ka'ba but gave it a new meaning, so converts to Islam brought into it their own immemorial cults. The idea that certain places were the dwellings of gods or superhuman spirits had been widespread since very ancient times: stones of an unusual kind, ancient trees, springs of water gushing spontaneously from the earth, were looked on as visible signs of the presence of a god or spirit to whom petitions could be addressed and offerings made, by the hanging of votive rags or the sacrifice of animals. All over the world where Islam spread, such places became associated with Muslim saints and thus acquired a new significance.

Some of the tombs of saints had become the centres of great public liturgical acts. The birthday of a saint, or some day specially associated with him, was celebrated by a popular festival during which Muslims from the surrounding district or further afield would gather to touch the tomb or pray before it and take part in festivities of various kinds. Some of these gatherings were of only local importance, but others would draw visitors from further afield. Such 'national' or universal shrines were those of Mawlay Idris (d. 791), reputed founder of the city of Fez; Abu Midyan (*c.* 1126–97) at Tlemçen in western Algeria; Sidi Mahraz, patron saint of sailors, in Tunis; Ahmad al-Badawi (*c.* 1199–1276) at Tanta in the Egyptian delta, subject of a cult in which scholars have seen a survival in a new form of the ancient Egyptian worship of Bubastis; and 'Abd al-Qadir, after whom the Qadiri order was named, in Baghdad.

In course of time the Prophet and his family came to be seen in the perspective of sainthood. The intercession of the Prophet on the Day of Judgement would, it was commonly believed, work for the salvation of those who had accepted his mission. He came to be regarded as a *wali* as well as a prophet, and his tomb at Madina was a place of prayer and petition, to be visited for itself or as an extension of the Hajj. The birthday of the Prophet (the *mawlid*) became an occasion of popular celebration: this practice appears to have begun to grow by the time of the Fatimid caliphs in Cairo, and it was widespread by the thirteenth and fourteenth centuries.

A living or dead saint could generate worldly power, particularly in the countryside where the absence of organized bureaucratic government allowed the free play of social forces. The residence or tomb of a saint was neutral ground where people could take refuge, and members of different groups which elsewhere were distant or hostile could meet to transact business. The festival of a saint was also a country fair where goods were bought and sold, and his tomb could be the guardian of a permanent market, or of the granary of a nomadic tribe. The saint, or his descendants and the guardians of his tomb, could profit from his reputation for sanctity; offerings from pilgrims would give them wealth and prestige, and they might be called upon to act as arbitrators in disputes.

Men of learning and piety, with a reputation for working miracles and resolving disputes, could be the point around which there could gather political movements, in opposition to rulers regarded as unjust or illegitimate. In some circumstances, the prestige of such a religious teacher could draw strength from a widespread popular idea, that of the *mahdi*, the man guided by God and sent by him to restore the rule of justice which would come before the end of the world. Examples of this process can be found throughout Islamic history. The most famous and successful of those recognized by their followers as the *mahdi* was perhaps Ibn Tumart (*c.* 1078–1130), a religious reformer born in Morocco who, after studying in the Middle East, returned to the Maghrib and began to call for a restoration of the original purity of Islam. He and those who gathered around him founded the Almohad Empire, which at its height extended throughout the Maghrib and the Muslim parts of Spain, and the memory of which was to confer legitimacy upon later dynasties, in particular the Hafsids of Tunisia.

CHAPTER 10

The Culture of the *Ulama*

THE *'ULAMA* AND THE *SHARI'A*

At the heart of the community of those who accepted Muhammad's message stood the religious scholars (*'ulama*), men learned in Qur'an, Hadith and law, who claimed to be the guardians of the community, the successors of the Prophet.

The struggle for the political succession to the Prophet during the first Islamic century had carried with it implications for the question of religious authority. Who had the right to interpret the message conveyed in the Qur'an and the life of Muhammad? For the Shi'is, and the various groups which sprang from them, authority lay with a line of *imams*, infallible interpreters of the truth contained in the Qur'an. From early Islamic times, however, a majority of Muslims in the Arabic-speaking countries were Sunnis: that is to say, they rejected the idea of an infallible *imam* who could, in a sense, prolong the revelation of God's Will. For them, that Will had been revealed finally and completely in the Qur'an and the *sunna* of the Prophet, and those who had the capacity to interpret it, the *'ulama*, were keepers of the moral conscience of the community.

By the eleventh century there was a clear distinction between the various *madhhabs* or 'schools' of moral and legal interpretation, and in particular the four most widespread and lasting of them, the Shafi'is, Malikis, Hanafis and Hanbalis. The relations between followers of the different *madhhabs* had been stormy at times; in Baghdad during the 'Abbasid period, Shafi'ism and Hanafism had given their names to urban factions which fought with one another. Later, however, the differences became less controversial. In some regions, one or other of the *madhhabs* was almost universal. The Malikis came to be almost the only school in the Maghrib, the Shafi'is were widespread in Egypt, Syria, Iraq, Iran and Hijaz, the Hanafis in central Asia and India. The Hanbalis were an important element in Baghdad, and in the Syrian cities from the twelfth century onwards. Just as schools of theology came to accept each other, so did schools of law. Even when, as was to happen, a dynasty would appoint members of a certain school to legal positions, the others would have their judges and juridical specialists.

Some of the differences between the *madhhabs* concerned the precise definition and relative weight of the principles of legal thought (*usul al-fiqh*). In regard to *ijma'*, the Hanbalis accepted only that of the Companions of the Prophet, not that of later scholars, and therefore gave a broader scope to *ijtihad*, provided it was exercised by scholars in accordance with the strict rules of analogy. Another school, that of the Zahiris, which was strong in Andalus for a time but later became extinct, clung only to the literal meaning of the Qur'an and Hadith, as interpreted by the Companions, and rejected later *ijtihad* and consensus. A rather similar doctrine was taught by Ibn Tumart, the founder of the Almohad movement and dynasty, but he claimed for himself the position of being the sole infallible interpreter of the Qur'an and Hadith. Two of the schools allowed some flexibility in the use of *ijtihad*: the Hanafis maintained that strict analogy need not always be used, and scholars could exercise a limited power of individual preference in interpreting the Qur'an and Hadith (*istihsan*); the Malikis too believed that a scholar could go beyond strict analogy in the interests of human welfare (*istislah*).

These principles were not developed and discussed simply for their own sake, but because they formed the basis of *fiqh*, the attempt by responsible human effort to prescribe in detail the way of life (*shari'a*) which Muslims should follow in order to obey the Will of God. All human actions, in direct relationship to God or to other human beings, could be examined in the light of the Qur'an and *sunna*, as interpreted by those qualified to exercise *ijtihad*, and classified in terms of five norms: they could be regarded as obligatory (either for the community as a whole, or for every single member of it), recommended, morally neutral, reprehensible, or forbidden.

Gradually, scholars of the different *madhhabs* drew up codes of human conduct, covering all human acts in regard to which guidance could be derived from the Qur'an and Hadith. One typical code, that of Ibn Abi Zayd al-Qayrawani (d. 996), a scholar of the Maliki school, begins with those essential truths 'which the tongue should express and the heart believe', a kind of profession of faith. It then deals with those acts which are immediately directed towards God, acts of worship ('*ibadat*): prayer and the ritual purification which is a preliminary to it, fasting, the giving of alms, the performance of the pilgrimage, and the duty of fighting in the cause of Islam (*jihad*). After the *'ibadat*, it proceeds to acts by which human beings are related to each other (*mu'amalat*): first of all, matters of intimate human relations, marriage and the ways in which it can be contracted and ended; then relations of broader scope and less personal intimacy, sales and similar contracts, including agreements for the pursuit of profit, inheritance and bequests, the creation of *waqfs*; then criminal matters, and certain forbidden acts, such as adultery and the drinking of wine, in regard to which the Qur'an lays down precise penalties. It then gives regulations for the procedure to be followed by judges who adjudicate on matters which are forbidden, and concludes with a section of moral exhortation:

It is an obligation for every believer to keep always in mind, in every word or pious act, the love of God: the words or acts of him who has some other aim in view than the love of God are not acceptable. Hypocrisy is a lesser polytheism. To repent of every sin is an obligation, and this involves not persevering in wrongdoing, reparation of injustices committed, abstention from forbidden acts, and the intention of not backsliding. Let the sinner invoke God's pardon, hoping for His forgiveness, fearing His punishment, mindful of His benefits, and expressing gratitude to Him . . . Man should not despair of the divine mercy.[1]

On matters of substance as well as on principles of interpretation there were some differences between the various *madhhabs*, but most of them were of minor importance. Even within a particular *madhhab* there could be differences of opinion, for no code, however detailed and precise, could cover all possible situations. A maxim often repeated declared that from the tenth century onwards there could be no further exercise of individual judgement: where consensus had been reached, 'the door of *ijtihad* is closed'. There seems to be no clear evidence, however, that this precept was ever formulated or generally accepted, and within each *madhhab ijtihad* was in fact carried on, not only by judges who had to make decisions, but by jurisconsults (*muftis*). A *mufti* was essentially a private scholar known for his learning and his ability to give rulings on disputed questions by means of the exercise of *ijtihad*. The opinions (*fatwa*) given by famous *muftis* could be incorporated in authoritative books of *fiqh* after a time, but the activity of giving *fatwas* had to continue. From perhaps the thirteenth century onwards rulers appointed official *muftis*, who might receive salaries, but the private scholar, who was paid a fee by those who sought a ruling from him, and was under no obligation to the ruler, had a position of special respect in the community.

It is customary to refer to the product of *fiqh*, the *shari'a*, as 'Islamic law', and this is justified, since from the times of the 'Abbasids onwards it served as the body of thought on which *qadis* appointed by the rulers relied in making judgements or reconciling disagreements. In reality, however, it was both more and less than what is now usually regarded as law. It was more, because it included private acts which concerned neither a man's neighbour nor his ruler: acts of private worship, of social behaviour, of what would be called 'manners'. It was a normative code of all human acts, an attempt to classify them, and by so doing to give guidance to Muslims about the way in which God willed them to live. It was less than law, because some of its provisions were theoretical only, never or rarely observed in practice, and also because it ignored whole fields of action which would be included in other legal codes. It was most precise in regard to matters of personal status – marriage and divorce, bequests and inheritance; less so in regard to contracts and obligations, and all that concerned economic activity; it did not cover the whole field of what would now be called criminal law – homicide was regarded as a private matter between the families of those involved, rather than one in which the community should intervene through the judges; and it said virtually nothing about 'constitutional' or administrative law.

Even in those fields in which it was most precise, its authority could be challenged by the power of the ruler or the actual practice of society. In most regimes, the ruler or his officials dealt with many criminal acts, in particular those in which the security of the state was involved; the procedure and punishments were decided by him. In the countryside, similarly, matters were decided in accordance with *'urf*, the custom of the community, preserved and applied by the elders of the village or tribe. In some places there seem to have been written codes of custom, and in some there may have been regular courts or councils; this may have been true in particular of Berber communities in the Maghrib. These were probably exceptional, however.

Just as the *shari'a* had grown up by a slow and complicated process of interaction between the norms contained in the Qur'an and Hadith and the local customs and laws of the communities brought under the rule of Islam, so there was a continuing process of mutual adjustment between the *shari'a*, once it took its definitive form, and the practices of Muslim societies. It has been shown, for example, that the precepts of Hanafi law, in regard to commercial practices, correspond with the practices of Egyptian merchants as they are revealed in documents of quite a different kind. What the *shari'a* said about contracts was modified by the acceptance into the Hanafi code of certain *hiyal,* or legal stratagems, by which such practices as the taking of interest were brought within the scope of the law.[2] Similarly, the issuing of regulations and the exercise of jurisdiction by rulers and their officials was justified by the principle of *siyasa shar'iyya* (statecraft within the bounds of the *shari'a*): since the ruler had been placed by God in human society in order to preserve religion and morality, and since his power was given sanction by being accepted by the community, he had the right to issue those regulations and take those decisions which were necessary in order to preserve a just social order, provided he did not infringe the limits imposed by the *shari'a.* The ruler was regarded as having the right to decide which cases should be sent to the *qadi* for judgement, and which he should keep for his own decision.

Although *'urf* and *shari'a* were often placed in opposition to one another for rhetorical purposes, they were not necessarily in conflict. Whatever in *'urf* was not opposed to *shari'a* was accepted by it as permissible. In parts of the Maghrib, indeed, there was an attempt to interpret the *shari'a* in the light of custom. From at least the fifteenth century onwards, there are records in Morocco of the use by *qadis* of a procedure known as *'amal*: the *qadi* was entitled to choose, among the opinions of jurists, those which best conformed with local custom or interest, even if they were not those which had the support of the majority of scholars.

We know little about customary law in the countryside during this period, but studies of what has happened in more modern times suggest that the opposite process may have taken place, that of a certain penetration of custom by the *shari'a.* Marriage might be solemnized in accordance with Islamic terminology, but its rights and duties, and questions of divorce and inheritance which arose from it, would be decided by custom; in many places the inheritance of land by daughters was contrary to custom, although it is in accordance with the *shari'a.* Disputes about property or partnerships might be taken to a *qadi* in the nearest town for decision or conciliation; contracts or agreements to which the parties wished to give a certain solemnity or permanence might also be taken to the *qadi,* to be expressed formally in the language of the *shari'a,* but the document might thereafter be interpreted in the light of local custom. To use the words of a scholar who has studied such documents from the Jordan valley: 'Custom mostly provides the substance and the *shari'a* the form'.[3]

THE TRANSMISSION OF LEARNING

The doctors of the law, those who developed and preserved the consensus of the community, were the nearest equivalent to a teaching authority in Sunni Islam, and it was essential for them to make sure that the understanding of *fiqh* and of its bases was fully transmitted from one generation to another.

From an early time there seems to have been a formal procedure for the transmission of religious learning. In mosques, and especially in the large congregational ones, circles of students would group themselves around a teacher sitting against a pillar and expounding a subject through reading and commenting upon a book. From at least the eleventh century, however, there grew up a kind of institution devoted largely to legal learning, the *madrasa*: its origin is often ascribed to Nizam al-Mulk (1018–92), the *wazir* of the first Saljuq ruler of Baghdad, but in fact it goes back to an earlier time. The *madrasa* was a school, often although not always attached to a mosque; it included a place of residence for students. It was established as a *waqf* by an individual donor; this gave it an endowment and ensured its permanence, since property of which the income was devoted to a pious or charitable purpose could not be alienated. The endowment was used for the upkeep of the building, the payment of one or more permanent teachers, and in some instances stipends or the distribution of food to students. Such *waqfs* might be established by any person of wealth, but the greatest and most lasting of them were those created by rulers or high officials, in Iraq and Iran under the Saljuqs, in Syria and Egypt under the Ayyubids and Mamluks, and in the Maghrib under the Marinids and Hafsids.

Some institutions were established for the teaching of the Qur'an or Hadith, but the main purpose of most of them was the study and teaching of *fiqh*. To take an example: the Tankiziyya *madrasa* in Jerusalem, endowed during the Mamluk period, had four halls (*iwan*) opening off a central courtyard, one each for the teaching of Hadith, Hanafi law and Sufism, while the fourth was a mosque. The endowment provided for fifteen students of law, twenty of Hadith and fifteen of Sufism, and for teachers of each subject; the students were to sleep in the *madrasa*, and there was also a hospice for twelve widows.[4] A *madrasa* could be endowed for the purpose of teaching one only of the *madhhabs*, or more than one, or all four; such a one was the *madrasa* of Sultan Hasan in Cairo, where four schools, one for each *madhhab*, opened off a central court. A more or less regular course of teaching was offered by the *mudarris*, the holder of an endowed chair, and by his assistants who taught subsidiary subjects. A student who came to a *madrasa* would normally have been already to a school of lower standing, a *maktab* or *kuttab*, where he would have learned the Arabic language and probably memorized the Qur'an. At the *madrasa* he would study ancillary subjects – Arabic grammar, and the annals of the early period of Islam – but his main study would be of the sciences of religion: how to read and interpret the Qur'an, Hadith, the bases of religious belief (*usul al-din*), jurisprudence (*usul al-fiqh*), and *fiqh*. The main method of teaching was the exposition of a text by a *mudarris*, perhaps amplified later by his teaching assistants; the emphasis was upon the memorizing of what was taught, but also upon an understanding of what was remembered.

In the first phase of study, usually lasting for several years, the student would learn the legal code on which there was a consensus of the doctors of a particular *madhhab*. Many students would not go further than this, and not all of them would be training for positions in the legal service; sons of merchants and others might have some years of this kind of education. At a higher level, there was a range of legal questions on which there were differences of opinion even within a single *madhhab*, since the variety of circumstances to which legal principles had to be applied was limitless. Students who wished to be teachers of law, or *qadis* at a high level, or *muftis*, would pursue their studies for longer. At this higher level, training in *ijtihad* took place by the method of formal logical disputation: the putting forward of a thesis, which had to be answered by a counter-thesis, which would be followed by a dialogue of objections and answers.

When a student had finished reading a book with a teacher, he could ask him for an *ijaza*, a certificate to the effect that A. had studied the book with B. At a higher level, he could ask for an *ijaza* of a different kind, certifying that he was competent to exercise *ijtihad* as a *mufti*, or to teach a certain book or subject. At this higher level, it was customary for a student to go from one teacher to another, in one city after another, and to ask for *ijazas* from all those whose courses he attended; such a procedure had its justification in the *hadith* which enjoined Muslims to seek learning wherever it was to be found.

An *ijaza* could be an elaborate document, mentioning a whole chain of transmission from teacher to student over the generations, and so inserting the recipient into a long chain of intellectual ancestors. By implication it could express a certain idea of what the life of a concerned and learned Muslim should be. No doubt there were many abuses of the system: we read of indolence and ignorance, of endowments embezzled or perverted to another use. Nevertheless, the scholar was one of the ideal types of Muslim man which persisted over the centuries. This is the way in which a legal and medical scholar of Baghdad, 'Abd al-Latif (1162/3–1231), describes what a scholar should be:

I commend you not to learn your sciences from books unaided, even though you may trust your ability to understand. Resort to professors for each science you seek to acquire; and should your professor be limited in his knowledge take all that he can offer, until you find another more accomplished than he. You must venerate and respect him . . . When you read a book, make every effort to learn it by heart and master its meaning. Imagine the book to have disappeared and that you can dispense with it, unaffected by its loss . . . One should read histories, study biographies and the experiences of nations. By doing this, it will be as though, in his short life space, he lived contemporaneously with peoples of the past, was on intimate terms with them, and knew the good and the bad among them . . . You should model your conduct on that of the early Muslims. Therefore, read the biography of the Prophet, study his deeds and concerns, follow in his footsteps, and try your utmost to imitate him . . . You should frequently distrust your nature, rather than have a good opinion of it, submitting your thoughts to men of learning and their works, proceeding with caution and avoiding haste . . . He who has not endured the stress of study will not taste the joy of knowledge . . . When you have finished your study and reflection, occupy your tongue with the mention of God's name, and sing His praises . . . Do not complain if the world should turn its back on you, it would distract you from the acquisition of excellent qualities . . . know that learning leaves a trail and a scent proclaiming its possessor; a ray of light and brightness shining on him, pointing him out . . . [5]

An important and distinctive type of Islamic writing sprang from an impulse similar to that which led to the giving of *ijazas*: the biographical dictionary. Its origin is to be found in the collection of *hadiths*. In order to verify a *hadith*, it was necessary to know who had transmitted it, and from whom he had himself learned it; it was important to be sure that the transmission had been continuous, but also that those who had transmitted it were honest and reliable. Gradually the collection of biographies was extended from the narrators of *hadiths* to other groups – legal scholars, doctors, Sufi masters, and so on. A distinctive type of work was the local dictionary, devoted to notable men, and sometimes women, of a certain city or region, with an introduction on its topography and history. The first important example of this genre was that compiled for Baghdad in the eleventh century by al-Khatib al-Baghdadi (1002–71). Some cities had a succession of such works; for Damascus, we have dictionaries of important persons for the ninth, tenth, eleventh, twelfth and thirteenth Islamic centuries (the fifteenth–nineteenth centuries AD). The most ambitious authors were those who tried to cover the whole of Islamic history, in particular Ibn Khallikan (1211–82).

Ibn Khallikan's work encompassed rulers and ministers, poets and grammarians, as well as religious scholars. In such books, however, the scholars of mosque and *madrasa* had a central place, as if to show that the history of the Muslim community was essentially that of the unbroken transmission of truth and high Islamic culture. A biography of a scholar might begin with his ancestry and the place and date of his birth. It would give details of his education: what books he studied and with whom, and what *ijazas* he received. It would thus place him in two lines of descent, the physical and intellectual: the two were not always different from each other, since a boy might begin to study with his father, and there were long dynasties of scholars. It would describe his work and travels, what books he wrote and whom he taught, and there might be some personal anecdotes. It would contain an encomium of his qualities, designed not so much to distinguish him from other scholars as to insert him into the framework of an ideal type.

KALAM

Those who studied *fiqh* in the *madrasa* also studied the basic tenets of religious belief, although the process by which they had evolved and the ways in which they could be defended do not seem to have played a large part in the curriculum. By the time the system of schools was fully grown, the great discussions through which the Sunni creed has been defined had largely come to an end.

Even after the period during which Mu'tazilism enjoyed the favour of the 'Abbasid caliphs, it continued to be a flourishing and important school of thought for another century or so. Its last important and systematic thinker was 'Abd al-Jabbar (c. 936–1025). It was only in the eleventh century that Mu'tazili teaching was suppressed in Baghdad and elsewhere, under the influence of the 'Abbasid caliphs and the Saljuq rulers. It continued to play an important part in the formation of Shi'i theology, and to be taught in Shi'i schools; in the Sunni world, however, it became a submerged current of thought until a certain revival of interest in it in modern times.

The decline of Mu'tazilism was caused partly by the continuing strength of the traditionalist teaching of Ibn Hanbal, particularly in Baghdad and Damascus, but also by the development of the line of thought which began with Ash'ari: the explanation and defence of what was given in the Qur'an and Hadith by rational argument based upon the principles of logic (dialectical theology, '*ilm al-kalam*). It was a sign of the spread of Ash'arism, or even a cause of it, that it came to be accepted by many of the doctors of the law as providing a basis of faith on which their *fiqh* could rest. This was particularly true of Shafi'i scholars.

This combination of Ash'ari *kalam* and *fiqh* was by no means universally accepted, however. The Hanbalis were opposed to *kalam*, and so were some of the Shafi'is. In the Maghrib, too, the dominant Maliki school discouraged theological speculation, and the Almoravids banned the teaching of theology; Ibn Tumart and the Almohads, however, encouraged *kalam*, mainly in its Ash'ari form, although in jurisprudence they were strict literalists of the Zahiri school. In the north-east of the Muslim world, another version of *kalam*, which traced its origin to al-Maturidi (d. 944), was more generally accepted in the Hanafi law schools. It differed from Ash'arism on a number of points, in particular the question of man's free will and its relationship with the omnipotence and justice of God: human actions, the Maturidis taught, occur by God's power, but those which are sinful do not occur with His pleasure or love. The early Saljuq sultans, who themselves came from the region where the combination of Maturidi *kalam* and Hanafi *fiqh* was widespread, made some attempt to bring it with them as they moved westwards. There was not, however, any lasting tension or hostility between Ash'ari and Maturidi thinkers, and the differences between them were not of permanent importance. In the Sunni *madrasas* of later centuries, the textbooks which summarized the basic tenets of the faith expressed a general consensus of scholars.

AL-GHAZALI

Even if the main line of Sunni thought accepted Ash'ari theology and the conclusions to which it led, it did so with reservations and within limits. Such reservations were expressed in a classic form by al-Ghazali, a writer of lasting influence and with a comprehensive view of all the main currents of thought in his time. Himself a master of Ash'ari *kalam*, he was aware of the dangerous paths into which it might lead him. He tried to define the limits within which *kalam* was licit. It was essentially a defensive activity: discursive reason and argumentation should be used in order to defend right belief derived from the Qur'an and Hadith against those who denied it, and also against those who tried to give false and speculative interpretations of it. It should not, however, be practised by those whose faith might be troubled by it, nor should it be used to build a structure of thought which went beyond what was given in the Qur'an and Hadith. It was a matter only for specialists, working independently outside the schools.

That Muslims should observe the laws derived from the Will of God as expressed in Qur'an and Hadith was the principle of Ghazali's thought; to abandon them was to be lost in a world of undirected human will and speculation. That human beings should obey the Will of God, but should do so in a way which would lead them nearer to Him, was the theme of one of the greatest and most famous of Islamic religious works, Ghazali's *Ihya 'ulum al-din* (*Revivification of the Sciences of Religion*).

In a work, *al-Munqidh min al-dalal* (*The Deliverer from Error*), which is often described – not very accurately – as his autobiography, Ghazali traced the path which led him to this conclusion. After his early studies in Khurasan, at Tus and Nishapur, he became a teacher in the famous Baghdad *madrasa* founded by Nizam al-Mulk, the *wazir* of the Saljuq sultan. There he became convinced that external observance of the *shari'a* was not sufficient, and found himself plunged into a search for the right path in life: 'Worldly desires began tugging me with their claims to remain as I was, while the herald of faith was crying out, "Away! Up and away!" '[6]

He became convinced that he could not find what he needed through the use of his intellect alone. To follow the path of the philosophers and construct the truth of the universe from first principles was to be lost in a morass of illicit innovations. The Shi'i path, that of following the teaching of an infallible interpreter of the faith, was dangerous: it might lead to an abandonment of what had been given in revelation, for the sake of some inner truth, and an acceptance that he who knows that inner truth is free from the restraints of the *shari'a*.

The only infallible teacher, Ghazali came to believe, was Muhammad, and the right path was to accept his revelation by faith, that 'light which God casts into the hearts of His servants, a gift and present from him',[7] and to follow the way it prescribes, but to do so with sincerity and the presence of the heart, and with an abandonment of all except the service of God.

The *Ihya 'ulum al-din* is concerned with the intimate relationship between acts and dispositions of the soul, or – to put it in other terms –

between external observances and the spirit which gives them meaning and value. There was, he believed, a reciprocal relationship: virtues and good character were formed and strengthened by right action:

He who wishes to purify his soul, to perfect and sweeten it by good acts, cannot do it by a single day's worship, nor prevent it by one day's rebellion, and that is what we mean when we say that a single sin does not deserve eternal punishment. But one day's abstention from virtue leads to another, and then the soul degenerates little by little, until it sinks in sloth.[8]

Acts had value, however, only if they were performed by minds and souls directed towards the goal of knowing and serving God.

It is the desire to illuminate this relationship which determines the contents and arrangement of the *Ihya*. The first of its four parts examines the Pillars of Islam, the basic duties of religion, prayer, fasting, almsgiving and pilgrimage, and in regard to each of them it goes beyond external observances – the precise rules of how the duty was to be performed – to explain its meaning, and the benefits to be derived from it if carried out in the right spirit. Prayer has its full value only if it is performed with the presence of the soul: with an understanding of the words which are used, and with an inner purification, a renunciation of all thoughts except of God, with veneration, fear and hope. Fasting is of value if it is so carried out as to make the soul free to turn towards God. Almsgiving should be performed out of a desire to obey God, and to regard the goods of the world as being of little worth. The pilgrimage should be undertaken in purity of intention, and with thoughts of the end of life, of death and judgement.

The second part of the book goes beyond ritual observances to other acts with moral implications, in particular those which bind human beings to each other: eating and drinking, marriage, the acquisition of material goods, listening to music. In regard to each of them, the question whether it is right to act, and if so within what limits and in what circumstances, is reviewed in the light of man's chief aim, which is to draw nearer to God. Marriage, for example, is seen as showing a balance of advantages and disadvantages. It provides a man with progeny, saves him from illicit carnal passions, and may give him 'a foretaste of paradise'; on the other hand, it can distract him from seeking knowledge of God through the proper performance of his religious duties.

The third part contains a systematic review of those human passions and desires which, if improperly indulged, will prevent a man from gaining spiritual benefit from the external acts of religion, and lead him towards perdition. The Devil enters the human heart through the five senses, the imagination and the carnal appetites. Ghazali passes in review the idols of the stomach, of concupiscence, of the tongue – its use in conflict, indecency, lies, mockery, calumny and flattery; anger, hatred and jealousy; the desire for wealth or worldly glory, and that for spiritual glory which leads to hypocrisy; pride of knowledge or piety, or birth, physical health or beauty.

Such impulses can be held in check by supplication to God – preferably at times of ritual observance, prayer, fasting and pilgrimage – by repetition of the name of God, meditation and self-knowledge, and with the help of a friend or spiritual director. In such ways, the path which the soul is taking can be reversed, and it can be set on another path which leads towards knowledge of God.

The last part of the book deals with this path towards God, of which the final goal is 'total purification of the soul from everything other than God Most High . . . utter absorption of the heart in the remembrance of God'.[9] Here Ghazali's thought reflects that of the Sufi masters. The path towards God is marked by a series of stages (*maqam*). The first of them is repentance, the turning away of the soul from its imprisonment in false gods; then come patience, fear and hope, renunciation even of those things which are not sinful but may be hindrances on the path, reliance on God and compliance with Him. To each station there correspond certain revelations and visions, spiritual comforts for the traveller; if they come, it is by the grace of God, and they do not remain.

As the soul moves up the path, its own efforts count for less, and more and more it is led by God. Its own task is 'purification, purgation and burnishing, then readiness and waiting, nothing more'. At every stage there is a danger, of remaining there and going no further, or being lost in illusions; but it may come about that God takes over and grants the soul the gift of contemplating Him. This is the highest point in the ascent, but it comes only as a grace which may be given and taken away:

Gleams of the truth will shine in his heart. In the beginning it will be like the rapid lightning, and will not remain. Then it will return and it may tarry. If it return it may remain, or may be snatched away.[10]

It is at this highest point, when a man has lost his awareness of himself in the contemplation of the God who has revealed Himself through love, that he understands the true meaning of the duties commanded by the *shari'a* and is able to perform them in the proper manner. It may be, however, that he also becomes aware of another reality. Ghazali hints at another kind of knowledge (*ma'rifa*) – of angels and devils, Heaven and Hell, and of God himself, His essence, attributes and names – a knowledge which is unveiled by God to man in his inmost soul. He does not write of it in this work, although there are other books attributed to him in which he elaborates on it. This state is not one of complete absorption in God or union with Him; at its highest it is a momentary proximity to Him, a foretaste of the afterlife, when man may have the vision of God from near, but still at a distance.

CHAPTER 11

Divergent Paths of Thought

ISLAM OF THE PHILOSOPHERS

In mosques and *madrasas*, *fiqh* and its ancillary sciences were the main objects of study, but outside them other kinds of thought were carried on. One which was of lasting importance was the thought of the philosophers, those who believed that human reason, working according to the rules of operation laid down in Aristotle's logic, could lead to the attainment of a truth which could be demonstrated.

This line of thought, of which the forerunners in the Islamic world had been al-Kindi and al-Farabi, reached its culmination in the work of Ibn Sina (Avicenna, 980–1037), whose influence on the whole of later Islamic culture was to be profound. In a brief fragment of autobiography he described his education, that which had by now become traditional, in the Qur'an and the sciences of the Arabic language, in jurisprudence, and the rational sciences, logic, mathematics and metaphysics: 'When I had reached the age of eighteen I was finished with all of these sciences . . . today my knowledge is more mature, otherwise it is the same; nothing has come to me since.'[1]

He was to make contributions to more than one of these sciences, but what was to have the most general and widespread influence on later thought was his attempt to articulate the truths of Islam in terms drawn from Aristotelian logic and later Greek metaphysics. The basic problem posed by Islamic revelation, for those who sought demonstrable truth, lay in the apparent contradiction between the unity of God and the multiplicity of created beings; for practical reasons, this dilemma could be stated in terms of the contradiction between the absolute goodness of God and the apparent evil of the world. The line of philosophers which culminated in Ibn Sina found the answer to such questions in the Neo-Platonic version of Greek philosophy, made more acceptable by the fact that a major work of the school, a kind of paraphrase of part of Plotinus's *Enneads*, was generally regarded as being a work of Aristotle (the so-called 'Theology of Aristotle'). This school conceived of the universe as being formed by a series of emanations from God, and in this way it was able to reconcile the unity of God with multiplicity. In Ibn Sina's formulation, God was the First Cause or Creator, the necessary Being in whom essence and existence were one. From Him there emanated a series of ten intelligences, ranging from the First Intelligence down to the Active Intelligence which governed the world of embodied beings. It was from the Active Intelligence that ideas were communicated to the human body by a radiation of the divine light, and thus the human soul was created.

The symbolism of light, which was common in Sufi as in other mystical thought, could derive authority from the Qur'an:

> God is the Light of the heavens and the earth:
> the likeness of His light is as a niche
> wherein is a lamp
> (the lamp is a glass,
> the glass as it were a glittering star)
> kindled from a Blessed Tree,
> an olive that is neither of the East nor of the West
> whose oil wellnigh would shine, even if no fire touched it:
> Light upon Light
> (God guides to His Light whom He will).[2]

Just as the soul was created by this process of descent from the First Being, a process animated by the overflowing of divine love, so human life should be a process of ascent, a return through the different levels of being towards the First Being, by way of love and desire.

If the divine light is radiated into the human soul, and if the soul by its own efforts can return towards its Creator, what need is there of prophecy, that is to say, special revelations of God? Ibn Sina accepted the need for prophets as teachers, imparting truths about God and the future life, and enjoining upon men those acts which make them aware of God and immortality – prayer and the other acts of ritual worship. He believed, however, that prophecy was not simply a grace of God; it was a kind of human intellect, and indeed the highest kind. The prophet would participate in the life of the hierarchy of Intelligences, and could rise as high as the First Intelligence. This was not an exclusive gift to prophets only, however; the man of high spiritual gifts could also attain to it by the way of ascesis.

Such a scheme of thought seemed to run counter to the content of divine revelation in the Qur'an, at least if it was taken in its literal sense. In the most famous controversy in Islamic history, Ghazali criticized with force the main points at which such a philosophy as that of Ibn Sina ran counter to his understanding of the revelation given in the Qur'an. In his *Tahafut al-falasifa* (*Incoherence of the Philosophers*), he laid emphasis upon three errors, as he thought them, in the philosophers' way of thought. They believed in the eternity of matter: the emanations of the divine light infused matter but did not create it. They limited the knowledge of God to universals, to the ideas which formed particular beings, not to the particular beings themselves; this view was incompatible with the Qur'anic image of a God concerned for every living creature in its individuality. Thirdly, they believed in the immortality of the soul but not of the body. The soul, they thought, was a separate being infused into the material body by the operation of the Active Intelligence, and at a certain point in its return towards God the body to which it was attached would become a hindrance; after death, the soul would be liberated from the body and would not need it.

What Ghazali was saying was that the God of the philosophers was not the God of the Qur'an, speaking to every man, judging him and loving him. In his view, the conclusions to which discursive human intellect could reach, without guidance from outside, were incompatible with those revealed to mankind through the prophets. This challenge was met, a century later, by another champion of the way of the philosophers, Ibn Rushd Averroes (1126–98). Born and educated in Andalus, where the tradition of philosophy had come late but had taken firm root, Ibn Rushd set himself to a detailed refutation of Ghazali's interpretation of philosophy in a work entitled, by reference to Ghazali's own book, *Tahafut al-tahafut* (*The Incoherence of the Incoherence*). In another work, *Fasl al-maqal* (*The Decisive Treatise*), he dealt explicitly with what had appeared to Ghazali to be the contradiction between the revelations through the prophets and the conclusions of the philosophers. Philosophical activity was not illegitimate, he maintained; it could be justified by reference to the Qur'an: 'Have they not considered the dominion of the heaven and the earth, and what things God has created?'[3] It was clear from such words of God that there could be no opposition between the conclusions of the philosophers and the statements of the Qur'an:

Since this religion is true and summons to the study which leads to knowledge of the Truth, we the Muslim community know definitely that demonstrative study does not lead to [conclusions] conflicting with what Scripture has given us; for truth does not oppose truth but accords with it and bears witness to it.[4]

How to explain, then, that they might appear to contradict each other? Ibn Rushd's answer was that not all the words of the Qur'an should be taken literally. When the literal meaning of Qur'anic verses appeared to contradict the truths to which philosophers arrived by the exercise of reason, those verses needed to be interpreted metaphorically. Most human beings, however, were incapable of philosophical reasoning or of accepting the metaphorical interpretation of the Qur'an. It should not be communicated to them, but only to whose who could accept it:

Anyone who is not a man of learning is obliged to take these passages in their apparent meaning, and allegorical interpretation of them is for him unbelief because it leads to unbelief ... Anyone of the interpretative class who discloses such [an interpretation] to him is summoning him to unbelief ... Therefore allegorical interpretations ought to be set down only in demonstrative books because if they are in demonstrative books they are encountered by no one but men of the demonstrative class.[5]

Philosophy was for the élite (*khass*); for the generality (*'amm*), the literal meaning was sufficient. Prophecy was necessary for both: for the *khass* in order to keep them on the right moral path, and for the *'amm* to express truths in acceptable images. Dialectical reasoning, *kalam*, was for minds in an intermediate position, since it used logic in order to support the level of truth appropriate to the *'amm*; but it had its dangers, since its rational principles were not adequately proved.

The work of Ibn Rushd does not appear to have had a widespread and lasting influence upon subsequent Islamic thought, although the Latin translations of some of his books were to have a deep impact upon western Christian philosophy. The thought of Ibn Sina, however, remained of central importance in religious as well as in philosophical thought. By the twelfth century there was beginning, in spite of Ghazali, a kind of rapprochement between *kalam* and philosophy. From the time of Fakhr al-Din al-Razi (1149–1209) onwards, works on *kalam* began with the explanations of logic and the nature of being, and proceeded from there to a rational articulation of the idea of God; in this way a logical structure was erected to defend and explain the revelations of the Qur'an, and it was only after this that such works dealt with matters which should be accepted entirely on the basis of revelation.

IBN 'ARABI AND THEOSOPHY

In Ibn Sina's writings there are references to *ishraq*, that radiation of divine light by which men are able to attain to contact with the hierarchy of Intelligibles. By some later writers the term *ishraq* was taken to refer to the ancient esoteric wisdom of the east (*sharq* is the Arabic word for 'east'), and used as a term for the systematic formulation of the ultimate Reality which lay behind the words of the Qur'an and gave meaning to the experiences of the Sufis.

An attempt to formulate such a theosophy was made by al-Suhrawardi and caused scandal which led to his execution by the Ayyubid ruler of Aleppo in 1191. The most elaborate and lasting formulation was that of Ibn 'Arabi (1165–1240). He was an Arab of Andalus, whose father was a friend of Ibn Rushd, and who himself met the philosopher and was present at his funeral. After studies of the normal kind in Andalus and the Maghrib, he embarked on a period of travel in the eastern lands. He made the pilgrimage to Mecca, and this seems to have been decisive in the formation of his thought; he became aware, through a vision, of the Ka'ba as being the point where the ultimate reality impinges upon the visible world, and it was here that he began writing his most elaborate work, *al-Futuhat al-makkiyya (The Meccan Revelations)*. After living for a time in the Saljuq sultanate in Anatolia, he settled in Damascus, where he died; his tomb on the Qasiyun mountain, which overshadows the city from the west, was to become a place of pilgrimage.

In the *Futuhat* and other works he tried to express a vision of the universe as an endless flow of existence from and back towards the Divine Being: a flow of which the primary symbol was that of Light. This process could be regarded, in one of its aspects, as an overflowing of love from God, the desire of the Necessary Being to know itself by seeing its Being reflected back on itself. As a tradition of the Prophet, frequently quoted by Sufi writers, had it: 'I was a hidden treasure and I desired to be known, therefore I created the creatures in order that I might be known.'[6]

This creation took place by a manifestation of God's Being through His Names or attributes. The Names could be seen in three aspects: in themselves as being part of the essence of the Divine Being, as eternal archetypes or forms, and as realized in specific and limited existent beings. In their active form the Names were known as Lords: they manifested themselves in images produced by the creative imagination of God, and concrete beings were an embodiment of these images.

All created things therefore were manifestations of particular Names through the mediation of images, but Man was capable of manifesting all of them. This idea of the privileged status of human beings was linked with that covenant (*mithaq*) which, according to the Qur'an, God had made with them, before the world was created. The archetype through which man was made was called by Ibn 'Arabi and other writers the 'Light of Muhammad' or 'Truth of Muhammad'. This was the 'clear mirror' in which the Divine Being could see itself fully reflected. In a sense, then, all human beings could be regarded as perfect manifestations of God, but there was another sense in which this was the privilege of certain men only. The idea of the 'Perfect Man' (*al-insan al-kamil*) put forward by Ibn 'Arabi was carried further by one of his followers, al-Jili (d. *c.* 1428). Such a man is one who most fully manifests the nature of God, is most fully made in His likeness; he is a visible embodiment of the eternal archetype, the 'Muhammadan Light'.

The prophets are such privileged human beings, who manifest the Names of God; in a famous work, *Fusus al-hikam* (*The Gems of Wisdom*), Ibn 'Arabi wrote of the sequence of prophets from Adam to Muhammad, and showed which of the Names was exemplified by each of them. Muhammad, the Seal of the Prophets, was the most perfect of these prophetic manifestations. There were also saints, however, who by ascesis and the possession of inner knowledge (*ma'rifa*) could attain to the position of being mirrors in which the Light of God was reflected. Prophets were also saints, but there could be saints who were not prophets, because they did not have the specific function of mediating the revelation of truth or of a law. There was an invisible hierarchy of saints, who preserved the order of the world, and at the head of them there was a 'pole' (*qutb*) for each age. (Ibn 'Arabi clearly thought of himself as being a *qutb*, and indeed as being the Seal or most perfect of them.)

The possessor of *ma'rifa*, like the ordinary unenlightened man, must still live within the limits of a law revealed by a prophet; Ibn 'Arabi himself adhered to the Zahiri school of strict and literal interpretation of the law revealed in the Qur'an and Hadith. He believed, however, that all revelations through prophets and lawgivers were revelations of the same Reality; all men worshipped the same God in different forms.

The outflow from God can also be seen, in its other aspect, as an inflow; creatures are mirrors which reflect the knowledge of God back to Him; the descent of creatures from the necessary Being is also an ascent towards Him. The path of ascent, illuminated by *ma'rifa*, leads through various stages, permanent advances in the spiritual progress. These are stages in his knowledge of himself: 'he who knows himself, knows his Lord'. On the way he can reach the archetypal images, sensible manifestations of the Names of God in the intermediate 'world of images' ('alam al-mithal). Beyond that, he may be given a vision of God, in which the veil is momentarily lifted and God shows Himself to the seeker. There are two moments in such a vision: that in which the seeker ceases to be aware of his own personality and those of other creatures in the radiance of the vision of God (fana), and that in which he sees God in His creatures (baqa), lives and moves among them but remains conscious of the vision.

In his attempts to describe the reality of the universe as it is revealed in the moments of vision. Ibn 'Arabi used the expression *wahdat al-wujud* (unity of being or existence), and there was later much controversy about its meaning. It could be taken to mean that there exists nothing except God, and all else is either unreal or is a part of God. It could also, however, be taken to refer to the distinction, common to the philosophers, between Necessary and Contingent Being: only God is Necessary Being, existing by His own nature; all other beings owe their existence to an act of creation or a process of emanation. It could also refer to those momentary experiences of vision when the seeker loses consciousness of himself in the awareness of the manifestation of God: he is present in God or God is present in him, momentarily replacing his human attributes by those of God.

Interpreted in some of these ways, it would be difficult to reconcile the idea of *wahdat al-wujud* with that separation between God and His creatures, the infinite distance between them, which seems to be the clear teaching of the Qur'an. A scholar has listed a large number of critical works on Ibn 'Arabi written in subsequent ages; they are divided more or less equally between those who opposed his basic conceptions as being incompatible with the truth of Islam, and those who defended them. Numerous *fatwas* were issued by doctors of religion and law, mainly in opposition to him, but not always so.[7] The most striking vindication of his orthodoxy was given by the Ottoman Sultan Selim I (1512–20), who restored Ibn 'Arabi's tomb in Damascus after the conquest of Syria in 1516; on this occasion a *fatwa* in his favour was issued by a famous Ottoman scholar, Kamal Paşa-zade (1468/9–1534). Even among Sufi masters, the work of Ibn 'Arabi remained a subject of dispute. While some of the Sufi orders accepted it as a valid expression of the *ma'rifa* which was the goal of their search, the Shadhilis in the Maghrib and the Naqshbandis in the eastern Muslim world were more doubtful of it.

IBN TAYMIYYA AND THE HANBALI TRADITION

Sunni Islam had no authoritative teaching body supported by the power of the ruler, and throughout its history there persisted a current of thought both hostile to philosophers and theosophists, and alien from the attempts of *kalam* to give a rational defence of the deposit of faith.

The tradition of thought which derived from the teaching of Ibn Hanbal remained alive in the central Muslim countries, and particularly in Baghdad and Damascus. With many divergences among them, those who traced their intellectual ancestry to Ibn Hanbal were united in their attempt to maintain what they regarded as the true Islamic teaching, that of those who adhered strictly to God's revelation through the Prophet Muhammad. For them, God was the God of the Qur'an and Hadith, to be accepted and worshipped in His reality as He had revealed it. The true Muslim was he who had faith: not simply acceptance of the revealed God, but action in accordance with God's revealed Will. All Muslims formed a community, which should remain united; no one should be excluded from it, except those who excluded themselves by refusing to obey the prescriptions of religion or spreading doctrines which were incompatible with the truths revealed through the prophets. Within the community, controversies and speculations which might lead to dissension and conflict should be avoided.

In thirteenth-century Syria, under Mamluk rule, this tradition was expressed once more by a powerful and individual voice, that of Ibn Taymiyya (1263–1328). Born in northern Syria, and living most of his life between Damascus and Cairo, he faced a new situation. The Mamluk sultans and their soldiers were Sunni Muslims, but many of them were of recent and superficial conversion to Islam and it was necessary to remind them of the meaning of their faith. In the community at large, what Ibn Taymiyya regarded as dangerous errors were widespread. Some touched the safety of the state, like those of Shi'is and other dissident groups; some might affect the faith of the community, like the ideas of Ibn Sina and Ibn 'Arabi.

Against such dangers, Ibn Taymiyya took it as his mission to reassert the middle path of the Hanbalis: uncompromising in their affirmation of the principles of revealed truth, but tolerant of diversity within the community of those who accepted that truth:

The Prophet has said, 'The Muslim is brother of the Muslim' . . . How then can it be permitted to the community of Muhammed to divide itself into such diverse opinions that a man can join one group and hate another one simply on the basis of presumptions or personal caprices, without any proof coming from God? . . . Unity is a sign of divine clemency, discord is a punishment of God.[8]

God was one and many: one in His essence, many in His attributes, which should be accepted just as the Qur'an described them. The most significant of His attributes for human life was His Will. He had created all things out of nothing by an act of will, and had made Himself known to human beings by the expression of His Will in the scriptures revealed to the line of prophets which ended in Muhammad. He was both infinitely distant from His creatures and close to them, knowing particulars as well as universals, seeing the inner secrets of the heart, loving those who obeyed Him.

Human life should be lived in the service of God under the guidance of the Prophet, by acceptance of His revealed word, and a sincere conformity of one's life to the human ideal implied by it. How should the Will of God be interpreted? Like Ibn Hanbal, Ibn Taymiyya looked first of all to the Qur'an, understood strictly and literally, then to the Hadith, then to the Companions of the Prophet, whose consensus had a validity equal to that of Hadith. Beyond this, the maintenance of truth depended on the transmission of religious knowledge by the body of concerned and well-informed Muslims. There was a continuing need for *ijtihad* by individuals who were capable of it; they could practise it with a certain flexibility, giving approval to certain acts which were not strictly enjoined by the *shari'a*, but the performance of which would have beneficial results, provided they were not forbidden by the *shari'a*. Ibn Taymiyya did not think of those who practised *ijtihad* as forming a corporate body; the consensus of the scholars of an age had a certain weight, but could not be regarded as infallible.

His version of Islam ran counter to some of the ideas put forward by Ibn Sina: the universe has been created from nothing by an act of Divine Will, not by emanations; God knows human beings in their particularity; they know Him not by the exercise of their reason but by His revelation to them. Ibn Taymiyya's opposition to Ibn 'Arabi's ideas was stronger still, because they posed graver and more urgent problems for the community as a whole. For him as for other Hanbalis, the existence of saints or 'friends of God' was not difficult to accept. They were those who had been given truths by inspiration, but not by the communication of a prophetic mission. They could be the recipients of divine graces through which they could appear to go beyond the habitual limits of human action. Such men and women should be respected, but there should be no external forms of devotion to them: no visits to their tombs or prayers performed there. The Sufi ritual of *dhikr*, repetition of the name of God, was a valid form of worship, but inferior in spiritual worth to ritual prayer and recitation of the Qur'an. The speculative theosophy by which Ibn 'Arabi and others interpreted mystical experience was to be totally rejected: man was not the manifestation of the Divine Light, but a created being. He could not be absorbed into God's Being; the only way by which he could draw nearer to God was obedience to His revealed Will.

Ibn Taymiyya played an important role in the Muslim society of his own time, and after his death his formulation of the Hanbali tradition remained an element in the religious culture of the central Islamic regions, but it was on the whole a submerged element, until awareness of it was heightened in the eighteenth century by a religious movement with political implications, that of the Wahhabis which led to the creation of the Saudi state in central Arabia. In spite of the strict contradiction between his view of Islam and that of Ibn 'Arabi, the instinct of the Sunni community for comprehensive toleration made it possible for them to live together, and some Muslims indeed were able to reconcile the two. A scholar has recorded his meeting in Aleppo with a group of Naqshbandi Sufis, who were studying the works of Ibn 'Arabi and Ibn Taymiyya side by side. Ibn Taymiyya, they argued, was the *imam* of the *shari'a,* Ibn 'Arabi that of the *haqiqa,* the truth to which seekers on the Sufi path aspired; the perfect Muslim ought to be able to unite in himself these two aspects of the reality of Islam.[9]

THE DEVELOPMENT OF SHI'ISM

Living among the majority of Arab-speaking Muslims who accepted the Sunni version of the faith, sometimes in conflict with them and sometimes at peace, were communities of 'Twelver' Shi'is. Gradually they developed their own view of what had happened in history, and what should have happened. The claims of 'Ali and his successors were supported, and the first three caliphs were reviled and regarded as usurpers. The external history of the Muslims, the story of political power, was seen as diverging from the true inner history.

For Shi'is, this inner history was that of the preservation and transmission of revealed truth by the line of *imams*. According to the theory of the *imamate* which was gradually developed from the tenth century onwards,

God had placed the *imam* as His proof (*hujja*) in the world at all times, to teach authoritatively the truths of religion and govern mankind in accordance with justice. The *imams* were descendants of the Prophet through his daughter Fatima and her husband 'Ali, the first *imam*; each was designated by his predecessor; each was infallible in his interpretation of the Qur'an and the *sunna* of the Prophet, through the secret knowledge given him by God; each was without sin.

Shi'is of the main branch held that the known lines of *imams* had come to an end with the twelfth, Muhammad, who had disappeared in 874. This event was known as the 'lesser occultation', because for a number of years the hidden *imam* was believed to communicate with the faithful through his representative. Then there came the 'greater occultation', when this regular communication came to an end, and the hidden *imam* was only seen occasionally, in fleeting appearances or in dreams or visions. He would emerge in the fullness of time to bring in the reign of justice; in this reappearance he would be the *mahdi*, the 'guided one' (this was a term which had a more precise meaning in Shi'i thought than in popular Sunni tradition).

Until the *imam* should emerge, mankind would still need guidance. Some Shi'is believed that the Qur'an and Hadith, as handed down and interpreted by the *imams*, were adequate as guides: others, however, maintained that there was a continuing need for interpretation and leadership, and from the thirteenth century they looked to the men of learning who were competent by intellect, character and education to interpret the deposit of faith through intellectual effort, *ijtihad* (hence the name by which they were known, that of *mujtahid*). They were not infallible, and had no direct guidance from God, but could simply interpret the teaching of the *imams* according to their best abilities; in every generation new *mujtahids* were needed, and ordinary Muslims were obliged to follow the teaching of the *mujtahids* of their age.

In time there grew up a rational theology to explain and justify the faith of Shi'i Muslims. The early Shi'is appear to have been traditionalists, but at the end of the tenth century al-Mufid (*c.* 945–1022) maintained that the truths of revelation should be defended by *kalam* or dialectical theology, and a follower of his, al-Murtada (966–1044) claimed that the truths of religion could be established by reason. From this time on the most widely accepted Shi'i teaching contained elements derived from the Mu'tazili school.

Later Shi'i thinkers incorporated into their system elements taken from the Neo-Platonic theories given Islamic form by Ibn Sina and others. Muhammad, Fatima and the *imams* were seen as embodiments of the Intelligences through which the universe was created. The *imams* were seen as spiritual guides on the path to knowledge of God: for Shi'is they came to have the position which the 'friends of God' had for Sunnis.

The same emphasis on the use of human reason to elucidate the faith led to the development of a Shi'i school of jurisprudence. This was the product of a group of scholars in Iraq, in particular those known as al-Muhaqqiq (1205–77) and al-'Allama al-Hilli (1250–1325). Their work was carried further by Muhammad ibn Makki al-'Amili (1333/4–84), known as the 'First Martyr' because of the manner of his death in Syria. For the most part the principles of Shi'i jurisprudence were taken from that of the Sunnis, but there were some significant differences which arose from the specific Shi'i view of religion and the world. Only those *hadiths* of the Prophet which had been transmitted by a member of his family were accepted; *hadiths* of what the *imams* had said or done were regarded as having the same status as those of the Prophet, although they could not abrogate the Qur'an or a prophetic *hadith*. The consensus of the community did not have the same importance as in Sunnism; if there was an infallible *imam*, the only *ijma'* which was valid was that of the community gathered around the *imam*. *'Aql*, reason used in a responsible way by those competent to use it, had an important position as a source of law.

The work of successive *mujtahids* upon the sources produced in course of time a body of Shi'i law which differed in some repsects from that of the four Sunni schools. A species of temporary marriage was permitted, in which the rights and obligations of the two parties were not the same as in full marriage; the rules of inheritance also differed from those of Sunni law. Certain matters remained in dispute among scholars, in particular the obligations of Shi'is towards those who ruled the world in the absence of the *imam*. They could not be regarded as having legitimate authority in the sense in which the *imams* had it, but was it lawful to pay taxes to them or enter their service if they used their power in support of justice and the law? In the absence of the *imam*, were the Friday prayers, and the sermon which was part of it, valid? Could *jihad* be proclaimed, and if so by whom? Legal scholars argued that the *mujtahids* could proclaim *jihad*, and also serve as collectors and distributors of *zakat*, the canonical alms; it was this task which gave them a certain independent social role, and made their integrity a matter of concern to the community as a whole.

From at least the tenth century, the tombs of the *imams* were places of pilgrimage. Four of them were buried in Madina, six in Iraq – at Najaf (where was the tomb of 'Ali), Karbala (which had the tomb of Husayn), Kazimayn and Samarra – and one at Mashhad in Khurasan. Around their shrines there grew up schools, hostels, and cemeteries to which dead Shi'is were brought to be buried. The tombs of the children of the *imams*, Companions of the Prophet and famous scholars were also held in reverence.

The distinction between Sunni and Shi'i places of worship should not be made too strictly, however. All alike made the pilgrimage to Mecca and visited the Prophet's tomb at Madina. Shi'is went to shrines of Sufi saints, and in some places the Sunni population gave reverence to the *imams* and their families; in Cairo, the shrine where the head of the Imam Husayn was supposed to be buried was a centre of popular devotion.

There was one annual celebration, however, which had a special meaning for Shi'is. This was the *'ashura*, the commemoration of the battle of Karbala at which the Imam Husayn had been killed on the tenth day of the month of Muharram in the year 680. For the Shi'is this was one of the most significant days in history. It marked the point at which the visible course of the world had diverged from that which God had willed for it. The death of Husayn was seen as a martyrdom, a voluntary sacrifice for the good of the community, and a promise that in the end God would restore the right order of things. On that day Shi'is wore signs of mourning, and sermons were preached in the mosques, narrating the sacrifice of Husayn and explaining its meaning. At a certain period the telling of the story of Husayn developed into a dramatic re-enactment of it.

From an early stage in the development of Shi'ism, reverence for the *imams* had tended to turn them into more than human figures, visible manifestations of the spirit of God, and behind the clear external meaning of the Qur'an there was believed to be a hidden truth. Such ideas had the support of the Fatimids when they ruled Egypt and Syria. The Isma'ilis, the Shi'i group from which the Fatimids came, or to which they claimed to be affiliated, held beliefs which were later obscured by a system of thought evolved by scholars under Fatimid patronage and spread with the help of Fatimid power.

The doctrine which the Fatimids favoured was one which gave legitimacy to their claim that the *imamate* had passed from Ja'far al-Sadiq to his grandson Muhammad as the seventh *imam*, and the last visible *imam* of his line. To justify and explain this belief, a definition of what it was to be *imam*, based on a certain view of history, was put forward. All through history, it was claimed, mankind needed a teacher divinely guided and sinless, and there were seven cycles of such teachers. Each cycle began with a messenger (*natiq*) who revealed a truth to the world; he was followed by an interpreter (*wasi*), who taught the chosen few the inner meaning of the messenger's revelation. This meaning was one which underlay the external forms of all religions: God was One and unknowable, from Him there proceeded the Universal Intelligence which contained the forms of all created beings, and these forms manifested themselves through a process of emanation. Each *wasi* was followed by a succession of seven *imams*, the last of whom was the messenger of the next era. The *natiq* of the seventh and last era would be the expected *mahdi*, who would reveal the inner truth to all; the era of external law would end, and that of undisguised knowledge of the nature of the universe would begin.

For a time the version of Shi'ism which the Fatimids encouraged was widespread, although more in Syria than in Egypt or the Maghrib. When Fatimid power declined and was finally replaced by that of the Ayyubids, Isma'ili communities shrank, but they continued to exist in the mountains along the northern Syrian coast and in Yemen, as well as in Iran. Mingled with them in the coastal mountains of Syria were two other communities professing other varieties of Shi'i belief. The faith of the Druzes sprang from the teaching of Hamza ibn 'Ali; he carried further the Isma'ili idea that the *imams* were embodiments of the Intelligences which emanated from the One God, and maintained that the One Himself was present to human beings, and had been finally embodied in the Fatimid Caliph al-Hakim (996–1021), who had disappeared from human sight but would return. The other community, the Nusayris, traced their descent from Muhammad ibn Nusayr, who taught that the One God was inexpressible, but that from Him there emanated a hierarchy of beings, and 'Ali was the embodiment of the highest of them (hence the name 'Alawis by which they were often known).

Of more obscure origins were two communities to be found mainly in Iraq. The Yazidis in the north had a religion which included elements drawn from both Christianity and Islam. They believed that the world was created by God, but was sustained by a hierarchy of subordinate beings, and human beings would gradually be perfected in a succession of lives. The Mandaeans in southern Iraq also preserved relics of ancient religious traditions. They believed that the human soul ascended by way of an inner illumination to reunion with the Supreme Being: an important part of their religious practice was baptism, a process of purification.

Cut off from the sources of power and wealth in the great cities, and living in most places under some suspicion if not the hostility of Sunni rulers, such communities withdrew into themselves and developed practices different from those of the majority. While Ibadi and Zaydi doctrines and laws were not very different from those of the Sunnis, among the Druzes and Nusayris the divergences reached a point where they were regarded by Sunni jurists as lying at best on the very margins of Islam, and under the Mamluks there was a period when they were persecuted. They had their own places of religious observance, which were different from those of Sunnis and Shi'is: the simple *khalwa* of the Druzes, lying on a hilltop above a town or village, where the men of religious knowledge and piety lived in seclusion, or the *majlis* of the Isma'ilis. The tradition of learning was handed on by religious scholars in schools or in their homes, and in the absence of the *imams* it was they who held moral authority in their communities.

JEWISH AND CHRISTIAN LEARNING

Until early modern times, the main centres of Jewish population and religious culture lay in the countries ruled by Muslims. Most of the Jews belonged to the main stream of Jewish life which accepted the authority of the Talmud, the body of interpretation and discussion of Jewish law which had been collected in Babylonia or Iraq, although there were smaller communities: the Karaites who held that the Torah, God's revealed teaching embodied in scripture, was the only source of law, and every scholar should study it for himself; and the Samaritans who had separated from the main body of Jews in ancient times.

During the early part of the Islamic period Iraq continued to be the main centre of Jewish religious learning. In its two great academies there worked the scholars who were regarded as guardians of the long oral tradition of the Jewish religion, and to whom questions about matters of interpretation were sent from all over the Jewish world. Later, however, as the 'Abbasid Empire disintegrated, independent authority was exercised by colleges (*yeshivot*) which grew up in the main centres of Jewish population, Cairo, Qayrawan and the cities of Muslim Spain.

At an early date in the Islamic period, the Jews living in countries where Arabic became the main language of government and Muslim population adopted it as their language of secular life, although they continued to use Hebrew for liturgical and religious purposes. The influence of Jewish religious and legal ideas upon the articulation of Islam into a system of thought had its reflection in Judaism, and there developed a Jewish theology and philosophy which were strongly influenced by *kalam* and Islamic philosophy. There was also a flowering of Hebrew poetry, both religious and secular, in Andalus, under the stimulus of Arabic poetic conventions and styles. With the coming of the Almohads in the twelfth century, however, the full development of Jewish culture and life in Andalus came to an end. The greatest figure of medieval Judaism, Musa ibn Maymun (Maimonides, 1135–1204) found a freer environment in Cairo under the Ayyubids than in the Andalus from which he came. His *Guide of the Perplexed*, written in Arabic, gave a philosophical interpretation of the Jewish religion, and other works, in Arabic and Hebrew, expounded Jewish law. He was court physician to Salah al-Din and his son, and his life and thought give evidence of easy relations between Muslims and Jews of education and standing in the Egypt of his time. In the following centuries, however, the distance widened, and although some Jews continued to be prosperous as merchants and powerful as officials in Cairo and other great Muslim cities, the creative period of Jewish culture in the world of Islam came to an end.

As with the Jews, the early period of Islamic rule had been one in which relations between Christians and Muslims were fruitful. Christians had still formed the majority of the population, at least in the part of the world of Islam which lay to the west of Iran.

The coming of Islam improved the position of the Nestorian and Mono-physite Churches, by removing the disabilities from which they had suffered under Byzantine rule. The Nestorian Patriarch was an important person-ality in Baghdad of the 'Abbasid caliphs and the Church of which he was the head extended eastwards into inner Asia and as far as China. As Islam developed, it did so in a largely Christian environment, and Christian scholars played an important part in the transmission of Greek scientific and philosophical thought into Arabic. The languages which the Christians had previously spoken and written continued to be used (Greek, Syriac and Coptic in the east, Latin in Andalus) and some of the monasteries were important centres of thought and scholarship: Dayr Za'faran in southern Anatolia, Mar Mattai in northern Iraq, and Wadi Natrun in the western desert of Egypt. As time went on, however, the situation changed. The dominant Muslim minority turned into a majority, and acquired a strong autonomous and self-confident intellectual and spiritual life. In the east, the worldwide Nestorian Church was almost extinguished by the conquests of Timur; in the Maghrib, Christianity disappeared; in Andalus, the gradual expansion of the Christian states from the north led to an increase of tension between Muslims and Christians. Both in Andalus and in the eastern countries where Christians lived – Egypt, Syria and Iraq – most of them abandoned their own languages for Arabic; but Arabic was not to have the same vivifying effect among them as in Jewish communities until the nineteenth century.

However easy and close relations between Muslims, Jews and Christians might be, there remained a gulf of ignorance and prejudice between them. They worshipped separately and had their own high places of worship and pilgrimage: Jerusalem for the Jews, another Jerusalem for Christians, and local shrines of saints. The differences may have been greater in the cities than in the countryside, however. Communities dwelling close to each other, in particular in regions where the hand of the urban government was not felt directly, might live in a close symbiosis based upon mutual need, or common obedience and loyalty to a local lord. Springs, trees and stones which had been regarded as places of intercession or healing since before the rise of Islam or even of Christianity were sometimes holy to adherents of different faiths. Some examples of this have been noted in modern times: in Syria, the *khidr*, the mysterious spirit identified with St George, was revered in springs and other sanctified places; in Egypt, Copts and Muslims alike celebrated the day of St Damiana, martyred during the last persecution of Christians in the Roman Empire; in Morocco, Muslims and Jews took part together in festivals at the shrines of Jewish and Muslim holy men.

CHAPTER 12

The Culture of Courts
and People

RULERS AND PATRONS

The disintegration of the 'Abbasid caliphate and its final extinction removed the central institution of power and patronage which had made possible the growth of a universal Arab Islamic culture. Poets and men of religious and secular learning had met together in Baghdad, and different cultural traditions had mingled with each other to produce something new. The political division of the lands of the caliphate brought with it a certain dispersion of energy and talent, but led also to the rise of a number of courts and capital cities to serve as focuses of artistic and intellectual production. The division was less than complete: by now there was a common language of cultural expression, and the movement of scholars and writers from one city to another preserved and developed it. In course of time, however, differences of style and emphasis which had always existed between the main regions of the Arab Muslim world grew wider. To put it too simply, Iraq remained within the sphere of radiation of Iran; Syria and Egypt formed a cultural unit, of which the influence extended to parts of the Arabian peninsula and of the Maghrib; and in the far west there developed an Andalusian civilization which was different in some ways from what existed in the east.

Andalusian society was formed by a fruitful mixture of different elements: Muslims, Jews and Christians; Arabs, Berbers, indigenous Spaniards, and soldiers of fortune from western and eastern Europe (the Saqaliba or 'Slavs'). It was held together by the Umayyad caliphate in Cordoba, and surrounding the court of the caliph was an Andalusian élite of families claiming Arab origin, descended from early settlers and with wealth and social power derived from official positions and the control of land. It was in and around the court of the later Umayyads that there first appeared a distinctive high culture. Theologians and lawyers were mainly of the Maliki *madhhab,* but some of them adhered to the Zahiri *madhhab* which taught a literalist interpretation of the faith and was later to disappear; doctors and officials studied philosophy and the natural sciences; the power of the rulers and the élite was expressed in splendid buildings and in poetry.

This culture continued to flourish around some of the courts of the small kingdoms into which the Umayyad caliphate split, the *muluk al-tawa'if* or 'party kings'. The Almoravids, who came from the desert fringes of the Maghrib, brought an austere temper of strict adherence to Maliki law and suspicion of free rational speculation. The power of their successors, the Almohads, was also created by an impulse of revival of piety, with an emphasis on the unity of God and observance of the law; but it drew its sustenance from the religious thought of the eastern Muslim world, where its founder, Ibn Tumart, had studied and formed his mind, and those who carried it throughout the Maghrib and to Andalus came from the settled Berber peoples of the Atlas mountains. Theirs was the last great age of Andalusian culture, and in a sense its culmination: the thought of Ibn Rushd was the final expression in Arabic of the philosophical spirit; that of Ibn 'Arabi was to exercise an influence over the Sufi tradition in west and east for many centuries. After the Almohads, the process of Christian expansion extinguished one centre of Arab Muslim life after another until only the kingdom of Granada was left. The tradition it had created was carried on, however, in various ways in the cities of the Maghrib, and of Morocco in particular, to which Andalusians migrated.

Buildings, the most lasting of human artefacts, have always been the expressions of the faith, wealth and power of rulers and élites. The great mosques were the permanent marks left by the early Muslim rulers in the lands they conquered, and the emergence of local centres of power and wealth, as the 'Abbasid hold grew weaker and then disappeared, gave rise to a proliferation of buildings, devoted, in different ways, to the preservation of religion and with it of civilized life. The development of the system of *waqfs* encouraged the creation of such buildings: *madrasas*, *zawiyas*, mausoleums, hospitals, public fountains, and caravanserais for merchants. Some were established by rich and powerful subjects, but the greatest by rulers, who also built palaces and citadels. The city centres of which vestiges still remain in Cairo and Tunis, Aleppo and Damascus, and Fez, and the centres of pilgrimage such as Jerusalem, were largely the creations of the later centuries of this era. Cairo was the greatest and largest of them, with the Citadel and the palaces of the Mamluks on a low spur of the Muqattam hills, the tomb mosques of sultans in the vast cemeteries outside the city walls, and complexes such as the mosque and *madrasa* of Sultan Hasan built on four sides of a courtyard.

By the tenth century the basic form of major public buildings had been created: the mosque with its *qibla, mihrab* and minarets, approached through a walled courtyard in which was a fountain for ablutions; and the palace of the ruler, cut off by walls or distance from the city, and carrying on its own life in a sequence of halls and kiosks lying in gardens. In such buildings of the earlier period, the external façade counted for little, it was the inner walls which expressed power or belief, decorated in vegetal or geometrical patterns or with inscriptions. In the later period, buildings in cities far apart continued to share, to some extent, a language of decoration: from Baghdad to Cordoba, walls of stucco, tiles or carved wood carried patterns or inscriptions in the Arab language. In some ways, however, distinctive styles emerged. More emphasis was placed upon external appearance – façades, monumental doorways, domes and minarets – and here there were significant differences. In the Syrian and Egyptian cities under Ayyubid and then Mamluk rule, façades were faced with stone in alternate bands of colour; this was the *ablaq* style, a Roman legacy which was used in Syria, spread to Egypt, and can also be seen in churches in Umbria and Tuscany in Italy. The dome became more prominent; externally, it might be decorated with a variety of geometrical or other designs; internally, the transition from the square hall to the round dome posed a problem which was solved by the use of a squinch or pendentive, often with stalactites for decoration.

In the far west of the Arab Muslim world, a distinctive style of mosque construction was initiated by the great mosque of Cordoba, with its many aisles, its decoration of sculpted marble, and its columns of a distinctive shape, with straight pillars surmounted by a horseshoe arch. The Almoravid and Almohad dynasties left their memorials in great mosques in Andalus, Morocco, Algeria and Tunisia. The Qarawiyyin mosque in Fez, a creation of the Almoravids, can be taken as an example of that style, with its narrow, long courtyard, the two minarets placed symmetrically at the ends, its prayer hall with rows of pillars parallel to the wall on which the *mihrab* lay, and the green tiles on the roof. The minaret in the Maghrib tended to be square, with a smaller square rising out of a platform at the top. Some were very tall and prominent: the Giralda at Seville, the Kutubiyya at Marrakish.

The most impressive surviving monument in the Andalusian style was not a mosque but a palace, the Alhambra at Granada. Built mainly in the fourteenth century, it was not just a palace, rather a royal city separate from the main city lying below it. Within its walls was a complex of buildings: barracks and fortifications at the outside, and at the centre two royal courtyards, the Court of Myrtle and that of the Lions, where sheets of water were surrounded by gardens and buildings, and at their ends lay ceremonial halls. The material used was brick, richly decorated with stucco or tiles, bearing inscriptions from the Qur'an and from Arabic poems specially written for them. The presence of water indicates a common feature of the Andalusian and Maghribi style: the importance of the garden. At the heart of a garden there lay a water-course or pool, surrounded by a rectangle of gardens and pavilions; flowers and bushes were chosen and planted carefully; the whole was enclosed by high walls of masonry covered with stucco.

The main adornment of the inside of buildings was the decoration of the walls, in tiles, stucco or wood. In palaces and bath-houses there appear to have been wall-paintings, with depictions of human beings and animals, engaged in hunting, war or parties of pleasure: themes which would have been impossible to illustrate in mosques, because strict religious doctrine disapproved of the portrayal of living beings, regarding it as an attempt to imitate the unique creative power of God. Walls were not hung with pictures, but books might be illustrated. There are manuscripts of *Kalila wa Dimna* from the twelfth and thirteenth centuries which contain pictures of birds and animals; those of the *Maqamat* of al-Hariri have scenes from life – the mosque, the library, the bazaar and the home; others again illustrate scientific devices. This tradition continued in the Mamluk period, but was not so strong as that in Iran further east.

Most prominent in the adornment of private houses and public buildings alike were works of glass, ceramic and metal, important not only for use or for beauty of form, but as the carriers of images which might be symbols of the truths of religion or of royal power: trees, flowers, words, animals or rulers. The earlier ceramics were made of glazed earthenware, but later lustre-ware was produced. Chinese blue-and-white porcelain was imported and was imitated from the fourteenth century. Egypt was the main centre of production, but after the destruction of Fustat in the twelfth century artisans migrated to Syria and beyond. In Mosul, Damascus, Cairo and elsewhere inland copper, bronze and brass vessels were made. Elaborate glass lamps were produced for hanging in the mosques.

POETRY AND STORY

Poetry played an important role in the culture of rulers and the wealthy. Wherever there were patrons there were poets to praise them. Often the praise took a familiar form: that of the *qasida* as it had been developed by poets of the 'Abbasid period. In Andalus, however, in and around the courts of the Umayyads and some of their successors, new poetic forms developed. The most important was the *muwashshah*, which had appeared by the end of the tenth century and was to continue to be cultivated for hundreds of years, not only in Andalus but in the Maghrib. This was a strophic poem: that is to say, one where every line did not end in the same rhyme, but there was a pattern of rhymes in each strophe or series of lines, and this was repeated throughout the poem. The metres and language used were basically the same as those of the *qasida*, but each strophe ended with an envoi (*kharja*), about the origin of which there has been much speculation by scholars; it was written in languages nearer the vernacular, and sometimes not in Arabic but in the Romance vernacular of the time; it expressed, often, sentiments of romantic love, in language put into the mouth of someone other than the poet. The subjects of the *muwashshah* included all those of Arabic poetry: descriptions of nature, praise of rulers, love, and exaltation of God and the path to mystical knowledge of Him. Rather later there appeared another form, the *zajal*, also a strophic poem, but composed in the colloquial Arabic of Andalus.

In some Andalusian love poems the personal note is strong, the expression of an individual destiny, as in the poems of Ibn Zaydun (1003–71). Brought up in Cordoba, at the time of the decline of the Umayyad caliphate, he was deeply involved in the political life of his age. Imprisoned by the caliph's government, he sought refuge first with one local ruler, then with another in Seville; when the ruler of Seville conquered Cordoba he returned there for a time. Most of his life, however, was spent in exile from his own city, and laments for his lost birthplace, mingling with regrets for youth that has passed, echo some of the traditional themes of the classical *qasida*, but in a way which reveals his personality. In a poem about Cordoba, he recalls the city and his youth:

God has sent showers upon the abandoned dwelling-places of those we loved. He has woven upon them a striped, many-coloured garment of flowers, and raised among them a flower like a star. How many girls like images trailed their garments among such flowers, when life was fresh and time was at our service . . . How happy they were, those days that have passed, days of pleasure, when we lived with those who had black, flowing hair and white shoulders ... Now say to Destiny whose favours have vanished – favours I have lamented as the nights have passed – how faintly its breeze has touched me in my evening. But for him who walks in the night the stars still shine: greetings to you, Cordoba, with love and longing.[1]

The same personal note of regret and anguish can be heard in his love poems addressed to Wallada, the Umayyad princess whom he had loved in his youth but who had left him for someone else:

Yes, I have remembered you with longing, at al-Zahra, when the horizon was bright and the face of the earth gave pleasure, and the breeze was soft in the late afternoon, as if it had pity on me. The garden was shining with its waters of silver, as if necklaces had been cast into it from breasts. It was a day like the days of our pleasures which have now left us. We passed the night like thieves stealing that pleasure while fortune slept ... A rose shone in its bed exposed to the sun, and the noonday grew more radiant at the sight of it; a water-lily passed, spreading its fragrance, a sleeper whose eyes had been opened by the dawn ... My most precious, most brilliant, most beloved possession – if lovers can have possessions – would not compensate for the purity of our love, in the time we wandered free in the garden of love. Now I thank God for my time with you; you have found consolation for it, but I have remained a lover.[2]

This was the last flowering of an original and personal lyrical poetry before modern times. Poetry continued to be written in abundance, as an activity for educated men, but few of its products have held the attention of later ages. The main exception to this is some of the poetry inspired by Sufism, such as that of 'Umar ibn al-Farid (1181–1235), with its images of love and intoxication, capable of more than one meaning.

One of the reasons for the flowering of Andalus may have been the mixture of peoples, languages and cultures. At least five languages were used there. Two were colloquial, the distinctive Andalusian Arabic and the Romance dialect which was later to develop into Spanish; both these were used in varying degrees by Muslims, Christians and Jews. There were also three written languages: classical Arabic, Latin and Hebrew; Muslims used Arabic, Christians Latin, Jews both Arabic and Hebrew. Jews who wrote on philosophy or science used mainly Arabic, but poets used Hebrew in a new way. For almost the first time, poetry in Hebrew was used for other than liturgical purposes; under the patronage of wealthy and powerful Jews who played an important part in the life of courts and cities, poets adopted forms of Arabic poetry such as the *qasida* and *muwashshah*, and used them for secular as well as liturgical purposes. The poet who has won the most lasting fame is Judah Halevi (1075–1141).

The high poetry was written in strictly grammatical language, celebrated certain recognized themes and resounded with echoes of past poems, but surrounding it there was a more widely diffused literature which it would be too simple to call 'popular', but which may have been appreciated by wide strata of society. Much of it was ephemeral, composed more or less impromptu, not written down, handed on orally and then lost in the recesses of time, but some has survived. The *zajal*, first emerging in Andalus in the eleventh century, spread throughout the Arabic-speaking world. There is also a tradition of play-acting. Certain shadow-plays, written by a thirteenth-century author, Ibn Daniyal, to be performed by puppets or hands in front of a light and behind a screen, are still extant.

The most widespread and lasting genre was that of the romance. Great cycles of stories about heroes grew up over the centuries. Their origins are lost in the mists of time, and different versions can be found in several cultural traditions. They may have existed in oral tradition before being committed to writing. They included the stories of 'Antar ibn Shaddad, the son of a slave girl, who became an Arabian tribal hero; Iskandar or Alexander the Great; Baybars, the victor over the Mongols and founder of the Mamluk dynasty in Egypt; and the Banu Hilal, the Arab tribe who migrated to the countries of the Maghrib. The themes of the cycles are varied. Some are stories of adventure or travel told for their own sake; some evoke the universe of supernatural forces which surround human life, spirits, swords with magical properties, dream-cities; at the heart of them there lies the idea of the hero or heroic company, a man or group of men pitted against the forces of evil – whether men or demons or their own passions – and overcoming them.

These compositions were recited in a mixture of poetry, rhymed prose (*saj'*) and ordinary prose. There were reasons for this: rhyme was an aid to memory, and also set the narrative apart from ordinary life and discourse; the mixture of different styles enabled the narrator to move from one register to another, in accordance with the audience and the impression he wished to leave upon it – a rural audience might have different expectations from those of city-dwellers, and the educated from the illiterate. In course of time the stories were written down, by writers of some literary skill, and those who recited them may have had knowledge of the written texts, but there was always scope for improvisation or adaptation to the needs of a particular time or place.

The history of the growth of these cycles has not been much studied, and perhaps cannot be. It is clear, however, that they grew gradually over the centuries and varied from one country to another. A study of the cycle of 'Antar has shown that its origins lay in some lost folk-stories of pre-Islamic Arabia, but it gradually accumulated other material as it moved from place to place; the text as we now have it was formed not later than the end of the fourteenth century. It has been suggested that such a process of development had more than a purely literary significance; it served to give a legitimacy to newly islamized or arabized peoples by fitting their history into an Arabian pattern; the nomadic tribesmen of the Sahara, telling their version of the story of 'Antar or Banu Hilal, were claiming an Arabian origin for themselves.

The cycle of stories known as the *Thousand and One Nights*, or in Europe as the *Arabian Nights*, although different from the romances in many ways, echoes some of their themes and seems to have grown in a rather similar way. It was not a romance built around the life and adventures of a single man or group, but a collection of stories of various kinds gradually linked together by the device of a single narrator telling stories to her husband night after night. The germ of the collection is thought to have lain in a group of stories translated from Pahlavi into Arabic in the early Islamic centuries. There are some references to it in the tenth century, and a fragment of an early manuscript, but the oldest full manuscript dates from the fourteenth century. The cycle of stories seems to have been formed in Baghdad between the tenth and twelfth centuries; it was expanded further in Cairo during the Mamluk period, and stories added or invented then were attributed to Baghdad in the time of the 'Abbasid Caliph Harun al-Rashid. Additions were made even later; some of the stories in the earliest translations into European languages in the eighteenth century, and in the first Arabic printed versions in the nineteenth, do not appear at all in the earlier manuscripts.

A narrative work quite different from these was produced in the last great age of Andalusian culture, that of the Almohads: *Hayy ibn Yaqdhan* by Ibn Tufayl (d. 1185/6): A philosophical treatise in the form of a story, it tells of a child brought up in isolation on an island. By the solitary exercise of reason he rises through the various stages of understanding the universe, each stage taking seven years and having its appropriate form of thought. Finally he reaches the summit of human thought, when he apprehends the process which is the ultimate nature of the universe, the eternal rhythm of emanation and return, the emanations of the One proceeding from level to level down to the stars, the point at which spirit takes material form, and the spirit striving to move upwards towards the One.

Such apprehension is only for the few, however. When Hayy finally meets another human being and both go for a time from the island to the inhabited world, he understands that there is a hierarchy of human intellects. Only the few can attain to truth by the use of reason alone; another minority can attain to it by using their reason to decipher what is given to them through the symbols of religious revelation; others again accept the laws based on those symbols but cannot interpret them by reason. The mass of mankind cares neither for the rational truth nor for the laws of religion, but only for the things of this world. Each of the first three groups has its own perfection and its own limits, and should not strive for more. Speaking, on his visit to the mainland, to men of the third group,

Hayy told them that he was of their opinion, and accepted that it was necessary for them to remain within the limits of the divine laws and external observance, refrain from going deeply into what does not concern them, have faith in what was obscurely understood and accept it, avoid innovation and subjective fancies, model themselves upon the pious ancestors and leave aside new-fangled ideas. He exhorted them to avoid the ways of ordinary folk who neglect the paths of religion and accept the world . . . This was the only path for such people as they, and if they tried to rise above it to the heights of insight what they possessed would be disturbed: they would not be able to reach the level of the blessed, but would waver and fall.[3]

MUSIC

In most ages and places music has been an adornment of the life of the powerful and wealthy, and an accompaniment to poetry of a certain kind. The *muwashshah* of Andalus were written to be sung, and they prolonged a tradition which had begun to grow up in early Islamic times, and which was itself a continuation of an older Iranian trandition. By Umayyad times the musician was a figure of the court, playing for the ruler, who marked his distance by concealment behind a curtain. A famous anthology, *Kitab al-aghani (The Book of Songs)*, records such an occasion at the ʿAbbasid court. The composer of a song is speaking:

I was led into a large and splendid saloon, at the end of which there hung a gorgeous silk curtain. In the middle of the room were several seats facing the curtain, and four of these seats had already been taken by four musicians, three female and one male, with lutes in their hands. I was placed next to the man, and the command was given for the concert to commence. After these four had sung, I turned to my companion and asked him to accompany me with his instrument . . . I then sang a melody of my own composition . . . Finally the door opened; Fadl ibn Rabi' cried, 'The Commander of the Faithful', and Harun appeared.[4]

At a certain point the art was carried by a musician from the court of the 'Abbasids to that of the Umayyads in Cordoba; there grew up an Andalusian and Maghribi tradition which was different from the Iranian tradition of the eastern courts.

Since music was handed on by direct oral transmission, there are virtually no records of what was played or sung until later centuries, but something can be learnt from the works of writers on musical theory. In accordance with the Greek thinkers, Muslim philosophers looked on music as one of the sciences: the ordering of sounds could be explained according to mathematical principles. To explain it was particularly important for them, because they thought of sounds as being echoes of the music of the spheres: of those celestial movements which gave rise to all movements in the world beneath the moon. In addition to their philosophical speculations, such works on music as those of Ibn Sina give details about styles of composition and performance and about instruments. Court music, they show, was primarily vocal. Poems were sung to the accompaniment of instruments: stringed instruments both plucked and bowed, flutes, percussion. Sounds were organized according to a number of recognized 'modes', but within these fixed patterns there was room for the improvising of variations and ornaments. Music was also an accompaniment of dancing, performed by professional female dancers in palaces and private houses.

All strata of society, in desert, countryside and city, had their music for important occasions: war and harvest, work and marriage. Each region had its own traditions, its songs sung unaccompanied or accompanied on drums, reed-pipes, or one-stringed fiddles; some occasions were celebrated too with dances, performed not by professional dancers but by men or women in lines or groups. The migration of peoples and the spread of the Arabic language and all that went with it may have moved these traditions in the direction of uniformity, but the differences remained, from one village or tribe to another.

Court music was associated with the worldliness of court life, and the music of the people, too, might be an accompaniment of worldly celebrations. The men of religion disapproved of it, but they could not condemn music altogether, since it soon came to play a part in religious practice: the call to prayer had its own rhythm, the Qur'an was chanted in formal ways, and the *dhikr*, the solemn ritual of repetition of the name of

God, was accompanied by music, and even by bodily movements, in some of the Sufi brotherhoods. It was important therefore for those writing within the legal tradition to define the conditions on which performing and listening to music were permitted. In a famous section of the *Ihya 'ulum al-din*, Ghazali recognized the power of music over the human heart:

There is no entry into the heart except through the antechamber of the ears. Musical tones, measured and pleasing, bring forth what is in the heart and make evident its beauties and defects . . . whenever the soul of the music and singing reaches the heart, then there stirs in the heart that which preponderates in it.[5]

It is necessary therefore to regulate the use of this powerful force. Poetry and music are not forbidden in themselves, but according to circumstances. They are permissible when they arouse the longing for pilgrimge, or urge men to warfare in situations in which warfare is licit, or evoke praiseworthy sorrow – 'the sorrow of a man for his own shortcomings in matters of religion, or for his sins'[6] – or love when the subject of love is permissible, or the love of God: 'no sound strikes upon a man's ear but he hears it from Him and in Him'.[7] They are forbidden, however, if the reciter or singer is one who arouses to temptation, or the song is obscene or blasphemous or gives rise to lust; certain instruments – pipes and stringed instruments – are forbidden because they are associated with those who are drunkards or effeminate.

UNDERSTANDING THE WORLD

Not only religious scholars and students in the *madrasas* but also members of urban families which had acquired literacy read books. By now there was a great mass of works written in Arabic for them to read, and there developed a kind of cultural self-consciousness, a study of and reflection on the accumulated culture expressed in Arabic.

The precondition of such activity was that books were easily available. The spread of the manufacture and use of paper from the ninth century onwards had made it easier and cheaper to copy books. A book would be dictated to scribes by its author or a scholar of repute, and he would then listen to or read the copy and authenticate it with an *ijaza*, a certificate of authentic transmission. This process propagated itself, as those who had copied a book gave authority to others to copy it. Copies were sold by booksellers, whose shops often lay near the main mosques of a city, and some of them were acquired by libraries.

The first large libraries of which we have record had been created by rulers: the 'House of Wisdom' (*Bayt al-hikma*) in Baghdad by the Caliph Ma'mun (813–33) and then the 'House of Learning' (*Dar al-'ilm*), founded in the early eleventh century in Fatimid Cairo. Both of these were more than repositories of books; they were also centres for the study and propagation of ideas favoured by the rulers: those of the rational sciences under Ma'mun, those of the Isma'ilis in Cairo. Later, libraries multiplied, partly because it came to be accepted that books which contributed to the study and teaching of religion could be constituted into religious endowments (*waqf*). Many mosques and *madrasas* had libraries attached to them, not only for the use of scholars in their private studies, but as centres for copying manuscripts and so transmitting them further.

The religious lawyers recognized only books conducive to religious knowledge as being the objects of *waqf*, but rulers and wealthy people did not necessarily make such distinctions. Palaces and large houses had libraries, some of them containing books written in beautiful calligraphy and illustrated with pictures.

Much of the production of those who read books and wrote them belonged to what a modern scholar has called the 'literature of recollection': dictionaries, commentaries upon literature, manuals of administrative practice, above all historiography and geography. The writing of history was a feature of all urban literate Muslim societies, and what was written seems to have been widely read. Works of history and cognate subjects provide the largest body of writing in the main languages of Islam, apart from religious literature. Although not forming part of the central curriculum of the *madrasa*, history books seem to have been much read by scholars and students as well as by a broader literate public. For one section of the reading public they were of special importance: for rulers and those in their service, history provided not only a record of the glories and achievements of a dynasty, but also a collection of examples from which lessons in statecraft could be learned.

As the unity of the caliphate disappeared and dynasties emerged, with their courts, bureaucracies and bourgeoisie which clustered round them, all over the world of Islam traditions of local history-writing also developed. Scholars, officials or court historians wrote the annals of a city or a region. In such works there might be a summary of universal history taken from the great historians of the 'Abbasid period, but this would be followed by a chronicle of local events or of a dynasty, recorded year by year; the biographies of those who died in that year might be added. Thus in Syria

Ibn al-Athir (1163–1233) placed the events of his own time and place in the context of a universal history. In Egypt, local histories written by al-Maqrizi (d. 1442) and Ibn Iyas (d. 1524) covered the period of the Mamluks. In the Maghrib, Ibn Khaldun's history of the Arab and Berber dynasties was preceded by his famous *Muqaddima* (*Prolegomena*) in which the principles of selection and interpretation of responsible history-writing are set forth:

Many competent persons and expert historians have erred in regard to such stories and opinions, and have accepted them without critical examination . . . and therefore history has been confused . . . He who practises this science needs to know the rules of statecraft, the nature of existing things, and the difference between nations, regions and tribes in regard to way of life, qualities of character, customs, sects, schools of thought, and so on. He must distinguish the similarities and differences between the present and past, and know the various origins of dynasties and communities, the reasons for their coming into existence, the circumstances of the persons involved in them, and their history. He must go on until he has complete knowledge of the causes of every event, and then he will examine the information which has been handed down in the light of his principles of explanation. If they are in harmony, this information is sound, otherwise it is spurious.[8]

The concern for the variety of human experience was shown also in another kind of writing, that of geography and travel. Those who wrote on geography combined knowledge derived from Greek, Iranian and Indian writing with the observations of soldiers and travellers. Some of them were concerned mainly to tell the story of their own travels and what they observed; those of Ibn Battuta (d. 1377) were the most far-reaching, and conveyed a sense of the extension the world of Islam and the variety of human societies within it. Others set themselves systematically to study the countries of the world in their relations with each other, to record the varieties of their natural properties, peoples and customs, and to trace also the routes which linked them and the distances between them. Thus al-Muqaddasi (d. 1000) wrote a compendium of the physical and human geography of the known world, based upon his own observations and those of reliable witnesses, and al-Yaqut (d. 1229) composed a kind of geographical dictionary.

The tastes of the bourgeoisie may not have been quite the same as those of religious scholars and students in the *madrasas*. In particular, families which provided secretaries, accountants and doctors to rulers had an attraction, by the nature of their work, to the kind of thought which was the product of observation and logical deduction from rational principles. The speculations of the philosophers were regarded with suspicion by some schools of religious law and some rulers, but other ways of using reason to elucidate the nature of things aroused less suspicion and had practical uses.

Astronomy was of practical value because it provided the means of calculating dates and times. This was one of the spheres in which the use of the Arabic language over a wide area from the Mediterranean Sea to the Indian Ocean made it possible to bring together the Greek scientific tradition with those of Iran and India.

Another science was of even more general use. Medical doctors were persons of great importance in Muslim societies; through their care of the health of rulers and powerful people, they could acquire much political influence. They could not do their work without some understanding of the nature and activities of the human body, and of the natural elements of which the body was made up. The core of Muslim medical knowledge was taken from Greek medical and physiological theory, and in particular from the work of Galen, the great synthesizer. The basis of this theory was the belief that the human body was made up of the four elements of which the whole material world was composed: fire, air, earth and water. These elements could be mixed in more ways than one, and the various mixtures gave rise to different temperaments and 'humours'. The proper balance of elements preserved the health of the body, and a lack of balance led to illness which called for the doctor's healing art.

The principles of the medical art had been expounded during the 'Abbasid period in two great works of synthesis: the *Hawi* (*Comprehensive Book*) by Abu Bakr Muhammad al-Razi (863–925) and the *Qanun* (*Principle of Medicine*) of Ibn Sina. Based as they were on the works of the great Greek scientists, they showed nevertheless the development of a distinctive Islamic tradition which in some ways carried the science of medicine further; Ibn Sina's book, translated into Latin and other languages, was to be the main textbook of European medicine until at least the sixteenth century.

The art of medicine, as Muslim doctors understood it, was taught not in the *madrasas* but by apprenticeship or in *bimaristans*, the hospitals endowed as *waqf* which existed in the main cities. It was as practitioners of the art of healing that Muslim doctors made their most important contributions. They carried further the techniques of surgery. They observed the course of diseases and described them; Ibn al-Khatib (1313–74) was perhaps the first to understand the way in which plague spread by contagion. They studied the making of drugs from medical plants and their effects on human bodies, and the pharmacopoeia was extensive; it has been said that the pharmacy as an institution is an Islamic invention. They also understood the importance of those factors which could prevent that imbalance of the elements which, as they believed, led to illness: healthy diet, fresh air and exercise.

In the later centuries an attempt was made to create an alternative system of medical science, 'prophetic medicine' (*tibb nabawi*). This represented a reaction against the tradition which came from Galen. Its system was built upon what the Hadith recorded of the practices of the Prophet and his Companions in regard to health and sickness. It was not created by medical men, however, but by lawyers and traditionalists who held the strict view that the Qur'an and Hadith contained all that was necessary for the conduct of human life. It was the view of a minority even among religious scholars, and a critical opinion was expressed, with his robust good sense, by Ibn Khaldun. This kind of medicine, he asserted, could occasionally and accidentally be correct, but it was based upon no rational principle. Events and opinions which happened to be recorded in connection with the life of the Prophet did not form part of the divine revelation:

The Prophet (peace be upon him) was sent to teach us the religious law, not medicine or any other ordinary matter . . . None of the statements about medicine that occur in sound traditions should be considered to have the force of law.[9]

Around the formal teaching of the religious sciences, and the speculations of the philosophers, was a wide penumbra of beliefs and practices by which human beings hoped to be able to understand and control the forces of the universe. Such beliefs reflected fear and bewilderment in the face of what might seem to be an incomprehensible and at times cruel fate, but they could be more than that. The line between 'science' and 'superstition' was not drawn in the same place as it is today, and many educated men and women accepted such beliefs and practices because they were based on ideas which were widely held, and which only some of the philosophers and theologians rejected, for different reasons.

The claims of astrology were based upon an idea which was widely accepted and had a respectable ancestry: that the celestial world determined the affairs of the sublunary, human world. The frontier between the two worlds was represented by the planets and stars, and a study of their configuration, and of the movements of the planets, would not only explain what was happening in the world of coming-to-be and passing-away, but might make it possible to change it. This had been an idea common among the Greeks, and it was taken over by some Muslim thinkers and given a specifically Islamic form by the Sufi theosophists: the objects of the celestial world were seen as emanations of God. Muslim astrologers developed techniques of prediction and influence: for example, by the solemn inscribing of figures or letters in certain arrangements on materials of various kinds. Even some distinguished thinkers accepted the claims of the astrologers, and thought that the stars might have influence over the body's health. Strict jurists and rational philosophers, however, condemned it; Ibn Khaldun thought that it had no basis in revealed truth, and that it denied the role of God as the sole agent.

Widely held also was the belief of the alchemists, that gold and silver could be produced out of base metals, if only a way to do so could be found. The practices of alchemy also had their basis in a scientific theory taken from the Greeks: the idea that all metals formed a single natural species, and were distinguished from one another only by their accidents, and that those accidents were slowly changing in the direction of becoming more precious. To try to turn them into gold and silver, therefore, was not to go against the laws of nature, but to expedite, by human intervention, a process which was already taking place. Once more there was controversy about this among the learned. Ibn Khaldun believed that it was possible to produce gold and silver by sorcery or by a divine miracle, but not by human craft; even if it were possible it would be undesirable, since, if gold and silver were no longer scarce, they could not serve as measures of value.

More widespread, and in fact virtually universal, was the belief in spirits and the need to find some way of controlling them. The *jinns* were spirits with bodies of vapour or flame which could appear to the senses, often in the form of animals, and could have an influence on human lives; they were sometimes evil, or at least mischievous, and it was therefore necessary to try to control them. There could also be human beings who had power over the actions and lives of others, either because of some characteristic over which they had no control – the 'evil eye' – or through the deliberate exercise of certain crafts, for example the performance of solemn ritual acts in special circumstancs, which could arouse supernatural forces. This was a distorted reflection of that power which the virtuous, the 'friends of God' might acquire by divine grace. Even the sceptical Ibn Khaldun believed that sorcery did exist, and certain human beings could find ways of exercising power over others, but he thought it was reprehensible. There was a general belief that such powers could be controlled or controverted by charms and amulets placed upon certain parts of the body, magical arrangements of words or figures, incantations or rites of exorcism or propitiation, such as the *zar*, a ritual of propitiation, still widespread in the Nile valley.

It was commonly held, in all cultures before the modern age, that dreams and visions could open a door into a world other than that of senses. They might bring messages from God; they might disclose a hidden dimension of a person's own soul; they might come from *jinns* or devils. The desire to unravel the meaning of dreams must have been widespread, and was generally regarded as legitimate; dreams told us something which it was important to know. Ibn Khaldun indeed regarded the interpretation of dreams as one of the religious sciences: when ordinary sense-perception was removed by sleep, the soul could catch a glimpse of its own reality; released from the body, it could receive perceptions from its own world, and when it had done so it could return to the body with them; it could pass its perceptions on to the imagination, which would form the appropriate pictures, which the sleeper would perceive as if by the senses. Muslim writers took over the science of dream-interpretation from the Greeks, but added something of their own; it has been said that the Islamic literature of dreams is the richest of all.

PART III

THE OTTOMAN AGE

(Sixteenth–Eighteenth Century)

During the fifteenth and sixteenth centuries the greater part of the Muslim world was integrated into three great empires, those of the Ottomans, Safavids and Mughals. All the Arabic-speaking countries were included in the Ottoman Empire, with its capital at Istanbul, except for parts of Arabia, the Sudan, and Morocco; the empire also included Anatolia and south-eastern Europe. Turkish was the language of the ruling family and the military and administrative élite, which was largely drawn from converts to Islam coming from the Balkans and the Caucasus; the legal and religious élite was of mixed origins, trained in the great imperial schools of Istanbul and transmitting a corpus of legal literature expressed in Arabic.

The empire was a bureaucratic state, holding different regions within a single administrative and fiscal system. It was also, however, the last great expression of the universality of the world of Islam. It preserved the religious law, protected and extended the frontiers of the Muslim world, guarded the holy cities of Arabia and organized the pilgrimage to them. It was also a multi-religious state, giving a recognized status to Christian and Jewish communities. Muslim inhabitants of the provincial cities were drawn into the system of government, and in the Arab countries there developed an Arab Ottoman culture, preserving the heritage and to some extent developing it in new ways. Beyond the frontiers, Morocco developed in rather different ways, under its own dynasties which also claimed an authority based on their protection of religion.

In the eighteenth century the balance between Ottoman central and local governments changed, and in some parts of the empire local Ottoman ruling families or groups had relative autonomy, but remained faithful to the major interests of the Ottoman state. There was a change also in the relations between the empire and the states of Europe. Whereas the empire had expanded into Europe in its earlier centuries, by the later part of the eighteenth century it was under military threat from the west and north. There were also the beginnings of a change in the nature and direction of trade, as European governments and merchants grew stronger in the Indian Ocean and Mediterranean Sea. By the end of the century the Ottoman ruling élite were becoming conscious of a relative decline in power and independence, and were beginning to make their first tentative responses to the new situation.

CHAPTER 13

The Ottoman Empire

THE LIMITS OF POLITICAL POWER

The acceptance of the ruler by the *'ulama* and those for whom they spoke was a two-edged weapon. So long as the ruler had the power to maintain himself, and to defend the urban interests which were associated with his own, he could hope for the acquiescence of the cities and their dependent hinterlands, for recognition by the doctors of the law and some degree of co-operation; despite the caution about frequenting princes uttered by Ghazali and others, there were always *'ulama* who were eager to serve the ruler as judges or officials and to justify his acts. If his power should fail, however, the city might do nothing to save him, and might transfer its allegiance to a new ruler who had effective power. The moment when a city fell was the one point at which the city might act autonomously: the *qadi* and other leaders might go out to meet the new ruler and hand the city over to him.

During the half-millennium after the 'Abbasid Empire began to disintegrate and before the assumption of power over most of the western Islamic world by the Ottomans, the rise and fall of dynasties were repeated again and again. Two kinds of explanation are needed for this, one in terms of the weakening of the power of an existing dynasty, the other in terms of the accumulation of power by its challenger. Contemporary observers and writers tended to lay the emphasis on the inner weaknesses of the dynasty, and to explain these in moral terms. For Nizam al-Mulk, there was an endless alternation in human history. A dynasty could lose the wisdom and justice with which God had endowed it, and then the world would fall into disorder, until a new ruler, destined by God and endowed with the qualities that were needed, appeared.

The most systematic attempt to explain why dynasties fell victim to their own weaknesses was that of Ibn Khaldun. His was a complex explanation:

the 'asabiyya of the ruling group, a solidarity oriented towards the acquisition and maintenance of power, gradually dissolved under the influence
of urban life, and the ruler began to look for support to other groups:

A ruler can obtain power only with the help of his own people . . . He uses them to
fight against those who revolt against his dynasty. They fill his administrative
offices and he appoints them as *wazirs* and tax-collectors. They help him to achieve
his ascendancy and share in all his important affairs. This is true so long as the first
stage of a dynasty lasts, but with the approach of the second stage the ruler shows
himself to be independent of his own people: he claims all the glory for himself and
pushes his people away from it . . . As a result they become his enemies, and to
prevent them from seizing power he needs other friends, not of his own kind,
whom he can use against his people.[1]

In time, too, the ruler ceases to maintain the *shari'a*, the basis of urban
prosperity and of his compact with the city population. Those around him
fall victims to the desire for luxury and lavish expenditure which over-tax
the resources of the people, and they in their turn fall into 'that apathy
which comes over people when they lose control over their own affairs and
become the instrument of others and dependent upon them.'[2]

When the ruler's demands went beyond the ability of society to meet
them, it was not necessarily because of an increase in the profligacy of the
palace; it might also be because of limits on the productive capacity of
society. For a state to be stable, the countryside under its control needed to
produce both sufficient food to feed its population and that of the cities,
and raw materials for manufacture; those who reared livestock, cultivated
the land and manufactured goods needed also to produce a surplus sufficient to maintain, by means of taxation, the ruler's court, government
and army. Whether this was possible depended on many factors, some of
which might change. There could be alterations in the techniques of
production: improvements – for example by the introduction of new crops
or methods of irrigation – which would make possible an increase in
production and in the surplus, or else a loss of technical skill which could
have the opposite effect. Changes in the size of the surplus would in their
turn affect the ability to invest in production, by taking new land into
production or cultivating it in new ways. The demand for products of the
land or the city, coming from other countries, could increase or diminish,
and alterations in the methods or cost of transportation, or in the security
of travel by land or sea, could affect the ability of a country to meet such
demands. In the medium or long run, the birthrate or death-rate could

increase or decrease, because of changes in medical science or in the manners and morals of society.

All these were processes of which the effects would be seen over a lengthy period. There might also, however, be sudden events with cataclysmic results: a war which disrupted trade-routes, destroyed cities and their crafts, and devastated the countryside; a bad harvest, or a succession of them, due to drought in the areas irrigated by rainfall, or an inadequate flow of water in the great rivers. A contagious disease could kill a large part of the population. In a period when the spread of disease can be largely controlled, and some have virtually disappeared, it is difficult to understand the sudden and devastating effect of epidemics, and particularly of the great epidemic disease of these centuries, bubonic plague. Carried by the black rat, it was brought from certain areas in which it was endemic, such as northern Iraq and parts of India, either by the land-routes or by sea to the Mediterranean world, where it could spread rapidly in cities and villages, killing a large proportion of the population and their livestock. (In 1739–41, a period of which we have more reliable statistical knowledge, the eastern Mediterranean seaport of Izmir lost 20 per cent of its population in an epidemic of plague, and more than that proportion of its people in another one thirty years later.)

Such processes interacted with each other, and some of them were cumulative and perpetuated themselves. They help to explain the changes in the relationship between the demands of the holders of power and the ability of society to satisfy them, and the appearance of challenges from leaders or groups which were able to generate power and use it to extend their control over resources. Such a change could take place within an existing system of government: a ruler's soldiers could seize effective power from him. They could also occur by means of an accumulation of power outside the area of a ruler's effective control. A leader would mobilize the manpower of the mountains or steppe, by means of some personal appeal or else that of a religious idea. Whether the seizure of power was from within or without, the motive power tended to come from soldiers drawn from outside the central regions of the state, from the mountains or steppes, or from across the frontiers. They had the hardiness and the skill in handling horses and weapons which were needed in the warfare of the time, before the decisive arms came to be artillery, and infantry trained to use firearms. There is some evidence that, until the coming of modern medical care, the people of the mountains and steppe were healthier than others and produced a surplus of young men who could be enrolled in armies. A leader who aspired to become a ruler would prefer to recruit soldiers from outside the society which he wished to control, or at least from its distant regions; their interests would be linked with his. Once he had established himself, the army might lose its cohesion or begin to acquire interests different from that of the dynasty, and he might try to replace them with a new professional army and a household of personal retainers, and for this too he would look to the distant countryside or beyond the frontiers. The soldiers who were trained in his household would be regarded as his *mamluks*, or slaves in a sense which implied not personal degradation but the sinking of their personalities and interests in that of their master. In due course, a new ruler might emerge within the army or household and found a new dynasty.

This is the context within which what may seem to be the meaningless procession of dynasties in Islamic history can be understood. In the first centuries, a new ruling group coming from the towns of western Arabia was able to create and maintain an army, a bureaucracy and a system of law which enabled settled and civilized life to flourish. Order was maintained in the hinterlands of the great imperial cities: irrigation works were restored or expanded, new products and techniques were introduced, the incorporation of lands lying round the Mediterranean and those lying around the Indian Ocean in a single political and cultural area generated a vast international trade. What little evidence there is points to an increase in population. This was a period of stable regimes in flourishing cities and the countryside around them: Baghdad in southern Iraq, the cities of Khurasan, Damascus in Syria, Fustat in Egypt, Qayrawan in Tunisia, Cordoba in Spain.

From the tenth or eleventh century onwards, however, there was a long period of dislocation, of which the obvious symptoms are the disintegration of the 'Abbasid caliphate, the formation of rival caliphates in Egypt and Andalus, and the coming into the world of Islam of new dynasties drawing their strength from other ethnic elements, some of them moved by religious fervour: the Christians in Spain, expanding at the expense of the Muslim states into which the western Umayyad caliphate had dissolved; the Almoravids and Almohads in the Maghrib and Andalus, springing from religious movements which mobilized Berbers from the mountains and desert fringes of Morocco; Turks and Mongols in the east. These changes may have been symptoms of a deeper disturbance in the balance between government, population and production, arising from other causes: the shrinking of areas of settled population in Iraq and Tunisia, because of the breakdown of ancient systems of irrigation or the extension of the area of movement of pastoral peoples; perhaps a decline in population in some places; a decline in demand for the products of the Muslim cities, linked with the revival of urban life and production in Italy.

There was a moment of recovery in the thirteenth century. While the power and wealth of Iraq shrank, with the destruction caused by the Mongol invasions and the end of the 'Abbasid caliphate, some dynasties were able to establish a stable order, unchallenged by powerful forces from outside the settled Islamic world: in particular, the Hafsids in Tunis, a successor-state of the Almohad Empire, and the Mamluks in Egypt and Syria, a self-perpetuating military élite which had grown up in the service of the previous dynasty, the Ayyubids. Cultivation was carried on over a wide and perhaps expanding area, the servants of the government were able to bring in the rural surplus to the cities, and urban production and trade flourished within the framework of a generally accepted Sunni *shari'a*; a certain symbiosis was maintained between ruling groups and urban populations.

It was a fragile order, however, and by the fourteenth century it was beginning to be shaken by a number of forces. Perhaps the most important of them was the great epidemic of plague known in European history as the Black Death, which attacked most countries in the western part of the world in the mid-fourteenth century, but continued for almost a century afterwards in recurrent outbursts. At a rough estimate, one-third of the people of Cairo died in the first epidemic, and by the middle of the fifteenth century the population of the city was little more than half what it had been a hundred years earlier (approximately 150,000 instead of 250,000). The reason for this was not only that the first coming of the plague was followed by others, but also that the plague affected the countryside as well as the city, so that rural migrants were not able to replenish the urban population. Because of the decline of the rural people and their livestock, agricultural production, and thus the resources available to the government through taxation, shrank.

To the cumulative effects of the plague were added other factors. The growth of textile production in Italy and other European countries, and the expansion of European navigation in the Mediterranean, affected the balance of trade and thus made it more difficult for Muslim governments to obtain the resources they needed. There were also changes in the arts of war, in shipbuilding and navigation, and the new use of gunpowder in artillery and firearms.

In these changed circumstances, the existing political order in the Mamluk state and in those of the Maghrib was open to challenge by new dynasties which were able to find the resources, in manpower and wealth, to create large and effective armies, control a productive countryside and take its surplus, and foster the manufacture and trade of cities. In the western Mediterranean the challenge was to the religious as well as the political order, from the Christian kingdoms of Spain, united into one shortly before the extinction of the last Muslim dynasty in 1492, and soon to have the wealth generated by the conquest of an empire in America. In the eastern Mediterranean, the new and rising power was that of a Muslim dynasty, named after its founder, 'Uthman or (in its Turkish spelling) Osman: hence its Islamic name of Osmanli or some equivalent, anglicized as Ottoman.

OTTOMAN GOVERNMENT

By origin, the Ottoman state was one of the Turkish principalities generated by the expansion of the Saljuqs and of Turkish immigrants westwards into Anatolia. On the disputed and shifting frontier with the Byzantine Empire there grew up a number of such principalities, nominally accepting the suzerainty of the Saljuqs but in fact autonomous. That founded by Osman was situated in the north-west of Anatolia, at the main point of contact with the Byzantines. It attracted to itself fighters in the wars on the frontiers and Turkish nomads moving westwards in search of lands for pasturage, but it also had within its frontiers comparatively extensive and productive agricultural lands, and market towns, some of them important points on the trade-routes running from Iran and further Asia to the Mediterranean. As it expanded its resources grew, and it was able to make use of the new weapons and techniques of warfare and create an organized army. By the end of the fourteenth century its forces had crossed the straits into eastern Europe and expanded rapidly there. Its eastern European empire added to its strength in more than one way. It came into contact and diplomatic relations with the states of Europe, and acquired new sources of manpower: former ruling groups were incorporated into its system of government, and conscripts from Balkan villages were taken into its army. With its increased strength it was then able to turn eastwards in Anatolia, in spite of a temporary check when its army was defeated by that of another Turkish conqueror from the east, Timur (Tamerlane). In 1453 it absorbed what was left of the Byzantine Empire and took Constantinople as its new capital, Istanbul.

In the east, however, its power was challenged by the Safavids, another rising dynasty of uncertain origin, around whom Turkish tribesmen had gathered. There was a long struggle for control of the frontier regions lying between their main centres of power, eastern Anatolia and Iraq; Baghdad was conquered by the Ottomans in 1534, lost to the Safavids in 1623, and not taken by the Ottomans again until 1638. It was partly as a consequence of the struggle with the Safavids that the Ottomans moved south into the lands of the Mamluk sultanate. Largely because of their superior fire-power and military organization, they were able to occupy Syria, Egypt and western Arabia in 1516–17.

The Ottoman Empire was now the principal military and naval power in the eastern Mediterranean, and also in the Red Sea, and this brought it into potential conflict with the Portuguese in the Indian Ocean and the Spaniards in the western Mediterranean. In the Red Sea area its policy was one of defence, to prevent the Portuguese advancing, but in the Mediterranean it used its naval power to check Spanish expansion and establish a chain of strong points at Algiers (in the 1520s), Tripoli (in the 1550s) and Tunis (1574), but not further west in Morocco. Maritime warfare continued for some time between Ottomans and Spaniards, but by now Spanish energies were mainly directed towards the new world of America. A more or less stable division of naval power in the Mediterranean grew up, and from 1580 onwards Spain and the Ottomans had peaceful relations.

In a sense, the formation of the Ottoman state was one more example of the process which had taken place many times in the history of Muslim peoples, the challenge to established dynasties by a military force drawn from largely nomadic peoples. Its origin was similar to that of the two other great states which rose at roughly the same time, those of the Safavids in Iran and the Mughals in India. All three drew their strength in the beginning from areas inhabited by Turkish tribesmen, and all owed their military success to their adoption of weapons using gunpowder which had been coming into use in the western half of the world. All succeeded in creating stable and lasting polities, militarily powerful, centralized and bureaucratically organized, able to collect taxes and maintain law and order over a wide area for a long time. The Ottoman Empire was one of the largest political structures that the western part of the world had known since the Roman Empire disintegrated: it ruled eastern Europe, western

Asia and most of the Maghrib, and held together lands with very different political traditions, many ethnic groups – Greeks, Serbs, Bulgarians, Romanians, Armenians, Turks and Arabs – and various religious communities – Sunni and Shi'i Muslims, Christians of all the historic Churches, and Jews. It maintained its rule over most of them for 400 years or so, and over some of them for as many as 600.

At the apex of the system of control of this vast empire there stood the ruler and his family, the 'house of Osman'. Authority resided in the family rather than in any clearly designated member of it. There was no rigid law of succession, but certain customs of the family led on the whole to peaceful successions and long reigns. Until the early seventeenth century the ruler was usually succeeded by one of his sons, but from then onwards it came to be generally accepted that when a ruler died or otherwise ceased to rule he should be followed by the oldest living member of the family. The ruler lived in the midst of a vast household which included the women of the *harim* and those who guarded them, personal attendants, gardeners and palace guards.

At the head of the system of government through which he maintained his control was the *sadr-i azam*, the high official whose most familiar English title was that of grand vizir. After the first Ottoman period he was regarded as having absolute power beneath the ruler. Under him there were a number of other *vizirs*. They controlled the army and the provincial governments as well as the civil service.

In the first phase of expansion, the Ottoman army had been largely a cavalry force drawn from Turks and other inhabitants of Anatolia and the Balkan countryside. Cavalry officers (*sipahis*) were given the right to collect and keep the tax on certain agricultural lands in return for service in times of need with a specified number of soldiers; this is known as the *timar* system. As time went on this force became less effective and important, both because of changes in the art of warfare and because the holder of a *timar* would be less eager to absent himself from his land for long campaigns in distant parts of the growing empire. From an early period another army was created, a highly disciplined standing force of infantry (janissaries) and cavalry, formed by means of the *devşirme*, that is to say, the periodical conscription of boys from the Christian villages of the Balkans converted to Islam.

In the course of the sixteenth century an elaborate bureaucracy grew up (the *kalemiye*). It consisted mainly of two groups: the secretaries who drew up documents – orders, regulations and replies to petitions – in due form, and preserved them; and those who kept the financial records, the assessment of taxable assets and accounts of how much was collected and how it was used. (Documents and accounts were carefully preserved, and they form an archive without parallel in the world of Islam, and of major importance for the history of much of the western half of the world; the systematic exploration of it has begun only in recent decades.)

The highest officials of army and government met regularly in the palace in a council (*divan*) which made decisions of policy, received foreign ambassadors, drew up orders, investigated complaints and responded to petitions, particularly those dealing with abuses of power; in early times the ruler himself presided at meetings of the council, but later it was the grand vizir who was its head.

This system of control was reproduced throughout the empire. As new lands were annexed, governors were appointed for important cities and their hinterlands, and garrisons of imperial troops were placed in them; later, the numerous local governments (*sancak*) were brought together in a smaller number of larger provinces (*eyalet*). The provincial government was like that of the central one in miniature: the governor had his elaborate household, his secretaries and accountants, and his council of high officials meeting regularly.

Among the main duties of the government was that of collecting the taxes on which it depended. The financial records, kept carefully at least during the early period and preserved in the archives, contain details of tax-assessment on households and on cultivable land, and regular budgets of income and expenditure. As in previous Muslim states, there were three kinds of regular tax. First were taxes on the produce of the countryside, crops, fisheries and livestock; in some places taxes on grain and other agricultural produce were levied as a proportion of the crop (in principle a tenth, although in practice much more), in others they were assessed on the cultivable area; some taxes were collected in money, others in kind, particularly those on grain, which could be stored for a long time. Secondly, there were various taxes and dues on urban activities: on produce sold in the markets, on shops, baths and *khans*, on industrial activities (weaving, dyeing, tanning) and on goods imported and exported; there were tolls levied on the main roads to pay for their upkeep. Thirdly, there were the personal taxes (*jizya*) paid by Christians and Jews; Muslims paid no regular personal taxes. In addition to these regular taxes, there were occasional levies in times of need. In the early ages of the empire, these taxes were carefully assigned to various purposes: the ruler's own privy purse or those of members of his family, the salaries and expenses of governors of *eyalets* and *sancaks*, the recompense to holders of *timars*. By the seventeenth century, however, this system was declining, because the fiscal needs of the government (and of its army in particular) were too great to allow the proceeds of taxation to be assigned in these ways. It was therefore replaced by a system of tax-farms, by which individuals, whether merchants or officials, undertook to collect a certain tax and send the proceeds for such purposes as the government might decide, after deducting a certain proportion of it as a commission. By the end of the seventeenth century, some tax-farms had become virtually hereditary possessions.

In the early period of the empire, the controlling positions in the government were largely held by commanders of the army, members of former ruling groups of states incorporated into the empire, and the educated population of the cities. By the sixteenth century, however, the commanding positions – *vizirs*, heads of the army, provincial governors – were mainly drawn from the ruler's own household. Members of the household came from among those recruited into the army by the *devşirme*, from slaves brought from the Caucasus, or from members of former ruling families. It was also possible for sons of those who held important positions in the government to enter the household; whatever their origin, however, all were regarded as the ruler's 'slaves'. They were carefully trained for service in the palace, then promoted to positions there or in the army or government. Promotion depended partly on patronage (*intisap*): a powerful official could obtain positions for those linked with him by family or marriage or ethnic origin or in other ways. Secretaries and financial officials seem to have been trained by a system of apprenticeship, after a basic formal education in a *madrasa*, and there was a hereditary element in the *kalemiye*; sons were brought into the service by their fathers.

In this way, the ruler was able to maintain his control over the whole system of government. His doing this, however, depended on his ability to exercise control, and in the first part of the seventeenth century there was a period during which his power was weakened. There were several reasons for this; one of them was the inflation caused by debasement of the currency and by the import into the Mediterranean area of precious metals from the Spanish colonies in America. This was followed by a revival in the strength of the government, but in a different form: the grand vizir became more powerful, and the road of promotion led less through the household of the ruler than through those of the grand vizir and other high officials. The empire tended to become less of an autocracy, more of an oligarchy of powerful officials linked by the 'asabiyya of having been brought up in the same household, by a common education and often by kinship or marriage.

The organization and modes of activity of the government reflected that Persian ideal of kingship which had been expressed by Nizam al-Mulk and other writers of the kind. The just and wise ruler should stand apart from the different orders of society to enable him to regulate their activities and maintain the harmony of the whole. In principle, Ottoman society was divided sharply into rulers (*asker*, literally soldiers) and subjects (*reaya*, literally the flock). The *asker*, by definition, included the high officials, holders of *timars*, and members of the various armed corps, both regular and auxiliary. They were exempt from the occasional special levies which became a kind of personal tax, and had their own judicial regime. In principle, only those who had this status could be appointed to positions in the government. The janissaries, in particular, were kept under a strictly separate regime. They were not allowed to marry while on active service, nor to carry on a trade; if they married after retirement, their sons could not enter the corps. This separation was shown in the life of the ruler, secluded in the inner courts of his Topkapi palace on a hill overlooking the Bosphorus, living among his slaves and *harim*, never – after the reign of Süleyman (1520–66) – contracting marriages with Ottoman families which might in this way be given too much influence. It was expressed too in the existence of a court culture: a refined code of manners, an Ottoman Turkish language enriched by borrowings from Persian as well as Arabic, an education which included the polite literature of Persian as well as the religious literature of Arabic.

At a certain level, however, order could not be maintained or taxes collected without the collaboration of the *reaya*. The ruler and his *asker* looked at the *reaya* not as a collection of individuals to be dealt with directly, but rather as a number of groups (in Turkish, *taife* or *cemaat*). If a certain category of subjects had to be dealt with separately, for purposes of taxation or other service to the state, they were regarded as a unit, and one of their number was recognized as an intermediary through whom the government could deal with the unit as a whole. He would normally be someone acceptable to the group as well as the government, and might therefore possess a certain moral position and even some autonomy of action, both mediating the orders and requirements of the government to the group, and expressing their grievances and requests to the government. He would help to preserve peace and order in the group, and settle its disputes and conflicts by arbitration before they reached the point where intervention by the government would be necessary.

These units were of different kinds. For purposes of taxation, the *sancak* was divided into smaller units, a small town, village or pastoral tribe. The cities were divided into quarters (*mahalle, hara*), although the use of the term seems to have varied greatly: a quarter could include a few hundred people or several thousands. Both for taxation and for skilled manpower, the different trades and crafts were organized separately; on certain state occasions they would form solemn processions; in the Ottoman period it is possible to talk of these craft groups as being roughly equivalent to the guilds of medieval Europe, having some functions beyond those of raising taxes or providing skilled labour. They were not self-sufficient, however; in a sense they were constituted by Ottoman recognition.

The various Jewish and Christian communities had a special position, because they paid the poll tax and had their own legal systems of personal law, and also because the government had to be assured of their loyalty. In the capital and the provinces, the government recognized a spiritual head of each community as having a certain legal jurisdiction and being responsible for collecting the *jizya* and maintaining order. In this way, the non-Muslims were integrated into the body politic. They did not fully belong to it, but an individual might rise to a position of power or influence: Jews were important in the financial service in the sixteenth century, and towards the end of the seventeenth Greeks became chief interpreters in the grand vizir's office and governors of the two Romanian provinces, Wallachia and Moldavia. They do not seem to have lived in isolation or under pressure, however: they belonged to trade or craft *cemaats*, and worship and education were free within limits. They could carry on most economic activities; Jews were important as bankers, Greeks in the sea-trade, and by the sixteenth century Armenians were beginning to be important in the trade in Iranian silk.

THE OTTOMANS AND ISLAMIC TRADITION

Such titles of the Ottoman ruler as *padishah* or sultan marked his link with the Persian tradition of kingship, but he was also the heir to a specifically Islamic tradition, and could claim to exercise legitimate authority in Islamic terms. This double claim is shown in the titles used in official documents:

His Majesty, the victorious and successful sultan, the ruler aided by God, whose undergarment is victory, the *padishah* whose glory is high as Heaven, king of kings who are like stars, crown of the royal head, the shadow of the Provider, culmination of kingship, quintessence of the book of fortune, equinoctial line of justice, perfection of the spring-tide of majesty, sea of benevolence and humanity, mine of the jewels of generosity, source of the memorials of valour, manifestation of the lights of felicity, setter-up of the standards of Islam, writer of justice on the pages of time, sultan of the two continents and of the two seas, ruler of the two easts and of the two wests, servant of the two holy sanctuaries, namesake of the apostle of men and of *jinns*, Sultan Muhammad Khan.[3]

The Ottomans did on occasion use the title of caliph also, but it carried with it at that time no claim to the kind of universal or exclusive authority which earlier caliphs had been acknowledged to possess. It had rather the implication that the Ottoman sultan was more than a local ruler, and used his power for purposes sanctioned by religion. On occasion, Ottoman writers claimed for the sultan a predominant position in the world of Islam, an 'exalted caliphate'.

The Ottomans defended the frontiers of Islam and expanded them when possible. They were faced by a threat from several sides. On the east stood the Safavids of Iran; the struggle of Ottomans and Safavids for control of Anatolia and Iraq gradually acquired religious overtones, for the Safavids proclaimed Shi'ism as the official religion of the dynasty, while the Ottomans became more strictly Sunni as their empire expanded to include the main centres of the high urban culture of Islam. On the other side of them stood the powers of Christian Europe. The Byzantine Empire had vanished with the fall of Constantinople in 1453; the Orthodox state growing up in Russia, and claiming to be the heir of Byzantium, did not begin to advance southwards towards the Black Sea until the end of the seventeenth century. The main challenge came not yet from there but from the three great Catholic powers of the northern and western Mediterranean basin: Spain, the Holy Roman Empire with its southern extension into Italy, and Venice with its eastern Mediterranean colonies. During the sixteenth century there was a struggle with Spain for control of the western Mediterranean and the Maghrib, with Venice for the islands of the eastern Mediterranean, and with the Holy Roman Empire for control of the Danube basin. By the end of the century a more or less stable frontier had been created: Spain controlled the western Mediterranean Sea (but only a few small points on the coast of the Maghrib); the Ottomans ruled the Danube basin as far as Hungary; Venice had lost Cyprus and other islands but retained Crete. This balance was partly changed during the seventeenth century: the

Ottomans conquered Crete, the last great Venetian outpost, but lost Hungary to the Holy Roman Empire, and other parts of its European lands in a war which ended with the Treaty of Carlowitz (1699).

The sultan was not only the defender of the frontiers of Islam, he was also the guardian of its holy places. Mecca and Madina in Hijaz, Jerusalem and Hebron in Palestine. As ruler of Mecca and Madina he had the proud title of Servant of the Two Sanctuaries. He also controlled the main routes by which pilgrims went to them. To organize and lead the annual pilgrimage was one of his main functions; conducted with great formality and as a major public act, the pilgrimage was an annual assertion of Ottoman sovereignty in the heart of the Muslin world.

Every year thousands of pilgrims came to the holy cities from all over the world of Islam; a European traveller who was in Mecca during the pilgrimage of 1814 estimated that there were some 70,000 pilgrims there. Groups of pilgrims went to the holy cities from Yemen, from central Africa by way of the ports of the Sudan, and from Iraq through central Arabia, but the main organized caravans of pilgrims continued to go from Cairo and Damascus. Of the two, that from Damascus had a greater importance in the Ottoman period, because it was linked with Istanbul by a major land-route and could be more firmly controlled. Every year a special delegate appointed by the sultan would leave Istanbul for Damascus, accompanied by high officials or members of the Ottoman family who intended to make the pilgrimage, and carrying with him the *surra*, money and provisions intended for the populations of the holy cities, and paid for partly by the proceeds of imperial *waqfs* dedicated to the purpose. (Until the eighteenth century, this *surra* was sent by sea to Egypt, and carried with the Cairo pilgrimage.) In Damascus they would join the pilgrim caravan organized by the governor of the city and led by an official appointed as leader of the pilgrimage (*amir al-hajj*); from the early eighteenth century this office was held by the governor of Damascus himself. Centuries later, in the last Ottoman age, and shortly before new means of communication were to change the way in which the pilgrimage was made, an English traveller, C. M. Doughty, described its setting out from Damascus.

The new dawn appearing we removed not yet. The day risen the tents were dismantled, the camels led in ready to their companies, and halted beside their loads. We waited to hear the cannon shot which should open that year's pilgrimage. It was near ten o'clock when we heard the signal gun fired, and then, without any disorder, litters were suddenly heaved and braced upon the bearing beasts, their charges laid upon the kneeling camels, and the thousands of riders, all born in the caravan countries, mounted in silence. As all is up the drivers are left standing upon their feet, or sit to rest out the latest moments on their heels: they with other camp and tent servants must ride those three hundred leagues upon their bare soles, although they faint; and are to measure the ground again upward with their weary feet from the holy places. At the second gun, fired a few moments after, the Pasha's litter advances and after him goes the head of the caravan column: other fifteen or twenty minutes we, who have places in the rear, must halt, that is until the long train is unfolded before us; then we strike our camels and the great pilgrimage is moving.[4]

The pilgrims would move out of the city in solemn procession, carrying with them the *mahmal*, a wooden frame covered by an embroidered cloth, and the Prophet's standard, which was kept in the citadel of Damascus. They would move down a line of resting-places, provided with fortresses, garrisons and provisions, until they reached Mecca; once there, the governor of Damascus was regarded as having a general supervision over the whole pilgrimage. To organize and lead the pilgrim caravan was in fact one of his most important tasks, and to pay for it was a main demand on the revenues of Damascus and the other Syrian provinces. The caravan which started from Cairo was no less important. It included pilgrims from the Maghrib, who came to Egypt by land or sea, as well as Egyptians. Led also by an *amir al-hajj*, and carrying with it its own *mahmal* and a *kiswa*, a veil to cover the outside of the Ka'ba, it went through Sinai and western Arabia to Mecca. It brought with it subsidies for the tribes on the route. It was not always possible, however, to prevent attacks by tribesmen on one or other of the caravans, either because the subsidies had not been paid, or because of drought, which impelled the beduin to try to raid the caravan's water-supply.

The most fundamental duty of a Muslim ruler, and that which both expressed and strengthened his alliance with the Muslim population, was to maintain the *shari'a*. In the Ottoman period, the institutions through which the *shari'a* was preserved were drawn into closer union with the ruler than before. The school of law favoured by the Ottomans was the Hanafi, and the judges who administered it were appointed and paid by the government. The Ottomans created a corps of official *'ulama* (the *ilmiye*) parallel with the political politico-military and bureaucratic corps; there was an equivalence between the ranks in the different corps. These official *'ulama* played an important part in the administration of the empire. At the head of them were the two military judges (*kadiasker*), who were members of the sultan's *divan*. Beneath them were the *qadis* of the great cities, and beneath them again those of the smaller towns or districts; for judicial purposes a province was divided into districts (*qada*) each with a resident *qadi*. His functions were more than judicial: he dealt with civil cases, trying to reach agreement or make decisions in disputes; he recorded financial transactions – sales, loans, gifts, contracts – in a form consistent with the *shari'a*; he dealt with inheritances, dividing up estates among the heirs in accordance with the provisions of the *shari'a*. He was also the intermediary through whom the sultan and his governors issued orders and proclamations. (All these documents of various kinds were carefully registered and preserved in the archives of the *qadi*'s courts; they are our most important source for the administrative and social history of the lands ruled by the Ottomans, and historians are now beginning to use them.)

Hanafi *muftis* were appointed by the government to interpret the law. At their head stood the *mufti* of Istanbul, the *shaykh al-islam*, who acted as the religious adviser of the sultan. He was regarded as the most exalted personage in the whole religious order: it was a sign of his freedom of judgement and his power to curb and rebuke the holders of power that he was not a member of the sultan's *divan* of high officials.

Those who were appointed to high positions in the legal hierarchy were trained in imperial schools, in particular those in the capital: a great complex of schools was established by Mehmet II, the sultan who conquered Constantinople in the fifteenth century, and another created by Süleyman 'the Magnificent', as European sources call him, in the sixteenth. Virtually all the high officials in the service were graduates of these schools. Here as in the other services there was an element of patronage and hereditary privilege which became more important as time went on; sons of high officials were allowed to jump stages on the path of promotion. It was possible also for those educated for service in the *ilmiye* to move into the bureaucracy, or even into the politico-military service, by patronage or in other ways.

In principle, the sultan used his power to uphold the *shari'a*, and it was an expression of this that those who administered the law were regarded as *asker*, members of the ruling élite and possessors of financial and judicial privileges; so too were the *sayyids*, those recognized as descendants of the Prophet, whose names were kept on a register maintained by one of their number, the 'marshal of the nobility', *naquib al-ashraf*, appointed by the sultan in each major city. The head of the order of *sayyids*, the *naqib* in Istanbul, was a great personage of the empire.

In fact, the *shari'a* was not the only law of the empire. Like previous rulers, the Ottoman sultan found it necessary to issue his own orders and regulations in order to preserve his authority or ensure that justice was done. He claimed to do this by virtue of the power which the *shari'a* itself gave to rulers, so long as they exercised it within the bounds of the *shari'a*. All Muslim rulers had issued rules and made decisions, but what seems to have been unique in the Ottoman system was that they formed an accumulating tradition which was embodied in codes (*kanun-name*), which were usually associated with the names of Mehmet II or of Süleyman, known in Ottoman tradition as *Kanuni* (the lawgiver). These codes were of various kinds. Some of them regulated the traditional tax-systems of the various provinces as they were conquered; others dealt with criminal matters, and attempted to bring the laws and customs of conquered provinces into conformity with a single code of Ottoman justice; others again concerned the system of promotion in government, court ceremonial, and the affairs of the ruling family. The *qadis* administered such codes, but more important criminal matters, and in particular those touching the security of the state, were brought to the *divan* of the sultan or his provincial governor. In later times this criminal code seems to have fallen into disuse.

GOVERNMENT IN THE ARAB PROVINCES

The Ottoman Empire was a European, Asian and African power, with vital interests to protect and enemies to face in all three continents. During most of its existence, a large part of its resources and energy were devoted to expansion into eastern and central Europe and the control of its European provinces, which held much of the population of the empire and provided much of its revenue; from the late seventeenth century onwards, it was concerned with defence against Austrian expansion from the west and Russian from the north, in the area around the Black Sea. The place of the Arab provinces in the empire must be seen in the context of this preoccupation with the Balkans and Anatolia. They had their own importance, however. Algiers in the west was a strong point against Spanish expansion, and Baghdad in the east against that of the Safavids. Syria, Egypt and Hijaz were not so far exposed to the same kind of threat from foreign powers, once Portuguese attempts in the sixteenth century to extend their maritime power to the Red Sea had ceased. They were important in other ways, however. The revenues of Egypt and Syria were a major part of the Ottoman budget, and they were the places where the annual pilgrimage to Mecca was marshalled. Possession of the holy cities gave the Ottomans a kind of legitimacy and a claim on the attention of the world of Islam which no other Muslim state possessed.

It was important therefore for the sultan's government to keep the Arab provinces under its control, but there was more than one way of doing this. In provinces lying a long way from Istanbul, too far for the regular sending of imperial armies, the method could not be the same as in those lying nearer, and on the great imperial roads. In course of time, after the first conquests, different systems of government grew up, with varying balances between central control and local power.

The Syrian provinces of Aleppo, Damascus and Tripoli had to be controlled directly, because of their tax-revenues, the place of Aleppo in the international trading system, that of Damascus as one of the centres from which the pilgrimage was organized, and that of Jerusalem and Hebron as holy cities (Jerusalem the place from which the Prophet was believed to have ascended to Heaven on his night journey, Hebron the burial-place of the patriarch Abraham). The government in Istanbul was able to retain direct control both by the roads through Anatolia and by sea, but this was limited to the great cities and the grain-producing plains around them, and the ports of the coast. In the mountains and desert, control was more difficult because of the terrain, and less important because the land produced less revenue. It was enough for the Ottoman government to give recognition to local families of lords, provided they collected and transmitted revenue and did not threaten the routes by which trade and armies passed. In the same way, chiefs of pastoral tribes in the Syrian desert, and those lying on the pilgrims' route to Mecca, were given formal recognition. A policy of manipulation, of setting one family or one member of a family against another, was usually sufficient to preserve the balance between imperial and local interests, but sometimes it could be threatened. In the early seventeenth century, a rebellious governor of Aleppo and an over-powerful lord in the Shuf mountains of Lebanon, Fakhr al-Din al-Ma'ni (d. 1635), with some encouragement from Italian rulers, were able to challenge Ottoman power for a time. Fakhr al-Din was finally captured and executed, and after that the Ottomans established a fourth province with its capital at Sayda, to keep a watch over the lords of Lebanon.

Iraq was mainly important as a stronghold against invasion from Iran. The wealth of the countryside was much diminished since the system of irrigation had declined, and vast areas were under the control of pastoral tribes and their chieftains, not only east of the Euphrates but in the land lying between it and the Tigris. Direct Ottoman control was largely limited to Baghdad, the centre from which the defence of the frontier with Iran could be organized, and to the main cities on the route which ran from Istanbul to Baghdad, in particular Mosul on the upper Tigris. In the north-west, a number of Kurdish families were recognized as local governors or tax-collectors, in order to hold the frontier against the Iranians; an Ottoman provincial governor of Shahrizor was maintained in order to keep some control over them. In the south, Basra was important as a naval base so long as there was a Portuguese or Dutch threat to the Gulf, but later the Ottoman navy there was allowed to decay. There was a weak point in the Ottoman system, however: the Shi'i holy cities of Najaf and Karbala, which were closely linked with the Shi'i centres of Iran, and were points from which Shi'ism radiated over the surrounding countryside.

Egypt like Syria was important for strategic, financial and religious reasons: it was one of the bastions of Ottoman control of the eastern Mediterranean, a country which produced large tax-revenues, an ancient centre of Islamic learning, and a point from which the pilgrimage was organized. It was more difficult than Syria to hold, however, because of its distance from Istanbul and the length of the land-route lying through Syria, and because it had the resources to support an independent centre of power: a rich countryside producing a large surplus for the use of the government, and a great city with a long tradition as a capital. From the beginning the Ottoman government was reluctant to give too much power to its governor in Cairo. He was replaced frequently, and his power was hedged around with restrictions. When the Ottomans conquered Egypt they established a number of military corps. By some time in the seventeenth century these corps had been drawn into Egyptian society: soldiers inter-married with Egyptian families and entered trades or crafts. Egyptians acquired rights of membership in the corps. Although the commanders of the corps were sent from Istanbul, other officers were local Ottomans, with a local solidarity.

In the same way, a solidarity grew up among some *mamluk* groups. When the Ottomans occupied Cairo, they absorbed some of the former military élite of the Mamluk state into their sytem of government. It is not clear whether these *mamluks* were able to perpetuate their households by importing new recruits from the Caucasus, or whether it was military officers who created new households by using a similar system of recruitment and training; whatever their origin, by the seventeenth century there had emerged groups of military *mamluks* from the Caucasus and elsewhere who were strong enough to hold some of the leading positions in the government and obtain control of much of the urban and rural wealth of Egypt. From about 1630, *mamluk* households held predominant power. In the 1660s the governors were able to restore their position, but this was once more challenged by high officers of one of the military corps, the janissaries, at the end of the century.

The process of devolution of power had therefore begun in Egypt, and it was carried further in some of the more peripheral regions of the empire. In Hijaz, it was enough for the Ottomans to retain control of the port of Jidda, where there was an Ottoman governor, and to assert their authority in the holy cities once a year when the pilgrimage came, led by a high official of the government and carrying subsidies for the inhabitants of Mecca and Madina and the tribes on the routes. The province was too poor to furnish revenue to Istanbul, too remote and difficult to be closely and permanently controlled; local power in the holy cities was left in the hands of appointed members of a family of *sharifs* or descendants of the Prophet. Further south, in Yemen, even that degree of control could not be maintained permanently. From the middle of the seventeenth century there was no Ottoman presence, even in the ports of the coast where the coffee trade was of increasing importance. In the mountains, the absence of Ottoman power made it possible for a new line of Zaydi *imams* to establish themselves.

In the Maghrib, the area under Ottoman rule was first controlled by the governor of Algiers, but from the 1570s there were three provinces, with their capitals at Tripoli, Tunis and Algiers. Here a typical Ottoman form of provincial government was set up: a governor sent from Istanbul with his household, an administration in which local Ottomans served, a corps of professional janissaries recruited in Anatolia, a Hanafi *qadi* (although most of the inhabitants were Malikis), and a navy recruited from various sources, including European converts to Islam, and used mainly for privateering against the commercial shipping of European states with which the Ottoman sultan or the local governors were at war.

Within a century, however, the balance between central government and local powers had begun to change in favour of the latter. In Tripoli, the janissaries seized effective power by the beginning of the seventeenth century, and their elected spokesman or *dey* shared power with the governor. It was a precarious power, however. The scale of life in the province was such as to make it impossible to maintain a large, permanent administration and army: the towns were small, the settled and cultivated countryside was limited. It was scarcely possible for the government to control the naval captains, whose privateering led more than once to the bombardment of Tripoli by European navies.

In Tunis, direct Ottoman rule lasted for an even shorter time. Before the end of the sixteenth century the lower officers of the janissaries revolted, formed a council, and elected a leader (*dey*) who shared power with the governor. In the middle of the seventeenth century a third person, the *bey* who commanded the janissary corps which collected rural taxes, seized a share of the power; at the beginning of the eighteenth century, one of them was able to found a dynasty of *beys*, the Husaynids. The *beys* and their government were successful in striking local roots and creating an alliance of interests with the population of Tunis, a city of considerable size, wealth and importance. The main political and military positions were largely in the hands of an élite of Circassian and Georgian *mamluks*, with some Greek and western European converts to Islam, trained in the *bey*'s household. This élite was, however, tending to become more Tunisian, through intermarriage or in other ways, and members of local Tunisian families held office as secretaries or administrators. Both the Turco-Tunisian ruling élite and members of local families of standing had a common interest in control of the countryside and its surplus of production. The easily accessible area of productive plain land, the Sahil, was large, and the *beys* had a local army by which they extracted the annual taxes from it. Government and city also had a common interest in the activity of privateering. The captains and sailors came mainly from European converts, or from the eastern provinces of the empire, but the ships were provided and equipped partly by the local government and partly by the wealthy families of Tunis.

Of the three centres of Ottoman power in the Maghrib, Algiers was the most important. It was essential for the Ottoman sultan to maintain a strong western frontier post in the age of Spanish expansion: even when the main Spanish attention was diverted from the Mediterranean region to the colonies in America, there was still a danger that Spain would seize ports on the coast of the Maghrib; Wahran (Oran) was under Spanish rule for much of the period from 1509 to 1792. Algiers was the seat of an Ottoman naval force which defended Ottoman interests in the western Mediterranean and engaged in privateering against European merchant ships in times of war. (European states equally engaged in privateering, and used captured Algerians as galley slaves.) It was also the seat of an important janissary force, perhaps the largest in the empire outside Istanbul. With these strong forces, the governor of Algiers could exercise influence over the whole littoral of the Maghrib. Here too, however, the balance shifted. Until the middle of the seventeenth century power remained formally in the hands of the governor, sent from Istanbul and replaced every few years. The naval captains were scarcely under his control, however, and the janissaries were obedient only to the extent to which he could collect taxes and pay their stipends. By the middle of the seventeenth century a council of high janissary officers was able to take control of the collection of taxes, and to choose a *dey* to collect them and make sure they received what was due to them. At the beginning of the eighteenth century the process came to its logical conclusion and the *dey* was able to obtain from the central government the office and title of governor.

As in Tripoli and Tunis, common interests united the governing élite and the merchants of Algiers; together they equipped the privateering activities of the sea-captains, and shared the profit from the sale of captured goods and the ransoming of captives. In the seventeenth century, Algerian ships went as far as the coasts of England and even Iceland. Algiers was not the centre of an ancient urban culture like Tunis, Cairo, Damascus or Aleppo, or of a rich indigenous bourgeoisie. It was dominated by three groups: the janissaries, mainly brought from Anatolia and other eastern parts of the empire; the sea-captains, many of them Europeans; and the merchants, many of them Jews, who disposed of the goods captured by the privateers through their contacts in the Italian port of Livorno. The centres of Algerian urban life lay inland, in and around the towns lying on the great plateaux. Here, governors appointed by the *dey* of Algiers retained their own armed forces, recruited from Algerians or from members of janissary families who were not permitted to enter the janissary corps in Algiers; here too there existed a local bourgeoisie closely linked with the government. Beyond the hinterland of these towns, the rule of Algiers was mediated through rural chieftains, who collected taxes and brought the proceeds to the annual tax-gathering expedition. There were districts, however, where even such mediated control did not exist, and at most there was a certain acquiescence in the authority of Ottoman Algiers and Istanbul; such were the principalities of the Kabyle mountains (Kabylia), the areas of the camel-breeding nomads of the Sahara, and the towns of the Mzab oasis, peopled by Ibadis and living under the rule of a council of learned and pious elders.

CHAPTER 14

Ottoman Societies

POPULATION AND WEALTH IN THE EMPIRE

The many countries incorporated into the Ottoman Empire, living within its system of bureaucratic control and under the jurisdiction of a single law, formed a vast trading area, in which persons and goods could move in relative safety, along trade-routes maintained by imperial forces and provided with *khans*, and without paying customs duties, although various local dues had to be paid. This area was linked on the one side with Iran and India, where the rule of Safavids and Mughals also maintained a framework of stable life, and where the coming of Europeans into the Indian Ocean – Portuguese, Dutch, French and English – had not yet disrupted traditional patterns of trade and navigation. On the west it was linked with the countries of western Europe, which were in process of economic expansion because of the existence of strong centralized monarchies, the growth of population and agriculture, and the import of precious metals from the new world of Spanish and Portuguese America. New kinds of goods of high value, in addition to the older staples of international trade, were carried over the long trade-routes. The spice trade still passed through Cairo, until, at some time in the seventeenth century, the Dutch began to carry a large part of it round the Cape of Good Hope; Persian silk was brought along a chain of trading cities from the Safavid empire of Iran, through Anatolia, to Istanbul, Bursa or Aleppo; coffee, first introduced in the sixteenth century, was imported to Cairo from Yemen, and from there distributed over the Mediterranean world; in the Maghrib, slaves, gold and ivory were brought from the grasslands south of the Sahara.

The manufactures of the Ottoman cities were no longer so important in the world market as they had been, but the textiles of Syria and the *shashiya*, the distinctive headgear made in Tunis, were in demand in the empire itself. In some parts of this trade western European merchants were playing an increasingly large role, but the most important trade was still that with the countries of the Indian Ocean, and here Ottoman merchants had the leading part.

Strong government, public order and flourishing trade were connected with two other phenomena of the period of Ottoman power. One of them was the growth of population. This was common to the whole Mediterranean world in the sixteenth century, partly as it recovered from the long decline caused by the Black Death, but also because of other changes of the time. A rough estimate, which seems to be generally accepted, is that the population of the empire may have increased by around 50 per cent in the course of the century. (In Anatolia, the tax-paying population doubled, but this may be partly explained not by natural increase but by a firmer control, which made it possible to register and collect taxes from more of the population.) By the end of the century, the total population may have been of the order of 20–30 millions, more or less evenly divided between the European, Asian and African parts of the empire; by this time the population of France was perhaps 16 millions, that of the Italian states 13, and that of Spain 8. Istanbul grew from a comparatively small city in the period immediately before and after the Ottoman conquest to one of 700,000 by the seventeenth century; it was larger than the largest European cities, Naples, Paris and London. This increase does not, however, appear to have continued in either the Muslim or Christian parts of the Mediterranean basin during the seventeenth century.

The rural as well as the urban population appears to have grown. Such evidence as exists points to an extension of agriculture and an increase in rural production in some parts of the empire at least; this was a result of better order, a more equitable system of taxation, increased demand from the urban population, and the generation of capital for investment by the prosperity of the cities. In the seventeenth century, however, there is evidence of a dislocation of settled rural life. The disturbances in part of Anatolia during the early years of the century, known as the *celali* risings, may have been a sign of rural over-population, as well as of a decline in the ability of the government to maintain order in the countryside.

As always, it was the cities which were the main beneficiaries of Ottoman order and economic growth, or at least some classes in the cities. When Mehmet II entered Constantinople, little remained of what had been a great imperial city. He and his successors encouraged or even compelled

Muslims, Christians and Jews from other places to settle there, and endowed the new Istanbul with great complexes of buildings. On the hill overlooking the Golden Horn was the palace of Topkapi. In the outer court public business was carried on; in the inner courts there lived the sultan and his household. The palace was in fact an inner city with many thousands of inhabitants, surrounded by walls. Beyond it lay the heart of the productive city, the central group of markets and the imperial foundations, complexes of mosques, schools, hospices and libraries; characteristic signs of the great Ottoman city were the imperial *waqfs*, by which the proceeds of shops and markets were devoted to religious and charitable uses. A third pole of activity lay across the Golden Horn, in the suburb of Pera where the foreign merchants lived, and which was virtually an Italian city.

The provisioning of the city was a major concern of the government. The urban population had to have grain for bread, sheep for meat, and other necessities of life, and to have them at prices it could pay. In principle, the grain produced in a district was to be consumed there, but an exception was made for regions serving a large city. To feed the enormous population of Istanbul, the European coastal regions of the Black Sea, Thrace and northern Anatolia were particularly important. Certain merchants were authorized to trade in grain, to buy it at fixed prices under the supervision of the *qadi*, transport it, to a great extent by sea, and sell it at prices fixed by the government; ships and ports were strictly supervised to make sure the grain was not sent elsewhere.

The wealth of the vast area of production and trade which was the empire flowed partly as revenue into the hands of the government, to support the army and bureaucracy, and partly into private hands. The dominant élite of the city continued to be that combination of large merchants and higher *'ulama* which was a distinctive feature of cities in the world of Islam. The merchants who engaged in long-distance trade, the manufacturers of fine textiles, the *sarrafs* or bankers who lent money to government or merchants profited from the greater volume of trade and the greater ease with which it could be carried on. They had a relatively protected and privileged position, because it was to them that the government would look if it needed to raise money for exceptional purposes. The higher *'ulama* profited not only from the salaries and consideration which they received from the sultan, but also from the *waqfs* which they administered and which augmented their stipends. Their wealth, and that of the merchants, was surpassed, however, by that of the high military and civil officials; they profited from the tax-units assigned to them. Their wealth was precarious, liable to be seized by the sultan if they fell from favour, for they were regarded officially as his slaves, and so not capable of inheriting, but with luck and skill they could pass it on to their families. As the system of tax-farms came in, there seems to have grown up a combination between the holders of rural and urban wealth – officials, merchants and others – to obtain the grant of tax-farms; by the eighteenth century, holders of *malikanes* – grants of farms for life – had become a new landowning class, cultivating land on a commercial basis.

THE ARAB PROVINCES

So far as the history of the Arabic-speaking provinces of the empire has been studied, it seems to show many of the same features as those of the European and Anatolian regions. The population appears to have increased in the period immediately after the Ottoman conquest, because of better security and the general prosperity of the empire, but after that to have remained stationary or even to have declined a little. After Istanbul, the great Arab cities were the largest in the empire. The population of Cairo had increased to perhaps 200,000 by the middle of the sixteenth century and 300,000 by the end of the seventeenth. By the same time Aleppo was a city of some 100,000 inhabitants, Damascus and Tunis possibly smaller but of the same order of magnitude. Baghdad had never recovered from the decline of the irrigation system of southern Iraq, the Mongol invasion, and the movement of the trade of the Indian Ocean from the Gulf to the Red Sea; it had a rather smaller population than the great Syrian cities. Algiers was largely an Ottoman creation, as a strong point against the Spaniards; it had between 50,000 and 100,000 inhabitants by the end of the seventeenth century.

The growth of population was linked with the physical change and expansion of cities. Ottoman rule maintained urban order, with separate police forces for day and night and guards in the various quarters, careful supervision of public services (water supply, cleaning and lighting of streets, fighting of fires), and control of the streets and markets, supervised by the *qadi*. Following the example of the sultan in Istanbul, Ottoman governors and military commanders initiated great public works in the city centres, particularly in the sixteenth century. Mosques and schools, with commercial buildings of which the income was used to maintain them, were built: for example, the foundation of Duqakin-zade Mehmet Pasha in Aleppo, in ·

which three *qaysariyyas*, four *khans* and four *suqs* provided for the upkeep of a great mosque; the Takiyya in Damascus, a complex of mosque, school and hostel for pilgrims built by Süleyman the Magnificent; rather later, the complex built by the military notable Ridwan Bey in Cairo.

The walls of most of the great cities were no longer useful, both because of the order which the Ottomans maintained in the surrounding countryside, and because the development of artillery made them ineffective for defence. Some were pulled down, some fell into disuse; the cities expanded into suburbs of residence for the growing populations. The rich lived in the centre of the city, near the seat of power, or in a quarter where they had influence, or else on the outskirts where the air was fresh and land plentiful. Craftsmen, small traders and proletariat lived in the popular quarters which spread out along the lines of trade: in Aleppo, Judayda, Bab Nayrab and Banqusa; in Damascus, Suq Saruja and the Maydan, stretching along the road leading south, by which grain was brought from Hawran and pilgrims left for the holy cities; in Cairo, Husayniyya lying to the north of the old city centre, along the line by which the Syrian caravans came and went, and Bulaq, the port on the river.

In these quarters of residence, there is some evidence that families, apart from the poorest, owned their own houses, and therefore that population was stable. There seems to have been a tendency in the Ottoman period for the quarters to separate themselves along religious or ethnic lines; Judayda in Aleppo was mainly Christian, there was a Kurdish quarter in Damascus, the district around the Ibn Tulun mosque in Cairo was largely inhabited by people from the Maghrib. Clustered around its mosque, public fountain and small market, the quarter was the focus of life for its inhabitants, united by ceremonies, whether public (the departure and return of pilgrims, Passover or Easter) or private (birth, marriage and death), protected at night by its watchmen and gates. In their economic activities, however, the men at least crossed frontiers and all sections of the population met in the marketplace.

Ottoman fiscal policy and the growth of trade with Europe led to a growth in the importance of Christians and Jews in the life of the cities. Jews were influential as money-lenders and bankers to the central government or provincial governors, and as managers of tax-farms; at another level, as craftsmen and dealers in precious metals. Jewish merchants were important in the trade of Baghdad, and in Tunis and Algiers Jews, many of them of Spanish origin, were prominent in the exchanges with the northern and western Mediterranean countries. The Greek families who lived in the

Phanar quarter of Istanbul controlled much of the trade with the Black Sea, in grain and furs. Armenians played an important part in the silk trade with Iran. In Aleppo and other places where European merchants lived, Christians acted as their intermediaries, helping them to buy goods for export and distribute those brought in from Europe; Syrian Christians were important in the trade between Damietta and the Syrian coast; Coptic Christians worked as accountants and managers for officials and tax-farmers in Egypt.

As the Ottoman government acquired permanent roots in the great provincial centres, there grew up local Ottoman ruling groups. In provinces under direct Ottoman control, the governor and *qadi* were appointed from Istanbul, and changed frequently. Local chancery officials, however, tended to be drawn from Ottoman families who were settled in the provincial cities and handed on their special expertise from father to son. Local janissary forces also were drawn into the community, passing on their privileges from generation to generation, although attempts were made to prevent this by sending new detachments from Istanbul. Governors or leaders of armed forces could, if they remained a long time in the city, create their own households of *mamluks* and install them in important positions.

These local groups were drawn into alliance with merchants and *'ulama*. The greatest owners of urban wealth were the money-changers and bankers and the merchants engaged in the long-distance trade. In spite of the rise in importance of foreign European and of Christian and Jewish merchants, the most important and lucrative trade, that between different parts of the empire or with the countries of the Indian Ocean, was in the hands of Muslim merchants: they controlled the coffee trade of Cairo, that which accompanied the pilgrimage to Mecca, and the caravan-routes which crossed the Syrian and Sahara deserts. Few merchant fortunes seem to have survived many generations; more permanent were the families with a tradition of religious learning. They were an important class numerically: in Egypt by the eighteenth century, *'ulama* in the broadest sense, including all those who exercised functions in law, education or worship, are esti- mated to have numbered as many as 4,000 out of an adult male population of 50,000. In the Arab cities they had a character different from those of Istanbul. The higher *'ulama* of Istanbul were very much a part of the machine of government, trained in imperial schools, appointed into the imperial service and hoping to rise to high positions in it. Those of the Arab cities were of local provenance, however. Many of them were of ancient lineage, going back to Mamluk or even earlier times, and some of them claiming (not always with reason) to be *sayyids*, descendants of the Prophet. They were for the most part educated in local schools (the Azhar in Cairo, the Zaytuna in Tunis, the schools of Aleppo and Damascus), and inherited a language and cultural tradition which went back far beyond the coming of the Ottomans. While retaining a certain independence, they were nevertheless willing to be drawn into the local service of the sultan. The Hanafi *qadi* of the greater cities was normally sent from Istanbul, but his deputies, most of the *muftis*, the *naqib al-ashraf*, and teachers in the *madrasas*, were mainly appointed from the body of the local *'ulama*. In cities where the Muslim population belonged to more than one *madhhab*, each of them would have its *qadi* and *mufti*. In Tunis the whole Muslim population, apart from those of Turkish origin, was Maliki by *madhhab*, and the Maliki *qadi* had an official position comparable to that of the Hanafi.

Between local Ottomans, merchants and local *'ulama*, relations of various kinds existed, giving to each of the groups a permanence and status it might not otherwise have had. To some extent they had a common culture. Sons of merchants were sent to the *madrasa*. Officials and military men might also send their sons there, and so give them a chance of a less precarious future: Bayram, a Turkish officer in the province of Tunis, founded a line of famous scholars; al-Jabarti, the historian of eighteenth-century Egypt, came from a family of merchants. They intermarried with each other, and also had financial connections, entering into partnership in commercial ventures. As the system of tax-farms spread, officials and merchants might co-operate in bidding for them. On the whole, it was the military men and officials who controlled the farms of rural taxes, because these could not be collected without the power and support of the governors. The merchants and *'ulama* had a larger share in the farms of local taxes and dues. *'Ulama* were administrators of important *waqfs*, and so could obtain capital to invest in business ventures or tax-farms.

At another level, a different alliance existed. In spite of the attempt by the sultan to keep his professional army apart from the local population, in course of time they began to mingle. By the end of the seventeenth century janissaries were pursuing crafts and trades, and membership of the corps became a kind of property, conferring a right to privileges and pensions, which could be handed on to sons, or be bought by members of the civil population. The alliance of interests could at times express itself in violent movements, with the coffee houses serving as the point where talk exploded in action. Such action could be of two kinds. At times it was political. In Istanbul, factions in the palace or the civil or military service struggling for power used the janissaries to mobilize an urban mass. In 1703 a rebellion of part of the army turned into a movement of political revolt, in which high officials of some of the great households, janissaries, *'ulama* and merchants – each group with its own interests but all united in the demand for justice – brought about the downfall of the *shaykh al-islam*, whose influence over Sultan Mustafa II they disliked, and then the deposition of the sultan himself. In the provincial cities there could be similar movements, and also spontaneous explosions, when food was short and prices high, and officials of the governor or holders of rural tax-farms were accused of causing artificial shortages by holding back grain until the prices rose. Such movements might have an immediate success, in the replacement of an unpopular governor or official, but the élite of the city viewed them with mixed feelings. The higher *'ulama*, as spokesmen of the urban population, might join the protest, but in the end their interests and sentiments were on the side of settled order.

THE CULTURE OF THE ARAB PROVINCES

The Ottoman conquest left its mark on the cities of the Arabic-speaking provinces in great architectural monuments, some created by the sultans themselves as signs of their grandeur and piety, some by local patrons moved by the force of imitation which is aroused by power and success. In the provincial capitals, mosques were built in the sixteenth and seventeenth centuries in the Ottoman style: a large courtyard led to a domed prayer hall, above which rose one, two or four minarets, long, thin and pointed. The hall might be decorated with coloured tiles in the Iznik style which was in favour at the Ottoman court, with flower designs in green, red and blue. Such were the Khusrawiyya mosque in Aleppo, designed by the greatest of Ottoman architects, Sinan; the mosque of Sulayman Pasha in the Citadel in Cairo; that over the shrine of Sidi Mahraz in Tunis; and the 'New Mosque' in Algiers. The most spectacular of Ottoman provincial creations was the Takiyya in Damascus, a great complex of buildings, also designed by Sinan, and devoted to the needs of the pilgrimage. It was in Damascus that one of the two great pilgrims' caravans assembled, and in a sense it was the more important of the two, because it was there that emissaries of the sultan came, and sometimes members of his family. A chain of caravanserais lay along the pilgrims' route from Istanbul through

Anatolia and northern Syria, and the Takiyya was the most elaborate of them: a domed mosque with two tall minarets symmetrically arranged on either side of it, built in stone with the alternating black and white bands which had long been a feature of the Syrian style; around the courtyard were rooms, refectories and kitchens for pilgrims. In the holy city of Jerusalem, too, Sultan Süleyman left his mark, in the tiles on the external walls of the Dome of the Rock, and the great walls which surrounded the city. Only in Baghdad, among the great Ottoman cities, was the influence of the new style scarcely felt; the older Persian style continued to be dominant. In the other cities, too, smaller mosques and public buildings continued to be constructed in traditional styles, although some Ottoman elements gradually entered into schemes of decoration.

Under Ottoman rule, the place of the Arabic language was not diminished but rather reinforced. The sciences of religion and law were taught in Arabic in the great schools of Istanbul no less than those of Cairo and Damascus. Ottoman authors writing books of certain kinds would tend to write in Arabic. Poetry and secular works might be written in the Ottoman Turkish language which developed in this period as a medium of high culture, but works of religion and law, and even of history and biography, might use Arabic. Thus Hajji Khalifa (1609–57), a government official in Istanbul, wrote in both languages, but his most important works were written in Arabic: a universal history, and a bibliographical dictionary of Arabic authors, *Kashf al-zunun*.

In the great Arab cities the literary tradition continued: not so much poetry and *belles-lettres* as local history, biography and the compilation of works of *fiqh* and *hadith*. The great schools continued to be centres for study of the sciences of religion, but with a difference. With some exceptions, the highest offices in the legal service were held not by graduates of the Azhar or the schools of Damascus and Aleppo, but by those of the imperial foundations in Istanbul; even the chief Hanafi *qadis* of the provincial capitals were for the most part Turks sent from Istanbul, and the highest official positions to which local graduates could aspire were those of deputy judge (*na'ib*) or *mufti*. (In Tunis, however, the strength of the local tradition of Maliki law was such that there were two *qadis*, one Hanafi and one Maliki, equally influential and close to the local ruler, and the latter was a graduate of the great school of Tunis, that of the Zaytuna mosque.)

The coming of the Ottomans brought encouragement to some of the Sufi orders, but also control over them. One of the first acts of Sultan Selim

II after the occupation of Syria was to erect a lavish tomb over the grave of Ibn ʿArabi in Damascus. One of the brotherhoods whose teaching was influenced by that of Ibn ʿArabi, the Khalwatiyya, spread from Anatolia throughout the Ottoman Empire, and gave rise to branches in Syria, Egypt and elsewhere. The Shadhiliyya too was widespread, probably because of the influence of Sufis from the Maghrib; one of the ʿAlami family from Morocco who settled in Jerusalem was the Shadhili deputy there, and his tomb on the Mount of Olives became a place of pilgrimage.

At the end of the seventeenth century, a new influence came from the eastern Islamic world. The Naqshbandi brotherhood had been present in Istanbul and elsewhere from an early period, but in 1670 or thereabouts a Sufi teacher from Samarkand, Murad, who had studied in India, came to live in Istanbul and then Damascus, and brought with him the new Naqshbandi teaching which had been developed by Ahmad al-Sirhindi in northern India in the earlier part of the century. He received favours from the sultan and founded a family in Damascus. Of writers who were touched by this new Naqshbandi teaching, the most famous was ʿAbd al-Ghani al-Nabulsi (1641–1731), a Damascene whose voluminous works included commentaries on the teaching of Ibn ʿArabi and a number of descriptions of journeys to shrines, which are also records of spiritual progress.

Outside the Sunni culture of the great cities, which was patronized by the Ottoman authorities, other forms of religious culture continued to exist. As the Ottomans became more strictly Sunni, the position of Shiʿis in Syria became more difficult. Their tradition of learning had by now receded to the small towns and villages of southern Lebanon, but was still carried on there by families of scholars. One writer of the early Ottoman period, Zayn al-Din al-ʿAmili (d. 1539), was summoned to Istanbul and executed; he is known in Shiʿi tradition as 'the second martyr' (al-shahid al-thani). Shiʿi learning continued to flourish, however, beyond the range of direct Ottoman authority, in the holy cities of Iraq and in the districts of al-Hasa and Bahrayn on the western side of the Gulf. It was given a new strength by the proclamation of Shiʿism as the official religion of the Safavid Empire: the shah's government needed judges and teachers, and could not find them in Iran itself; scholars therefore went from Iraq, Bahrayn and southern Lebanon to the shah's court, and some of them held important positions. One of them, Nur al-Din ʿAli al-Karaki from Lebanon (c. 1466–1534), wrote extensive and influential works on the problems created by the adoption of Shiʿism as a state religion: whether the faithful should pay taxes to the ruler, whether the *'ulama* should serve him, and whether the Friday prayers should be celebrated in the absence of the *imam*.

In the seventeenth century the world of Shi'i scholarship was torn by a conflict about the place of *ijtihad* in the formation of law. While the dominant position had been that of the Usulis, who accepted the need for rational argument in interpretation and application of the precepts of the Qur'an and Hadith, there now rose another school of thought, that of the Akhbaris, who wished to limit the use of rational interpretation by means of *qiyas* (analogy), and laid emphasis upon the need to accept the literal meaning of the tradition of the *imams*. This school was dominant in the holy cities during the second part of the century.

Influences coming from outside were also felt in the Jewish communities of the Ottoman Empire, but they were of another kind. The Christian reconquest of Andalus led to the destruction of the Jewish communities there. They went into exile, some in Italy and elsewhere in Europe, but many of them in Istanbul and other cities of the Ottoman Empire. They brought with them the distinctive traditions of Sephardic or Andalusian Jewry, and in particular the mystical interpretation of the faith, the Kabbala, which had been developed there. From the middle of the sixteenth century onwards, the most creative centre of mystical thought was Safad in Palestine. A thinker of great originality, Isaac Luria (1534-72), came to Safad at the end of his life and had a deep influence on the followers of the Kabbala there.

One of the marks of his teaching was a certain doctrine about the universe. Its life had become disordered, and it was the task of human beings, but particularly of Jews, to help God in the work of redemption, by living a life in accordance with the Will of God. Such teaching created an apocalyptic expectation, that redemption was near, and the atmosphere was propitious for the emergence of a redeemer. In 1665 Sabbatai Sevi (1626-76), born in Izmir and known as one who performed strange acts while in a state of illumination, was recognized by a local prophet as the Messiah while on a visit to the Holy Land. His fame spread almost at once throughout the Jewish world, even in northern and eastern Europe, where Jewish communities were disturbed by massacres in Poland and Russia. The return of the Jews to the Holy Land seemed near, but the hopes collapsed almost at once: summoned to appear before the sultan's *divan*, Sabbatai Sevi was given the choice between death and conversion to Islam. He chose conversion, and, while some of his followers remained faithful, most could no longer believe in him.

Among the Christian populations of the Arabic-speaking provinces, and particularly those of Syria, some change in ideas and knowledge took place during these centuries. This was brought about by the spread of Roman Catholic missions. They had been in the area intermittently for a long time; the Franciscans had been there since the fifteenth century as custodians of the Catholic shrines in the Holy Land; Jesuits, Carmelites, Dominicans and others came later. From the late sixteenth century a number of colleges were set up by the Papacy in Rome for training priests of the eastern Churches: the Maronite and Greek Colleges in 1584, the College of the Congregation for the Propagation of the Faith in 1627. In the seventeenth century the number of missionary priests in countries of the Middle East increased. This process had two results. It expanded the numbers of those in the eastern Churches who accepted the authority of the Pope while wishing to retain their own liturgies, customs and religious law. The Maronites had been in this position since the time of the Crusades, and in the early eighteenth century they made a concordat with the Papacy by which their relations were defined. In the other Churches, the question of papal supremacy was more divisive; in Aleppo in northern Syria, in particular, there were conflicts between Catholic and non-Catholic groups for control of the Churches. By the early eighteenth century a virtual separation had taken place. From that time there were two lines of patriarchs and bishops in the Orthodox Patriarchate of Antioch, one recognizing the primacy of the Ecumenical Patriarch of Constantinople, the other 'Uniate' or 'Greek Catholic', that is to say, accepting the authority of the Pope. Similar developments occurred at different times in the Nestorian, Syrian Orthodox, Armenian and Coptic Churches, although it was not until the early nineteenth century that the Ottoman sultan formally recognized the Uniates as separate *millets* or communities.

The second result was the development of a distinctive Christian culture expressed in Arabic. Something of this had long existed, but now it changed its nature. Priests educated in the colleges in Rome came back with a knowledge of Latin and Italian; some of them took to the serious study of Arabic; some established monastic orders on the western model, especially in the untrammelled atmosphere of the Lebanese mountains, and these became centres both for cultivation of the soil and for the study of theology and history.

BEYOND THE EMPIRE: ARABIA, THE SUDAN, MOROCCO

Beyond the Ottoman frontiers in Arabia lay regions with small merchant towns or ports and sparse countryside, where urban resources were limited and government could be only on a small scale: the principalities of the oasis towns of central and eastern Arabia, and the ports of the west coast of the Gulf. One of them was more important than the others. In the south-eastern corner of the peninsula, Oman, there was a comparatively stable and prosperous rural community in the fertile seaward mountain valleys of Jabal Akh-ar. The inhabitants were Ibadis, and their *imamate*, which was restored in the early seventeenth century under a dynasty from the Ya'ribi tribe, gave a certain precarious unity to the society of the mountain valleys. On the coast, the port of Masqat became an important centre for the trade of the Indian Ocean; it was captured by the Omanis from the Portuguese in the mid-seventeenth century, and Omani merchants established themselves along the east African coast. In these Arabian fringes the Ottomans did not exercise suzerainty, but one of the ports of the Gulf, Bahrayn, was under Iranian rule from 1602 to 1783. Here, and in other parts of the Gulf, much of the population was Shi'i; the region of al-Hasa north of Bahrayn was indeed an important centre of Shi'i learning. In the south-west of the peninsula, Yemen was no longer under Ottoman control; here too the ports had trade with India and south-east Asia, particularly in coffee, and southern Arabian emigrants served in the armies of Indian rulers.

South of Egypt, Ottoman authority was limited: it extended up the Nile valley as far as the Third Cataract, and on the Red Sea coast there were garrisons at Sawakin and Massawa, subject to the governor of Jidda. Beyond them, there arose a sultanate of comparatively great power and stability, that of the Funj, established in the area of settled cultivation lying between the Blue and White Niles; this was to last for more than three centuries (from the early sixteenth century to 1821).

Beyond the western frontier of the empire, in the far west of the Maghrib, there lay a state of a different kind – the ancient empire of Morocco. Ottoman naval operations did not extend beyond the Mediterranean into the waters of the Atlantic, and the Ottoman government did not implant itself in the coastal parts of Morocco, or impose control over the mountains and plateaux of the Rif and Atlas. Here local authorities, some of them with a religious sanction, held sway; in certain conditions a crystallization of local forces around a leadership with a religious sanction could produce a larger political entity. In the fifteenth century there emerged a new factor which changed the nature of such movements: the Christian reconquest of Spain and Portugal threatened to spill over into Morocco and also led to the immigration of Muslims from Andalus into the Moroccan cities. Any movement which seemed able and willing to defend the country against the new crusaders had therefore a special appeal. Such movements from now onwards tended to claim legitimacy by inserting themselves into a central spiritual lineage of the Muslim world. In 1510 a family which claimed descent from the Prophet, that of the Sa'did *sharifs*, was able to found a state in the southern region of Sus, obtain control of the market town of Marrakish, and then move northwards. The Sa'dids created a system of government which was able to rule most of the country, although in a limited way. The court and central administration, the *makhzan*, were to some extent modelled on those of the Ottomans. The sultan had two kinds of force to rely on: his personal army of black soldiers drawn from the inhabitants of slave status in the southern oases and the valley of the Niger river, and certain Arab groups in the plains, the *jaysh* or 'military' tribes; these were exempted from taxation on condition they collected the taxes and kept order in the countryside and, on occasion, in the cities. This was a time of increasing prosperity: the trading cities of the north, the Atlantic ports and the inland cities of Fez and Titwan revived, partly because of the coming of the Andalusians, who brought industrial skills and contacts with other parts of the Mediterranean world. After a period in the mid-sixteenth century when Spain, Portugal and the Ottomans struggled for control of the country, the Sa'dids were able to maintain a certain independence, and even to expand southwards. From their stronghold in Marrakish the sultans were able to control the west African trade in gold and slaves; at the end of the sixteenth century they conquered and held for a short time the towns on the Saharan trade-routes as far as Timbuktu.

The government of the *sharifs* was always weaker than that of the Ottoman sultans, however. Urban wealth and power were more limited. The most important urban centre, Fez, was a city with a considerable tradition of urban learning, but only half the size of Aleppo, Damascus or Tunis, and very much smaller than Istanbul or Cairo. Of the other towns, the ports of the Atlantic coast were centres of foreign trade and privateering; the captains of the twin ports of Rabat and Salé were for a time in rivalry with those of Algiers. Neither the trade of the towns nor the production of the countryside was sufficient, however, to enable the sultan to maintain an elaborate bureaucracy or a large standing army. Beyond certain limited regions, he exercised some power by occasional military expeditions, political manipulation, and the prestige of his lineage from the Prophet. He and his *makhzan* resembled less the centralized bureaucratic governments of the Ottoman Empire and some European states of his time than that of a wandering medieval monarchy: the ruler, his court and ministers, his few secretaries and treasury, and his personal troops, made a regular progression through the nearer country districts, collecting enough money to pay the army and trying by delicate political manoeuvres to retain at least a final sovereignty over as wide an area as possible. Even in the cities his hold was precarious. He had to control Fez, Maknas and others in order to survive: their *'ulama* gave him legitimacy, and he needed the income from dues on trade and industry. To some extent he could rule them through appointed officials, or by giving or withholding favours, but in a sense he remained external to the cities. The people of the city did not want the sultan's power to be wholly absent, for they needed it to protect trade-routes and defend them from European attacks on the coast, but they wished the relationship to be on their own terms: not to pay taxes, not to be overawed by the *jaysh* tribes around them, to have a governor and *qadi* of their own choosing or at least acceptable to them. At times they were able to mobilize their forces for these purposes.

With such limits upon their resources and power, the Sa'did *sharifs* were not able to create a permanent, self-perpetuating system of government like that of the Ottomans and Safavids. After a century or so, there was a rift in the family, and once more there arose local combinations of forces around leaders claiming legitimacy in religious terms. After a period of conflict, in which the Ottomans in Algiers and European merchants in the ports intervened, another family of *sharifs*, the Filalis or 'Alawis from the Tafilalt oasis, were able to unite the whole country by political skill and with the help of some of the Arab tribes: first the east, where they acted as leaders of opposition to the spread of Ottoman power, then Fez and the north, then the centre and south by 1670. (This dynasty has continued to rule Morocco until today.)

Under one of the early rulers of the dynasty, Mawlay Isma'il (1672–1727), the government took the form it was to retain more or less until the beginning of the twentieth century: a royal household composed largely of black slaves or others from the south; ministers drawn from leading families of Fez or the *jaysh* tribes; an army of European converts, blacks of slave origin, the *jaysh* tribes of the plains; and urban levies in times of need. The sultan carried on a struggle against two dangers: the lingering fear of attack from Spain and Portugal, and the expansion of Ottoman power from Algiers. With its army, its religious legitimacy and its successful resistance of such dangers, it was able for a time to generate the power which enabled it to move the balance between government and city in its favour, and to exercise political control over much of the countryside.

The Christian conquest of Andalus impoverished the civilization of Morocco. The final expulsion of Muslims from Spain in the seventeenth century brought more Andalusian settlers into the Moroccan cities, but they no longer carried with them a culture which would enrich the Maghrib. At the same time, contacts with the eastern parts of the Muslim world were limited by distance and the barrier of the Atlas mountains. Some Moroccans did indeed go eastwards, for trade or on pilgrimage; gathering in the oasis of Tafilalt, they would proceed along the North African coast or by sea to Egypt, where they would join the pilgrims' caravan which assembled in Cairo. Some of the merchants might remain there, and some of the scholars stay to study in the mosques and schools of Cairo, Madina or Jerusalem. A few of them became teachers themselves, and founded learned families; such was the 'Alami family in Jerusalem, reputed to be descended from a scholar and Sufi teacher from Jabal 'Alam in northern Morocco. Few scholars from the east, however, visited the far west or settled there.

The culture of Morocco by this time was therefore a distinctive and limited one. Poets and men of letters were few and without distinction. The tradition of writing history and biography continued, however. In the eighteenth century al-Zayyani (1734–c. 1833), a man who had held important posts and travelled widely, wrote a universal history, the first to be written by a Moroccan, which showed some knowledge of European history and more of Ottoman.

In the schools, the main discipline studied was Maliki *fiqh*, with its ancillary sciences. It was taught in the great mosque of al-Qarawiyyin in Fez, with its attached *madrasas*, and also at Marrakish and elsewhere; a compendium of Maliki law, the *Mukhtasar* of al-Khalil, was particularly important. In these cities, as elsewhere in the world of Islam, there were great families of scholars which preserved the tradition of high learning from one generation to another; such a one was the Fasi family, of Andalusian origin but settled in Fez since the sixteenth century.

The influence of the jurists of the cities was extended to some degree into the countryside, where *'ulama* might act as notaries, to give formal expression to contracts and agreements. The main source of intellectual sustenance, however, was provided by teachers and spiritual guides belonging to Sufi brotherhoods, and in particular those linked with the Shadhiliyya. This had been founded by al-Shadhili (d. 1258), a Moroccan by birth who had settled in Egypt. It spread widely in Egypt, and was brought back to Morocco by al-Jazuli in the fifteenth century (d. *c.* 1465); it was a member of the Fasi family who brought it to Fez. The influence of the way taught by the Shadhiliyya and other brotherhoods was felt at every level of society. Among the learned, it provided an explanation of the inner meaning of the Qur'an and an analysis of the spiritual states on the path which led towards experiential knowledge of God. Teachers and holy men, whether affiliated with a brotherhood or not, held out hopes of intercession with God to assist men and women in the trials of life on earth. Here as elsewhere, the tombs of holy men were centres of pilgrimage; among the most famous were those of Mawlay Idris, reputed founder of Fez, in a shrine city named after him, and of his son, also called Idris, in Fez itself.

Here as elsewhere, too, men of learning and piety tried to preserve the idea of a just Muslim society against the excesses of superstition or worldly ambition. A study by a French scholar has revealed the life and teaching of one such, al-Hasan al-Yusi (1631–91). A man of the south, he was drawn into the learned order and taught in Fez for a time, by way of the schools in Marrakish and elsewhere. His writings are varied, and include a series of conversations (*muhadarat*) in which he tried to define and preserve the middle way of the learned and pious *'ulama* between opposing temptations. On the one hand stood the temptations and corruptions of power. In a famous essay, in which he expressed the *'ulama*'s own view of their role, he warned Sultan Isma'il against the tyranny practised in his name by his officials. The earth, he proclaimed, belonged to God, and all men are His slaves: if the ruler treats his people with justice, he is God's deputy on earth, the shadow of God over His slaves. He has three tasks: to collect taxes justly, to pursue *jihad* by maintaining the strength of the kingdom's defences, and to prevent oppression by the strong over the weak. All three are neglected in his kingdom: tax-collectors are exercising oppression, the defences are neglected and officials oppress the people. The lesson which he draws is a familiar one: once prophecy is ended, the *'ulama* remain as guardians of the truth; let the sultan do as the caliphs did, and take the advice of trustworthy exponents of the holy law.[1]

On the other side of the middle way there was the spiritual corruption brought to ordinary people in the countryside by false and ignorant Sufi teachers:

In earlier times, the words of such men as those of the Qadiri and Shadhili orders, and of the masters of spiritual states, struck the ears of the common folk and touched their hearts. These words enthralled crowds, which have thrown themselves into imitation of them. But what can you expect of an ignorant man who gives rein to his own fancies and does not even know the externals of the holy law, let alone understanding its inner meaning, and who occupies no high spiritual station? You find him talking vehemently, referring to knowledge both rational and revealed. You find this above all among the sons of holy men, who wish to adorn themselves with the graces of their fathers, and make their adherents follow them without any right or truth, but solely for the sake of the vanities of this world . . . Such a man will not allow people to love anyone for the sake of God, or know or follow anyone except himself . . . He promises them paradise, whatever their acts may have been, because of his intercession for them on the Day of Judgement . . . The ignorant folk are satisfied with this, and remain in his service, son after father.[2]

CHAPTER 15

The Changing Balance of Power
in the Eighteenth Century

CENTRAL AND LOCAL AUTHORITIES

In the seventh century the Arabs created a new world into which other peoples were drawn. In the nineteenth and twentieth, they were themselves drawn into a new world created in western Europe. This of course is too simple a way of describing a very complicated process, and the explanations of it can be too simple too.

One explanation which is commonly given would run like this: by the eighteenth century the ancient kingdoms of the Muslim world and the societies they ruled were in decline, while the strength of Europe was growing, and this made possible an expansion of goods, ideas and power which led to the imposition of European control, and then to a revival of the strength and vitality of Arab societies in a new form.

The idea of decline is a difficult one to use, however. Some Ottoman writers themselves used it. From the late sixteenth century onwards, those who compared what they saw around them with what they believed to have existed earlier often said that things were not what they had been in an earlier age of justice, and the institutions and code of social morality on which Ottoman strength had rested were in decay. Some of them read Ibn Khaldun; in the seventeenth century the historian Naima reflected some of his ideas, and in the eighteenth part of his *Muqaddima* was translated into Turkish.

For such writers, the remedy lay in a return to the institutions of the real or imagined golden age. For Sari Mehmed Pasha (d. 1717), at one time treasurer or *defterdar*, writing at the beginning of the eighteenth century, what was important was that the old distinction between rulers and ruled should be restored and that the rulers should act justly:

The entering of the *reaya* into the military class must be avoided carefully. Disorder is sure to come when those who are not sons or grandsons of *sipahis* are all at once made into *sipahis* . . . Let [the officials] neither oppress the poor *reaya* nor cause them to be vexed by the demand for new impositions in addition to the well-known yearly taxes which they are accustomed to give . . . The people of the provinces and dwellers in the towns should be protected and preserved by the removal of injustices and very great attention should be paid to making prosperous the condition of the subjects . . . Yet too much indulgence must not be shown to the *reaya*.[1]

Rather than speaking of decline, it might be more correct to say that what had occurred was an adjustment of Ottoman methods of rule and the balance of power within the empire to changing circumstances. By the end of the eighteenth century the Ottoman dynasty had existed for 500 years and had been ruling most of the Arab countries for almost 300; it was only to be expected that its ways of government and the extent of its control would change from one place and time to another.

There were two kinds of change which were particularly important by the eighteenth century. In the central government of Istanbul, power had tended to move from the household of the sultan to an oligarchy of high civil officials in or around the offices of the grand vizir. Although different groups among them competed for power, they were linked with each other, and with the high dignitaries of the judicial and religious service, in more than one way. They had a common culture, in which there were Arabic and Persian as well as Turkish elements. They shared a concern for the strength and welfare of the empire and the society which it protected. They were not held aloof from society, as the household slaves had been, but were involved in its economic life through their control of religious endowments and tax-farms, and association with merchants for investment in trade and land.

The professional army also had been drawn into society; janissaries became merchants and artisans, and merchants and artisans acquired membership or affiliation with janissary corps. This process was connected, as cause and as effect, with the other important change: the emergence in the provincial capitals of local ruling groups, which were able to control the tax-resources of the provinces and use them to form their own local armies. Such groups existed in most provincial capitals, except those which could be easily controlled from Istanbul. They could be of different kinds. In some places there were ruling families, with their households and dependants; their members were able to obtain recognition from Istanbul from one generation to another. In others, there were self-perpetuating groups of *mamluks*: these were men from the Balkans or Caucasus who had come to a city as military slaves or apprentices in the household of a governor or army commander, had risen to important positions in the local government or army, and been able to pass their power on to other members of the same group. Such local rulers were able to make alliances of interests with merchants, land-holders and *'ulama* of the city. They maintained the order which was necessary for the prosperity of the city, and in return they profited from it.

This was the situation in most of the Ottoman provinces in Anatolia and Europe, except for those which could be easily reached from Istanbul, and in virtually all the Arab provinces. Aleppo in northern Syria, lying as it did on a major imperial road, and with comparatively easy access from Istanbul, remained under direct control; but in Baghdad and at Acre on the coast of Palestine members of *mamluk* groups held the post of governor; in Damascus and Mosul, families which had risen in the Ottoman service were able to fill the office of governor for several generations. In Hijaz, the *sharifs* of Mecca, a family claiming descent from the Prophet, ruled the holy cities, although there was an Ottoman governor at Jidda on the coast. In Yemen, there was no longer an Ottoman presence, and such central authority as did exist was in the hands of a family of *imams* recognized by the Zaydi inhabitants.

In Egypt the situation was more complicated. There was still a governor sent from Istanbul, and not allowed to remain too long in case he should acquire too much power; but most high offices, and control of the tax-farms, had fallen into the hands first of rival groups of *mamluks* and army officers, and then of one of them. In the three Ottoman provinces in the Maghrib, leaders of the local armies had seized power in one way or another. In Tripoli and Tunis, military commanders created dynasties, recognized by Istanbul as governors but holding the local title of *bey*. In Algiers, the military corps appointed successive rulers (the *deys*); but in time the *dey* was able to create a group of high officials which was able to perpetuate itself and keep the office of *dey* in its hands. In all three, officials, army officers and merchants had been united at first by the common interest of equipping privateering ships (the 'Barbary pirates') to capture the ships of European states with which the Ottoman sultan was at war and sell their goods; but this practice had virtually come to an end by the late eighteenth century.

However great these changes, they should not be exaggerated. In Istanbul the sultan still had final power. Even the strongest official could be deposed and executed, and his goods confiscated; the sultan's officials were still regarded as his 'slaves'. With some exceptions, even the strongest local rulers were content to remain within the Ottoman system; they were 'local Ottomans', not independent monarchs. The Ottoman state was not alien to them, it was still the embodiment of the Muslim community (or at least of a large part of it). Local rulers could have their own dealings with foreign powers, but they would use their strength to further the major interests and defend the frontiers of the empire. Moreover, the central government still had a residue of strength in most parts of the empire. It could give or withhold formal recognition; even the *bey* of Tunis and the *dey* of Algiers wished to be formally invested by the sultan as governor. It could make use of rivalries between different provinces, or different members of a family or a *mamluk* group, or between the provincial ruler and local notables. Where it could use the great imperial roads or the sea-routes of the eastern Mediterranean, it could send an army to reassert its power; this happened in Egypt, briefly, in the 1780s. The pilgrimage, organized by the governor of Damascus, carrying gifts from Istanbul to the inhabitants of the holy cities, guarded by an Ottoman force, moving down a road maintained by Ottoman garrisons, was still an annual assertion of Ottoman sovereignty all along the way from Istanbul through Syria and western Arabia to the heart of the Muslim world.

A new balance of forces had been created in the empire. It was precarious, and each party to it tried to increase its power when it could; but it was able to maintain an alliance of interests between central government, provincial Ottomans, and the social groups which possessed wealth and prestige, the merchants and *'ulama*. There is evidence that in some regions this combination of strong local governments and active urban élites maintained or increased agricultural production, the basis of urban prosperity and of the strength of governments. This seems to have happened in the European provinces; the growth of population in central Europe increased the demand for foodstuffs and raw materials, and the Balkan provinces were able to meet it. In Tunisia and Algeria grain and hides were produced for export to Marseille and Livorno; in northern Palestine and western Anatolia cotton production increased to meet the demand from France. In most provinces, however, control by the local government and its urban allies did not extend far from the cities. In the Maghrib, Ottoman power did not spread far inland into the high plateau. In the Fertile Crescent, some tribes of camel-breeding nomads had moved northwards from central Arabia; the area used for pasture expanded at the expense of that used for cultivation, and so did the area in which tribal leaders rather than urban officials controlled the cultivators who remained.

In lands beyond the frontier of the empire processes of the same kind had taken place. In Oman a new ruling family, which at first claimed the *imamate* of the Ibadis, established themselves at Masqat on the coast, and an alliance of rulers and merchants was able to spread Omani trade around the coasts of the Indian Ocean. In other ports of the Gulf, Kuwait, Bahrayn and some smaller ones, ruling families linked closely with merchant communities emerged. In the Sudan, to the south of Egypt, there were two longlived sultanates: one, that of the Funj, lay in the fertile land between the Blue and White Niles, where trade-routes running from Egypt to Ethiopia crossed those going from west Africa to the Red Sea; the other was that of Darfur, lying west of the Nile, on a trade-route which went from west Africa to Egypt.

In Morocco, the extreme Maghrib, the 'Alawis had been ruling since the middle of the seventeenth century, but without the firmly based military or bureaucratic strength which even the local Ottoman rulers could rely on. Like their predecessors, they could never wholly dominate the city of Fez with its powerful merchant families, its *'ulama* clustered around the Qarawiyyin mosque, and its saintly families guarding the shrines of their ancestors; outside the cities they could at best manage to control parts of the countryside by political manipulation and the prestige of their descent. Being insecurely based, their strength fluctuated; great at the beginning of the eighteenth century, it then grew weaker, but was reviving in the second half of the century.

ARAB OTTOMAN SOCIETY AND CULTURE

In the eighteenth century, the imprint of Ottoman power and culture upon the Arab provinces appears to have gone deeper. It took root in the cities by way of what have been called 'local Ottoman' families and groups. On the one hand, military commanders and civil officials settled in provincial capitals and founded families or households which were able to retain positions in the Ottoman service from one generation to another; the local ruling families and Mamluk groups were only the upper level of a phenomenon which also existed at other levels. Some of them held positions in the local administration, some acquired wealth through the acquisition of tax-farms, and some sent their sons to local religious schools and from there into the legal service. On the other hand, members of local families with a tradition of religious learning tended increasingly to obtain posts in the religious and legal service, and through this to acquire control over *waqfs*, including the most lucrative ones which had been established for the benefit of the holy cities or of institutions founded by the sultans; many of these were diverted from their original purpose to private use. It has been estimated that, while there were seventy-five official positions in the religio-legal system in Damascus in the early eighteenth century, by the middle of the century the number had risen to over three hundred. A concomitant of this was that many local families which by tradition adhered to the Shafi'i or Maliki *madhhabs* came to accept the Hanafi code, the one which was officially recognized by the Ottoman sultans. (This does not appear to have occurred in the Maghrib, however; there the bulk of the population, except for those of Turkish origin, remained Maliki.)

By the late eighteenth century, therefore, there existed, at least in some of the great Arab cities, powerful and more or less permanent families of local 'notables', some of them more Turkish and others more Arab. An expression of their power and stability was the construction of elaborate houses and palaces in Algiers, Tunis, Damascus and elsewhere. One of the most magnificent was the 'Azm palace in Damascus, a group of rooms and suites built around two courtyards, one for the men of the family and their visitors, the other for women and domestic life. On a smaller scale, but still splendid, were the houses built in Judayda, a Christian quarter in Aleppo, by families enriched through the growing trade with Europe. In the mountains of south Lebanon the palace of the *amir* of Lebanon, Bashir II, was built by artisans from Damascus: an unexpected urban palace on a distant hillside. Such houses were built by local architects and craftsmen, and architectural design and style were expressions of local traditions, but here too, as in the mosques, the influence of Ottoman decorative styles was to be seen, particularly in the use of tiles; mingled with this there was a certain imitation of European styles, as in wall-paintings, and the use of Bohemian glass and other goods manufactured in Europe for the Middle Eastern market. In Tunis, a French traveller in the early part of the century found that the ancient palace of the *beys*, the Bardo, had been provided with furniture in the Italian style.

The survival and social power of the families of notables were bound up with the local schools. A study of Cairo has suggested that a considerable part of the male population – perhaps as many as half – may have been literate, but few of the women. This implies that the elementary schools, the *kuttabs*, were numerous. At a higher level, a historian of the time mentions about twenty *madrasas* and the same number of mosques where higher teaching was carried on. The central institution, the Azhar mosque, seems to have flourished at the expense of some of the smaller and less well-endowed mosques and *madrasas*; it drew students from Syria, Tunisia, Morocco and the regions of the upper Nile. In the same way, in Tunis the Zaytuna mosque grew in size and importance during the century; its library was enlarged, and its endowments were supplemented by the proceeds of the *jizya*, the poll tax on non-Muslims.

In such higher schools, the ancient curriculum was still followed. The most important studies were Qur'anic exegesis, Hadith and *fiqh*, for which collections of *fatwas* as well as formal treatises were used; linguistic subjects were studied as an introduction to them. The basic doctrines of religion were taught mainly in later compendia, and the works of Ibn 'Arabi and other Sufis seem to have been widely read. Such rational sciences as mathematics and astronomy were studied and taught for the most part outside the formal curriculum, but there seems to have been great interest in them.

Within the limits of a rather rigid and unchanging curriculum, there was still room for literary production of high quality. In Tunis, a family founded by a Turkish soldier who had come to the country with the Ottoman expeditionary force in the sixteenth century produced four men in successive generations, all of them called Muhammad Bayram, who were well-known scholars and Hanafi *muftis*. In Syria, the family founded by Murad, the Naqshbandi from central Asia, also held the office of Hanafi *mufti* for more than one generation. One of them, Muhammad Khalil al-Muradi (1760–91), carried on a specifically Syrian tradition of collecting biographies of men of learning and renown; his biographical dictionary covers the twelfth Islamic century.

For help in collecting biographies, Muradi turned to a famous scholar resident in Egypt, Murtada al-Zabidi (1732–91). His letter expresses the self-consciousness of one who is aware that he stands at the end of a long tradition which must be preserved:

When I was in Istanbul with one of its great men . . . there was talk of history, and its decline in our age, and the lack of concern for it among the men of this time, although it is the greatest of the arts; we lamented it sadly.[2]

Of Indian origin, Zabidi had lived for a time in Zabid in Yemen, an important stopping-place on the route from south and south-east Asia to the holy cities, and a significant centre of learning at the time; he had moved to Cairo, and from there his influence radiated far and wide, because of his reputation for having the power of intercession, and through his writings. Among them were works on Hadith, a commentary on Ghazali's *Ihya 'ulum al-din*, and a great Arabic lexicon.

Murtada al-Zabidi in his turn asked a younger scholar, 'Abd al-Rahman al-Jabarti (1753–1825) to help him in collecting biographical material, and this was the impulse which turned his mind to the writing of history; in due course he was to produce the last great chronicle in the traditional style, covering not only political events but also the lives of scholars and famous men.

In the Shi'i world, too, the tradition of high learning continued, but scholars were sharply divided. Throughout most of the century the Akhbari school of thought was dominant among the scholars of the holy cities, but towards the end there was a revival of the Usuli school, under the influence of two important scholars, Muhammad Baqir al-Bihbihani (d. 1791) and Ja'far Kashif al-Ghita (c. 1741–1812); supported by the local rulers in Iraq and Iran, for whom the flexibility of the Usulis offered some advantages, this was to become once more the leading school. The Akhbariyya continued to be strong in some regions of the Gulf, however. Towards the end of the century both Usulis and Akhbaris were challenged by a new movement, the Shaykhiyya, which grew out of the mystical tradition, that of spiritual interpretation of the holy books, which was endemic in Shi'ism: this was condemned by both the other schools, and regarded as outside the bounds of *imami* Shi'ism.

There is no indication that the thought either of Sunnis or of Shi'is was penetrated at this time by the new ideas which were emerging in Europe. Some of the Syrian and Lebanese priests who had acquired a knowledge of Latin, Italian or French were aware of the Catholic theology and the European scholarship of their time. A few of them taught in Europe, and became scholars of European reputation: the most famous was Yusuf al-Sim'ani (Joseph Assemani, 1687–1768), a Maronite from Lebanon, a student of Syriac and Arabic manuscripts who became librarian of the Vatican Library.

THE WORLD OF ISLAM

Whether they lived within the Ottoman Empire or outside its frontiers, those who professed faith in Islam and lived through the medium of the Arabic language had something in common which was deeper than political allegiance or shared interests. Among them, and between them and those who spoke Turkish or Persian or the other languages of the Muslim world, there was the common sense of belonging to an enduring and unshaken world created by the final revelation of God through the Prophet Muhammad, and expressing itself in different forms of thought and social activity: the Qur'an, the Traditions of the Prophet, the system of law or ideal social behaviour, the Sufi orders oriented towards the tombs of their founders, the schools, the travels of scholars in search of learning, the circulation of books, the fast of Ramadan, observed at the same time and in the same way by Muslims everywhere, and the pilgrimage which brought many thousands from all over the Muslim world to Mecca at the same moment of the year. All these activities preserved the sense of belonging to a world which contained all that was necessary for welfare in this life and salvation in the next.

Once more, a structure which lasts for ages must be expected to change, and the Abode of Islam as it existed in the eighteenth century was different in many ways from what it had been earlier. One wave of change came from the far east of the Muslim world, from northern India, where the other great Sunni dynasty, the Mughals, ruled Muslims and Hindus. Here a number of thinkers, of whom the most famous was Shah Waliullah of Delhi (1703–62), were teaching that rulers should rule in accordance with the precepts of Islam, and that Islam should be purified by teachers using their *ijtihad* on the basis of the Qur'an and Hadith; the different *madhhabs* should be merged in a single system of morality and law, and the devotions of the Sufis should be kept within its bounds. Scholars and ideas moving westwards from India met and mingled with others in the great schools and in the holy cities at the time of pilgrimage, and from this mingling there came a strengthening of that kind of Sufism which laid its emphasis on strict observance of the *shari'a*, no matter how far advanced a Muslim might be on the road which led to experience of God. The Naqshbandiyya had spread earlier from central Asia and India into the Ottoman countries, and its influence was growing. Another order, the Tijaniyya, was founded in Algeria and Morocco by a teacher returning from Mecca and Cairo, and spread into west Africa.

There was another movement which might have seemed of less importance at the time, but was to have wider significance later. It arose in central Arabia in the early eighteenth century, when a religious reformer, Muhammad ibn 'Abd al-Wahhab (1703–92), began to preach the need for Muslims to return to the teaching of Islam as understood by the followers of Ibn Hanbal: strict obedience to the Qur'an and Hadith as they were interpreted by responsible scholars in each generation, and rejection of all that could be regarded as illegitimate innovations. Among these innovations was the reverence given to dead saints as intercessors with God, and the special devotions of the Sufi orders. The reformer made an alliance with Muhammad ibn Sa'ud, ruler of a small market town, Dir'iyya, and this led to the formation of a state which claimed to live under the guidance of the *shari'a* and tried to bring the pastoral tribes all around it under its guidance too. In so doing it asserted the interests of the frail urban society of the oases against the pastoral hinterland, but at the same time it rejected the claims of the Ottomans to be the protectors of the authentic Islam. By the first years of the nineteenth century the armies of the new state had expanded; they had sacked the Shi'i shrines in south-western Iraq and occupied the holy cities of Hijaz.

CHANGING RELATIONS WITH EUROPE

Living, growing, self-sufficient and unchallenged as the world of Islam may have seemed to most of those who belonged to it, by the last quarter of the eighteenth century at least some members of the Ottoman élite knew that it was threatened by forces which were bringing about a change in its relations with the world around it. The Ottoman government had always been aware of a world beyond itself: to the east, the Shi'i Empire of Iran and beyond that the empire of the Mughals; to the north and west, the Christian states. From an early time it had been brought into contact with western and central Europe; it controlled the eastern and southern shores of the Mediterranean, and its western frontier lay in the basin of the Danube. The contacts were not only those of enmity. That certainly existed, when the Ottoman fleet fought the Venetians and Spaniards for control of the Mediterranean, and the army came to the gates of Vienna; to that extent, the relationship could be expressed in terms of crusade on the one side and *jihad* on the other. There were other kinds of relationship, however. Trade was mainly carried on by European merchants, Venetians and Genoese in the earlier Ottoman centuries, British and French in the eighteenth. There were alliances with European kings who shared a common enemy with the sultan; in particular with France against the Habsburgs of Austria and Spain. In 1569 France was given concessions (Capitulations), regulating the activities of merchants and missionaries; these were modelled upon earlier privileges given to merchants of some of the Italian cities, and were later given to other European powers. The main states of Europe had permanent embassies and consulates in the empire, which became part of the states-system of Europe, although it did not itself send permanent missions to European capitals until much later. (In the same way, Morocco and England had good relations when both were hostile to Spain.)

Until the middle of the eighteenth century, the relationship could still be regarded by the Ottomans as being broadly one of equal strength. In the late fifteenth the disciplined professional army of the sultan, using firearms, had been a match for any in Europe. In the seventeenth the Ottomans made their last great conquest, the island of Crete, taken from the Venetians. By the early eighteenth, they were dealing with European states on a level of diplomatic equality, instead of the superiority which they had been able to maintain at an earlier time, and their army was regarded as having fallen behind others in organization, tactics and the use of weapons, although not so far behind that efforts could not be made to strengthen it within the existing system of institutions. Trade was still carried on within the bounds of the Capitulations.

In the last quarter of the century, however, the situation began to change rapidly and dramatically, as the gap between the technical skills of some western and northern European countries and those of the rest of the world grew wider. During the centuries of Ottoman rule there had been no advance in technology and a decline in the level of scientific knowledge and understanding. Apart from a few Greeks and others educated in Italy, there was little knowledge of the languages of western Europe or of the scientific and technical advances being made there. The astronomical theories associated with the name of Copernicus were mentioned for the first time, and even then only briefly, in Turkish at the end of the seventeenth century, and the advances in European medicine were only slowly coming to be known in the eighteenth.

Some countries of Europe had now moved on to a different level of power. Plague had ceased to ravage the cities of Europe as quarantine systems took effect, and the introduction of maize and the extension of cultivated land ended the threat of famine and made it possible to feed a larger population. Improvements in the construction of ships and the art of navigation had taken European sailors and merchants into all the oceans of the world, and led to the establishment of trading points and colonies. Trade and the exploitation of the mines and fields of the colonies had given rise to an accumulation of capital, which was being used to produce manufactured goods in new ways and on a larger scale. The growth of population and wealth made it possible for governments to maintain larger armies and navies. Thus some of the countries of western Europe – England, France and The Netherlands in particular – had embarked on a process of continuous accumulation of resources, while the Ottoman countries, like other parts of Asia and Africa, were still living in a situation in which population was held down by plague and famine, and in some places had decreased, and production did not generate the capital necessary for fundamental changes in its methods or any increase in the organized power of the government.

The growth in the military power of western Europe was not yet felt directly. In the western Mediterranean, Spanish power had waned, and the *dey* of Algiers was able in 1792 to capture Oran, which had been in Spanish hands; in the eastern Mediterranean, Venetian power was in decline, and that of England and France was not yet felt. The danger seemed to come from the north and east. Russia, whose army and government had been reorganized on western lines, was advancing southwards. In a decisive war with the Ottomans (1768–74), a fleet under Russian command sailed the eastern Mediterranean, and a Russian army occupied the Crimea, which was annexed to the Russian Empire a few years later. From this time the Black Sea ceased to be an Ottoman lake; the new Russian port of Odessa became a centre of trade.

Far to the east, in India, something no less ominous was beginning. European ships had first rounded the Cape of Good Hope in the late fifteenth century, and European trading posts had gradually been established on the coasts of India, in the Gulf and on the islands of south-east Asia, but for the next century or more their trade was limited. The Cape route was long and hazardous, and spices and other Asian goods were still sent by the Gulf or Red Sea to the cities of the Middle East, to be sold in the local markets or distributed further west and north. Europe wanted to buy spices but had little to offer in return, and its ships and merchants in the Indian Ocean were largely occupied in buying and selling between Asian ports. In the early seventeenth century the spice trade was diverted round the Cape by the Dutch; but to some extent the loss to Ottoman merchants was made up by the new trade in coffee, grown in Yemen and distributed over the western world by merchants in Cairo. Later, European trading companies began to expand beyond their ports and become tax-collectors and virtual rulers of wide areas. The Dutch East India Company extended its control in Indonesia, and the British company took over the administration of a large region of the Mughal Empire, Bengal, in the 1760s.

By the last years of the eighteenth century, the nature of European trade with the Middle East and the Maghrib was clearly changing. Some groups of Arab merchants and sailors were still able to keep their position in the trade of the Indian Ocean, in particular those of Oman, whose activities and power spread on the east African coast. In general, however, exchanges between different regions of the world fell into the hands of European merchants and shipowners; English ships came to Mokha on the coast of Yemen to buy coffee; spices of Asia were brought to the Middle East by European merchants. Not only merchants but also producers felt the challenge. Goods produced in Europe, or under European control in the colonies of Asia and the New World, began to compete with those of the Middle East both in the European and in the Middle Eastern market. The coffee of Martinique was cheaper than that of Yemen, and the merchants who handled it had better commercial techniques than those of Cairo; they also had a monopoly of the European markets. By the late eighteenth century Mokha coffee had virtually lost the European trade, and was facing the competition of coffee from the Antilles in Cairo, Tunis and Istanbul. Sugar from the Antilles, refined in Marseille, was threatening the sugar industry of Egypt. French textiles of good quality were being bought by ordinary men and women as well as courts. In return, Europe was buying for the most part raw materials: silk of Lebanon and cotton of northern Palestine, grain of Algeria and Tunisia, hides of Morocco.

So far as trade with Europe was concerned, the countries of the Middle East and the Maghrib were moving into the position of being mainly suppliers of raw materials and buyers of finished products. The effects of this were still limited, however. Trade with Europe was less important for the economies of the Arab countries than that with the countries further east, or that which passed by the Nile or Saharan routes between the Mediterranean coastlands and Africa; the main effect may have been to lessen the trade between different parts of the Ottoman Empire in those goods in which Europe was becoming a competitor.

However limited, it was a sign of a displacement of power. If British ships came as far as Mokha, they might come further up the Red Sea and threaten the security of the holy cities and the revenues of Egypt; the expansion of British power in Bengal, a region with a large Muslim population and part of the Mughal Empire, was known at least to the Ottoman ruling group. The Russian occupation of the Crimea, a land of mainly Muslim population, ruled by a dynasty closely connected with the Ottomans, and the movements of the Russian fleet in the Mediterranean were more widely known. By the end of the century there was a growing awareness of the dangers. Among ordinary people it found expression in Messianic prophecies, among the Ottoman élite in the idea that something must be done. Occasional embassies to the courts of Europe, meetings with European diplomats and travellers, had brought some knowledge of the changes taking place in western Europe. It became clear to some of the high Ottoman officials that the defences of the empire needed to be strengthened. Some attempts were made to introduce corps with a modern training and equipment into the army and navy, and in the 1790s, on the initiative of a new sultan, Selim III (1789–1807), a more sustained effort was made to create a new model army; but in the end it came to nothing, because the creation of a new army, and the fiscal reforms which it involved, threatened too many powerful interests.

PART IV

THE AGE OF EUROPEAN EMPIRES

(1800–1939)

The nineteenth century was the age when Europe dominated the world. The growth of large-scale factory production and the changes in methods of communication – the coming of steamships, railways and telegraphs – led to an expansion of European trade. This was accompanied by an increase in the armed power of the great European states; the first major conquest of an Arabic-speaking country was that of Algeria by France (1830–47). Muslim states and societies could no longer live in a stable and self-sufficient system of inherited culture; their need was now to generate the strength to survive in a world dominated by others. The Ottoman government adopted new methods of military organization and adminis-tration and legal codes modelled upon those of Europe, and so did the rulers of two of the virtually autonomous provinces of the empire, Egypt and Tunisia.

In the capitals of these reforming governments, and in the ports which grew as a result of expanding trade with Europe, a new alliance of interests was formed between reforming governments, foreign merchants and an indigenous élite of landowners and merchants engaged in the trade with Europe. It was an unstable balance, however, and in due course Egypt and Tunisia fell under European control, followed by Morocco and Libya. The Ottoman Empire also lost most of its European provinces, and became more of a Turkish–Arab state.

While the religious and legal culture of Islam continued to be preserved, a new kind of thought emerged, trying to explain the reasons for the strength of Europe and show that Muslim countries could adopt European ideas and methods without being untrue to their own beliefs. Those who developed this new kind of thought were to a great extent graduates of schools created by reforming governments or foreign missionaries, and they could express their ideas through the new media of the newspaper and the periodical. Their dominant ideas were those of the reform of Islamic law; the creation of a new basis for the Ottoman Empire, that of equal citizenship; and – at the end of the nineteenth century – nationalism. Apart from rare moments of upheaval, the new ideas scarcely touched the lives of people in the countryside and desert.

The First World War ended with the final disappearance of the Ottoman Empire. Out of the ruins of the empire a new independent state of Turkey emerged, but the Arab provinces were placed under British and French control; the whole of the Arabic-speaking world was now under European rule, except for parts of the Arabian peninsula. Foreign control brought administrative change and some advance in education, but also encouraged the growth of nationalism, mainly among the educated strata of society. In some countries agreement was reached with the dominant power on the extension of self-rule within limits, but in others the relationship remained one of opposition. The encouragement given by the British government to the creation of a Jewish national home in Palestine created a situation which was to affect nationalist opinion in all Arabic-speaking countries.

CHAPTER 16

European Power and Reforming Governments (1800–1860)

THE EXPANSION OF EUROPE

The first attempts to recover the strength of the imperial government were given urgency by the wars between the France of the Revolution and then of Napoleon, and the other European powers, which convulsed Europe from 1792 to 1815 and were carried on wherever European armies could march or navies sail. French, Russian and Austrian armies at different times occupied parts of the sultan's European provinces. For the first time, British and French naval power was shown in the eastern Mediterranean. At one point a British fleet tried to enter the straits leading to Istanbul. In 1798 a French expeditionary force commanded by Napoleon occupied Egypt as an incident in the war with England; the French ruled Egypt for three years, tried to move from there into Syria, but were compelled to withdraw by British and Ottoman intervention, after the first formal military alliance between the Ottomans and non-Muslim states.

This was a brief episode, and its importance has been disputed by some historians; others have thought of it as opening a new era in the Middle East. It was the first major incursion of a European power into a central country of the Muslim world, and the first exposure of its inhabitants to a new kind of military power, and to the rivalries of the great European states. The Islamic historian al-Jabarti was living in Cairo at the time and recorded the impact made by the invaders at length and in vivid detail, and with a sense of the discrepancy of strength between the two sides, and the inadequacy of the rulers of Egypt to meet the challenge. When the news of the French landing at Alexandria first came to the leaders of the Mamluks in Cairo, he tells us, they thought nothing of it: 'relying on their strength, and their claim that if all the Franks came they would not be able to stand against them, and they would crush them beneath their horses' hooves'.[1] This was followed by defeat, panic, and attempts at revolt. Mingled with Jabarti's opposition to the new rulers, however, there was a certain admiration for the scholars and scientists who came with them:

if any of the Muslims came to them in order to look round they did not prevent him entering their most cherished places . . . and if they found in him any appetite or desire for knowledge they showed their friendship and love for him, and they would bring out all kinds of pictures and maps, and animals and birds and plants, and histories of the ancients and of nations and tales of the prophets . . . I went to them often, and they showed me all that.[2]

Such events disturbed the life of the Ottoman and Arab lands. The French armies in the Mediterranean bought grain from Algeria, and the British army in Spain bought it from Egypt. British and French merchant ships could not move easily in the eastern Mediterranean, and this gave an opening for Greek merchants and ship-owners. The creation of republics by the French in parts of the Balkans did not go unnoticed by Greeks and Serbs; some echoes of the rhetoric of the Revolution were caught by Christian subjects of the sultan, although not to any significant extent by Turkish or Arab Muslims.

Once the Napoleonic wars were ended, European power and influence spread even further. The adoption of new techniques of manufacture and new methods of organization of industry had been given an impetus by the needs and energies which wars release. Now that the wars were over and merchants and goods could move freely, the world lay open to the new, cheap cotton and woollen cloths and metal goods which were being produced, first and mainly in England, but also in France, Belgium, Switzerland and western Germany. In the 1830s and 1840s there began a revolution in transport, with the coming of steamships and railways. Previously, transport, especially by land, had been costly, slow and risky. Now it became quick and reliable, and the proportion which it represented of the total price of goods was smaller; it became possible to move not only luxuries but bulky goods for a large market over long distances. Men and news could move quickly too, and this made possible the growth of an international money market: banks, stock exchanges, currencies linked with the pound sterling. The profits of trade could be invested to generate new productive activities. Behind the merchant and the sailor there stood the armed power of the European states. The Napoleonic wars had shown their superiority, not so much in weapons, for the great changes in military technology were to come rather later, as in the organization and use of armies.

Connected with these changes was the continuing growth in population. Between 1800 and 1850 the population of Great Britain increased from 16 to 27 millions, and that of Europe as a whole increased by about 50 per cent. London became the largest city in the world, with a population of 2½ millions by 1850; other capital cities also grew, and there emerged a new kind of industrial city dominated by offices and factories. By the middle of the century more than half the population of England was urban. This concentration in cities provided manpower for industry and armies, and a growing domestic market for the products of the factories. It both required and made possible governments which would intervene more directly in the life of society. At the same time the spread of literacy and newspapers helped the expansion of ideas generated by the French Revolution and created a new kind of politics, which attempted to mobilize public opinion in active support of a government or in opposition to it.

The repercussions of this vast expansion of European energy and powers were felt everywhere in the world. Between the 1830s and 1860s regular steamship lines connected the ports of the southern and eastern Mediterranean with London and Liverpool, Marseille and Trieste, and textiles and metal goods found a wide and growing market. British exports to the eastern Mediterranean countries increased 800 per cent in value between 1815 and 1850; by that time beduin in the Syrian desert were wearing shirts made of Lancashire cotton. At the same time, the need of Europe for raw materials for the factories and food for the population which worked in them encouraged the production of crops for sale and export: the export of grain continued, although it became less important as Russian grain exports grew; Tunisian olive oil was in demand for the making of soap, Lebanese silk for the factories of Lyon, above all Egyptian cotton for the mills of Lancashire. By 1820 a French engineer, Louis Jumel, had begun to cultivate a long-staple cotton suitable for high-class textiles, which he had found in an Egyptian garden. From that time an increasing amount of Egypt's cultivable land was turned over to the production of cotton, almost all of it for export to England. In the forty years which followed Jumel's beginning, the value of exports of Egyptian cotton increased from almost nothing to approximately 1.5 million Egyptian pounds by 1861. (The Egyptian pound was roughly equivalent to the pound sterling.)

Faced with this explosion of European energy, the Arab countries, like most of Asia and Africa, could generate no countervailing power of their own. The population did not change much during the first half of the nineteenth century. Plague was gradually controlled, at least in the coastal cities, as quarantine systems under European supervision were introduced, but cholera came in from India. The Arab countries had not yet entered the railway age, except for small beginnings in Egypt and Algeria; internal communications were bad and famine could still occur. While the population of Egypt increased, from 4 millions in 1800 to 5.5 in 1860, in most of the other countries it remained stationary, and in Algeria, for special reasons, it went down considerably, from 3 millions in 1830 to 2.5 in 1860. Some of the coastal ports grew in size, particularly Alexandria, the main port for the export of Egyptian cotton, which increased from some 10,000 in 1800 to 100,000 by 1850. Most of the cities, however, remained roughly the same size as before, and there had not grown those specifically modern cities which generated the power of modern states. Apart from areas which produced crops for export, agricultural production remained at subsistence level, and could not lead to an accumulation of capital for productive investment.

THE BEGINNINGS OF EUROPEAN EMPIRE

Behind the merchants and ship-owners of Europe stood the ambassadors and consuls of the great powers, supported in the last resort by the armed might of their governments. During the first half of the nineteenth century they were able to work in a way which had been impossible before, acquiring influence with governments and officials, and using it in order to further the commercial interests of their citizens and the major political interests of their countries, and also to extend help and protection to communities with which their governments had a special connection. France had a special relationship, going back to the seventeenth century, with the Uniate Christians, those parts of the eastern Churches which accepted the primacy of the Pope, and more specifically with the Maronites in Lebanon; by the end of the eighteenth century, Russia was putting forward a similar claim to protect the Eastern Orthodox Churches.

With their new power, not only France and Russia but the European states in general now began to intervene collectively in the relations between the sultan and his Christian subjects. In 1808 the Serbs in what is now Yugoslavia revolted against the local Ottoman government, and the outcome, after many vicissitudes, was the establishment, with European help, of an autonomous Serbian state in 1830. In 1821 something of more general importance occurred: an uprising among the Greeks, who had long held a comparatively favoured position among the subject peoples, and whose wealth and contacts with Europe had been expanding. In part this was a series of risings against local rulers, in part a religious movement against Muslim domination, but it was also moved by the new spirit of nationalism. The idea that those who spoke the same language and shared the same collective memories should live together in an independent political society had been spread by the French Revolution, and among Greeks it was connected with a revival of interest in ancient Greece. Here too the outcome was European intervention, both military and diplomatic, and the creation of an independent kingdom in 1833.

In some places, European states were able to impose their own direct rule. This took place not in the central parts of the Ottoman world, but on the margins where one European state was able to act without deference to the interests of others. In the Caucasus, Russia expanded southwards into lands inhabited largely by Muslims and ruled by local dynasties which had lived within the Ottoman sphere of influence. In the Arabian peninsula, the port of Aden was occupied by the British from India in 1839, and was to become a staging-post on the steamship route to India; in the Gulf, there was a growing British presence based upon naval power and embodied in some places in formal agreements with the small rulers of the ports, by which they bound themselves to maintain truces with each other at sea (hence the term by which some of them were known, the 'Trucial States': these included Abu Dhabi, Dubai and Sharja).

What happened in the Maghrib was more important than this. In 1830 a French army landed on the Algerian coast and occupied Algiers. There had been a number of European naval expeditions to check a revival of privateering during and after the Napoleonic wars, but this was to be an event of a different kind. Its origins lay partly in the internal politics of France under the restored monarchy, partly in an obscure question of debts arising from the supply of grain to France during the wars, but more deeply in the new expansive dynamism created by economic growth: the merchants of Marseille wanted a strong trading position on the Algerian coast. Once installed in Algiers, and soon afterwards in some other coastal towns, the French did not at first know what to do. They could scarcely withdraw, because a position of strength could not be surrendered lightly, and because they had dismantled the local Ottoman administration. Soon they were led inexorably to expand into the interior. Officials and merchants saw prospects of gain through acquisition of land; military men wished to make their position more secure and safeguard the food supply and trade with the interior; and the removal of the local Ottoman government had weakened the traditional system of relationships among local authorities. The *dey*'s government had stood at the apex of that system, regulating as far as it could the extent to which each local authority could extend his power; once it was removed, the various leaders had to find their own balance with each other, and this led to a struggle for supremacy. The most successful contestant was 'Abd al-Qadir (1808–83) in the western region. Deriving prestige from belonging to a family with a religious position, connected with the Qadiri order, he became the point around which local forces could gather. For a time he ruled a virtually independent state, with its centre lying in the interior, and extending from the west into the eastern part of the country. This inevitably brought him into conflict with French power expanding from the coast. The symbols of his resistance to the French were traditional ones – his war was a *jihad*, he justified his authority by the choice of the *'ulama* and respect for the *shari'a* – but there were modern aspects of his organization of government.

'Abd al-Qadir was finally defeated and sent into exile in 1847; he spent his later years in Damascus, much respected by the population and on good terms with the representatives of France and other European powers. In the process of defeating him, French rule had extended southwards across the high plateau to the edge of the Sahara, and its nature had changed. French and other immigrants had begun to come in and take over land, made available by confiscation, the sale of state domain, and in other ways. In the 1840s the government began more systematically to take part of what was regarded as the collective land of a village for settlement by immigrants (*colons*). This went largely to those who had the capital to cultivate it, using either immigrant peasants from Spain or Italy or Arab labour. What remained was assumed to be sufficient for the needs of the villagers, but the partition in fact destroyed ancient modes of land-use and led to the dispossession of small cultivators, who became sharecroppers or landless labourers on the new estates.

By 1860 the European population of Algeria was almost 200,000, among a Muslim population of approximately 2.5 millions (less than before, because of losses sustained in the war of conquest, epidemics, and famine in years of bad harvests). Algiers and other coastal towns had become largely European, and agricultural settlement had spread southwards beyond the coastal plain and into the high plateaux. Economic life had come to be dominated by an alliance of interests between officials, those landowners with the capital to practise commercial agriculture, and merchants who managed the exchanges between Algeria and France, some of them Europeans, some indigenous Jews. This economic process had a political dimension. The growth of colonization raised in an urgent form the question of what France should do in Algeria. The fully conquered and intensively settled districts were assimilated into the French administrative system in the 1840s; they were ruled directly by officials, with local government in the hands of the immigrant population, and the indigenous notables, who had previously acted as intermediaries between the government and the Muslim population, were reduced to the position of subordinate officials. Areas where settlement was not so far advanced remained under military rule, but these grew smaller in size as colonization expanded. The immigrants wanted this situation to continue, and the country to become fully French: 'there is no longer an Arab people, there are men who talk another language than ours'. They were becoming numerous enough, and sufficiently well-connected with French politicians, to form an effective lobby.

This policy posed a problem, that of the future of the Muslim population, Arab and Berber, and by the beginning of the 1860s the ruler of France, the Emperor Napoleon III, was beginning to look with favour on another policy. In his view, Algeria was an Arab kingdom, a European colony and a French camp; there were three separate interests to be reconciled: those of the French state, the *colons*, and the Muslim majority. This idea found expression in a decree of 1863 (the *senatus consultus*), which laid down that the policy of dividing village lands should end, the rights of the cultivators to the land be recognized, and the social position of the local leaders be strengthened in order to win them over to support of French authority.

REFORMING GOVERNMENTS

From more than one direction European political and economic power was drawing nearer to the heartlands of the Arab Muslim world, but in those lands there was still some freedom of reaction, partly because the conflicting interests of the European states would not permit any of them to move too far. It was therefore possible for a number of indigenous governments to try to create their own framework, within which Europe could pursue its interests but its interventions would be limited, and their subjects, Muslims and non-Muslims alike, would continue to accept their rule.

After the tentative attempts of Selim III had come to nothing, it was not until the 1820s that another sultan, Mahmud II (1808–39), and a small group of high officials convinced of the need for change were strong enough to take decisive action Their new policy involved the dissolution of the old army and the creation of a new one raised by conscription and trained by European instructors. With this army it was possible gradually to establish direct control over some of the provinces in Europe and Anatolia, Iraq and Syria, and Tripoli in Africa. The plan of reform went further than that, however. The intention was not only to restore the strength of the government but to organize it in a new way. This intention was proclaimed in a royal decree (the Hatt-i şerif of Gülhane), issued in 1839, shortly after the death of Mahmud:

All the world knows that since the first days of the Ottoman state, the lofty principles of the Qur'an and the rules of the *shari'a* were always perfectly preserved. Our mighty sultanate reached the highest degree of strength and power, and all its subjects of ease and prosperity. But in the last one hundred and fifty years, because of a succession of difficult and diverse causes, the sacred *shari'a* was not obeyed nor were the beneficent regulations followed; consequently, its former strength and prosperity have changed into weakness and poverty. It is evident that countries not governed by the *shari'a* cannot survive . . . Full of confidence in the help of the Most High, and certain of the support of our Prophet, we deem it necessary and important from now on to introduce new legislation in order to achieve effective administration of the Ottoman government and provinces.[3]

Officials should be free from the fear of arbitrary execution and seizure of property; they should govern in accordance with regulations drafted by high officials meeting in council. The subjects should live under laws derived from principles of justice, and which enabled them to pursue their economic interests freely; the laws should recognize no difference between Muslims, Christian and Jewish Ottomans. New commercial laws would enable foreign merchants to trade and travel freely. (The reorganization which followed this decree was known as the Tanzimat, from the Arabic and Turkish word for order.)

Central control, conciliar bureaucracy, the rule of law, equality: behind these guiding ideas there lay another one, that of Europe as the exemplar of modern civilization and of the Ottoman Empire as its partner. When the reformers issued the Gülhane decree, it was communicated to the ambassadors of friendly powers.

In two of the Arab provinces, rather similar policies were started by local Ottoman rulers. In Cairo, the disturbance of the local balance of power brought about by the French invasion led to the seizure of power by Muhammad 'Ali (1805–48), a Turk from Macedonia who had come to Egypt with the Ottoman forces sent against the French; he rallied support among the townspeople, outwitted his rivals, and virtually imposed himself on the Ottoman government as governor. Around him he formed his own local Ottoman ruling group of Turks and *mamluks*, a modern army and an élite of educated officials, and he used them to impose his control over the administration and tax-collection of the whole country, and to expand beyond it into the Sudan, Syria and Arabia. Egyptian rule in Syria and Arabia did not last long; he was forced to withdraw by a combined effort of the European powers, which did not wish to see a virtually independent Egyptian state weakening that of the Ottomans. In return for withdrawal, he obtained in 1841 recognition of his family's right to rule Egypt under Ottoman suzerainty (the special title his successors took was that of *khedive*). Egyptian rule continued, however, in the Sudan, which for the first time constituted a single political unit.

In some ways, what Muhammad 'Ali tried to do was simpler than what the statesmen of Istanbul were attempting. There was no explicit idea of citizenship or change in the moral basis of government. In other respects, however, the changes introduced in Egypt went beyond those in the rest of the empire, and from this time Egypt was to follow a separate line of development. There was a sustained attempt to train a group of officers, doctors, engineers and officials in new schools and by missions to Europe. In a smaller and simpler society than that of the main body of the empire, the ruler was able to bring all agricultural land under his control, by confiscating tax-farms and religious endowments, and to use his power to extend the cultivation of cotton, buy the produce at a fixed price and sell it to exporters in Alexandria; this involved a new kind of irrigation, the building of dams to divert water from the river into canals which would carry it where and when it was needed. At first he tried to manufacture textiles and other goods in factories, but the smallness of the internal market, the scarcity of power, and the lack of technical skill made these ineffective, although there was some export of textiles for a time. In the later years of his reign, pressure from Europe obliged him to give up his monopoly over the sale of cotton and other products, and Egypt moved into the position of a plantation economy supplying raw materials and importing finished products at prices fixed in the world market. By this time also land was being granted by the ruler to members of his family and entourage, or others who would bring it into cultivation and pay the land-tax, and so a new class of landowners was being created.

In Tunis there were the beginnings of change in the reign of Ahmad Bey (1837–55), who belonged to the family which had held power since the early eighteenth century. Some members of the ruling group of Turks and Mamluks were given a modern training, the nucleus of a new army was formed, direct administration and taxation were extended, some new laws were issued, and the ruler tried to create a monopoly of certain goods. Under his successor, in 1857, a proclamation of reform was issued: security, civil liberty, regular taxation and conscription, the right of Jews and foreigners to own land and carry out all kinds of economic activity. In 1861 a kind of constitution was enacted, the first in the Muslim world: there would be a council of sixty members whose approval would be necessary for laws, and the *bey* pledged himself to govern within its limits.

Beyond the frontiers of the empire, in the Arabian peninsula, the impact of European power was scarcely felt. In central Arabia, the Wahhabi state was destroyed for a time by the expansion of Egyptian power, but soon revived, on a smaller scale; in Oman the ruling family which had established itself in Masqat was able to extend its rule to Zanzibar and the east African coast. In Morocco, an expansion of European trade did take place, consulates were opened and regular steamship services began. The power of the government remained too limited to control these changes. Sultan 'Abd al-Rahman (1822–59) tried to create a monopoly of imports and exports, but under foreign pressure the country was opened to free trade.

Even at best, the indigenous governments which tried to adopt new methods of rule and preserve their independence could act only within narrow limits. The limits were imposed first of all by the European states. Whatever their rivalries, they had certain common interests and could unite to further them. They were concerned first of all to widen the field in which their merchants could work. They all opposed the attempts of rulers to maintain monopolies over trade. By a series of commercial conventions, they brought about a change in customs regulations: in the Ottoman Empire the first of these was the Anglo-Ottoman convention of 1838; in Morocco a similar one was made in 1856. They obtained the right of merchants to travel and trade freely, to maintain direct contacts with producers, and to have commercial disputes decided in special tribunals, not in Islamic courts under Islamic law. Because of the influence of ambassadors and consuls, the Capitulations were turning into a system by which foreign residents were virtually outside the law.

Beyond this, the powers were concerned with the situation of the sultan's Christian subjects. In the years after the Gülhane decree, they intervened collectively more than once to ensure that his undertakings to the non-Muslims were carried out. Running counter to this sense of the 'Concert of Europe', however, were the struggles of the various powers to secure paramount influence. In 1853 these led to the Crimean War, in which the Ottomans received help from England and France against Russia; but it ended in a reassertion of the 'Concert of Europe'. The Treaty of Paris in 1856 included a further statement by the sultan reaffirming his guarantees to his subjects. In a sense, then, the relationship of ruler and ruled was placed under the official notice of Europe. From this time the sultan was treated formally as a member of the community of European monarchs, but with overtones of doubt: while England and France thought it might be possible for the Ottoman Empire to become a modern state on European lines, Russia was more doubtful and believed the future would lie in the grant of broad self-government to the Christian provinces of Europe. No power, however, wished actively to encourage the break-up of the empire, with its consequences for the peace of Europe; memories of the Napoleonic wars were still alive.

Even within the limits imposed by Europe, the reforms could have only a limited success. They were the acts of individual rulers with small groups of advisers, encouraged by some of the foreign ambassadors and consuls. A change of rulers, a shift in the balance between different groups of officials, the conflicting ideas and interests of European states could bring about a change in the direction of policy. In Istanbul, the élite of high officials was strong and stable enough, and sufficiently devoted to the interests of the empire, to ensure a certain continuity in policy, but in Cairo, Tunis and Morocco everything depended on the ruler; when Muhammad 'Ali died, some lines of policy were reversed by his successor, 'Abbas I (1849–54), but then restored by the next ruler, Sa'id (1854–63).

In so far as the reforms were carried out, they might have unexpected results. Some changes did take place in the methods by which governments worked: offices were organized in new ways, and officials were supposed to act in accordance with new regulations; some new laws were issued; armies were trained in different ways, and raised by conscription; taxes were supposed to be collected directly. Such measures were intended to make for greater strength and justice, but in the first phase they tended also to weaken the relationship between governments and societies. The new methods and policies, carried out by officials trained in a new way, were less comprehensible to the subjects, and had no roots in a moral system hallowed by long acceptance. They also disturbed an ancient relationship between governments and certain elements in society.

Who profited from the new ways of government? Clearly the ruling families and their higher officials did so. Greater security of life and property made it possible to accumulate wealth and hand it on to their families. Stronger armies and administrations enabled them to extend the power of the government over the land. In Egypt and Tunisia this led to the formation of large estates by members of ruling families or those close to them. In the central Ottoman countries, an analogous process took place. The new administration and army needed to be paid for, but it was not yet strong enough to collect taxes directly; the old system of tax-farming continued, and tax-farmers could take their share of the rural surplus.

Beyond the ruling élites, the new policies favoured merchants engaged in trade with Europe. Import and export trade was growing, and merchants engaged in it were playing an increasingly large part not only in trade but in the organization of production, advancing capital to landowners or cultivators, deciding what they should produce, buying it, processing it – ginning cotton and winding silk – and then exporting it. The largest merchants were Europeans, who had a clear advantage because they knew the European market and had access to credit from banks. Others were local Christians and Jews: Greeks and Armenians, Syrian Christians, Jews of Baghdad, Tunis and Fez. They knew the local markets and were well placed to act as intermediaries with foreign merchants. By the middle of the nineteenth century many of them had a knowledge of foreign languages, acquired in schools of a new kind, and some also had foreign nationality or protection, by an extension of the right of embassies and consulates to appoint a number of local subjects as agents or translators; a few had established their own offices in centres of European business, Manchester or Marseille. In some places long-established groups of Muslim merchants were able to make the change to the new kind of trade: Arabs from southern Arabia were active in south-east Asia; Muslim merchants from Damascus and Fez had settled in Manchester by 1860; some Moroccan Muslims had even become protégés of foreign consulates.

On the other hand, groups on which governments had formerly depended, and with which their interests had been linked, now found themselves to an increasing extent excluded from a share of power. The 'ulama who had controlled the legal system were challenged by the creation of new legal codes and courts. The notable families of the cities, who had served as intermediaries between government and urban population, saw their influence waning. Even if those who retained possession of land might in some places make profits by growing crops for sale and export, their position, and their hold over the cultivators, were threatened by the extension of direct government and the expanding activities of the merchants in the ports. Old-established industries, like textile weaving in Syria, sugar refining in Egypt, and the making of the *shashiya* headgear in Tunisia, suffered from the competition of European goods, although in some cases they were able to adjust themselves to the new conditions and even to expand. Little is known about the condition of the rural population, but it does not seem to have improved, and in some places may have grown worse. The production of food probably increased in general, but bad harvests and poor communications could still cause famine, although less often than before. In two ways their condition may have worsened: conscription took a proportion of their young men for armies; taxes were heavier and were more effectively raised.

The dislocation of the economy, the loss of power and influence, the sense of the political world of Islam being threatened from outside: all these expressed themselves in the middle of the century in a number of violent movements directed against the new policies, against the growing influence of Europe, and in some places against the local Christians who profited from it. In Syria, these came to a head in 1860. In the mountain valleys of Lebanon there was an ancient symbiosis between the main religious communities, the Maronite Christians and Druzes. A member of a local family, that of Shihab, was recognized by the Ottomans as chief tax-farmer, and the Shihabs had become in effect hereditary princes of the mountain, and heads of a hierarchy of land-holding families, both Christian and Druze, between whom there were common interests, alliances and formal relationships. From the 1830s onwards, however, the symbiosis broke down, because of shifts in population and local power, the discontent of peasants with their lords, Ottoman attempts to introduce direct control, and British and French interference. In 1860 there was a civil war in Lebanon, and this touched off a massacre of Christians in Damascus, an expression of opposition to the Ottoman reforms and the European interests linked with them, at a moment of commercial depression. This in turn led to intervention by the European powers, and the creation of a special regime for Mount Lebanon.

In Tunisia in 1864, in a period of bad harvests and epidemics, there was a violent revolt against the rule of the *bey* and the classes which profited from it, the *mamluks* and foreign merchants, and against the increase of taxation necessary to pay for the reforms. Beginning among the tribes, it spread to the towns of the olive-growing coastal plain, the Sahil; the rebels demanded a decrease in taxation, an end to *mamluk* rule, and justice according to the *shari'a*. The *bey*'s power was threatened for a moment, but the unity of interests between government and foreign communities held, and he was able to wait until the alliance of rebels fell apart and then suppress it.

CHAPTER 17

European Empires and Dominant Élites
(1860–1914)

THE LIMITS OF INDEPENDENCE

The Treaty of Paris of 1856 created a kind of balance between European interests and those of the indigenous ruling group in the Ottoman Empire dedicated to reform. The powers which signed the treaty, while 'recognizing the high value' of the sultan's reform decree, promised to respect the independence of the empire. In fact, however, they could not avoid intervention in its internal affairs because of the discrepancy of military strength between them and the Ottomans, the way in which various groups of officials looked for help to the embassies, the relations of different states with various Christian communities, and their common concern for European peace. It was their intervention which brought about a settlement in Lebanon after the civil war of 1860. A few years later, in 1866, the two Romanian provinces became united and virtually independent. In the next decade, however, a long-drawn-out 'eastern' crisis showed the limits upon effective intervention. Unrest in the European provinces of the empire was met with severe repression: European governments protested, and finally Russia declared war in 1877. The Russian army advanced towards Istanbul, and the Ottomans signed a peace treaty which gave autonomy to the Bulgarian regions of the empire. This seemed likely to give Russia a preponderant position of influence and aroused a strong British reaction. For some time a European war appeared possible, but in the event the powers negotiated the Treaty of Berlin (1878), under the terms of which two separate Bulgarian districts were given different degrees of autonomy, the Ottoman government promised to improve conditions in the provinces with large Christian populations, and the powers undertook once more not to intervene in the internal affairs of the empire.

It was clear that no European state would allow another to occupy Istanbul and the Straits, and none of them wished to risk the explosion which would result from an attempt to dismantle the empire. The process by which frontier regions split off did indeed continue. The two Bulgarian districts united in an autonomous state in 1885; the island of Crete was given autonomy in 1898 and incorporated in Greece in 1913. In that year, after a war with the Balkan states created by its former subjects, the empire lost most of its remaining European territories. On the other hand, as European rivalries grew more intense and the rise to power of Germany added one more element to the European balance, the Ottoman government acquired a little more freedom of action in its central regions. This was shown in the 1890s, when nationalist parties in another Christian community, the Armenians, began to work actively for independence; the Ottomans were able to suppress the movement with great loss of life, and without effective European action, although Armenian nationalism continued to be strong beneath the surface.

The loss of most of the European provinces changed the nature of the empire. Even more than before it appeared to its Muslim citizens, whether Turks or Arabs, as the last manifestation of the political independence of a Muslim world beleaguered by enemies. It was more urgent than ever to carry on the policies of reform. The bureaucracy and army were modernized further: officers and officials were trained in the military and civil schools. Improved communications enabled direct control to be extended. With the coming of steamships, Ottoman garrisons could be reinforced quickly in regions near the Mediterranean and Red Seas. The telegraph, an essential channel of control, was extended throughout the empire in the 1850s and 1860s. By the end of the nineteenth century railways had been built in Anatolia and Syria. In the early years of the twentieth, the Hijaz railway was laid down from Damascus to Madina; this enabled pilgrims to be carried to the holy cities, and also made it possible for the Ottoman government to keep more control over the *sharifs* of Mecca. It was able to restore its direct presence in Yemen too. In central Arabia, a dynasty supported by the Ottomans, that of Ibn Rashid, was able for a time to suppress the Saudi state, which was then revived by a young and vigorous member of the family, 'Abd al-'Aziz, and by 1914 was challenging the power of Ibn Rashid. In eastern Arabia, however, its expansion was limited by British policy. To prevent the growing influence of other states, Russia, France and Germany, the British government was giving more formal expression to its relations with the rulers of the Gulf; agreements were made by which the rulers of Bahrayn, Oman, the Trucial States and Kuwait placed their relations with the outside world in the hands of the British government. These agreements had the effect of preventing Ottoman expansion, although the Ottomans did maintain a claim to sovereignty over Kuwait.

Even within its narrower frontiers, the power of Istanbul was not so firm as might have appeared. The coalition of forces within the ruling élite, which had made the reform possible, was breaking up. There was a split between those who believed in government by officials in council, guided by their own consciences and principles of justice, and those who believed in representative government, responsible to the will of the people as expressed through elections; many of the older officials thought that this would be dangerous in a state without an educated public, and one in which different national or religious groups could use their political liberties in order to work for independence from the empire. In 1876, at the height of the 'eastern crisis', a constitution was granted and a parliament was elected and met, but it was suspended by the new sultan, Abdülhamid II (1876–1909) as soon as he felt strong enough. From then on a deeper split opened. Power moved from the élite of high officials to the sultan and his entourage, and this weakened the link between the dynasty and the Turkish element on which the empire ultimately depended.

In 1908 a revolution supported by part of the army restored the constitution. (Romania and Bulgaria took advantage of this to declare their formal independence.) At first it appeared to many that this revolution would be the beginning of a new era of freedom and of co-operation between the peoples of the empire. An American missionary long resident in Beirut wrote that the revolution was taken to be a transition

from an irresponsible rule of hungry and bribe-taking pashas, to a parliament of representatives from all parts of the empire, elected by people from all sects, Moslems, Christians and Jews! The whole empire burst forth in universal rejoicing. The press spoke out. Public meetings were held, cities and towns decorated, Moslems were seen embracing Christians and Jews.[1]

In the next few years, however, power over the government was seized by a group of Turkish officers and officials (the Committee of Union and Progress, or 'Young Turks') who tried to strengthen the empire by increasing central control.

Although the Ottoman government was able to preserve its freedom of political action, another kind of European intervention became more important. From the 1850s onwards the Ottoman government had been increasingly in need of money to pay for the army, the administration and some public works, and it had found a new source of money in Europe, where the development of industry and trade had led to an accumulation of capital which was channelled, through a new kind of institution, the banks, into investment all over the world. Between 1854 and 1879 the Ottoman government borrowed on a large scale, and on unfavourable terms; of a nominal amount of 256 million Turkish pounds (the Turkish pound was equivalent to £0.9 sterling) it received only 139 millions, the remainder being discounted. By 1875 it was unable to carry the burden of interest and repayment, and in 1881 a Public Debt Administration representing foreign creditors was set up; it was given control of a large part of the Ottoman revenues, and in that way had virtual control over acts of government which had financial implications.

THE PARTITION OF AFRICA: EGYPT AND THE MAGHRIB

A similar process took place in Egypt and Tunisia but ended differently, in the imposition of direct control by a European state; both these were countries where, for various reasons, a single state was able to intervene decisively. In Tunisia, the growth of indebtedness to European banks had the same immediate result as in the empire: the creation of an international financial commission in 1869. There followed a further attempt to reform the finances, reorganize justice and extend modern education. The more the country was opened to foreign enterprise, however, the more it attracted the interest of foreign governments, in particular that of France, already installed across the western frontier in Algeria. In 1881 a French army occupied Tunisia, partly for financial reasons, partly to forestall the growth of a rival influence, that of Italy, and partly to secure the Algerian frontier. Two years later an agreement was made with the *bey* by which France would assume an official protectorate and take responsibility for administration and finance.

In Egypt too larger openings for foreign enterprise gave greater incentives to intervention. Under the successors of Muhammad 'Ali, and particularly under Isma'il (1862–79), the attempt to create the institutions of a modern society continued. Egypt became virtually independent of the empire. Education was extended, some factories were opened, above all the process by which the country became a plantation producing cotton for the English market was carried further. The American civil war of 1861–5, which cut off the supply of cotton for a time, was an incentive to increased production. This continued after the war, and involved expenditure on irrigation and on communications; Egypt entered the railway age early, from the 1850s onwards. Another great public work was carried out: the Suez Canal, built with mainly French and Egyptian capital and Egyptian labour, was opened in 1869. Its opening was one of the great occasions of the century. The Khedive Isma'il took the opportunity to show that Egypt was no longer part of Africa, but belonged to the civilized world of Europe. The guests included the Emperor of Austria, the Empress Eugénie, wife of Napoleon III of France, the Crown Prince of Prussia, French writers and artists – Théophile Gautier, Émile Zola, Eugène Fromentin – Henrik Ibsen, and famous scientists and musicians. Ceremonies were conducted by Muslim and Christian men of religion, and the Empress in the imperial yacht led the first procession of boats through the new canal; at almost the same time, the Opera House in Cairo was opened with a cantata in honour of Isma'il and a performance of Verdi's *Rigoletto*. The opening of the canal inevitably drew to Egypt the attention of Britain, with its maritime trade with Asia and its Indian Empire to defend.

The export and processing of cotton were profitable for European financiers, and so too were the canal and other public works. Between 1862 and 1873 Egypt borrowed £68 millions, but received only two-thirds of it, the rest being discounted. In spite of efforts to increase its resources, including the sale of its shares in the canal to the British government, by 1876 it was unable to meet its obligations, and a few years later Anglo-French financial control was imposed. The growth of foreign influence, the increasing burden of taxation to meet the demands of foreign creditors, and other causes led to a movement to limit the power of the *khedive*, with overtones of nationalism, and with an army officer, Ahmad 'Urabi (1839–1911), as its spokesman; a law creating a Chamber of Deputies was issued in 1881, and when the Chamber met it tried to assert its independence of action. The prospect of a government less malleable by foreign interests led in its turn to European intervention, first diplomatic by Britain and France jointly, then military by Britain alone in 1882. The pretext for the British invasion was the claim that the government was in revolt against legitimate authority, and that order had broken down; most contemporary witnesses do not support this claim. The real reason was that instinct for power which states have in a period of expansion, reinforced by the spokesmen of European financial interests. A British bombardment of Alexandria, followed by the landing of troops in the canal zone, aroused religious even more than national feelings, but Egyptian opinion was polarized between the *khedive* and the government, and the Egyptian army could offer no effective resistance. The British army occupied the country, and from then onwards Britain virtually ruled Egypt, although British domination was not expressed in formal terms because of the complexity of foreign interests; it was not until 1904 that France recognized Britain's paramount position there.

The occupations of Tunisia and Egypt were important steps in the process by which the European powers defined their respective spheres of interest in Africa, as an alternative to fighting each other, and they opened the way to other steps. British rule was extended southwards along the Nile valley into Sudan. The explicit reason for this was the rise of a religious movement, that of Muhammad Ahmad (1844–85), regarded by his followers as the *mahdi*, with the aim of restoring the rule of Islamic justice. Egyptian rule over the country was ended by 1884, and an Islamic form of government was created, but it was not so much the fear of its expansion as fear of other European governments moving in that led to an Anglo-Egyptian occupation which destroyed the Islamic state and in 1899 set up a new system of government, formally an Anglo-Egyptian 'condominium', but in fact with a mainly British administration.

Soon afterwards, the growth of European influence in the kingdom of Morocco reached a similar conclusion. The attempts of the sultan to keep the country free from intervention virtually ended in 1860, when Spain invaded the country, partly to extend its influence beyond the two ports of Ceuta and Melilla, which had been in Spanish hands for centuries, and partly to oppose the spread of British influence. The invasion ended in a treaty by which Morocco had to pay a financial indemnity which was beyond its means. Efforts to pay it, and the commercial agreements made with the European states, led to a rapid increase of European activity. Under Sultan Hasan (1873–94), the government tried to carry out reforms similar to those attempted in other countries in order to provide a framework within which European penetration could be contained: a new army, a reformed administration, a more effective means of raising and using revenue. The policy had only limited success, since the government did not possess sufficient control over the country to make it possible. The rural lords, with their position rooted in religious or tribal solidarities, were virtually independent, and in the south their power was increasing; in the cities, the new measures of taxation and administration weakened the moral authority of the ruler. Local chiefs established direct relationships with foreign representatives, and merchants put themselves under their protection. In order to survive, the government began to take loans from

European banks; this increased foreign interests, and the logical conclusion came in 1904, when England and Spain, two of the three powers most deeply involved, recognized the predominant interest of the third, France (Britain in return for a free hand in Egypt, Spain for a share in the eventual control). In 1907 the main European states agreed upon virtual Franco-Spanish control over the administration and finances. The two powers occupied parts of the country, Spain in the north, and France on the Atlantic coast and the Algerian frontier. There was a rebellion against the sultan, who placed himself under French protection, but the expansion of French power continued and in 1912 a new sultan signed an agreement accepting a French protectorate; the most important of the southern chieftains also accepted it. By Franco-Spanish agreement, part of the north was to be administered by Spain; and Tangier, the centre of foreign interests, was to remain under a special international regime.

At about the same time the partition of the Maghrib reached its conclusion. In 1911 Italy, coming late to the 'Scramble for Africa', declared war on the Ottoman Empire, landed a force on the coast of Tripoli and, in spite of Ottoman resistance, was able to occupy the ports and obtain some recognition of its position from the Ottoman government.

THE ALLIANCE OF DOMINANT INTERESTS

By the outbreak of the First World War, the implications of Italian control in Libya and French and Spanish in Morocco were scarcely to be seen, but French rule had left its mark on Algeria and Tunisia, and British rule on Egypt and the Sudan. In some ways, they marked a break with the past and with what was happening in the Ottoman Empire: the major strategic and economic interests of a single European state were paramount, and although in Egypt, Tunisia and Morocco the indigenous governments existed in name, they gradually lost power as the hold of European officials expanded, and they did not possess even the limited scope for independent action which enabled the government in Istanbul to play off one power against another and pursue what it regarded as the national interest.

In other ways, the policies followed by England and France could be regarded in a sense as continuations, in a more effective form, of those of the indigenous reformers. Beneath the façade of indigenous government, more foreign officials were introduced, and they gradually acquired a wide control; the balance between them and the native officials shifted. (In the Sudan there was no such façade, but direct administration of a colonial type, with almost all senior posts in British hands and Egyptians and others in subordinate ones.) Governments worked more effectively, but also more distantly. Foreign soldiers, or native ones under foreign command, and disciplined police enabled the control of the government to be pushed further into the countryside. Better communications brought the provinces nearer to the capital: railways in both Tunisia and Egypt, in Tunisia roads as well. Secular courts administering codes of European style were created or extended. Stricter financial control and more efficient collection of taxes led to a reduction of foreign debts to manageable proportions. More buoyant finances and access to foreign capital on more favourable terms made it possible to carry out some public works: in particular, irrigation works in the Nile valley, culminating in the Aswan Dam, through which perennial irrigation was introduced in upper Egypt. A limited number of schools was established, or retained from the previous period: enough to train officials and technicians at the level at which it was judged feasible to employ them, but not enough to produce a large class of discontented intellectuals.

In the areas ruled from Istanbul, Cairo, Tunis and Algiers, the alliance of interests around the new kinds of government was extended and strengthened during the second half of the nineteenth century. In addition to the officials, two groups were particularly favoured by the policies of governments. The first was that which was linked with commerce and finance. The growth of population and industry in Europe, the improvement of ports, the building of railways and (in Lebanon, Algeria and Tunisia) of roads, all led to an expansion of trade with Europe, as well as between different parts of the Middle East and the Maghrib, in spite of periods of depression. In general it was on the same lines as before: export to Europe of raw materials (Egyptian cotton, Lebanese silk, wool and hides of the Maghrib, Tunisian phosphates) and foodstuffs (oranges from Palestine and wine from Algeria, olive oil from Tunisia); import of textiles, metal goods, tea, coffee and sugar. In general, there was an unfavourable balance of trade with Europe; this was largely offset by the import of capital for public works and, in some places, remittances from emigrants to the New World and an outflow of gold and silver.

The main share of the trade was in the hands of European companies and merchants, primarily British and French, with a growing share for Germans as the population and industry of Germany expanded. But indigenous merchant groups also played a considerable part in international trade, and a dominant one in local trade: in the Middle East, Syrian and

Lebanese Christians, Syrian and Iraqi Jews, and Egyptian Copts in the Nile trade; in the Maghrib, local Jews and also certain others with a long tradition of trade, merchants of Sus in Morocco, the Mzab oasis in Algeria, and the island of Jarba off the Tunisian coast.

European financial interests extended beyond trade. The first large investments were in those loans to governments which led to the establishment of foreign financial control; after that further loans were raised by governments, but the existence of foreign control made it possible to raise them on less onerous terms than before. Investment now extended beyond loans to governments, to public utilities for which foreign companies were given concessions. After the Suez Canal, concessions were granted, in various regions, for ports, tramways, water, gas, electricity and, above all, railways. Compared with this, there was little investment in agriculture, except in those parts of Egypt and Algeria where a large and regular demand for certain products, and an administration under European control, guaranteed a large and safe return. There was little investment in industry too, except for small-scale consumer industries, and in a few places mineral extraction (phosphates in Tunisia, oil in Egypt).

Not only wholly European banks and companies, but some now established in Istanbul, Cairo and elsewhere, such as the Ottoman Bank, took part in the investment. The capital in these local banks, however, was largely European, and a major part of the profits of investment was not held in the countries concerned in order to generate further wealth and national capital, but was exported to the countries of origin to swell their wealth and capital.

CONTROL OF THE LAND

The other groups whose interests were associated with those of the new governments were the landowners. Both in the main body of the Ottoman Empire and in Egypt the legal basis of landownership was changed in the middle years of the nineteenth century. In the empire, the Land Law of 1858 defined the various categories of land. Most cultivated agricultural land was regarded, in accordance with long-standing tradition, as belonging to the state, but those who cultivated it, or undertook to do so, could obtain a title which enabled them to enjoy full and unchallenged use of it, and to sell it or transmit it to their heirs. A purpose of the law seems to have been to encourage production and to strengthen the position of the actual cultivators. In some places it may have had this result: in parts of

Anatolia, and in Lebanon where smallholdings on silk-producing land increased, partly because of remittances sent back by emigrants to their families. In most places, however, the results were different. In regions near the cities, engaged in producing foodstuffs and raw materials for the cities or for export, land tended to fall into the hands of urban families. They could make better use of the administrative machinery for registering title; they were in a better position than peasants to obtain loans from commercial banks or mortgage companies, or from the government's agricultural bank; they could advance money to the peasants to enable them to pay their taxes or finance their operations; in areas producing for export, urban merchants having links with the foreign markets could control production, deciding what should be grown, advancing the money to grow it, and buying the produce. Some were in a position of monopoly: the purchase of silk and tobacco throughout the empire was the monopoly of concessionary companies with foreign capital. In these ways a class of absentee owners, essentially city-dwellers, was created, who were in a position to call upon the government to support their claims to a share of the produce; the peasants who cultivated it were either landless labourers or sharecroppers, obtaining enough of the product to survive. Of these private estates, perhaps the largest, and among the best administered, were those of the Sultan Abdülhamid himself.

In the more distant countryside, beyond the effective control of the cities, another kind of large landowner appeared. Much of the land, particularly in areas used for grazing, had always been regarded, both by the government and by those who lived on it, as belonging collectively to a tribe; now much of it was registered by the leading family of the tribe in its own name. If the area was large, however, effective control of the land might lie not with the tribal leader but with an intermediate group of agents, closer to the land and the process of cultivation than a city landowner or a large tribal *shaykh* could be.

These new landowners included Christian and Jewish merchants and money-lenders, but few foreigners in most parts of the empire still ruled from Istanbul. The main exception to this was Palestine, where from the 1880s there was growing a Jewish community of a new kind: not the long-established oriental Jews but Jews from central and eastern Europe, and not coming to Jerusalem to study, pray and die, but coming in accordance with a new vision of a restored Jewish nation rooted in the land. In 1897 this aspiration was expressed in the resolution of the first Zionist Congress calling for the creation for the Jewish people of a home in Palestine secured by public law. In spite of opposition from the Ottoman government, and growing anxiety among part of the local Arab population, by 1914 the Jewish population of Palestine had increased to approximately 85,000, or 12 per cent of the total. About a quarter of them were settled on the land, some of it bought by a national fund and declared to be the inalienable property of the Jewish people, on which no non-Jews could be employed. Some were living in agricultural settlements of a new kind (the *kibbutz*), with collective control of production and communal life.

In Egypt the process by which land passed from the ruler into private hands, which had begun in the later years of Muhammad 'Ali, was carried further between 1858 and 1880, by a series of laws and decrees which led in the end to full private ownership, without such limitations as the Ottoman law retained. Here again, the intention may not have been to create a class of large landowners, but this in fact was what happened, because of a number of interrelated processes. Until the British occupation in 1882, much land was handed out by the *khedive* in grants to members of his family or high officials in his service; much was kept in his own hands as private domain; important village families also were able to extend their lands as the demand for cotton increased. After the occupation, land which was handed over by the ruler to service the foreign debt, and land newly brought into cultivation, fell into the hands of large owners or of land and mortgage companies. Small owners fell into debt to urban money-lenders and lost their land; even if they retained it they could not easily obtain access to credit in order to finance improvements; the laws of inheritance led to fragmentation of holdings to the point where they could no longer support a family. By the time of the First World War, over 40 per cent of the cultivated land was in the hands of large owners (those owning more than fifty *feddans*), and about 20 per cent was owned in smallholdings of less than five *feddans*. (One *feddan* is approximately equal to one acre or 0.4 hectares.) About one-fifth of the large estates were owned by foreign individuals or companies, particularly in the north. The normal pattern had come to be that of the large proprietor whose land was cultivated by peasants, who provided labour and were allowed to rent and cultivate a piece of land for themselves; beneath them was a growing number of landless labourers, about one-fifth of the working population.

In Tunisia, the appropriation of the land by foreign owners was carried even further. There was already a large French and Italian community by the time of the French occupation. For the first ten years or so of the protectorate, measures taken by the government were in favour of large interests which wished to buy land: land cases were to be settled by mixed courts with a European component; those who leased *waqf* land were permitted to buy it. From 1892 a new policy was adopted, of encouraging immigration and settlement, partly under pressure from the *colons*, partly to increase the French element among them. A large amount of land was made available for purchase: *waqf* land, state domain, collective land of tribes where the same policy was adopted as had been followed in Algeria, of squeezing the inhabitants into a smaller proportion of it. Favourable terms were offered for purchasers: rural credit, equipment, roads. Economic conditions also were favourable: the demand for grain continued, that for wine and olive oil grew. Thus the amount of land in European hands increased, particularly in the grain-growing areas of the north and the olive-growing region of the Sahil; by 1915 *colons* owned about one-fifth of the cultivated land. Comparatively few of them were smallholders; the typical pattern was that of the large landowner cultivating with the help of Sicilian, southern Italian or Tunisian labourers, or taking rent from Tunisian peasant farmers. There was an abundant supply of labour, because the process of expropriating the land had worsened the condition of the peasants; they were deprived of access to capital, and of the protection which indigenous landowners had given them. The economic shift brought with it a change in political power. The *colons* were claiming a larger share in the determination of policy; they wished the government to move in the direction of annexing the country to France, dominating the indigenous population by force, and maintaining it within a traditional culture and way of life which would prevent it from sharing effectively in the exercise of power. They had some success in this: a large proportion of government officials were French; the consultative conference for financial and economic affairs consisted mainly of *colons*. On the other hand, the government in Paris, and the higher officials who were sent from there, wished to maintain the protectorate on the basis of co-operation between French and Tunisians.

French policy in Tunisia by 1914 had reached a stage similar to that of Algeria in the 1860s, but meanwhile in Algeria things had changed. The defeat of France in the Franco-Prussian war of 1870–71 and the fall of Napoleon III weakened the authority of the government in Algiers. The *colons* took over power for a moment, but in the east of the country something different occurred – a widespread revolt among Arabs and Berbers, with many causes: on the part of the nobility, a desire to recover their political and social position, which had been weakened as direct administration expanded; on the part of the villagers, opposition to the loss of their land and the growing power of the *colons*, and destitution after a period of epidemics and bad harvests; among the population at large, the desire for independence, not yet expressed in nationalist terms, but rather in those of religion, and given leadership and direction by one of the Sufi orders. The risings were suppressed, with grave results for the Algerian Muslims. Collective fines and confiscation of land were imposed as punishment; it has been estimated that those districts involved in the rebellion lost 70 per cent of their capital.

The long-term results were even graver. The destruction of the indigenous leadership and the change of regime in Paris removed the barriers against the spread of European landownership. By sale or grant of state domain and confiscated lands, by seizure of collective lands and legal subterfuges, large tracts of land passed into the hands of *colons*. By 1914 Europeans owned approximately one-third of the cultivated land, and it was the most productive land, yielding grain as before, or else vines, for Algerian wine now found a large market in France. Much of the cultivation on wine-producing land was carried on by European immigrants, Spanish and Italian as well as French, but it belonged mainly to comparatively wealthy owners with access to capital. Confined to smaller areas of unfavoured land, without capital, and with shrinking resources of livestock, Algerian smallholders tended to become sharecroppers or labourers on European estates, although in some places a new class of Muslim landowners was coming into existence.

Partly because of the new opportunities on the land, the European population of Algeria increased rapidly, from 200,000 in 1860 to approximately 750,000 by 1911; this last figure includes the Algerian Jews who had all been given French nationality. The indigenous population had by now grown to 4,740,000; Europeans therefore formed 13 per cent of the total population. In the large cities they were an even larger element: by 1914 three-quarters of the inhabitants of Algiers were European.

This growing European population virtually controlled the local government by 1914. By now they had representatives in the French parliament and formed an important political lobby in Paris. Gradually, as a new generation born in Algeria grew up, and immigrants from other countries took French citizenship, they developed a separate identity and a separate interest which the lobby could advance: to have Algeria assimilated as much as possible to France, but to have the local French administration under their control. On the whole they succeeded in this. The vast majority of local officials were French, and almost all those in the higher ranks. The areas which were administered by municipal councils with a French majority expanded, and in these areas Muslims had virtually no power. They paid direct taxes far higher than those of the *colons*, but the revenues were used mainly for the benefit of the Europeans; they were subject to a special penal code administered by French magistrates; little was spent on their education. By the end of the century the government in Paris was becoming aware of the 'Arab problem': of the importance of ensuring that the administration remained independent of pressure from the *colons*, and could use its power to 'safeguard the dignity of the defeated'.[2] Something was now done for Muslim education at the elementary level, but by 1914 the number of Algerians with a secondary or higher education was to be counted in dozens or hundreds, not thousands.

THE CONDITION OF THE PEOPLE

In those parts of the Middle East and Maghrib where government control had become more effective, public works had been constructed, new land laws gave assured property rights, banks or land-mortgage companies offered access to capital, and products found a market in the industrialized world, the area of cultivation grew and crop yields were increased in the years between 1860 and 1914. It is clear, in spite of the poverty of statistics, that this took place in Algeria, and in Tunisia where the cultivable area doubled. In Egypt conditions were particularly favourable. By this time government control was unchallenged even in upper Egypt, the market for cotton was expanding, in spite of the fluctuations to which it was subject, and the great irrigation works made it possible to increase the yield of land; the cropped area increased by approximately one-third between the 1870s and 1914. This increase was not without its dangers: the profitability of growing cotton for export was so great that more and more land was given over to it, and by about 1900 Egypt had become a net importer of foodstuffs as well as of manufactured goods.

For Syria, Palestine and Iraq, statistics are more imperfect, but such indications as do exist point in the same direction. In Syria and Palestine, peasants of the hill villages were able to extend their area of cultivation into the plains, and produce grain and other crops which had a market in the outside world: olive oil, sesame seed, oranges of the Jaffa district. In Lebanon, the cultivation of silk spread. In Iraq, the important factor was neither the extension of the power of the state nor the improvement of irrigation; the first large-scale work, the Hindiyya barrage on the Euphrates, was not opened until 1913. It was rather the way in which the land laws worked; when tribal leaders registered land in their names, they had an inducement to shift their tribesmen from pastoralism towards settled agriculture, producing grain or, in the south, dates for export.

Such a change in the balance between settled agriculture and nomadic pastoralism took place wherever two factors co-existed. The first was expansion in the area of control by government, which always preferred settled peasants who could be taxed and conscripted to nomads living outside the political community and who might be a danger to order. This expansion was taking place wherever governments were strong and communications were improving. In Algeria, the French army moved southwards from the high plateau into the oases of the Sahara and the lands where the Tuareg lived. In Syria, the building of railways made it possible to move the frontier of cultivation into the steppe. Every railway station with its officials, garrison and market became a centre from which agriculture and trade spread. Certain elements in the population were used to keep the countryside in order: Kurdish regiments were recruited in the north; Circassians who had left their homes in the Caucasus when the Russians conquered it were settled in a line of villages in southern Syria.

The second factor was a decreasing demand for the main products of the steppe, or the shrinking profits from them compared with those from crops produced for sale and export. The market for camels began to shrink as modern communications came in (but the decisive change, the arrival of the motor car, had scarcely begun). The demand for sheep continued, and may have increased as population grew, but capital was more profitably invested in the growing of crops, and what evidence there is suggests that numbers of livestock in proportion to population decreased: in Algeria there had been 2.85 sheep per head of the population in 1885, and thirty years later the figure had shrunk to 1.65.

In general, this period was one of increasing population, at rates varying greatly from one country to another. The countries where statistics are most reliable, and where the increase can be most clearly seen, are Algeria and Egypt. In Algeria, the Muslim population doubled in fifty years, from 2 millions in 1861 to 4.5 in 1914. In Tunisia, the increase was of the same order, from 1 to 2 millions. In Egypt, growth had been continuous throughout the nineteenth century: from 4 millions in 1800 to 5.5 in 1860 and 12 in 1914. In the Sudan, the population seems to have grown steadily from the beginning of the British occupation. In the Fertile Crescent, we are still in the period of guesswork. The population of Syria in the broader sense may have grown by something like 40 per cent between 1860 and 1914, from 2.5 to 3.5 millions; on the other side, there was a large outflow from Lebanon to North and South America and elsewhere, and by 1914 about 300,000 Lebanese are said to have left. The increase in Iraq may have been on a similar scale. It might be roughly estimated that the population of the Arab countries as a whole increased from some 18–20 millions in 1800 to some 35–40 millions by 1914.

It was still mainly a rural population. Some cities grew rapidly, in particular ports specializing in trade with Europe: the Algerian coastal towns, Beirut, and Alexandria (which by 1914 was the second largest city of the Arab countries). Others, in particular the national and provincial capitals, grew roughly in proportion to the growth of the total population. Cairo, for example, more or less doubled in size, and remained the largest of Arab cities, but the population of Egypt as a whole also grew; the degree of urbanization remained more or less what it had been, and the flow of rural migrants into the cities had scarcely begun.

The rise in population was the result of a number of factors. In Egypt it may have been linked with the spread of cotton cultivation: small children could help in the fields from an early age, so there was an inducement to marry early and have large families. In most countries it was a result of a decline in the strength of two factors which had limited population in the past: epidemic and famine. Improved quarantine arrangements, under the control of European doctors and with the backing of foreign governments, had more or less stamped out plague in the Mediterranean countries by 1914, and had limited the incidence of cholera. A combination of increased production of food and better communications made it possible to compensate for local failures of crops which in previous ages would have caused famine. In some countries – Algeria, Tunisia and the Sudan – the increase did not so much raise the population to new and unprecedented heights, as compensate for a sharp decrease earlier. In Algeria the war of conquest and the revolts, epidemics and famine had decreased the population considerably in the middle years of the nineteenth century; in Tunisia, there had been a gradual decrease over a long period; in the Sudan the disturbances caused by the Mahdist movement, followed by a succession of bad harvests, had led to a serious decline in the 1890s.

An increase in population does not, of course, necessarily mean that living standards are rising, and it can mean the opposite. Nevertheless, there is reason to think that in some places the standard did rise. This was certainly true of the upper strata of the urban population, those who were linked with the new governments or with the expanding sectors of the economy; they had higher earnings, better housing and medical care, and a wider range of goods to buy. In the countryside, increased production of food and better communications improved nutrition in some places at least: not in the countries of European colonization where the peasants had lost the best land, but in Egypt and parts of Syria, where there was a balance between production and population. (In Egypt, however, improvement in health because of better nutrition was balanced by the spread of a debilitating infection, bilharzia, carried by water and increasing as irrigation was extended.)

Even in the most favourable circumstances, however, the possibility of improvement in the life of cultivators was limited, not only by the continuing growth of population but by the shift in the balance of social power in favour of those who owned or otherwise controlled land. They had the power of the law and government to support their claims; they had access to the capital without which production could not be carried on, and the produce could not be taken to the market. For the most part, they did not have to work within the restraints of a moral bond between themselves and those who worked for them: the *colon*, the urban money-lender, the tribal *shaykh* turned landowner, did not have the same relationship with those who worked for them as some of their predecessors had had. In such circumstances, the peasants lacked the power to obtain from the rural product more than the minimum they needed for subsistence, and lacked also the protection of the powerful in times of oppression or hardship.

THE DUAL SOCIETY

By 1914 the Arab countries of the Ottoman Empire and the Maghrib showed, in varying degrees, a new kind of stratification: European commercial and financial groups, and in some places settler communities, protected by the influence and favoured by the power of their governments; indigenous merchant and landowning classes whose interests were to some extent assimilated to those of the foreign communities, but who in some circumstances might be in rivalry with them; and a growing rural population and a poor population in the cities, with limited access to power, and excluded to a great extent from the benefits of administrative, legal and economic change.

The altered relationship of social forces was expressed in the changes which began to take place in urban life in the second half of the nineteenth century. Economic activity and power moved from the great cities of the interior to the sea-ports, in particular those of the Mediterranean coast. These became not only places of trans-shipment of goods but the main centres of finance and commerce, where goods were collected from the interior and imports distributed over it, and where the business of importation and exportation, and to a great extent agricultural production, were organized and financed. Some of the ports were ancient towns which took on a new size and importance: Beirut replacing Sayda and Acre as the main port for southern Syria; Alexandria taking the place of Damietta and Rosetta in the maritime trade of Egypt, as trade with Europe increased and that with Anatolia and the Syrian coast declined; Basra, the main place of export of Iraqi dates and grain; Jidda, the main port of Hijaz, and becoming more important as western Arabia came to be supplied with foreign goods by sea rather than by caravan from Syria; Tunis and the ports of Algeria. Others were virtually new creations as centres of international traffic: Port Said at the northern end of the Suez Canal; Aden as a port of call and coaling for ships on the steamship route from Europe by way of the canal to India; Casablanca on the Atlantic coast of Morocco.

The centres of the ports were dominated by warehouses, banks, offices of shipping companies, built in the monumental style of southern Europe; they had residential quarters with villas surrounded by gardens; they were planned with public gardens, squares, hotels, restaurants and cafés, shops and theatres. Their principal streets were broad enough to permit the passage of trams, horse-carriages and, by 1914, the first motor cars. The cities of the interior too were changing their appearance in much the same way. At first, attempts were made to insert new streets and buildings into the heart of the old cities: a broad avenue was driven through Cairo to the foot of the Citadel; bazaars were straightened and widened in Damascus to make Suq Hamidiyya and Suq Midhat Pasha. In the long run, however, the new quarters grew up outside the walls (if they still remained) of the old cities, on land unencumbered by buildings and property rights, and which could therefore be developed according to a plan. New Damascus expanded to the east of the old, up the slopes of the Jabal Qasiyun; new Cairo was built first to the north of the old city, then to the west on land stretching to the Nile, which had been marshy but by now had been drained and made ready for building: new Tunis grew up partly on land reclaimed from the lake lying to the west of it; Khartoum, the capital of the Sudan under the Egyptians and then under the Condominium, was a new creation, with streets symmetrically laid out, near the point where the Blue and White Niles meet. At the end of the period, similar changes were taking place in Morocco: the capital of the protectorate and principal residence of the sultan lay in the new part of Rabat on the coast; a new Fez was being designed, outside the walls of the old city and carefully avoiding all intrusion into it.

The new cities gradually drained the life away from the old ones. It was here that banks and companies had their offices, and palaces and government offices grew up. In Cairo, the new ministries were built in the western quarters, the foreign consuls had their residences there, and the *khedive* moved from the Citadel to a new palace built in European style; the British army controlled Cairo from Qasr al-Nil barracks on the banks of the Nile.

A large part of the population of the new cities and quarters was foreign: officials, consuls, merchants, bankers, professional men. Algiers and Oran, the largest cities of Algeria, had European majorities; in Cairo 16 per cent of the population was foreign, in Alexandria 25 per cent. They led a secluded and privileged life, with their own schools, churches, hospitals and places of recreation, their lawsuits judged by consular European or mixed courts, their economic interests protected by the consulates and, in countries under European control, the government. The attraction of power and new ways of life drew to the new cities also indigenous merchants – mainly Christians and Jews – engaged in the international trade, and some of them enjoying foreign protection and virtually absorbed into the foreign communities. By 1914 Muslim families of government officials or landowners were beginning to leave their ancestral homes in the old cities for the amenities of the new quarters.

In the new cities a different kind of life grew up, a reflection of that of Europe. Men and women dressed in a different way. One significant aspect of the modernizing reforms of the time of Mahmud II had been a change in formal dress. The sultan and his officials abandoned the flowing robes and wide turbans of their predecessors for the formal frock-coat of Europe and a new headdress, the red fez or tarbush with a black tassel. Soldiers of the new armies, Ottoman, Egyptian and Tunisian, wore uniforms of European style. Travel, the sight of foreign residents, and new schools accustomed merchants and professional men and their families to the new clothes; Jews and Christians took to them rather earlier than Muslims. By the end of the century some of their wives and daughters too were wearing clothes of French or Italian style, learned from illustrated periodicals, the shops of the new cities, travel and schools; by 1914, however, few Muslim women went out without some kind of covering over the head if not over the face.

Houses too were visible expressions of changed ways of living. The buildings of the new quarters, whether for business or residence, were largely designed by French or Italian architects or in their style: stone-built, stuccoed, richly decorated with wrought iron. Public buildings presented imposing façades to the outer world, and some of them expressed new visions of life in society: in Cairo, the Opera House, the museum, the Khedivial Library. Houses also reflected a different view of family life. The separation of living rooms on the ground floor and bedrooms above was difficult to reconcile with the older and rigid division between the salons where the men of the family received visitors and the *harim* where the life of the family was carried on. Changes in economic life and social customs, as well as Ottoman, Egyptian and British actions against the slave-trade, had more or less brought an end to domestic slavery by 1914, and outside some palaces the black eunuch, the guardian of the sanctity of the *harim*, had almost disappeared. Chairs and tables, made in imitation of French eighteenth-century furniture, implied a different way of receiving guests and eating together. Houses were surrounded by gardens, not built round inner courtyards; their windows faced outwards to the street – it was possible to look out and for others to look in. In the broader streets or on the outskirts of the town, women of good family could take the air in horse-drawn carriages. Theatres offered new ways of seeing, if not – for women – of being seen; by 1914 aristocratic ladies of Cairo could attend performances by touring companies of French classical drama or Italian opera, discreetly hidden behind gauze screens in the boxes of the grand tier at the Opera House.

CHAPTER 18

The Culture of Imperialism
and Reform

THE CULTURE OF IMPERIALISM

In the new cities, and especially in the lands under European occupation, Europeans and Arabs now confronted each other in a new way, and their views of each other changed. In the eighteenth century, the curiosity of the European mind had expanded, under the impact of travel and trade, to include the whole world. In the nineteenth, the curiosity was deepened, and it had more to feed on, as trade, residence and war brought increasing numbers of Europeans and Americans into the Middle East and North Africa; organized tourism began in the middle of the century, with pilgrimages to the Holy Land and tours on the Nile.

Universal curiosity expressed itself in a new kind of scholarship, which tried to understand the nature and history of the societies of Asia through a study of what they had left of written records or artefacts. The first European translation of the Qur'an goes back much further, to the twelfth century, but this early effort left little behind it, and the systematic attempt to understand the basic texts of Muslim belief and history begins in the seventeenth century, with the creation of chairs of Arabic at the universities of Paris and Leiden, Oxford and Cambridge, the collection of manuscripts for the great libraries, and the first careful editions and translations of them. By the time Edward Gibbon wrote his *Decline and Fall of the Roman Empire* (1776–88), he had a considerable body of sources and learned works to use.

The organized study and teaching of things Arabic and Islamic, and the creation of institutions through which the results could be transmitted from one generation to another, began later. In the new British territory of Bengal, Sir William Jones (1746–94) established the Asiatic Society for the study of the Muslim as well as the Hindu culture of India, the first of many such learned societies. In Paris, the French scholar, Silvestre de Sacy

(1758–1838), started a line of teachers and research workers which extended by a kind of apostolic succession to other generations and other countries. A special part in the growth of this tradition was played by German-speaking scholars, in Germany and the Habsburg Empire, looking at the religion and culture of Islam with minds formed by the great intellectual disciplines of their time: cultural history, the study of the continuity of human development from one epoch and people to another; comparative philology, which tried to trace the natural history and family relationships of languages, and of the cultures and collective personalities expressed through them; the application of critical methods to sacred texts in order to reveal the early development of religious traditions. The recording and interpretation of the life, customs and beliefs of the peoples of Asia and Africa, now brought within the range of European travel and rule, gave rise to the science of anthropology. By the end of the century another kind of science had come to cast light upon the study of texts: archaeology, the endeavour to discover and interpret the relics of human settlements. In this way, knowledge of the history of countries where Arabs lived, especially Egypt and Iraq, was carried back before the rise of Islam.

The romantic imagination, the cult of the past, distant and strange, working on the knowledge or half-knowledge derived from travel and scholarship, produced a vision of the Orient, mysterious, enticing and threatening, cradle of wonders and fairy tales, which fertilized the arts. Translations of the *Arabian Nights* became part of the western heritage. Images from them and other books provided subordinate themes on European literature: Goethe wrote poems on Islamic themes, the *Westöstliche Diwan*; Sir Walter Scott made Saladin an epitome of medieval chivalry in *The Talisman*. The influence on the visual arts was greater. Islamic motifs appeared in the design and decoration of some buildings. An 'orientalist' style of painting was practised by great artists, Ingres and Delacroix, as well as minor ones. Certain images recurred in their work: the Arab horseman as savage hero, the seductiveness of beauties in the *harim*, the charm of the bazaar, the pathos of life continuing among the ruins of ancient grandeur.

Interwoven with the desire to know and the imaginative evocation of a mysterious attraction there was another theme. Defeat goes deeper into the human soul than victory. To be in someone else's power is a conscious experience which induces doubts about the ordering of the universe, while those who have power can forget it, or can assume that it is part of the natural order of things and invent or adopt ideas which justify their possession of it. Several kinds of justification were put forward in the Europe of the nineteenth century, and particularly in Britain and France, since these were the two countries mainly involved in rule over Arabs. Some were expressions in more secular language of attitudes which western Christians had held towards Islam and Muslims since they were first faced with Muslim power: Islam was seen as a danger, both moral and military, to be opposed. Translated into secular terms, this provided both a justification for rule and a warning: the fear of a 'revolt of Islam', of a sudden movement among the unknown peoples whom they ruled, was present in the minds of British and French rulers. In the same way, memories of the Crusades could be used to justify expansion.

Other ideas were plucked from the intellectual air of the epoch. Seen in the perspective of Hegel's philosophy of history, the Arabs belonged to a past moment in the development of the human spirit: they had fulfilled their mission of preserving Greek thought, and handed on the torch of civilization to others. Seen in that of comparative philology, those who lived through the medium of the Semitic languages were judged incapable of the rationality and higher civilization which lay open to the Aryans. A certain interpretation of Darwin's theory of evolution could be used to support the claim that those who had survived in the struggle for existence were superior, and therefore had the right to dominate. On the other hand, power could be regarded as bringing with it obligations. The phrase 'the White Man's burden' expressed an ideal which, in one way or another, inspired officials, doctors and missionaries, or even those who read about Asia and Africa from afar. The sense of worldwide responsibility found expression in the beginnings of aid to victims of disaster; money given in Europe and America for the victims of the Lebanese civil war of 1860, and distributed by the consuls, provided one of the first examples of organized international charity.

The idea of human identity and equality, beneath all differences, did sometimes break through. At the beginning of the nineteenth century, Goethe proclaimed that 'Orient and Occident can no more be severed';[1] but by the end of it the dominant voice was that of Kipling, asserting that 'East is East and West is West'[2] (although he may not himself have meant exactly what others read into his words).

THE RISE OF THE INTELLIGENTSIA

Such discussions were not taking place over a body which could not overhear them. By the later part of the nineteenth century, the awareness of the strength of Europe which already existed in the Ottoman ruling élite had become widespread. There had grown up a new educated class looking at itself and the world with eyes sharpened by western teachers, and communicating what it saw in new ways.

A few exceptions apart, this class was formed in schools of a new kind. The most influential were those established by reforming governments for their own purposes. To begin with, these were specialized schools training officials, officers, doctors and engineers, in Istanbul, Cairo and Tunis. By the end of the century, however, the official systems had grown. Primary and secondary schools existed in Ottoman provincial cities, and the improvement of communications made it possible for boys to go on from them to the higher colleges in Istanbul, and from there to be drawn into the imperial service; in Istanbul a university also had been established. In Egypt some developments took place outside the official network; Cairo had a French law school training lawyers for work in the mixed courts, and the first university was founded by private enterprise. In the Sudan, a government college, Gordon College, educated boys for the minor roles in government administration for which they were needed. In Tunisia, similarly, encouragement by the government was limited: there were some 'Franco-Arab' primary schools, some higher schools for teachers; the Sadiqiyya, a secondary school set up on the model of a *lycée*, was reformed and controlled by the French. In Algeria, elementary schools were gradually extended from the 1890s, but slowly and at a low level, and against the will of the *colons*, who were not eager to see Algerian Muslims acquire a knowledge of French and the ideas expressed in it; three *madrasas*, teaching both modern and traditional subjects at secondary level, were maintained; few Algerians entered French secondary schools, or the schools of law, medicine or letters of the University of Algiers, partly because few were able to reach the level needed, partly because Algerians were reluctant to send their sons to French schools.

Side by side with government schools were a small number set up by indigenous bodies, and a larger number maintained by European and American missions. In Lebanon, Syria and Egypt, some of the Christian communities had their own schools, in particular the Maronites with their long tradition of higher education; a few modern schools were established by Muslim voluntary organizations too. Catholic mission schools expanded, with financial support from the French government and under its protection. In 1875, the Jesuits founded their Université St-Joseph in Beirut, and a French Faculty of Medicine was attached to it in 1883.

It was a French initiative too which led to the creation of the Alliance Israélite, a Jewish organization which founded schools for Jewish communities stretching from Morocco to Iraq. From the beginning of the century, the work of Catholic missions was supplemented in one sense and challenged in another by that of Protestant missions, mainly American, which created a small Protestant community, but provided education for other Christians and later for some Muslims too; at the apex of their schools stood the Syrian Protestant College in Beirut, founded in 1866 and later to become the American University of Beirut. Russian schools for members of the Eastern Orthodox Church were also founded by the Imperial Russian Orthodox Palestine Society.

In all these systems there were schools for girls, not yet reaching as high a standard as those for boys, but spreading literacy and producing women who could earn their living in a few professions: as school-teachers or nurses, and more rarely as journalists or writers. A few were government schools, but most were mission schools; Catholic nuns' schools were favoured by Muslim parents, as giving their daughters the French language, good manners, feminine accomplishments, and protection.

There grew up a new generation accustomed to reading. Many of them read in foreign languages. By the middle of the nineteenth century French had replaced Italian as the *lingua franca* of trade and the cities; knowledge of English scarcely existed in the Maghrib and was less widespread than French further east. Bilingualism was common, and in some families, particularly in Cairo, Alexandria and Beirut, French or English was replacing Arabic in the family. For those who had been educated to a high level in Arabic, a new literature was being produced. Printing in Arabic had scarcely existed before the nineteenth century, but it spread during the century, particularly in Cairo and Beirut, which were to remain the principal centres of publishing: government schools in Cairo and mission schools in Beirut had produced a comparatively large reading public. Apart from school texts, books were less important in this period than newspapers and periodicals, which began to play a large part in the 1860s and 1870s. Among the periodicals of ideas, opening windows on to the culture, science and technology of the West, were two produced by Lebanese Christians in Cairo: *al-Muqtataf* by Ya'qub Sarruf (1852–1927) and Faris Nimr

(1855–1951), and *al-Hilal* by Jurji Zaydan (1861–1914). A similar venture
was an encyclopaedia published in periodical parts, produced by Butrus
Bustani (1819–83) and his family, a compendium of modern knowledge
which shows what was known and understood in Beirut and Cairo in the
last quarter of the nineteenth century. Its articles on modern science and
technology are accurate and clearly expressed; articles on Greek history,
mythology and literature extend far beyond what had been known of
classical antiquity in the Islamic culture of an earlier age; a work edited
and written mainly by Arab Christians, it speaks of Islamic subjects in
tones not clouded by reserve or fear. The earliest newspapers were those
published under official sponsorship in Istanbul, Cairo and Tunis, containing texts and explanations of laws and decrees. The unofficial newspaper
of opinion developed later, when a new generation of readers wished to
know what was happening in the world, and the telegraph made it possible
to satisfy their curiosity. The size of the reading public and the greater
extent of intellectual freedom made Cairo the centre of the daily press, and
once more the first successful journalists were immigrants from Lebanon;
al-Ahram, founded by the Taqla family in 1875, was later to become the
foremost newspaper of the Arab world.

THE CULTURE OF REFORM

Books, periodicals and newspapers were channels through which knowledge of the new world of Europe and America came to the Arabs. Much
of what they published was translated or adapted from the French or
English; the movement of translation began under Muhammad 'Ali, who
needed manuals for his officials and officers and textbooks for schools.
Some of those who had been trained in Europe and had learnt French or
another language wrote descriptions of what they had seen and heard.
Thus Rifa'a al-Tahtawi (1801–73), who had been sent by Muhammad 'Ali
with an educational mission to Paris, wrote a description of the city and its
inhabitants:

The Parisians are distinguished among the people of Christendom by the sharpness
of their intellects, the precision of their understanding, and the immersion of their
minds in deep matters . . . they are not prisoners of tradition, but always love to
know the origin of things and the proofs of them. Even the common people know
how to read and write, and enter like others into important subjects, every man
according to his capacity . . . It is of the nature of the French that they are curious
and enthusiastic about what is new, and love change and alteration in things,

particularly in clothes . . . Change and caprice also are of their nature; they will change immediately from joy to sadness, or from seriousness to joking or vice versa, so that in one day a man will do all manner of contradictory things. But all this is found in small matters; in great things, their views of politics do not change; every man remains in his beliefs and opinions . . . They are nearer to miserliness than generosity . . . They deny miracles, and believe it is not possible to infringe natural laws, and that religions came to point men to good works . . . but among their ugly beliefs is this, that the intellect and virtue of their wise men are greater than the intelligence of the prophets.[3]

As time went on, however, there emerged a new kind of literature, in which Arab writers tried to express in Arabic their consciousness of themselves and their place in the modern world. One of the main concerns of the new literature was the Arabic language itself. Those who had been brought within the sphere of radiation of the new learning and literature of Europe began to look at their own past in a new way. Texts of classical Arabic works were printed in Cairo as well as Europe. Old literary genres were revived; the foremost Lebanese writer of his time, Nasif al-Yaziji (1800–71), wrote a work in the style of the *maqamat*, a series of stories and anecdotes about a resourceful hero, narrated in elaborate rhymed prose. Others set themselves to adapt the language so that it could express new ideas and new forms of artistic sensibility. Butrus Bustani, and those who learned from him, used a new kind of expository prose, not departing from the basic rules of Arabic grammar but with simpler modes of expression and new words and idioms, either developed from within the resources of the Arabic language or else adapted from English or French. There was also a revival of Arabic poetry, still using the classical system of metres and rhyme, but gradually coming to express new ideas and feelings. Ahmad Shawqi (1868–1932) can be regarded as a late classical poet, using high language to commemorate public events or express national sentiments, or in praise of rulers; he came from the Turco-Egyptian élite which clustered around the Egyptian court. Among his contemporaries, however, Khalil Mutran (1872–1949) wrote poetry in which traditional forms and language were used not for their own sake but to give precise expression to a reality, whether in the external world or in the author's feelings. Hafiz Ibrahim (1871–1912) expressed the political and social ideas of Egyptians of his time with a more common touch, and more widespread appeal than Shawqi. Wholly new kinds of writing also began to come in: the drama, the short story, the novel. The first important novel, Husayn Haykal's *Zaynab*, published in 1914, expressed a new way of looking at the countryside, human life as rooted in nature, and the relationships of men and women.

The other main concern of the new writing was with the expanding social and intellectual power of Europe, seen not only as an adversary but as a challenge, and in some ways an attractive one. The power and greatness of Europe, modern science and technology, the political institutions of the European states, and the social morality of modern societies were all favourite themes. Such writing raised a fundamental problem: how could Arab Muslims, and how could the Ottoman Muslim state, acquire the strength to confront Europe and become part of the modern world?

The first clear attempts to answer such a question appear in the writings of officials connected with the reform of the mid-century in Istanbul, Cairo and Tunis. Some were written in Turkish, but a few were in Arabic, in particular a work by Khayr al-Din (d. 1889), who was the leader of the last attempt to reform the Tunisian government before the French occupation. In the introduction to his book, Khayr al-Din explained its purpose:

First, to urge those who are zealous and resolute among statesmen and men of religion to adopt, as far as they can, whatever is conducive to the welfare of the Islamic community and the development of its civilization, such as the expansion of the bounds of science and learning and the preparation of the paths which lead to wealth . . . and the basis of all this is good government. Secondly, to warn those who are heedless among the generality of Muslims against persistence in closing their eyes to what is praiseworthy and what conforms with our own religious law in the practice of adherents of other religions, simply because they have the idea fixed in their minds that all the acts and institutions of those who are not Muslims should be avoided.[4]

In the view of such authors, the Ottoman Empire should acquire the strength of a modern state by changes in laws, methods of administration and military organization; the relationship of sultan and subject should be changed into that of modern government and citizen, and loyalty to a ruling family should be transmuted into the sense of membership of a nation, the Ottoman nation, which would include Muslims and non-Muslims, Turks and non-Turks. All this could be done without disloyalty to Islam or the traditions of the empire, if only they were understood correctly.

As the century went on, and with the rise of the new educated class in the 1860s and 1870s, a split appeared among those who supported the reforms. It was a division of opinion about the bases of authority: whether it should lie with officials responsible to their own sense of justice and the interests of the empire, or with a representative government produced by elections.

The split between the generations went deeper than this, however. The second generation, in all three countries, was aware of a problem implicit in the changes which were taking place. Reform of institutions would be dangerous unless rooted in some kind of moral solidarity: what should this be, and how far could it be derived from the teachings of Islam? Such a question became more pressing as the new schools began to produce a generation not grounded in the traditional Islamic learning, and exposed to winds of doctrine blowing from the West.

The problem did not, of course, arise for the Arabic-speaking Christians of Lebanon and Syria, who played a large part in the intellectual life of this period. For most of them, the civilization of the West did not appear wholly alien; they could move towards it without any sense of being untrue to themselves. They had their own equivalent of the problem, however. The power of the hierarchies of the Churches, recognized and supported by the state, could be an obstacle to their thinking and expressing themselves as they pleased. Some of them moved in the direction of secularism, or of Protestantism, which was as near as they could go to secularism in a society where identity was expressed in terms of membership of a religious community.

For Muslims, however, the problem was inescapable. Islam was what was deepest in them. If to live in the modern world demanded changes in their ways of organizing society, they must try to make them while remaining true to themselves; and this would be possible only if Islam was interpreted to make it compatible with survival, strength and progress in the world. This was the starting-point of those who can be called 'Islamic modernists'. Islam, they believed, was not only compatible with reason, progress and social solidarity, the bases of modern civilization; if properly interpreted, it positively enjoined them. Such ideas were put forward by Jamal al-Din al-Afghani (1839–97), an Iranian whose writings were obscure but whose personal influence was considerable and farflung. They were developed more fully and clearly in the writings of an Egyptian, Muhammad 'Abduh (1849–1905), whose writings were to have a great and lasting influence throughout the Muslim world. The purpose of his life, as he stated it, was:

to liberate thought from the shackles of imitation [*taqlid*] and understand religion as it was understood by the community before dissension appeared; to return, in the acquisition of religious knowledge, to its first sources, and to weigh them in the scale of human reason, which God has created in order to prevent excess or adulteration in religion, so that God's wisdom may be fulfilled and the order of the human world preserved; and to prove that, seen in this light, religion must be accounted a friend to science, pushing man to investigate the secrets of existence, summoning him to respect established truths and to depend on them in his moral life and conduct.[5]

In his work a distinction emerges between the essential doctrines of Islam and its social teachings and laws. The doctrines have been transmitted by a central line of thinkers, the 'pious ancestors' (*al-salaf al-salih*, hence the name often given to this kind of thought, *salafiyya*). They are simple – belief in God, in revelation through a line of prophets ending in Muhammad, in moral responsibility and judgement – and they can be articulated and defended by reason. Law and social morality, on the other hand, are applications to particular circumstances of certain general principles contained in the Qur'an and acceptable to human reason. When circumstances change they too should change; in the modern world, it is the task of Muslim thinkers to relate changing laws and customs to unchanging principles, and by so doing to give them limits and a direction.

Such a view of Islam was to become part of the furnishing of the mind of many educated Arab Muslims, and of Muslims far beyond the Arab world. It could be developed along more than one line, however. 'Abduh's most prominent follower, the Syrian Rashid Rida (1865–1935), in his periodical *al-Manar*, tried to remain true to both sides of his master's teaching. In defending the unchanging doctrines of Islam against all attacks he was to draw closer to the Hanbali interpretation of it, and later to Wahhabism; in a series of *fatwas*, he tried to bring the laws appropriate to the modern world within the framework of a revised *shari'a*.

THE EMERGENCE OF NATIONALISM

Both 'Abduh and Rida were *'ulama* of traditional education, concerned not only to justify change but to impose limits on it; but for those educated in modern schools the attraction of 'Abduh's view of Islam was that it released them to accept the ideas of the modern west without any sense of betraying their own past. A series of writers, some of whom claimed allegiance to him, began to put forward new ideas about the way in which society and the state should be organized. It was in this generation that the idea of nationalism became explicit among Turks, Arabs, Egyptians and Tunisians. There had been some stirrings of national self-consciousness earlier, and behind them there lay something older and stronger, the wish of long-established societies to continue their lives without interruption, but as an articulate idea animating political movements it became important only in the last two decades before the First World War.

The various national movements arose in response to different challenges. Turkish nationalism was a reaction to the continuing and growing pressure from Europe, and to the breakdown of the ideal of Ottoman nationalism. As the Christian peoples of the empire seceded one by one, Ottoman nationalism acquired more of an Islamic colouring, but when, under Abdülhamid, the alliance between the throne and the Turkish ruling élite broke down, the idea of a Turkish nation emerged: the idea, that is, that the empire could survive only on the basis of the solidarity of a nation united by a common language.

Since by this time the empire had become largely a Turco-Arab state, any attempt to emphasize the paramountcy of the Turkish element was bound to upset the balance between them and the Arabs, and by reaction Arab nationalism gradually became explicit. In the first phase this was a movement of sentiments among some educated Muslims in Syria, mainly in Damascus, and a few Syrian and Lebanese Christian writers. Its roots lay in the revival of consciousness of the Arab past in the new schools, and the emphasis placed by Islamic reformers on the early period of Islamic history, the period when Arabs had been predominant. It became an important political force only after the revolution of 1908 weakened the position of the sultan, the traditional focus of loyalty, and led ultimately to the seizure of power by the 'Young Turks'. Since their policy was one of strengthening central control and laying emphasis upon the national unity of the empire, by implication it tended in the direction of Turkish nationalism. Some Arab officers and officials, mainly Syrians from Damascus, who for various reasons were opposed to this group, began to put forward the demand, not yet for an independent Arab state, but for a better position for the Arab provinces inside the empire, a decentralization going even as far as autonomy. Within the Arabic-speaking area, some Lebanese Christians began to hope for a greater measure of Lebanese autonomy under the protection of a European power.

Turkish and Arab nationalism at this stage were not primarily directed against the encroachments of European power so much as towards problems of identity and the political organization of the empire: what were the conditions on which the Ottoman Muslim community could continue to exist? They could in principle extend beyond the empire to all who spoke Turkish or Arabic. Egyptian, Tunisian and Algerian nationalism were different in these ways. All three were faced with specific problems of European rule, and all three were concerned with these problems within a clearly delimited country. Egypt and Tunisia had been virtually separate political entities for a long time, first under their own dynasties, then under British or French rule; Algeria too had been a separate Ottoman territory and had by now been virtually integrated into France.

Thus when Egyptian nationalism emerged it arose as an attempt to limit or end the British occupation, and it had a specifically Egyptian rather than an Arab or Muslim or Ottoman content. The resistance to the British occupation of 1882 had already had a nationalist element in it, but it was not yet fully articulated, and it was not until the first years of the new century that it became an effective political force, and one which could serve as a focus for other ideas about the way in which society should be organized. It was not a united force: there was a division between those who called for a British withdrawal and those who, under the influence of the ideas of Islamic modernism, thought that the first need was for social and intellectual development, and that Egypt could profit in this way from the British presence. Similarly, in Tunis there was an overtone of nationalist feeling in the resistance to the French invasion in 1881, but the first clearly distinguished nationalist group, the 'Young Tunisians', a small number of men with a French education, appeared around 1907. Here too the prevailing sentiment was not so much in favour of an immediate French withdrawal as of a change in French policy, which would give Tunisians greater access to French education and greater opportunities in government service and agriculture; this was a policy which was opposed by the *colons*. In Algeria too, on the surface of the deep and continuing resistance to French colonization, still expressed in mainly traditional terms, there appeared a small 'Young Algerian' movement with the same basis of 'modernist' ideas, and the same kind of demand for education in French, financial and judicial reforms, and wider political rights within the existing framework. In Morocco, however, the opposition to the French protectorate, widespread in city and countryside, still found its leaders among the urban *'ulama* and its symbols in the traditional ways of Islamic thought.

THE CONTINUITY OF ISLAMIC TRADITION

Ottomanism, Islamic reformism and nationalism were the ideas of an educated urban minority, expressing a new relationship with the state and the external world in terms of new concepts. Beyond this minority, there may well have been some stirrings of thought and feeling which would in a later generation articulate themselves in nationalist form and give national-ist movements a new strength, but for the most part Islam as traditionally conceived still provided the motives which could urge men to action and the symbols in terms of which they gave it meaning. What is called 'tradition', however, was not unchanging; it was following its own path at its own pace.

The old system of schools had lost something of its position in society. Study in them no longer led to high office in government service; as new methods of administration were introduced, a new kind of expertise was needed, and knowledge of a European language became almost indispens-able. Their graduates no longer controlled the judicial system. New criminal and commercial codes, modelled upon those of western Europe, limited the effective scope of the *shari'a*; the civil code of the Ottoman Empire, while still retaining its basis in the *shari'a*, was also remodelled. With the new laws there came new courts: mixed courts or foreign courts for cases involving foreigners, courts of a new kind – and in Algeria French courts – for most cases involving local subjects. The *qadi*'s court was confined to matters of personal status. Judges and lawyers of a new kind were therefore needed, and they were trained in a new way. In Egypt and Algeria an attempt was made to give students trained in the traditional way an education in modern subjects: the *madrasas* in Algeria and Dar al-'Ulum in Egypt. Sons of wealthy and eminent families, however, were increasingly sent to schools of the new type.

Nevertheless, the old schools continued, and so did the production of scholarly works on theology and law within the cumulative traditions of Islamic learning. The most alert of their students were beginning to express disappointment with the kind of teaching they received there. As one of them wrote, the student's life was one of

unrelieved repetition, in which he found nothing new from the year's beginning to its end . . . all through his studies he heard reiterated words and talk which did not touch his heart or rouse his appetite or nourish his mind, or add anything to what he knew.[6]

Some attempts were made to reform them, in particular the Azhar under the influence of 'Abduh, but without great success. They still, however, had great power in society, as channels through which clever boys from poor rural families could find their level, and as forming and articulating a kind of collective conscience. For this reason, reforming governments tried to exercise closer control over them. By the end of the nineteenth century, the head of the Azhar had been given greater authority than before over the teachers and students there, but he in his turn had been brought more strictly under the control of the *khedive*; the French authorities in Tunisia were trying to bring the Zaytuna under their control.

As yet there was no appreciable decline in the influence of Sufi orders. The opposition of the Wahhabis to them had little influence outside central Arabia. Some modernists criticized what they regarded as the abuses of Sufism – the authority exercised by Sufi masters over their pupils, the belief in miracles worked by the intercession of the 'friends of God' – but most believed that a purified Sufism was possible and indeed necessary for the health of the community. In general, a large part of the population continued to have some affiliation to one or other of the orders. Older ones like the Shadhiliyya and Qadiriyya continued to give rise to sub-orders; those like the Naqshbandiyya and Tijaniyya which laid emphasis on observance of the *shariʿa* went on spreading; some new ones appeared of a similar kind, like the Sanusiyya, established in Cyrenaica in the 1840s by an Algerian who had studied in Fez and Mecca.

New methods of maintaining urban order, by officials, police and garrisons (foreign ones in Egypt and the Maghrib), limited the social influence of the orders in the cities, and indeed of all forces which might instigate or express popular discontent. The later nineteenth century was a period almost without urban disorder, after the great outbreaks of the 1860s and 1870s and the disturbances at the time of the foreign occupations. In the countryside, however, teachers who had some claim to spiritual authority could still exercise the same power as before. In the age of imperial expansion, the spokesmen and leaders of rural resistance came largely from the men of religion. In Algeria, 'Abd al-Qadir's position in the local Qadiri order had provided him with a starting-point from which his power could expand; in the later revolt of 1871, the Rahmaniyya order played an important part. Similarly, in Egypt, Tunisia and Morocco resistance to the growth of European influence could be mobilized by use of Islamic symbols, and the Italian attempt to conquer Libya was to find its main opposition in the Sanusiyya, which by that time had a network of local centres in the oases of the Cyrenaican desert. Not all Sufi orders, however, took the path of resistance: in Algeria, the Tijaniyya made their peace with the French; in Egypt, most of the orders took the side of the *khedive* in the crisis of 1882.

The most striking example of the political power of a religious leader was provided by the Sudan in that movement which ended Egyptian rule in the 1880s. It drew some of its strength from opposition to the foreign governors, but had far deeper roots. Muhammad Ahmad, who founded it, drew his inspiration from his Sufi training, and was regarded by his followers as the *mahdi*, the one guided by God to restore the reign of justice in the world. His movement spread quickly, in a country where government control was limited, the towns were small and the Islam of the *'ulama* was too weak to counterbalance the influence of a rural teacher. After ending Egyptian rule he was able to create a state based upon the teachings of Islam, as interpreted by him, and consciously modelled upon the ideal community of the Prophet and his Companions. This state was carried on by his *khalifa* after his death, but was ended by the Anglo-Egyptian occupation at the end of the century.

Such movements gave fuel to the fear of the 'revolt of Islam' which reforming and foreign governments felt, and led to attempts to oppose or at least control them. In Egypt, from the time of Muhammad 'Ali there had been an attempt to control the Sufi orders by the appointment of the head of a family associated with one of them, the Bakriyya, to be head of them all; his powers and functions were formally defined later in the century. Leadership in an order became an office formally recognized by the government, and through the leaders some of the excesses of popular practice, which were coming under increasing criticism, could be restrained. In Algeria, after the revolt of 1871 the orders were regarded by the French with suspicion, and an attempt was made to repress those which seemed to be hostile, and win over the leaders of others by giving them favours.

In the Ottoman Empire, the sultan was in a position to canalize popular religious feeling in his own interests. From the middle of the nineteenth century there was a sustained effort by the government to lay emphasis on the role of the sultan, as defender of the state which was virtually the last relic of the political power and independence of Sunni Islam. The claim of the sultan to be caliph had not hitherto been put forward with much emphasis, except in the sense in which any powerful Muslim ruler could be called caliph. From the middle of the nineteenth century, however, it began to be pressed more systematically, both as a rallying call to Muslims in the empire and outside to gather around the Ottoman throne, and a warning to European states which had millions of Muslim subjects. Sultan Abdülhamid made use of Sufi confidants and protégés to emphasize his religious claims; the building of the Hijaz railway, with Muslim capital and for the purpose of taking pilgrims to the holy cities, was an expression of the same policy. Islamic modernists criticized the policy, on the ground that the kind of Islam he was encouraging was not the true Islam; they might also dispute his claim to be caliph and hope that the caliphate would return to the Arabs. Nevertheless, the policy did arouse feelings and loyalties in the world of Islam, Arab and Turkish and beyond: in India where the Mughal Empire had finally been extinguished after the 'Indian Mutiny' of 1857, in the Caucasus and central Asia where the expansion of Russian power was destroying the ancient monarchies, and in the regions of British and French control in northern Africa.

CHAPTER 19

The Climax of European Power

(1914–1939)

THE SUPREMACY OF GREAT BRITAIN AND FRANCE

By 1914 the rivalries of the European powers were breaking out of the limits imposed by the sense of common destiny and by memories of the Napoleonic wars, and the Ottoman Empire was the point at which they were most acute, because of its weakness and the importance of the interests which were at stake there. In some parts, the allocation of railway concessions had created a kind of division into spheres of interest, but in others – parts of the Balkans, Istanbul and the Straits, and Palestine – the interests of the powers clashed directly with each other. It was the Balkan rivalry of Austria and Russia which was the immediate cause of the outbreak of the First World War in 1914, and when the Ottoman Empire entered the war in November on the side of Germany and Austria, and against England, France and Russia, its own lands became a battle-ground. The Ottoman army, reinforced by its allies, had to fight Russia on its north-eastern frontier, and a mainly British force in its Arab provinces. At first the Ottoman army threatened the British position in Egypt, but later a British and allied army advanced into Palestine, and by the end of the war was in occupation of the whole of Syria. In the meantime, another British and Indian force had landed in Iraq at the head of the Gulf, and by the time the war ended it held the whole of Iraq.

By 1918, then, the military control of Britain and France in the Middle East and the Maghrib was stronger than ever before, and, what was even more important, the great imperial government under which most of the Arab countries had lived for centuries, and which had served as some kind of protection against European rule, was eclipsed and soon to disappear. The Ottoman Empire had lost its Arab provinces and was confined to Anatolia and a small part of Europe; the sultan was under the control of navies and representatives of the Allies in his capital, and was compelled to sign an unfavourable peace treaty (the Treaty of Sèvres, 1920) imposing a virtual foreign tutelage over his government; but a movement of rejection by the Turkish population of Anatolia, led by army officers and strengthened by Allied encouragement to the Greeks to occupy part of western Anatolia, resulted in the creation of a Turkish republic and the abolition of the sultanate. These changes were accepted by the allies in the Treaty of Lausanne (1923), which can be regarded as bringing the Ottoman Empire to a formal end.

The political structure within which most Arabs had lived for four centuries had disintegrated; the capital of the new Turkish state was not Istanbul but Ankara in the Anatolian highlands, and the great city which had been the seat of power for so long had lost its attractive force; the dynasty which, whether or not its claims to the caliphate were accepted, had been regarded as the guardian of what was left of the power and independence of Sunni Islam had vanished into history. These changes had a deep effect on the way in which politically conscious Arabs thought of themselves and tried to define their political identity. It posed questions about the way in which they should live together in political community. Wars are catalysts, bringing to consciousness feelings hitherto inarticulate and creating expectations of change. The idea of a world to be remade on the basis of the self-determination of national entities had been encouraged by statements made by Woodrow Wilson, President of the United States, and by other allied leaders, and wartime events had aroused a desire among some strata of some Arab peoples for a change in their political status. In the Maghrib, Algerian and Tunisian soldiers, many of them volunteers, had fought in the French army on the western front, and could expect changes which would recognize what they had done. Egyptians, although not directly involved as combatants in the war, had suffered hardships: forced labour, high prices and shortage of foodstuffs, the humiliations of being occupied by a large alien army. In the Arab parts of the Ottoman Empire the change was of a different kind. In 1916 Husayn, the *sharif* of Mecca of the Hashimite family (1908–24), came out in revolt against the Ottoman sultan, and an Arab force, recruited partly from beduin of western Arabia and partly from prisoners or deserters from the Ottoman army, fought alongside the allied forces in the occupation of Palestine and Syria. This movement had followed correspondence between the British and Husayn, acting in contact with Arab nationalist groups, in which the British had encouraged Arab hopes of independence (the McMahon–Husayn correspondence, 1915–16). A possible line of reasoning which led to this

British action is explained by the man whose name is most often associated with it, T. E. Lawrence:

We could see a new factor was needed in the East, some power or race which would outweigh the Turks in numbers, in output and in mental activity. No encouragement was given us from history to think that these qualities could be supplied ready-made from Europe . . . Some of us judged that there was latent power enough and to spare in the Arabic peoples (the greatest component of the old Turkish Empire), a prolific Semitic agglomeration, great in religious thought, reasonably industrious, mercantile, politic, yet solvent rather than dominant in character.[1]

In a way which perhaps exaggerated his own role, he claimed: 'I meant to make a new nation, to restore a lost influence'.[2] Whether anything was actually promised, and if so what, and whether the *sharif*'s revolt played a significant part in the allied victory, are matters in dispute, but what is clear is that for the first time the claim that those who spoke Arabic constituted a nation and should have a state had been to some extent accepted by a great power.

Hopes, grievances and the search for an identity all came up against the power and policies of England and France in the years after the war. In Algeria some changes were indeed made by the French government, and Muslims were henceforth to pay the same taxes as European settlers, and to have more representatives in local assemblies; but a movement led by a descendant of 'Abd al-Qadir, and asking that Muslims should be represented in the French parliament without having to abandon the Islamic laws of personal status, was suppressed. In Morocco, an armed movement of resistance to French and Spanish rule, led by 'Abd al-Karim al-Khattabi, a former judge in the Spanish zone of northern Morocco (1882–1963), in the Rif mountains in the north, was defeated in 1926, and French conquest of the whole country was virtually complete by the end of the 1920s; similarly, Italian rule had been extended from the Libyan coast into the desert by 1934. In Egypt, a British declaration had put an end to Ottoman sovereignty in 1914 and placed the country under British protectorate; the *khedive* had taken the title of sultan. In 1919, the refusal by the British government to allow an Egyptian government to present its case for independence at the peace conference touched off a widespread national rising, centrally organized and with popular support. It was suppressed, but led to the creation of a nationalist party, the Wafd, with Sa'd Zaghlul (1857–1927) as its leader, and then to the issue by the British in 1922 of a 'declaration of independence', which reserved control of strategic and economic interests to the British pending an agreement between the two countries. The declaration made it possible for an Egyptian constitution to be promulgated; the sultan changed his title once more and became king. To the south, in the Sudan, a movement of opposition in the army was suppressed, and Egyptian soldiers and officials, who had shared with the British in controlling the country under the condominium agreement, were expelled from it.

In the other Arab provinces of the Ottoman Empire, the situation was more complicated. An Anglo-French agreement of 1916, while accepting the principle of Arab independence laid down in the correspondence with the *sharif* Husayn, divided the area into zones of permanent influence (the Sykes–Picot Agreement, May 1916); and a British document of 1917, the Balfour Declaration, stated that the government viewed with favour the establishment of a Jewish national home in Palestine, provided this did not prejudice the civil and religious rights of the other inhabitants of the country. After the war ended, the Treaty of Versailles provided that the Arab countries formerly under Ottoman rule could be provisionally recognized as independent, subject to the rendering of assistance and advice by a state charged with the 'mandate' for them. It was these documents, and the interests reflected in them, which determined the political fate of the countries. Under the terms of the mandates, formally granted by the League of Nations in 1922, Britain would be responsible for Iraq and Palestine and France for Syria and Lebanon. In Syria, an attempt by supporters of Husayn's revolt – with some temporary support from the British – to create an independent state under Husayn's son Faysal was suppressed by the French, and two political entities were set up: the state of Syria, and that of Lebanon, an enlargement of the privileged region created in 1861. In 1925 a combination of specific grievances against French administration in the Druze region of Syria with nationalist opposition to the French presence led to a revolt, which was suppressed only with difficulty. To the south of the French mandated area, in Palestine and the land to the east of it, Britain held the mandate. Because of the obligation undertaken in the Balfour Declaration and repeated in the mandate, to facilitate the creation of a Jewish national home, the British ruled Palestine directly; but to the east of it a principality of Transjordan was established, ruled by another son of Husayn, 'Abdullah (1921–51), under British mandate but with no obligation in regard to the creation of the Jewish national home. In the third area, Iraq, a tribal revolt in 1920 against British military occupation, with overtones of nationalism, was followed by an attempt to set up institutions of self-government under British control. Faysal, who had been expelled from Syria by the French, became king of Iraq (1921–33), under British supervision and within the framework of the mandate; the provisions of the mandate were embodied in an Anglo-Iraqi treaty.

Of all the Arab countries, only parts of the Arabian peninsula remained free from European rule. Yemen, once the Ottoman occupation ended, became an independent state under the *imam* of the Zaydis, Yahya. In Hijaz, the *sharif* Husayn proclaimed himself king and ruled for a few years, but in the 1920s his rule, ineffective and deprived of British support, was ended by an expansion of the power of the Saudi ruler, 'Abd al-'Aziz (1902–53), from central Arabia; it became part of the new kingdom of Saudi Arabia, stretching from the Gulf to the Red Sea. Here too, however, it was confronted to the south and east by British power. The protectorate over the small states of the Gulf continued to exist; an area of British protection was extended eastwards from Aden; and in the south-western corner of the peninsula, with British help the power of the sultan of Oman in Masqat was extended into the interior at the expense of that of the Ibadi *imam*.

Without known resources, with few links with the outside world, and surrounded on all sides by British power, Yemen and Saudi Arabia could be independent only within limits. In the former Ottoman territories, the only truly independent state which emerged from the war was Turkey. Built around the framework of the Ottoman administration and army, and dominated until his death by a remarkable leader, Mustafa Kemal (Atatürk, 1881–1938), Turkey embarked on a path which led it away from its past, and from the Arab countries with which its past had been so closely connected: that of re-creating society on the basis of national solidarity, a rigid separation of state and religion, and a deliberate attempt to turn away from the Middle Eastern world and become part of Europe. The ancient tie between Turks and Arabs was dissolved, in circumstances which left some bitterness on both sides, exacerbated for a time by disputes about frontiers with Iraq and Syria. Nevertheless, the example of Atatürk, who had defied Europe with success and set his nation on a new path, was to have a profound effect upon national movements throughout the Arab world.

THE PRIMACY OF BRITISH AND FRENCH INTERESTS

Once the movements of opposition in the 1920s had been checked, Britain and France faced no serious challenge from within to their power in the Middle East and the Maghrib, and for some years there was no challenge from outside either. The other great European states – the Russian, German and Austro-Hungarian Empires – had collapsed or withdrawn into themselves at the end of the war, and this meant that the Middle East, which for long had been the field of common action or rivalry for five or six European powers, was now the domain of Britain and France, and more of Britain than of France, which had emerged formally victorious but much weakened from the war; in the Maghrib, however, France continued to be the supreme power.

For Britain and France, control over the Arab countries was important not only because of their interests in the region itself, but because it strengthened their position in the world. Britain had major interests in the Middle East: the production of cotton for the factories of Lancashire, of oil in Iran and later in Iraq, investment in Egypt and elsewhere, markets for manufactured goods, the moral interests which grew up around the obligation to help in creating a Jewish national home. There were also more extended interests: Britain's presence in the Middle East helped to maintain her position as a Mediterranean power and a world power. The sea-route to India and the Far East ran through the Suez Canal. Air-routes across the Middle East were also being developed in the 1920s and 1930s: one went by way of Egypt to Iraq and India, another through Egypt southwards into Africa. These interests were protected by a series of bases which reinforced and were reinforced by others in the Mediterranean basin and the Indian Ocean: the port of Alexandria, and other ports which could be used, military bases in Egypt and Palestine, and air-fields in those countries and in Iraq and the Gulf.

Similarly, the Maghrib was important to France not only for itself but for its place in the French imperial system. The Maghrib provided manpower for the army, minerals and other materials for industry; it was the field of vast investment, and the home of more than a million French citizens. Routes by land, sea and air to French possessions in west and central Africa passed by it. These interests were protected by the French army spread across the Maghrib, and the navy at Bizerta, Casablanca and, later, at Mers el-Kebir. Compared with this, interests in the Middle East were limited, but still considerable: investments in Egypt and Lebanon; the oil from Iraq which, by 1939, was providing half of what France needed; some degree of moral commitment to the Christians of the mandated territory. Moreover, France's military presence in Syria and Lebanon strengthened her position as a Mediterranean power and a world power; her army could use its land, her navy its ports, and a military air-route went by way of Lebanon to France's empire in Indo-China.

Until the later 1930s these positions went virtually untouched. The first serious challenge – and it was difficult to say how serious it would be – came from Italy. In 1918 Italy was already established in the Dodecanese Islands (taken from the Ottoman Empire in 1912) and on the Libyan coast, and by 1939 it occupied the whole of Libya, Albania in the Mediterranean, and Ethiopia in east Africa; it was therefore able to threaten the French position in Tunisia, where many of the European residents were of Italian origin, and that of Britain in Egypt, the Sudan and Palestine. Italy exerted some influence over Arab movements of opposition to British or French rule, and so, by 1939, did Germany, although there were as yet no clear signs of a direct German challenge to British or French interests there. Russia also had done little to assert its presence since the Revolution of 1917, although British and French officials were inclined to ascribe their difficulties to communist influence.

Firmly placed in their positions of power, Britain and France were able in the period 1918–39 to expand their control over the trade and pro-duction of the region. The Arab world was still primarily important for Europe as a source of raw materials, and a large proportion of British and French investment was devoted to creating the conditions for extracting and exporting them. It was a period of scarcity of capital for both countries, but French capital went into the Maghrib to improve the infrastructure of economic life – irrigation, railways, roads, the generation of electricity (from water where it was available, or from imported coal or oil) – and to exploit the mineral resources, in particular phosphates and manganese, of which the Maghrib countries came to be among the largest exporters. British investment extended the cultivation of cotton for export in Egypt and in the parts of the Sudan lying between the Blue and White Nile; in Palestine it developed the port of Haifa, and there was a large import of capital by Jewish institutions concerned with building the Jewish national home.

Compared with the investment of European capital in agriculture and mining, that in industry was small, and for the most part confined to building materials, food-processing and textiles. The main exception to this was the oil industry. Already by 1914 oil was being extracted in Iran, and, on a small scale, in Egypt. By 1939 it was also being produced in large quantities in Iraq, and exported to European countries – mainly to France – through a pipeline with two branches which came to the Mediterranean coast at Tripoli in Lebanon and Haifa in Palestine; it was being produced on a small scale in Saudi Arabia and Bahrayn as well. The companies had mostly British, French, American and Dutch owners, and their agreements with the producing countries reflected the unequal balance not only of financial but of political strength, with British power supporting, in the last resort, the position of the companies; the concessions under which they operated gave them control of exploration, production, refining and export, over wide areas and for long periods, subject to payment of limited royalties to the host governments and the provision of limited quantities of oil for their use.

With this exception, the Arab countries were still dependent on Europe for most manufactured goods: not only textiles but also fuels, metals and machinery. Import and export were carried out mainly by British and French ships. Egypt secured greater control over its tariffs, however, and in Morocco France was bound by an agreement made by the European states in 1906 to maintain an 'open door'.

IMMIGRANTS AND THE LAND

In countries where Europeans had immigrated on a large scale, they controlled not only finance, industry and foreign trade, but, to a large extent, the land. The *colons* of Algeria were already well established by 1914, but in the years after the war the French government tried to encourage further immigration and settlement on the land in Tunisia and Morocco. As Morocco was gradually brought under French control in the 1920s, state domain and lands held under collective title were thrown open to settlers. These efforts were successful in the sense that they led to a considerable immigration, and to an extension of the cultivated area and the yield of produce, but they did not succeed in keeping most of the immigrants on the land. From 1929 onwards the Maghrib was involved in the world economic crisis which depressed the prices of foodstuffs. The governments of the three countries, and French banks, arranged for the extension of credit to landowners, but it was in fact the large landowners who were able to make use of it. By 1939, the pattern of settlement was one of large estates, using tractors and up-to-date techniques, employing

Spanish, Berber or Arab labourers, and producing cereals and wine for the French market. Although what one writer has called 'the symbol of the red-roofed farmhouse'[3] still played an important part in the self-image of the European population, the typical immigrant was not a small cultivator but a government official, an employee of a company, a shopkeeper or mechanic. Europeans formed rather less than 10 per cent of the total population (roughly 1½ millions out of 17 millions), but they dominated the large towns: Algiers and Oran had European majorities, and Europeans formed half the population of Tunis and almost half that of Casablanca.

In two other countries the appropriation of land by immigrants was important during the period 1918–39. In Cyrenaica, the eastern part of Libya, there was official colonization on lands expropriated for the purpose, and with funds supplied by the Italian government. Here too, however, the experience of other parts of the Maghrib was repeated, and by 1939 only some 12 per cent of the Italian population of 110,000 were living on the land; the typical Italian of Libya was a dweller in Tripoli or some other coastal town.

In Palestine, the acquisition of land for European Jewish immigrants, which had begun during the late nineteenth century, continued within the new system of administration established by Britain as mandatory government. Jewish immigration was encouraged, within limits determined partly by the administration's estimate of the number of immigrants the country could absorb at any moment, and partly by the amount of pressure which Zionists or Arabs could bring to bear upon the government in London. The structure of the country's population changed dramatically during this period. In 1922 Jews had formed about 11 per cent of a total population of three-quarters of a million, the rest being mainly Arabic-speaking Muslims and Christians; by 1949 they formed more than 30 per cent of a population which had doubled. By this time there had been considerable investment, both by individual Jews and by institutions formed to help in the creation of the national home. Much of it had gone to immediate needs of immigration, some to industrial projects: electrification (for which a Jewish company was given an exclusive concession), building materials, food-processing. Much also went into the buying of land and agricultural projects. By the early 1940s Jews owned perhaps 20 per cent of the cultivable land, and a large part of this was possessed by the Jewish National Fund, which held it as the inalienable property of the Jewish people, on which no non-Jew could be employed. As in the Maghrib, the land held and cultivated by immigrants included a large proportion of the most productive areas; but again as in the Maghrib, the immigrant population had become mainly urban. By 1939 only 10 per cent of the Jewish population lived on the land, because immigration by then was too great to be absorbed in agriculture. The typical Palestinian Jew was a town-dweller living in one of the three large towns, Jerusalem, Haifa or Tel Aviv; but the farmer living in the collective settlement, the *kibbutz*, was an important symbol.

THE GROWTH OF THE INDIGENOUS ÉLITE

For the settler communities, and for the European governments, the use of their power to defend their own interests was paramount, but power is not comfortable unless it can turn itself into legitimate authority, and the idea that they were there in order to carry out a civilizing mission was strong among Europeans who ruled or conducted their business in Arab countries, whether it expressed itself as the idea of a superior civilization bringing a lower or a moribund one to its own level, or of the creation of justice, order and prosperity, or the communication of a language and the culture expressed in it. Such ideas, of which the logical conclusion was the ultimate absorption of Arabs on a level of equality into a new, unified world, were crossed by others: a sense of an unbridgeable difference, of an innate superiority which conferred the right to rule, and, among the settler groups, something else. In the Maghrib there had emerged what by now was almost a separate nation of settlers: the higher élite might belong socially and culturally to metropolitan France, but the mass of *petits blancs* were different. Of mixed Italian, Spanish and French origin, largely born in the Maghrib, speaking a French of their own, not quite at home in France, conscious of an alien and hostile world all around them, which both attracted and repelled them, they looked to France to protect their own interests, which might be different from its greater ones. Similarly, in Palestine a new Jewish nation was emerging, consciously different from that on which it had turned its back by emigration, living through the medium of the Hebrew language, which had been revived as a language of ordinary life, separated from the Arab population by differences of culture and social customs, by the aspiration to create something totally Jewish, and by growing anxiety for the fate of the Jews in Europe, and looking to England to defend its interests until it was able to maintain itself.

Major interests, as well as pressures from the settler peoples, strengthened the determination of England and France to remain in control, but on the other hand that determination was affected by doubts, if not about the morality of imperial rule, at least about its cost. Among the French there were from the beginning doubts about the profitability of the Syrian mandate, but few of them would have contemplated any kind of withdrawal from the Maghrib; even French communists would have thought rather in terms of a more complete and equal absorption of Algeria into another kind of France, although they could hope for a different relationship with the Muslims and could lend their weight to protests against specific acts of injustice. In England there was an increasing tendency to question the justice of imperial rule and to argue that essential British interests could be safeguarded in another way, by agreement with those elements in the ruled peoples which were willing to make a compromise with the imperial ruler.

The stimulus towards a change in the relationship was the greater because there seemed to be those on the other side who would make it possible: members of a new élite who, by interest or formation of mind, were committed to the kind of political and social organization which was regarded as necessary in order to live in the modern world, and who might safeguard the essential interests of the imperial powers.

By the 1920s there was in most Arab countries a class of landowners whose interests were bound up with the production of raw materials for export, or with the maintenance of imperial rule. Some of the lords of the countryside had been able to make the transition into becoming modern landowners, sometimes with the help of foreign rulers who looked to them for support. In Morocco, the way in which French control was extended inland, and the nature of the countryside, made it expedient to reach agreement with some of the powerful lords of the High Atlas, in particular Thami al-Glawi, a Berber chieftain who controlled the mountain area east of Marrakish. In Iraq, the process by which tribal land was registered as the property of leading families of the tribes, which had begun in the nineteenth century, was carried further by the British mandatory government; in the Sudan, the government for a number of years followed a policy of 'indirect rule', control of the countryside by means of tribal leaders, whose power was altered and increased by official backing. In other places, however, the landowners belonged largely to a new class brought into existence by the new conditions of commercial agriculture. The cotton-growing landowners of Egypt were the first class of this kind, and they continued to be the richest, largest and most influential in national life. Similar groups existed in Syria and Iraq, and even in the countries of European settlement in the Maghrib a new class of indigenous landowners was emerging: Tunisians cultivating olive trees in the Sahil, and Algerians buying land from *colons* who were leaving for the cities, and developing economic aspirations similar to theirs.

International trade remained largely in the hands of Europeans or members of Christian and Jewish communities who were closely connected with them, but there were some exceptions. Some Egyptian landowners were engaged in the export of cotton; the merchants of Fez, some of them now installed in Casablanca, still imported textiles from England. Again, there were some exceptions to the general rule that industry was in European hands. The most important of them was Egypt, where in 1920 a bank was established with the purpose of providing the finance for industrial enterprises; the capital of Banque Misr came mainly from large landowners seeking a more profitable investment than agriculture could now give, and in the next few years it was used to create a group of companies, in particular for shipping, making films, and spinning and weaving cotton. That it should have been established was a sign of several changes: the accumulation of national capital seeking investment, the decreasing yield of investment in land, the desire for national strength and independence. The new conditions were precarious, however, and in the late 1930s the Misr group ran into difficulties, and was saved only by government intervention.

Another kind of élite was no less important: those who had had an education of European type. Schooling in this period was still mainly confined to those who could afford it, or possessed some other advantage; even within that group, it might still be limited by the reluctance of society to send its boys (and even more its girls) to schools which would alienate them from their families and traditions, or the reluctance of the foreign rulers to educate a class which could not be absorbed into government service and might therefore go into opposition. Nevertheless education did expand, at different paces in different countries.

In Morocco, modern schools were just beginning, with the creation of a number of 'Franco-Muslim' secondary schools, and some higher institutions in Rabat. In Algeria, by 1939 the number of holders of secondary certificates was still in the hundreds, of university graduates even less; the University of Algiers, one of the leading French schools, was mainly for Europeans, but an increasing number of Muslims were finding their way to Paris, Tunis or Cairo. In Tunisia too the number of those going to *lycées* of French type was growing, and a group who were later to be leaders of their nation were going to France on scholarships to pursue higher studies.

In Egypt, the number of students in secondary schools increased from less than 10,000 in 1913–14 to more than 60,000 thirty years later; the small private university founded in the early years of the century was absorbed in 1925 into a larger, government-financed Egyptian University, with schools of arts and sciences, law, medicine, engineering and commerce. When political changes gave the Egyptian government greater control over educational policy, schools expanded rapidly at every level. The same was true of Iraq, although the process started from a lower level.

Much of the education at secondary and higher level in Egypt was in the hands of European or American religious or cultural missions. This was true also in Syria, Lebanon and Palestine. There was a small government university in Damascus, and a teachers' training college in Jerusalem, but the main universities were privately owned: in Beirut the Jesuit Université St-Joseph, supported by the French government, and the American University; and in Jerusalem the Hebrew University, which was mainly a centre for the creation of a new national culture expressed in Hebrew, and scarcely attracted any Arab students at the time. In these countries secondary education too was largely in foreign hands, which in Lebanon were mainly French.

The fact that so many of the higher institutions were foreign had several implications. For an Arab boy or girl to study in one of them was itself an act of social and psychological displacement; it involved studying in accordance with a method and a curriculum alien to the traditions of the society from which he came, and doing so through the medium of a foreign language, which became the first or perhaps the only language in which he could think of certain subjects and practise certain vocations. A further implication was that the number of girls receiving higher secondary or higher education was larger than it would have been had the only schools been state schools. Few girls went to state schools above the elementary level, many to schools kept by French Catholic nuns or American Protestant schoolteachers. In the Maghrib, where mission schools were fewer and closely associated with the immigrant population, the education of girls beyond elementary level was only just beginning. In the Arab east, more Christian and Jewish than Muslim girls went to the foreign schools; they tended to be more fully absorbed into the foreign culture, and alienated from the traditions of their society.

The graduates of the new schools found certain roles waiting to be filled in their changing societies. Women could still scarcely find a public role except that of schoolteacher or nurse, but men could become lawyers and doctors, although not to a great extent engineers or technicians; scientific and technological education was backward, and so, at a lower level, was the training of farmers and artisans. Above all, they could hope to become government officials, at levels which varied according to the degree and nature of foreign control of society: most of all in Egypt and Iraq, least in Palestine and the Sudan, where for different reasons the high positions were kept in British hands, and in the Maghrib where officials from France held the controlling positions, and intermediate and even lower ones were largely occupied by local Europeans.

Indigenous landowners and merchants needed to control the machinery of government in their own interests; educated young men wished to become government officials. These aspirations gave strength and direction to the movements of national opposition to foreign rule which marked this period, but blended with them was something else: the desire and need to live in society in a new way.

ATTEMPTS AT POLITICAL AGREEMENT

Educated men and women wanted more scope in government service and the professions, and landowners and merchants needed to be able to control the machinery of government; at times they could mobilize support among the urban masses, when they could appeal to their practical grievances, or their sense of a community in danger. Nationalism of this kind could also offer the foreign rulers the possibility of a compromise, and mobilize enough support to compel them to consider it.

In most countries, the level of political organization was not high, either because the imperial powers would not permit too serious a threat to their own position, or because traditional patterns of political behaviour persisted. In Morocco a group of younger educated men, largely drawn from the bourgeoisie of Fez, drew up a 'plan of reform' in 1934, and began to demand a change in the French protectorate. In Algeria, some members of the French-educated professional class began to put forward claims for a better position within French Algeria and for the preservation of their own culture, with independence still a distant hope; the public celebrations in 1930 of the centenary of the French occupation of the country gave a new urgency to their movement. In Syria, Palestine and Iraq, former officials and officers of the Ottoman service, some of them belonging to old families of urban notables, others having risen through the Ottoman army, pressed claims for a greater measure of self-government; their position was the more difficult for them to accept because they had so recently been members of a ruling élite. In the Sudan, a small group of graduates of the higher schools was beginning by 1939 to demand a larger share in the administration.

In two countries, however, leaders were able to create more highly organized political parties. These were Tunisia and Egypt, in both of which there was a long tradition of domination of a great city over a settled countryside. In Tunisia, the Destour party, which was the same kind of loose grouping of leaders as existed in other countries, was replaced in the 1930s by one of another kind, the Neo-Destour; founded by Habib Bourguiba (b. 1902), it was led by younger Tunisians with a French higher education, but it managed also to strike roots in the provincial towns and villages of the olive-growing coastal plain, the Sahil. The same was true of Egypt, where the Wafd party, formed in the struggle against British policy after the end of the war, created a permanent organization throughout the country. It drew support from the professional élite and other parts of the bourgeoisie, from some but not all sections of the landowning class, and at moments of crisis from the urban population as a whole; the charisma of Zaghlul survived his death in 1927, so that, in spite of splits among the leadership, the Wafd could still in 1939 claim to speak for the nation.

Whatever the ultimate hopes of such groups and parties, their immediate aim was to achieve a greater measure of self-government within imperial systems which they could not hope to overturn. In Britain rather more than in France, political and official opinion in the period gradually moved in the direction of trying to protect British interests through agreement with such groups, so that ultimate control would remain in British hands but responsibility for local government, and a limited measure of independent international action, would be given to governments representing nationalist opinion.

This policy was pursued in Iraq and Egypt. In Iraq, British mandatory control had almost from the beginning been exercised through King Faysal and his government; the scope of action of the government was extended in 1930 by an Anglo-Iraqi Treaty, by which Iraq was given formal independence in return for an agreement to co-ordinate its foreign policy with that of Britain and to allow Britain two air-bases and the use of communications in time of need; Iraq was accepted as a member of the League of Nations, a symbol of equality and admission into the international community. In Egypt, the existence on the one hand of a well-organized nationalist party and behind it a powerful landowning class and an expanding bourgeoisie not anxious for violent change, and British fears of Italian ambitions on the other, made possible a similar compromise by the Anglo-Egyptian Treaty of 1936. The military occupation of Egypt was declared to be ended, but Britain would still be able to keep armed forces in a zone round the Suez Canal; soon afterwards, the Capitulations were abolished by international agreement, and Egypt entered the League of Nations. In both countries, the balance thus achieved was a fragile one: Britain was willing to concede self-government within limits narrower than those which nationalists would permanently accept; in Iraq the ruling group was small and unstable and had no solid basis of social power to rest on; in Egypt, a time would come in the 1940s when the Wafd would not be able permanently to control and lead all the political forces in the country.

In countries under French rule, the harmony of perceived interests was not such as to make possible even the attainment of so fragile a balance. France was weaker in the world than Britain. Even when control was relaxed in Iraq and Egypt, they would still remain surrounded on all sides by British military and financial power. Their economic life would still be dominated by the City of London and the cotton-manufacturers of Lancashire. France, on the other hand, with an unstable currency, a stagnant economy and its armed forces concentrated on its eastern frontier, could not be sure of keeping independent countries within its sphere. Its essential interests in the Maghrib were different from those of Britain in Egypt. The European population had a claim on the French government, and was in a position to make its claim accepted: in Algeria and Tunisia, the large European businessmen and landowners controlled the local councils which advised the governments on budgetary and other financial matters; in Paris, the representatives of the French of Algeria in parliament, and the great financial interests which controlled the banks, industries and trading companies of the Maghrib, formed a powerful lobby against which the weak French governments of the period could not stand. This was shown clearly when the Popular Front government of 1936 tried to make concessions; it proposed that a limited electorate of Algerian Muslims should be represented in parliament, and began to talk with nationalist leaders in Tunisia and Morocco; but opposition from the lobby prevented change, and the period ended with disorders and repression through the Maghrib.

The influence of powerful lobbies opposed to change was felt also in the French mandated territories of Syria and Lebanon. In 1936 the Popular Front government negotiated treaties with them similar to that of Britain with Iraq: they were to become independent, but France would have the use of two air-bases in Syria for twenty-five years, and of military facilities in Lebanon. These were accepted by the dominant alliance of nationalist leaders in Syria, and by the mainly Christian political élite in Lebanon, but they were never ratified by France, since the Popular Front government broke up and the weak coalitions which followed it gave in to pressure from various lobbies in Paris.

The same absence of a viable balance of interests existed in Palestine. From an early point in the administration of the British mandate, it became clear that it would be difficult to create any kind of structure of local government which would accommodate both the interests of the indigenous Arab inhabitants and those of the Zionists. For the latter, the important point was to keep the doors open to immigration, and this involved maintaining direct British control until the Jewish community had become large enough and had secured enough control of the economic resources of the country to be able to look after its own interests. For the Arabs, what was essential was to prevent Jewish immigration on a scale that would endanger the economic development and ultimate self-determination, and even the existence, of the Arab community. Caught between these two pressures, the policy of the British government was to retain direct control, permit immigration within limits, favour on the whole the economic development of the Jewish community, and assure the Arabs from time to time that what was happening would not be allowed to lead to their subjection. This policy was more in the interests of the Zionists than of the Arabs, since, no matter what assurances were given, the growth of the Jewish community did bring nearer the time when it could take matters into its own hands.

By the middle 1930s, it was becoming more difficult for Britain to maintain a balance. The coming to power of the Nazis in Germany increased pressure from the Jewish community and their supporters in England to permit larger immigration; and immigration in its turn was changing the balance of population and power in Palestine. In 1936 the opposition of the Arabs began to take the form of armed insurrection. Political leadership lay with an association of urban notables, with Amin al-Husayni, *mufti* of Jerusalem, as the dominant figure, but a popular military leadership was beginning to appear, and the movement was having repercussions in surrounding Arab countries, at a moment when the threat to British interests from Italy and Germany made it desirable for Britain to have good relations with the Arab states. Faced with this situation, the

British government made two attempts to resolve it. In 1937 a plan to divide Palestine into Jewish and Arab states was put forward after an inquiry by a Royal Commission (the Peel Commission); this was acceptable to the Zionists in principle, but not to the Arabs. In 1939, a White Paper provided for the ultimate establishment of a government with an Arab majority, and limitations on Jewish immigration and purchase of land. This would have been acceptable to the Arabs with some changes, but the Jewish community would not agree to a solution which would shut the gates of Palestine to most immigrants and prevent the emergence of a Jewish state. Armed Jewish resistance was beginning to show itself, when the outbreak of a new European war ended formal political activity for the moment.

CHAPTER 20

Changing Ways of Life and Thought
(1914–1939)

POPULATION AND THE COUNTRYSIDE

Even at their strongest and most successful, understandings between the imperial powers and local nationalists would have expressed only a limited confluence of interests, and by the 1930s there were taking place changes in Arab societies which would in due course alter the nature of the political process.

Wherever it is possible to estimate it, there was a rapid increase of population. It was perhaps greatest, and is easiest to estimate reliably, in Egypt, where population increased from 12.7 millions in 1917 to 15.9 in 1937: an annual increase of 12 per thousand. On a rough guess, the total population of the Arab countries was of the order of 55–60 millions by 1939; in 1914 it had been 35–40 millions. A small part of the growth was due to immigration: Europeans in Morocco and Libya, Jews in Palestine, Armenian refugees from Turkey during and after the First World War in Syria and Lebanon. This was counterbalanced by emigration: Syrians and Lebanese going to west Africa and Latin America (but no longer to the United States in large numbers, as they had gone before 1914, because of the new American immigration laws); Algerian workers going temporarily to France. The main increase was natural, however. The birthrate does not appear to have decreased, except perhaps among sections of the bourgeoisie practising birth control, and having expectations of a rising standard of living. For most people, to have children, and male children in particular, was both unavoidable – since effective means of birth control were not generally known – and a source of pride; and the pride expressed an interest, for children could work in the fields from an early age and to have many children was a guarantee, in a society where the expectation of life was low and there was no national welfare system, that some of them would survive to look after their parents in old age. It was above all a decline in the death rate, because of control of epidemics and better medical care, which was responsible for the growth of population. This was true of all parts of society, but particularly significant in the cities, where for the first time epidemics did not play their historic role of devastating the urban masses from time to time.

Partly as a result of the growth in population, but also for other reasons, the balance between different sectors of society also changed. The 1920s and 1930s were the period when nomadic pastoralists virtually disappeared as an important factor in Arab society. The coming of the railway and the motor car struck at the activity on which the long-distance pastoral economy depended: the rearing of camels for transport. Even in areas where pasturage was still the best or the only use for sparse vegetation and scarce water, the freedom of movement of the beduin was restrictd by the use of armed forces enlisted from the nomads themselves. The market for sheep still existed, but in the sheep-rearing districts on the slopes of mountains or on the margins of the steppe the extension of control by governments and changes in urban demand were causing mainly nomadic and pastoral groups to move nearer to becoming sedentary cultivators; this was happening, for example, in the Jazira district lying between the Tigris and Euphrates rivers.

It was in this period that, perhaps for the last time, the armed force of the nomads was used in the political process. When the *sharif* Husayn revolted against the Turks, his first forces were drawn from the beduin of western Arabia, but any effective military action in the later stages of the movement came from officers or conscripts who had served in the Ottoman army. The forces with which 'Abd al-'Aziz ibn Sa'ud conquered most of Arabia were also drawn from beduin animated by a religious doctrine, but the man who led them belonged to an urban family, and an essential part of his policy was to persuade the beduin to settle. In Iraq, a conflict between groups of urban politicians in the 1930s could still be fought by means of stirring tribes in the Euphrates valley to revolt, but the government was able to use the new method of aerial bombardment against them.

In the settled countryside, the changes were not due, as they were in the pastoral areas, to a weakening of the economic basis. In most countries the area of cultivation expanded; in some of them – Morocco and Algeria, Egypt and the Sudan, and Iraq – irrigation was extended. In Egypt, it is true, the most fertile land had already been brought under cultivation, and expansion was into more marginal land, but this was not true of most of the other countries, and where capital was available it was possible to increase the yield of land. Even an expanded area of cultivation could no longer support the rural population in some countries. Not only was the population growing by natural increase, but the most productive land no longer needed so much labour. Large landowners were able to obtain capital resources and use them for mechanization, and this meant that less labour was needed. In some places (Morocco and Palestine) the import of capital was linked with the settlement of foreign workers on the land.

In a number of countries, therefore, there took place a process of polarization in the countryside. On one side there were large estates of fertile and irrigated land producing for export (cotton, cereals and wine, olive oil, oranges and dates), using tractors and fertilizers where appropriate, and cultivated by wage-labourers (crop-sharing was now becoming somewhat less common); a large proportion of them were owned by foreign companies or individuals, and in Palestine, and to a lesser extent in the Maghrib, the labour also was provided by immigrants. On the other side were smallholdings or land owned communally by a village, usually less fertile and less well watered, where small indigenous farmers with no capital resources and no access to credit produced cereals, fruit or vegetables by less advanced methods, either for consumption or for a local market, and where the increase of population was causing a decline in the ratio of land to labour and in per capita income. The situation of these farmers was made worse by the system of inheritance, which fragmented smallholdings into even smaller ones. In the 1930s it was harmed also by the world economic crisis, which led to a lowering of prices of agricultural produce. This touched all cultivators, but those who were already in a weak position were worst affected; governments or banks stepped in to rescue the large landowners who had political influence or whose production was linked to the international economy.

The surplus population of the countryside moved into the cities. This had always happened, but now it took place faster and on a larger scale and with different results. In previous ages, villages moving into the town had replenished an urban population ravaged by epidemics. Now the rural immigrants came to swell an urban population which was itself increasing because of improvements in public health. The cities, and in particular those where the possibility of employment was highest, grew more rapidly than the country as a whole; the proportion of the population living in large cities was greater than it had been. Cairo grew from a city of 800,000 in 1917 to one of 1,300,000 in 1937. In 1900 less than 15 per cent of the total population of Egypt had lived in cities of more than 20,000; by 1937 the figure was more than 25 per cent. Similarly, in Palestine the Arab population of the five largest towns more than doubled in twenty years. In the mixed cities of the Maghrib too the Arab element increased rapidly.

LIFE IN THE NEW CITIES

The result was a change in the nature and form of cities. Certain changes which had begun before 1914 were carried further after the war. Outside the *madina* there grew up new bourgeois quarters, not only of villas for the rich, but apartment blocks for the growing middle classes, government officials, professional men, and rural notables moving in from the country-side. In some places they were planned, in others they grew haphazardly at the cost of the destruction of the old. The most careful planning was in Morocco, where a French resident-general with taste, Lyautey, placed the new Fez some distance away from the old walled city. His purpose was to preserve the life of the old city, but what happened in the end was not quite what he had planned. Families of wealth and standing began to move out of their old houses in the *madina* for the greater convenience of the new quarters, and their place was taken by rural immigrants and the poor; hence a certain degradation in the physical appearance and life of the *madina*.

Not all the immigrants found shelter in the *madina*. There were also new popular quarters. Most of those who settled in them were Arabs, or, in the Maghrib, Berbers, but there were others also: *petits blancs* in Algeria drifting away from the land which they had not the capital to develop, Armenian refugees from Turkey in Beirut and Aleppo, Jewish immigrants in Palestine. Some of these quarters grew up on the outskirts of cities, where workshops and factories offered employment. In Cairo, the expansion of bourgeois quarters westwards to the Nile and across it was balanced by an expansion of poorer quarters to the north, where more than a third of the population lived by 1937; in Casablanca, the poor quarters grew up all around the city, but especially in the industrial zones. In these parts, but also in others, there were *bidonvilles*, villages with houses made of reeds or of tin cans (*bidon* in French, hence the name), appearing wherever there was an empty space.

In cities with a large foreign population, European and indigenous quarters tended to be separate, although they might be near each other. In Casablanca, which in this period changed from being a small port to the largest city in the Maghrib, around the *madina* there was a European city, and beyond it there was a new Muslim city with the characteristics of a *madina*: *suqs*, mosques, a palace for the ruler, villas for the bourgeoisie and popular dwellings. In the Middle Eastern city the separation was less complete, particularly in Syria and Lebanon where the bourgeoisie was mainly indigenous and the foreign population small; but in Palestine a sharp line divided Arab from Jewish quarters, and a wholly Jewish city, Tel Aviv, grew up side by side with Arab Jaffa.

Rural migrants tended to settle among their own people and, at least in the first phase, to preserve their own social ways. They would leave their families behind in the village to begin with, and, if they prospered enough to bring them, their life in the city would be a continuation or reconstruction of that which they had left. They brought the life of the Nile delta into Cairo, the Tigris valley into Baghdad, the Kabyle mountains into Algiers, the Shawiya and Anti-Atlas into Casablanca.

In the end, however, they would be drawn into a way of life which was different not only from that of the village but from that of the *madina*. Going to shops was not quite the same as going to the *suq*, although there was still a preference for small shops where a personal relationship was possible; restaurants, cafés and cinemas offered new kinds of recreation and new places for meeting; women could go out more freely, and the younger generation of educated Muslim women began to go unveiled, or very lightly covered. The amenities of domestic life were greater. Modern water and drainage systems, electricity and telephones spread in the 1920s; gas had come earlier. Means of transport changed. A Belgian company had laid down tramways in some of the coastal cities by the end of the nineteenth century, and then the motor car appeared; the first one was seen in the streets of Cairo in 1903, in most other cities later. By the 1930s, private cars, buses and taxis were common, and the horse-drawn carriage had virtually disappeared in all except the smaller provincial towns. Motor traffic demanded better roads and bridges, and these in their turn made it possible to enlarge the area of cities: Baghdad extended for miles along the banks of the Tigris; Cairo spread to the two islands in the Nile, Rawda and Gazira, and across to the west bank of the river.

These means of transport integrated the urban population in new ways. Men and women no longer lived entirely within a quarter. They might live a long way from their work; the extended family might be spread across a city; people of one ethnic origin or religious community might live in the same quarters as those of others; the range of marriage choices might be extended. Invisible lines of division still existed, however; intermarriage across the lines of religious communities remained difficult and rare; in cities under foreign rule barriers were created not only by religious and national difference, but by the consciousness of power and impotence. In some ways the barriers were higher than before: as European communities grew, the greater was the possibility for them to lead a separate life, similar to that in the home country; if more Arabs spoke French or English, few Europeans knew Arabic or had any concern for Islamic culture. Many Arab students returning from study abroad brought with them foreign wives, who were not always fully accepted in either community.

Just as the bourgeois need not live within his own quarter, so he was no longer as limited to his city as he had been. The changes in transportation linked city to city, country to country, in new ways. The railway network, which already existed in 1914, was extended further in some countries; in most, good roads for the first time connected the main cities. The most spectacular change was the conquest of the desert by the motor car. In the 1920s two Australian brothers whom the fortunes of war had brought to the Middle East started a regular service by taxi, and later by coach, from the Mediterranean coast by way of Damascus or Jerusalem to Baghdad; the journey from Iraq to Syria, which had taken a month before the war, could now be done in less than a day. A student from northern Iraq, who in the early 1920s had travelled to the American University of Beirut by way of Bombay, could now go there overland. In the same way, lorries and coaches could cross the Sahara from the Mediterranean coast.

Contacts were not only wider than they had been, but they could take place at a deeper level. New media of expression were creating a universe of discourse which united educated Arabs more fully than the pilgrimage and the travels of scholars in search of learning had been able to do. Newspapers multiplied, and those of Cairo were read outside Egypt; the older cultural periodicals of Egypt continued, and new ones grew up, in particular literary ones such as *al-Risala* and *al-Thaqafa* which published the work of poets and critics. The publishing houses of Cairo and Beirut produced textbooks for the increasing numbers of students, and also poetry, novels and works of popular science and history, which circulated wherever Arabic was read.

By 1914 there were already cinemas in Cairo and some other cities; in 1925 the first authentic Egyptian film was made, and appropriately it was based on the first authentic Egyptian novel, *Zaynab*. In 1932 the first 'talkie' was produced in Egypt, and by 1939 Egyptian films were shown all over the Arab world. By that time too there were local radio stations broadcasting talks, music and news, and some of the European countries were broadcasting to the Arab world, in competition with each other.

Travel, education and the new media all helped to create a shared world of taste and ideas. The phenomenon of bilingualism was common, at least in the countries on the Mediterranean coast; French and English were used in business and in the home; among women educated in French convent schools, French might virtually replace Arabic as the mother tongue. The news of the world could be gathered from foreign newspapers or broadcasts; intellectuals and scientists needed to read more in English or French than in Arabic; the habit of going to Europe for summer holidays spread, particularly among rich Egyptians who might spend several months there; Algerians, Egyptians and Palestinians grew used to seeing and meeting European or American tourists. Such movements and contacts led to changes in tastes and attitudes, not always easy to define: different ways of furnishing a room, hanging pictures on walls, eating at table, entertaining friends; different modes of dressing, particularly for women whose fashions reflected those of Paris. There were different recreations: large cities had racecourses, and in a sense this was a new form of enjoying an old sport, but tennis, a bourgeois sport, and football, enjoyed by all and played by many, were newcomers.

The example of Europe and the new media also made for changes in artistic expression. The visual arts on the whole were in an intermediate phase between old and new. There was a decline in standards of craftsmanship, both because of competition from mass-produced foreign goods, and for internal reasons: the use of imported raw materials and the need to cater to new tastes, including those of tourists. Some painters and sculptors began working in a western style, but without producing much of great interest to the outside world; there were virtually no art galleries where tastes could be formed, and picture books were not so common as they were later to become. The large architectural commissions for government buildings were given for the most part to British or French architects, some of whom (particularly the French in the Maghrib) worked in a pastiche of 'oriental' style which could be pleasing. Some Arab architects trained abroad also began to build villas of Mediterranean style, *art nouveau* mansions in Garden City in Cairo, and the first buildings of what was then the 'modern' school.

The first gramophone records of Arabic music were made in Egypt very early in the century, and the exigencies of broadcasting and of the musical film gradually brought about changes in musical conventions: from the improvised to the written and rehearsed performance, from the performer taking inspiration from an audience which applauds and encourages, to the silence of the studio. Singers performed to the accompaniment of orchestras which combined western with traditional instruments; some of the compositions they sang had become, by the 1930s, nearer to Italian or French café music than to traditional music. The older styles continued to exist, however: there were attempts to study them in Cairo, Tunis and Baghdad; Umm Kulthum, a great singer in the traditional manner, chanted the Qur'an and sang poems written by Shawqi and other poets, and the new media made her known from one end of the Arab world to the other.

THE CULTURE OF NATIONALISM

It was in literature that the most successful fusion of western and indigenous elements took place. Newspapers, radio and films spread a modern and simplified version of literary Arabic throughout the Arab world; thanks to them, Egyptian voices and intonations became familiar everywhere. Three academies, in Baghdad, Damascus and Cairo, were founded to watch over the heritage of the language. With a few exceptions, there was no challenge to the primacy of the literary language, but writers were using it in new ways. A school of Egyptian poets born in or near the 1890s, the 'Apollo' group, used traditional metres and language, but tried to express personal feelings in a way which would give unity to a whole poem; among the best known was Zaki Abu Shadi (1892–1955). The influence of English and French poetry could be seen in their work and in that of a group in the next generation: Romantics, believing that poetry should be the sincere expression of emotion, giving an attention to the natural world which was not traditional in Arabic poetry, and which became nostalgia for a lost world in the work of Lebanese poets who had emigrated to North or South America. They were Romantics too in their view of the poet as the seer who gave voice to truths received by inspiration from outside. The revolt against the past could go as far as the total rejection expressed in the writing of one of the most original of them, the Tunisian Abu'l-Qasim al-Shabbi (1909–34): 'Everything the Arab mind has produced in all the periods of its history is monotonous and utterly lacking in poetic inspiration.'[1]

The breach with the past was shown also in the development of certain literary forms virtually unknown in the classical literature. Plays had been written in the nineteenth century, and in this period some more were written, but theatres to perform them were still rare, apart from the appearance in Egypt of Najib Rihani's theatre of humorous social comment and his creation 'Kish-Kish Bey'. More significant was the development of the novel and short story, pre-eminently in Egypt, where a number of writers born in the last decade of the nineteenth century and the first of the twentieth created a new medium for the analysis and criticism of society and the individual; in their stories they depicted the poverty and oppression of the poor in village and city, the struggles of the individual to be himself in a society which tried to confine him, the conflict of the generations, the disturbing effects of western ways of life and values. Among them were Mahmud Taymur (1894–1973) and Yahya Haqqi (b. 1905).

The writer who best expressed the problems and hopes of his generation was the Egyptian Taha Husayn (1889–1973). He was not only the representative, but perhaps the most original of them, and the writer of one of the books most likely to survive as part of the literature of the world: his autobiography *al-Ayyam*, a narrative of how a blind boy became aware of himself and his world. His writings include novels, essays, works of history and literary criticism and an important work, *Mustaqbil al-thaqafa fi Misr* (*The Future of Culture in Egypt*). They show, in this period, a sustained attempt to hold in balance the three essential elements, as he sees them, of the distinctive Egyptian culture: the Arab element, and above all the classical Arabic language; the elements brought in from outside at different periods, and above all that of Greek rationalism; and the basic Egyptian element, persisting throughout history:

Three elements have formed the literary spirit of Egypt since it was arabicized. The first of them is the purely Egyptian element which we have inherited from the ancient Egyptians . . . and which we have drawn perpetually from the land and sky of Egypt, from its Nile and its desert . . . The second element is the Arab element, which came to us through its language and religion and civilization. Whatever we do, we shall not be able to escape from it, or weaken it, or diminish its influence in our life, because it is mingled with that life in a way which has formed it and shaped its personality. Do not say that it is a foreign element . . . The Arabic language is not a foreign language among us, it is *our* language, and a thousand times closer to us than the language of the ancient Egyptians . . . As for the third element, it is the foreign element which has always influenced Egyptian life, and will always do so. It is what has come to Egypt from its contacts with the civilized peoples in the east and west . . . Greeks, and Romans, Jews and Phoenicians in ancient times, Arabs, Turks and Crusaders in the Middle Ages, Europe and America in the modern age . . . I should like Egyptian education to be firmly based on a certain harmony between these three elements.[2]

His assertion that Egypt was part of the world of culture formed by Greek thought aroused most attention at the time, but perhaps his most lasting contribution lay in his care for the Arabic language, and his demonstration that it could be used to express all the nuances of a modern mind and sensibility.

He wrote also about Islam, but at least in the 1920s and 1930s what he wrote was in the form of an imaginative re-creation of the life of the Prophet, of a kind which could satisfy the emotions of ordinary people. Later he was to write in a different vein, but for the moment the unifying principle of his thought was not Islam so much as the collective identity of the Egyptian nation. In one form or another, this was to be characteristic of educated Arabs of his generation. The central theme was that of the nation; not only how it could become independent, but how it could have the strength and health to prosper in the modern world. The definition of the nation might vary: since every Arab country was facing a different problem in relation to its European rulers, there was a tendency, at least among the political leaders, to develop a separate national movement in each, and an ideology to justify it. This was particularly true of Egypt, which had had its own political destiny since the time of Muhammad 'Ali. In some cases, the fact of a separate existence was given legitimacy by a theory of history. Nationalist movements were revolts against the present and the immediate past, and they could appeal to the memory of a more distant, pre-Islamic past, to which the discoveries of archaeologists and the opening of museums gave a visible reality. The discovery of the tomb of Tutankhamen in 1922 aroused great interest, and encouraged Egyptians to lay emphasis upon the continuity of Egyptian life from the time of the Pharaohs.

Ahmad Shawqi, who had been the poet of the Egyptian court, emerged in the 1920s as a spokesman of an Egyptian nationalism which drew inspiration and hope from the monuments of the immemorial past of Egypt. In one of his poems, written for the unveiling of a monument in a public garden in Cairo, he portrays the Sphinx as looking down unchanged on the whole of Egyptian history:

Speak! and perhaps your speech will guide us. Inform us, and perhaps what you tell us will console us. Have you not seen Pharaoh in his might, claiming descent from the sun and moon, giving shade to the civilization of our ancestors, the high edifices, the great relics? . . . You have seen Caesar in his tyranny over us, making us slaves, his men driving us before them as one drives donkeys, and then defeated by a small band of noble conquerors . . . [the Sphinx speaks:] I have preserved for you something that will strengthen you, for nothing preserves sweetness like stone . . . The morning of hope wipes out the darkness of despair, now is the long-awaited daybreak.[3]

Deeply rooted in such movements, whether it was explicit or not, was an Arab element. Since the aim of the nationalist movements was to create an autonomous and flourishing modern society, the revival of the Arabic language as a medium of modern expression and a bond of unity was a central theme.

For the same reason, there was inevitably an Islamic element in nationalism. It tended to be implicit and submerged among the educated classes in this period, both because the separation of religion from political life seemed to be a condition of successful national life in the modern world, and because in some of the eastern Arab countries – Syria, Palestine, Egypt – Muslims and Christians lived together, and the emphasis was therefore on their common national bonds. (Lebanon was a partial exception to this. The larger Lebanon created by the French included more Muslims than the privileged Ottoman district had had. Most of the Muslims thus incorporated in it believed it should be absorbed in a larger Arab or Syrian entity; for most of the Christians, it was essentially a Christian state. It was only towards the end of the 1930s that the idea of a state based on accord between the various Christian and Muslim communities began to gain strength.)

The idea that a group of people form a nation, and that the nation should be independent, is a simple one, too simple to be able by itself to provide guidance for the way in which social life should be organized. In this period, however, it served as a focus for a cluster of other ideas. In general, the nationalism of this period was secularist, believing in a bond which could embrace people of different schools or faiths, and a policy based upon the interests of state and society, and it was constitutionalist, holding that the will of the nation should be expressed by elected governments responsible to elected assemblies. It placed great emphasis on the need for popular education, which would enable the nation to participate more fully in its collective life. It stood for the development of national industries, since industrialization seemed to be the source of strength.

The idea of Europe as the exemplar of modern civilization, which had animated the reforming governments of the previous century, was powerful in these national movements. To be independent was to be accepted by European states on a level of equality, to have the Capitulations, the legal privileges of foreign citizens, abolished, to be admitted to the League of Nations. To be modern was to have a political and social life similar to those of the countries of western Europe.

Another component of this cluster of ideas deserves more than a passing mention. Nationalism gave an impetus to the movement for the emancipation of women. The opening of schools for girls, by governments and foreign missions, had given a stimulus to this during the second half of the nineteenth century; travel, the European press and the example of European women all encouraged it; it found a theoretical justification in the writings of a few writers connected with the Islamic reform movement (but by no means all of them).

The autobiography of a member of a prominent Sunni Muslim family of Beirut conveys some idea of the ferment of change. Born in the last years of the nineteenth century, brought up in the warm certainties of a traditional family life, and wearing the veil in public until her twenties, 'Anbara Salam received a full modern education. Her mother and grandmother were literate and read books of religion and history, and she herself was sent to school: for a time to a Catholic school, from which she kept a lasting memory of the humility and sweetness of the nuns, then to one established by a Muslim benevolent association. She also took lessons in Arabic from one of the leading scholars of the day. A visit to Cairo in 1912 revealed some of the marvels of modern civilization: electric lights, lifts, automobiles, the cinema, theatres with special places for women. Before she was out of her teens she had begun to write in the press, to speak at women's meetings, and to have a new idea of personal independence: she refused to be betrothed to a relation at an early age, and decided she could not marry someone whom she did not already know. When she married, it was with a member of a prominent family of Jerusalem, Ahmad Samih al-Khalidi, a leader in the promotion of Arab education, with whom she shared in the life and misfortunes of the Palestinian Arabs, while playing her own part in the emancipation of Arab women.[4]

The desire to generate all the potential strength of the nation gave a new meaning to the emancipation of women: how could the nation flourish while half its power was unused; how could it be a free society so long as there was inequality of rights and duties? The excitement of nationalist activity gave a new kind of courage. As the leading Egyptian feminist of her time, Huda Sha'rawi (1878–1947), arrived at the main railway station of Cairo on her return from a women's conference in Rome in 1923, she stepped on to the running-board of the train and drew back the veil from her face; it is said that the women present broke into applause and some of them copied her. Her example was followed by some of her generation, while those of the next may never have worn the veil.

By 1939, however, the changes had not gone very deep. There were more girls in schools and a few in universities, an expanding freedom of social intercourse, but no effective change in the legal status of women; some women participated in political activities, the movement of the Wafd in Egypt and resistance to British policy in Palestine, but few professions were open to them. Egypt, Lebanon and Palestine had moved furthest on this road; in some other countries, like Morocco, the Sudan and the countries of the Arabian peninsula, almost no change could be seen.

ISLAM OF THE ÉLITE AND THE MASSES

The old-established populations of cities, of whatever level of income, had been formed by the experience of living together in urban community. A system of customs, a shared possession of things regarded as sacred, had held them together; notables and bourgeoisie, living among craftsmen and shopkeepers, controlled their production and acted as their protectors. The religion of the city and the countryside, although differing, had been linked by common observance of prayer, Ramadan and pilgrimage, and reverence for common places of devotion. Most urban *'ulama* belonged to one or other of the Sufi orders, whose ramifications spread throughout the countryside; even if the villagers lived by custom, they respected the *shari'a* in principle and might use its forms to express important agreements and common undertakings. Now, however, the two worlds of thought and practice were becoming more distant from each other. In cities of the new kind, physical separation was a sign of a deeper divorce of attitudes, tastes, habits and faith.

By the 1930s a large part of the educated élite was no longer living within the bounds of the *shari'a*. In the new Turkish republic it was formally abolished and replaced by positive laws derived from European models. No Arab country, and no European power ruling Arabs, went to such lengths, but in countries affected by the reforms of the nineteenth century, whether introduced by reforming autocrats or by foreign rulers, a duality of legal systems was by now well established. Criminal, civil and commercial cases were decided according to European codes and procedures, and the authority of the *shariʿa*, and of the judges who dispensed it, was confined to matters of personal status. The main exception was the Arabian peninsula: in Saudi Arabia, the Hanbali version of the *shariʿa* was the only recognized law of the state, and religious obligations, those of prayer and fasting, were rigorously enforced by state officials. In countries where the pace of change was greatest, even the religious prescriptions of the *shariʿa* were less widely observed than before. They still governed the great moments of human life – birth and circumcision, the contract of marriage, death and inheritance – but in the new bourgeois quarters the ritual of the five daily prayers, announced by the call from the minaret, was less important as a measure of time and life; perhaps Ramadan was less fully observed than in the past, when life was freed from the social pressures of the *madina* where everyone watched his neighbours; the use of alcoholic drinks was more widespread. The number of those for whom Islam was an inherited culture rather than a rule of life increased.

Those among the educated élite for whom Islam was still a living faith tended to interpret it in a new way. The position of the *ʿulama* in high urban society had changed. They no longer filled important positions in the system of government; not they but leaders of political parties were now the spokesmen for the aspirations of the bourgeoisie. The education they offered was no longer so attractive to the young and ambitious who had a possibility of choice; it did not lead to advancement in government service, and it did not appear to offer any help in understanding or mastering the modern world. In Syria, Palestine and Lebanon, in Egypt and Tunisia, the young man (and to some extent the young woman) of good family would go to a modern secondary school, official or foreign, to the universities in Cairo or Beirut, or to France, England or the United States. Even in Morocco, which had been slower to change, the new school set up by the French in Fez, the Collège Moulay Idris, was drawing students away from the Qarawiyyin.

The Islam of those educated in the new fashion was no longer that of the Azhar or the Zaytuna, but that of the reformists of the school of ʿAbduh. Those who interpreted his thought in the direction of a separation *de facto* between the spheres of religion and social life found a new topic of discussion in the 1920s: the abolition of the Ottoman caliphate by the new Turkish Republic gave rise to thought about the nature of political authority, and one of ʿAbduh's followers, ʿAli ʿAbd al-Raziq (1888–1966), wrote a famous book, *al-Islam wa usul al-hukm* (*Islam and the Bases of Political Authority*), in which he argued that the caliphate was not of divine origin, and that the Prophet had not been sent to found a state and had not in fact done so:

In reality, the religion of Islam is innocent of that caliphate which Muslims have come to know . . . It is not a religious institution, nor is the office of judge or any of the offices of state . . . These are all purely political offices. Religion has nothing to do with them; it neither knows nor denies them, neither commands nor forbids them, it has left them to us, to consult in regard to them the principles of reason, the experience of nations, and the laws of statecraft.[5]

His ideas were badly received by religious conservatives, but their implication, that the caliphate should not be restored, was generally accepted.

The other line of thought which derived from 'Abduh was that which laid emphasis on the need to go back to the bases of the faith and derive from them, by responsible reasoning, a social morality which would be acceptable in modern times. This kind of reformism began to have a large influence in the Maghrib, and one which in the end would take a political form. In Algeria, an Association of Algerian 'Ulama was founded in 1931 by Muhammad Ben Badis, with the aim of restoring the moral supremacy of Islam, and with it of the Arabic language, among a people whom a century of French rule had torn from their roots. This it sought to do by putting forward an interpretation of Islam based on the Qur'an and Hadith and tending to break down the barriers between different sects and schools of law, by creating non-governmental schools teaching in Arabic and by working for the release of Islamic institutions from state control. Its work drew upon it the hostility of Sufi leaders and the suspicion of the French government, and by 1939 it had become more fully involved in political life, and identified with the nationalist demand that Muslims should have equal rights within the French system, without having to give up their distinctive laws and social morality.

In Morocco also reformist teachings took root in the 1920s, with similar results. To try to purge Moroccan Islam from the corruptions of later times was, by implication, to attack the position which the leaders of Sufi orders had held in Moroccan society; and to call for a society and state based upon a reformed *shari'a* was to oppose the rule of the foreign occupiers of the country. Such teachings pointed the way towards political action, and when a nationalist movement emerged it was led by a disciple of the reformers, 'Allal al-Fasi (1910–74). The moment for action came in 1930, when what was believed to be an attempt by the French to replace the *shari'a* by customary law in Berber districts was interpreted by the nationalists as an attempt to split Berbers from Arabs, and provided an issue on which they could mobilize urban opinion.

These were movements among the educated élite, but the urban masses, and the rural population which was swelling them, still held to traditional ways of beliefs and behaviour. Prayer, fast and pilgrimage still gave shape to the stream of days and years; the preacher in the mosque on Friday and the Sufi teacher who guarded the tomb of a saint were still those who formed and expressed public opinion on questions of the day. Sufi orders were still widespread among the masses in city and countryside, but their nature and role were changing. Under the influence of reformism and Wahhabism, fewer of the 'ulama and the educated class joined them, and Sufi thought and practice were no longer held within the restraints of the high urban culture. When the government controlled the countryside firmly, the political role of the Sufi leader was more limited than it had been, but where such control was weak or lacking he could still become the head of a political movement. During the Italian conquest of Libya, resistance in the eastern region, Cyrenaica, was led and directed by the heads of the Sanusi order.

Even within the world of popular Islam the more activist, political version was spreading. Among Algerian workers, in France and Algeria itself, a popular movement spread in the 1930s: the Étoile Nord-Africaine, led by Messali al-Hajj, more openly nationalist than the movements of the French-educated élite, and appealing more openly to Islamic sentiment. Of more general significance was a movement in Egypt which was to serve as a prototype of similar groups in other Muslim countries: the Society of the Muslim Brothers. Founded in 1928 by an elementary-school teacher, Hasan al-Banna (1906–49), it was not specifically or exclusively political:

You are not a benevolent society, nor a political party, nor a local organization having limited purposes. Rather, you are a new soul in the heart of this nation to give it life by means of the Qur'an . . . When asked what it is for which you call, reply that it is Islam, the message of Muhammad, the religion that contains within it government, and has as one of its obligations freedom. If you are told that you are political, answer that Islam admits no such distinction. If you are accused of being revolutionaries, say, 'We are voices for right and for peace in which we dearly believe, and of which we are proud. If you rise against us or stand in the path of our message, then we are permitted by God to defend ourselves against your injustice.'[6]

The Muslim Brothers began as a movement for the reform of individual and social morality, based on an analysis of what was wrong with Muslim societies, similar to, and in part derived from, that of the Salafiyya. Islam, it believed, had declined because of the prevalence of a spirit of blind imitation and the coming in of the excesses of Sufism; to these had been added the influence of the West, which, in spite of its social virtues, had brought alien values, immorality, missionary activity and imperial domination. The beginning of a cure was for Muslims to return to the true Islam, that of the Qur'an as interpreted by genuine *ijtihad*, and to try to follow its teachings in every sphere of life; Egypt should become an Islamic state based upon a reformed *shari'a*. This would have implications in every aspect of its life. Women should be educated and allowed to work, but some kind of social distance between them and men should be maintained; education should be based upon religion; the economy too should be reformed in the light of principles deduced from the Qur'an.

This teaching had political implications too. Although the Brothers did not at first claim that they themselves should rule, they would recognize as legitimate rulers only those who acted according to the *shari'a* and were opposed to a foreign rule which threatened the *shari'a* and the community of believers. They were primarily concerned with Egypt, but their view extended over the whole Muslim world, and their first active involvement in politics came with the revolt of the Palestinian Arabs in the late 1930s. By the end of the decade they were a political force to be reckoned with, and were spreading in the urban population – among neither the poor nor the very highly educated, but among those in an intermediate position: craftsmen, small tradesmen, teachers and professional men who stood outside the charmed circle of the dominant élite, had been educated in Arabic rather than in English or French, and read their scriptures in a simple, literal way.

The belief of such movements as the Muslim Brothers that the doctrines and laws of Islam could provide the bases of society in the modern world was encouraged by the creation of a state which had such a basis: that of Saudi Arabia. The attempts of King 'Abd al-'Aziz and his Wahhabi supporters to maintain the predominance of the *shari'a* in its Hanbali form, against tribal custom on the one hand and innovations from the West on the other, was to have a greater influence at a later time, when the kingdom came to occupy a more important position in the world, but even in this period it had a certain resonance; however poor and backward, Saudi Arabia contained the holy cities of Islam.

PART V

THE AGE OF NATION-STATES

(since 1939)

The Second World War changed the structure of power in the world. The defeat of France, the financial burdens of the war, the emergence of the USA and USSR as super-powers, and a certain change in the climate of opinion were to lead, in the next two decades, to the end of British and French rule in the Arab countries. The Suez crisis of 1956 and the Algerian war of 1954–62 marked the last major attempts of the two powers to reassert their position. In one place, Palestine, British withdrawal led to a defeat for the Arabs when the state of Israel was created. Elsewhere, the former rulers were replaced by regimes of one kind or other committed to the cluster of ideas which had gathered around that of nationalism: the development of national resources, popular education and the emancipation of women. They had to try to carry out their policies within societies in process of rapid change: populations were growing fast; cities were expanding, in particular the capital cities; societies were stratified in different ways; and the new mass media – the cinema, radio, television and cassette – made possible a different kind of mobilization.

The dominant idea of the 1950 and 1960s was that of Arab nationalism, aspiring towards a close union of Arab countries, independence from the super-powers, and social reforms in the direction of greater equality; this idea was embodied for a time in the personality of Jamal 'Abd al-Nasir, ruler of Egypt. The defeat of Egypt and Syria and Jordan in the war of 1967 with Israel, however, halted the advance of this idea, and opened a period of disunity and increasing dependence on one or other of the super-powers, with the USA in the ascendant. At other levels, contacts between the Arab peoples were growing closer: the media, both old and new, transmitted ideas and images from one Arab country to another; in some

351

of the Arab countries the exploitation of oil resources made possible rapid economic growth, and this attracted migrants from other countries.

In the 1980s, a combination of factors added a third idea to those of nationalism and social justice as a force which might give legitimacy to a regime, but might also animate movements of opposition to it. The need of uprooted urban populations to find a solid basis for their lives, the sense of the past implicit in the idea of nationalism, an aversion from the new ideas and customs which were coming in from the western world, and the example of the Iranian revolution of 1979 all led to the rapid growth of Islamic feelings and loyalties.

CHAPTER 21

The End of the Empires (1939–1962)

The Second World War came upon an Arab world which seemed to be firmly held within the British and French imperial systems. Nationalists might hope for a more favoured position within them, but the military, economic and cultural ascendancy of England and France seemed unshakeable. Neither the United States nor the Soviet Union had more than a limited concern with the Middle East or the Maghrib. German and Italian power and propaganda had some influence over the younger generation, but until the war broke out a structure so firmly based seemed able to resist the challenge. Once more, however, war was a catalyst, bringing rapid changes in power and social life, and in the ideas and hopes of those affected by it.

For the first few months the war was a northern European one, with French armies in the Maghrib and British and French in the Middle East on the alert but not engaged. The situation changed in 1940, when France was defeated and withdrew from the war and Italy entered it. Italian armies threatened the British position in the western desert of Egypt, and in Ethiopia on the southern frontier of the Sudan. In the early months of 1941 the German occupation of Yugoslavia and Greece aroused fears that Germany might move further eastwards, into Syria and Lebanon which were ruled by a French administration receiving its orders from France, and into Iraq, where power had fallen into the hands of a group of army officers and politicians headed by Rashid 'Ali al-Gaylani (1892–1965) and having some relations with Germany. In May 1941 Iraq was occupied by a British force which restored a government favourable to Britain, and in June Syria was invaded by British and imperial forces, together with a French force formed from those who had responded to the call of General de Gaulle that France had not lost the war and Frenchmen should continue to take part in it.

From the middle of 1941 the war between European states became a world war. The German invasion of Russia opened the possibility that Germany might advance into the Middle East through the Caucasus and Turkey, and the wish to send British and American supplies to Russia led to a joint occupation of Iran by British and Soviet armies. At the end of the year, the Japanese attack upon the American navy brought the United States into the war, against Germany and Italy as well as Japan. The years 1942–3 were the turning-point in the Middle East. A German army had reinforced the Italians in Libya, and in July 1942 they advanced into Egypt and stood not far from Alexandria; but the war in the desert was one of rapid movement, and before the end of the year a counterattack brought the British forces far westwards into Libya. Almost at the same time, in November, Anglo-American armies landed in the Maghrib and rapidly occupied Morocco and Algeria. The Germans fell back on their last stronghold in Tunisia, but finally abandoned it under attack from both east and west in May 1943.

The active war was now more or less ended so far as the Arab countries were concerned, and it might have seemed to end with a reassertion of British and French predominance. All the countries which had previously been under British control remained so, and British armies were in Libya, Syria and Lebanon as well. French rule still continued formally in Syria and Lebanon and in the Maghrib, where the French army was being remade to take an active part in the last stages of the war in Europe.

In fact, however, the bases of British and French power had been shaken. The collapse of France in 1940 had weakened its position in the eyes of those it ruled; although it had emerged on the side of the victors, and with the formal status of a great power, the problems of re-creating a stable national life and restoring a damaged economy would make it more difficult to hold on to an empire that reached from Morocco to Indo-China. In Britain, the efforts of the war had led to an economic crisis which could be overcome only gradually and with help from the United States; fatigue and the consciousness of dependence strengthened the doubt whether it was possible or desirable to rule so large an empire in the same way as before. Overshadowing Britain and France were the two powers whose potential strength had been made actual by the war. The United States and the Soviet Union had greater economic resources and manpower than any other states, and in the course of the war had established a presence in many parts of the world. Henceforth they would be in a position to claim that their interests should be taken into account everywhere, and the economic dependence of Europe upon American aid gave the United States a powerful means of pressure upon its European allies.

Among the Arab peoples, the events of the war aroused hopes of a life made new. The movements of armies (particularly rapid and extensive in the desert), the fears and expectations of occupation and liberation, the prospects held out by competing services of propaganda, the spectacle of Europe tearing itself to pieces, the declarations of high principle by the victorious Anglo-American alliance, and the emergence of communist Russia as a world power: all these encouraged the belief that life might be different.

Among many other changes, the circumstances of the war strengthened the idea of closer unity between the Arab countries. Cairo was the main centre from which the British organized the struggle for the Middle East, and also its economic life; the need to conserve shipping led to the creation of the Middle East Supply Centre (British at first, and later Anglo-American), which went beyond regulating imports to encouraging changes in agriculture and industry which would make the Middle East more fully self-supporting. The fact that Cairo was the centre of military and economic decision-making gave an opportunity to the Egyptian government (with rather vague encouragement from Britain) to take the initiative in creating closer links between Arab states. In early 1942 a British ultimatum to the king of Egypt compelled him to ask the Wafd to form a government; at this critical moment of the war it seemed desirable to Britain to have an Egyptian government which could control the country and was more ready to co-operate with the British than the king and those who surrounded him. The authority which this gave the Wafd government enabled it to undertake discussions with other Arab states about the possibility of closer and more formal unity between them. There were differences of sentiment and interest: in Syria and Iraq, the leaders still had memories of the lost unity of the Ottoman Empire, and wished for some closer bond; Lebanon was precariously balanced between those who thought of themselves as Arabs and those, mainly Christians, who saw Lebanon as a separate country closely linked with western Europe; the governments of Egypt, Saudi Arabia and Yemen had some sense of Arab solidarity, but a strong conception of their national interest; all of them wished to create an effective support for the Arabs of Palestine. Two conferences held at Alexandria in 1944 and Cairo in 1945 resulted in the creation of the

League of Arab States. This brought together seven states which had some freedom of action (Egypt, Syria, Lebanon, Transjordan, Iraq, Saudi Arabia and Yemen), along with a representative of the Palestinian Arabs, with the door left open for other Arab countries to join if they should become independent. There was to be no interference in the sovereignty of each country, but it was hoped that they would act together in matters of common concern – in particular, the defence of the Arabs in Palestine and the Maghrib – and in whatever international organization would emerge from the war. When the United Nations was formed in 1945, the independent Arab states became members of it.

NATIONAL INDEPENDENCE (1945–1956)

After the end of the war, the Middle East and the Maghrib, which for a generation had been the almost exclusive field of influence of two European states, became one where four or more could exercise power of influence, and where relations between them were not so stable as they had been in the period of the 'Concert of Europe'. In this situation, it was possible for nationalist parties and the local interests they represented to press for changes in the status of their countries.

France was in a weaker position than Britain, and the pressure upon it was the greater. At the end of the war it was able to restore its position in Indo-China and the Maghrib, after severe repression of disturbances in eastern Algeria in 1945, but was obliged to leave Syria and Lebanon. When British and Free French forces occupied the country in 1941, an arrangement was made by which the French had administrative authority but the British had strategic control; Britain recognized France's position as paramount European power, subject to the grant of independence to the two countries. The possibilities of a clash of interests were strong. The Free French were unwilling to grant self-government immediately; their claim to be the real France would not seem plausible in French eyes if they surrendered a French territory not, as they believed, to its inhabitants, but to be drawn into the British sphere of influence. For the British, on the other hand, to fulfil the pledge of independence would be to their advantage among Arab nationalists hostile to their policy in Palestine. The politicians of Beirut and Damascus were able to make use of this disagreement in order to obtain independence before the war should end and they be left to the unrestrained rule of the French. There were two crises, one in 1943 when the Lebanese government tried to limit French authority, and the second in 1945 when a similar attempt by the Syrians led to a French bombardment of Damascus, a British intervention, and a process of negotiation which ended in an agreement that the French and British should withdraw simultaneously and completely by the end of 1945. Thus Syria and Lebanon obtained complete independence, without the limitations that the treaties with Britain had imposed upon Egypt and Iraq. Henceforth it would be difficult for any nationalist party to settle for less than that.

The British position in the Middle East appeared to be unshaken and in some ways strengthened by the end of the war. The campaigns in the desert had brought one more Arab country, Libya, under British rule. In the Arab parts of the Middle East, the United States seemed to have no wish to replace Britain as the paramount power, although there were overtones of rivalry for markets and for control of oil production. The beginning of the 'Cold War', however, led to greater American involvement. In 1947 the United States took over responsibility for defending Greece and Turkey against any Russian threats to them, and the implication of this was that further south, in the Arab countries, Britain would be mainly responsible for protecting western political and strategic interests in the new era of Cold War.

This implicit understanding was to last for ten years or so, and during the earlier part of that period there was a sustained effort by the Labour government in Britain to put its relations with the Arab countries on a new footing. The British withdrawal from India in 1947 might have appeared to make it less important than before for Britain to remain in the Middle East, but this was not the government's view; investments, oil, markets, communications, the strategic interests of the western alliance, and the sense that the Middle East and Africa remained the only parts of the world where Britain could take the initiative seemed to make it more important to retain its position, but on a new basis.

The general line of British policy was one of support for Arab independence and a greater degree of unity, while preserving essential strategic interests by friendly agreement, and also of helping in economic development and the acquisition of technical skills to the point where Arab governments could take responsibility for their own defence. This policy rested on two assumptions: that Arab governments would regard their major interests as being identical with those of Britain and the western alliance; and that British and American interests would coincide to the extent that the stronger party would be willing to leave the defence of its interests to the weaker. In the next ten years, however, both these assumptions were proved to be invalid.

The first country where a decision had to be made was Libya. At the end of the war there was a British military administration in two of the three regions of the country, Cyrenaica and Tripolitania, and a French in the third, Fazzan. In the eastern region, Cyrenaica, forces loyal to the head of the Sanusi order had helped in the conquest and been given promises about the future. In discussions among the major powers and other interested parties and at the United Nations, the idea was put forward that Libya might be a country in which the new concept of a 'trusteeship' of 'more advanced' countries could be applied. In one of the first expressions of that hostility to imperial rule which was to become one of the marks of the United Nations, the majority was reluctant to allow Britain or France to remain in Libya, or Italy to return as trustee. Various local groups asked for independence, although they disagreed about the future relationship between the three regions, and in 1949 the United Nations passed a resolution supporting independence and set up an international commission to supervise the transfer of power. In 1951 the country became independent, with the head of the Sanusi order as King Idris, but for a number of years Britain and the United States kept military bases there.

In another country, Palestine, the resolution of conflicting interests proved to be impossible, and this was to cause lasting damage to relations between the Arab peoples and the western powers. During the war, Jewish immigration to Palestine had been virtually impossible, and political activity had for the most part been suspended. As the war drew near its end, it became clear that the relationships of power had changed. The Arabs in Palestine were less capable than before of presenting a united front, because of the exile or imprisonment of some leaders during and after the revolt of 1936–9 and the tensions and hostilities generated by violent movements; the formation of the Arab League, with its commitment to support for the Palestinians, seemed to offer them a strength which in the end turned out to be illusory. The Palestinian Jews for their part were united by strong communal institutions; many of them had had military training and experience in the British forces during the war; they had wider and more determined support from Jews in other countries, stirred by the massacres of Jews in Europe, and resolved to create not only a refuge for those who had survived but a position of strength which would make such an event impossible in future. The British government, while conscious of the arguments in favour of rapid and large-scale Jewish immigration, was aware also that it would lead to a demand for a Jewish state, and that this would arouse strong opposition from the Arabs, who were fearful of being subjected or dispossessed, and from the Arab states. It was no longer so free to act as it had been before 1939, because of its close relations with the United States and economic dependence on it; the American government, having as yet smaller interests of its own in the Middle East, and being under some pressure from its large and politically active Jewish community, was inclined to use its influence in favour of the Zionist demands for immigration and statehood. The question of Palestine now became an important issue in Anglo-American relations. Attempts to agree upon a joint policy, by means of an Anglo-American committee of inquiry (1945–6) and then bilateral discussions, came to no conclusion, for no policy suggested met with the approval of both Jews and Arabs, and the British government was not willing to carry out a policy which did not have that approval. American pressure upon Britain increased, and Jewish attacks upon British officials and installations in Palestine came near the point of open revolt.

In 1947 Britain decided to hand the matter over to the United Nations. A special committee of the United Nations sent out to study the problem produced a plan of partition on terms more favourable to the Zionists than that of 1937 had been. This was accepted by the General Assembly of the United Nations in November 1947, with very active support from the United States and from Russia, which wanted the British to withdraw from Palestine. The Arab members of the United Nations and the Palestinian Arabs rejected it, and, faced once more with the impossibility of finding a policy which both Arabs and Jews would accept, Britain decided to withdraw from Palestine on a fixed date, 14 May 1948. This followed a precedent recently set by the British withdrawal from India, and it may have been hoped that, as in India, the imminence of withdrawal would bring the two parties to some kind of agreement. As the date came nearer, British authority inevitably decreased and fighting broke out, in which the Jews soon gained the upper hand. This in turn led to a decision by the neighbouring Arab states to intervene, and thus a series of local conflicts turned into a war. On 14 May the Jewish community declared its independence as the state of Israel, and this was immediately recognized by the United States and Russia; and Egyptian, Jordanian, Iraqi, Syrian and Lebanese forces moved into the mainly Arab parts of the country. In a situation where there were no fixed frontiers or clear divisions of population, fighting took place between the new Israeli army and those of the

Arab states, and in four campaigns interrupted by cease-fires Israel was able to occupy the greater part of the country. From prudence to begin with, later because of panic and the deliberate policy of the Israeli army, almost two-thirds of the Arab population left their homes and became refugees. At the beginning of 1949 a series of armistices was made between Israel and its Arab neighbours under the supervision of the United Nations, and stable frontiers were created. About 75 per cent of Palestine was included within the frontiers of Israel; a strip of land on the southern coast, stretching from Gaza to the Egyptian frontier, was taken under Egyptian administration; the remainder was annexed by the Hashimite Kingdom of Jordan (the name taken by Transjordan in 1946 after a treaty with Britain redefined the relations between the two countries). Jerusalem was divided between Israel and Jordan, although many other countries did not formally recognize the division.

Public opinion in the Arab countries was much affected by these events. They were regarded as a defeat for the Arab governments, and this was to lead to a number of upheavals in the next few years. They were also generally thought of as a defeat for the British, who had succeeded in withdrawing their officials and soldiers from the country without loss, but in circumstances which aroused suspicion and hostility on both sides. In Arab countries the prevalent opinion was that British policy in effect had helped the Zionists: having encouraged Jewish immigration, the government had not been willing to accept its implications for the Arabs, and either stop it before it would lead to their subjection or dispossession, or at least try to limit the damage it would cause. The United States for its part was seen to have acted throughout in support of the Zionists.

Nevertheless, both the British and the American positions remained strong. The Israeli government, in which the dominant figure was David Ben Gurion (1886–1973), refused to take back any substantial number of Arab refugees; but it was generally accepted by the British, American and Israeli governments that they would sooner or later be absorbed into the population of the countries where they had found refuge, and that if not peace, then at least a stable *modus vivendi* between Israel and its neighbours might be achieved. In the meantime, the main energies of the government of Israel were given to the task of absorbing large numbers of Jewish immigrants, not only from eastern Europe but also from the Arab countries. This changed the structure of the population; by 1956, out of a total of 1.6 million, Arab Muslims and Christians numbered 200,000, or some 12.5 per cent. Much of the land which had belonged to Arabs was taken, by different legal means, for Jewish settlement. Although Arab citizens of Israel had legal and political rights, they did not fully belong to the national community which was taking shape. The movement of population into Israel had an impact in Arab states as well. In the generation after 1948 the ancient Jewish communities of the Arab countries virtually ceased to exist; those from Yemen and Iraq moved mainly to Israel; those from Syria, Egypt and the Maghrib to Europe and North America as well as to Israel; only the Jewish community of Morocco continued to be of significant size.

In the next few years the centre of political conflict and discussion lay not in the Arab–Israeli conflict but in other countries in which Britain still had a special position: Iran beyond the eastern boundary of the Arab world, where nationalization of the British-owned oil company caused an international crisis, and Egypt. Here Britain still had much freedom of action. Having differed from British policy in Palestine, the United States was not disposed to weaken the position of Britain as guardian of western interests in other parts of the Arab world, although the large investment of American capital in the oil fields of Saudi Arabia did lead to the replacement of British by American influence there. The Soviet Union for its part was too fully occupied with other regions to follow an active policy in the Arab countries. The Arab states, although committed in principle to the defence of the interests of the Palestinians, were mainly concerned with their own problems.

The basis of British power in the Middle East had always been the military presence in Egypt, and it was here that Britain found itself faced with the most urgent problem. As soon as the war ended, there was a demand by the Egyptian government for a change in the agreement which had been reached in 1936. Negotiations between the two governments took place from 1946 onwards, but failed on two points: first, the Egyptian claim to sovereignty over the Sudan, a claim which the British government did not accept, in the belief that most Sudanese would not accept it and that Britain had obligations to them; and secondly, the question of the British strategic position in the country. In pursuance of the treaty of 1936, British forces were withdrawn from Cairo and the delta, but there was a deadlock in regard to the Canal Zone; British statesmen and strategists thought it was essential to remain there in strength, both for the defence of western interests in the Middle East and for that of British interests in the eastern Mediterranean and Africa. In 1951 serious fighting broke out between British forces and Egyptian guerillas, and in January 1952 this touched off a popular movement in Cairo in which installations associated with the British presence were destroyed; the breakdown of order in its turn gave the opportunity for the seizure of power in July 1952 by a secret society of Egyptian officers of middle rank, at first with a corporate leadership and then under the domination of Jamal 'Abd al-Nasir (1918–70). The break with the past, which was to show itself in many spheres, was symbolized by the deposition of the king and the proclamation of Egypt as a republic.

Having firmer control over the country than previous governments, the military rulers were able to resume negotiations with the British. Of the two main issues, that of the Sudan was removed when the Egyptian government reached a direct agreement with the main Sudanese parties in 1953. Political movements in the Sudan had been able to express themselves more freely after an elected Legislative Assembly was created in 1947, and three main forces had appeared: those who wished for independence and the preservation of a link with Britain, those who wished for independence and a closer link with Egypt, and those who spoke for the non-Muslim, non-Arab peoples of the south. The agreement made with Egypt involved the first two of these, and it was accepted by Britain, although with some reluctance. It was agreed that power should be transferred from the Anglo-Egyptian condominium to the Sudanese under international supervision. Elections were held in the same year, and by 1955 the process was completed; the administration was in Sudanese hands and British and Egyptian armed forces were withdrawn. The largest shadow over the future was thrown by the beginning of revolt and guerilla warfare in the southern provinces, where the population, being neither Arab nor Muslim, was apprehensive of the results of being transferred from British to Arab rule.

With the Sudanese problem resolved, negotiations on the other issue, that of Britain's strategic position, went ahead, and agreement was reached in 1954. British forces were to be withdrawn from the Canal Zone, and more than seventy years of British occupation would come to an end; but it was agreed that the base could be brought into active use if there were an attack on Egypt, another Arab state, or Turkey. The inclusion of Turkey was an expression of British and American concern for the defence of western interests in the Middle East against a possible threat from Russia; various plans for a Middle Eastern defence pact were being discussed, and Egypt's willingness to include mention of Turkey in the agreement seemed to indicate that it might be willing to join in.

The end of foreign occupation in Syria, Lebanon, Egypt and the Sudan made it difficult for Iraq and Jordan to accept less than what they had obtained. In Iraq, the regime which had been restored by British intervention in 1941 was anxious to retain a strategic link with the western powers; it was more aware of the proximity of Russia than were other Arab countries. In 1948 an attempt was made to renegotiate the Anglo-Iraqi Treaty of 1930 on these lines, but failed because of opposition from those who wished Iraq to be less committed to the western alliance. Then in 1955 the government made an agreement with Turkey to set up a common defence and economic pact (the Baghdad Pact); Pakistan, Iran and Britain joined it, and the United States later began to participate in its work. In the context of this pact, an agreement was made with Britain by which the two British air-bases were handed over to Iraq, but Britain agreed to give assistance if there were an attack on Iraq, or the threat of one, and if Iraq asked for help.

In Jordan there was a similar situation, of a regime anxious for help against dangers from outside – from its Arab neighbours and also from Israel – but under pressure from nationalist public opinion. After 1948 the country had a majority of Palestinians, who looked upon Israel as their main enemy and watched for any sign that the regime was making concessions to it. In 1951 King 'Abdullah was assassinated, a mark of nationalist suspicion that he was more accommodating towards the Israelis and their western sponsors than seemed wise and right. The uneasy balance shifted for a time in favour of complete independence. In 1957 the treaty with Britain was brought to an end by agreement and British forces were withdrawn from the bases which they had occupied; but it was a sign of the precarious position of Jordan and of the Hashimite regime that in the same year the British and American governments declared that the independence and integrity of the country were of vital interest to them.

In the Maghrib, it was more difficult for France to come to terms with the demand for independence. The French presence there was not only a matter of armies or the domination of metropolitan economic interests, but of the large French communities who lived there, controlled the profitable sectors of the economy and held the greater number of positions in the government at all except the lowest levels. To bring about any change in the relations of French and Arabs involved a greater effort and met with stronger resistance. The efforts began in Tunisia and Morocco as soon as the war was over. In Tunisia, the Neo-Destour party had the moral advantage that its leader, Bourguiba, had given unequivocal support to the Free French and their allies while in exile or prison during the war, and the material strength derived from the combination of the party and the trade-union federation, founded after the war when Tunisians were allowed to join unions for the first time. In Morocco, strength came from a combination of several elements. The small nationalist groups which had appeared in the 1930s organized themselves into the Independence Party (Istiqlal), and established relations with the sultan, Muhammad V (1927–62), who began discreetly to demand the end of the French protectorate. The idea of independence began to touch wider strata of society: a trade-union federation was formed and the Istiqlal party was able to establish control over it; the rural migration into Casablanca and other cities created stronger links between city and countryside and encouraged the spread of nationalist ideas. The presence of foreign commercial interests protected by international treaty since the beginning of the century, and a new American strategic interest, gave the nationalists some hope of a certain sympathy from outside.

The weak French governments of the years after the war, based upon shifting coalitions and attentive to a public opinion which had not recovered from the humiliation of defeat, could offer no more than repression or 'co-sovereignty', which meant that the European community would have equal weight with the indigenous population in local institutions and that the decisive voice would still be that of the French metropolitan government. In 1952 Bourguiba and a number of others were arrested in Tunisia, and a movement of active resistance began, which evoked a similar movement of violence among European settlers. In the next year matters came to a crisis in Morocco. Contacts between the palace and the Istiqlal party had grown closer, and the sultan demanded total sovereignty. In reply, the French authorities used, perhaps for the last time, a traditional mode of political action. They brought in the forces of rural chieftains whose power they had built up and whose position was threatened by the stronger central control which was implicit in the nationalist vision of the future. In 1953 the sultan was deposed and exiled; the effect of this was to make him a unifying symbol for most Moroccans, and turn the agitation into armed insurrection.

In 1954, however, French policy changed. The French position in Indo-China was under severe threat from a new kind of popular nationalist movement in arms, and in Algeria a similar movement was emerging. A new and more decisive French government opened negotiations with the Neo-Destour and with the sultan of Morocco, who was brought back from exile. Both countries were given independence in 1956. In Morocco, the Spanish zone and the international city of Tangier were fully incorporated into the independent state. Independence strengthened the hand of the sultan (who became king in 1957), but in Tunisia the *bey*, who had played little part in the political process, was deposed and Bourguiba became president. In both countries, however, independence and relations with France remained precarious for the next few years, since by this time Algeria was engulfed in a war of independence: the first shots were fired in November 1954, and soon its repercussions were felt all over the Maghrib.

THE SUEZ CRISIS

By the middle of the 1950s, most Arab countries which had been under European rule had become formally independent; foreign military bases remained in some of them, but would soon be abandoned. French rule remained only in Algeria, where it was being actively challenged by a popular nationalist revolt. British rule or protection remained in the eastern and southern fringes of the Arabian peninsula. The main state of the peninsula, Saudi Arabia, had never had a period of foreign rule, but British influence had been considerable. The discovery and exploitation of oil had led to a replacement of British by American influence, but had also made it possible for the patriarchal rule of the Sa'udi family to begin the process of turning itself into a more fully developed system of government; by the time King 'Abd al-'Aziz died in 1953, the state he had founded was becoming more central and important in the political life of the region. Yemen, on the other hand, remained isolated from other countries under its *imam*, in spite of becoming a member of the Arab League.

The ambiguities of policy in Iraq and Jordan, however – the desire to end the presence of British forces, but at the same time to have some military relationships with the western powers – showed that formal withdrawal of foreign military forces did not by itself necessarily create a different relationship with the former imperial rulers, but rather restated the problem of independence in a new form. The Arab countries found themselves faced by the growing power and influence, in all aspects of economic and political life, of another western state, the United States, which now, in the period of the Cold War and economic expansion, believed that its interests in the Middle East could be protected only through close relations with local governments prepared to link their policy with that of the western alliance. Many politicians and political groups argued, however, that the only guarantee of independence in the post-colonial world would lie in maintaining neutrality between the two armed camps. Since the western camp was linked with memories of imperial rule, and with the problems of Palestine and Algeria which still festered, and since it was from this side that the main pressure to make defence agreements came, the desire for neutrality carried with it a tendency to incline more in the direction of the other camp.

The polarization of the western and eastern blocs, and the conflict of policies between neutrality and the western alliance, gave a new dimension to the relationships between the Arab states. The desire for a closer union between them had become part of the common language of Arab politics; it was now a matter in dispute whether such unity should be brought about within the framework of a close agreement with the western powers, or independently of them.

The future of the relationship between the Arab states and Israel also became linked with the general question of alignment. In the 1950s the British and American governments discussed plans for a resolution of the problem: there should be some adjustment of the frontiers of 1949 in favour of the Arabs, the return of some of the refugees to their homes and the absorption of most of them in the surrounding Arab countries; if the Arab states had a close links with the western powers, this would imply an acceptance of such a solution and some kind of recognition of the existence of Israel. On the other hand, the formation of a neutral group of Arab states which had positive relations with the eastern and western blocs might be used to increase the political weight of the Arab countries and strengthen their armed forces, so bringing about a radical change in the situation established by the armistice agreements of 1949.

As these differences of approach and policy became acute, they came to be linked with the personality of Jamal 'Abd al-Nasir, leader of the military group that now ruled Egypt. The signature of the agreement under which British forces were to leave the Canal Zone did not in fact lead to the entry of Egypt into the western defence system. On the contrary, it gave Egypt the freedom to follow a policy of non-alignment, and to form around itself a bloc of similarly non-aligned Arab states that the outside world would have to deal with as a whole. One expression of this policy was the close relationship established with the leading supporters of the idea of non-alignment, India and Yugoslavia; another and more dramatic one was an agreement made in 1955 for the supply of arms to Egypt from the Soviet Union and its allies, an agreement which broke the control over arms supplies to Israel and its Arab neighbours which the United States, Britain and France had tried to maintain.

This policy of neutralism almost inevitably drew Egypt and its allies into enmity with those whose interests would be affected by it. The western powers would at least have to expect obstacles and limits to the pursuit of their political and economic interests; they could no longer control the development of the problem of Israel, or other problems, as they might have hoped to do; for the United States government in the era of the Cold War, refusal to join a western defence alliance in the Middle East was in effect to join the eastern bloc. The appeal for neutralism and closer unity under Egyptian leadership, made by 'Abd al-Nasir to Arab peoples over the heads of their governments, was a threat to those Arab regimes which stood for different policies: in particular, that of Iraq, which after the formation of the Baghdad Pact became the chief protagonist of the western alliance; its political life in this period was dominated by Nuri al-Sa'id (1888–1958), who had played an important part in Arab national politics since the Arab revolt during the First World War. The rise of a strong Egyptian government, having its own source of arms and appealing strongly to the feelings of Palestinians and other Arabs, was seen by Israel as a threat to its position. These local antagonisms in turn deepened the hostility of the western powers: the United States because of its link with Israel, Britain because of its membership of the Baghdad Pact, and France because of the encouragement and help which Egypt, with its vision of an independent and non-aligned Arab world, was thought to be giving to the Algerian revolution.

Between 1955 and 1961 there was a series of crises in which all these factors were involved. In 1956, the United States, which had held out hopes that it would give Egypt financial aid for a very large irrigation project (the High Dam at Aswan), suddenly withdrew its offer. In response to this, the Egyptian government no less suddenly nationalized the Suez Canal Company and took over the administration of the canal. This caused alarm to users of the canal, who feared that the freedom to use it might be subject to political considerations. To the British and French governments it seemed like an act of hostility, both because of the British and French stake in the company which had built and owned the canal, and because it increased 'Abd al-Nasir's standing in the Arab countries. The Israelis saw it as an opportunity to weaken an over-powerful and hostile neighbouring state, the frontier with which had been disturbed for some time. The result was a secret agreement between France, Britain and Israel to attack Egypt and overturn the rule of 'Abd al-Nasir.

In October Israeli forces invaded Egypt and moved towards the Suez

Canal. In accordance with their previous agreement, Britain and France sent an ultimatum to both Israel and Egypt to withdraw from the Canal Zone, and 'Abd al-Nasir's refusal gave a pretext for British and French forces to attack and occupy part of the zone. This action, however, was a threat not only to Egypt and those Arab states which supported it, but to the United States and Soviet Union, which as great powers could not accept that such decisive steps should be taken in an area in which they had interests without those interests being taken into account. Under American and Soviet pressure, and faced with worldwide hostility and the danger of financial collapse, the three forces withdrew. This was one of those rare episodes when the structure of power in the world stood clearly revealed: the hostility of local forces drew in world powers of the second rank pursuing interests of their own, only to come up sharply against the limits of their strength when they challenged the interests of the super-powers.

The results of this crisis were to increase the standing of 'Abd al-Nasir in the surrounding Arab countries, since he was generally thought to have emerged from the crisis as the political victor, and also to deepen the split between those who supported him and those who regarded his policies as dangerous. This division now entered as a factor into the internal affairs of other Arab states. In 1958 it combined with local rivalries to cause an outbreak of civil war in Lebanon. In the same year a struggle for power between political groups in Syria led one of them to take the initiative in calling for union with Egypt; the union took place, and in February the two countries were merged in the United Arab Republic. The two Hashimite kingdoms, Iraq and Jordan, set up a rival union, but later in the year, in July, the same combination of internal discontents with the hopes raised by Egyptian leadership of a new Arab world led to the seizure of power in Iraq by a group of army officers. The king and most of his family were killed, and so was Nuri al-Sa'id. Iraq became a republic, and the Hashimite dynasty could no longer hope to play the leading role in Arab politics (although the other branch of it continued to rule in Jordan). The news of the revolution led to the sending of American troops to Lebanon and British to Jordan to stabilize an uncertain situation, but they soon withdrew, and so far as Britain was concerned this marked the end of its playing an active and major part in Arab politics.

At first the revolution appeared to open the prospect of Iraq joining the union of Egypt and Syria, but the division of interests between Baghdad and Cairo soon showed itself. Within the United Arab Republic itself, the differing interests of Damascus and Cairo also led, in 1961, to a military *coup* in Syria and the dissolution of the union. In spite of these setbacks, however, 'Abd al-Nasir still appeared, in the eyes of most Arabs and much of the outside world, as the symbol of the movement of Arab peoples towards greater unity and genuine independence.

THE ALGERIAN WAR

The years of crisis in the Middle East were also those of the final crisis of imperial rule in the Maghrib, where the Arabs of Algeria fought a long and finally successful battle to obtain independence from France.

Algerians faced greater difficulties than most other Arab peoples in their struggle for independence. Officially their country was not a colony but an integral part of metropolitan France, and the demand that it should break away met with the resistance of those to whom the land of France was indivisible. Moreover, the European settlers had now become almost a nation of their own, rooted in Algeria, where 80 per cent of them had been born. They would not willingly give up their position of strength: they controlled the most fertile land and most productive agriculture, improved by mechanization and still expanding; the main cities, Algiers and Oran, were more French than Algerian Muslim; they held the vast majority of positions in the government and in the professions; their strong and long-standing influence over the local administration and the government in Paris could prevent any changes which were to their disadvantage. A manifesto issued by a group of educated Algerians in 1943, calling for an autonomous republic linked with France, met with no response except the abolition of some legal disadvantages; a more violent movement in 1945 was suppressed ruthlessly. Some changes were then made: Algerian Muslims would be represented in the French parliament, and they would have the same number of members as the Europeans in the Algerian Assembly; but the elections to the Assembly were managed by the administration in order to produce a docile majority.

Beneath the surface of unshaken French control, however, Algerian society was changing. The Muslim population was growing at a high rate; by 1954 it had risen to almost 9 millions, of whom more than half were less than twenty years old; the European population was almost a million. The greater part of the Muslim population was crowded into the less productive part of the land, without the capital to develop it, and with limited facilities for credit, in spite of small and late attempts by the government to provide them. As a result, living standards were low and the rate of rural unemployment high. There was a growing migration of peasants from the depressed and over-populated countryside into the plains, to work as labourers on European farms, and into the cities of the coast, where they formed an unskilled, underemployed proletariat; by 1954 almost a fifth of the Muslims were town-dwellers in Algeria, and about 300,000 had gone overseas to France. Opportunities for education were larger than they had been, but still small; 90 per cent of the population were illiterate. Only a few thousands went from primary to secondary schools, only a few dozens into higher education; by 1954 there were less than 200 Muslim doctors and pharmacists, and a smaller number of engineers.

Among migrants living away from their families in alien cities, soldiers in the French army, students with limited opportunities, there was an awareness of the great changes occurring in the world: French defeats in the war and in Indo-China, the independence of Asian and African countries, the changes in ideas about colonial rule. Independence began to seem a possibility, but at a price: the repression of the disturbances of 1945 had shown that it would not be given easily. In the years after 1945, the party of those who were prepared to settle for a better position within the French political system lost much of its influence, and within the nationalist party there was gradually formed a revolutionary group: men for the most part of limited education but with military experience in the French army, although later they were to attract members of the educated élite to them. In 1954 they formed the Front de Libération Nationale (FLN), and in November of that year they fired the first shots in the revolution.

To begin with it was a limited movement, and its chances of success could be doubted. The momentum of revolution and the actions of the French government, however, gradually turned it into a national movement with widespread support in the world. The first reaction of the government was one of military repression; when a government more inclined to the left came to power it seemed prepared to make concessions, but then gave in to the opposition of the army and the Europeans of Algeria. At the end of 1956 an attempt to negotiate a settlement through the help of Morocco and Tunisia came to nothing, when some of the Algerian leaders flying from Rabat to Tunis had their plane diverted to Algiers and were there arrested; the French government accepted an act which seems to have been one of local initiative.

By now effective power had been transferred from the government in Paris to the army and the Europeans of Algeria; on the other side, the greater part of the Algerian Muslim population had rallied to the FLN. A well-informed and sympathetic French scholar observed that, after two years of war, 'almost all of Muslim society found itself solidly and effectively supported by a clandestine structure . . . the men in control came not only from the revolutionary ranks . . . they represented the entire range of the élite of the Algerian population'.[1] The outlines of a future independent Algerian nation began to appear, with the fervour generated by revolution oriented towards social equality and the reappropriation of the land. The war reached its military climax in 1957, when there was a sharp and lengthy struggle for control of Algiers itself. The army re-established its control over the capital, and in the countryside followed a policy of large-scale displacement of the population. The nature of the conflict gradually changed: the FLN operating from Morocco, Tunisia and Cairo proclaimed itself the 'Provisional Government of the Algerian Republic' in 1958, receiving support and conducting negotiations all over the world, and with encouragement also from some radical elements in France. An attempt by the French army to expand the war into Tunisia was stopped by American and other objections, and it was because of the fear that international pressure would overwhelm the weak government of post-war France that the army, the Europeans and their supporters in France virtually imposed a change of regime; the Fourth Republic came to an end and in 1958 De Gaulle returned to power, with a new constitution which gave the president of the republic wider powers.

It was the hope of those who brought De Gaulle to power that he would use his position to strengthen the French hold over Algeria. It soon became clear, however, that he was moving, in obscure and indirect ways, towards a settlement with the Algerians, although it is not certain that he envisaged from the first the grant of complete independence. In the first phase, his policy was one of continuing the military measures to suppress the revolt, but of acting independently of the army and the Europeans of Algeria in order to improve the conditions of the Muslims. A plan of economic development was announced: industry would be encouraged, land would be distributed. Elections were to be held for the Algerian Assembly, and it was hoped that they would produce an alternative leadership with which France could negotiate without needing to come to terms with the FLN. This hope proved vain, however, and there was no alternative to negotiating with the FLN. The first talks in 1960 came to nothing. By the next year De Gaulle had greater freedom of manoeuvre: a referendum in France showed that there was a majority in favour of granting self-determination to

371

Algeria; an attempt by the army in Algeria to carry out a *coup d'état* against De Gaulle was suppressed. Negotiations were resumed, and two problems proved the most difficult to resolve: that of the European community, and that of the Algerian Sahara, which France wished to retain because by now important resources of oil and natural gas had been discovered there and were being exploited by a French company. In the end the French conceded both points: the Europeans were to be free to stay or to leave with their possessions; the whole of Algeria, including the Sahara, was to become a sovereign state, which would receive French aid. An agreement was signed in March 1962. Independence had been secured, but at great human cost to all concerned. A large part of the Muslim population had been displaced, perhaps 300,000 or more had been killed, many thousands who had been on the French side were killed or forced to emigrate after independence. The French had lost perhaps 20,000 dead. In spite of guarantees, the vast majority of the settler population left the country; too much blood had flowed to be forgotten; an activist group among the settlers had taken to acts of violence in the last stages of the war, and this helped to make the position of the Europeans precarious.

CHAPTER 22

Changing Societies (1940s and 1950s)

POPULATION AND ECONOMIC GROWTH

These years of political stress were also a time when societies were changing rapidly. First of all, the growth of population and its pressure upon the means of subsistence were now to be observed almost everywhere, and were beginning to be recognized as the source of problems of many kinds.

In Egypt the increase had been continuing for more than a century, with ever-growing momentum. While the rate of increase in the 1930s had been a little more than 1 per cent a year, by 1960 it was between 2.5 and 3 per cent; the total population had increased from 16 millions in 1937 to 26 in 1960. The change was caused primarily by a decrease in the death-rate, from 27 per thousand in 1939 to 18 per thousand in 1960; infant mortality in particular had decreased in that time from 160 to 109 per thousand. Compared with this there had been little change in the birthrate. Similar rates of growth existed by now in other countries, although the process had started later than in Egypt. In Morocco, there seems to have been little natural increase before 1940, but in the twenty years after that the population grew from 7 to 11.5 millions. In Tunisia, the increase in these years was from 2.6 to 3.8 millions; in Syria, from 2.5 to 4.5 millions; in Iraq from 3.5 to 7 millions.

The result of such a rapid increase was that the age-distribution of the people changed, by 1960, more than half the population in most countries was under the age of twenty. There were other changes too in the structure of the population. The foreign element, which had played so large a part in the modern sector of the economy, had shrunk as political conditions changed and economic privileges were whittled away. The number of foreign residents in Egypt shrank from 250,000 in 1937 to 143,000 by 1960; in Libya from 100,000 to half as much in the same period; in Tunisia from 200,000 to less than 100,000; in Morocco from 350,000 to 100,000;

in Algeria from almost a million to less than 100,000. As against this, there was a large movement of Jews both from Europe and from the countries of the Middle East and the Maghrib to the new state of Israel, of which the Jewish population grew from 750,000 in 1948 to 1.9 million by 1960; the ancient Jewish communities of the Arab countries dwindled in a corresponding degree, through emigration to Israel, Europe and America.

A change of more general significance was the movement of population away from the land. This came about mainly as a result of the increase of the rural population above the capacity of the land to support it, but in some places it was caused also by changes in agricultural techniques: the introduction of tractors on grain-producing land meant that fewer labourers were needed; the owners of land which was intensively cultivated for commercial purposes might prefer skilled workers to sharecroppers. In one country, Palestine, the displacement was more directly a result of political changes. Rural over-population was already to be seen in Arab villages by 1948, but the events of that year led to the dispossession of more than half the villagers, and most of them became landless refugees in camps or slums in Jordan, Syria and Lebanon.

For peasants who could not survive in the villages, the centres of power and trade had a positive attraction: they could hope for work in the growing industrial and service sectors of the economy, and for a higher standard of living and better opportunities for the education of their children. Many thousands of peasants from Kabylia in Algeria and from Morocco and Tunisia emigrated from their countries to the great cities of France, and to a lesser extent of Germany; by 1960 there were approximately half a million North Africans in France. Most of the rural migrants, however, went to the cities of their own or neighbouring countries. In Morocco, Casablanca grew more rapidly than the other cities: from being a city of a quarter of a million in 1936 it had become one of a million by 1960. Cairo had had 1.3 million inhabitants in 1937; by 1960 it had 3.3 millions, more than half of whom had been born outside the city. The population of Baghdad grew from half a million in the 1940s to 1.5 million by the 1960s. The most spectacular growth was that of Amman, from 30,000 in 1948 to a quarter of a million by 1960; most of the growth was the result of the movement of refugees from Palestine.

Because of these internal migrations, most of the Arab countries were changing from mainly rural societies to societies where a large and growing part of the population was concentrated in a few large cities. In Egypt, almost 40 per cent of the population lived in cities by 1960; almost 13 per

374

cent were in Cairo (and more than that, if the town of Giza, now virtually incorporated in it, was included). Casablanca held 10 per cent of all Moroccans, Baghdad 20 per cent of all Iraqis.

If the growing populations were to be fed, and living standards improved, more would need to be produced in countryside and city. This need gave a new urgency to the idea of economic growth, which attracted governments for other reasons as well. In the last phase of imperial rule, both Britain and France began to look to rapid economic growth as a possible way of creating a common interest between rulers and ruled, and when nationalist governments took over they too looked upon economic development as the only way of achieving the strength and self-sufficiency without which nations could not be really independent.

This was therefore a period when governments intervened more strongly in the economic process in order to encourage growth. In the countryside, it was an era of large-scale irrigation works in a number of countries: Morocco, Algeria, Tunisia, Syria and above all Egypt and Iraq. In Egypt, more than a century of changes in the system of irrigation reached its conclusion in the late 1950s, when work started on the High Dam at Aswan, to be built with financial and technical assistance from the Soviet Union, which stepped in when the United States withdrew. Previous irrigation schemes in the Nile valley had aimed at holding up the annual flood and distributing the water in such a way as to irrigate a larger area of land perennially, and so to make possible the production of more than one crop a year, but the High Dam was to do more than this. The purpose of building it was to store successive floods in a vast lake and release the water where and when it was needed. In this way fluctuations in the volume of water from one year to another could be ignored, and for the first time in the long history of settled life in the Nile valley the annual flood would no longer be the central event of the year. It was hoped in this way to increase the cultivated area by 1 million *feddans*, and the crop area by even more, because of the extension of perennial irrigation to land which was already under cultivation. The dam would also be used for generating electric power, and there was a possibility of developing fisheries in the lake. On the debit side, however, the rate of evaporation of the water would be high, and there might be a change in the climate; the retention of water in the lake would mean that its silt would be deposited there and not in the more northern parts of Egypt.

In Iraq, an increase in the revenues of the government because of greater production of oil made it possible for the first time to carry out works of irrigation and flood-control on a large scale and in accordance with a plan. In 1950 a development board was created, with control over the larger part of the revenues from oil, and it planned and carried out large schemes of flood-control on both the Tigris and Euphrates, and the building of dams on tributaries of the Tigris in the north.

This was a period too when tractors were introduced on a large scale. They had already been in use by 1939 on European-owned land in the Maghrib and Jewish-owned land in Palestine, but scarcely anywhere else. Now they were imported into Iraq, Syria, Jordan and Egypt, where over 10,000 were in use by 1959. The use of chemical fertilizers was not so widespread, except in Egypt, Lebanon and Syria, nor were improved seeds and breeds.

The result of these changes was an extension of the cultivated area in a few countries, and of crop areas almost everywhere, and in most places a change from the production of cereals intended for local consumption to that of cash crops to be marketed in the cities or exported. In Morocco, the French authorities in the last phase of their rule made a systematic effort at the 'modernization of the peasantry': indigenous cultivators grouped in large units were instructed in new methods and the production of cash crops, and provided with co-operative facilities for credit and marketing. In Syria and northern Iraq, the changes were brought about by private enterprise. In the region lying between the Tigris and Euphrates rivers, merchants with capital began leasing land from tribal *shaykhs* and growing grain with the help of tractors; for the first time, land in this region of uncertain rainfall could be cultivated on a large enough scale and with sufficient economy of manpower to make cultivation profitable. The result was a further shift in the balance between settled agriculture and the rearing of livestock – which previously had been the safest and most profitable use of land – and the extension of cultivation: in Syria, the area under grain was more than doubled in twenty years, from 748,000 hectares in 1934 to 1,890,000 in 1954. In the valley of the Euphrates and elsewhere in Syria cotton cultivation also expanded.

Important as it might be, the expansion of agriculture was not the first priority for most governments with resources to invest. The rapid development of industry seemed more urgent. Most governments gave attention to creating the infrastructure without which industry could not grow: roads, railways, ports, telecommunications and hydroelectric power. In the three countries of the Maghrib, the French made systematic efforts to improve transport and communications, the generation of electricity and works of irrigation.

Investment by governments, and to a lesser extent by private individuals (mainly Europeans in the Maghrib, and landowners with money to spare further east) led to some expansion of industry. For the most part it was consumer industry: food-processing, building materials, and textiles, particularly in Egypt and Syria which had their own supplies of cotton. In countries with mineral resources mining became important, especially phosphates in Jordan, Morocco and Tunisia.

In some ways, economic growth increased the dependence of most Arab states upon the industrialized countries. The accumulation of national capital for investment was not sufficient for their needs, and growth depended on investment and aid from abroad. In the years after the Second World War some countries were able to draw upon sterling balances accumulated from the expenditure of armies during the war, and those of the Maghrib had funds provided by the French government, out of the aid given to France under the Marshall Plan. There was little private foreign investment, except in Morocco, which was attractive to French capitalists during the post-war years because of fear of what might happen in France. Later, American loans were given to countries whose policies were in harmony with those of the United States, and by the end of the 1950s Russian loans were being made to Egypt and Syria.

Foreign aid was given, partly at least, for political reasons and, when it was not used to expand the armed forces of newly independent countries which found themselves involved in complicated and often hostile relations with each other, it was used mainly to finance the importation of capital goods or materials which were needed in order to improve the infrastructure or to develop industry. The result tended to be that dependence on the countries from which aid came was increased. Countries which received aid remained in debt to those which gave it, and their main trading relations continued to be those with the industrial nations of Europe, and to an increasing extent with the United States; an exception was Egypt, which by the end of the 1950s was sending more than 50 per cent of its exports to countries of the eastern bloc and buying about 30 per cent of its imports from them. The pattern of exchanges remained much as it had been before, with raw materials being exported and manufactured goods coming in. There were two significant changes, however: the import of textiles became less important, as local textile factories were created; the import of wheat increased, since local production could no longer feed the growing population of the cities.

One kind of export grew rapidly in importance in these years, that of oil, and it provided the most striking example of economic interdependence between the countries which possessed oil and the industrialized world. After a small beginning before the Second World War, the oil resources of countries of the Middle East and the Maghrib proved to be among the most important in the world. By 1960 these countries were producing 25 per cent of the world's crude oil and – because of the small size of the local market – were collectively the world's biggest exporters. The largest production was in Iran and, among the Arab countries, in Iraq, Kuwait and Saudi Arabia, but there was also production in other countries of the Gulf and in Egypt, and by 1960 large deposits had been discovered also in Libya and Algeria. In the future, Middle Eastern oil seemed likely to become more important still: in 1960 the reserves were estimated to form some 60 per cent of the known reserves of the world.

The concessions to explore for oil, and to extract and export it when discovered, were held everywhere by western companies, for the most part controlled by the small number of great oil companies who between them held a virtual monopoly over the industry. In Iraq exploitation was in the hands of a company with joint British, French, Dutch and American ownership, in Saudi Arabia in American hands; in Kuwait in British and American; in Libya in the hands of a large number of companies; and in Algeria in those of a French company with government funds invested in it. Their capital came mostly from private western investors, and this indeed was the most important example of western private investment in Arab countries during this period. The higher technology too was provided mainly by European and American officials. The bulk of the oil was exported to western countries. Apart from the oil itself, the contribution of the host countries lay for the most part in the lower ranks of labour, skilled and unskilled, and this was limited in amount, since the extraction and processing of oil did not demand much labour.

By the beginning of the 1960s the situation was changing, however. More local men were being employed in highly skilled jobs and, although the total labour force was still not large, those trained in the industry were moving into other sectors of the economy. More important still, the division of profits between the companies and the host countries was changing. In 1948, 65 per cent of the gross receipts of the industry went to the companies, and the countries' share was limited to a royalty, a small percentage on a price which the companies themselves fixed. From 1950, pressure from the producing countries secured changes in the agreements, until their share came to 50 per cent of the net income of the companies. In 1960 the main producing countries (not only in the Middle East) came together in the Organization of Petroleum Exporting Countries (OPEC), an alliance with the aim of presenting a common front in negotiations with the great oil companies, which themselves worked closely together. The way was therefore open for a new process which would end in the countries' taking over the functions of the companies, at least in production.

THE PROFITS OF GROWTH: MERCHANTS AND LANDOWNERS

With the coming of independence, indigenous merchants and landowners were able to take a large part of the profits of economic growth. Merchants were able to use their access to the independent governments in order to obtain a larger share of the import–export trade; even in the Egyptian cotton trade, which for so long had been in the hands of foreign firms and banks, some very large Egyptian companies, working in close collaboration with politicians, played an important part. In Iraq, the greater part of the Jewish bourgeoisie, which had been prominent in the trade with England and India, left when their position became difficult after the creation of the state of Israel, and their place was mainly taken by Iraqi Shi'i merchants. Most of the new industries also were in local hands, because of a certain accumulation of capital by merchants and landowners, but also because of the need for young industries to have access to the government. In some countries, however, collaboration between indigenous and foreign capitalists existed. This was true of Morocco, where mixed Franco-Moroccan companies continued to be important after independence, and up to a certain date of Egypt too. Indigenous or mixed banks also were becoming important; the holding and investment of royalties and private profits from the oil industry were largely in the hands of banks managed by Lebanese and Palestinians in Beirut.

In most places, too, the expansion of agriculture in the years after the war was primarily in the interest of those who owned or controlled land, and in particular of large landowners who had access to credit from banks and mortgage companies and could accumulate capital for investment. In Morocco and Tunisia, land which had been in the hands of foreign owners was bought after independence either by indigenous capitalists or by the government. In Egypt, the position of the large landowners remained strong

379

until 1952. The 400-odd members of the royal family were collectively the largest landowners; around them there was a group of some 2,500 Egyptian families and companies, and about 200 foreign ones, who owned more than 100 *feddans* each; between them, these large owners held 27 per cent of the cultivated land. They virtually controlled the government; on average, half the ministers, senators and deputies came from this class. They were therefore able to obtain advantages in irrigation and to keep the tax-system favourable to them. Because of their accumulated capital and access to credit they were able to buy land when it became available, and their control of the best land made it possible to impose high rents on the tenants who cultivated most of it. Some economists were urging the need for a reform of land-tenure, and the sense of injustice was strong among the cultivators, but before 1952 scarcely a voice was raised in favour of reform in the public assemblies of the nation.

The power of the landowners also increased in Syria and Iraq during this period. In Syria, the great plains of the interior, given over to grain cultivation, had always been in the possession of leading families in the cities, but now the class of large owners was swollen by those who grew cotton on irrigated land in the Euphrates valley and those (whether they were owners or leaseholders) who grew grain in the Jazira. In Iraq, the class of large landowners to a great extent was created by changes which had occurred since the late nineteenth century: the extension of farming with the help of tractors, pumps and irrigation works, the transition from pastoralism to settled agriculture, and the registration of title to land. The policy of the British mandatory government, and later of the independent government, worked in favour of the landowners, and in particular of those of them who were tribal *shaykhs* and could use their authority in favour of the British and the monarchy. By 1958, over 60 per cent of privately owned land was in the hands of those who owned more than 1,000 *dunums*, and 49 families owned more than 30,000 *dunums* each. (The Iraqi *dunum* is equivalent to approximately 0.25 of a hectare and 0.6 of an acre.) Holdings were larger than in Egypt, because cultivation was extensive and land was plentiful, and excessive salinity tended to exhaust it quickly. Apart from tribal *shaykhs*, the landowning class included families of urban notables who had obtained land through government service or religious prestige, and Muslim merchants with capital to invest. As in Egypt, the landowners had a strong political position, through membership of ministries and parliament and because the monarchy and ruling group needed them.

THE POWER OF THE STATE

The triumph of nationalism may therefore have appeared at first to be that of the indigenous possessing classes, but in most countries this was short-lived, and the victor was the state itself, those who controlled the government and those in the military and civil service through whom its power was exercised. The basic social process by which the government assumed direct control over all its territories had been completed in most countries by the time the foreign rulers left, even in those like Morocco where the authority of urban governments had hitherto been weak; the independent governments inherited the means of control, armies, police forces and bureaucracies. In Saudi Arabia too the stronger and better organized government which 'Abd al-'Aziz bequeathed to his sons held a number of different regions in a unified political society. Only on the southern fringes of the peninsula was the process still incomplete. In Yemen, the rule of the *imam* scarcely yet extended over the whole country. The British administration in Aden had created a loose grouping of small chieftains under British protection in the surrounding countryside, but did not govern them directly. In Oman, too, the power of the ruler, supported by the British, did not yet reach the whole of the interior from his capital at Masqat on the coast.

The activities of governments now began to extend beyond the maintenance of law and order, collection of taxes and provision of some basic services. Almost everywhere, public utilities were taken into public ownership: banks of issue, railways, telephones, the provision of water, gas and electricity. This was in conformity with what was happening all over the world, but there was a special reason for it here: in most countries the utilities had been owned by foreign companies, and nationalization meant both a change from private to public ownership and one from foreign to indigenous.

The movement of nationalization had its own momentum. The new governments feared the continuation or growth of independent centres of economic power, which might generate political power or link themselves with the former rulers. Moreover, rapid industrialization would be difficult and slow if left to private enterprise: the accumulation of private capital for investment had been limited under foreign rule and was still inadequate; its direction into productive investment was difficult so long as there was no organized money-market; private investors might hesitate to put their money into new and untried industries rather than urban buildings or land;

even if they did so, the factories they set up might not be those to which a national plan would give priority.

These were arguments for the intervention of the government in the economic process, and such intervention was now possible because of the accumulation of resources in its hands. The withdrawal of the foreign rulers meant that revenues from taxes were now under full control of the governments, and the revenues were all the greater because the fiscal privileges which foreign enterprises had enjoyed were cut down. In some countries, resources for investment were now provided by the increased revenues from oil; even countries which did not possess oil might profit from payments made by companies for transit rights, or from loans or grants given them by the richer countries. By 1960, 61 per cent of government revenues in Iraq came from oil, 81 per cent in Saudi Arabia, almost 100 per cent in the small states of the Gulf; in Syria, 25 per cent of revenue came from the pipelines which carried oil from Iraq and Arabia to the Mediterranean coast, and in Jordan 15 per cent. Loans for development also came from the industrialized countries and from international agencies.

Even before independence some economic activities had been brought under state control. The extraction of phosphates in Morocco had been under the control of a government agency ever since it became important; in the Sudan, the concession given to British companies to cultivate cotton in the Jazira district lapsed in 1951. After independence the process quickened. Tunisia took over the phosphates industry, and in Jordan too the phosphates company had a large degree of government participation. In Egypt, the policy of the military government which took power in 1952 moved increasingly in the direction of nationalizing factories, until it culminated in 1961 in the taking over by the state of all banks and insurance companies and almost all large industrial companies. In the previous year the first five-year plan had been issued, with the aim of rapid industrial and agricultural growth under the control of the government. The main exception to this trend was Morocco, where by 1960 there had appeared a clear choice between a controlled economy, with rapid industrialization and restrictions upon consumption, and an economy dependent upon private enterprise and investment. The choice involved a struggle for power between a nationalist party pressing for rapid change and the more conservative forces gathered around the king; it ended in the assumption of direct power by the king, and a choice in favour of private enterprise.

The most spectacular example of state intervention in economic processes was given not by industry but by the reform of the system of landownership.

This had the greatest political and social importance, because most of the population of the Arab countries still lived in the countryside and also because almost everywhere the large landowners formed the most powerful class, the one which possessed most influence over the government and the most capital; to strike at its property would be to destroy a power which could control the government, and to release capital for investment elsewhere.

The first and most far-ranging scheme of land reform was announced by the new military government in Egypt soon after it took power in 1952. That a detailed plan could be put forward so soon after the seizure of power, although the matter had scarcely been discussed by previous governments or in parliament, was a sign both of the independent power of the government and of the emergence of a new ruling group with ideas very different from those whom it had displaced. The most prominent part of the plan was the limitation of the maximum size of estates to 200 *feddans* for an individual, with an additional 100 *feddans* for his children; the maximum was lowered to 100 *feddans* in 1961, and 50 in 1969. Land above the maximum would be bought by the government at a fixed price in government bonds, and distributed to small cultivators; in addition, land belonging to the royal family was confiscated without compensation. The amount of rent which an owner could charge a tenant was limited, and tenancy agreements would last for at least three years. Tenants and smallholders would be helped to obtain credit and market their produce by co-operatives to be established by the government. In the decade which followed, about half a million *feddans* were compulsorily purchased by the state, and a part of these was distributed. The effects were far-reaching, but not always what had been expected: politically, the power of the large landowners and the royal family was broken; economically, income was redistributed from large owners to smallholders and tenant–cultivators, while the intermediate group of medium-sized owners was scarcely touched.

In Syria a similar measure was initiated in 1958: the maximum size of holdings was limited, agricultural contracts were redefined in the interests of the tenant or sharecropper, and a minimum wage was fixed for agricultural labourers. In the first years it could not be applied as effectively as in Egypt, because the bureaucracy was not adequate to the task, there was no full survey of title to land and the political power of the landowners was as yet unbroken. In Iraq, too, a similar measure was adopted after the military *coup* in 1958, but before there had emerged from the revolution a stable ruling group with clear and agreed ideas about how society should be organized; for the first few years there was disagreement among the rulers over whether the land which was taken over by the state should be held and developed by it, or should be distributed in smallholdings.

RICH AND POOR IN THE CITY

The increasing size of the population, the migration from the countryside into the city and the growing numbers and power of the national bourgeoisie – landowners, merchants, owners and managers of factories, civil servants and army officers – affected the nature of urban life in many ways. With the coming of independence, the indigenous middle class moved into quarters which formerly had been inhabited mainly by Europeans, and the rural migrants moved into quarters they had vacated, or into new ones. In each case, there was a change in customs and ways of life: the middle class took to living in a way which formerly had been typical of the foreign residents, and the rural migrants adopted the ways of the urban poor.

In the Maghrib, the process by which the classes with a modern education took over the centre of their cities from the foreigners had already begun before independence, in the 1940s and early 1950s. The urban segregation which had been the policy of the French protectorate in Morocco, and which existed too in Algeria and to a lesser extent in Tunisia, was breaking down, and the coming of independence carried the process further. Europeans left with their capital, and the new rulers, the officials and the landowning and merchant classes associated with them moved in. In Cairo and Alexandria the segregation had never been so complete, but there had been quarters which had been more European than Egyptian, and the nature of these changed. The opening of the Gazira Sporting Club more fully to Egyptians, and the burning of certain buildings associated with foreigners during the riots of 1952 in Cairo, were symbols of a social change. In Lebanon, Syria and Iraq, foreign colonies had never been so large or exclusive, but in Palestine the dispossession of most of the Arab population in 1948 meant that what had formerly been mixed cities became cities mainly populated by Jews of European origin; Jewish immigrants from Arab countries settled mainly in new towns or villages. In Jerusalem, now divided between Israel and Jordan, the Jordanian half, which included the Old City, was almost completely Arab, but a large part of the Arab bourgeoisie of Jerusalem, as of Haifa and Jaffa, settled in cities outside

Palestine, and it was their capital and energy which were the main cause of the rapid growth of Amman.

In their new quarters the bourgeoisie lived much as the Europeans had done, in the same kind of houses and wearing the same kind of clothes, although there might be some compromises between an old and a new way of life; a Moroccan in Casablanca might wear European clothes at business but the traditional costume, the *jallaba*, at the mosque on Fridays; a modern house might have a room furnished in the oriental style, with low divans, copper trays and wall-hangings. In some of the new quarters, members of different religious communities mingled more than they would have done in the *madina*; they lived in the same apartment blocks or streets, and their children went to the same schools; intermarriage between Muslims and Christians and Jews was still rare, but perhaps a little less so than before.

In the openness of the new quarters, wealth could show itself more freely than in the old cities, where fear of the ruler or the neighbours led people to hide evidence of their prosperity. Houses presented a bolder front to the street, rooms were more lavishly furnished, jewellery more openly displayed. One particular symbol of status became important in this period – the private automobile. Comparatively rare before the Second World War, it now became more common; in Cairo, the number almost doubled between 1945 and 1960. The increase in the number of cars, and also of trucks and buses, made new and wider roads necessary in city and countryside. To drive a wide boulevard through a quarter of the old city became almost a symbolic act of modernity and independence. It had first happened in the 1870s when Isma'il Pasha made Muhammad 'Ali Street in Cairo, and was now repeated elsewhere in the Middle East, although not in the Maghrib. Private automobiles, and the roads made for them, changed the way in which the wealthier classes lived. Their lives were no longer confined to their quarter; they could possess the whole city and its rural hinterland, and they could live far from their places of work.

The quarters which the bourgeois were leaving were being taken over by rural migrants. Some of them went to the *madina*, drawn by the attraction of a famous shrine or mosque, or the existence of available lodgings: in the mixed cities, some settled in what had formerly been the quarters of the European petty bourgeoisie, such as Shubra in Cairo. In some cities, the *bidonvilles* which already existed grew and multiplied wherever there was vacant land; but this did not happen in Cairo, where the 'City of the Dead', the vast cemeteries outside the old city, served the same purposes of housing the overflow of population. The *bidonvilles* were moved from place to place by the authorities, but in course of time some of them acquired the permanent buildings and amenities of the city; the Palestinian refugee camps on the outskirts of Beirut, Damascus and Amman became virtual quarters of the city. In a few countries governments began programmes of building low-cost popular housing, on the outer rim of the city or near the new industrial zones. In the last decade of French rule in Morocco, a gifted city-planner tried to set up a programme of this kind; in Egypt, a five-year plan of housing was announced in 1960, including the building of a new satellite city near Cairo, Madinat Nasr. In these years an Egyptian architect, Hasan Fathi (1900–89), was asking important questions about the ways in which such schemes were designed and carried out. Instead of adopting the current methods and shapes of western architecture, he suggested, it was possible to learn much from the traditions of Islamic town-planning and building.

In Cairo, Beirut and a few other cities, the ways characteristic of 'modernity', and the income needed to support them, had spread beyond a small class, and between rich and poor quarters there lay a 'transitional belt', where a petty bourgeoisie of shopkeepers, small officials and skilled artisans tried to maintain middle-class standards. In most cities, however, there was a gulf between rich and poor. The rural migrants tended to adopt the habits of the urban masses at a point where the city-dwellers might be giving them up, and so a traditional way of life was perpetuated. Women who in the countryside had worked unveiled in the fields or drawn water from the well now veiled and secluded themselves. Even at this level of society, however, there were some changes. Polygamy, which had been practised to some extent in certain social strata, became rarer, because of the difficulties of life in small apartments, or a different conception of family life. The rate of divorce was high, but may have diminished. The birthrate, although high compared with industrial countries, was lower in the city than the countryside, because girls who went to school tended to marry later, and men would try to obtain a fixed employment and save some money before marrying, and also because of the spread of birth control; in Egypt, by the late 1950s more than 50 per cent of those with higher education practised it, and about 10 per cent of the urban poor, but virtually none of the rural poor. By this time the problems of the exploding population were widely known and discussed in Egypt, and some of the *'ulama* declared that birth control was legitimate.

Life continued to be hard for the urban poor. A large proportion of them was unemployed. Of the population of Cairo, it was estimated that in 1960 7.5 per cent worked in industry, 23 per cent in services, and 66 per cent were without fixed or regular work. In the overcrowded tenements or shanties where most of them lived, disease was widespread: the great epidemics of plague and cholera which had decimated cities in former times had now more or less disappeared, but tuberculosis, typhoid, malaria and eye diseases were common. Infant mortality was high; in the *bidonvilles* of Baghdad, it was estimated that the infant death-rate in 1956 was 341 in every 1,000 pregnancies.

There is some evidence, however, that conditions of life were improving among at least some of the poor. Tea and sugar, which had been beyond their means, had by now become staples of life in Morocco and Iraq; the consumption of food in Egypt rose from an average of 2,300 calories a day at the beginning of the 1950s to one of 2,500 a decade later. Social services were expanding, clinics provided health services, better water supplies lowered the incidence of some diseases, in some towns public transport was improved, a larger proportion of children went to elementary school, and anti-illiteracy campaigns were mounted. More women went to work, mainly as domestic workers or in factories; they were for the most part young and unmarried and living in the family home, and the fact that they worked outside it and earned money did not yet cause much of a change in the structure of family life; it increased the income of their families, but did not necessarily make the women workers themselves more prosperous or independent.

Such changes affected some strata of the population more than others. The gap between industrial workers and unskilled casual workers probably grew wider. Governments began to intervene more actively in industry, to regulate conditions of work; in Egypt, a maximum working day and week were fixed by law. In most countries trade unions were now authorized; the change took place for the most part in the 1940s, under the impact of the war, then of the Labour government in Britain and left-wing parties in French coalition governments. The number of workers enrolled in unions increased as industry expanded. In Morocco and Tunisia the unions formed an integral part of the nationalist movement, and in Egypt too workers' organizations were active in the opposition to British control after 1945. Once independence was attained, governments tried to limit the political activities of unions, but in some places they were effective in obtaining better conditions of work.

The inequalities between city and countryside were even greater than those within the city. All urban classes profited to some extent from the changing conditions of urban life, but the improvements had scarcely begun to affect life in the villages. Most villagers in most parts of the Arab countries lived as they had always done, producing many children but seeing most of them die in infancy or youth, without medical care and with only rudimentary education, without electricity, enmeshed in a system of cultivation in which the surplus of agricultural production was taken by landowners and tax-collectors, and in conditions of overpopulation such as to deprive them of a strong bargaining position. Some attempts were made by governments in the 1940s to improve their conditions without changing the pattern of social relations: in particular, the 'rural combined units' in Egypt, which provided health and other services for groups of villages. The first serious attempt to change the relationships of rural classes, and to redistribute income from agriculture, did not appear until the measures of land reform introduced in some countries in the 1950s. Some things were changing, however: migrants into the city could send money back to their families, and the horizons of the village life were being widened by the movement to the cities, the extension of roads for cars and trucks, the circulation of newspapers, the spread of the radio and of elementary schools.

CHAPTER 23

National Culture (1940s and 1950s)

PROBLEMS OF EDUCATION

Changes in society and the coming to power of an indigenous élite between them led to a rapid spread of education. The exigencies of life in cities made literacy and the acquisition of skills more necessary; nationalist governments were committed to the making of strong nations, and this involved the use of all human potentialities; modern centralized governments needed to communicate with their subjects more fully than had been necessary in the past.

The creation of an educated élite by means of higher education was, of course, a process which had begun long before in some of the Arab countries, but the pace increased with the winning of independence. In 1939 there had been half a dozen universities, most of them small and foreign-controlled; by 1960 there were some twenty full universities, three-quarters of them national, and several other institutions of higher learning. The number of university students was of the order of 100,000, excluding those studying in Europe or America. Far the largest number were in Egypt, with Syria, Lebanon and Iraq coming next. The increase was less rapid in the Maghrib, however. When the French left Tunisia, there were only 143 indigenous doctors and 41 engineers; in Morocco, there were only 19 Muslim and 17 Moroccan Jewish doctors, 15 Muslim and 15 Jewish engineers, but rather more lawyers, teachers and officials. The training of an élite therefore had to start from a lower level.

The logic of nationalism led beyond the formation of élites to the education of a whole people. Mass popular education was one of the first tasks which the new governments set themselves, and to which they devoted a high proportion of their revenues. Almost everywhere schools were opened on a large scale, in poor quarters of the towns and in some villages. In Egypt by 1960, 65 per cent of children of primary age were attending schools and there was a school population of 3 millions, 200,000 of them in secondary schools. In Morocco, only 12 per cent of Muslim children were in school in 1954, in spite of efforts made by the French during the last years of the protectorate, but by 1963 the figure had risen to 60 per cent, and to almost 100 per cent of children aged seven. In Tunisia, the increase over the same period was from 11 to 65 per cent. This increase in school population, together with efforts for adult education, brought some countries nearer to the goal of complete literacy, although still far from it. In Egypt, 76 per cent of men had been illiterate in 1937, and by 1960 the figure had decreased to 56 per cent. In the countries of the Arabian peninsula, however, the change was slower. The conservative regimes with a religious sanction in Saudi Arabia and Yemen were more cautious than others about opening schools of a new kind and exposing the students to the winds of new ideas; apart from the holy cities of Mecca and Madina, they did not possess great centres from which urban literate culture could radiate over the countryside. In the British-controlled or protected states on the fringes, resources were small, and neither the British nor the rulers they protected had an active desire for rapid change with all the problems it would bring; the exception was Kuwait, where increasing revenues from the export of oil were being used to create a modern society.

The proportion of women who were uneducated and illiterate was much higher than that of men; in Egypt, 94 per cent were illiterate in 1937 and 83 per cent in 1960, and in most countries the figures were higher still. The aim of national governments was to educate girls as well as boys, however, since otherwise half of the potential strength of the nation would not be used in the wage-economy. In Egypt, 50 per cent of girls of school age were in school by 1960; in Tunisia approximately 30 per cent. The proportion of girls in secondary or higher education was smaller, but growing: in the University of Baghdad, 22 per cent of the students were girls by 1960/61, in that of Rabat 14 per cent, in that of Tunis 23 per cent; in the Sudan, where female education had started later, a private college for women had been created, and a few girls were studying at the University of Khartoum by 1959/60.

Some of the problems of rapidly expanding education were those which were common to all countries at this stage of change and growth. The rapid increase in population meant that, even if the proportion of children of school age who were at school grew, the total number of children who were still not in school did not necessarily diminish. To accommodate as many as possible, schools were opened rapidly, classes were too large for effective teaching and most teachers were not well trained for their work. The results were seen at every level; in particular, Arab education tended to be inadequate at secondary level, and students who went to university were on the whole not well trained for higher study. There was a tendency to concentrate on academic education which would lead to government service or the liberal professions, rather than upon technical or vocational training; the use of the hands as well as the mind was alien to the concept of education in Islamic as in most other pre-modern cultures. The growth of the oil industry was making a difference, however; Arab workers in it acquired skill and knowledge which they could use in other sectors of the economy.

There were some problems, however, which expressed the specific historical experience of Arab societies. When they became independent they inherited a variety of schools: some public, some private; some modern, some traditionally Islamic; some teaching through the medium of Arabic, others through that of a European language, usually English or French. The tendency of independent governments was to unify the systems and to bring them all under control of the state. Traditional Islamic schools were either closed or incorporated in the state system; the ancient teaching mosque of the Azhar in Cairo became part of a university of a modern kind, the Zaytuna in Tunis became the school of *shari'a* of the University of Tunis, the Qarawiyyin in Fez virtually ceased to exist as a teaching institution, but the schools in Madina and those of the Shi'i shrine cities in Iraq continued without much change.

In some countries, foreign schools were brought under state control and taught according to the national school programme, but there were exceptions: in Lebanon the two foreign universities, the American and the French, still flourished, although side by side with them a state university was created, and in Egypt the American University in Cairo and the Catholic mission schools which had the diplomatic protection of the Vatican were able to preserve their independence. The main tendency was to arabize schools: those foreign schools which had taught through the medium of foreign languages now used Arabic to a greater extent. This was now the general rule at primary level. In Syria, it was followed to the point where no foreign language was studied before the age of eleven, with consequences for secondary and higher education. In the Maghrib, however, where the presence of a large foreign population which controlled government and the economy had led to the penetration of a knowledge of French to a lower level of society than in the Arab east, the independent governments, while emphasizing the importance of Arabic, regarded bilingualism as part of their cultural capital. In some universities efforts were made to teach all subjects in Arabic, including the natural sciences, but this raised difficulties: textbooks in Arabic could be produced, but a student who could not read scholarly or scientific works in the main languages of higher learning was at a disadvantage. Many thousands of students were sent abroad to study on government scholarships and they needed to go with a foreign language thoroughly learnt.

As in all societies, those who had wealth, access to power or a family tradition of culture could overcome or evade these problems. In every country there were some schools which were better than the rest, controlled by foreign or private organizations and with smaller classes and better teachers, such as the *lycées* in the Maghrib, Egypt and Lebanon which the French government supplied with teachers. Students from such schools could study abroad successfully on family or government funds, and the result was to perpetuate a gap between two cultures, but in a rather different form from that which had existed formerly. An élite which tended to perpetuate itself lived, not – as it had done in an earlier generation – in an English or American or French cultural milieu, but in an Anglo-Arab or Franco-Arab one, knowing two or three languages well, at home in Arabic but acquiring its high culture and knowledge of the world through English or French (and increasingly through English, except in the Maghrib). A much larger class, however, was at home only in Arabic, and drew its knowledge of world politics, its ideas about society and its understanding of science from books, newspapers and broadcasts in Arabic.

LANGUAGE AND SELF-EXPRESSION

By now there was an increasing mass of material to feed the minds of those who saw the world through the medium of the Arabic language, and most of it was material which was common to all the Arab countries.

This was the great age of the cinema. By the early 1960s television was only just beginning to appear in the Arab countries, but cinemas were numerous: there had been 194 in Egypt in 1949, and by 1961 there were 375; the increase in most other countries was of the same order. American films were popular, as they were almost everywhere in the world, and French ones in the Maghrib, but films made in Egypt also were shown widely. In 1959 sixty feature films were produced in Cairo; most of them were romantic musical films of a kind which had been made since the beginning, but there were a few more serious films of social realism. They increased the common consciousness of Arabs, spreading everywhere a stock of images, a familiarity with Egyptian voices, Egyptian colloquial Arabic and Egyptian popular music, which was replacing the Andalusian music in the Maghrib.

This was the age of radio too. Radio sets were imported on a large scale in the 1940s and 1950s. By 1959 there were 850,000 in Egypt and half a million in Morocco, and each set might be listened to by dozens of people, in cafés or village squares; the events of the war and the post-war period, victories and defeats, promises, hopes and fears, became known more widely and more quickly than ever before. Every government had its radio station, and the great powers with interests in the Arab countries also had their short-wave transmissions in Arabic. A large proportion of the programmes sent out by all stations – talks, music and plays – originated in Cairo, and they too spread a knowledge of Egypt and its ways of speech. The most influential of all stations in this period was 'The Voice of the Arabs', beamed from Egypt to the surrounding countries, expressing in strident tones the aspirations of the Arabs as Egypt saw them. Certain Egyptian voices became familiar everywhere – that of the country's ruler, Jamal 'Abd al-Nasir, and that of the most famous of Egyptian singers, Umm Kulthum; when she sang, the whole Arab world listened.

With the spread of literacy and of concern for public affairs, newspapers circulated more widely and became more important in forming public opinion. Once more, those of Cairo were the most widely read and influential. *Al-Ahram* continued to be the most famous, with a circulation in hundreds of thousands. The Egyptian press was comparatively free until the coming to power of the military politicians in 1952, but after that it came under control of the state, until it was nationalized in 1960 at the same time as other large enterprises. Even after that, Egyptian newspapers were still widely read because they showed how the rulers of the country saw the world; the articles of Hasanayn Haykal, the editor of *al-Ahram*, were important political events. In most other countries too newspapers were strictly controlled as regards news and opinions, but there were a few where news could be freely given and opinions of all kinds expressed. The freest press was that of Beirut: its educated public was large and varied, and drawn from other countries as well as Lebanon, and the delicate balance of political forces made the emergence of a strong and oppressive government impossible. The newspapers and periodicals of Beirut, like those of Cairo, were read far beyond the frontiers of the country.

Cairo and Beirut were also the main centres of book publishing for the Arab countries, and in both places the number of books issued and of copies printed increased vastly, to feed a growing public of students and general readers. By the 1960s, about 3,000 books a year were being published in Egypt. There were books of all kinds: textbooks at every level, works of popular science and literature, the beginnings of a special literature for children (the concept of a child's world, formulated in Europe in the nineteenth century, was now becoming universal), and also pure literature.

Of greatest significance were those books in which Arab writers explored their relations with their own society and its past. By now there was a well-established tradition of historical research in some of the universities – Tunis, Cairo, the American University of Beirut – and some original interpretations of Arab and Islamic history were produced, such as 'Abd al-'Aziz Duri's (b. 1919) *Nash'at 'ilm al-tarikh 'ind al-'arab* (*The Rise of Historical Writing among the Arabs*) and Abdullah Laroui's (b. 1933) *Histoire du Maghreb*, an attempt to win back the interpretation of Maghribi history from French writers who, in his view, had failed to understand its essence:

We can distinguish a long period during which the Maghrib is a pure object and can be seen only through the eyes of its foreign conquerors . . . the history of this period ceases to be anything more than a history of foreigners on African soil . . . On several occasions the social mechanism has stopped in the Maghrib. Individuals and groups have often concluded a separate peace with destiny. What can we do to prevent this happening again, now that the end of colonization has offered us an opportunity to make a fresh start? . . . What each one of us wants to know today is how to get out of ourselves, how to escape from our mountains and sand-dunes, how to define ourselves in terms of ourselves and not of someone else, how to stop being exiles in spirit.[1]

The novel and short story continued to be the main forms in which Arab writers explored their relations with their society. To the novel which expressed nationalist themes, and the predicament of the educated Arab torn between his own inherited culture and that of Europe, there was now added that of social analysis and implied criticism. As before, the most interesting fiction was produced in Egypt. In a series of novels of urban life, set in Cairo and written in the 1940s and 1950s, Najib Mahfuz (b. 1911) depicted the lives of the petty bourgeoisie of Egypt with their anxieties and confusions in a world becoming strange to them; he was given the Nobel Prize for Literature in 1988. 'Abd al-Rahman al-Sharqawi

(b. 1920) described the lives of the rural poor in his novel, *al-Ard* (*The Earth*). Such works helped, at least by implication, to explain the alienation of society from its rulers, but also that of the individual from society. A new note was heard with the appearance of a number of women novelists, whose work dealt with the efforts of women to live more freely; the title of Layla Ba'albaki's first novel, *Ana ahya* (*I Live*), was symbolic of their aims. In some novelists a new kind of revolt could be observed: against the present, in the name of some 'authentic' past before the dislocations of modern life had begun to show themselves. Writers of this kind looked at religion in a different light; the Islam they showed was not that of the modernists, nor that of the real or imagined first age of purity, but Islam as it had in fact developed, the cult of saints and reverence for their shrines, the Sufi practices of the village.

In Egypt, and to a lesser extent in other countries, such themes were also expressed in a comparatively new medium, the drama. Plays were becoming a popular form of entertainment: the cinema and radio accustomed the audience to seeing and hearing the tension of human relationships expressed in words and gestures, and also provided patronage for writers of plays. The poetic drama, written in high classical language and designed to be read rather than acted, was still written, for example by Tawfiq al-Hakim (1899–1987), but side by side with it there appeared the drama of modern society, intended to be acted, and performed in the small theatres of Cairo and other cities. To an increasing extent these plays were written in the colloquial, or a language which approached it, and the reasons have been explained by a literary scholar. The classical language lends itself to static declamation rather than dramatic action; it is a public language which cannot easily become the voice of an individual temperament; it is abstract, without reference to a specific environment. The colloquial language, on the other hand, may lack the resonance needed to rise to the height of a dramatic or a tragic moment.

Something of the same discontent with the frozen, impersonal nature of the classical language and the forms of expression associated with it could be found in the poetry of the period. From the late 1940s there was a poetic revolution, particularly among the younger poets of Lebanon, Syria, Palestine and Iraq, living mainly in Baghdad and Beirut, where their mouthpiece, the periodical *Shi'r*, was published. It was a multiple change which they tried to bring about. There was a change in the intention and content of the poem. The Romantics of the previous generation had tried to replace the poetry of rhetoric and public events by one which expressed personal emotion and saw the natural world as an external sign of that emotion. Now the new poets tried to break with the subjectivism of the Romantics, while preserving something which they had learned from them. Poetry should express the reality of things, but reality could not be learnt by the intellect alone; it had to be apprehended by the total personality of the poet, by his imagination as well as his mind. Individual poets differed in their emphasis on various aspects of the many-sided reality. Some were concerned with problems of their own identity in an age of anxiety; others, taking from the French literary discussions of the 1950s the idea that a writer should be 'committed', were concerned with the theme of the Arab nation and its weaknesses. A new Arab nation, a new Arab individual, needed to be brought into being, and the poet should be the 'creator of a new world'. A leading poet of this group, the Syrian Ahmad Sa'id (b. 1929), who wrote under the name of Adunis, said that poetry should be 'a change in the order of things'.[2]

In the poetry of Badr Shakir al-Sayyab (1926–64), the Iraqi village where he was brought up becomes a symbol of life – not only individual life, but that of the Arab people – hemmed in by the streets of the city, the sterile prison of the human spirit:

Streets of which tales told by the fireside say, No one returns from them, as no one returns from the shore of death . . . who shall make the water burst out from them in springs, so that our villages will be built around them? . . . Who has shut the doors of Jaykur against its son who knocks at them, who has diverted the roads from it, so that, wherever he goes, the city rears up its head towards him? . . . Jaykur is green; the dusk has touched the tips of its palm trees with a mournful sun. My path went to it like a flash of lightning; it sprang up, then vanished, and then light returned and caused it to blaze, until it lit up the city.[3]

A new world needed a new language, and these poets tried to break away from accepted views of how poetry should be written. The basic unit of poetic language should not be the line composed of a fixed number of feet, but the single foot; the accepted system of rhymes – and rhyme itself – could be abandoned; strict syntactical relations between words could give way to looser groupings. Words and images which had been emptied of meaning by repetition should be changed for others and a new system of symbols created. Some of these were private, others drawn from the common stock of symbols of modern French or English poetry.

One of the distinctive marks of the group was the extent to which their poetic intelligence and sensibility had been formed by European poetry.

They tried to enlarge the poetic awareness of the Arab reader to include the heritage of the whole world's culture: images of fertility taken from Eliot's *The Waste Land*, that of the death and resurrection of Tammuz (Adonis), taken from classical mythology but given a local resonance because of its association with the Syrian countryside. (The adoption by Ahmad Sa'id of the pen-name Adunis (Adonis) was significant.)

In the Maghrib, there appeared at this time a group of writers publishing novels, plays and poems in French, but expressing a specific sensibility and mode of thought. In Algeria, writers of the 'generation of 1952' such as Kateb Yacine (1929–89), Mouloud Feraoun (1913–62) and Mouloud Mammeri (1917–88) used their mastery of French to explore problems of personal liberation and national identity. That they wrote in French did not mean that they were torn from their roots; it was a result of their education and the position of their communities; some of the Algerians were Berbers from Kabylia who were more at home in French than in Arabic. Some took part in the national struggle and all were marked by it; the best known in France, Kateb Yacine, gave up writing in French after 1970 and devoted himself to creating drama in colloquial Arabic.

ISLAMIC MOVEMENTS

The new poetry was written to be read and thought about, and was different in significant ways from the poetry written to be recited to large audiences at the poetic festivals which were a distinctive feature of this period. It was read by a minority who could understand its allusions, but it did nevertheless express a general *malaise*, a discontent of the Arabs with themselves and their world.

In wider strata of the population, such feelings, and the desire for change, were expressed in words and images associated with Islam, in one or other of its many forms. The modernist attempt to reformulate Islam in ways which would make it a viable response to the demands of modern life was still perhaps the most widespread form of Islam among the educated élite who had led the nationalist movements and now dominated the new governments. In a less intellectually rigorous form it was expressed for a larger audience by popular writers who were widely read: for example, the Egyptian Khalid Muhammad Khalid (b. 1920), whose formulation carried with it a sharp rejection of the religion taught in the Azhar. The Islam of the 'priesthood', he asserted, was a religion of reaction, attacking the freedom of the human intellect, supporting the interests of the powerful and rich, and justifying poverty. The true religion was rational, humane, democratic and devoted to economic progress; the legitimate government was not a religious one, but one based on national unity and aiming at prosperity and justice. Some of the leading writers of the age began in this period to write in a more explicitly Islamic idiom, and here too their main emphasis was on social justice; for Taha Husayn, the Caliph 'Umar was a social reformer whose ideas were similar to those of the modern age.

With such voices were now mingled others, proclaiming that social justice could be achieved only under the leadership of a government which took Islam as the basis of its policy and laws. After the war the movement of the Muslim Brothers became a major political factor in Egypt, and a considerable one in Syria and some other countries. During the years between 1945 and 1952, years of the disintegration of the Egyptian political system, the teachings of the Brothers seemed to offer a principle of united action in terms of which the struggle against the British and against corruption could be carried on in unity and trust. After the seizure of power by the officers in 1952, the Brothers, with whom some of the officers had close connections, seemed to provide a goal towards which the policies of the new government could be directed. They were the only political organization exempted at first from the decree dissolving political parties. Relations soon became hostile, however, and after an attempt on 'Abd al-Nasir's life in 1954 some of the leaders of the Brothers were executed; after that it served as the most effective channel of clandestine opposition and continued to provide an alternative model of a just society.

The founder, Hasan al-Banna, had been assassinated in the disturbed years after the war, but other writers connected with the movement were now expressing the idea of a specifically Islamic just society: Mustafa al-Siba'i in Syria and Sayyid Qutb (1906–66) in Egypt. In a famous book, *al-'Adala al-ijtima'iyya fi'l-islam (Social Justice in Islam)*, Sayyid Qutb put forward a powerful interpretation of the social teaching of Islam. For Muslims, as distinct from Christians, there was, he suggested, no gap between faith and life. All human acts could be seen as acts of worship, and the Qur'an and Hadith provided the principles on which action should be based. Man was free only if he was released from subjection to all powers except that of God: from the power of priesthood, fear, and the domination of social values, human desires and appetites.

Among the principles to be derived from the Qur'an, he maintained, was that of the mutual responsibility of men in society. Although human beings were fundamentally equal in the eyes of God, they had different tasks corresponding to their different positions in society. Men and women were equal spiritually but different in function and obligation. Rulers too had special responsibilities: to uphold law, which must be rigorously applied in order to preserve rights and lives; to enforce morality; to uphold a just society. This involved maintaining the right to property, but making sure it was used for the good of society: wealth should not be used for luxury or usury, or in dishonest ways; it should be taxed for the benefit of society; the necessities of communal life should not be in the hands of individuals, but owned in common. So long as the rulers upheld the fabric of a just society they should be obeyed, but if they ceased to do so the duty of obedience lapsed. The great age of Islamic justice had been the first age; after that, rulers not approved of by the people had brought successive disasters on the Muslim community. A true Islamic society could be restored only through the creation of a new mentality by means of proper education.

In Egypt and other countries, the leaders of such movements tended to be men of comparatively high education and standing in society, but their followers were drawn largely from a lower stratum, of those who had acquired a certain education through the medium of Arabic rather than French or English, and who held intermediate positions in urban society but were shut out of the higher ranks. For them, movements of this type offered a possible moral basis for life in the modern world. They provided a system of principles which was relevant to all social problems and accessible to all men and women, as distinct from the Islam of saints and shrines which by its nature was related to a certain place and a limited group. It was therefore appropriate to a society in which social and political action had extended to the whole national community, and it could even hope to transcend national boundaries and extend to the whole world of Islam.

There were still wide strata of society which had not been drawn into the new life on a larger scale; for the villagers, and the new urban proletariat of migrants from the countryside, the tomb of the local saint still held its place as the embodiment of an assurance that life had a meaning; for the rural migrants into the cities, the great places of pilgrimage – Mawlay Idris in Fez, Sayyida Zaynab in Cairo, Ibn 'Arabi in Damascus – were familiar signs in an alien world. The guardian of the tomb might have lost some of his social functions, to the doctor, gendarme or government official, but he could still be an effective mediator in the problems of everyday life, for those who were touched by misfortune, women who were childless, victims of theft or of neighbours' spite. It was possible for a *tariqa* growing from the memory of a holy man not long dead to extend its hold by the use of modern methods of organization in the interstices of urban bourgeois society.

CHAPTER 24

The Climax of Arabism
(1950s and 1960s)

POPULAR NATIONALISM

A certain Islamic element would always remain important in that combination of ideas which made up the popular nationalism of the age, extending beyond the highly educated élite to the larger stratum of those, mainly in the cities, who were brought by education and the mass media into some kind of political participation. Whether it was the Islam of the modernists or that of the Brothers, however, it remained on the whole a subordinate element in the system. The main elements which set the tone of popular nationalism came from other sources. This was the period when the idea of the 'Third World' became important: the idea, that is, of a common front of countries in process of development, mainly belonging to the former colonial empires, keeping themselves uncommitted to either of the two blocs, that of the 'West' and that of the communist 'East', and exercising a certain collective power through acting together, and in particular through their command of a majority in the General Assembly of the United Nations. A second element was the idea of Arab unity: that the newly independent Arab states had enough in common, in shared culture and historical experience as well as shared interests, to make it possible for them to come into close union with each other, and such a union would not only give them greater collective power but would bring about that moral unity between people and government which would make government legitimate and stable.

To these elements another one was now added – that of socialism: that is to say, the idea of the control of resources by government in the interests of society, of state-ownership and direction of production, and equitable distribution of income through taxation and the provision of social services. The increasing strength of this idea was partly a reflection of what was happening elsewhere in the world: the strength of socialist and communist parties in western Europe, the growing influence in the world of the USSR and its allies, the coming to power of the Communist Party in China, the blend of nationalist and socialist ideas in the programmes of some of the parties which assumed power in the newly independent states of Asia. Specifically it was shown in the articulation of Marxist ideas in Arabic. Once more, the centre of this activity was Egypt. Historians began to interpret Egyptian history in Marxist terms, so that what appeared to be nationalist movements were now seen as movements of particular classes pursuing their own interests. A socialist critique of Egyptian culture was written by Mahmud Amin al-'Alim and 'Abd al-'Azim Anis. Culture, they declared, must reflect the whole nature and situation of a society, literature must try to show the relationship of the individual with the experience of his society. A literature which flees from that experience is empty; thus the writing which reflected bourgeois nationalism is now devoid of meaning. New writing must be judged by whether it adequately expresses the struggle with the 'octopus of imperialism' which is the basic fact about Egyptian life, and whether it mirrors the life of the working class. Seen in this light, the question of forms of expression becomes important. A gap between expression and content, they suggest, is a sign of a flight from reality; Najib Mahfuz, writing about popular life but avoiding the use of colloquial Arabic, seems to them to show a certain alienation from real life.

The ways in which these various elements were integrated into popular movements varied from country to country. In the Maghrib, the circumstances of the struggle against French rule had led to the creation of nationalist movements with wider popular support and better organization than those further east. Since the French had been present not simply as an alien government but as a privileged group of residents controlling the productive resources, the only way of opposing them successfully had been by means of a popular revolt, well organized and spreading from beyond the cities into the countryside. In Tunisia, independence had been achieved and the new government was dominated by a combination of trade unions and the Neo-Destour party, led by an educated élite whose roots lay for the most part in the small towns and villages of the Sahil and with branches throughout the country. Similarly in Algeria: the organization which launched the revolt against French rule in 1954, the Front de Libération Nationale (FLN), led mainly by men of humble origin but with a military training, gradually under the pressure of war attracted to itself wide support in every stratum of society. When it changed from a revolutionary force to a government, its leadership was a mixture of the historic military chiefs of the revolution and the highly educated technocrats without whom a modern government could not be carried on, and it drew its strength from a nationwide network of party branches in which small merchants, landowners and teachers played a part. In Morocco, a similar coalition of interests – between king, Istiqlal party and trade unions – had achieved independence, but did not prove itself to be as stable and unified as in the other countries of the Maghrib. The king could claim, as against the Istiqlal party, to be the authentic embodiment of the national community, and was able too to establish his control over the new army. The Istiqlal, without the popular support to be derived from a generally accepted claim to express the national will, tended to break up into factions along class lines; from it there emerged a new movement, the Union Nationale des Forces Populaires, directed by leaders from the countryside and mountains, and claiming to speak for the interests of the proletariat of the cities.

In most countries of the Middle East, independence had been achieved by manipulation of political forces, both internal and external, and by negotiations which were relatively peaceful, in spite of moments of popular disturbance. Power in the newly independent states came in the first instance into the hands of ruling families or educated élites who had had the social position and political skill which had been needed during the period of transfer of power. Such groups did not on the whole, however, possess the skill and appeal needed to mobilize popular support in the new circumstances of independence, or to create a state in the full sense. They did not speak the same political language as those whom they claimed to represent, and their interests lay in the preservation of the existing social fabric and distribution of wealth, rather than in changes in the direction of greater social justice. In these countries political movements tended to break up after independence, and the way lay open to new movements and ideologies, which would blend the elements of nationalism, religion and social justice in a more appealing fashion. The Muslim Brothers were such a movement, particularly in Egypt, the Sudan and Syria. Communist and socialist groups also began to play a significant role in opposition both to imperial rule in its last phase and to the new governments which took its place.

In Egypt, the communist movement was split into small groups which managed nevertheless to play a part at certain moments of crisis. In particular, during the confrontation with the British in the years following the end of the war, the communist-dominated Committee of Workers and Students gave leadership and direction to the popular forces which were roused. In Iraq, a similar role was played by communists in the movement which compelled the government to withdraw from the agreement on defence which it signed with Britain in 1948. The agreement had the support of most of the established political leaders, and it offered some advantages to Iraq, by the provision of arms for the army and the possibility of British support in the struggle then beginning in Palestine, but it seemed to imply a permanent link between Iraq and Britain, and therefore in the last resort a permanent subordination of Iraqi to British interests. The opposition to it served as a focus around which a number of different interests could coalesce: those of peasants alienated from their *shaykhs* who had become landowners; of the urban proletariat faced with high prices for food; of students; and of nationalist leaders of a different complexion. In this situation, the Communist Party played an important part in providing a link between different groups. In the Sudan, again, the ruling group which inherited the British position was linked with two parties, each of which was associated with a traditional religious leadership, and which were similar in social composition, although they differed on the extent to which they wished to link the Sudan with Egypt; there was a popular role which they could not play, and which the Communist Party, formed largely by students who had studied in Egypt, tried to fill.

In the face of this fragmentation of political forces, there were several attempts to create movements of a new kind which could combine all the important elements. Two were of particular importance in the 1950s and 1960s. One was the Ba'th (Resurrection) party, which grew up in Syria. It was a party which presented a challenge to the domination of Syrian politics by a small number of great urban families and by the parties or loose associations of leaders which expressed their interests. Its appeal was primarily to the new educated class, created by the rapid increase in education, who came from the less dominant classes in society, and to a large extent from communities outside the Sunni Muslim majority: 'Alawis, Druzes and Christians. Its origin lay in intellectual debates about the national identity of the Syrians, and their relations with other Arabic-speaking communities: a debate which was more urgent in Syria than elsewhere, because the frontiers drawn by Britain and France in their own interests corresponded less than in most Middle Eastern countries to natural and historical divisions.

The answer which the main theorist of the Ba'th, Michel 'Aflaq (1910–89), a Christian from Damascus, gave to this question was expressed in uncompromisingly Arab terms. There was a single Arab nation, with the right to live in a single united state. It had been formed by a great historical experience, the creation by the Prophet Muhammad of the religion of Islam and the society which embodied it. This experience belonged not only to Arab Muslims, but to all Arabs who appropriated it as their own, and regarded it as the basis of their claim to have a special mission in the world and a right to independence and unity. They could achieve these aims only by means of a double transformation: first of the intellect and soul – an appropriation of the idea of the Arab nation through understanding and love – and then of the political and social system.

In this system of ideas the element of social reform and socialism was at first of less importance, but in the middle 1950s the Ba'th party amalgamated with a more explicitly socialist party. In this form its influence spread in Syria, and in the surrounding countries, Lebanon, Jordan and Iraq, and also in the countries of the Arabian peninsula. Its appeal extended beyond students and intellectuals who were troubled by questions of identity; it was particularly great among the generation of army officers of humble provincial origin, and the urban working class of migrants from the countryside. In the 1950s there were alternations of military rule and parliamentary government in Syria; in a situation of fragmented power, a party which had a clear policy and a popular appeal could play a role which exceeded its numbers, and the Ba'th was important both in the movement which led to the formation of the United Arab Republic in 1958 and in its break-up in 1961. Similarly in Iraq, after the revolution of 1958 it had a growing influence.

The Ba'th was an ideology which became a political force, but the other important movement of the period was a regime which gradually developed a system of ideas in terms of which it claimed to be legitimate. The Egyptian army officers who took power in 1952, and of whom 'Abd al-Nasir soon emerged as the unquestioned leader, had a limited programme of action to begin with, and no common ideology beyond an appeal to the national interest as standing above the interests of parties and factions, and a feeling of solidarity with the peasant masses from which most, although not all, of them sprang. In course of time, however, they acquired a characteristic ideology, which was generally identified with the personality of 'Abd al-Nasir. In this Nasirist ideology there were a number of elements which at that time had the power to move opinion. The language of Islam was the natural language which the leaders used in appeals to the masses. In general they stood for a reformist version of Islam which did not oppose but rather endorsed the kinds of secularizing and modernizing change which they were introducing. In this period the Azhar came more strictly under the control of the government.

On the whole, however, the appeal to Islam was emphasized less than the appeal to Arab nationalism and unity. Arab unity had been accepted by previous governments of Egypt as an important strand in foreign policy, but the separate historical development of Egypt and the distinctive culture which had grown up in the Nile valley had kept it somewhat distant in feeling from its neighbours. Now, however, the regime of ʿAbd al-Nasir began to think of the country as part of the Arab world, and its natural leader. Its leadership, they believed, should be used in the direction of social revolution: state-ownership or control of the means of production, and the redistribution of income, were essential in order to maximize national strength and to generate mass support for the regime.

The programme of social reform was justified in terms of the idea of a specifically 'Arab socialism', a system halfway between Marxism, which stood for the conflict of classes, and capitalism, which meant the primacy of individual interests and the domination of the classes which owned the means of production. In 'Arab socialism', the whole of society was thought to rally round a government which pursued the interests of all. This idea was put forward in the 'National Charter', issued in 1962:

Revolution is the way in which the Arab nation can free itself of its shackles, and rid itself of the dark heritage which has burdened it . . . [It] is the only way to overcome underdevelopment which has been forced on it by suppression and exploitation . . . and to face the challenge awaiting the Arab and other underdeveloped nations: the challenge offered by the astounding scientific discoveries which help to widen the gap between the advanced and backward countries . . . Ages of suffering and hope have finally produced clear objectives for the Arab struggle. These objectives, which are the true expression of Arab consciousness, are freedom, socialism and unity . . . Freedom today means that of the country and of the citizen. Socialism has become both a means and an end: sufficiency and justice. The road to unity is the popular call for the restoration of the natural order of a single nation.[1]

Political democracy was declared to be impossible without social democracy, and this involved public ownership of communications and other public services, banks and insurance companies, heavy and medium industry, and – most important – foreign trade. There should be equality of opportunity, health care and education for all, men and women alike; family planning was to be encouraged. Class divisions should be resolved within the national unity, and so should the divisions between the Arab countries: Egypt must call for Arab unity without accepting the argument that this would be interference in the affairs of other countries. In the next few years measures of social reform were carried out vigorously: limitations on hours of work, a minimum wage, extension of public health services, a proportion of the profits of industry distributed in insurance and welfare services. These measures were made possible by the rapid growth of Egypt in the early 1960s. By 1964, however, growth had ceased and per capita private consumption was no longer rising.

Even at its highest point, the regime of 'Abd al-Nasir did not succeed in canalizing all the political forces of the Egyptian people. Its mass political movement, the Arab Socialist Union, was a channel through which the intentions of the government were communicated to the people rather than one by which popular desires, suggestions and complaints could be expressed. The Muslim Brothers accused it of using the language of Islam in order to cover a basically secular policy; Marxists criticized 'Arab socialism' as being different from 'scientific' socialism based upon a recognition of the differences and conflicts of classes.

In other Arab countries, however, 'Nasirism' met with a vast and continuing public acceptance. The personality of 'Abd al-Nasir, the successes of his regime – the political victory of the Suez crisis of 1956, the building of the High Dam, the measures of social reform – and the promise of strong leadership in defence of the Palestinian cause: all these seemed to hold out the hope of a different world, of a united Arab nation rejuvenated by genuine social revolution and taking its rightful place in the world. Such hopes were encouraged by skilful use of the press and radio, which appealed above the heads of other governments to the 'Arab people'. These appeals deepened conflicts between Arab governments, but Nasirism remained a potent symbol of unity and revolution, and embodied itself in political movements of wide scope, such as the Movement of Arab Nationalists which was founded in Beirut and was popular among Palestinian refugees.

THE ASCENDANCY OF NASIRISM

Throughout the 1960s the public life of the Arab countries continued to be dominated by this idea of a socialist, neutralist, form of Arab nationalism, with 'Abd al-Nasir as its leader and symbol.

With the achievement of independence by Algeria in 1962, the age of the European empires virtually came to an end, but there were still some areas of the Middle East where British power remained, embodied in forms of government and based in the last resort upon the possibility of using armed force. In Aden and the protectorate around it, British interests had become more significant in the 1950s. The oil refinery of Aden was important and so was the naval base, because of the fear that the USSR might establish its control in the Horn of Africa on the opposite shore of the Red Sea. The loose protectorate over the surrounding country was being transformed into a more formal system of control.

The stirrings of political consciousness in Aden, encouraged by the rise of 'Nasirism' and certain changes which were taking place in Yemen, made it necessary for the British to extend the degree of local participation in government. A legislative assembly was set up in Aden, and the surrounding protected states were formed into a federation in which Aden itself was incorporated. Limited concessions brought new demands, however, from the small educated class and the workers in Aden, and from those opposed to the domination of the rulers in the federation, with encouragement from Egypt. Unrest broke out, and in 1966 the British government decided to withdraw. By this time the opposition had split into two groups, and when withdrawal took place in 1967 it was an urban group with a Marxist orientation which was able to seize power.

In the Gulf, it was not local pressure so much as a changed conception of Britain's position in the world which led to withdrawal. In 1961 Kuwait was granted full independence: a stable ruling class of merchant families clustered around a ruling family was now able to create a new kind of government and society by exploitation of its oil. Further down the Gulf, a review of British resources and strategy led in 1968 to the government's decision to withdraw its military forces and therefore its political control throughout the Indian Ocean area by 1971. In a sense, this decision ran counter to a local British interest. The discovery of oil in various parts of the Gulf, and its exploitation on a large scale in Abu Dhabi, gave a new importance to what had been a very poor area and led to a certain extension of British control from the small ports of the coast into the interior, where precise delimitation of frontiers now became important. Through British influence, a loose federation, the United Arab Emirates, was set up to take the unifying role which the British had exercised. This consisted of seven small states (Abu Dhabi, Dubai, Sharja and four others), but neither Bahrayn nor Qatar joined it. For a time the independence of Bahrayn was threatened by Iranian claims to sovereignty, based on historical arguments, but these were withdrawn in 1970.

After that, the only part of the peninsula where a British presence continued was one where it had never officially existed. The ruler of Oman had been for a long time under the virtual control of a small number of British officials. His rule had scarcely extended into the interior, where actual power was held by the *imam* of the Ibadi sect. In the 1950s, however, the prospect of finding oil in the interior led to an extension of the sultan's power, backed by the British. This in turn gave rise to a local revolt, supported by Saudi Arabia, which had its own territorial claims; behind the conflict there lay the clashing interests of British and American oil companies. The uprising was suppressed, with British help, and the *imamate* extinguished, but in 1965 a more serious revolt broke out in the western part of the country, Dhufar. This continued into the 1970s, again with support from outside. The sultan was unwilling to make any concessions to change, and in 1970 he was deposed at British instigation in favour of his son.

By the 1960s, the main attention of those concerned with what appeared to be the emergence of an Arab nation was no longer given to the vestiges of imperial rule, but to two other kinds of conflict: that between the two 'super-powers'; and that between states ruled by groups committed to rapid change or revolution on broadly Nasirist lines and those ruled by dynasties or groups more cautious about political and social change and more hostile to the spread of Nasirist influence. In Syria, power was seized by the Ba'th party in 1963: first by its civilian leaders, then by army officers affiliated with it. In Iraq, the government of officers set up by the revolution of 1958 was overturned in 1963 by one more inclined to the Ba'th and to Nasirism; but discussions about unity between Iraq, Syria and Egypt showed the differences of interest and ideas between the three of them. In the Sudan, a military *coup* took place in 1958, and the government which resulted from it followed a policy of neutralism and economic development, until parliamentary government was restored in 1964 by popular pressure. In Algeria the first government established after independence, with Ahmad Ben Bella at its head, was replaced in 1965 by one more fully committed to socialism and neutralism, led by Hawari Boumediene. On the other side, however, there stood the monarchies of Morocco, Libya, Jordan and Saudi Arabia, with Tunisia in an ambiguous position, ruled as it was by Bourguiba as the leader of a mass nationalist party committed to far-reaching reform but hostile to the extension of Egyptian influence and to many of the current ideas of Arab nationalism.

The sense of a nation in process of formation was strengthened in this period by the new wealth and other changes created by the exploitation of oil. The oil resources of the Arab and other Middle Eastern countries had now become really important in the world economy, and this was having a deep impact on the societies of the oil-producing countries. By the mid-1960s, the five largest Arab oil-producing countries – Iraq, Kuwait, Saudi Arabia, Libya and Algeria – between them had government revenues of some $2 billions a year. The revenues were being used – with greater responsibility in Iraq, Kuwait, Libya and Algeria, and less in Saudi Arabia, until a family revolution replaced Sa'ud, the eldest son of 'Abd al-'Aziz, who had become king on his father's death, by his abler brother Faysal (1964–75) – to build the infrastructure of modern societies, to extend social services, but also to create more elaborate structures of administration and the defence and security forces on which they were based.

These developments were beginning to change the place of the Arabian peninsula in the Arab world, in two different ways. On the one hand, the rulers of Saudi Arabia and the countries of the Gulf were able to use their wealth to obtain a position of greater influence in Arab affairs; in this period they began giving aid on a large scale to the poorer states. On the other, their rapidly changing societies began to attract great numbers of migrants from other Arab countries. This was less true of Algeria and Iraq, which had large populations and could produce their own skilled and educated workers, but in Saudi Arabia, Kuwait and other countries of the Gulf, and in Libya, populations were too small to meet the need to develop resources, and the educated classes were smaller still. The migrants were for the most part Palestinians, Syrians and Lebanese; except in Libya, fewer came from Egypt, where the needs of a large standing army and a growing state-controlled economy made the government reluctant to allow emigration on a large scale. By the beginning of the 1970s there may have been approximately half a million migrants. Most of them were educated or trained workers, and they brought with them to the countries of immigration the ideas which were current in the countries from which they came: ideas of Nasirist revolution or Ba'thist nationalism, and the unending longing of the Palestinians to regain their country. Their ideas and aspirations seemed to support the interest of the Egypt of 'Abd al-Nasir in using the wealth of the oil states as an instrument for creating a strong bloc of Arab countries under Egyptian leadership.

THE CRISIS OF 1967

Already in the early 1960s there were signs that the claims and pretensions of Nasirism went beyond its power. The dissolution of the union between Egypt and Syria in 1961, and the failure of the later talks on unity, showed the limits of 'Abd al-Nasir's leadership and of the common interests of Arab states. More significant were events occurring in Yemen. In 1962 the Zaydi *imam*, the ruler of the country, died, and his successor was almost at once deposed by a movement in which educated liberals who had been in exile joined with officers of the new regular army, with some limited tribal support. The ancient *imamate* became the Yemen Arab Republic (now often referred to as North Yemen, to distinguish it from the state established after the British withdrawal from Yemen and the protectorate around it, known officially as the People's Democratic Republic of Yemen, but often called South Yemen). The group which seized power asked at once for Egyptian help and Egyptian army units were sent. Even with this support, however, the task of ruling a country which had been directly controlled, but had been held together by the accumulated skill and contacts of the *imamate*, proved too much for the new government. Parts of the country-side, which still accepted the authority of the *imam*, or were opposed to the kind of control which the government was trying to create, rose in revolt. They had support from Saudi Arabia, and there followed several years of civil war, in which the conflict between local groups and that between Egypt and the 'traditional' Arab monarchies were intertwined. Neither side was able to overcome the other; those whom the Egyptians backed could just control the main cities and the roads between them, but not the greater part of the countryside, and a large Egyptian army, fighting in unfamiliar conditions, was held down there for a number of years.

The limitations of Egyptian and Arab power were shown more decisively in a greater crisis which occurred in 1967, bringing Egypt and other Arab states into direct and disastrous confrontation with Israel. It was inevitable that the dynamics of Nasirist policy should impel 'Abd al-Nasir into the position of leading champion of the Arabs in what for most of them was the central problem: that of their relations with Israel. At first cautious in its approach to the problem, by 1955 the military government of Egypt had begun to assert its leadership. The events of 1956 and subsequent years turned 'Abd al-Nasir into the symbolic figure of Arab nationalism, but behind that there lay a certain line of Egyptian policy: to make Egypt the leader of an Arab bloc so closely united that the outside world could deal with it only by way of an agreement with Cairo. The task of acting as leader and spokesman of the Palestinian cause had obvious dangers, and until 1964 Egypt performed it with care; in that year it refused to be drawn into confrontation with Israel over Israeli plans to use the Jordan waters for irrigation. From that time, however, 'Abd al-Nasir was exposed to pressure from various sides. The 'conservative' regimes, with which he was already in conflict because of the civil war in Yemen, asserted that his caution was a sign that he did not really believe in the cause he was claiming to support. In Syria, power had fallen into the hands of a group of Ba'thists which believed that only through social revolution and direct confrontation with Israel could the problem of Palestine be settled and a new Arab nation created.

Into the web of inter-Arab relations a new strand was now woven. Since 1948 the Palestinians themselves had not been able to play an independent part in the discussions about their own destiny: their leadership had collapsed, they were scattered between a number of states, and those who had lost their homes and work had to make a new life for themselves. They had been able to play a part only under the control of the Arab states and with their permission. In 1964 the Arab League did create a separate entity for them, the Palestine Liberation Organization (PLO), but it was under Egyptian control and the armed forces connected with it formed part of the armies of Egypt, Syria, Jordan and Iraq. By this time a new generation of Palestinians was growing up, in exile but with a memory of Palestine, educated in Cairo or Beirut and responsive to currents of thought there. Gradually in the late 1950s distinctively Palestinian political movements of two kinds began to emerge: Fatah, committed to remaining fully independent of Arab regimes, whose interests were not the same as those of the Palestinians, and to direct military confrontation with Israel; and a number of smaller movements which emerged from the pro-Nasirist Arab nationalist groups in Beirut and gradually moved in the direction of a Marxist analysis of society and social action, and a belief that the path to the recovery of Palestine lay through a fundamental revolution in the Arab countries.

By 1965, such groups were beginning to take direct action inside Israel, and the Israelis were beginning to retaliate, not against the Syrian Ba'th which was backing the Palestinians, but against Jordan. These Israeli actions were not simply a response to what the Palestinians were doing, but sprang from the dynamics of Israeli policy. The population of Israel had continued to grow, mainly by immigration; by 1967 it stood at some

2.3 millions, of whom the Arabs formed roughly 13 per cent. Its economic strength had increased, with the help of aid from the United States, contributions from Jews in the outside world, and reparations from West Germany. It had also been building up the strength and expertise of its armed forces, and of the air force in particular. Israel knew itself to be militarily and politically stronger than its Arab neighbours; in the face of threats from those neighbours, the best course was to show its strength. This might lead to a more stable agreement than it had been able to achieve; but behind this there lay the hope of conquering the rest of Palestine and ending the unfinished war of 1948.

All these lines converged in 1967. Faced with Israeli retaliation against other Arab states, and with reports (which may have been unfounded) of a coming Israeli attack on Syria, 'Abd al-Nasir asked the United Nations to withdraw the forces which had been stationed on the frontier with Israel since the Suez war of 1956, and when this was done he closed the straits of 'Aqaba to Israeli shipping. It may have appeared to him that he had nothing to lose: either the United States would intervene at the last moment to negotiate a political settlement which would be a victory for him, or, if it came to war, his armed forces, equipped and trained by the USSR, were strong enough to win. His calculations might have proved correct had the United States had full control over Israeli policy, for there was a movement inside the American government to resolve the problem peacefully. The relations between great powers and their clients are never simple, however. The Israelis were not prepared to give Egypt a political victory which did not correspond to the balance of power between them, and they too had nothing to lose; they believed their armed forces to be the stronger, and in the event of an unexpected reverse they could be sure of support from the United States. As tension mounted, Jordan and Syria made military agreements with Egypt. On 5 June Israel attacked Egypt and destroyed its air force; and in the next few days of fighting the Israelis occupied Sinai as far as the Suez Canal, Jerusalem and the Palestinian part of Jordan, and part of southern Syria (the Jawlan or 'Golan Heights'), before a cease-fire agreed on at the United Nations ended the fighting.

The war was a turning-point in many different ways. The conquest of Jerusalem by the Israelis, and the fact that Muslim and Christian holy places were now under Jewish control, added another dimension to the conflict. The war changed the balance of forces in the Middle East. It was clear that Israel was militarily stronger than any combination of Arab states, and this changed the relationship of each of them with the outside world. What was, rightly or wrongly, regarded as a threat to the existence of Israel aroused sympathy in Europe and America, where memories of the Jewish fate during the Second World War were still strong; and the swift Israeli victory also made Israel more desirable as an ally in American eyes. For the Arab states, and in particular for Egypt, what had happened was in every sense a defeat which showed the limits of their military and political capacity; for the USSR it was also a kind of defeat, but one which made the Russians more resolute to prevent their clients from incurring another defeat of the same magnitude. At a very deep level, the war left its mark on everyone in the world who identified himself as either Jew or Arab, and what had been a local conflict became a worldwide one.

The most important result in the long run was the Israeli occupation of what was left of Arab Palestine: Jerusalem, Gaza and the western part of Jordan (usually known as the 'West Bank'). More Palestinians became refugees, and more came under Israeli rule. This strengthened the sense of Palestinian identity, and the conviction among them that in the end they could rely only on themselves; and it also posed a problem for Israelis, Arab states and great powers. Should Israel remain in occupation of what it had conquered, or trade land for some kind of peaceful settlement with the Arab states? Should there be some kind of political entity for the Palestinians? How could the Arab states win back the land they had lost? How could the powers achieve a settlement which would not result in another war, into which they might be drawn?

It is possible that some initiative by the victors might have opened the way to answering some of these questions; but the initiative did not come, perhaps because it took some time for the Israelis to digest the results of so sudden and complete a victory, and all parties entrenched themselves in new positions. The Palestinians, finding themselves for the most part united under Israeli rule, demanded a separate and independent national existence. The Israelis began to administer the conquered lands virtually as parts of Israel. The Security Council of the United Nations finally succeeded in November in agreeing on Resolution 242, by the terms of which there was to be peace within secure and recognized frontiers, Israel would withdraw from territories it had conquered and provision would be made for the refugees. There was disagreement, however, about the way in which this should be interpreted: whether Israel should withdraw from all or some of the territories; whether the Palestinians should be regarded as a nation or a mass of individual refugees. The heads of Arab states adopted their own resolution in a conference held at Khartoum in September 1967: no recognition of the Israeli conquests, and no negotiations. Here too, however, there could be different interpretations: for Egypt and Jordan at least, the way was still open to a negotiated settlement.

CHAPTER 25

Arab Unity and Disunity (since 1967)

THE CRISIS OF 1973

'Abd al-Nasir lived for three years after his defeat. His position in the world had been badly shaken by it; his relationships with the United States and Britain were soured by his accusation and belief that they had helped Israel militarily during the war, and by the American insistence that Israel would withdraw from conquered territories only in return for peace. His position in regard to other Arab rulers was weakened as the limitations of his power became clear. One immediate result of the war of 1967 was that he cut his losses in Yemen, and made an agreement with Saudi Arabia by which his forces were withdrawn.

Inside Egypt, however, his position was still strong. At the end of the fateful week in June 1967 he announced his resignation, but this aroused widespread protests in Egypt and some other Arab countries, perhaps because of skilful organization, but perhaps because of a feeling that his resignation would be a deeper defeat and humiliation. His hold over popular sentiment in other Arab countries also remained strong. Both because of his own stature and because of the recognized position of Egypt, he was the indispensable broker between the Palestinians and those among whom they lived. In the years after 1967, the growth of Palestinian national feeling and the increasing strength of Fatah, which controlled the PLO from 1969, led to a number of incidents of guerilla action against Israel, and Israeli reprisals against the lands where the Palestinians had some freedom of action. In 1969, Egyptian intervention brought about an agreement between the Lebanese government and the PLO, which set the limits within which the PLO would be free to operate in southern Lebanon. In the next year, 1970, severe fighting broke out in Jordan between the army and Palestinian guerilla groups which seemed on the point of taking over power in the country. The Jordanian government was able to impose its authority and end the freedom of action of the Palestinian groups, and once more it was the mediation of 'Abd al-Nasir which made peace between them.

Immediately after this, 'Abd al-Nasir suddenly died. The extraordinary scenes at his funeral, with millions weeping in the streets, certainly meant something; at least for the moment, it was difficult to imagine Egypt or the Arab world without him. His death was the end of an era of hope for an Arab world united and made new.

'Abd al-Nasir was succeeded by a colleague of long standing, Anwar Sadat (1918–81). It seemed, at first, that Egypt would continue as before. In other Arab countries, too, changes in 1969 and 1970 brought to power people who seemed likely to follow a policy roughly similar to Nasirism or at least consistent with it. In Morocco and Tunisia, it is true, there was no basic change at this time; King Hasan and those around him, and Bourguiba and the Neo-Destour, remained in power. In Algeria too the change within the ruling group had come a few years earlier. Further east, the rule of King Faysal in Saudi Arabia, King Husayn in Jordan, and the dynasties of the Gulf states continued. In Libya, however, a familiar combination of army officers and radical intellectuals overthrew the monarchy in 1969; after a time, there emerged in the new ruling group the dominant figure of an officer, Mu'ammar al-Qadhafi. In the Sudan a similar group, led by Ja'far al-Numayri, overturned the constitutional regime in 1969. In Syria, the Ba'thist regime which had been deeply involved in the defeat of 1967, was replaced in 1970 by a group of army officers led by Hafiz al-Asad, also belonging to the Ba'th but more cautious in policy. In Iraq, too, a period of rather shaky rule by coalitions of army officers and civilians was ended when a more cohesive group linked with the Ba'th took power in 1968; Saddam Husayn gradually emerged as its strongest figure. In South Yemen, too, 1969 was a critical year. The coalition of forces which had taken power with the coming of independence was replaced by a more strictly Marxist group. In North Yemen, however, these years did not mark a decisive change: the end of the civil war brought to power a coalition of elements from the two sides, whose relationships with each other still remained to be defined. It was not until 1974 that a more or less stable regime was established, with support from the army and some powerful tribal leaders.

In 1973 there took place events no less dramatic than those of 1967, and which seemed to mark a new stage on the path of Arab unity and the reassertion of independence in the face of the great powers. Once more there was a confrontation with Israel. Already before 'Abd al-Nasir died, the desire to compensate for the defeat of 1967 had shown itself in a 'war of attrition' along the Suez Canal and in the rearming of the Egyptian and Syrian armies by the USSR. Early in the 1970s the new ruler of Egypt, Sadat, made a certain change in policy when he asked for the withdrawal of Russian advisers and technicians, but the army remained one which the Russians had equipped and trained, and in October 1973 it launched a sudden attack upon the Israeli forces on the east bank of the Suez Canal; at the same moment, and by agreement, the Syrian army attacked the Israelis in the Jawlan.

In the first rush of fighting, the Egyptian army succeeded in crossing the canal and establishing a bridgehead, and the Syrians occupied part of the Jawlan; weapons supplied by the Russians enabled them to neutralize the Israeli air force, which had won the victory of 1967. In the next few days, however, the military tide turned. Israeli forces crossed the canal and established their own bridgehead on the west bank, and drove the Syrians back towards Damascus. Apart from their own skill, their success was due partly to the equipment which was quickly sent them by the Americans, and partly to differences of policy between Egypt and Syria which soon revealed themselves. The campaigns showed once more the military superiority of the Israelis, but neither in the eyes of the Arabs nor in those of the world did the war seem to be a defeat. The attacks had shown careful planning and serious determination; they had attracted not only sympathy but financial and military help from other Arab countries; and they ended in a cease-fire imposed by the influence of the super-powers which showed that, while the USA would not allow Israel to be defeated, neither it nor the USSR would allow Egypt to be defeated, and that they did not wish to allow the war to escalate in a way which would draw them in.

Part of the reason for the intervention of the powers was the use by the Arab states of what appeared to be their strongest weapon – the power to impose an embargo on the export of oil. For the first and perhaps the last time, this weapon was used successfully. The Arab oil-producing countries decided to cut down their production so long as Israel remained in occupation of Arab lands, and Saudi Arabia imposed a total embargo on exports to the USA and The Netherlands, which was regarded as the most favourable to Israel of western European countries and was also a centre of the free market in oil.

The effects of these decisions were all the greater because they more or less coincided with another change towards which the oil-exporting countries had been moving for some time. The demand for Middle Eastern oil had been increasing, as the needs of the industrial countries grew faster than production, and the organization of oil exporting countries (OPEC) had been growing stronger and more determined to increase their share of the profits, which were a smaller proportion of the price than was the amount taken in taxation by the consumer countries which imported oil. At the end of 1973 OPEC decided to increase the prices at which oil was sold by some 300 per cent; Iran and the Arab countries were the prime movers in this decision. (The increase in the price paid by the consumer was less than this, however, since taxes and other costs did not rise as much.)

THE PREDOMINANCE OF AMERICAN INFLUENCE

Within a few years, however, it became clear that what might have seemed to be a declaration of political and economic independence was in fact a first step towards greater dependence on the United States. The lead was taken, as it had been in every Arab enterprise for the last twenty years or so, by Egypt. For Sadat, the war of 1973 had not been fought to achieve military victory, but in order to give a shock to the super-powers, so that they would take the lead in negotiating some settlement of the problems between Israel and the Arabs which would prevent a further crisis and a dangerous confrontation. This indeed is what happened, but in a way which increased the power and participation of one of the super-powers, the USA. America had intervened decisively in the war, first to supply arms to Israel and prevent its being defeated, and then to bring about a balance of forces conducive to a settlement. In the next two years, American mediation led to an Israeli–Syrian agreement by which Israel withdrew from some of the Syrian territory it had conquered in 1967 and 1973, and two similar agreements between Israel and Egypt. There was a brief and abortive attempt to bring together the super-powers, Israel and the Arab states in a general conference under the auspices of the United Nations, but the main line of American policy was so far as possible to exclude Russia from the Middle East, to support Israel politically and militarily, to bring it into agreements with Arab countries by which it would withdraw from conquered territories in exchange for peace, but to keep the PLO out of the discussions, in deference to Israeli wishes, at least so long as the PLO did not recognize Israel.

This policy changed for a short time in 1977, when a new American

President, Jimmy Carter, tried to formulate a joint approach to the problem by the USA and the USSR, and to find a way by which the Palestinians could be drawn into the process of negotiation. These efforts, however, came to nothing for two reasons: Israeli opposition, which increased when a more strongly nationalist government took power in Israel, with Menahem Begin as prime minister; and Sadat's sudden decision, in November 1977, to go to Jerusalem and offer Israel an opening for peace by direct negotiations.

It was clearly in Sadat's mind to try to put an end to the sequence of wars which, he believed, the Arabs could not win, but there were also wider perspectives: direct negotiations, sponsored by the USA, would eliminate the Soviet Union as a factor in the Middle East; once at peace with Israel, Egypt might become a more important ally for America, with all the consequences which might follow in the way both of economic support and of a more favourable American attitude towards the claims of the Palestinian Arabs. In the mind of the Israeli government of the time, the aim was different: to make peace with Egypt, their most formidable enemy, even at the price of withdrawing from Sinai, and therefore to free their hands for the essential aim of their policy – to implant Jewish settlers in the conquered territories of the West Bank and gradually annex them, and to be able to deal effectively with any opposition from Syria or the PLO. In the discussions which followed Sadat's journey, therefore, the central question was that of the connection to be established between an Israeli–Egyptian peace and the future status of the West Bank. When agreement was finally reached, with American mediation, in 1978 (the 'Camp David Agreement'), it was clear that in this essential matter the Israeli opinion had prevailed against that of Egypt, and up to a point that of the United States. According to the agreement, there was to be formal peace between Egypt and Israel, and there was to be some kind of autonomy, to be defined later, for the West Bank and Gaza, leading after five years to discussions about its definitive status; but there was no formal link between the two. In later discussions on autonomy it soon became clear that Israeli ideas were very different from those of Egypt or America, and Israel refused to suspend its policy of Jewish settlement in the conquered territories.

President Sadat was assassinated in 1981 by members of a group who opposed his policy and wished to restore the Islamic basis of Egyptian society, but the main lines of his policy were continued by his successor, Husni Mubarak. In the course of the next few years, Egypt's relations with the United States grew closer, and it received large amounts of financial and military aid. The agreement with Israel, however, was repudiated not only by the Palestinians but by most other Arab states, with greater or lesser degrees of conviction, and Egypt was formally expelled from the Arab League, which moved its headquarters from Cairo to Tunis. Nevertheless, the advantages to be derived from a closer alignment with the United States policy were so great and obvious that a number of other Arab states also moved in that direction: Morocco, Tunisia, Jordan, and in particular the oil-producing countries of the Arabian peninsula, for, after the climax of their influence in 1973, it soon became clear that the wealth derived from oil could generate weakness rather than strength.

Judged by all prevous standards, that wealth was very great indeed. Between 1973 and 1978, annual revenues from oil in the main Arab producing countries grew enormously: in Saudi Arabia from $4.35 to $36.0 billions; in Kuwait from $1.7 to $9.2 billions; in Iraq from $1.8 to $23.6 billions; in Libya from $2.2 to $8.8 billions. Some other countries also increased their production greatly, in particular Qatar, Abu Dhabi and Dubai. The control of the countries over their resources also expanded. By 1980 all the main producing states had either nationalized the production of oil or else taken a major stake in the operating companies, although the great multinational companies still had a strong position in transport and selling. The increase in wealth led to an increase in dependence on the industrialized countries. Producing countries had to sell their oil, and the industrial countries were their main customers. In the course of the 1970s the excess of demand over supply came to an end, because of economic recession, attempts to economize in the consumption of fuel, and increased production by countries which were not members of OPEC; the bargaining position and unity of OPEC grew weaker, and a high and uniform level of prices could not be maintained. Those countries which had larger revenues than they could spend on development, because of the limits of population and natural resources, had to invest the surplus somewhere, and did so for the most part in the industrial countries. They had to go to those countries too for the capital goods and technical expertise which they needed for economic development and for building their armed forces.

The increasing dependence had another aspect. The use by the Arab countries of the weapon of embargo in 1973 had brought home to the industrial states the extent of their dependence upon Middle Eastern oil, and there were indications as the decade went on that the United States might intervene in force if supplies of oil were interrupted again, either because of revolutions in the producing countries, or – as the Americans saw it – because of the danger of an extension of Soviet influence in the countries of the Gulf. Intervention would be a last resort, however, and for the most part the United States depended on its main allies in the region of the Gulf, Saudi Arabia and Iran. At the end of the 1970s, however, the situation changed. The Russian occupation of Afghanistan in 1979 aroused fears, whether justified or not, that the USSR might intend to extend its control further into the world of the Indian Ocean. The Iranian revolution of 1978–9 destroyed the position of the shah, the strongest ally of the United States, and replaced his government by one committed to making Iran into a truly Islamic state, as the first step towards a similar change in other Muslim countries; there was some danger that the revolution would spread westwards into neighbouring countries, which would disrupt the political system of the Gulf countries and their relations with the United States. Such considerations led to the formulation of American plans for the defence of the Gulf in case of need, in agreement with such Middle Eastern states as were prepared to co-operate. Most of the Gulf states tried, however, to keep some distance from a full American alliance, and in 1981 Saudi Arabia and the smaller states created their own Gulf Co-operation Council.

The opening to the west was more than a change in foreign or military policy; it was also a change in the attitudes and policies of most Arab governments towards the economy. It was a change known in Egypt, significantly, as the *infitah* (policy of the open door), after a law promulgated in 1974. A number of causes led up to it: the power of the United States, as shown in the war of 1973 and its aftermath; the need for foreign loans and investment in order to develop resources and acquire strength; perhaps also an increasing awareness of the limitations of state control over the economy; and the pressure of private interests.

The *infitah* consisted of two processes, closely concerned with each other. On the one hand there was a shift in the balance between the public and private sectors of the economy. Apart from Lebanon, which had virtually no public sector, even the countries most committed to private enterprise retained some areas of public control, for there was no possibility of rapid development except through investment and direction by the state; in Saudi Arabia, for example, the oil industry was nationalized and the largest new industrial enterprises were owned by the state. In most countries, however, a wider scope was now given to private enterprise, in agriculture, industry and commerce. This was most noticeable in Egypt, where the 1970s saw a rapid and far-reaching change from the state socialism of the 1960s. In Tunisia, an attempt at state control of imports and exports, of industrial production and internal distribution, ran into difficulties and was ended in 1969. In Syria and Iraq, too, in spite of the socialist principles of the Ba'th party, a similar change took place.

Secondly, *infitah* meant an opening to foreign, and specifically to western, investment and enterprise. In spite of the accumulation of capital from the production of oil, the capital resources of most Arab countries were not adequate for the rapid and large-scale developments to which most governments were committed. Investment from the United States and Europe, and from international bodies, was encouraged by guarantees and tax-privileges, and restrictions upon imports were lowered. The results on the whole were not what had been hoped for. Not very much private foreign capital was attracted into countries where, for the most part, regimes seemed unstable and the chances of profit uncertain. Most aid came from governments or international agencies, and was used for armaments, the infrastructure, and costly and over-ambitious schemes. Some aid was given on conditions, explicit or implied; pressure by the International Monetary Fund on Egypt to reduce its deficit led to an attempt to raise food prices, which aroused serious disturbances in 1977. Moreover, the easing of restrictions upon imports meant that young indigenous industries faced competition from the well-established industries of America, western Europe and Japan, at least in those lines of production where a high level of technical expertise and experience was needed. The result would be to keep the Arab countries, like those in most of the Third World, in a situation in which they would produce consumer goods for themselves but would continue to import products of the higher technology.

THE INTERDEPENDENCE OF ARAB COUNTRIES

The death of 'Abd al-Nasir and the events of the 1970s weakened what may have been an illusion of independence, and also an illusion of unity, but in some ways the links between different Arab countries grew closer during this period. More inter-Arab organizations were in existence than ever before, and some of them were effective. The Arab League lost much of what had always been a limited authority when Egypt was expelled, but its membership increased: Mauritania in west Africa and Djibouti and Somalia in east Africa were accepted as members, although none of them had previously been regarded as Arab countries, and their acceptance was a sign of the ambiguity of the term 'Arab'. At the United Nations and in other international bodies, the members of the League often succeeded in following a common policy, particularly where the problem of Palestine was concerned.

The differences of interest between the states which had resources of oil and those which did not were lessened by the creation of economic institutions through which part of the wealth of the richer countries could be given or loaned to the poorer. Some of these institutions were supranational: the special fund created by OPEC, that set up by the organization of Arab oil-exporting countries (OAPEC), the Arab Fund for Economic and Social Development. Others were set up by individual countries, Kuwait, Saudi Arabia and Abu Dhabi. By the end of the 1970s the volume of aid was very large. In 1979 some \$2 billions were given by oil-producing countries to other developing countries, through various channels; this was 2.9 per cent of their GNP.

Other kinds of links were even more important, because they were links between individual human beings as well as between the societies of which they formed part. A common culture was in process of formation. The rapid expansion of education which had begun when countries became independent continued with accelerated speed, in all countries to a greater or lesser extent. By 1980 the proportion of boys of elementary school age who attended school was 88 per cent in Egypt and 57 per cent in Saudi Arabia; that of girls was 90 per cent in Iraq and 31 per cent in Saudi Arabia. The literacy rate in Egypt was 56.8 per cent for men and 29 per cent for women. In Egypt and Tunisia almost a third of university students were women and in Kuwait over 50 per cent; even in Saudi Arabia the proportion was almost a quarter. Schools and universities were of varying quality; the need to educate as many as possible as soon as possible meant that classes were large, teachers inadequately trained and buildings unsuitable. A common factor in most schools was the emphasis on the teaching of Arabic, and the teaching of other subjects through the medium of Arabic. For the greater number of those who came out of the schools, and of graduates of the new universities, Arabic was the only language in which they were at home, and the medium through which they saw the world. This strengthened the consciousness of a common culture shared by all who spoke Arabic.

This common culture and awareness were now spread by a new medium. Radio, cinemas and newspapers continued to be important, but to their influence there was added that of television. The 1960s were the decade during which Arab countries established television stations, and the TV set became a part of the household scarcely less important than the cooker and the refrigerator, in all classes except the very poor or those who lived in villages not yet reached by electricity. By 1973 there were estimated to be some 500,000 TV sets in Egypt, a similar number in Iraq and 300,000 in Saudi Arabia. What was transmitted included news, presented in such a way as to win support for the policy of the government, religious programmes in most countries to a greater or lesser extent, films or serials imported from Europe or America, and also plays and musical programmes made in Egypt and Lebanon; plays transmitted ideas, images and that most fragile of transplants, humour, across the frontiers of Arab states.

Another link between Arab countries which grew closer in these ten years was that created by the movement of individuals. This was the period when air transport came within the range of possibility of large strata of the population. Airports were built, most countries had their national airlines, air-routes connected Arab capitals with each other. Road travel also increased as roads were improved and automobiles and buses became more common: the Sahara and the Syrian and Arabian deserts were crossed by well-maintained roads. In spite of political conflicts which might close frontiers and hold up travellers or goods, these routes carried increasing numbers of tourists and businessmen; efforts made by the Arab League and other bodies to strengthen commercial links between the Arab countries had some success, although inter-Arab trade still accounted for less than 10 per cent of the foreign trade of Arab countries in 1980.

The most important movement along the air- and land-routes, however, was not that of goods but of migrants from the poorer Arab countries to those made rich by oil. The movement of migration had begun in the 1950s, but in the late 1960s and the 1970s the flow became greater because of two different kinds of factor. On the one hand, the vast increase in profits from oil and the creation of ambitious schemes of development raised the demand for labour in the oil-producing states, and the number of those states grew; apart from Algeria and Iraq, none of them had the manpower needed, at various levels, to develop their own resources. On the other hand, the pressure of population in the poorer countries grew greater, and the prospects of migration became more attractive. This was particularly true of Egypt after 1967; there was little economic growth, and the government encouraged migration in the period of *infitah*. What had been mainly a movement of educated younger men now became a mass migration of workers at every level of skill, to work not only in the civil service or professions, but as building workers or in domestic service. Mostly it was a movement of single men or, increasingly, of women who left their families behind; but the Palestinians, having lost their homes, tended to move as whole families and to settle permanently in the countries of migration.

Estimates of the total number of workers cannot be accurate, but by the end of the 1970s there may have been as many as 3 million Arab migrants, perhaps half of them in Saudi Arabia, with large numbers also in Kuwait, the other Gulf states and Libya. The largest group, perhaps a third of the whole number, came from Egypt, and a similar number from the two Yemens; half a million were Jordanians or Palestinians (including the dependants of workers), and smaller numbers came from Syria, Lebanon, the Sudan, Tunisia and Morocco. There was some migration also between the poorer countries: as Jordanians moved to the Gulf, Egyptians took their places in some areas of the Jordanian economy.

The increased knowledge of peoples, customs and dialects which was brought about by this large-scale migration must have deepened the sense of there being a single Arab world within which Arabs could move with comparative freedom and understand each other. It did not necessarily, however, increase the desire for closer union; there was an awareness of differences also, and migrants were conscious of being excluded from the local societies into which they moved.

ARAB DISUNITY

In spite of the strengthening of such ties, in the political sphere the main trend of the 1970s was towards difference and even hostility rather than greater union. Although the personality of 'Abd al-Nasir had aroused hostilities and led to divisions between Arab states and conflicts between governments and peoples, it had nevertheless generated a kind of solidarity, a feeling that there was such a thing as an Arab nation in the making. For the first few years after his death something of this continued, and its last manifestation was in the war of 1973 when there seemed for a moment to be a common front of Arab states irrespective of the nature of their regimes. The common front disintegrated almost at once, however; and although attempts at union between two or more Arab states were still discussed and announced from time to time, the general impression which the Arab states gave their peoples and the world by the end of the 1970s was one of weakness and disunity.

The weakness was shown most obviously in regard to what all Arab peoples regarded as their common problem: that of Israel and the fate of the Palestinians. By the end of the 1970s, the situation in the regions occupied by Israel during the war of 1967 was changing rapidly. The policy of Jewish settlement, begun soon after the war of 1967 for reasons which were partly strategic, had taken on a new meaning with the coming to power in Israel of the more rigidly nationalist government led by Begin; settlement took place on a larger scale, with expropriation of land and water from the Arab inhabitants, and with the ultimate aim of annexing the area to Israel; the Arab part of Jerusalem, and the Jawlan region conquered from Syria, were in fact formally annexed. In the face of such measures both the Palestinians and the Arab states seemed to be powerless. The PLO and its chairman, Yasir 'Arafat, were able to speak for the Palestinians in the occupied areas and to obtain international support, but not to change the situation in any appreciable way. Neither of the paths of action which, in theory, were open to the Arab states seemed to lead anywhere. Active opposition to Israel was impossible, given the superior armed might of the Israelis, and the separate interests of the Arab states, which they were not prepared to place in jeopardy. The path tried by Egypt under Sadat did result in an Israeli withdrawal from Sinai, but it soon became clear that Egypt had not obtained sufficient influence over Israel to persuade it to change its policy, or over the USA to persuade it to oppose Israeli policy in more than a formal way.

Military weakness, the growth of separate interests and of economic dependence all led to a disintegration of whatever common front had seemed to exist until the war of 1973. The obvious line along which it disintegrated was that which divided the states whose ultimate inclination was towards the USA, a political compromise with Israel, and a free capitalist economy, and those which clung to a policy of neutralism. Those in this second camp were usually thought to include Algeria, Libya, Syria, Iraq and South Yemen, together with the PLO, which was formally regarded by the Arab states as having the status of a separate government.

In practice, however, the lines were not so clearly drawn, and alliances between individual countries might cut across them. Within each camp, relations were not necessarily close or easy. Among those which were 'pro-western', the independent policy adopted by Egypt in its approach to Israel caused hesitations and embarrassment, and virtually all Arab states formally severed relations with it, although they did not cut off the flow of migrants' remittances back to their families. In the other camp, there were varying relations with the other super-power; Syria, Iraq and South Yemen obtained military and economic aid from the USSR. There was also a deep antagonism between the two Ba'thist regimes of Syria and Iraq, caused both by rivalry for leadership of what appeared for a time to be a powerful and expanding nationalist party and by different interests between countries which had a common frontier and shared the water-system of the Euphrates. There was, moreover, endless friction with Libya, whose dominant figure, Qadhafi, seemed at times to be trying to take up the mantle of 'Abd al-Nasir, without any basis of strength except what money could provide.

In this period there were three armed conflicts which gravely affected the relations between Arab states. The first occurred in the far west of the Arab world. It concerned a territory known as the Western Sahara, a thinly populated western extension of the Sahara desert to the Atlantic coast south of Morocco. It had been occupied and ruled by Spain since the late nineteenth century, but was of little strategic or economic importance until the discovery in the 1960s of important deposits of phosphates, which a Spanish company extracted. In the 1970s Morocco began to put forward claims to it, because the authority of the sultan had formerly run there. These claims were opposed by Spain, and also by Mauritania, the country immediately to the south, which had been under French rule since the early years of the twentieth century, had become independent in 1960, and itself put forward claims to part at least of the territory. After a long diplomatic process Spain, Morocco and Mauritania reached agreement in 1975, by which Spain would withdraw and the territory be divided between the other two. This did not end the crisis, however; by this time the people of the territory itself had organized their own political movements, and after the agreement of 1975 one of them, known by the acronym 'Polisario', emerged as an opponent of Moroccan and Mauritanian claims and called for independence. Mauritania gave up its claims in 1979, but Morocco continued to be involved in a long struggle with Polisario, which had the support of Algeria, a country which also shared a frontier with the territory and did not wish to see Moroccan power extended. There began a conflict which was to continue in one form or another for a number of years, and to complicate relations not only between Morocco and Algeria, but also within organizations of which they both formed part: the Arab League and the Organization for African Unity.

Another conflict, which broke out in Lebanon at roughly the same time, drew into it, in one way or another, the main political forces in the Middle East: the Arab states, the PLO, Israel, western Europe and the super-powers. Its origins lay in certain changes in Lebanese society which called in question the political system. When Lebanon became independent in the 1940s, it included three regions with different kinds of population and traditions of government: the region of Mount Lebanon, with a population mainly Maronite Christian in the north and mixed Druze and Christian in the south, the coastal cities with a mixed Muslim and Christian population, and certain rural areas to the east and south of Mount Lebanon where the population was mainly Shi'i Muslim. The first of these areas had a long tradition of separate administration under its own lords, and later as a privileged district of the Ottoman Empire; the second and third had been integral parts of the empire, and were incorporated into Lebanon by the French mandatory government. The new state had a democratic consti-tution, and by the time the French left the country there was an agreement between the leaders of the Maronites and the Sunni Muslims that the president of the republic should always be a Maronite, the prime minister a Sunni, and other posts in government and administration be distributed among the different religious communities, but in such a way as to preserve effective power in Christian hands.

Between 1945 and 1958 the system succeeded in maintaining a balance and a certain degree of co-operation between the leaders of the different communities, but within a generation its bases were growing weaker. There was a demographic change: the Muslim population grew faster than the Christian, and by the 1970s it was generally accepted that the three communities collectively regarded as Muslim (Sunnis, Shi'is and Druzes) were larger in numbers than the Christian communities, and some of their leaders were less willing to accept a situation in which the presidency and ultimate power were in the hands of the Christians. Moreover, the rapid economic changes in the country and the Middle East led to the growth of Beirut into a great city in which half the population lived and more than half worked. Lebanon had become an extended city-state; it needed control by a strong and effective government. The gap between rich and poor had grown, and the poor were mainly Sunni or Shi'i Muslims; they needed a redistribution of wealth through taxation and social services. A government based on a fragile agreement between leaders was not well placed to do what was required, for it could survive only by not pursuing any policy which would disturb powerful interests.

In 1958 the balance broke down, and there were several months of civil war, which ended with a reassertion of the balance under the slogan 'No victors, no vanquished'. The underlying conditions which had led to the breakdown continued to exist, however, and in the next decade and a half another factor was added to them – the larger role which Lebanon played in the confrontation between the Palestinians and Israel. After the power of the Fatah and other guerilla organizations in Jordan was broken in 1970, their main efforts were concentrated in southern Lebanon, whose frontier with Israel was the only one across which they could hope to operate with some freedom, and with the support of the large Palestinian refugee population. This aroused the alarm of important elements among the Christians, and in particular their best-organized political party, the Kata'ib (Phalanges): both because Palestinian activities in the south were leading to a strong Israeli response, which might threaten the independence of the country, and because the presence of the Palestinians gave support to those groups, mainly Muslim and Druze, which wanted to change the political system in which power lay mainly in Christian hands.

By 1975 there was a dangerous confrontation of forces, and each protagonist found arms and encouragement from abroad: the Kata'ib and their allies from Israel, the Palestinians and their allies from Syria. Serious fighting broke out in the spring of that year, and continued, with varying fortunes, until late 1976, when a more or less stable truce was agreed. The chief instigator of this was Syria, which had changed its policy during the period of fighting. It had supported the Palestinians and their allies at the beginning, but had then moved closer to the Kata'ib and their allies when they seemed to be in danger of losing: its interest lay in maintaining a balance of forces which would restrain the Palestinians and make it difficult for them to pursue a policy in southern Lebanon that might draw Syria into a war with Israel. To preserve these interests, it sent armed forces into Lebanon, with some kind of approval from the other Arab states and the USA, and they remained there after the end of the fighting. There followed some five years of uneasy truce. Maronite groups ruled the north, the Syrian army was in the east, the PLO was dominant in the south. Beirut was divided between an eastern section controlled by the Kata'ib, and a western section controlled by the PLO and its allies. The authority of the government had more or less ceased to exist. The unrestrained power of the PLO in the south brought it into intermittent conflict with Israel, which in 1978 mounted an invasion; this was brought to a halt by international pressure, but left behind it a local government under Israeli control in a strip along the frontier. The invasion and the disturbed situation in the south led the Shi'i inhabitants of the area to create their own political and military force, Amal.

In 1982 the situation acquired a more dangerous dimension. The nationalist government in Israel, having secured its southern frontier by the peace treaty with Egypt, now tried to impose its own solution of the problem of the Palestinians. This involved an attempt to destroy both the military and the political power of the PLO in Lebanon, to install a friendly regime there, and then, freed from effective Palestinian resistance, to pursue its policy of settlement and annexation of occupied Palestine. With some degree of acquiescence from the USA, Israel invaded Lebanon in June 1982. The invasion culminated in a long siege of the western part of Beirut, mainly inhabited by Muslims and dominated by the PLO. The siege ended with an agreement, negotiated through the US government, by which the PLO would evacuate west Beirut, with guarantees for the safety of Palestinian civilians given by the Lebanese and US governments. At the same time, a presidential election resulted in the military head of the Kata'ib, Bashir Jumayyil, becoming president; he was assassinated soon afterwards and his brother Amin was then elected. The assassination was taken by Israel as an opportunity to occupy west Beirut, and this allowed the Kata'ib to carry out a massacre of Palestinians on a large scale in the refugee camps of Sabra and Shatila.

The withdrawal of the PLO, while it ended the fighting for a time, moved the conflict into a more dangerous phase. The gulf beween local groups grew wider. The new government, dominated by the Kata'ib and supported by Israel, tried to impose its own solution: concentration of power in its hands, and an agreement with Israel by which Israeli forces would withdraw in return for a virtual political and strategic control of the country. This aroused strong opposition from other communities, the Druzes and Shi'is, with support from Syria. Although the invasion had shown the impotence either of Syria or of other Arab countries to take concerted and effective action, Syrian troops were still in parts of the country, and Syrian influence was strong with those who opposed the government. Syria and its allies could draw upon some support from the USSR, while the USA was in a position to give both military and diplomatic support to the Kata'ib and their Israeli backers. As one of the conditions under which the PLO left Beirut, a multinational force with a strong American element had been sent to Lebanon. It had been quickly withdrawn, but returned after the massacre of Sabra and Shatila. From that time, the American component of the multinational force gradually enlarged its functions, from defence of the civilian population to active support of the new Lebanese government and of a Lebanese–Israeli agreement which it helped to negotiate in 1983. By the later months of that year it was engaged in military operations in support of the Lebanese government, but, after attacks on US marines and under pressure of American public opinion, it withdrew its forces. Without effective American or Israeli support and faced with strong resistance from Druzes, Shi'is and Syria, the Lebanese government cancelled the agreement with Israel. One result of this episode was the emergence of Amal and other Shi'i groups as major factors in Lebanese politics. In 1984 Amal took effective control of west Beirut; it was partly under its pressure that Israeli forces withdrew from all Lebanon except for a strip along the southern frontier.

A third conflict in these years involved an Arab with a non-Arab state, and threatened to draw in other Arab states; this was the war between Iraq and Iran which began in 1980. There were certain frontier questions at issue between them, and these had been resolved in favour of Iran in 1975, when the shah was at the height of his power in the world. The Iranian revolution, and the period of confusion and apparent weakness which followed it, gave Iraq an opportunity to redress the balance. Something more important than this was at stake, however. The new Iranian regime appealed to Muslims everywhere to restore the authority of Islam in society, and might seem to have a special attraction to the Shi'i majority in Iraq; the Iraqi regime faced a double challenge, as a secular nationalist government and as one dominated by Sunni Muslims. In 1980 the Iraqi army invaded Iran. After its first successes, however, it was not able to occupy any part of the country permanently, and after a time Iran was able to take the offensive and invade Iraq. The war did not split Iraqi society, for the Shi'is of Iraq remained at least quiescent, but to some extent it split the Arab world. Syria supported Iran, because of its own disagreement with Iraq, but most other Arab states gave financial or military support to Iraq, because an Iranian victory would upset the political system in the Gulf and might also affect the order of society in countries in which Muslim, and particularly Shi'i, sentiment was strong.

The fighting finally came to an end with a cease-fire negotiated by the United Nations in 1988. Neither side had won territory, and both had lost heavily in human lives and economic resources. In a sense, however, both had salvaged something: neither regime had collapsed under the stress of war, and the Iranian revolution had not spread to Iraq or the Gulf.

The end of the war between Iraq and Iran opened prospects of a change in the relations between Arab states. It seemed likely that Iraq, with its energies released and with an army well tried in war, would play a more active role in other spheres: in the Gulf, and in the general politics of the Arab world. Its relations with Egypt and Jordan had been strengthened by the help they had given it during the war; its relations with Syria were bad because Syria had helped Iran, and as an opponent of Syria it might intervene more actively in the tangled affairs of Lebanon.

The problem of Palestine also moved into a new phase in 1988. At the end of the previous year, the population of the territories under Israeli occupation, the West Bank and Gaza, had erupted in a movement of resistance, almost universal, at times peaceful and at times violent, although avoiding the use of firearms; the local leadership had links with the PLO and other organizations. This movement, the *intifada*, continued throughout 1988, changing the relationship of Palestinians with each other and with the world outside in the occupied territories. It revealed the existence of a united Palestinian people, and re-established the division between the territories under Israeli occupation and Israel itself. The Israeli government was unable to suppress the movement, increasingly on the defensive against foreign criticism, and faced with a deeply divided public. King Husayn of Jordan, finding himself unable to control the rising or to speak for the Palestinians, withdrew from active participation in the search for a settlement. The PLO was in a position to step into the vacuum, but its own nature was changed. It had to take into account the opinion of those in the occupied territories, and their desire to end the occupation. The Palestine National Council, the representative body of Palestinians, met in Algiers and produced a charter proclaiming its willingness to accept the existence of Israel and to negotiate a final settlement with it. These developments were taking place in a new context: a certain reassertion of Arab unity in regard to the problem, the return of Egypt as an active participant in Arab affairs, and a change in the relationship between the United States and the USSR. The former declared its willingness to talk directly to the PLO for the first time, and the latter began to intervene more actively in the affairs of the Middle East.

CHAPTER 26

A Disturbance of Spirits (since 1967)

ETHNIC AND RELIGIOUS DIVISIONS

The conflicts in Lebanon and Iraq showed how easily enmities between states could be intertwined with those of discordant elements within a state. In this period, some of the internal discords which exist in all states became more significant. In Iraq there was the opposition of Arabs and Kurds. The Kurdish minority in the north-east of the country had for long been neglected in the measures of economic and social change which were carried out mainly in districts nearer to the large cities. As inhabitants of mountain valleys, or members of transhumant tribes, they did not want close control by urban bureaucracies; they were touched too by the idea of Kurdish independence, which had been in the air since the later Ottoman period. From the time of the British mandate there were intermittent Kurdish revolts, and they became more persistent and better organized, and had more support from states which were hostile to Iraq, from the time of the 1958 revolution. For some years the revolt had support from Iran, but this was withdrawn when the two countries reached agreement on various questions in 1975. After that the revolt ended, and the government took some measures to give the Kurdish areas a special administration and a programme of economic development, but the situation remained uneasy, and revolt flared up once again in the late 1980s, during the war between Iraq and Iran.

A similar situation existed, potentially, in Algeria. Part of the population of the mountain areas of the Atlas in Morocco and Kabylia in Algeria were Berbers, speaking dialects of a language different from Arabic and with a long tradition of local organization and leadership. In the period of French rule, the government had tended to maintain the difference between them and the Arabic-speaking inhabitants, partly for political reasons, but also because of a natural tendency of local officials to preserve the special nature of the communities they ruled. When nationalist governments came to power after independence, their policy was one of extending the control of the central government and also the sway of Arabic culture. In Morocco, this policy was strengthened by two factors, the long and powerful tradition of the sultan's sovereignty, and the prestige of the Arabic culture of the great cities; Berber was not a written language of high culture, and as Berber villagers came within the sphere of radiation of urban life they tended to become Arabic-speaking. In Algeria, however, the situation was different: the tradition of Arabic culture was weaker, for Algeria had had no great cities or schools, and that of French culture was stronger and seemed to offer an alternative vision of the future. The authority of the government, too, was not so firmly rooted; its claim to legitimacy was based upon its leadership in the struggle for independence, and in that struggle Berbers from Kabylia had played a full part.

Ethnic differences, then, could give a new depth to differences of interest, and so too could differences of religion. The example of Lebanon showed how a struggle for power could easily express itself in religious terms. In the Sudan an analogous situation existed. The inhabitants of the southern parts of the country were neither Arabs nor Muslims; some of them were Christians, converted by missionaries during the period of British rule. They had memories of a period when they had been liable to slave raids from the north, and after independence, with power in the hands of a ruling group which was mainly Arab and Muslim, they were apprehensive about the future: the new government might try to extend Islam and Arabic culture southwards and would be more conscious of the interests of regions near the capital than of those further away. Almost as soon as the country became independent a revolt broke out in the south, and it continued until 1972, when it was ended by an agreement which gave the south a considerable degree of autonomy. Mutual tensions and suspicions continued to exist, however, and they came to the surface in the early 1980s when the government began to follow a more explicitly Islamic policy: a revolt against rule from Khartoum continued on a large scale through the 1980s, and the government was unable either to suppress it or to come to terms with it.

A situation of great danger and complexity existed in countries with large Shi'i populations: Iraq, Kuwait, Bahrayn, Saudi Arabia, Syria and Lebanon. The Iranian revolution seemed likely to arouse a stronger sense of Shi'i identity, and this could have political implications in countries where government was firmly in the hands of Sunnis. On the other hand, however, a sense of common nationality or of common economic interest could work in the opposite direction. In Syria, a different situation existed, at least temporarily. The Ba'thist regime which had held power since the 1960s had been dominated since 1970 by a group of officers and politicians, with Asad at their head, drawn largely from the 'Alawi community, a dissident branch of the Shi'is; opposition to the government therefore tended to take the form of a strong assertion of Sunni Islam by the Muslim Brothers or similar bodies.

RICH AND POOR

A gap of another kind was growing wider in most Arab countries – that between rich and poor. It had of course always existed, but it took on a different meaning in a time of rapid economic change. It was a period of growth rather than of fundamental structural change. Mainly because of the increase in profits from oil, the rate of growth was high not only in the oil-producing countries but also in others, which profited from loans and grants, investments and remittances from migrant workers. The annual rate in the 1970s was over 10 per cent in the United Arab Emirates and Saudi Arabia, 9 per cent in Syria, 7 per cent in Iraq and Algeria, 5 per cent in Egypt. Growth did not, however, take place equally in all sectors of the economy. A large part of the increase in government revenues was spent on acquiring armaments (mainly from the USA and western Europe) and on expanding the machinery of administration; the sector of the economy which grew most rapidly was the service sector, particularly government service; by 1976 civil servants formed 13 per cent of the economically active population of Egypt. The other important field of expansion was that of consumer industries: textiles, food-processing, consumer goods and construction. This expansion was encouraged by two developments in the period: the loosening in most countries of restrictions upon private enterprise, which resulted in the proliferation of small companies, and the vast increase in the volume of remittances from migrants. By 1979 the total volume of these was in the region of $5 billions a year; they were encouraged by governments because they eased the problem of the balance of payments, and they were used largely for real estate and consumer durables.

On the whole, private investors had no reason to put their money in heavy industry, where both capital outlay and risks were high, and foreign investment in it was limited as well. Virtually the only new heavy industries were those in which governments chose to invest, if they had the necessary resources. A number of the oil-producing countries tried to develop petro-chemical industries, and also steel and aluminium; on the whole the developments were on a larger scale than the likely market would justify. The most ambitious industrial plans were those in Saudi Arabia, where two large complexes were built, one on the Red Sea coast and the other on the Gulf coast, and in Algeria. Under Boumediene the policy of the Algerian government was to devote the larger part of its resources to heavy industries like steel, and to industries which involved high technology, with the hope of making the country independent of the powerful industrial countries and then at a later stage using the new technology and the products of heavy industry to develop agriculture and the production of consumer goods. After the death of Boumediene in 1979, however, this policy was changed, and greater emphasis laid on agriculture and social services.

Almost everywhere the most neglected sector was the agricultural. The main exception was Syria, which devoted more than half of its investment to agriculture, and in particular to the Tabqa Dam on the Euphrates, begun in 1968 with help from the USSR and by the end of the 1970s producing hydroelectric power as well as permitting the extension of irrigation in the river valley. The result of this general neglect of agriculture was that, although a large part of the population of every country lived in the villages, agricultural production did not increase in most countries, and in some of them it declined. In Saudi Arabia, 58 per cent of the economically active population lived in the countryside, but they produced only 10 per cent of the Gross Domestic Product. Circumstances were exceptional here, because of the overriding importance of oil-production, but in Egypt the proportions were not very different: 52 per cent lived in the countryside and produced 28 per cent of the GDP. By the end of the 1970s, a large proportion of the food consumed in the Arab countries was imported.

Economic growth did not raise the standard of living so much as might have been expected, both because the population grew faster than ever, and because the political and social systems of most Arab countries did not provide for a more equal distribution of the proceeds of production. Taking the Arab countries as a whole, the total population, which had been some 55–60 millions in 1930 and had increased to some 90 millions by 1960, had reached some 179 millions by 1979. The rate of natural growth in most countries was between 2 and 3 per cent. The reason for this was not primarily an increase in births; if anything, the birthrate was declining as methods of birth control began to spread and as urban conditions led young people to marry later. The main reason was an increase in life expectancy and in particular a decline in infant mortality.

As before, the growth of population swelled the cities, both because the natural increase of the urban population was higher than before, as health conditions improved, and because of immigration from the countryside. By the middle of the 1970s more or less half the population of most Arab countries lived in cities: more than 50 per cent in Kuwait, Saudi Arabia, Lebanon, Jordan and Algeria, and between 40 and 50 per cent in Egypt, Tunisia, Libya and Syria. The increase took place in the smaller towns as well as the larger, but it was most remarkable in the capital cities and the main centres of trade and industry. By the mid-1970s there were eight Arab cities with populations of more than a million: Cairo had 6.4 million inhabitants and Baghdad 3.8 million.

The nature of economic growth, and of rapid urbanization, led to a greater and more obvious polarization of society than had previously existed. The beneficiaries of growth were in the first instance members of ruling groups, army officers, government officials of the higher ranks, technicians, businessmen engaged in construction, import and export, or consumer industries, or having some connection with multinational enterprises. Skilled industrial workers also reaped some benefits, particularly where political circumstances allowed them to organize themselves effectively. Other segments of the population benefited less or not at all. In the cities, there was a population of small employees, small traders and those giving services to the rich, and around them was a larger floating population of those employed in the 'informal sector', as itinerant vendors or casual workers, or not employed at all. In the countryside, medium-sized landowners, or large ones in countries which had not had land reform, could cultivate their land profitably because they had access to credit, but the poorer peasants, who owned a little land or none at all, could scarcely hope to improve their position. The migrant workers in the oil-producing countries might earn more than they could hope to in their own countries, but had no security and no possibility of improving their position by concerted action. They could be removed at will and there were others waiting to take their places. By the end of the 1970s they were even more vulnerable, since many of them no longer came from Arab countries but were brought in temporarily and on contract from further east – from South Asia, Thailand, Malaysia, the Philippines or Korea.

Some governments, under the influence of ideas current in the outside world, were now creating social services which did result in some redistribution of income: popular housing, health and education services, and systems of social insurance. Not all the population was able to benefit from them, even in the richest countries. In Kuwait, all Kuwaitis had full advantage of them, but the non-Kuwaiti part of the population much less; in Saudi Arabia large towns had their *bidonvilles* around them, and the villages were not affluent. The situation was most difficult in the large cities which had grown rapidly through immigration and natural increase. If the *bidonvilles* there were being eliminated, the cheap housing which replaced them was not necessarily much better, lacking as it did material facilities and the sense of community which could exist in the *bidonville*. Public transport facilities were almost everywhere defective, and there was a sharp distinction between those who owned private transport and those who did not. In most cities the water and drainage systems had been constructed for smaller communities, and could not cope with the demands of the larger population; in Cairo the drainage system had virtually collapsed. In Kuwait and Saudi Arabia the problem of water-supply was being met by desalinization of seawater, an expensive but effective method.

WOMEN IN SOCIETY

This was also a period in which another kind of relationship within society became an explicit problem. The changing role of women, and changes in the structure of the family, raised questions not only for men who wished to build a strong and healthy national community, but for women conscious of their position as women.

Over the previous generations, various changes had taken place which were bound to affect the position of women in society. One of them was the spread of education: in all countries, even in the most conservative societies of the Arabian peninsula, girls were now going to school. At the primary level, in some countries there were almost as many girls as boys at school; at higher levels, the proportion was increasing fast. The degree of literacy among women was also increasing, although it was still lower than among men; in some countries virtually all women of the younger generation were literate. Partly for this reason, but also for others, the range of work available to women had grown wider. In the countryside, when men migrated to the cities or to the oil-producing countries, women often looked after the land and livestock while the men of the family were away. In the city, modern factories employed women, but work here was precarious; they were hired if there was a shortage of men workers, and in conditions of slump or overemployment they were the first to be dismissed. Unskilled women were more likely to find work as domestic servants; these were mainly young unmarried girls coming from the villages. Educated women worked in increasing numbers in government offices, particularly in clerical positions, and there was a growing number of professional women, lawyers, doctors and social workers. In some countries there was a small but increasing number of women at the higher levels of responsibility in government; this was particularly true of countries such as Tunisia, South Yemen and Iraq, which were making a deliberate effort to break with the past and create a 'modern' society. In spite of these changes, however, only a small proportion of women were employed outside the home, and at almost every level they were handicapped in competition with men.

The conditions of life in the city, and work outside the home, had some effect upon family life and the place of women in it. In the village, the migration of men workers meant that a wife might have greater responsibilities for the family and might have to make a range of decisions which formerly would have been left to the husband. In the town, the extended family could not have the same reality as in the village; the wife might no longer live in a large female community of sisters and cousins, under the domination of her mother-in-law; husbands and wives were thrown more directly into contact with each other; children might no longer be educated for social life within the extended family, and might be formed by the school and the street as much as by the home. The traffic of ideas and the extension of medical services led to the spread of contraception; urban families, out of economic necessity and because of new possibilities, tended to be smaller than rural ones. Because of education and employment, girls married in their late teens or twenties rather than in their middle teens. In the street and the place of work, seclusion was inevitably breaking down. Not only was the veil less common than it had been, but other forms of separation of men and women were disappearing. In Saudi Arabia an attempt was being made to prevent this: the veil was still generally worn in the streets, education was strictly segregated, and a separate sphere of women's work was defined – they could work as teachers or in women's clinics, but not in government offices or other places where they would mix with men.

These changes were taking place, however, within a legal and ethical framework which was still largely unchanged, and which upheld the primacy of the male. Some alterations were indeed being made in the ways in which Islamic laws of personal status were interpreted. Among Arab countries, only Tunisia had abolished polygamy, but it was becoming rarer elsewhere. In some countries, for example Tunisia and Iraq, it had become easier for women to request the dissolution of marriage, but everywhere the right of a husband to divorce his wife without giving reasons, and without process of law, was maintained; the right of the divorced husband to the custody of the children after a certain age was also untouched. In some countries the minimum age of marriage had been raised. In some, the laws of inheritance also had been reinterpreted, but in none of them was there a secular law of inheritance. Still less had any Arab country introduced secular laws of personal status to replace those derived from the *shari'a*, as had happened in Turkey.

Even when laws changed, social customs did not necessarily change with them. New laws could not always be enforced, particularly when they came up against deeply rooted social customs which asserted and preserved the domination of the male. That girls should marry early, that their marriages should be arranged by the family, and that wives could easily be repudiated were firmly rooted ideas, preserved by women themselves; the mother and the mother-in-law were often pillars of the system. A large number of women still accepted the system in principle, but tried to obtain for themselves a better position within it by more or less subtle manipulation of their menfolk. Their attitude was expressed, for example, in the stories of an Egyptian woman writer, Alifa Rifaat, depicting Muslim women whose lives were still punctuated by the call of the minaret to the five daily prayers:

She . . . raised her hand to her lips, kissing it back and front in thanks for His generosity. She regretted that it was only through such gestures and the uttering of a few simple supplications that she was able to render her thanks to her Maker. During Ahmed's lifetime she would stand behind him as he performed the prayers, following the movements as he bowed down and then prostrated himself, listening reverently to the words he recited and knowing that he who stands behind the man leading prayers and following his movements has himself performed the prayers . . . with his death she had given up performing the regular prayers.[1]

There were, however, an increasing number of women who did not accept the system and were claiming the right to define their own identity and bring about changes in their social status which reflected that new definition. They were not yet in positions of power; women ministers or members of parliament were little more than tokens of change. Their views were expressed through women's organizations and in the press. Apart from women novelists, there were a number of well-known polemical writers whose work was widely diffused, in the outside world through translations as well as in the Arab countries. The Moroccan Fatima Mernissi, in *Beyond the Veil*, argued that sexual inequality was based upon, or at least justified by, a specifically Islamic view of women as having a dangerous power which must be contained; this, she suggested, was a view which was incompatible with the needs of an independent nation in the modern world.

There was, it is true, a phenomenon of the late 1970s and the early 1980s which might seem to show a contrary tendency. In the streets and places of work, and particularly in schools and universities, an increasing proportion of young women were covering their hair if not their faces and avoiding social and professional mixing with men. By what might seem a paradox, this was more a sign of their assertion of their own identity than of the power of the male. Those who took this path often did not come from families where segregation was the rule, but took it as a deliberate act of choice, springing from a certain view of what an Islamic society should be, and one which was to some extent influenced by the Iranian revolution. Whatever the motives for such an attitude, however, in the long run it would tend to reinforce a traditional view of women's place in society.

A HERITAGE AND ITS RENEWAL

The events of 1967, and the processes of change which followed them, made more intense that disturbance of spirits, that sense of a world gone wrong, which had already been expressed in the poetry of the 1950s and 1960s. The defeat of 1967 was widely regarded as being not only a military setback but a kind of moral judgement. If the Arabs had been defeated so quickly, completely and publicly, might it not be a sign that there was something rotten in their societies and in the moral system which they expressed? The heroic age of the struggle for independence was over; that struggle could no longer unite the Arab countries, or the people in any one of them, and failures and deficiencies could no longer be blamed so fully as in the past upon the power and intervention of the foreigner.

Among educated and reflective men and women, there was a growing awareness of the vast and rapid changes in their societies, and of the ways in which their own position was being affected by them. The increase of population, the growth of cities, the spread of popular education and the mass media were bringing a new voice into discussion of public affairs, a voice expressing its convictions, and its grievances and hopes, in a traditional language. This in its turn was arousing consciousness among the educated of a gap between them and the masses, and giving rise to a problem of communication: how could the educated élite speak to the masses or on their behalf? Behind this there lay another problem, that of identity: what was the moral bond between them, by virtue of which they could claim to be a society and a political community?

To a great extent, the problem of identity was expressed in terms of the relationship between the heritage of the past and the needs of the present. Should the Arab peoples tread a path marked out for them from outside, or could they find in their own inherited beliefs and culture those values which could give them a direction in the modern world? Such a question made clear the close relationship between the problem of identity and that of independence. If the values by which society was to live were brought in from outside, would not that imply a permanent dependence upon the external world, and more specifically western Europe and North America, and might not cultural dependence bring with it economic and political dependence as well? The point was forcefully made by the Egyptian economist Galal Amin (b. 1935) in *Mihnat al-iqtisad wa'l-thaqafa fi Misr (The Plight of the Economy and Culture in Egypt)*, a book which tried to trace the connections between the *infitah* and a crisis of culture. The Egyptian and other Arab peoples had lost confidence in themselves, he maintained. The *infitah*, and indeed the whole movement of events since the Egyptian revolution of 1952, had rested on an unsound basis: the false values of a consumer society in economic life, the domination of a ruling élite instead of genuine patriotic loyalty. Egyptians were importing whatever foreigners persuaded them that they should want, and this made for a permanent dependence. To be healthy, their political and economic life should be derived from their own moral values, which themselves could have no basis except in religion.

In a rather similar way, another Egyptian writer, Hasan Hanafi, wrote about the relationship between the heritage and the need for renewal. Arabs like other human beings were caught up in an economic revolution, which could not be carried through unless there were a 'human revolution'. This did not involve an abandonment of the heritage of the past, for which the Arabs were no less responsible than they were for 'people and land and wealth', but rather that it should be reinterpreted 'in accordance with the needs of the age', and turned into an ideology which could give rise to a

443

political movement. Blind adherence to tradition and blind innovation were both inadequate, the former because it had no answer to the problems of the present, and the latter because it could not move the masses, being expressed in a language alien from that which they understood. What was needed was some reformation of religious thought which would give the masses of the people a new definition of themselves, and a revolutionary party which would create a national culture and so change the modes of collective behaviour.

Much of contemporary Arab thought revolved around this dilemma of past and present, and some writers made bold attempts to resolve it. The answer given by the Syrian philosopher Sadiq Jalal al-'Azm (b. 1934) sprang from a total rejection of religious thought. It was false in itself, he claimed, and incompatible with authentic scientific thought in its view of what knowledge was and its methods of arriving at truth. There was no way of reconciling them; it was impossible to believe in the literal truth of the Qur'an, and if parts of it were discarded then the claim that it was the Word of God would have to be rejected. Religious thought was not only false, it was also dangerous. It supported the existing order of society and those who controlled it, and so prevented a genuine movement of social and political liberation.

Few other writers would have taken this position, but more widespread was a tendency to resolve the body of religious belief into a body of inherited culture, and thus to turn it into a subject of critical treatment. For the Tunisian Hisham Djaït (b. 1935), national identity could not be defined in terms of religious culture. It should indeed be preserved; the vision of human life mediated through the Prophet Muhammad, and the love and loyalty which had gathered around him over the centuries, should be cherished, and both should be protected by the state. Social institutions and laws, however, should be wholly separated from religion and based upon 'humanistic' principles; the individual citizen should be free to abandon his inherited faith if he so wished.

We are for laicism, but a laicism which will not be hostile to Islam, and does not draw its motivation from anti-Islamic feeling. In our anguished journey we have preserved the very essential of faith, a profound and ineradicable tenderness for this religion which has lighted our childhood and been our first guide towards the Good and the discovery of the Absolute ... Our laicism finds its limits in the recognition of the essential relation between the state, certain elements of moral and social behaviour, the structure of the collective personality and the Islamic faith, and in our being for the maintenance of this faith and for its reform. Reform should not be made in opposition to religion, it should be made at one and the same time by religion, in religion and independently of it.[2]

For another Maghribi writer, Abdullah Laroui, a redefinition both of past and of present was essential. What was needed was genuine historical understanding, to 'take possession of our past' through an understanding of causality, of the way in which things developed out of one another. Beyond that, a genuine 'historicism' was necessary: that is to say, a willingness to transcend the past, to take what was needed from it by a 'radical criticism of culture, language and tradition', and use it to create a new future. This process of critical understanding could not itself give a direction for the future. It needed to be guided by the living thought of the age, and in particular by Marxism if correctly understood; with its sense that history had a direction and moved in stages towards a goal, it could provide the insights by which the past could be incorporated into a new system of thought and action.[3]

At the other end of the spectrum were those who believed that the Islamic heritage by itself could provide the basis for life in the present, and that it alone could do so, because it was derived from the Word of God. This was the attitude expressed in increasingly sharp terms by some of those associated with the Muslim Brothers in Egypt and elsewhere. In such movements there took place in the 1960s a certain polarization; some of the leaders and members were willing to make a compromise with the holders of power and to accept the existing regimes, at least for the present, in the hope that this would give them influence over policy. Others, however, moved in the opposite direction: a total rejection of all forms of society except the wholly Islamic one. In a work published earlier, in 1964, *Ma'alim fi'l-tariq (Signposts on the Path)*, Sayyid Qutb had defined the true Islamic society in uncompromising terms. It was one which accepted the sovereign authority of God; that is to say, which regarded the Qur'an as the source of all guidance for human life, because it alone could give rise to a system of morality and law which corresponded to the nature of reality. All other societies were societies of *jahiliyya* (ignorance of religious truth), whatever their principles: whether they were communist, capitalist, nationalist, based upon other, false religions, or claimed to be Muslim but did not obey the *shari'a*:

The leadership of western man in the human world is coming to an end, not because western civilization is materially bankrupt or has lost its economic or military strength, but because the western order has played its part, and no longer possesses

445

that stock of 'values' which gave it its predominance . . . The scientific revolution has finished its role, as have 'nationalism' and the territorially limited communities which grew up in its age . . . The turn of Islam has come.[4]

The path to the creation of a truly Muslim society, Sayyid Qutb had declared, began with individual conviction, transformed into a living image in the heart and embodied in a programme of action. Those who accepted this programme would form a vanguard of dedicated fighters, using every means, including *jihad*, which should not be undertaken until the fighters had achieved inner purity, but should then be pursued, if necessary, not for defence only, but to destroy all worship of false gods and remove all the obstacles which prevented men from accepting Islam. The struggle should aim at creating a universal Muslim society in which there were no distinctions of race, and one which was worldwide. 'The western age is finished': it could not provide the values which were needed to support the new material civilization. Only Islam offered hope to the world.

The implications of such teaching, if taken seriously were far-reaching. It led that part of the Muslim Brothers which supported Sayyid Qutb into opposition to 'Abd al-Nasir's regime; Qutb himself was arrested, tried and executed in 1966. In the following decade, groups emerging from the Brothers followed literally his teaching that the first stage towards creation of an Islamic society was withdrawal from the society of the *jahiliyya*, to live according to the *shari'a*, purify the heart, and form the nucleus of dedicated fighters. Such groups were prepared for violence and martyrdom; this was shown when members of one of them assassinated Sadat in 1981, and when Muslim Brothers in Syria tried to overthrow the regime of Hafiz al-Asad in the following year.

Somewhere in the middle of the spectrum were those who continued to believe that Islam was more than a culture: it was the revealed Word of God, but it must be understood correctly, and the social morality and law derived from it could be adapted to make it the moral basis of a modern society. There were many forms of this reformist attitude. Conservatives of the Wahhabi school, in Saudi Arabia and elsewhere, believed that the existing code of law could be changed slowly and cautiously into a system adequate to the needs of modern life; some thought that only the Qur'an was sacred, and it could be freely used as the basis of a new law; some believed that the true interpretation of the Qur'an was that of the Sufis, and a private mystical devotion was compatible with the organization of society on more or less secular lines.

A few attempts were made to show how the new moral and legal system could be deduced from Qur'an and Hadith in a way which was responsible but bold. In the Sudan, Sadiq al-Mahdi (b. 1936), the great-grandson of the religious leader of the later nineteenth century, and himself an important political leader, maintained that it was necessary to have a new kind of religious thought which would draw out of the Qur'an and Hadith a *shari'a* which was adapted to the needs of the modern world. Perhaps the most carefully reasoned attempt to state the principles of a new jurisprudence came from beyond the Arab world, from the Pakistani scholar Fazlur Rahman (1919–88). In an attempt to provide an antidote to the 'spiritual panic' of Muslims at the present time, he suggested a method of Qur'anic exegesis which would, he claimed, be true to the spirit of Islam but provide for the needs of modern life. The Qur'an was 'a divine response, through the Prophet's mind, to the moral–social situation of the Prophet's Arabia'. In order to apply its teaching to the moral and social situation of a different age, it was necessary to extract from that 'divine response' the general principle inherent in it. This could be done by studying the specific circumstances in which the response had been revealed, and doing so in the light of an understanding of the Qur'an as a unity. Once the general principle had been extracted, it should be used with an equally clear and meticulous understanding of the particular situation in regard to which guidance was needed. Thus the proper interpretation of Islam was a historical one, moving with precision from the present to the past and back again, and this demanded a new kind of religious education.[5]

THE STABILITY OF REGIMES

An observer of the Arab countries in the 1980s would have found societies in which the ties of culture, strong and perhaps growing stronger as they were, had not given rise to political unity; where increasing wealth, unevenly spread, had led to some kinds of economic growth but also to a wider gap between those who profited most from it and those who did not, in the swollen cities and the countryside; where some women were becoming more conscious of their subordinate position in the private and public worlds; where the urban masses were calling in question the justice of the social order and the legitimacy of governments out of the depths of their own inherited culture, and the educated élite was showing a deep disturbance of spirit.

The observer would also, however, have noticed something else which, in all the circumstances, might have surprised him: the apparent stability of political regimes. Although the Arab countries were often thought of as politically unstable, there had in fact been little change in the general nature of regimes or the direction of policy since the end of the 1960s, although there had been changes of personnel. In Saudi Arabia, the Gulf states, Jordan, Tunisia and Morocco, there had been no substantial change for a generation or more. In Algeria, the real change had taken place in 1965; in Libya, the Sudan, South Yemen and Iraq, the group which was to remain in power until the 1980s had taken over in 1969, and in Syria in 1970; in Egypt too, the change from 'Abd al-Nasir to Sadat in 1970, which might at first have seemed like a change of persons within a continuing ruling group, had soon turned out to signal a change of direction. Only in three countries were the 1970s a decade of disturbance; South Yemen, where there were conflicts within the ruling party; North Yemen, where a certain rather inconclusive change of regime took place in 1974; and Lebanon, which remained in a state of civil war and disturbance from 1975 onwards.

The apparent paradox of stable and enduring regimes in deeply disturbed societies was worth considering, although in the end it might turn out not to be a paradox. To borrow and adapt an idea from Ibn Khaldun, it could be suggested that the stability of a political regime depended upon a combination of three factors. It was stable when a cohesive ruling group was able to link its interests with those of powerful elements in society, and when that alliance of interests was expressed in a political idea which made the power of the rulers legitimate in the eyes of society, or at least of a significant part of it.

The cohesion and persistence of the regimes could partly be explained in obvious ways. Governments now had means of control and repression at their disposal such as had not been available in the past: intelligence and security services, armies, in some places mercenary forces recruited from outside. If they wished, and if the instruments of repression did not break in their hands, they could crush any movement of revolt, at whatever cost; the only check was imposed by the fact that the instruments were not wholly passive and might turn against the rulers or dissolve, as happened in Iran in the face of the massive rising of the people in 1979–80. They had also a direct control over the whole of society such as no government had had in the past. First the Ottoman reformers and then the European colonial rulers had extended the power of government far beyond the cities and their dependent hinterlands, into the remotest parts of the countryside, the mountain valleys and steppes. In the past, authority had been exercised in these remoter parts by political manipulation of intermediate powers, lords of the valleys, tribal chiefs or saintly lineages; now it was exercised by direct bureaucratic control, which extended the hand of the government into every village and almost every house or tent; and where the government came it was not concerned only, as in the past, with defending the cities, roads and frontiers and raising taxes, but with all the tasks which modern governments perform: conscription, education, health, public utilities and the public sector of the economy.

Beyond these obvious reasons for the strength of governments there were others, however. Ruling groups had been successful in creating and maintaining their own *'asabiyya*, or solidarity directed towards acquiring and keeping power. In some countries – Algeria, Tunisia, Iraq – this was the solidarity of a party. In others it was that of a group of politicians who were held together by links established in early life and strengthened by a common experience, as with the military politicians in Egypt and Syria. In others again it was that of a ruling family and those closely associated with it, held together by ties of blood as well as common interests. These various kinds of group were not so different from each other as might appear. In all of them, ties of interest were reinforced by those of neighbourliness, kinship or intermarriage; the tradition of Middle Eastern and Maghribi society was that other kinds of relationship were stronger if expressed in terms of kinship.

Moreover, the ruling groups now had at their disposal a machinery of government larger and more complex than in the past. A vast number of men and women were connected with or dependent upon it, and therefore willing (at least up to a point) to help it in maintaining its power. In earlier days the structure of government had been simple and limited. The sultan of Morocco until the later nineteenth century had been an itinerant monarch, raising taxes and showing his authority by progresses through his domains, with a personal army and a few dozen secretaries. Even in the Ottoman Empire, perhaps the most highly bureaucratic government the Middle East had known, the number of officials was comparatively small; at the beginning of the nineteenth century there had been approximately 2,000 civil officials in the central administration, but by the end of the century the number had grown to perhaps 35,000. By the early 1980s, there were almost twice as many government officials as workers employed in industry in Egypt, and the proportions were similar in other countries. This vast regiment of officials was distributed among a number of different structures controlling the various sectors of society: the army, the police, intelligence services, planning organizations, irrigation authorities, departments of finance, industry and agriculture, and the social services.

Personal interests were involved in the maintenance of the regimes; not only those of the rulers, but army officers, senior officials, managers of enterprises in the public sector, and technicians at a higher level without whom a modern government could not be carried on. The policies of most of the regimes favoured other powerful sections of society as well: those who controlled certain private sectors of the economy, industries in private ownership, import and export trade, often in connection with the great multinational corporations, which were of increasing importance in the period of the *infitah*. To these could be added, to a lesser extent, skilled workers in the larger industries, who in some countries had been able to organize themselves effectively in trade unions and could bargain for better working conditions and wages, although they could not use their collective power to exercise influence over the general policy of the government.

In the last decade or two there had emerged a new social group, of those who had prospered by migration to the oil-producing countries. Of the 3 million or more immigrants from Egypt, Jordan, the two Yemens and elsewhere into Libya, Saudi Arabia and the Gulf, most went without the intention of settling. Their interest therefore lay in the existence of stable governments which would allow them to move backwards and forwards easily, to bring home what they had saved and invest it, for the most part in land, buildings and durable consumer goods, and to remain in secure possession of what they owned.

Army officers, government officials, international merchants, industrialists and the new rentier class all, therefore, wanted regimes which were reasonably stable and able to maintain order, and on good enough terms with each other (in spite of political quarrels) to permit the free flow of workers and money, and which maintained a mixed economy with the balance shifting in favour of the private sector and permitted the import of consumer goods. By the end of the 1970s most regimes were of this nature; South Yemen with its strictly controlled economy was an exception, and Algeria a partial exception, although there too the emphasis had changed after the death of Boumediene.

There were other segments of society of which the interests were not favoured to the same extent by the policies of government, but which were not in a position to bring effective pressure upon it. Large landowners with a base in the city and with access to credit were able to obtain a profit from agriculture, but smallholders, sharecroppers and landless peasants were in a weak position. They formed a smaller proportion of the population than before, because of migration to the cities, although still a considerable one; they produced a lesser part of the GDP of every country, and were no longer able to supply the food needed by the urban populations, which were dependent upon the import of foodstuffs; they were neglected in the investment programmes of most regimes. On the whole they were in a depressed condition, but it was difficult to mobilize peasants for effective action.

In the cities there were vast strata of semi-skilled or unskilled workers: lower government employees, unskilled factory workers, those engaged in providing services, those working in the 'informal' section of the economy, as itinerant traders or casual workers, and the unemployed. Their position was fundamentally weak: engaged in the daily struggle for existence, in natural competition with each other, since supply greatly exceeded demand, splintered into small groups – the extended family, those from the same district or the same ethnic or religious community – in order not to be lost in the vast, anonymous and hostile city. They could erupt into effective and united action only in special circumstances: when the government's system of control broke down, or when there was an issue which touched their immediate needs or deeper loyalties, as with the food-riots in Egypt in 1977 or the Iranian revolution of 1979–80.

One of the signs of the new dominant position of governments in Arab societies was that they were able to appropriate to themselves the ideas which could move minds and imaginations, and extract from them a claim of legitimate authority. By this time, any Arab government which wished to survive had to be able to claim legitimacy in terms of three political languages – those of nationalism, social justice and Islam.

The first to emerge as a potent language was that of nationalism. Some of the regimes which existed at the beginning of the 1980s had come to power during the struggle for independence, or could claim to be the successors of those who had; this kind of appeal to legitimacy was particularly strong in the Maghrib, where the struggle had been bitter and memories of it were still fresh. Almost all regimes made use too of a different kind of nationalist language, that of Arab unity; they gave some kind of formal allegiance to it, and spoke of independence as if it were the first step towards closer union, if not complete unity; connected with the idea of unity was that of some concerted action in support of the Palestinians. In recent years there had taken place an extension of the idea of nationalism; regimes claimed to be legitimate in terms of economic development, or the full use of national resources, both human and natural, for common ends.

The second language, that of social justice, came into common political use in the 1950s and 1960s, the period of the Algerian revolution and the spread of Nasirism, with its idea of a specifically Arab socialism expressed in the National Charter of 1962. Such terms as socialism and social justice tended to be used with a specific meaning; they referred to reform of the system of land-tenure, extension of social services and universal education, for girls as well as boys, but in few countries was there a systematic attempt to redistribute wealth by means of high taxation of incomes.

The latest of the languages to become powerful was that of Islam. In a way, of course, it was not new. There had always existed a sense of common destiny among those who had inherited the religion of Islam – a belief, enriched by historical memories, that the Qur'an, the Traditions of the Prophet and the *shari'a* could provide the principles according to which a virtuous life in common should be organized. By the 1980s, however, Islamic language had become more prominent in political discourse than it had been a decade or two earlier. This was due to a combination of two kinds of factor. On the one hand, there was the vast and rapid extension of the area of political involvement, because of the growth of population and of cities, and the extension of the mass media. The rural migrants into the cities brought their own political culture and language with them. There had been an urbanization of the migrants, but there was also a 'ruralization' of the cities. Cut off from the ties of kinship and neighbourliness which made life possible in the villages, they were living in a society of which the external signs were strange to them; the sense of alienation could be counterbalanced by that of belonging to a universal community of Islam, in which certain moral values were implicit, and this provided a language in terms of which they could express their grievances and aspirations. Those who wished to arouse them to action had to use the same language. Islam could provide an effective language of opposition: to western power and influence, and those who could be accused of being subservient to them; to governments regarded as corrupt and ineffective, the instruments of private interests, or devoid of morality; and to a society which seemed to have lost its unity with its moral principles and direction.

It was factors of this kind which produced such movements as the Muslim Brothers, of which the leaders were articulate and educated men, but which appealed to those who were shut out of the power and prosperity of the new societies; and it was partly in self-defence against them or in order to appeal to a wider segment of their nations that most regimes began to use the language of religion more than before. Some regimes, it is true, used the language of Islam spontaneously and continuously, in particular that of Saudi Arabia, which had been created by a movement for the reassertion of the primacy of God's Will in human societies. Others, however, appeared to have been driven into it. Even the most secularist of ruling groups, those for example of Syria, Iraq and Algeria, had taken to using it more or less convincingly, in one way or another. They might evoke historical themes, of the Arabs as the carriers of Islam; the rulers of Iraq, caught in their struggle with Iran, appealed to a memory of the battle of Qadisiyya, when the Arabs had defeated the last Sasanian ruler and brought Islam into Iran. In most countries of mixed population, the constitution laid down that the president should be a Muslim, so linking the religion of Islam with legitimate authority. In legal codes there might be a reference to the Qur'an or the *shari'a* as the basis of legislation. Most governments which took this path tended to interpret the *shari'a* in a more or less modernist way, in order to justify the innovations which were inevitable for societies living in the modern world; even in Saudi Arabia, the principles of Hanbali jurisprudence were invoked in order to justify the new laws and regulations made necessary by the new economic order. Some regimes, however, resorted to certain token applications of the strict letter of the *shari'a*: in Saudi Arabia and Kuwait, the sale of alcohol was forbidden; in the Sudan, a provision of the *shari'a* that persistent thieves should have their hands cut off was revived in the last years of Numayri's period of rule. In some countries strict observance of the fast of Ramadan, which had been spreading spontaneously, was encouraged by the government; an earlier attempt by the Tunisian government to discourage it, because it interfered with the efforts needed for economic development, had met with widespread opposition.

THE FRAGILITY OF REGIMES

Cohesive ruling groups, dominant social classes and powerful ideas: the combination of these factors might help to explain why regimes had been stable throughout the 1970s, but if examined closely all three might also appear to be sources of weakness.

Ruling groups were subject not only to the personal rivalries which arose inevitably from conflicting ambitions or disagreements about policy, but also to the structural divisions which appeared as the machinery of government grew in size and complexity. The different branches of government became separate centres of power – the party, the army, the intelligence services – and ambitious members of the ruling group could try to control one or other of them. Such a process tended to occur in all complex systems of government, but in some it was contained within a framework of stable institutions and deeply rooted political habits. When not so contained, it could lead to the formation of political factions, and to a struggle for political power in which the leader of a faction would try to eliminate his rivals and prepare the way for his succession to the highest position. Such a struggle could be kept within limits only by constant exercise of the arts of political manipulation by the head of the government.

The link between the regime and the dominant social groups might also turn out to be fragile. What could be observed was a recurrent pattern in Middle Eastern history. The classes which dominated the structure of wealth and social power in the cities wanted peace, order and freedom of economic activity, and would support a regime so long as it seemed to be giving them what they wanted; but they would not lift a finger to save it, and would accept its successor if it seemed likely to follow a similar policy. By the middle of the 1980s, the situation of some of the regimes seemed to be precarious. Oil prices reached their peak in 1981; after that they declined rapidly, because of an excess of production, more careful use of energy in industrial countries and the failure of OPEC to maintain a united front on prices and volume of production. The decline in revenue from oil, together with the effects of the war between Iran and Iraq, had an impact on all the Arab countries, rich and poor alike.

If the support given by powerful segments of society to governments was passive, it was partly because they did not participate actively in the making of decisions. In most regimes this was done at a high level by a small group, and the results were not communicated widely; there was a tendency for rulers, as they settled into power, to become more secretive and withdrawn – guarded by their security services and surrounded by intimates and officials who controlled access to them – and to emerge only rarely to give a formal explanation and justification of their actions to a docile audience. Beneath this reason for the distance between government and society, however, there lay another one: the weakness of the conviction which bound them to each other.

Once political ideas were appropriated by governments, they were in danger of losing their meaning. They became slogans which grew stale by repetition, and could no longer gather other ideas around them into a powerful constellation, mobilize social forces for action, or turn power into legitimate authority. The idea of nationalism seemed to have suffered this fate. It would always exist as an immediate and natural reaction to a threat from outside; this was shown during the war between Iraq and Iran, when those parts of the Iraqi population which might have been expected to be hostile to the government gave it support. It was doubtful, however, whether it could serve as a mobilizing force for effective action, or as the centre of a system of ideas by which life in society could be organized. 'Arabism', the idea of a politically united Arab nation, might still be brought into action by a new crisis in the relations between Israel and its Arab neighbours; the quiescence of the Arab states during the Israeli invasion could be partly explained by the complexities of the Lebanese situation, and was not necessarily a foretaste of what would happen were Israel at war with other neighbours. In general, however, the main function of Arabism was as a weapon in conflicts between Arab states and a pretext for the interference of one state in the affairs of others; the example of 'Abd al-Nasir, appealing over the heads of governments to the Arab peoples, had not been forgotten. On the other hand, the strengthening of human ties between the Arab peoples, because of education, migration and the mass media, might in the long run have an effect.

About the other leading ideas, those of social justice and Islam, the contrary might be said: not that they had lost their meaning, but that they had too much meaning, and too great a power as motives for action, to be harnessed for long to the purposes of any regime. Their roots lay too deep in history and conscience for them to be made into the docile instruments of government.

Governments which appealed to such deeply rooted and powerful ideas did so at their own peril. They were caught in the ambiguities and compromises of power, and if they used languages with such a strong appeal their opponents could also do so, in order to show the gap between what the government said and what it did. They could use with deadly force such words as tyranny and hypocrisy which rang through the whole of Islamic history. The assassination of Sadat in 1981, and an episode in Saudi Arabia in 1979 when a group of convinced Muslims occupied the Great Mosque in Mecca, were signs of the strength of such movements of opposition, particularly when they could combine the appeal to social justice with that to Islam.

Even the most stable and the longest-lasting regimes, then, might prove to be fragile. There would certainly be shifts of power within ruling groups, because of death or palace revolutions; in 1985 Numayri, the ruler of the Sudan, was deposed by a military *coup* combined with widespread civil disturbance; in 1988, Bourguiba's long domination of the political life of Tunisia ended when he was deposed and replaced by an officer of the army, Zayn al-'Abidin Ben 'Ali. Such events might lead to changes in the direction of policy, as had happened when Sadat succeeded 'Abd al-Nasir; but were there likely to be more violent and radical changes?

In some countries there was a possibility that more lasting and formal institutions, which broadened the extent of participation in the making of decisions, would be restored. There was a general desire for this among the educated classes, and even some of the regimes themselves might decide that it was in their own interest; without some degree of participation effective social and economic development could not take place, and real stability was impossible without institutions – that is to say, known and accepted conventions about the way in which power should be obtained, used and transmitted.

Whether such a change occurred would depend on the level of education, the size and strength of the middle classes, and the confidence of the regime. It was not likely to occur in most Arab countries, but there were signs that it was taking place in some of them. In Kuwait, the parliament was restored in 1981 after a gap of several years, and showed itself to have independent opinions and the power to persuade government to take notice of them; but it was dissolved in 1986. In Jordan, an attempt was made in 1984 to revive the parliament which had been in abeyance for some time. In Lebanon, in spite of the civil war, the idea of parliament as the place where, in the end, differences could be reconciled, and of constitutional rule as the basis of legitimacy, was still alive.

The country where constitutional rule seemed most likely to be restored was Egypt, where the educated class was large and stood at a level of political understanding above that of most Arab countries. It had a social and cultural unity, and a surviving memory of the constitutional period, which had lasted for thirty years and had been a period when, within certain limits, opinions could be expressed freely; the memory had been revived in recent years by contrast with the relative lack of political freedom in the periods of 'Abd al-Nasir and Sadat. Under Sadat's successor Husni Mubarak, a cautious change began. Elections to the Assembly were held in 1984; the electoral system was devised in such a way as to ensure a large majority for the government, but the election took place in an atmosphere of comparatively free discussion, and some members of an opposition party, a revival of the Wafd, were elected. This might have been an indication that Egypt was moving into a position like that of Turkey or some Latin American countries, where periods of parliamentary rule and military dictatorship would alternate, and constitutional life would be always restored and always threatened.

If more radical changes took place, it seemed more likely in the 1980s that they would take place in the name of an Islamic idea of the justice of God in the world than in that of a purely secular ideal. There was not one idea of Islam only, but a whole spectrum of them. The word 'Islam' did not have a single, simple meaning, but was what Muslims made of it. For 'traditional' villagers, it might mean everything they thought and did. For more concerned and reflective Muslims, it provided a norm by which they should try to shape their lives, and by which their acts could be judged, but there was more than one norm. The term 'fundamentalism', which had become fashionable, carried a variety of meanings. It could refer to the idea that Muslims should try to return to the teaching and practice of the Prophet and the first generation of his followers, or to the idea that the Qur'an alone provided the norm of human life; this could be a revolutionary idea, if Muslims claimed – as the Libyan leader Qadhafi appeared to do – that they had the right to interpret the Qur'an freely. The word could also be used of an attitude which might better be called 'conservative': the attitude of those who wished to accept and preserve what they had inherited from the past, the whole cumulative tradition of Islam as it had in fact developed, and to change it only in a cautious and responsible way. This was the attitude of the Saudi regime and its supporters, and of the Iranian revolutionary regime, although the cumulative traditions they accepted were very different from each other.

The circumstances of the different Arab countries varied greatly. An Islamic movement in one country could have a different meaning from what might appear to be the same movement in another. For example, the Muslim Brothers in Syria did not have the same role as those in Egypt; to a great extent they served as a medium for the opposition of the Sunni urban population to the domination of a regime identified with the 'Alawi community. Similarly, the fact that the Iranian revolution had taken a certain form did not mean that it would take the same form in other countries. In part at least, the revolution could be explained in terms of factors which were specific to Iran: certain powerful social classes were particularly responsive to appeals expressed in religious language, and there was a religious leadership which was able to act as a rallying point for all movements of opposition; it was relatively independent of the government, generally respected for its piety and learning, and had always acted as the spokesman of the collective consciousness.

Such a situation did not exist in the Arab countries. In Iraq, where Shi'is formed a majority, their men of learning did not have the same intimate connection with the urban masses or the same influence on the government as in Iran. Sunni 'ulama had a less independent position. Under Ottoman rule they had become state functionaries, close to the government and compromised by their relations with it; by tradition and interests they were linked with the upper bourgeoisie of the great cities. Leadership of Islamic movements therefore tended to be in the hands of laymen, converted members of the modern educated élite. Such movements did not have the sanctity conferred by leaders of inherited and recognized piety and learning; they were political parties competing with others. On the whole they did not have clear social or economic policies. It seemed likely that they would be important forces of opposition, but would not be in a position to be able to form governments.

An observer of the Arab countries, or of many other Muslim countries, in the mid-1980s might well have come to the conclusion that something similar to the Iranian path would be the path of the future, but this might have been a hasty conclusion, even so far as Iran was concerned. In a sense the rule of men of religion was a reaffirmation of tradition, but in another sense it went against tradition. The inherited wisdom of the 'ulama was that they should not link themselves too closely with the government of the world; they should keep a moral distance from it, while preserving their access to the rulers and influence upon them: it was dangerous to tie the eternal interests of Islam to the fate of a transient ruler of the world. This attitude was reflected in a certain popular suspicion of men of religion who took too prominent a part in the affairs of the world; they were as susceptible as others to the corruptions of power and wealth, and perhaps they did not make very good rulers.

It might happen too that, at a certain stage of national development, the appeal of religious ideas – at least of ideas sanctified by the cumulative tradition – would cease to have the same force as another system of ideas: a blend of social morality and law which were basically secular, but might have some relationship to general principles of social justice inherent in the Qur'an.

The Maps

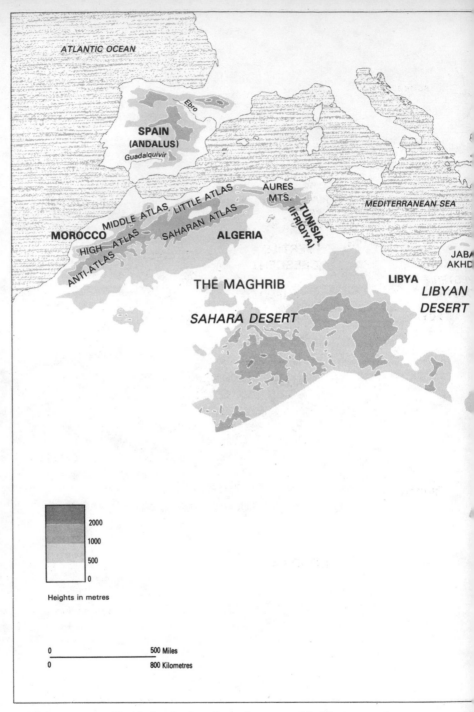

1 The area covered by the book, showing main geographical features and names frequently used.

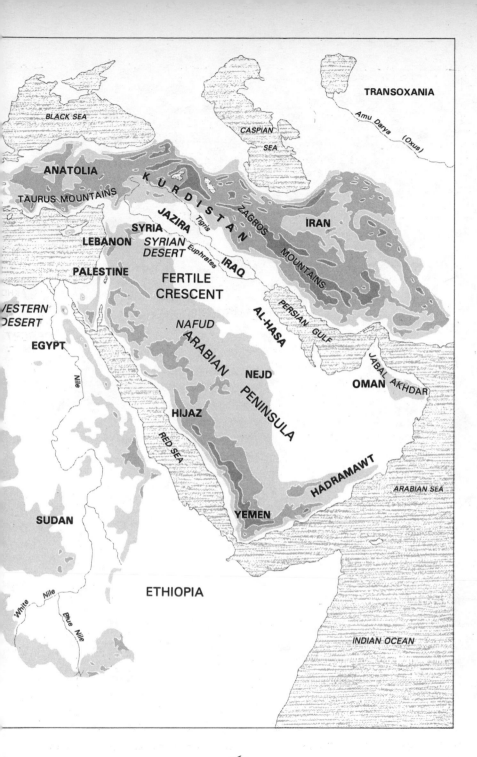

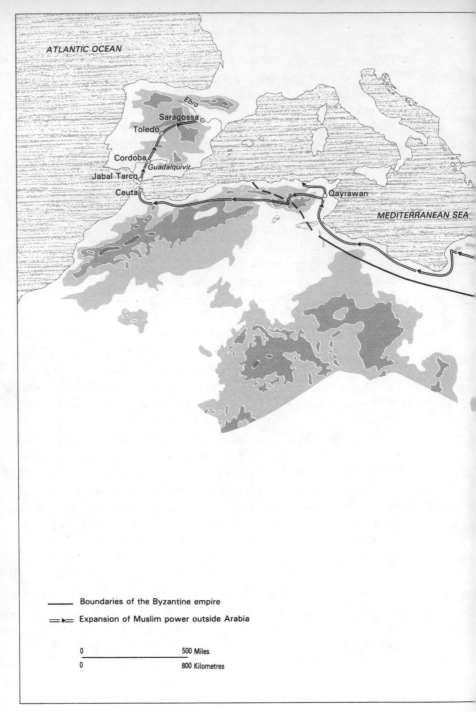

2 The expansion of the Islamic empire.

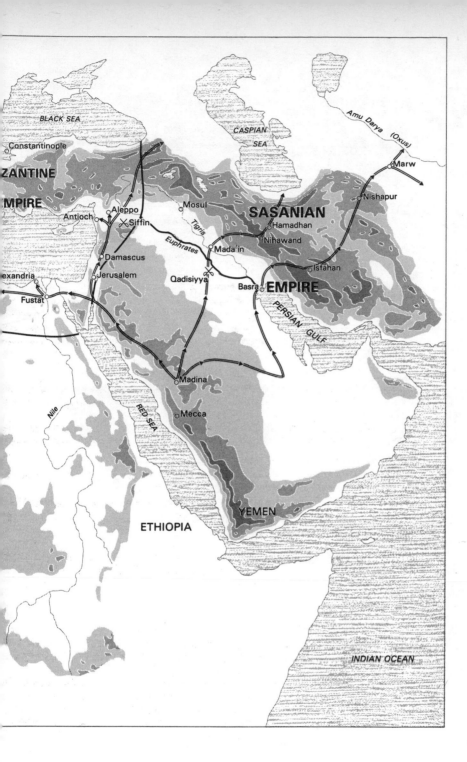

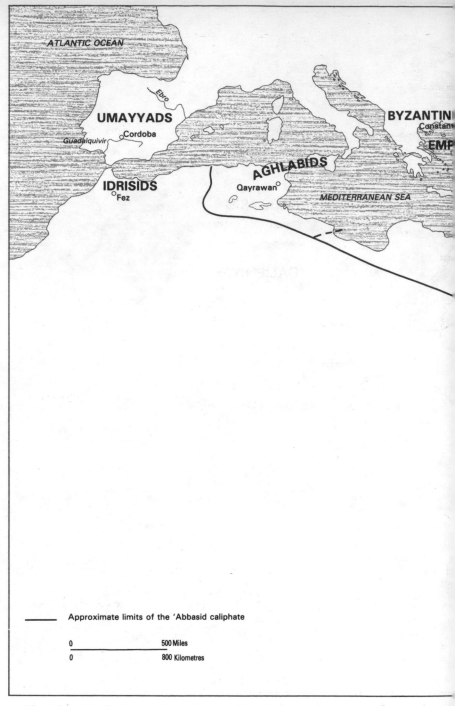

3 The 'Abbasid caliphate at the beginning of the ninth century.

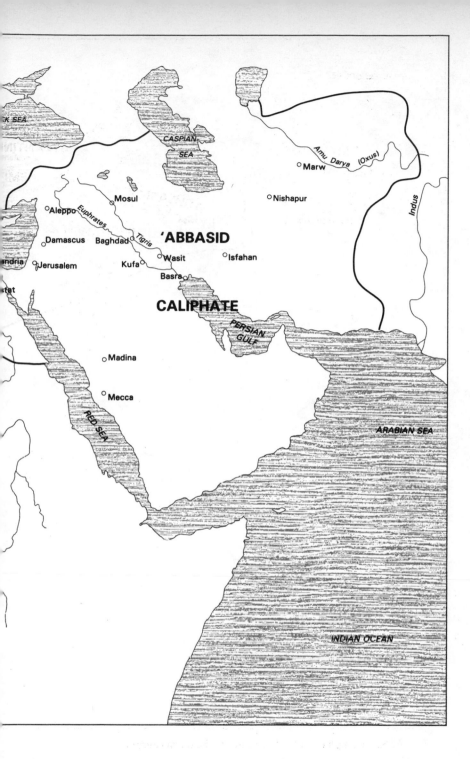

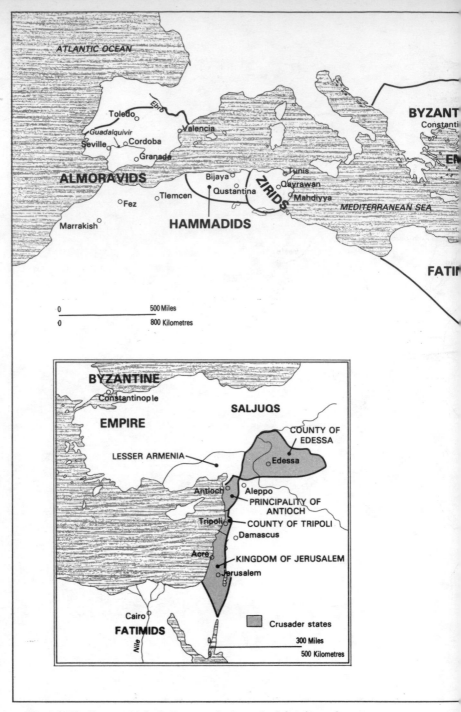

4 The Middle East and Maghrib towards the end of the eleventh century.

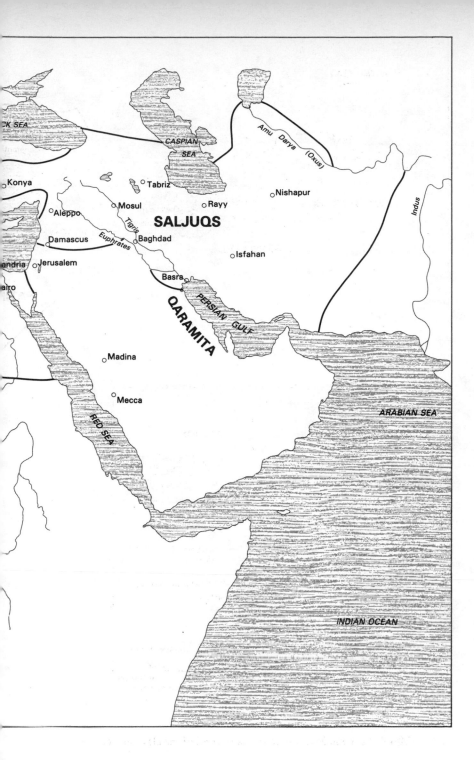

CK SEA

CASPIAN
SEA

Amu Darya (Oxus)

Konya

Tabriz

Nishapur

Indus

Aleppo

Mosul

Rayy

SALJUQS

Damascus

Tigris

Euphrates

Baghdad

andria

Jerusalem

Isfahan

airo

Basra

QARAMITA

PERSIAN GULF

Madina

Mecca

ARABIAN SEA

RED SEA

INDIAN OCEAN

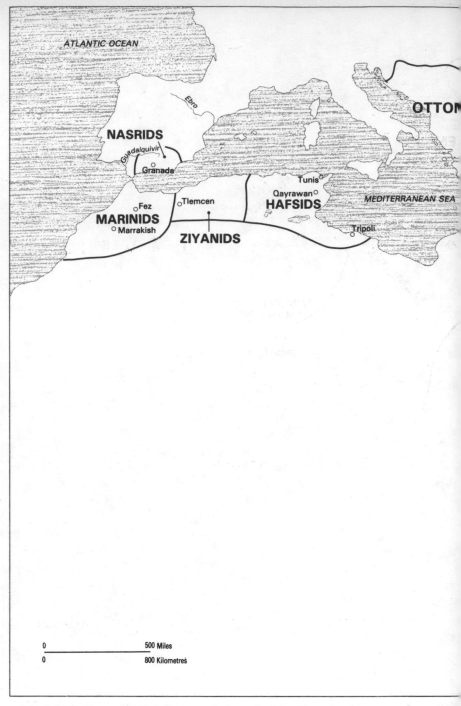

5 The Middle East and Maghrib towards the end of the fifteenth century.

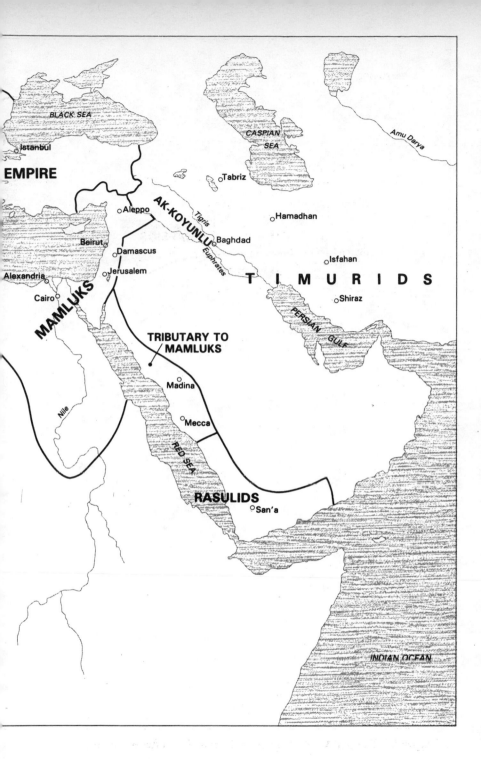

KINGDOM OF
NAVARRE

KINGDOM OF
ARAGON

Leon

Pamplona

KINGDOM OF LEON

COUNTY OF
BARCELONA

Ebro

Saragossa

Barcelona

Toledo

Cordoba

MEDITERRANEAN SEA

Seville

Guadalquivir

Granada

Algericas

Tangier

Ceuta

☐ Area of Umayyad Caliphate

IDRISIDS

0   200 Miles

0   300 Kilometres

Fez

Tlemcen

6 Muslim Spain: i) the Umayyad caliphate; ii) the Christian reconquest.

KINGDOM OF NAVARRE

KINGDOM OF
LEON AND CASTILE

KINGDOM OF
ARAGON

Ebro

KINGDOM OF
PORTUGAL

Barcelona

Toledo

Lisbon

Valencia

Cordoba
Seville   Guadalquivir

MEDITERRANEAN SEA

Granada

NASRIDS

———— Frontier at beginning of 13th century
═══════ Frontier at end of 13th century

MARINIDS

0   200 Miles

Fez

0   300 Kilometres

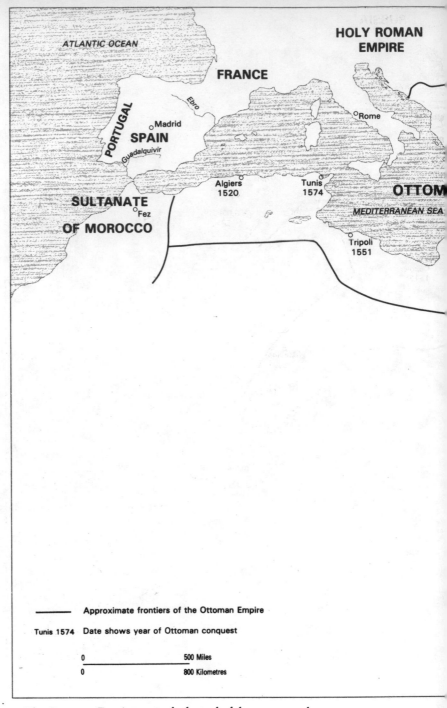

ATLANTIC OCEAN

HOLY ROMAN
EMPIRE

FRANCE

PORTUGAL

SPAIN
o Madrid

Guadalquivir

Ebro

Rome

Algiers
1520

Tunis
1574

OTTOM

MEDITERRANEAN SEA

SULTANATE
o Fez

OF MOROCCO

Tripoli
1551

Approximate frontiers of the Ottoman Empire

Tunis 1574   Date shows year of Ottoman conquest

0   500 Miles
0   800 Kilometres

7 The Ottoman Empire towards the end of the seventeenth century.

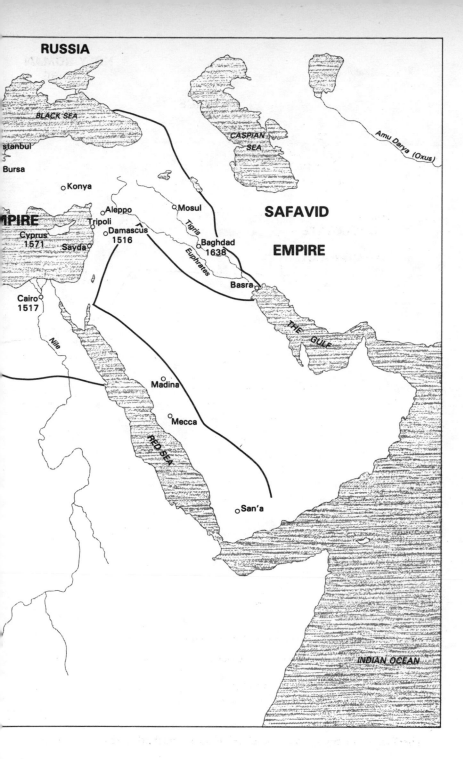

RUSSIA

BLACK SEA

stanbul

Bursa

Konya

Aleppo

Tripoli

Damascus
1516

Sayda

Cyprus
1571

MPIRE

Cairo
1517

Nile

Mosul

Tigris

Baghdad
1638

Euphrates

Basra

CASPIAN
SEA

Amu Darya (Oxus)

SAFAVID

EMPIRE

THE GULF

Madina

Mecca

RED SEA

San'a

INDIAN OCEAN

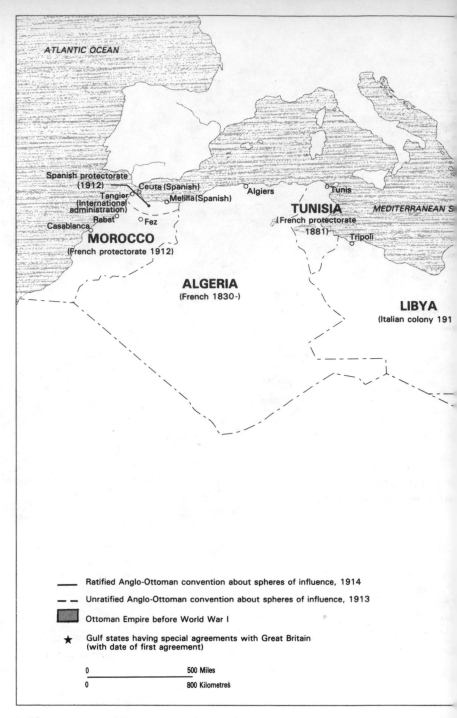

ATLANTIC OCEAN

Spanish protectorate
(1912)
Tangier
(International
administration)
Casablanca
Rabat
Fez
Ceuta (Spanish)
Melilla (Spanish)
Algiers
Tunis
MEDITERRANEAN S

MOROCCO
(French protectorate 1912)

TUNISIA
(French protectorate
1881)
Tripoli

ALGERIA
(French 1830-)

LIBYA
(Italian colony 191

——— Ratified Anglo-Ottoman convention about spheres of influence, 1914

– – – Unratified Anglo-Ottoman convention about spheres of influence, 1913

▨ Ottoman Empire before World War I

★ Gulf states having special agreements with Great Britain
(with date of first agreement)

0 — 500 Miles
0 — 800 Kilometres

8 The expansion of European empires until 1914

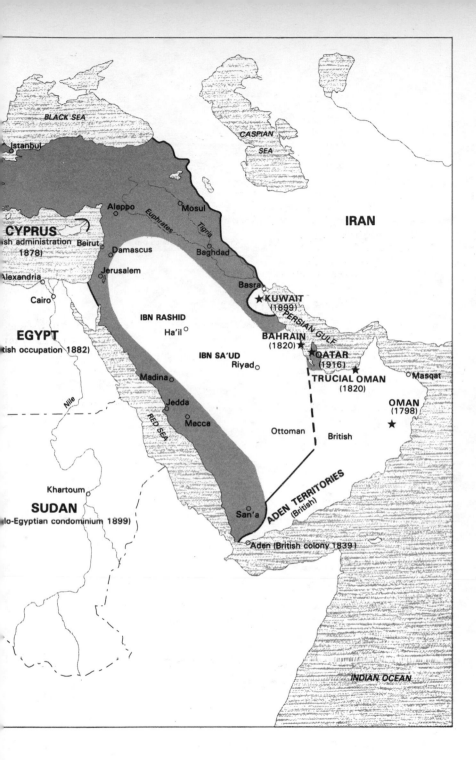

BLACK SEA

Istanbul

CASPIAN

SEA

Aleppo
Mosul
Euphrates
Tigris

IRAN

CYPRUS
sh administration   Beirut
(1878)

Damascus

Baghdad

Alexandria

Jerusalem

Cairo

Basra

★KUWAIT
(1899)

EGYPT
ish occupation 1882)

IBN RASHID
Ha'il

BAHRAIN
(1820) ★

PERSIAN GULF

★QATAR
(1916)

IBN SA'UD
Riyad

TRUCIAL OMAN
(1820)

Masqat

Nile

Madina

OMAN
(1798)
★

RED SEA

Jedda

Mecca

Ottoman

British

Khartoum

SUDAN
lo-Egyptian condominium 1899)

San'a

ADEN TERRITORIES
(British)

Aden (British colony 1839)

INDIAN OCEAN

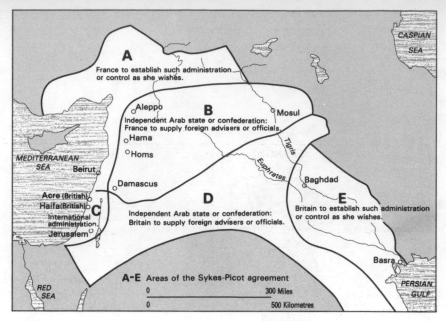

9 The post-war settlement, 1918–1923: i) the Sykes-Picot agreement, 1916

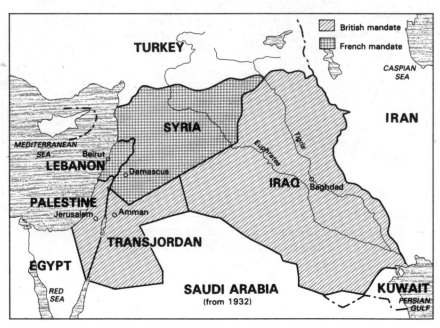

ii) the Mandates.

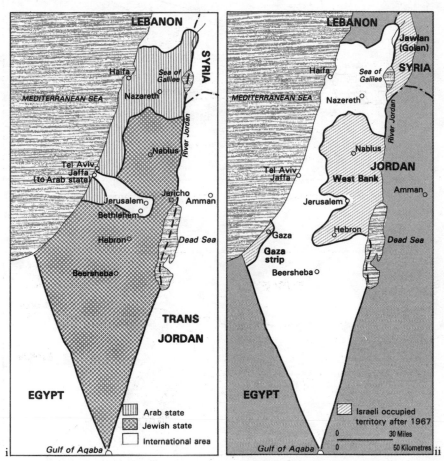

10 The partition of Palestine: i) the partition plan of the Royal Commission, 1937; ii) the armistice lines, 1949, and the Israeli occupation, 1967.

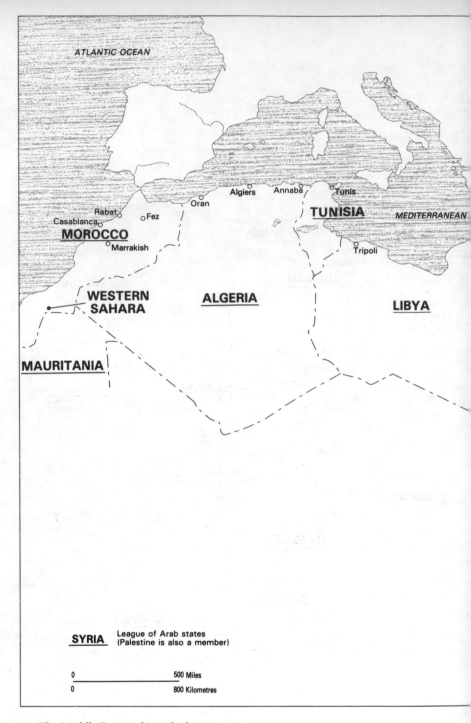

11 The Middle East and Maghrib in 1988.

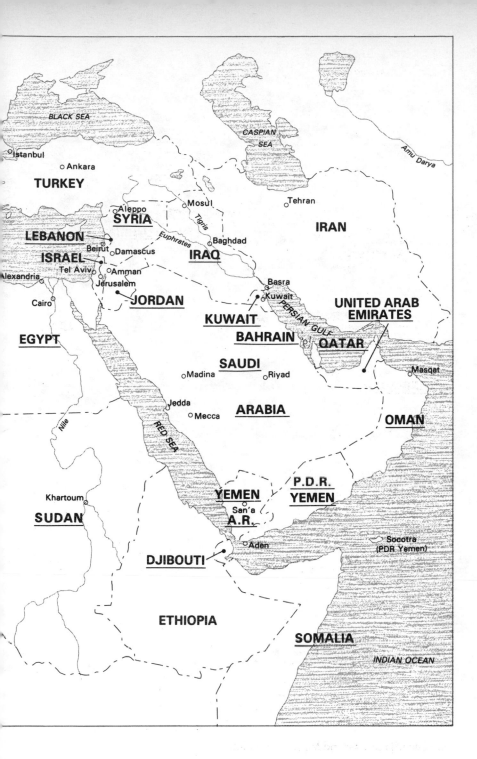

479

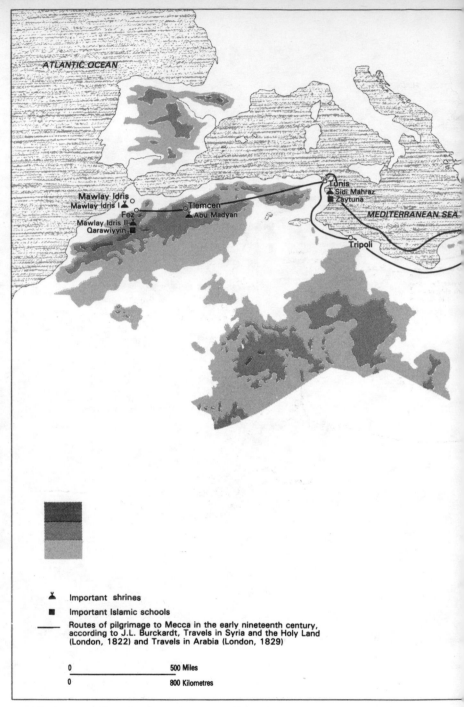

ATLANTIC OCEAN

MEDITERRANEAN SEA

Mawlay Idris
Mawlay Idris I
Fez
Mawlay Idris II
Qarawiyyin

Tlemcen
Abu Madyan

Tunis
Sidi Mahraz
Zaytuna

Tripoli

▲ Important shrines

■ Important Islamic schools

──── Routes of pilgrimage to Mecca in the early nineteenth century,
according to J.L. Burckardt, Travels in Syria and the Holy Land
(London, 1822) and Travels in Arabia (London, 1829)

0 ─────────── 500 Miles

0 ─────────── 800 Kilometres

12 Pilgrimage routes, shrines and centres of learning.

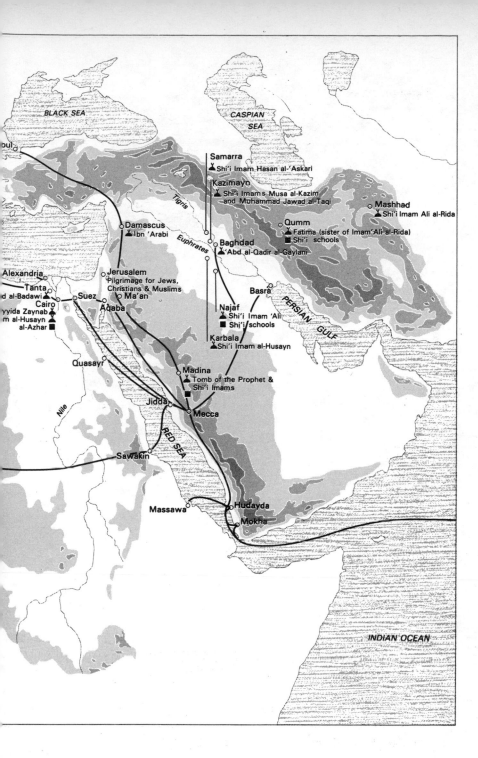

BLACK SEA

CASPIAN
SEA

Samarra
♔ Shi'i Imam Hasan al-'Askari

Kazimayn
♔ Shi'i Imams Musa al-Kazim
and Muhammad Jawad al-Taqi

Mashhad
♔ Shi'i Imam Ali al-Rida

Damascus
♔ Ibn 'Arabi

Qumm
♔ Fatima (sister of Imam 'Ali al-Rida)
■ Shi'i schools

Tigris

Euphrates

Baghdad
♔ 'Abd al-Qadir al-Gaylani

Alexandria

Tanta
d al-Badawi

Jerusalem
Pilgrimage for Jews,
Christians & Muslims
Ma'an

Basra

PERSIAN GULF

Cairo
yyida Zaynab
m al-Husayn
al-Azhar ■

Suez

Aqaba

Najaf
♔ Shi'i Imam 'Ali
■ Shi'i schools

Quasayr

Karbala
♔ Shi'i Imam al-Husayn

Nile

Madina
♔ Tomb of the Prophet &
Shi'i Imams ■

Jidda

Mecca

RED SEA

Sawakin

Massawa

Hudayda

Mokha

INDIAN OCEAN

Tables
Notes
Bibliography
Index of Terms
Index

The Family of the Prophet

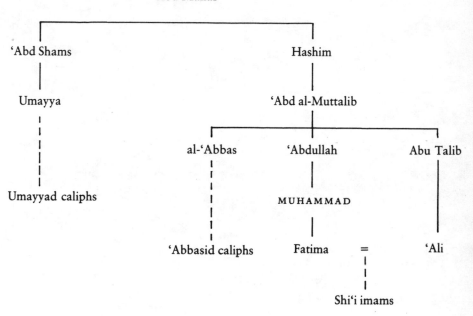

Adapted from J. L. Bacharach, *A Middle East Studies Handbook* (Seattle, 1984), p. 17.

The Shi'i Imams

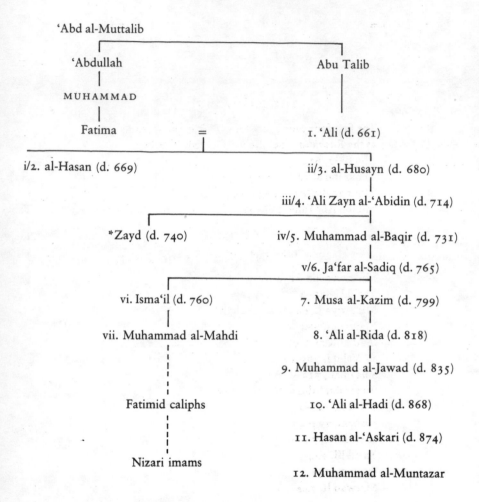

'Abd al-Muttalib

'Abdullah   Abu Talib

MUHAMMAD

Fatima   =   1. 'Ali (d. 661)

i/2. al-Hasan (d. 669)   ii/3. al-Husayn (d. 680)

iii/4. 'Ali Zayn al-'Abidin (d. 714)

*Zayd (d. 740)   iv/5. Muhammad al-Baqir (d. 731)

v/6. Ja'far al-Sadiq (d. 765)

vi. Isma'il (d. 760)   7. Musa al-Kazim (d. 799)

vii. Muhammad al-Mahdi   8. 'Ali al-Rida (d. 818)

9. Muhammad al-Jawad (d. 835)

Fatimid caliphs   10. 'Ali al-Hadi (d. 868)

11. Hasan al-'Askari (d. 874)

Nizari imams   12. Muhammad al-Muntazar

Arabic numerals indicate the line of succession recognized by the 'Twelver' Shi'is.
Roman numerals indicate the line recognized by the Isma'ilis.

*recognized as *imam* by the Zaydis.

Adapted from J. L. Bacharach, *A Middle East Studies Handbook* (Seattle, 1984), p. 21.

The Caliphs

THE RASHIDUN

The first four caliphs are known to Sunni Muslims
as the *Rashidun* (the 'Rightly Guided' Caliphs):
Abu Bakr, 632–4
'Umar ibn al-Khattab, 634–44
'Uthman ibn 'Affan, 644–56
'Ali ibn Abi Talib, 656–61

THE UMAYYADS

Mu'awiya ibn Abi Sufyan I, 661–80
Yazid I, 680–3
Mu'awiya II, 683–4
Marwan I, 684–5
'Abd al-Malik, 685–705
al-Walid I, 705–15
Sulayman, 715–17
'Umar ibn 'Abd al-'Aziz, 717–20
Yazid II, 720–4
Hisham, 724–43
al Walid II, 743–4
Yazid III, 744
Ibrahim, 744
Marwan II, 744–50

THE 'ABBASIDS

Abu'l-'Abbas al-Saffah, 749–54
al-Mansur, 754–75
al-Mahdi, 775–85
al-Hadi, 783–6
Harun al-Rashid, 786–809
al-Amin, 809–13
al-Ma'mun, 813–33
al-Mu'tasim, 833–42
al-Wathiq, 842–7
al-Mutawakkil, 847–61
al-Muntasir, 861–2
al-Musta'in, 862–6
al-Mu'tazz, 866–9
al-Muhtadi, 869–70
al-Mu'tamid, 870–92
al-Mu'tadid, 892–902
al-Muktafi, 902–8
al-Muqtadir, 908–32
al-Qahir, 932–4
al-Radi, 934–40
al-Muttaqi, 940–4
al-Mustakfi, 944–6
al-Muti', 946–74
al-Ta'i', 974–91
al-Qadir, 991–1031
al-Qa'im, 1031–75
al-Muqtadi, 1075–94
al-Mustazhir, 1094–1118
al-Mustarshid, 1118–35
al-Rashid, 1135–6
al-Muqtafi, 1136–60
al-Mustanjid, 1160–70
al-Mustadi, 1170–80
al-Nasir, 1180–1225
al-Zahir, 1225–6
al-Mustansir, 1226–42
al-Muzta'sim, 1242–58

Adapted from C. E. Bosworth,
The Islamic Dynasties (Edinburgh, 1967).

Important Dynasties

'Abbasids, 749–1258. Caliphs, claiming universal authority; main capital Baghdad.

Aghlabids, 800–909. Tunisia, eastern Algeria, Sicily.

'Alawis, 1631–today. Morocco.

Almohads (al-Muwahhidun), 1130–1269. Maghrib, Spain.

Almoravids (al-Murabitun), 1056–1147. Maghrib, Spain.

Ayyubids, 1169–1260. Egypt, Syria, part of western Arabia.

Buyids (Buwayhids), 932–1062. Iran, Iraq.

Fatimids, 909–1171. Maghrib, Egypt, Syria. Claimed to be Caliphs.

Hafsids, 1228–1574. Tunisia, eastern Algeria.

Hashimites of Iraq, 1921–58. Iraq.

Hashimites of Jordan, 1923–today. Transjordan, part of Palestine.

Idrisids, 789–926. Morocco.

Ilkhanids, 1256–1336. Iran, Iraq.

Mamluks, 1250–1517. Egypt, Syria.

Marinids, 1196–1464. Morocco.

Mughals, 1526–1858. India.

Muhammad 'Ali and successors, 1805–1953. Egypt.

Muluk al-tawa'if ('party kings'), eleventh century. Spain.

Nasrids, 1230–1492. Southern Spain.

Ottomans, 1281–1922. Turkey, Syria, Iraq, Egypt, Cyprus, Tunisia, Algeria, western Arabia.

Rassids, ninth–thirteenth century, end of sixteenth century–1962. Zaydi Imams of Yemen.

Rasulids, 1229–1454. Yemen.

Rustamids, 779–909. Western Algeria.

Sa'dids, 1511–1628. Morocco.

Safavids, 1501–1732. Iran.

Saffarids, 867–end of fifteenth century. Eastern Iran.

Samanids, 819–1005. North-eastern Iran, central Asia.

Sa'udis, 1746–today. Central, then western Arabia.

Saljuqs, 1038–1194. Iran, Iraq.

Saljuqs of Rum, 1077–1307. Central and eastern Turkey.

Timurids, 1370–1506. Central Asia, Iran.

Tulunids, 868–905. Egypt, Syria.

Umayyads, 661–750. Caliphs, claiming universal authority; capital Damascus.

Umayyads of Spain, 756–1031. Claimed to be caliphs.

Note: some of the dates are approximate, as it is not always easy to know when a dynasty began or ceased to reign. Names of countries indicate the main centres of power of dynasties; except for modern dynasties, they are used in a loose geographical sense.

Adapted from T. Mostyn (ed.), *The Cambridge Encyclopedia of the Middle East and North Africa* (Cambridge, 1988), p. 59.

Ruling Families in the Nineteenth and Twentieth Century

THE OTTOMAN SULTANS

Selim III, 1789–1807
Mustafa IV, 1807–8
Mahmud II, 1808–39
Abdülmecid I, 1839–61
Abdülaziz, 1861–76
Murad V, 1876
Abdülhamid II, 1876–1909
Mehmed V Reşad, 1909–18
Mehmed VI Vahideddin, 1918–22
Abdülmecid II, recognized as caliph but not sultan, 1922–4

THE KINGS OF SAUDI ARABIA

'Abd al-'Aziz, 1926–53
Sa'ud, 1953–64
Faysal, 1964–75
Khalid, 1975–82
Fahd, 1982–

THE DYNASTY OF MUHAMMAD 'ALI IN EGYPT

Muhammad 'Ali, *Vali* (governor) of Egypt, 1805–48
Ibrahim, *Vali*, 1848
'Abbas I, *Vali*, 1848–54
Sa'id, *Vali*, 1854–63
Isma'il, Khedive, 1863–79
Tawfiq, Khedive, 1879–92
'Abbas II Hilmi, Khedive, 1892–1914
Husayn Kamil, Sultan, 1914–17

Fu'ad I, Sultan, then King, 1917–36
Faruq, King, 1936–52
Fu'ad II, King, 1952–3

THE 'ALAWIS OF MOROCCO

Sulayman, Sultan, 1796–1822
'Abd al-Rahman, Sultan, 1822–59
Muhammad, Sultan, 1859–73
Hasan I, Sultan, 1873–94
'Abd al-'Aziz, Sultan, 1894–1908
'Abd al-Hafiz, Sultan, 1908–12
Yusuf, Sultan, 1912–27
Muhammad V, Sultan, then King, 1927–61
Hasan II, King, 1961–

THE HASHIMITES

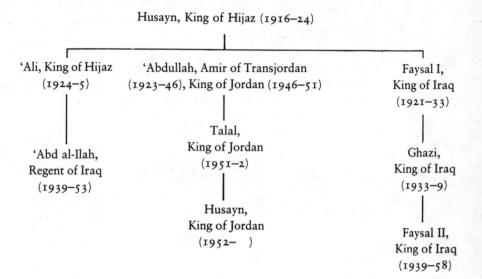

Husayn, King of Hijaz (1916–24)

'Ali, King of Hijaz (1924–5)

'Abdullah, Amir of Transjordan (1923–46), King of Jordan (1946–51)

Faysal I, King of Iraq (1921–33)

'Abd al-Ilah, Regent of Iraq (1939–53)

Talal, King of Jordan (1951–2)

Ghazi, King of Iraq (1933–9)

Husayn, King of Jordan (1952–)

Faysal II, King of Iraq (1939–58)

Notes

Notes have been kept to a minimum. For the most part they refer to direct quotations, but a few references are also given to other books where I have followed them closely. Where I know of a reliable English translation of a text, I have either quoted it or else used it as a basis for my translation. References to the Qur'an are to the translation by A. J. Arberry, *The Koran Interpreted* (London, 1955); the first figure given refers to the *sura* (chapter) and the second to the *aya* (verse).

Prologue
1. 'Abd al-Rahman Ibn Khaldun, *Muqaddima* (Cairo, n.d.), p. 33; English trans. F. Rosenthal, *The Muqaddimah* (London, 1958), Vol. 1, p. 65.
2. Ibid., p. 163; English trans. Vol. 1, p. 330.
3. Ibn Khaldun, *al-Ta'rif bi Ibn Khaldun*, ed. M. T. al-Tanji (Cairo, 1951), p. 246; French trans. A. Cheddadi, *Ibn Khaldun: le voyage d'occident et d'orient* (Paris, 1980), p. 148.

Chapter 1
1. R. B. Serjeant, '*Haram* and *hawta*: the sacred enclave in Arabia' in A. R. Badawi (ed.), *Mélanges Taha Hussein* (Cairo, 1962), pp. 41–58.
2. F. A. al-Bustani and others (eds.), *al-Majani al-haditha*, Vol. 1 (Beirut, 1946), p. 103; English trans. A. J. Arberry, *The Seven Odes* (London, 1957), p. 142.
3. Ibid., pp. 112–13; English trans. p. 147.
4. Ibid., p. 88; English trans. p. 118.
5. For these and later quotations from biographies of the Prophet, see A. Guillaume, *The Life of Muhammad* (London, 1955), a translation of Ibn Ishaq's *Sira* (life) of the Prophet.
6. Qur'an 96:1–8.

Chapter 2
1. O. Grabar, *The Formation of Islamic Art* (New Haven, 1973), pp. 45–74.
2. Muhammad ibn Jarir al-Tabari, *Tarikh*, ed. M. Ibrahim, Vol. 7 (Cairo, 1966), pp. 421–31; English trans. J. A. Williams, *The History of al-Tabari 27: The 'Abbasid Revolution* (Albany, New York, 1985), pp. 154–7.
3. Ibid., pp. 614–22; English trans. J. A. Williams, *Al-Tabari, the early 'Abbasi Empire 1: The reign of al-Ja'far al-Mansur* (Cambridge, 1988), p. 145.
4. al-Khatib al-Baghdadi, *Tarikh Baghdad*, Vol. 1 (Cairo, 1931), pp. 100 ff.; English trans. in J. Lassner, *The Topography of Baghdad in the Early Middle Ages* (Detroit, 1970), pp. 86 ff.

Chapter 3

1. R. W. Bulliet, *Conversion to Islam in the Medieval Period* (Cambridge, Massachusetts, 1979).
2. Abu'l-Tayyib al-Mutanabbi, *Diwan*, ed. A. W. al-'Azzam (Cairo, 1944), pp. 355–6; English trans. A. J. Arberry, *Poems of al-Mutanabbi* (Cambridge, 1967), p. 76.
3. Ibid., pp. 322–55; English trans. pp. 70–4.
4. 'Amr ibn Bahr al-Jahiz, *'al-nubl wa'l-tannabul wa dhamm al-kibr'* in C. Pellat, 'Une risala de Gahiz sur le "snobisme" et l'orgueil', *Arabica*, Vol. 14 (1967), pp. 259–83; English trans. in C. Pellat, *The Life and Works of Jahiz*, trans. D. Hawke (London, 1969), p. 233.
5. Muhammad Abu Rayhan al-Biruni, *Tahqiq ma li'l-Hind* (Hyderabad, 1958), p. 5; English trans. E. Sachau, *Alberuni's India* (London, 1888), Vol. 1, p. 7.
6. Ibid., p. 85; English trans. pp. 111–12.
7. Ibid., p. 76; English trans. p. 100.
8. Biruni, *Kitab al-saydana fi'l-tibb*, ed. and English trans. H. M. Said (Karachi, 1973), p. 12.
9. U. Haarmann, 'Regional sentiment in medieval Islamic Egypt', *Bulletin of the School of Oriental and African Studies*, Vol. 43 (1980), pp. 55–66; Haarmann, 'Die Sphinx: systematische Volkreligiosität im spätmittelaltischen Ägypten', *Saeculum*, Vol. 29 (1978), pp. 367–84.

Chapter 4

1. P. Crone and M. Hinds, *God's Caliph* (Cambridge, 1986).
2. Qur'an 8:20.
3. Muhammad ibn Idris al-Shafi'i, *al-Risala*, ed. A. M. Shakir (Cairo, 1940); English trans. M. Khadduri, *Islamic Jurisprudence: Shafi'i's Risala* (Baltimore, 1961).
4. Qur'an 26:192–5, 13:37.
5. Qur'an 7:171.
6. Ahmad ibn 'Ahd Allah al-Isbahani, *Hilyat al-awliya*, Vol. 2 (Cairo, 1933), pp. 132, 140; English trans. J. A. Williams, *Islam* (New York, 1961), p. 124.
7. Muhammad ibn 'Ali al-Tirmidhi, *Kitab khatm al-awliya*, ed. U. Yahya (Beirut, 1965), pp. 13–32.
8. al-Isbahani, *Hilyat al-awliya*, Vol. 10 (Cairo, 1938), p. 79; English trans. M. S. Smith, *An Early Mystic of Islam* (London, 1935), p. 243.
9. Ya'qub ibn Ishaq al-Kindi, 'Fi'l-falsafa al-ula' in M. A. Abu Rida (ed.), *Rasa'il al-Kindi al-falsafiyya* (Cairo, 1950), p. 103; English trans. R. Walzer in *Greek into Arabic* (Oxford, 1962), p. 12.
10. Ahmad ibn al-Qasim ibn Abi Usaybi'a, *'Uyun al-anba fi tabaqat al-atibba* (Beirut, 1979), Vol. 1, p. 43; English trans. in F. Rosenthal, *The Classical Heritage in Islam* (London, 1975), p. 183.
11. A. I. Sabra, 'The scientific enterprise' in B. Lewis (ed.), *The World of Islam* (London, 1976), p. 182.

Chapter 6

1. R. M. Adams, *Land behind Baghdad* (Chicago, 1965).
2. M. Brett, 'Ibn Khaldun and the arabisation of North Africa', *Maghreb Review*, Vol. 4, i (1979), pp. 9–16; and 'The Fatimid revolution (861–973) and its aftermath in North Africa' in J. D. Fage (ed.), *Cambridge History of Africa*, Vol. 2 (Cambridge, 1978), pp. 631–6.
3. L. Abu Lughod, *Veiled Sentiments* (Berkeley, 1986), p. 147.

Chapter 7

1. Ibn al-Hajj, *al-Madkhal* (Cairo, 1929), Vol. 1, pp. 245–6.
2. Qur'an 40:40; 16:97.
3. R. Le Tourneau, *Fès avant le protectorat* (Casablanca, 1949), pp. 565–6.
4. Muhammad ibn 'Abd Allah ibn Battuta, *Rihla*, ed. T. Harb (Beirut, 1987); English trans. H. A. R. Gibb, *The Travels of Ibn Battuta*, Vols. 1–3 (Cambridge, 1958–71).

Chapter 8

1. I. M. Lapidus, *Muslim Cities in the Later Middle Ages* (Cambridge, Massachusetts, 1967), pp. 199–206.
2. M. H. Burgoyne with D. S. Richards, *Mamluk Jerusalem* (London, 1987), p. 69.
3. 'Abd al-Wahhab ibn Ahmad al-Sha'rani, *Lata'if al-manan wa'l-akhlaq* (Cairo, 1972), p. 63.
4. Qur'an 4:59.
5. A. K. S. Lambton, *State and Government in Medieval Islam* (Oxford, 1981), p. 45.
6. Muhammad al-Ghazali, *Nasihat al-muluk* (Tehran, 1972), quoted in Lambton, p. 124.
7. Nizam al-Mulk, *The Book of Government or Rules for Kings*, English trans. H. Darke (London, 1978), p. 9.
8. Ibid.

Chapter 9

1. Qur'an 3:105.
2. Guillaume, *Life of Muhammad*, p. 651.
3. G. E. von Grunebaum, *Muhammadan Festivals* (New York, 1951), p. 28.
4. Ibn Battuta, *Rihla*, p. 153; English trans. Vol. 1, p. 189.
5. Qur'an 3:97.
6. Qur'an 9:125.
7. C. Padwick, *Muslim Devotions* (London, 1961), p. 252.
8. Qur'an 12:101.

Chapter 10

1. Ibn Abi Zayd al-Qayrawani; ed. and French trans. L. Bercher, *La Risala*, 3rd edn (Algiers, 1949), pp. 302–3.
2. A. L. Udovitch, *Partnership and Profit in Medieval Islam* (Princeton, 1970).
3. A. Layish and A. Shmueli, 'Custom and *shari'a* in the Beduin family according to legal documents from the Judaean desert', *Bulletin of the School of Oriental and African Studies*, Vol. 42 (1979), pp. 29–45.
4. Burgoyne, *Mamluk Jerusalem*, pp. 71–2.
5. Ibn Abi Usaybi'a, *'Uyun*, Vol. 3, pp. 342–4; English trans. in G. Makdisi, *The Rise of Colleges* (Edinburgh, 1981), pp. 89–91. This section owes much to Makdisi's book.
6. Ghazali, *al-Munqidh min al-dalal*, ed. J. Saliba and K. 'Ayyad, 3rd edn (Damascus, 1939), p. 127; English trans. R. J. McCarthy, *Freedom and Fulfilment* (Boston, 1980), p. 91.
7. Ghazali, *Faysal al-tafriqa bayn al-islam wa'l-zandaqa*, ed. S. Dunya (Cairo, 1961), p. 202; English trans. McCarthy, p. 167.
8. Ghazali, *Ihya 'ulum al-din*, Part 3, Book 2 (Cairo, 1334/1916), Vol. 2, p. 52.
9. Ghazali, *Munqidh*, p. 132; English trans. McCarthy, p. 94.
10. Ghazali, *Ihya*, Part 3, Book 1, Vol. 2, p. 17; English trans. R. J. McCarthy, p. 380.

Chapter 11

1. al-Husayn ibn 'Abd Allah ibn Sina, *The Life of Ibn Sina*, ed. and English trans. W. E. Gohlman (Albany, New York, 1974), pp. 36–9.
2. Qur'an 24:35–9.

3. Qur'an 8:85.
4. Muhammad ibn Ahmad Ibn Rushd, *Fasl al-maqal*, ed. G. F. Hourani (Leiden, 1959), p. 7; English trans. G. F. Hourani, *Averroes on the Harmony of Religion and Philosophy* (London, 1961), p. 50.
5. Ibid., p. 17; English trans. p. 61.
6. Muhyi al-Din ibn 'Arabi, *Shajarat al-kawn* (Beirut, 1984), p. 45; B. Furuzanfarr, *Ahadith-i Masnavi* (Tehran, 1955), p. 29. I owe these references to the kindness of Dr J. Baldick and Dr T. Gandjei.
7. O. Yahia, *Histoire et classification de l'œuvre d'Ibn 'Arabi* (Damascus, 1964), Vol. 1, pp. 113–35.
8. Ahmad Ibn Taymiyya, *Majmu'at al-rasa'il al-kubra* (Cairo, 1323/1905), Vol. 1, pp. 307–9; French trans. in H. Laoust, *Essai sur les doctrines sociales et politiques de Taki-d-Din b. Taimiya* (Cairo, 1939), pp. 256–7.
9. O. Yahia, Vol. 1, p. 19.

Chapter 12
1. Ahmed ibn 'Abd Allah ibn Zaydun, *Diwan*, ed. K. al-Bustani (Beirut, 1951), pp. 29–33.
2. Ibid., pp. 48–9; English trans. A. J. Arberry, *Arabic Poetry* (Cambridge, 1965), pp. 114–17.
3. Muhammad ibn 'Abd al-Malik ibn Tufayl, *Hayy ibn Yaqdhan*, ed. J. Saliba and K. 'Ayyad, 5th edn (Damascus, 1940), pp. 191–2; English trans. L. E. Goodman, *Hayy ibn Yaqzan* (New York, 1972), pp. 164–5.
4. Abu'l-Faraj al-Isbahani, *Kitab al-aghani* (Beirut, 1955), Vol. 6, pp. 294–8; English trans. in H. G. Farmer, *A History of Arabian Music* (London, 1929), pp. 102–3.
5. Ghazali, *Ihya*, Part 3, Book 8, Vol. 2, p. 237; English trans. D. B. Macdonald, 'Emotional religion in Islam as affected by music and singing', *Journal of the Royal Asiatic Society* (1901), p. 199.
6. Ibid., p. 244; English trans. p. 223.
7. Ibid., p. 249; English trans. p. 229.
8. Ibn Khaldun, p. 28, English trans. Vol. 1, pp. 55–6.
9. Ibn Khaldun, pp. 493–4; English trans. Vol. 3, p. 150.

Chapter 13
1. Ibn Khaldun, p. 183; English trans. Vol. 1, p. 372.
2. Ibid., p. 100; English trans Vol. 1, p. 300.
3. Quoted in T. W. Arnold, *The Caliphate*, new edn (London, 1965), p. 203.
4. C. M. Doughty, *Travels in Arabia Deserta*, new edn (London, 1921), pp. 6–8.

Chapter 14
1. Ahmad al-Nasiri al-Salawi, *Kitab al-istiqsa*, Vol. 7 (Casablanca, 1956), pp. 82–6; French trans. in J. Berque, *Al-Yousi* (Paris, 1958), pp. 91–2.
2. Ibid., Vol. 4 (Casablanca, 1955), pp. 163–4; French trans. I. Hamet, *Archives Marocaines*, Vol. 33 (1934), pp. 570–2.

Chapter 15
1. English trans. in W. L. Wright, *Ottoman Statecraft* (Princeton, 1935), pp. 117–18.
2. Quoted in 'Abd al-Rahman al-Jabarti, *'Aja'ib al-athar fi'l-tarajim wa'l-akhbar* (Cairo, 1965), Vol. 4, p. 214. I must thank Dr K. Barbir for drawing my attention to this letter.

Chapter 16
1. Jabarti, Vol. 4, p. 285.
2. Ibid., p. 348.

3. English trans. H. Inalcik in J. C. Hurewitz (ed.), *The Middle East and North Africa in World Politics* (New Haven, 1975), Vol. 1, pp. 269–71.

Chapter 17
1. H. H. Jessup, *Fifty-three Years in Syria*, Vol. 2 (New York, 1910), pp. 786–7.
2. J. Cambon, quoted in C. R. Ageron, *Les algériens musulmans et la France (1871–1919)* (Paris, 1968), p. 478.

Chapter 18
1. J. W. van Goethe, 'Aus dem Nachlass', *Westöstliche Divan*.
2. R. Kipling, 'A Ballad of East and West'.
3. Rifa'a Rafi'i al-Tahtawi, *Takhlis al-ibriz ila talkhis Bariz* in M. F. Hijazi (ed.), *Usul al-fikr al-'arabi al-hadith 'ind al Tahtawi* (Cairo, 1974), pp. 208 ff.
4. Khayr al-Din al-Tunisi, *Aqwam al-masalik fi ma'rifat ahwal al-mamalik* (Tunis, 1867–8), p. 5; English trans. L. C. Brown, *The Surest Path* (Cambridge, Massachusetts, 1967), p. 74.
5. Rashid Rida, *Tarikh al-ustadh al-imam al-shaykh Muhammad 'Abduh*, Vol. 1 (Cairo, 1931), p. 11.
6. Taha Husayn, *al-Ayyam*, Vol. 3, 19th edn (Cairo, 1972), pp. 3–4; English trans. K. Cragg, *A Passage to France* (Leiden, 1976), pp. 1–2.

Chapter 19
1. T. E. Lawrence, *Seven Pillars of Wisdom*, new edn (London, 1940), p. 56.
2. Ibid., p. 23.
3. J. Berque, *Le Maghreb entre deux guerres* (Paris, 1962), p. 60; English trans. *French North Africa* (London, 1967), p. 63.

Chapter 20
1. Abu'l-Qasim al-Shabbi, quoted in M. M. Badawi, *A Critical Introduction to Modern Arabic Poetry* (Cambridge, 1975), p. 159.
2. Taha Husayn, reply to Tawfiq al-Hakim, *al-Risala*, 15 June 1933, pp. 8–9; reprinted in *Fusul fi'l-adab wa'l-naqd* (Cairo, 1945), pp. 107–9.
3. Ahmad Shawqi, *al-Shawqiyyat*, Vol. 1 (Cairo, n.d.), pp. 153–66.
4. 'Anbara Salam al-Khalidi, *Jawla fi'l-dhikrayat bayn Lubnan wa Filastin* (Beirut, 1978).
5. 'Ali 'Abd al-Raziq, *al-Islam wa usul al-hukm*, 2nd edn (Cairo, 1925), p. 103.
6. Quoted in R. Mitchell, *The Society of the Muslim Brothers* (London, 1969), p. 30.

Chapter 21
1. G. Tillion, *Les ennemis complémentaires* (Paris, 1960); English trans. *France and Algeria: complementary enemies* (New York, 1961), p. 9.

Chapter 23
1. Abdullah Laroui, *L'histoire du Maghreb: un essai de synthèse* (Paris, 1970), pp. 15, 353–4; English trans. R. Manheim, *The History of the Maghreb: an interpretive essay* (Princeton, 1977), pp. 10, 384–5.
2. Adunis ('Ali Ahmad Sa'id), quoted in S. K. Jayyusi, *Trends and Movements in Modern Arabic Poetry* (Leiden, 1977), Vol. 2, p. 572.
3. Badr Shakir al-Sayyab, *Anshudat al-matar* (Beirut, 1960), pp. 103–7; English trans. in S. K. Jayyusi (ed.), *Modern Arabic Poetry* (New York, 1987), pp. 432–5.

Chapter 24
1. Department of Information, Cairo, *Mashru' al-mithaq* (Cairo, 1962), pp. 13 ff.; English trans. S. Hanna and G. H. Gardner (eds.), *Arab Socialism* (London, 1969), pp. 344–5.

Chapter 26

1. A. Rifaat, *Distant View of a Minaret*, English trans. D. Johnson-Davies (London, 1983), p. 109.
2. Hichem Djaït, *La personnalité et le devenir arabo-islamiques* (Paris, 1974), p. 140.
3. A. Laroui, *La crise des intellectuels arabes* (Paris, 1974), English trans. *The crisis of the Arab intellectual* (Berkeley, 1976); and *L'idéologie arabe contemporaire*, new edn (Paris, 1977).
4. Sayyid Qutb, *Ma'alim fi'l-tariq* (Cairo, 1964), pp. 4–5.
5. F. Rahman, *Islam and Modernity* (Chicago, 1982).

Bibliography

This is not an exhaustive bibliography. It does not attempt to include all the books and articles I have consulted, nor all those which a reader interested in a particular subject should know. All I have tried to do is to give hints on further reading, and to provide for different tastes. Most of the items are in English, but some are in French or Arabic, and a few in German, Italian or Turkish. I have given a few references to original sources in Arabic for readers who might wish to taste them.

The list is arranged according to the parts and chapters of the book, and, within each chapter, roughly according to the order of the various subjects which it covers. It is a cumulative bibliography: items mentioned in connection with one subject may of course be relevant to another which is mentioned later, but to have repeated them would have made the list too long.

I have given only such details as may be sufficient to enable a reader to identify items in a library catalogue. Subtitles of books are mentioned when they indicate the subject more fully than the title. When the book has been published in the United Kingdom, I have usually given the title and place and date of publication of the British edition: details of the American edition may, of course, be different.

GENERAL BIBLIOGRAPHY

Reference books
The Encyclopaedia of Islam, 2nd edn (Leiden, in progress: 5 vols. published 1960–86).
J. D. Pearson and others (eds.), *Index Islamicus 1906–1955* and regular supplements (Cambridge, 1958–).
W. H. Belan, *Index Islamicus 1665–1905* (Millersville, Pennsylvania, 1988).
D. Grimwood-Jones and others, *An Islamic Bibliography* (Hassocks, Sussex, 1977).
J. Sauvaget and C. Cahen, *Introduction to the History of the Muslim East: a bibliographical guide*, English trans. (Berkeley, 1965).
J. Bacharach, *A Middle East Studies Handbook*, revised edn (Cambridge, 1984).
C. E. Bosworth, *The Islamic Dynasties* (Edinburgh, 1967).
G. S. P. Freeman-Grenville, *The Muslim and Christian Calendars* (London, 1967).

Geography
R. Roolvink, *Historical Atlas of the Muslim Peoples* (Amsterdam, 1957).
F. Robinson, *Atlas of the Islamic World since 1500* (Oxford, 1982).

P. Birot and J. Dresch, *La Méditerranée et le Moyen-Orient* (Paris, 1956).
J. Despois, *L'Afrique du nord* (Paris, 1964).

Historical surveys
M. G. S. Hodgson, *The Venture of Islam*, 3 vols. (Chicago, 1974).
I. M. Lapidus, *A History of Muslim Societies* (Cambridge, 1988).
U. Haarmann (ed.), *Geschichte der arabischen Welt* (Munich, 1987).
J. M. Abun-Nasr, *A History of the Maghrib in the Islamic Period* (Cambridge, 1987).

Islam
H. A. R. Gibb, *Islam*, 2nd edn (Oxford, 1969).
F. Rahman, *Islam*, 2nd edn (Chicago, 1979).
M. Ruthven, *Islam in the World* (Harmondsworth, Middlesex, 1984).
J. A. Williams (ed.), *Themes of Islamic Civilization* (Berkeley, 1971).

Civilization and culture
J. Schacht and C. E. Bosworth (eds.), *The Legacy of Islam*, 2nd edn (Oxford, 1974).
B. Lewis (ed.), *The World of Islam* (London, 1976).
H. A. R. Gibb, *Studies on the Civilization of Islam* (London, 1962).
T. Khalidi, *Classical Arab Islam* (Princeton, 1985).
H. A. R. Gibb, *Arabic Literature*, 2nd edn (Oxford, 1963).
G. Brockelmann, *Geschichte der arabischen Literatur*, 2 vols. and 3 supplements (Leiden, 1938–49).
F. Sezgin, *Geschichte des arabischen Schrifttums* (Leiden, in progress: 9 vols. published 1967–84).
R. Ettinghausen and O. Grabar, *The Art and Architecture of Islam* (London, 1987).
D. Eickelman, *The Middle East: an anthropological approach* (Englewood Cliffs, New Jersey, 1981).
A. L. Udovitch (ed.), *The Islamic Middle East 700–1900: studies in economic and social history* (Princeton, 1981).

Periodicals (dates are those of first publication)
Arabica (Leiden, 1954).
Bulletin of the School of Oriental and African Studies (London, 1917).
Der Islam (Berlin, 1910).
International Journal of Middle East Studies (Cambridge, 1970).
Journal of the Economic and Social History of the Orient (Leiden, 1957).
Middle East Journal (Washington, 1947).
Middle Eastern Studies (London, 1964).
Oriente Moderno (Rome, 1921).
Revue des Études Islamiques (Paris, 1927).
Studia Islamica (Paris, 1953).

Prologue

Ibn Khaldun's Muqaddima
Text: E. Quatremère (ed.), *Les prologomènes d'Ebn Khaldun*, 3 vols. (Paris, 1858);
    Muqaddimat Ibn Khaldun (Bulaq, 1857; reprints, Cairo and Beirut).
English trans. F. Rosenthal, *Ibn Khaldun: the Muqaddimah*, 3 vols. (London, 1958).

Ibn Khaldun's History
Text: *Kitab al-'ibar wa diwan al-mubtada wa'l-khabar*, 7 vols. (Bulaq, 1867–8); reprint as
    Tarikh al-'allama Ibn Khaldun, 7 vols. (Beirut, 1956–61).

Partial French trans. M. de Slane, *Histoire des Berbères et des dynasties musulmanes de l'Afrique septentrionale*, 2 vols. (Algiers, 1847–51).

Autobiography
Text: M. al-Tanji (ed.), *Al-Ta'rif bi Ibn Khaldun wa rihlatuhu gharban wa sharqan* (Cairo, 1951); French trans. A. Cheddadi, *Ibn Khaldun: le voyage d'occident et d'orient* (Paris, 1980).

Studies
Bibliography in A. al-Azmeh, *Ibn Khaldun in Modern Scholarship* (London, 1981), pp. 231–318.
A. al-Azmeh, *Ibn Khaldun: an essay in reinterpretation* (London, 1982).
M. Mahdi, *Ibn Khaldun's Philosophy of History* (London, 1957).
M. A. al-Jabiri, *al-'Asabiyya wa'l-dawla* (Casablanca, 1971).

PART I THE MAKING OF A WORLD (SEVENTH–TENTH CENTURY)

Chronicles
Ahmad ibn Yahya al-Baladhuri, *Ansab al-ashraf*: Jerusalem edn, Vols. 4A, 4B, 5 (Jerusalem, 1936–); ed. A. Duri, Vols. 3, 4i (Wiesbaden, 1978–).
al-Baladhuri, *Futuh al-buldan*, ed. S. Munajjid, 3 vols. (Cairo, 1956–7); English trans. P. K. Hitti and F. C. Murgotten, *The Origins of the Islamic State*, 2 vols. (New York, 1916–24).
'Ali ibn al-Husayn al-Mas'udi, *Muruj al-dhahab*, ed. C. Pellat, 7 vols. (Beirut, 1966–79); French trans. C. Barbier and P. de Courtelle, 9 vols. (Paris, 1861–77).
Muhammad ibn Jarir al-Tabari, *Kitab tarikh al-rusal wa'l-muluk*: ed. M. J. de Goeje and others, *Annales*, 15 vols. (Leiden, 1879–1901); ed. M. A. Ibrahim, *Tarikh al-Tabari*, 10 vols. (Cairo, 1960–9); English trans. *The History of al-Tabari* (Albany, New York, in progress: 20 vols. published 1985–9).

Inscriptions
M. van Berchem and others, *Matériaux pour un corpus inscriptionum arabicorum*, Part 1 (Egypt), Part 2 (Syria), Part 3 (Asia Minor) (Paris, 1903–54), Part 4i (Arabia) (Cairo, 1985).
E. Combe and others, *Répertoire chronologique d'épigraphie arabe* (Cairo, in progress: 17 vols. published 1931–82).

Coins
M. Broome, *Handbook of Islamic Coins* (London, 1985).

Surveys
H. Kennedy, *The Prophet and the Age of the Caliphates* (London, 1986).
C. Cahen, *L'islam dès origines au début de l'empire ottoman* (Paris, 1970).
D. and J. Sourdel, *La civilisation de l'islam classique* (Paris, 1968).
C. A. Julien, *Histoire de l'Afrique du nord*, Vol. 2, revised edn R. Le Tourneau (Paris, 1956); English trans. *History of North Africa* (London, 1970).
E. Lévi-Provençal, *Histoire de l'Espagne musulmane*, revised edn, 3 vols. (Paris, 1950–3).
W. M. Watt and P. Cachia, *A History of Islamic Spain* (Edinburgh, 1965).
M. Amari, *Storia dei Musulmani di Sicilia*, revised edn C. Nallino, 3 vols. (Catania, 1933–9).

Chapter 1 A New Power in an Old World

The Middle East before Islam

P. Brown, *The World of Late Antiquity* (London, 1971).

P. Brown, 'The rise and function of the holy man in late antiquity', *Journal of Roman Studies*, Vol. 61 (1971), pp. 80–101.

J. Herrin, *The Making of Christendom* (Oxford, 1987).

J. M. Cook, *The Persian Empire* (London, 1983).

R. C. Zaehner, *The Dawn and Twilight of Zoroastrianism* (London, 1961).

I. Shahid, 'Pre-islamic Arabia' in P. M. Holt and others (eds.), *The Cambridge History of Islam*, Vol. 1 (Cambridge, 1970), pp. 3–29.

I. Shahid, *Rome and the Arabs* (Washington, 1984).

I. Shahid, *Byzantium and the Arabs in the Fourth Century* (Washington, 1984).

I. Shahid, *Byzantium and the Arabs in the Fifth Century* (Washington, 1989).

J. Ryckmans, *L'institution monarchique en Arabie méridionale avant l'islam* (Louvain, 1951).

G. Ryckmans, 'Les religions arabes preislamiques', *Le Muséon*, Vol. 26 (1951), pp. 6–61.

H. Pirenne, *Mahomet et Charlemagne* (Paris, 1937); English trans. *Mohammed and Charlemagne* (London, 1939).

D. Whitehouse and R. Hodges, *Mohammed, Charlemagne and the Origins of Europe* (London, 1983).

Pre-Islamic poetry

The Mu'allaqat, numerous editions; English trans. A. J. Arberry, *The Seven Odes* (London, 1957).

R. Blachère, *Histoire de la littérature arabe*, 3 vols. (Paris, 1952–66).

A. F. L. Beeston and others (eds.), *Arabic Literature to the End of the Umayyad Period* (Cambridge, 1983).

M. Zwettler, *The Oral Tradition of Classical Arabic Poetry* (Columbus, Ohio, 1975).

T. Husayn, *Fi'-l adab al-jahili* (Cairo, 1927).

A. A. Sa'id (Adunis), *Diwan al-shi'r al-'arabi*, Vols. 1–3 (Beirut, 1964–8).

Muhammad

'Abd al-Malik ibn Hisham, *al-Sira al-nabawiyya*, 2 vols. (Cairo, 1955); English trans. A. Guillaume, *The Life of Muhammad* (London, 1957).

W. M. Watt, *Muhammad at Mecca* (Oxford, 1953).

W. M. Watt, *Muhammad at Medina* (Oxford, 1956).

M. Rodinson, *Mahomet*, 2nd edn (Paris, 1968); English trans. *Mohammed* (London, 1971).

M. Cook, *Muhammad* (Oxford, 1983).

Muhammad ibn 'Umar al-Waqidi, *Kitab al-maghazi*, ed. J. M. B. Jones, 3 vols. (London, 1955).

A. Caetani, *Annali dell'Islam*, 10 vols. (Milan, 1905–26).

M. J. Kister, *Studies in Jahiliyya and Early Islam* (London, 1980).

P. Crone, *Meccan Trade and the Rise of Islam* (Princeton, 1987).

R. B. Serjeant, 'Haram and hawta: the sacred enclave in Arabia' in A. R. Badawi (ed.), *Mélanges Taha Hussein* (Cairo, 1962), pp. 41–58.

S. P. Brock, 'Syriac views of emergent Islam' in G. H. A. Juynboll (ed.), *Studies on the First Century of Islamic Society* (Carbondale, Illinois, 1982), pp. 9–21.

The Qur'an

English trans. A. J. Arberry, *The Koran Interpreted*, 2 vols. (London, 1961).

Commentaries: 'Abd Allah ibn 'Umar al-Baydawi, *Anwar al-tanzil*, 2 vols. (Cairo, AH 1330/1912).

Muhammad ibn Jarir al-Tabari, *Jami' al-bayan 'an ta'wil ay al-Qur'an*, ed. M. M. and A. M. Shakir, Vols. 1–16 (Cairo, 1955–69); English trans. J. Cooper, *Commentary on the Qur'an*, Vol. 1 (Oxford, 1987).

W. M. Watt (ed.), *Bell's Introduction to the Qur'an* (Edinburgh, 1970).

T. Izutsu, *Ethico-religious Concepts in the Qur'an* (Montreal, 1966).

F. Rahman, *Major Themes of the Qur'an* (Minneapolis, 1980).

J. Wansbrough, *Quranic Studies* (Oxford, 1977).

J. Wansbrough, *The Sectarian Milieu* (Oxford, 1978).

Chapter 2 The Formation of an Empire

Rashidun and Umayyads

J. Wellhausen, *Das arabische Reich und sein Sturz* (Berlin, 1902); English trans. *The Arab Kingdom and Its Fall* (Calcutta, 1927).

F. M. Donner, *The Early Islamic Conquests* (Princeton, 1981).

G. H. A. Juynboll (ed.), *Studies on the First Century of Islamic Society* (Carbondale, Illinois, 1982).

H. Lammens, *Études sur le siècle des Omayyades* (Beirut, 1975).

G. R. Hawting, *The First Dynasty of Islam: the Umayyad Caliphate A.D. 661–750* (London, 1986).

P. Crone, *Slaves on Horses* (Cambridge, 1980).

T. Nagel, *Rechtleitung und Califat* (Bonn, 1975).

'Abbasids

M. A. Shaban, *The Abbasid Revolution* (Cambridge, 1970).

H. Kennedy, *The Early Abbasid Caliphate* (London, 1981).

J. Lassner, *The Shaping of Abbasid Rule* (Princeton, 1980).

D. Sourdel, *Le vizirat 'abbasid de 749 à 936*, 2 vols. (Damascus, 1959–60).

Chapter 3 The Formation of a Society

The end of political unity

H. Busse, *Chalif und Grosskönig: die Buyiden in Iraq 945–1055* (Beirut, 1969).

W. Madelung, 'The assumption of the title Shahanshah by the Buyids and "the reign of Daylam" ', *Journal of Near Eastern Studies*, Vol. 28 (1969), pp. 84–108, 168–83.

G. Hanotaux (ed.), *Histoire de la nation égyptienne*, Vol. 4: G. Wiet, *L'Egypte arabe* (Paris, 1937).

M. Canard, *Histoire de la dynastie des Hamdanides* (Paris, 1953).

M. Talbi, *L'emirat aghlabide 184–296/800–909* (Paris, 1960).

Economic and social change

M. Morony, *Iraq after the Muslim Conquest* (Princeton, 1984).

H. Djait, *Al-Kufa: naissance de la ville islamique* (Paris, 1986).

J. Lassner, *The Topography of Baghdad in the Early Middle Ages* (Detroit, 1970).

S. al-'Ali, *al-Tanzimat al-ijtima'iyya wa'l-iqtisadiyya fi'l-Basra* (Baghdad, 1953).

A. al-Duri, *Tarikh al-'Iraq al-iqtisadi fi'l-qarn al-rabi'* (Baghdad, 1945).

Ya'qub ibn Ibrahim Abu Yusuf, *Kitab al-kharaj* (Cairo, 1933); French trans. E. Fagnan, *Le livre de l'impot foncier* (Paris, 1921).

M. A. Cook, 'Economic developments' in J. Schacht and C. E. Bosworth (eds.), *The Legacy of Islam*, 2nd edn (Oxford, 1974), pp. 210–43.

A. M. Watson, *Agricultural Innovation in the Early Islamic World* (Cambridge, 1983).

R. W. Bulliet, *Conversion to Islam in the Medieval Period* (Cambridge, Massachusetts, 1979).

R. W. Bulliet, *The Camel and the Wheel* (Cambridge, Massachusetts, 1975).

Buildings

O. Grabar, *The Formation of Islamic Art* (New Haven, 1973).

K. A. C. Creswell, *Early Muslim Architecture*, Vol. 1, 2nd edn (Oxford, 1969), Vol. 2 (Oxford, 1940).

R. W. Hamilton, *Khirbat al-Mafjar* (Oxford, 1959).

O. Grabar and others, *City in the Desert: Qasr al-Hayr East*, 2 vols. (Cambridge, Massachusetts, 1978).

Geography

A. Miquel, *La géographie humaine du monde musulman jusq'au milieu du 11e siècle*, 2nd edn, 3 vols. (Paris, 1973–80).

'Ali ibn al-Husayn al-Mas'udi, *Kitab al-tanbih wa'l-ashraf*, ed. M. J. de Goeje (Leiden, 1894/Beirut, 1965).

Abu'l Qasim ibn 'Ali ibn Hawqal, *Surat al-ard* (Beirut, 1979).

History

A. al-Duri, *Bahth fi nash'at 'ilm al-tarikh 'ind al-'arab* (Beirut, 1960); English trans. *The Rise of Historical Writing Among the Arabs* (Princeton, 1983).

T. Khalidi, *Islamic Historiography: the histories of Mas'udi* (Albany, New York, 1975).

F. Rosenthal, *A History of Muslim Historiography* (Leiden, 1952).

Muhammad Abu Rayhan al-Biruni, *Tahqiq ma li'l-Hind* (Hyderabad, 1958); English trans. E. Sachau, *Alberuni's India*, 2 vols. (London, 1888).

Literature

J. Pedersen, *The Arabic Book* (Princeton, 1984).

A. Hamori, *On the Art of Medieval Arabic Literature* (Princeton, 1974).

I. 'Abbas, *Fann al-shi'r* (Beirut, 1959).

J. E. Bencheikh, *Poétique arabe: essai sur les voies d'une création* (Paris, 1975).

Abu Tayyib al-Mutanabbi, *Diwan* (numerous editions); English trans. A. J. Arberry, *The Poems of al-Mutanabbi* (Cambridge, 1967).

T. Husayn, *Ma' al-Mutanabbi* (Cairo, 1962).

R. Blachère, *Un poète arabe du 4e siècle de l'Hegire: Abou-t-Tayyib al-Mutanabbi* (Paris, 1935).

C. Pellat, *Le milieu basrien et la formation de Gahiz* (Paris, 1953).

C. Pellat, *The Life and Works of Jahiz*, English trans. (London, 1969).

Regional identity

U. Haarmann, 'Regional sentiment in medieval Islamic Egypt', *Bulletin of the School of Oriental and African Studies*, Vol. 43 (1980), pp. 55–66.

A. al-Duri, *al-Takwin al-tarikhi li'l-umma al-'arabiyya* (Beirut, 1984); English trans. A. A. Duri, *The Historical Formation of the Arab Nation* (London, 1987).

Chapter 4 The Articulation of Islam

Caliphate and imamate

T. W. Arnold, *The Caliphate*, 2nd edn (London, 1965).

W. Madelung, 'Imama', *Encyclopaedia of Islam*, 2nd edn, Vol. 3, pp. 1163–9.

A. K. S. Lambton, *State and Government in Medieval Islam* (London, 1965).

T. Nagel, *Staat und Glaubensgemeinschaft in Islam*, 2 vols. (Zurich, 1981).

P. Crone and M. Hinds, *God's Caliph* (Cambridge, 1986).
J. C. Wilkinson, *The Imamate Tradition of Oman* (Cambridge, 1987).

Theology
I. Goldziher, *Vorlesungen über den Islam* (Heidelberg, 1910); English trans. A. and R. Hamori, *Introduction to Islamic Theology and Law* (Princeton, 1981).
H. Laoust, *Les schismes dans l'islam* (Paris, 1965).
W. M. Watt, *The Formative Period of Islamic Thought* (Edinburgh, 1973).
A. J. Wensinck, *The Muslim Creed* (Cambridge, 1982).
J. Van Ess, *Anfänge Muslimische Theologie* (Wiesbaden, 1977).
M. A. Cook, *Early Muslim Dogma* (Cambridge, 1981).
L. Gardet and M. M. Anawati, *Introduction à la théologie musulmane*, 2nd edn (Paris, 1970).
W. Madelung, *Religious Schools and Sects in Medieval Islam* (London, 1985).
R. J. McCarthy, *The Theology of Al-Ash'ari* (Beirut, 1953).
G. Makdisi, 'Ash'ari and the Ash'arites in Islamic religious thought', *Studia Islamica*, Vol. 17 (1962), pp. 37–80; Vol. 18 (1963), pp. 19–39.

Shi'ism and Isma'ilism
M. Momen, *An Introduction to Shi'i Islam* (New Haven, 1985).
S. M. Stern, *Studies in Early Isma'ilism* (Leiden, 1983).
W. Madelung, *Der Imam al-Qasim ibn Ibrahim und die Glaubenslehre der Zaiditen* (Berlin, 1971).
W. Madelung, 'Isma'iliyya', *Encyclopaedia of Islam*, 2nd edn, Vol. 4, pp. 198–206.

Hadith
Muhammad ibn Isma'il al-Bukhari, *al-Jami' al-sahih*, 8 vols. (Bulaq, AH 1296/1879), 3 vols. (Cairo, AH 1348/1930).
I. Goldziher, *Muhammedanische Studien*, Vol. 2 (Halle, 1890); English trans. ed. S. M. Stern, *Muslim Studies*, Vol. 2 (London, 1971).
G. H. A. Juynboll, *Muslim Tradition* (Cambridge, 1983).
W. A. Graham, *Divine Word and Prophetic Word in Early Islam* (The Hague, 1977).

Jurisprudence and law
J. Schacht, *The Origins of Muhammadan Jurisprudence* (Oxford, 1950).
J. Schacht, *An Introduction to Islamic Law* (Oxford, 1964).
P. Crone, *Roman, Provincial and Islamic Law* (Cambridge, 1987).
N. J. Coulson, *A History of Islamic Law* (Edinburgh, 1964).
Muhammad ibn Idris al-Shafi'i, *al-Risala*, ed. A. M. Shakir (Cairo, AH 1357/1938); English trans. M. Khadduri, *Islamic Jurisprudence* (Baltimore, 1961).
E. Tyan, *Histoire de l'organisation judiciaire en pays d'islam*, 2 vols. (Paris, 1938–43).

Sufism
M. Molé, *Les mystiques musulmans* (Paris, 1965).
J. Baldick, *Mystical Islam* (London, 1989).
A. M. Schimmel, *Mystical Dimensions of Islam* (Chapel Hill, North Carolina, 1975).
R. A. Nicholson, *The Mystics of Islam* (London, 1914).
R. A. Nicholson, *Studies in Islamic Mysticism* (Cambridge, 1921).
M. Smith, *Readings from the Mystics of Islam* (London, 1950).
L. Gardet and G. C. Anawati, *Mystique musulmane* (Paris, 1961).
Harith ibn Asad al-Muhasibi, *Kitab al-nufus* (Beirut, 1984).
J. van Ess, *Die Gedankenwelt des Harit al-Muhasibi* (Bonn, 1961).
Muhammad ibn 'Ali al-Tirmidhi, *Kitab Khatm al-awliya*, ed. U. Yahya (Beirut, 1965).

Ahmad ibn 'Abd Allah al-Isbahani, *Hilyat al-awliya*, 10 vols. (Cairo, 1932–8).

L. Massignon, *Essai sur les origines du lexique technique de la mystique musulmane* (Paris, 1922).

L. Massignon, *La passion de Husayn ibn Mansour Hallaj, martyr mystique de l'islam*, 2nd edn, 4 vols. (Paris, 1975); English trans. H. Mason, *The Passion of al-Hallaj, Mystic and Martyr of Islam*, 4 vols. (Princeton, 1982).

Philosophy

F. Rosenthal, *Das Fortleben der Antike in Islam* (Zurich, 1965); English trans. *The Classical Heritage in Islam* (London, 1975).

R. Walzer, *Greek into Arabic* (Oxford, 1962).

M. Fakhry, *A History of Islamic Philosophy*, 2nd edn (London, 1983).

G. F. Hourani, *Reason and Tradition in Islamic Ethics* (Cambridge, 1985).

PART II ARAB MUSLIM SOCIETIES (ELEVENTH–FIFTEENTH CENTURY)

Chronicles

'Izz al-Din 'Ali ibn al-Athir, *al-Kamil fi'l-tarikh*, 12 vols. (Cairo, 1884–5).

Ahmad ibn' 'Ali al-Maqrizi, *Kitab al-suluk li ma'rifat duwal al-muluk*, 8 parts (Cairo, 1934–72).

Muhammad Lissan al-Din al-Khatib, *Kitab a'mal al-'alam*: Vol. 3, *Tarikh al-Maghrib al-'arabi fi'l-'asr al-wasit* (Casablanca, 1964).

Geographers and travellers

Muhammad ibn 'Abd Allah Ibn Battuta, *Tuhfat al-nuzzar fi ghara'ib al-amsar wa 'aja' ib al-safar*, ed. T. Harb, *Rihlat Ibn Battuta* (Beirut, 1987); English trans. H. A. R. Gibb, *The Travels of Ibn Battuta*, 3 vols. (Cambridge, 1958–71).

Yaqut ibn 'Abd Allah al-Hamawi, *Mu'jam al-buldan*, 10 vols. (Cairo, 1906–7).

Leo Africanus, French trans. A. Epaulard, *Jean Leon, l'Africain, Description de l'Afrique*, 2 vols. (Paris, 1956); English trans. J. Pory, *The History and Description of Africa*, 3 vols. (London, 1896).

Documents

S. M. Stern (ed.), *Fatimid Decrees* (London, 1964).

S. M. Stern (ed.), *Documents from Islamic Chanceries* (Oxford, 1965).

D. Little, *A Catalogue of the Islamic Documents from al-Haram al-Šarif in Jerusalem* (Beirut, 1984).

Survey

G. E. von Grunebaum, *Medieval Islam* (Chicago, 1953).

Chapter 6 The Countryside

Agricultural production and irrigation

R. M. Adams, *Land behind Baghdad* (Chicago, 1965).

J. C. Wilkinson, *Water and Tribal Settlement in South-East Arabia* (Oxford, 1977).

J. Weulersse, *Paysans de Syrie et du proche-orient* (Paris, 1946).

H. M. Rabie, *The Financial System of Egypt A. H. 564–741/1169–1341* (London, 1972).

T. F. Glick, *Irrigation and Society in Medieval Valencia* (Cambridge, 1970).

M. Mundy, 'The Family, Inheritance and Islam' in A. al-Azmeh (ed.), *Islamic Law: Social and Historical Contexts* (London, 1988).

Tribes and authority
R. Montagne, *La civilisation du désert* (Paris, 1947).
C. Cahen, 'Nomades et sédentaires dans le monde musulman du moyen âge' in Cahen, *Les peuples musulmans dans l'histoire médiévale* (Damascus, 1947), pp. 423–37.
P. Dresch, *Tribes, Government and History in Yemen* (Oxford, 1989).
J. Berque, *Structures sociales du Haut Atlas*, 2nd edn (Paris, 1978).
E. E. Evans-Pritchard, *The Sanusi of Cyrenaica* (Oxford, 1949).
A. Musil, *The Manners and Customs of the Rwala Bedouins* (New York, 1928).
W. Lancaster, *The Rwala Bedouin Today* (Cambridge, 1981).
J. Pitt-Rivers (ed.), *Mediterranean Countrymen* (Paris, 1963).
J. G. Peristiany (ed.), *Honour and Shame* (London, 1965).
L. Abu Lughod, *Veiled Sentiments* (Berkeley, 1986).

Chapter 7 The Life of Cities

Cities in general
A. H. Hourani and S. M. Stern (eds.), *The Islamic City* (Oxford, 1970).
I. M. Lapidus, *Muslim Cities in the Later Middle Ages* (Cambridge, Massachusetts, 1967).

The size of cities
A. Raymond, 'La population du Caire de Maqrizi à la description de l'Egypte', *Bulletin d'Études Orientales*, Vol. 28 (1975), pp. 201–15.
J. C. Russell, *Medieval Regions and their Cities* (Bloomington, Indiana, 1972).
M. Dols, *The Black Death in the Middle East* (Princeton, 1977).

The growth and shape of cities
Cairo   J. Abu Lughod, *Cairo: 1001 years of the City Victorious* (Princeton, 1971).
J. M. Rogers, 'al-Kahira', *Encyclopaedia of Islam*, 2nd edn, Vol IV, pp. 424–41.
Damascus   J. Sauvaget, 'Esquisse d'une histoire de la ville de Damas', *Revue des Études Islamiques*, Vol. 8 (1934), pp. 421–80.
Aleppo   J. Sauvaget, *Alep* (Paris, 1941).
   H. Gaube and E. Wirth, *Aleppo: historische und geographische Beitrage* (Wiesbaden, 1984).
Jerusalem   M. Burgoyne and D. S. Richards, *Mamluk Jerusalem: an architectural study* (London, 1987).
Baghdad   G. Makdisi, 'The topography of eleventh century Baghdad', *Arabica*, Vol. 6 (1959), pp. 178–97, 281–309.
Qus   J. C. Garcin, *Un centre musulman de la Haute-Egypte médiéval: Qus* (Cairo, 1976).
San'a   R. B. Serjeant and R. Lewcock (eds.), *San'a, an Arabian Islamic City* (London, 1983).
Fez   R. Le Tourneau, *Fez in the Age of the Marinids* (Norman, Oklahoma, 1961).
   R. Le Tourneau, *Fès avant le protectorat* (Casablanca, 1949).

The life of a great city: Cairo
Ahmad ibn 'Ali al-Maqrizi, *al-Mawa'iz wa'l-i'tibar fi dhikr al-khitat wa'l-akhbar*, ed. G. Wiet, 5 vols. (Cairo, 1911); index: A. A. Haridi, *Index analytique des ouvrages d'Ibn Duqmaq et de Maqrizi sur le Caire*, 3 vols. (Cairo, 1983–4).
S. D. Goitein, *A Mediterranean Society*, 5 vols. (Berkeley, 1967–88).
E. W. Lane, *The Manners and Customs of the Modern Egyptians* (London, 1836 and reprints).

Trades and markets

G. Wiet and A. Raymond, *Les marchés du Caire* (Cairo, 1979).

E. Wirth, 'Zum probleme des bazars', *Der Islam*, Vol. 51 (1974), pp. 203–60; Vol. 52 (1975), pp. 6–46.

S. Y. Habib, *Handelsgeschichte Ägyptens im Spätmittelalten 1171–1517* (Wiesbaden, 1965).

R. Lopez, H. Miskimin and A. L. Udovitch, 'England to Egypt: long-term trends and long-distance trade' in M. A. Cook (ed.), *Studies in the Economic History of the Middle East* (London, 1970), pp. 93–128.

A. L. Udovitch, *Partnership and Profit in Medieval Islam* (Princeton, 1970).

M. Rodinson, *Islam et capitalisme* (Paris, 1966); English trans. *Islam and Capitalism* (London, 1974).

Elements of the population

B. Musallam, *Sex and Society in Islam* (Cambridge, 1983).

B. Lewis, *The Jews of Islam* (London, 1984).

R. Brunschvig, "Abd', *Encyclopaedia of Islam*, 2nd edn, Vol. 1, pp. 24–40.

G. Rotter, *Die Stellung des Negers in der islamisch–arabischer Gesellschaft bis zum 16ten Jahrhundert* (Bonn, 1967).

The life of houses

J. C. Garcin and others, *Palais et maisons du Caire: L'époque mamelouk (13e–16e siècle)* (Paris, 1982).

D. Waines, 'Cuisine' in T. Mostyn and A. Hourani (eds.), *The Cambridge Encyclopedia of the Middle East and North Africa* (Cambridge, 1988), pp. 240–3.

Chapter 8 Cities and Their Rulers

Armies

V. J. Parry and M. E. Yapp (eds.), *War, Technology and Society in the Middle East* (London, 1975).

D. Ayalon, *Gunpowder and Firearms in the Mamluk Kingdom* (London, 1956).

D. Ayalon, *The Mamluk Military Society* (London, 1979).

Loyalties

R. Mottahedeh, *Loyalty and Leadership in an Early Islamic Society* (Princeton, 1980).

C. Cahen, 'Mouvements populaires et autonomisme urbain dans L'Asie musulmane du moyen âge', *Arabica*: Vol. 5 (1958), pp. 225–50, Vol. 6 (1959), pp. 25–56, 233–65.

Adminstration

C. F. Petry, *The Civilian Élite of Cairo in the Later Middle Ages* (Princeton, 1981).

J. P. Nielsen, *Secular Justice in an Islamic State: mazalim under the Bahri Mamlukes* (Leiden, 1985).

R. Brunschvig, 'Urbanisme médiéval et droit musulman', *Revue des Études Islamiques* (1947), pp. 127–55.

B. Johansen, '*Amwal zahira wa amwal batina*: town and countryside as reflected in the tax-system of the Hanafite School' in W. al-Qadi (ed.), *Studia Arabica and Islamica* (Beirut, 1981), pp. 247–63.

B. Johansen, 'The all-embracing town and its mosques', *Revue de l'Occident Musulman et de la Méditerranée*, Vol. 32 (1981), pp. 139–61.

A. Raymond, 'Espaces publics et espaces privés dans les villes arabes traditionelles', *Maghreb Mashrek*, No. 123 (1989), pp. 194–201.

Control of the land
C. Cahen, 'L'évolution de l'iqta' du 9e au 13e siècle' in Cahen, *Les Peuples musulmans dans l'histoire médiévale* (Damascus, 1977), pp. 231–69.
A. K. S. Lambton, 'The evolution of the *iqta'* in medieval Iran', *Iran*, Vol. 5 (1967), pp. 41–50.

Political theory
'Ali ibn Muhammad al-Mawardi, *al-Ahkam al-sultaniyya* (Cairo, AH 1298/1881); French trans. E. Fagnan, *Les statuts gouvernementaux*, reprint (Paris, 1982).
Husayn ibn 'Ali, Nizam al-Mulk, *Siyaset-name*; English trans. H. Darke, *The Book of Government, or Rules for Kings*, 2nd edn (London, 1978).
Ahmad Ibn Taimiyya, *al-Siyasa al-shar'iyya fi islah al-ra'y wa'l-ra'iyya* (Baghdad, n.d.); French trans. H. Laoust, *Le traité de droit public d'Ibn Taimiya* (Beirut, 1948).
Muhammad al-Farabi, *Ara ahl al-madina al-fadila*; text and English trans. R. Walzer, *Al-Farabi on the Perfect State* (Oxford, 1985).

Chapter 9 Ways of Islam

Pillars of Islam
G. E. von Grunebaum, *Muhammadan Festivals* (New York, 1951).
M. Gaudefroy-Demombynes, *Le pélerinage à la Mekke* (Paris, 1923).
J. Jomier, *Le mahmal et la caravanne égyptienne des pélerins de la Mecque 13e–20e siècle* (Cairo, 1953).
'Ali ibn Abi Bakr al-Harawi, *Kitab al-isharat ila ma'rifat al-ziyarat* (Damascus, 1957); French trans. J. Sourdel-Thomine, *Guide des lieux de pélerinage* (Damascus, 1957).
R. Peters, *Islam and Colonialism: the doctrine of jihad in modern history* (The Hague, 1979), pp. 9–37.

Saints and Sufis
J. S. Trimingham, *The Sufi Orders in Islam* (Oxford, 1971).
C. Padwick, *Muslim Devotions* (London, 1961).
J. A. Williams (ed.), *Themes of Islamic Civilization* (Berkeley, 1971), 'The friends of God', pp. 307–70.
I. Goldziher, *Muhammedanische Studien*, Vol. 2 (Halle, 1890), pp. 277–378; English translation S. M. Stern, *Muslim Studies*, Vol. 2 (London, 1971), 'Veneration of saints in Islam', pp. 255–341.
T. Canaan, *Mohammedan Saints and Sanctuaries in Palestine* (London, 1927).
J. S. Macpherson, *The Mawlids of Egypt* (Cairo, 1941).
E. A. Westermarck, *Pagan Survivals in Mohammedan Civilization* (London, 1933).

Mahdism
W. Madelung, 'al-Mahdi', *Encyclopaedia of Islam*, 2nd edn, Vol. 5, pp. 1230–8.
I. Goldziher (ed.), *Le livre de Mohamed ibn Tumart, mahdi des Almohades* (Algiers, 1903).

Chapter 10 The Culture of the *'Ulama*

Codes of law
L. Milliot, *Introduction à l'étude du droit musulman* (Paris, 1953).
'Abd Allah ibn Abi Zayd al-Qayrawani, *Risala*; text and French trans. L. Bercher, *La Risala ou Epitre sur les éléments du dogme et de la loi de l'islam selon le rite malekite* (Algiers, 1949).

'Abd Allah ibn Ahmad ibn Qudama, *Kitab al-'umda fi ahkam al-fiqh* (Cairo, 1933); French trans. H. Laoust, *Le précis de droit d'Ibn Qudama* (Beirut, 1950).

J. Berque, "Amal', *Encyclopaedia of Islam*, 2nd edn, Vol. 1, pp. 427–8.

A. Layish and A. Shmueli, 'Custom and *shari'a* in the Beduin family according to legal documents from the Judaean desert', *Bulletin of the School of Oriental and African Studies*, Vol. 42 (1979), pp. 29–45.

Madrasas

G. Makdisi, *The Rise of Colleges: institutions of learning in Islam and the West* (Edinburgh, 1981).

J. Berque, 'Ville et université: aperçu sur l'histoire de l'école de Fès', *Revue Historique du Droit Français et Etranger*, Vol. 27 (1949), pp. 64–117.

Biographical dictionaries

H. A. R. Gibb, 'Islamic biographical literature' in B. Lewis and P. M. Holt (eds.), *Historians of the Middle East* (London, 1962), pp. 54–8.

Ahmad ibn Muhammad Ibn Khallikan, *Wafayat al-a'yan wa anba abna al-zaman*, ed. I. 'Abbas, 8 vols. (Beirut, 1968–72).

al-Ghazali

W. M. Watt, *Muslim Intellectual* (Edinburgh, 1963).

Muhammad al-Ghazali, *Ihya 'ulum al-din*, 4 vols. (Cairo, 1916).

G. H. Bousquet, *Ihya ouloum ed-din ou vivification des sciences de la foi: analyse et index* (Paris, 1955).

Muhammad al-Ghazali, *al-Munqidh min al-dalal*, ed. J. Saliba and K. 'Ayyad (Damascus, 1939); English trans. R. J. McCarthy, *Freedom and Fulfilment* (Boston, 1980).

F. Jabr, *La notion de la ma'rifa chez Ghazali* (Beirut, 1958).

Chapter 11 Divergent Paths of Thought

Philosophy

L. Gardet, *La pensée religieuse d'Avicenne* (Paris, 1955).

W. E. Gohlman (ed. and trans.), *The Life of Ibn Sina* (Albany, New York, 1974).

al-Husayn ibn 'Abd Allah ibn Sina, *Kitab al-isharat wa'l-tanbihat*, ed. S. Dunya, 4 vols. (Cairo, 1957–60); French trans. A. M. Goichon, *Livre des directives et remarques* (Paris, 1951).

A. M. Goichon, *Lexique de la langue philosophique d'Ibn Sina* (Paris, 1938).

Muhammad al-Ghazali, *Tahafut al-falasifa*, ed. S. Dunya, 3rd edn (Cairo, 1964).

Muhammad ibn Ahmad ibn Rushd, *Tahafut al-tahafut*, ed. S. Dunya (Cairo, 1964); English trans. S. van den Bergh (London, 1954).

Muhammad ibn Ahmad ibn Rushd, *Fasl al-maqal*, ed. G. F. Hourani (Leiden, 1959); English trans. G. F. Hourani, *Averroes on the Harmony of Religion and Philosophy* (London, 1961).

Ibn 'Arabi

Muhyi al-Din ibn 'Arabi, *Fusus al-hikam*, ed. A. 'Afifi (Cairo, 1946); English trans. R. J. W. Austin, *The Bezels of Wisdom* (London, 1980).

A. E. Affifi, *The Mystical Philosophy of Muhyid Din Ibnul Arabi* (Cambridge, 1939).

O. Yahia, *Histoire et classification de l'œuvre d'Ibn 'Arabi*, 2 vols. (Damascus, 1964).

T. Izutsu, *Sufism and Taosim: a comparative study of key philosophical concepts*, revised edn (Berkeley, 1984).

Ibn Taymiyya
H. Laoust, *Essai sur les doctrines sociales et politiques de Taki-d-Din Ahmad b. Taimiya* (Cairo, 1939).

Shiʻi thought
H. Modarressi Tabataba'i, *An Introduction to Shiʻi Law* (London, 1984).
D. M. Donaldson, *The Shiʻite Religion* (London, 1933).
E. Kohlberg, 'From Imamiyya to Ithnaʻashariyya', *Bulletin of the School of Oriental and African Studies*, Vol. 39 (1976), pp. 521–34.

Druzes
M. G. S. Hodgson, 'Duruz', *Encyclopaedia of Islam*, 2nd edn, Vol. 2, pp. 631–4.
D. Bryer, 'The origins of the Druze religion', *Der Islam*: Vol. 52 (1975), pp. 47–84, 239–62; Vol. 53 (1976), pp. 5–27.
N. M. Abu Izzeddin, *The Druzes* (Leiden, 1984).

Christians and Jews
A. S. Atiya, *A History of Eastern Christianity* (London, 1968).
G. Graf, *Geschichte der christliche arabischen Literatur*, 5 vols. (Vatican, 1944–53).
N. Stillman (ed.), *The Jews of Arab Lands* (Philadelphia, 1979).

Shared cults
F. W. Hasluck, *Christianity and Islam under the Sultans*, 2 vols. (Oxford, 1929).
N. Slousch, *Travels in North Africa* (Philadelphia, 1927).

Chapter 12 The Culture of Courts and People

Andalusian society and culture
E. Lévi-Provençal, *La civilisation arabe en Espagne* (Cairo, 1938).
T. F. Glick, *Islamic and Christian Spain in the Early Middle Ages* (Princeton, 1979).
R. I. Burns, *Islam under the Crusades: colonial survival in the thirteenth-century kingdom of Valencia* (Princeton, 1973).

Art and architecture
K. A. C. Creswell, *The Muslim Architecture of Egypt*, 2 vols. (Oxford, 1952–9).
G. Marçais, *L'architecture musulmane de l'occident* (Paris, 1954).
O. Grabar, *The Alhambra* (London, 1975).
R. Ettinghausen, *Arab Painting* (Lausanne, 1962).
O. Grabar, *The Illustrations of the Maqamat* (Chicago, 1984).
A. Lane, *Early Islamic Pottery* (London, 1947).
A. Lane, *Later Islamic Pottery*, 2nd edn (London, 1971).
J. W. Allan, *Islamic Metalwork: the Nuhad es-Said collection* (London, 1982).
J. Lehrman, *Earthly Paradise: garden and courtyard in Islam* (London, 1980).
J. Dickie, 'The Hispano-Arab garden', *Bulletin of the School of Oriental and African Studies*, Vol. 31 (1958), pp. 237–48.

Literature
I. 'Abbas, *Tarikh al-adab al-andalusi*, 2nd edn, 2 vols. (Beirut, 1969–71).
S. M. Stern, *Hispano-Arabic Strophic Poetry* (Oxford, 1974).
Ahmad ibn 'Abd Allah ibn Zaydun, *Diwan*, ed. K. al-Bustani (Beirut, 1951).
Abu Bakr ibn al-Tufayl, *Hayy ibn Yaqdhan*, ed. J. Saliba and K. 'Ayyad, 5th edn (Damascus, 1940); English trans. L. E. Goodman, *Hayy ibn Yaqzan* (New York, 1972).
D. Goldstein (ed.), *The Jewish Poets of Spain 900–1250* (Harmondsworth, Middlesex, 1971).

M. M. Badawi, 'Medieval Arabic drama: Ibn Daniyal', *Journal of Arabic Literature*, Vol. 13 (1982), pp. 83–107.
Y. Eche, *Les bibliothèques arabes* (Damascus, 1962).

Popular literature and romance
P. J. Cachia, *Narrative Ballads of Modern Egypt* (Oxford, 1988).
H. T. Norris, *The Adventures of Antar* (Warminster, Wiltshire, 1988).
H. T. Norris, *Saharan Myth and Saga* (Oxford, 1972).
A. Miquel and P. Kemp, *Majnun et Layla: l'amour fou* (Paris, 1984).
M. Mahdi, *Kitab alf layla wa layla* (Leiden, 1984).
D. B. Macdonald, 'The earlier history of the Arabian Nights', *Journal of the Royal Asiatic Society* (1924), pp. 353–97.
P. Heath, 'Romance as genre in *The Thousand and One Nights*', *Journal of Arabic Literature*: Vol. 18 (1987), pp. 1–21; Vol. 19 (1988), pp. 1–26.

Music
H. G. Farmer, *A History of Arabian Music* (London, 1929).
Abu'l-Faraj al-Isbahani, *Kitab al-aghani*, 30 vols. (Cairo, 1969–79).
Muhammad al-Ghazali, *Ihya 'ulum al-din* (Cairo, 1916), Vol. 2, pp. 236–69; English trans. D. B. Macdonald, 'Emotional religion in Islam as affected by music and singing', *Journal of the Royal Asiatic Society* (1901), pp. 198–252, 705–48; (1902), pp. 1–28.
O. Wright, 'Music', in J. Schacht and C. E. Bosworth (eds.), *The Legacy of Islam* (Oxford, 1974), pp. 489–505.
O. Wright and others, 'Arabic music' in S. Sadie (ed.), *The New Grove Dictionary of Music and Musicians* (London, 1980), Vol. 1, pp. 514–39.
E. Neubauer, 'Islamic religious music' in *The New Grove Dictionary of Music and Musicians*, Vol. 9, pp. 342–9.
O. Wright, *The Modal System of Arab and Persian Music A.D. 1250–1300* (Oxford, 1978).

Science and medicine
A. I. Sabra, 'The scientific enterprise' in B. Lewis (ed.), *The World of Islam* (London, 1976), pp. 181–200.
A. I. Sabra, 'The exact sciences' in J. R. Hayes (ed.), *The Genius of Arab Civilization* (London, 1976).
J. Vernet, 'Mathematics, astronomy, optics' in J. Schacht and C. E. Bosworth (eds.), *The Legacy of Islam* (Oxford, 1974), pp. 461–89.
M. Ullmann, *Islamic Medicine* (Edinburgh, 1978).
M. Ullmann, *Die Medizin in Islam* (Leiden, 1970).
P. Johnstone, 'Tradition in Arabic Medicine', *Palestine Exploration Quarterly*, Vol. 107 (1975), pp. 23–37.

The occult
L. Thorndike, *A History of Magic and Experimental Science*, Vol. 1, Parts 1 and 2 (New York, 1934).
M. Ullmann, *Die Natur und Geheimwissenschaften in Islam* (Leiden, 1972).
G. E. von Grunebaum and R. Caillois (eds.), *The Dream and Human Societies* (Berkeley, 1966).

PART III THE OTTOMAN AGE (SIXTEENTH–EIGHTEENTH CENTURY)

General histories
P. Kinross, *The Ottoman Centuries: the rise and fall of the Turkish empire* (London, 1977).
S. J. and E. Shaw, *A History of the Ottoman Empire and Turkey*, 2 vols. (Cambridge, 1976–7).
R. Mantran (ed.), *Histoire de l'empire ottoman* (Paris, 1989).
I. H. Uzunçarsılı, *Osmanli Tarihi*, Vols. 1–4, new edn (Ankara, 1982–3).
E. Z. Karal, *Osmanlı Tarihi*, Vols. 6–8, new edn (Ankara, 1983).
A. K. Rafiq, *Bilad al-Sham wa Misr 1516–1798*, 2nd edn (Damascus, 1968).

Chapter 13 The Ottoman Empire

The rise of Ottoman power
P. Wittek, *The Rise of the Ottoman Empire* (London, 1971).
R. P. Lindner, *Nomads and Ottomans in Medieval Anatolia* (Bloomington, Indiana, 1983).
A. Hess, *The Forgotten Frontier: a history of the sixteenth century Ibero-African frontier* (Chicago, 1978).
A. Hess, 'The evolution of the Ottoman seaborne empire in the age of the oceanic discoveries, 1453–1525', *American Historical Review*, Vol. 75 (1970), pp. 1892–1919.
R. H. Savory, *Iran under the Safavids* (London, 1980).
F. Braudel, *La Méditerranée et le monde méditerranéen à l'époque de Philippe II*, 2nd edn, 2 vols. (Paris, 1966); English trans. *The Mediterranean and the Mediterranean World in the Age of Philip II*, 2 vols. (London, 1972–3).

The structure of government
H. Inalcık, *The Ottoman Empire: the classical age, 1300–1600* (London, 1973).
H. Inalcık, *The Ottoman Empire: conquest, organization and economy* (London, 1976).
A. D. Alderson, *The Structure of the Ottoman Dynasty* (Oxford, 1956).
I. H. Uzunçarsılı, *Osmanlı Devletinin Teşkilâtından Kapukulu Ocakları*, 2 vols. (Ankara, 1943–4).
I. H. Uzunçarsılı, *Osmanlı Devletinin Saray Teşkilâtı* (Ankara, 1945).
N. Itzkowitz, *Ottoman Empire and Islamic Tradition* (New York, 1972).
C. Fleischer, *Bureaucrat and Intellectual in the Ottoman Empire* (Princeton, 1986).
M. Kunt, *The Sultan's Servants: the transformation of Ottoman provincial government, 1550–1650* (New York, 1983).
O. G. de Busbecq, *The Turkish Letters of Ogier Ghiselle de Busbecq*, English trans. (Oxford, 1927).
P. Rycaut, *The History of the Present State of the Ottoman Empire*, 4th edn (London, 1675).

Examples of Ottoman documents
Ö. L. Barkan, *Kanunlar* (Istanbul, 1943).
R. Mantran and J. Sauvaget, *Règlements fiscaux ottomans: les provinces syriennes* (Beirut, 1951).
R. Mantran, 'Règlements fiscaux: la province de Bassora', *Journal of the Economic and Social History of the Orient*, Vol. 10 (1967), pp. 224–77.
U. Heyd, *Documents on Palestine 1552–1615* (Oxford, 1960).
R. Mantran, *Inventaire des documents d'archive turcs du Dar-el-Bey (Tunis)* (Paris, 1961).
A. Temimi, *Sommaire des registres arabes et turcs d'Alger* (Tunis, 1979).

Religious and judicial organization
I. H. Uzunçarsılı, *Osmanlı Devletinin Ilmiye Teşkilâtı* (Ankara, 1965).
U. Heyd, *Studies in Old Ottoman Criminal Law* (Oxford, 1973).
U. Heyd, 'Some aspects of the Ottoman fetva', *Bulletin of the School of Oriental and African Studies*, Vol. 32 (1969), pp. 35–56.
R. C. Repp, *The Mufti of Istanbul* (London, 1986).
R. C. Repp, 'Some observations on the development of the Ottoman learned hierarchy' in N. Keddie (ed.), *Scholars, Saints and Sufis* (Berkeley, 1972), pp. 17–32.

Government in the Arab provinces
A. Raymond, 'Les provinces arabes 16e–18e siècle' in R. Mantran (ed.), *Histoire de l'empire ottoman* (Paris, 1989), pp. 341–420.
P. M. Holt, *Egypt and the Fertile Crescent 1516–1922* (London, 1962).
P. M. Holt, *Studies in the History of the Near East* (London, 1973).
S. H. Longrigg, *Four Centuries of Modern Iraq* (Oxford, 1925).
A. M. Al-'Azzawi, *Tarikh al-'Iraq bayn ihtilalayn*, 5 vols. (Baghdad, 1935–56).
A. Abu-Husayn, *Provincial Leadership in Syria 1575–1650* (Beirut, 1985).
K. S. Salibi, *The Modern History of Lebanon* (London, 1965).
A. Cohen and B. Lewis, *Population and Revenue in the Towns of Palestine in the Sixteenth Century* (Princeton, 1978).
W. D. Hütteroth and K. Abdelfattah, *Historical Geography of Palestine, Transjordan and Southern Syria in the Late 16th Century* (Erlangen, 1972).

Chapter 14 Ottoman Societies

Population
Ö. L. Barkan, 'Essai sur les données statistiques des registres de recensement dans l'empire ottoman aux 15e et 16e siècles', *Journal of the Economic and Social History of the Orient*, Vol. 1 (1958), pp. 9–36.
M. A. Cook, *Population Pressure in Rural Anatolia 1450–1600* (London, 1972).
D. Panzac, *La peste dans l'empire ottoman* (Louvain, 1985).

Trade
S. Faroghi, *Towns and Townsmen of Ottoman Anatolia: trade, crafts and food-production in an urban setting 1520–1620* (Cambridge, 1984).
S. Faroghi, *Peasants, Dervishes and Traders in the Ottoman Empire* (London, 1986).
R. Mantran, 'L'empire ottoman et le commerce asiatique aux 16e et 17e siècles' in D. S. Richards (ed.), *Islam and the Trade of Asia* (Oxford, 1970), pp. 169–79.

Istanbul
H. Inalcık, 'Istanbul', *Encyclopaedia of Islam*, 2nd edn, Vol. 4, pp. 224–48.
R. Mantran, *Istanbul dans la seconde moitié du 17e siècle* (Paris, 1962).
L. Güçer, 'Le commerce intérieur des céréales dans l'empire ottoman pendant la seconde moitié du 16e siècle', *Revue de la Faculté des Sciences Economiques de l'Université d'Istanbul*, Vol. 11 (1949–50), pp. 163–88.
L. Güçer, 'L'approvisionnement d'Istanbul en céréales vers le milieu du 18e siècle', ibid., pp. 153–62.

Arab cities
A. Raymond, *The Great Arab Cities in the 16th–18th centuries* (New York, 1984).
A. Raymond, *Les grandes villes arabes a l'époque ottomane* (Paris, 1985).
A. Tamimi (ed.), *al-Hayat al iqtisadi li'l-wilayat al-'arabiyya wa masadiruha fi'l-'ahd al-*

'uthmani, 3 vols.: Vols. 1 and 2 Arabic, Vol. 3 French and English (Zaghouan, Tunisia, 1986).

A. Abdel-Nour, *Introduction à l'histoire urbaine de la Syrie ottomane* (Beirut, 1982).

Buildings

G. Goodwin, *A History of Ottoman Architecture* (London, 1971).

J. Revault, *Palais et demeures de Tunis, 16e et 17e siècles* (Paris, 1967).

B. Maury and others, *Palais et maisons du Caire: époque ottomane, 16e–18e siècle* (Paris, 1967).

Religion and literature

N. Keddie (ed.), *Scholars, Saints and Sufis* (Berkeley, 1972).

L. W. Thomas, *A Study of Naima* (New York, 1972).

A. Abdesselam, *Les Historiens tunisiens des 17e, 18e et 19e siècles* (Paris, 1973).

J. Berque, *L'intérieur du Maghreb 15e–19e siècles* (Paris, 1978).

J. Berque, *Ulémas, fondateurs, insurgés du Maghreb* (Paris, 1982).

B. Braude and B. Lewis (eds.), *Christians and Jews in the Ottoman Empire*, 2 vols. (New York, 1982).

S. Runciman, *The Great Church in Captivity* (Cambridge, 1968).

G. Scholem, *Sabbatai Sevi: The Mystical Messiah, 1626–1676* (London, 1973).

Sudan

P. M. Holt and M. W. Daly, *A History of the Sudan*, 4th edn (London, 1988).

Morocco

Ahmad al-Nasiri al-Salawi, *Kitab al-istiqsa li akhbar duwal al-maghrib al-aqsa*, 9 vols. (Casablanca, 1954–6); French trans. 'Histoire des dynasties du Maroc', *Archives Marocaines*, Vols. 9 (1906), 10 (1907), 30 (1923), 31 (1925), 32 (1927), 33 (1934).

H. de Castries, *Les sources inédites de l'histoire du Maroc de 1530 à 1845*, 26 vols. (Paris, 1905–60).

E. Lévi-Provençal, *Les historiens des chorfa* (Paris, 1922).

J. Berque, *Al-Yousi: problèmes de la culture marocaine au 17e siècle* (Paris, 1958).

Chapter 15 The Changing Balance of Power in the Eighteenth Century

General introduction

T. Naff and R. Owen (eds.), *The Islamic World in the 18th Century* (Carbondale, Illinois, 1977).

The central government

I. Moradgea d'Ohsson, *Tableau générale de l'empire ottoman*, 7 vols. (Paris, 1788–1924).

H. A. R. Gibb and H. Bowen, *Islamic Society and the West*, Vol. 1, Part i (London, 1950).

N. Itzkowitz, 'Eighteenth century Ottoman realities', *Studia Islamica*, Vol. 16 (1961), pp. 73–94.

R. A. Abou-el-Haj, *The 1703 Rebellion and the Structure of Ottoman Politics* (Istanbul, 1984).

M. Aktepe, *Patrona Isyanı 1730* (Istanbul, 1958).

The Arab provinces

P. Kemp, *Territoires d'Islam: le monde vu de Mossoul au 18e siècle* (Paris, 1982).

H. L. Bodman, *Political Factors in Aleppo 1760–1826* (Chapel Hill, North Carolina, 1963).

A. Russell, *The Natural History of Aleppo*, 2nd edn, 2 vols. (London, 1794).

J. L Burckhardt, *Travels in Syria and the Holy Land* (London, 1822).

A. K. Rafeq, *The Province of Damascus 1723–1783* (Beirut, 1966).

K. K. Barbir, *Ottoman Rule in Damascus 1708–1758* (Princeton, 1980).

K. K. Barbir, 'From pasha to efendi: the assimilation of Ottomans into Damascene society 1516–1783', *International Journal of Turkish Studies*, Vol. 1 (1979–80), pp. 63–83.

A. Cohen, *Palestine in the Eighteenth Century* (Jerusalem, 1973).

A. al-Budayri al-Hallaq, *Hawadith Dimashq al-yawmiyya* (Cairo, 1959).

A. Raymond, *Artisans et commerçants au Caire au 18e siècle*, 2 vols. (Damascus, 1973–4).

A. Raymond, 'Problèmes urbains et urbanisme au Caire aux 17e et 18e siècles' in A. Raymond and others, *Actes du colloque internationale sur l'histoire du Caire* (Cairo, 1973), pp. 353–72.

A. Raymond, 'Essai de géographie des quartiers de résidence aristocratique au Caire au 18e siècle', *Journal of the Economic and Social History of the Orient*, Vol. 6 (1963), pp. 58–103.

Description de l'Egypte, 9 vols. text, 14 vols. plates (Paris, 1809–28).

C. F. Volney, *Voyages en Syrie et en Egypte*, 2 vols. (Paris, 1787); English trans. *Travels through Syria and Egypt*, 2 vols. (Dublin, 1793).

'Abd al-Rahman al-Jabarti, *'Aja'ib al-athar fi'l-tarajim wa'l-akhbar*, 4 vols. (Bulaq, 1879–80).

Arabia

C. Niebuhr, *Reisebeschreibung nach Arabien*, 3 vols. (Copenhagen, 1774–8); English trans. *Travels through Arabia*, 2 vols. (Edinburgh, 1792).

The Maghrib

L. Valensi, *Le Maghreb avant la prise d'Alger 1790–1830* (Paris, 1969); English trans. *On the Eve of Colonialism* (New York, 1977).

M. H. Chérif, *Pouvoir et société dans la Tunisie de Husain bin 'Ali*, 2 vols. (Tunis, 1984–6).

Muhammad ibn Tayyib al-Qadiri, ed. N. Cigar, *Nashr al-mathani* (London, 1981).

Economic change

A. Raymond, 'L'impact de la pénétration européenne sur l'économie de l'Egypte au 18e siècle', *Annales Islamologiques* 18 (1982), pp. 217–35.

R. Paris, *Histoire du commerce de Marseille*, Vol. 5: *Le Levant* (Paris, 1957).

R. Davis, *Aleppo and Devonshire Square* (London, 1967).

M. von Oppenheim, *Die Beduinen*, 4 vols. (Leipzig/Wiesbaden, (1939–67).

A. A. 'Abd al-Rahim, *al-Rif al-misri fi'l-qarn al-thamin 'ashar* (Cairo, 1974).

K. M. Cuno, 'The origins of private ownership of land in Egypt: a reappraisal', *International Journal of Middle East Studies*, Vol. 12 (1980), pp. 245–75.

L. Valensi, *Fellahs tunisiens: l'économie rurale et la vie des campagnes aux 18e et 19e siècles* (Paris, 1977); English trans. *Tunisien Peasants in the 18th and 19th Centuries* (Cambridge, 1985).

Architecture and art

J. Revault, *Palais et demeures de Tunis: 18e et 19e siècles* (Paris, 1971).

J. Carswell and C. J. F. Dowsett, *Kütahya Tiles and Pottery from the Armenian Cathedral of St James, Jerusalem*, 2 vols. (Oxford, 1972).

J. Carswell, 'From the tulip to the rose' in T. Naff and R. Owen (eds.), *Studies in Eighteenth Century Islamic History* (Carbondale, Illinois, 1977), pp. 325–55.

Religion and literature

H. A. R. Gibb and H. Bowen, *Islamic Society and the West*, Vol. 1, Part ii (London, 1957).

J. Heyworth-Dunne, *Introduction to the History of Education in Modern Egypt* (London, 1939).

A. Hourani, 'Aspects of Islamic culture: introduction' in T. Naff and R. Owen (eds.), *Studies in Eighteenth Century Islamic History* (Carbondale, Illinois, 1977), pp. 253–76.

N. Levtzion and J. O. Voll (eds.), *Eighteenth Century Revival and Reform in Islam* (Syracuse, New York, 1987).

J. O. Voll, *Islam: continuity and change in the modern world* (London, 1982).

Muhammad Khalil al-Muradi, *Silk al-durar fi a'yan al-qarn al-thani 'ashar*, 4 vols. (Bulaq, 1883).

M. H. Chérif, 'Hommes de religion et de pouvoir dans la Tunisie de l'époque moderne', *Annales ESC*, Vol. 35 (1980), pp. 580–97.

Wahhabism

H. St J. Philby, *Saudi Arabia* (London, 1955).

H. Laoust, *Essai sur les doctrines sociales et politiques de Taki-d-Din b. Taimiya* (Cairo, 1939), pp. 506–40.

PART IV THE AGE OF EUROPEAN EMPIRES (1800–1939)

The 'Eastern question'

M. S. Anderson, *The Eastern Question 1774–1923* (London, 1966).

J. C. Hurewitz (ed.), *The Middle East and North Africa in World Politics*, 2 vols. (New Haven, 1975).

L. C. Brown, *International Politics and the Middle East* (London, 1984).

General surveys

M. E. Yapp, *The Making of the Modern Middle East 1798–1923* (London, 1987).

B. Lewis, *The Emergence of Modern Turkey* (London, 1961).

W. R. Polk and R. L. Chambers (eds.), *Beginnings of Modernization in the Middle East* (Chicago, 1968).

Groupes de Recherches et d'Études sur le Proche-Orient, *L'Egypte au 19e siècle* (Paris, 1982).

Economic and social change

C. Issawi, *An Economic History of the Middle East and North Africa* (New York, 1982).

C. Issawi (ed.), *The Economic History of the Middle East 1800–1914* (Chicago, 1966).

C. Issawi (ed.), *The Fertile Crescent 1800–1914* (New York, 1988).

R. Owen, *The Middle East in the World Economy 1800–1914* (London, 1981).

S. Pamuk, *The Ottoman Empire and World Capitalism 1820–1913* (Cambridge, 1987).

G. Baer, *Studies in the Social History of Modern Egypt* (Chicago, 1969).

A. Barakat, *Tatawwur al-milkiyya al-zira'iyya fi Misr wa atharuha 'ala al-harakat al-siyasiyya 1813–1914* (Cairo, 1977).

Intellectual change

N. Berkes, *The Development of Secularism in Turkey* (Montreal, 1964).

A. Hourani, *Arabic Thought in the Liberal Age*, revised edn (Cambridge, 1983).

Chapter 16 European Power and Reforming Governments (1800–1860)

The expansion of Europe

F. Charles-Roux, *Bonaparte Governor d'Egypte* (Paris, 1936); English trans. *Bonaparte Gouverneur of Egypt* (London, 1937).

H. L. Hoskins, *British Routes to India* (New York, 1928).

J. B. Kelly, *Britain and the Persian Gulf 1795–1880* (Oxford, 1968).
C. A. Julien, *Histoire de l'Algérie contemporaine*, Vol. 1 1827–71 (Paris, 1964).
R. Danziger, *Abd al-Qadir and the Algerians* (New York, 1977).

The Tanzimat and local movements
Turkish Ministry of Education, *Tanzimat* (Istanbul, 1940).
Cevdet Paşa, *Tezâkir*, 4 vols. (Ankara, 1953–67).
C. V. Findley, *Bureaucratic Reform in the Ottoman Empire* (Princeton, 1980).
U. Heyd, 'The Ottoman 'ulama and westernization in the time of Selim III and Mahmud II'
    in Heyd (ed.), *Studies in Islamic History and Civilization* (Jerusalem, 1960), pp. 63–96.
R. Clogg (ed.), *The Movement for Greek Independence 1770–1821* (London, 1976).
L. S. Stavrianos, *The Balkans since 1453* (New York, 1958).
M. Maoz, *Ottoman Reform in Syria and Palestine 1840–1861* (Oxford, 1968).
A. Hourani, 'Ottoman reform and the politics of notables' in Hourani, *The Emergence of
    the Modern Middle East* (London, 1981), pp. 36–66.

Egypt
A. Lutfi al-Sayyid Marsot, *Egypt in the Reign of Muhammad 'Ali* (Cambridge, 1984).
E. R. Toledano, *State and Society in Mid-Nineteenth-Century Egypt* (Cambridge, 1990).
A. R. al-Rafi'i, *Tarikh al-haraka al-qawmiyya wa tatawwur nizam al-hukm fi Misr*, 14 vols.
    (Cairo, 1929–51).

Tunisia
L. C. Brown, *The Tunisia of Ahmad Bey 1837–1855* (Princeton, 1974).

Morocco
J. L. Miège, *Le Maroc et l'Europe*, 4 vols. (Paris, 1961–3).
J. L. Miège (ed.), *Documents d'histoire économique et sociale marocaine au 19e siècle*
    (Paris, 1969).

Chapter 17 European Empires and Dominant Élites (1860–1914).

The 'Eastern question'
W. L. Langer, *The Diplomacy of Imperialism 1890–1902*, 2nd edn (New York, 1951).
E. M. Earle, *Turkey, the Great Powers and the Baghdad Railway* (New York, 1966).

The Ottoman government and the provinces
R. H. Davison, *Reform in the Ottoman Empire 1856–1876* (Princeton, 1963).
R. Devereux, *The First Ottoman Constitutional Period* (Baltimore, 1963).
R. Abu Manneh, 'Sultan Abdulhamid II and Shaikh Abulhuda al-Sayyadi', *Middle Eastern
    Studies 15* (1979), pp. 131–53.
C. Findley, *Ottoman Civil Officialdom* (Princeton, 1989).
E. E. Ramsaur, *The Young Turks: prelude to the revolution of 1908* (Princeton, 1957).
F. Ahmed, *The Young Turks: the Committee of Union and Progress in Turkish politics
    1908–1914* (Oxford, 1969).
W. Ochsenwald, *Religion, Society and the State in Arabia: the Hejaz under Ottoman
    control 1840–1908* (Columbus, Ohio, 1984).
L. Nalbandian, *The Armenian Revolutionary Movement* (Berkeley, 1963).

Beginnings of Zionist immigration
W. Z. Laqueur, *A History of Zionism* (London, 1972).
N. Mandel, *The Arabs and Zionism before World War I* (Berkeley, 1976).

Egypt
R. Hunter, *Egypt under the Khedives 1805–1879* (Pittsburgh, 1984).
Nubar Pasha, *Mémoires* (Beirut, 1983).
D. Landes, *Bankers and Pashas* (London, 1958).
J. Marlowe, *The Making of the Suez Canal* (London, 1964).
A. Schölch, *Ägypten den Ägyptern!* (Zurich, 1972); English trans. *Egypt for the Egyptians!: the socio-political crisis in Egypt 1878–1882* (London, 1981).
Lord Cromer, *Modern Egypt*, 2 vols. (London, 1908).
J. Berque, *L'Egypte, impérialisme et révolution* (Paris, 1963); English trans. *Egypt, Imperialism and Revolution* (London, 1972).
A. Lutfi al-Sayyid, *Egypt and Cromer* (London, 1968).
T. Mitchell, *Colonising Egypt* (Cambridge, 1988).

Sudan
P. M. Holt, *The Mahdist State in the Sudan 1881–1898* (Oxford, 1958).
M. W. Daly, *Empire on the Nile: the Anglo-Egyptian Sudan 1898–1934* (Cambridge, 1986).
Abu Bakr (Babikr) Badri, *Tarikh hayati*, 3 vols. (Omdurman, 1959–61); English trans. *The Memoirs of Babikr Badri*: Vol. 1 (London, 1969), Vol. 2 (London, 1980).

France and the Maghrib
J. Ganiage, *Les Origines du protectorat français en Tunisie 1861–1881* (Tunis, 1968).
C. R. Ageron, *Histoire de l'Algérie contemporaine*, Vol. 2: *1871–1954* (Paris, 1979).
C. R. Ageron, *Les algériens musulmans et la France 1871–1919* (Paris, 1968).
E. Burke, *Prelude to Protectorate in Morocco* (Chicago, 1976).
D. Rivet, *Lyautey et l'institution du protectorat français au Maroc 1912–1925*, 3 vols. (Paris, 1988).

Population and economic change
A. Jwaideh, 'Midhat Pasha and the land system of lower Iraq' in A. Hourani (ed.), *St Antony's Papers: Middle Eastern Affairs 3* (London, 1963), pp. 106–36.
N. N. Lewis, *Nomads and Settlers in Syria and Jordan 1800–1980* (Cambridge, 1987).
R. Aboujaber, *Pioneers over Jordan* (London, 1989).
A. Schölch, *Palästina im Umbruch 1856–1882* (Stuttgart, 1986).
B. Labaki, *Introduction à l'histoire économique du Liban: soie et commerce extérieur . . . 1840–1914* (Beirut, 1984).
D. Chevallier, *La société du Mont Liban à l'époque de la révolution industrielle en Europe* (Paris, 1971).
E. J. R. Owen, *Cotton and the Egyptian Economy 1820–1914* (London, 1962).
G. Baer, *Introduction to the History of Landownership in Modern Egypt 1800–1950* (London, 1962).
J. Poncet, *La colonisation et l'agriculture européenne en Tunisie depuis 1881* (Paris, 1962).
X. Yacono, *La colonisation des plaines du Chelif*, 2 vols. (Algiers, 1955–6).
X. Yacono, 'Peut-on évaluer la population de l'Algérie vers 1830?' *Revue Africaine*, Vol. 98 (1954), pp. 277–307.
J. Ruedy, *Land Policy in Colonial Algeria* (Berkeley, 1967).

Social change

D. Quaetaert, *Social Disintegration and Popular Resistance in the Ottoman Empire 1881–1908* (New York, 1983).

L. T. Fawaz, *Merchants and Migrants in Nineteenth Century Beirut* (Cambridge, Massachusetts, 1983).

L. Schatkowski Schilcher, *Families in Politics: Damascus factions and estates of the 18th and 19th centuries* (Stuttgart, 1985).

R. Tresse, 'L'évolution du coutume syrien depuis un siècle' in Centre d'Études de Politique Étrangère, *Entretiens sur l'évolution des pays de civilisation arabe*, Vol. 2 (Paris, 1938), pp. 87–96.

A. Mubarak, *al-Khitat al-tawfiqiyya*, 4 vols. (Cairo, 1887–9).

J. P. Thieck, 'Le Caire d'après les *Khitat* de 'Ali pacha Mubarak' in Groupe de Recherche et d'Études sur le Proche-Orient, *L'Egypt au 19e siècle* (Paris, 1982), pp. 101–16.

A. Berque, 'Fragments d'histoire sociale' in Berque, *Écrits sur l'Algérie* (Aix-en-Provence, 1986), pp. 25–124.

K. Brown, *People of Salé: tradition and change in a Moroccan city 1830–1930* (Manchester, 1976).

Chapter 18 The Culture of Imperialism and Reform

Orientalism

M. Rodinson, *La fascination de l'islam* (Paris, 1980); English trans. *The Mystique of Islam* (London, 1989).

E. Said, *Orientalism* (London, 1978).

A. Hourani, *Europe and the Middle East* (London, 1980).

N. Daniel, *Europe, Islam and Empire* (Edinburgh, 1966).

Education

A. I. 'Abd al-Karim, *Tarikh al-ta'lim fi Misr*, 3 vols. (Cairo, 1945).

A. L. Tibawi, *British Interests in Palestine 1800–1901* (Oxford, 1961).

A. L. Tibawi, *American Interests in Syria 1800–1901* (Oxford, 1966).

A. L. Tibawi, *Islamic Education: its traditions and modernization into the Arab national systems* (London, 1972).

D. Hopwood, *The Russian Presence in Syria and Palestine 1843–1914* (Oxford, 1969).

H. Charles, *Jésuites missionaires dans la Syrie et le Proche-Orient* (Paris, 1929).

A. Chouraqui, *L'Alliance Israélite Universelle et la renaissance juive contemporaine 1860–1960* (Paris, 1965).

Journalism

P. de Tarazi, *Tarikh al-sahafa al-'arabiyya*, 4 vols. in 3 (Beirut, 1913–33).

I. 'Abduh, *Tarikh al-tiba'a wa'l-sahafa fi Misr* (Cairo, 1949).

N. Farag, 'The Lewis affair and the fortunes of *al-Muqtataf*', *Middle Eastern Studies*, Vol. 8 (1972), pp. 74–83.

Literature

M. M. Badawi, *A Critical Introduction to Modern Arabic Poetry* (Cambridge, 1975).

S. K. Jayyusi, *Trends and Movements in Modern Arabic Poetry*, 2 vols. (Leiden, 1977).

S. K. Jayyusi (ed.), *Modern Arabic Poetry: an anthology* (New York, 1987).

A. Shawqi, *al-Shawqiyyat*, 4 vols. (Cairo, 1961).

I. Shahid, *al-'Awda ila Shawqi* (Beirut, 1986).

A. Boudot-Lamotte, *Ahmad Šawqi, l'homme et l'œuvre* (Damascus, 1977).

M. M. Badawi, *Early Arabic Drama* (Cambridge, 1988).
M. M. Badawi, *Modern Arabic Drama in Egypt* (Cambridge, 1987).

Islamic reform
C. C. Adams, *Islam and Modernism in Egypt* (London, 1933).
N. Keddie, *Sayyid Jamal al-Din 'al-Afghani'* (Berkeley, 1972).
N. Keddie, *An Islamic Response to Imperialism* (Berkeley, 1968).
M. 'Abduh, *Risalat al-tawhid* (Cairo, numerous editions); English trans. *The Theology of Unity* (London, 1966).
M. R. Rida, *Tarikh al-ustadh al-imam al-shaykh Muhammad 'Abduh*, 3 vols. (Cairo, 1906–31).
J. Jomier, *Le commentaire coranique du Manar* (Paris, 1954).
A. H. Green, *The Tunisian Ulama 1873–1915* (Leiden, 1978).
F. de Jong, *Turuq and Turuq-linked Institutions in Nineteenth Century Egypt* (Leiden, 1978).
B. Abu Manneh, 'The Naqshbandiyya-Mujaddidiyya in the Ottoman lands in the early 19th century', *Die Welt des Islams*, Vol. 22 (1982), pp. 1–36.
O. Depont and X. Coppolani, *Les confréries religeuses musulmanes* (Algiers, 1897).
C. S. Hurgronje, 'Les confréries, la Mecque et le pan-islamisme' in Hurgronje, *Verspreide Geschriften*, Vol. 3 (Bonn, 1923), pp. 189–206.
C. S. Hurgronje, *Mekka in the Latter Part of the 19th Century*; English trans. (Leiden, 1931).
J. M. Abun-Nasr, *The Tijaniyya: a Sufi order in the modern world* (Cambridge, 1965).

Nationalism
S. Mardin, *The Genesis of Young Ottoman Thought* (Princeton, 1964).
S. Mardin, *Jön Türklerin siyasî Fikirleri 1895–1908* (Ankara, 1964).
Z. Gökalp, *Turkish Nationalism and Western Civilization*, ed. and trans. N. Berkes (London, 1959).
W. L. Cleveland, *The Making of an Arab Nationalist: Ottomanism and Arabism in the life and thought of Sati' al-Husri* (Princeton, 1971).
W. L. Cleveland, *Islam against the West: Shakib Arslan and the campaign for Islamic nationalism* (London, 1985).
S. al-Husri, *al-Bilad al-'arabiyya wa'l-dawla al-'uthmaniyya* (Beirut, 1960).
G. Antonius, *The Arab Awakening* (London, 1938).
S. Haim (ed.), *Arab Nationalism: an anthology* (Berkeley, 1962).
C. E. Dawn, *From Ottomanism to Arabism* (Urbana, Illinois, 1973).
Z. N. Zeine, *The Emergence of Arab Nationalism* (Beirut, 1966).
P. S. Khoury, *Urban Notables and Arab Nationalism: the politics of Damascus 1860–1920* (Cambridge, 1983).
J. M. Ahmed, *The Intellectual Origins of Egyptian Nationalism* (London, 1960).
I. Gershoni and J. P. Jankowski, *Egypt, Islam and the Arabs: the search for Egyptian nationhood 1900–1930* (New York, 1986).
L. C. Brown, 'Stages in the process of change' in C. A. Micaud (ed.), *Tunisia: the politics of modernization* (London, 1964), pp. 3–66.
A. Laroui, *Les origines sociales et culturelles du nationalisme marocaine 1830–1912* (Paris, 1977).

Chapter 19 The Climax of European Power (1914–1939)

The First World War and the peace settlement

E. Monroe, *Britain's Moment in the Middle East 1914–1956* (London, 1963).

B. C. Busch, *Mudros to Lausanne: Britain's frontier in Asia 1918–1923* (Albany, New York, 1976).

T. E. Lawrence, *Seven Pillars of Wisdom* (London, 1935).

E. Kedourie, *England and the Middle East: the destruction of the Ottoman Empire 1914–1921*, 2nd edn (London, 1987).

M. Vereté, 'The Balfour Declaration and its makers', *Middle Eastern Studies*, Vol. 6 (1970), pp. 48–76.

A. J. Toynbee, *Survey of International Affairs 1925*, Vol. 1: *The Islamic World after the Peace Conference* (London, 1927).

C. M. Andrew and A. S. Kanya-Forstner, *France Overseas: the Great War and the climax of French imperial expansion* (London, 1981).

P. Kinross, *Atatürk: the rebirth of a nation* (London, 1964).

A. Kazancigil and E. Özbudun (eds.), *Atatürk, Founder of a Modern State* (London, 1981).

Mandates and western interests

E. Monroe, *The Mediterranean in Politics* (London, 1938).

S. H. Longrigg, *Iraq 1900–1950* (London, 1953).

P. Sluglett, *Britain in Iraq 1914–1932* (London, 1976).

M. Khadduri, *Independent Iraq 1932–1958*, 2nd edn (London, 1960).

P. S. Khoury, *Syria and the French Mandate* (London, 1987).

M. C. Wilson, *King Abdullah, Britain and the Making of Jordan* (Cambridge, 1987).

L. Hirszowicz, *The Third Reich and the Arab East* (London, 1966).

The problem of Palestine

W. Z. Laqueur (ed.), *An Israel–Arab Reader* (London, 1969).

J. C. Hurewitz, *The Struggle for Palestine* (New York, 1950).

Palestine Royal Commission, *Report*, Cmd 5479 (London, 1937).

W. Khalidi, *From Haven to Conquest* (Beirut, 1971).

F. R. Nicosia, *The Third Reich and the Palestine Question* (London, 1985).

K. Stein, *The Land Question in Palestine 1917–1936* (Chapel Hill, North Carolina, 1984).

Y. M. Porath, *The Emergence of the Palestinian National Movement 1918–1929* (London, 1974).

Y. M. Porath, *The Palestinian Arab National Movement 1929–1939* (London, 1977).

Egypt

A. Lutfi al-Sayyid-Marsot, *Egypt's Liberal Experiment 1922–1936* (Berkeley, 1977).

M. Anis, *Dirasat fi thawrat sanat 1919* (Cairo, 1963).

M. H. Haykal, *Mudhakkirat fi'l-siyasa al-misriyya*, 3 vols. (Cairo, 1951–78).

M. Deeb, *Party Politics in Egypt: the Wafd and its rivals 1919–1939* (London, 1979).

The Maghrib

J. Berque, *Le Maghreb entre deux guerres* (Paris, 1962); English trans. *French North Africa: the Maghrib between two world wars* (London, 1962).

R. Le Tourneau, *Évolution politique de l'Afrique du nord musulmane 1920–1961* (Paris, 1962).

A. al-Fasi, *al-Harakat al-istiqlaliyya fi'l-maghrib al-'arabi* (Cairo, 1948).

Economic and social change

H. Batatu, *The Old Social Classes and the Revolutionary Movements of Iraq* (Princeton, 1978).

C. Issawi, *Egypt, an Economic and Social Analysis* (London, 1947).

R. L. Tignor, *State, Private Enterprise and Economic Change in Egypt 1918–1952* (Princeton, 1984).

A. Dasuqi, *Kibar mallak al-aradi al-zira'iyya wa dawruhum fi'l-mujtama' al-misri* (Cairo, 1975).

S. B. Himadeh (ed.), *The Economic Organization of Syria* (Beirut, 1936).

S. B. Himadeh (ed.), *al-Nizam al-iqtisadi fi'l-'Iraq* (Beirut, 1938).

E. Davis, *Challenging Colonialism: Bank Misr and Egyptian Industrialization 1920–1941* (Princeton, 1983).

J. Beinin and Z. Lockman, *Workers on the Nile: nationalism, communism, Islam and the Egyptian working class 1882–1954* (London, 1988).

R. Montagne, *Naissance du proletariat marocain* (Paris, 1951).

Chapter 20 Changing Ways of Life and Thought (1914–1939)

Urban life

M. Wahba, 'Cairo memories', *Encounter*, Vol. 62 v (May 1984), pp. 74–9.

A. Adam, *Casablanca*, 2 vols. (Paris, 1968).

J. Abu Lughod, *Rabat: urban apartheid in Morocco* (Princeton, 1980).

R. D. Matthews and M. Akrawi, *Education in Arab Countries of the Near East* (Washington, 1950).

R. F. Woodsmall, *Muslim Women Enter a New World* (London, 1936).

S. Graham-Brown, *Images of Women. . . . 1860–1950* (London, 1988).

Literature and art

P. Cachia, *Taha Husain* (London, 1956).

T. Husayn, *al-Ayyam*, 3 vols. (Cairo, 1929–73); English trans. Vol. 1: *An Egyptian Childhood* (London, 1932); Vol. 2: *The Stream of Days* (London, 1948); Vol. 3: *A Passage to France* (London, 1976).

T. Husayn, *Mustaqbil al-thaqafa fi Misr*, 2 vols. (Cairo, 1938).

A. Shabbi, *Diwan* (Beirut, 1971).

G. Sadoul (ed.), *The Cinema in the Arab Countries* (Beirut, 1966).

J. Racy, 'Arabic music and the effects of commercial recording', *The World of Music*, Vol. 20 (1978), pp. 47–55.

J. Racy, 'Music' in T. Mostyn and A. Hourani (eds.), *The Cambridge Encyclopedia of the Middle East and North Africa* (Cambridge, 1988), pp. 244–50.

J. Dickie, 'Modern Islamic Architecture in Alexandria', *Islamic Quarterly*, Vol. 13 (1969), pp. 183–91.

Islamic movements

H. A. R. Gibb, *Modern Trends in Islam* (Chicago, 1947).

C. Geertz, *Islam Observed* (New Haven, 1968).

R. P. Mitchell, *The Society of the Muslim Brothers* (London, 1969).

A. 'Abd al-Raziq, *al-Islam wa usul al-hukm* (Cairo, 1925); French trans. 'L'islam et les bases du pouvoir', *Revue des Études Islamiques*: Vol. 7 (1933), pp. 353–91; Vol. 8 (1934), pp. 163–222.

A. Merad, *Le réformisme musulman en Algérie de 1925 à 1940* (Paris, 1967).

W. Bennabi, *Mémoires d'un témoin du siècle* (Algiers, n.d.).

E. Gellner, 'The unknown Apollo of Biskra: the social base of Algerian puritanism' in Gellner, *Muslim Society* (Cambridge, 1981), pp. 149–73.
K. Brown, 'The impact of the *Dahir Berbère* in Salé' in E. Gellner and C. Micaud (eds.), *Arabs and Berbers* (Paris, 1967), pp. 201–15.

PART V THE AGE OF NATION-STATES (SINCE 1939)

Reference books
Europa Publications, *The Middle East and North Africa* (London, annual 1948–).
Centre de Recherches et d'Études sur les Sociétés Méditerranéennes, *Annuaire de l'Afrique du Nord* (Paris, annual 1962–).
T. Mostyn and A. Hourani (eds.), *The Cambridge Encyclopedia of the Middle East and North Africa* (Cambridge, 1988).
P. Mansfield, *The Middle East: a political and economic survey*, 4th edn (London, 1973).
W. Knapp, *North-west Africa: a political and economic survey*, 3rd edn (Oxford, 1977).

Statistics
United Nations, Department of Economic Affairs, *World Economic Survey* (New York, annual).
United Nations, Statistical Office, *Statistical Year-book* (New York, annual).
United Nations, Food and Agriculture Organization, *Production Year-book* (Rome, annual).
United Nations Educational, Social and Cultural Organization (UNESCO), *Statistical Year-book* (Paris, annual).

Countries and regions
P. Sluglett and M. Farouk-Sluglett, *Iraq since 1958* (London, 1987).
P. Marr, *The Modern History of Iraq* (London, 1985).
A. J. Cottrell and others, *The Persian Gulf States* (Baltimore, 1980).
R. S. Zahlan, *The Making of the Modern Gulf States* (London, 1989).
F. Heard-Bey, *From Trucial States to United Arab Emirates* (London, 1982).
A. Raymond (ed.), *La Syrie d'aujourd'hui* (Paris, 1980).
D. Hopwood, *Syria, 1945–1986: politics and society* (London, 1988).
P. Gubser, *Jordan* (London, 1983).
H. Cobban, *The Making of Modern Lebanon* (London, 1985).
N. Lucas, *The Modern History of Israel* (London, 1974).
Groupe de Recherches et d'Études sur le Proche-Orient, *L'Egypte d'aujourd'hui* (Paris, 1977).
D. Hopwood, *Egypt: politics and society 1945–1984*, 2nd edn (London, 1986).
Centre de Recherches et d'Études sur les Sociétés Méditerranéennes, *Introduction à l'Afrique du nord contemporaine* (Paris, 1975).
M. K. and M. J. Deeb, *Libya since the Revolution* (New York, 1982).
J.-C. Vatin, *L'Algérie politique: histoire et société*, 2nd edn (Paris, 1983).

Chapter 21 The End of the Empires (1939–1962)

The Second World War
I. S. O. Playfair and others, *History of the Second World War: the Mediterranean and the Middle East*, 6 vols. (London, 1954–73).
C. de Gaulle, *Mémoires de guerre*, 3 vols. (Paris, 1954–9); English trans. 3 vols. (London, 1955–60).

E. L. Spears, *Fulfilment of a Mission: the Spears Mission in Syria and Lebanon 1941–1944* (London, 1977).

H. Macmillan, *War Diaries: politics and war in the Mediterranean 1943–1945* (London, 1984).

Y. Porath, *In Search of Arab Unity 1930–1945* (London, 1986).

A. M. H. Gomaa, *The Foundation of the League of Arab States* (London, 1977).

Britain and the Middle East
W. R. Louis, *The British Empire in the Middle East 1935–1951* (Oxford, 1984).

W. R. Louis and J. A. Bill (eds.), *Musaddiq, Iranian Nationalism and Oil* (London, 1988).

W. R. Louis and R. Owen (eds.), *Suez 1956: the crisis and its consequences* (Oxford, 1989).

The problem of Palestine
W. R. Louis and R. W. Stookey (eds.), *The End of the Palestine Mandate* (London, 1986).

M. J. Cohen, *Palestine and the Great Powers* (Princeton, 1982).

B. Morris, *The Birth of the Palestine Refugee Problem 1947–1949* (Cambridge, 1987).

A. Shlaim, *Collusion across the Jordan: King Abdullah, the Zionist movement and the partition of Palestine* (Oxford, 1988).

M. 'Alami, *'Ibrat Filastin* (Beirut, 1949); English trans. 'The lesson of Palestine', *Middle East Journal*, Vol. 3 (1949), pp. 373–405.

France and the Maghrib
C.-A. Julien, *L'Afrique du nord en marche*, 3rd edn (Paris, 1972).

M. Bourguiba, *La Tunisie et la France* (Paris, 1954).

A. Nouschi, *La naissance du nationalisme algérien* (Paris, 1962).

M. Lacheraf, *L'Algérie, nation et société* (Paris, 1965).

A. Horne, *A Savage War of Peace: Algeria 1954–1962* (London, 1977).

J. Daniel, *De Gaulle et l'Algérie* (Paris, 1986).

Chapter 22 Changing Societies (1940s and 1950s)

Economic growth
Y. Sayigh, *The Arab Economy: past performance and future prospects* (Oxford, 1982).

D. Warriner, *Land Reform and Development in the Middle East* (London, 1957).

Lord Salter, *The Development of Iraq* (London, 1955).

C. Issawi, *Egypt at Mid-century* (London, 1954).

C. Issawi, *Egypt in Revolution* (London, 1963).

R. Mabro, *The Egyptian Economy 1952–1972* (Oxford, 1974).

A. Gaitskell, *Gezira: a study of development in the Sudan* (London, 1959).

S. Amin, *L'économie du Maghreb*, 2 vols. (Paris, 1966).

G. Leduc (ed.), *Industrialisation de l'Afrique du nord* (Paris, 1952).

W. D. Swearingen, *Moroccan Mirages: agricultural dreams and deceptions 1912–1986* (London, 1986).

Urbanization
L. C. Brown (ed.), *From Madina to Metropolis* (Princeton, 1973).

P. Marthelot, 'Le Cairo, nouvelle métropole', *Annales Islamologiques*, Vol. 8 (1969), pp. 189–221.

A. Raymond, 'Le Caire' in Centre de Recherches et d'Études sur le Proche-Orient, *L'Egypte d'aujourd'hui* (Paris, 1977), pp. 213–41.

Architecture

H. Fathy, *Architecture for the Poor: an experiment in rural Egypt* (Chicago, 1973).

S. S. Damluji, 'Islamic architecture in the modern world' in T. Mostyn and A. Hourani (eds.), *The Cambridge Encyclopedia of the Middle East and North Africa* (Cambridge, 1988), pp. 232–6.

Chapter 23 National Culture (1940s and 1950s)

Education

J. S. Szyliowicz, *Education and Modernization in the Middle East* (Ithaca, New York, 1973).

B. G. Massialas and S. A. Jarrar, *Education in the Arab World* (New York, 1983).

J. Waardenburg, *Les universités dans le monde arabe actuel*, 2 vols. (Paris, 1966).

A. B. Zahlan, *Science and Science Policy in the Arab World* (London, 1980).

Historiography

A. Laroui, *L'histoire du Maghreb: un essai de synthèse* (Paris, 1970); English trans. *The History of the Maghrib* (Princeton, 1977).

C. Zurayq, *Nahnu wa'l-tarikh* (Beirut, 1959).

Literature

J. Stetkevych, 'Classical Arabic on stage' in R. C. Ostle (ed.), *Studies in Modern Arabic Literature* (Warminster, Wiltshire, 1975), pp. 152–66.

Adunis (A. A. Sa'id), *al-athar al-kamila*, 2 vols. (Beirut, 1971).

B. S. al-Sayyab, *Diwan*, 2 vols. (Beirut, 1971–4).

D. Johnson-Davies (ed. and trans.), *Arabic Short Stories* (London, 1983).

N. Mahfuz, *Zuqaq al-midaqq* (Cairo, 1947); English trans. *Midaq Alley* (London, 1974).

N. Mahfuz, *Bayn al-qasrayn, Qasr al-shawq, al-Sukkariyya* (The 'Cairo Trilogy'; Cairo, 1956–7); English trans. of Vol. 1, *Palace Walk* (London, 1990).

A. al-Sharqawi, *al-Ard* (Cairo, 1954).

L. Ba'labakki, *Ana ahya* (Beirut, 1963).

J. Dejeux, *Littérature maghrebine de langue française*, 3rd end. (Sherbrooke, Quebec, 1980).

J. Dejeux and A. Memmi, *Anthologie des écrivains maghrebins d'expression française*, 2nd edn (Paris, 1965).

K. Yacine, *Nedjma* (Paris, 1956).

M. Feraoun, *Le fils du pauvre* (Paris, 1954).

A. Djebar, *Les alouettes naïves* (Paris, 1967).

Islamic movements

K. M. Khalid, *Min huna nabda* (Cairo, 1950); English trans. *From Here We Start* (Washington, 1953).

T. Husayn, *al-Fitna al-kubra*, 2 vols. (Cairo, 1947–56).

O. Carré and G. Michaud, *Les frères musulmans: Egypt et Syrie 1920–1982* (Paris, 1983).

O. Carré, *Mystique et politique: lecture révolutionnaire du Coran par Sayyid Qutb* (Paris, 1984).

S. Qutb, *Al-'Adala al-ijtima'iyya fi'l-islam*, 4th edn (Cairo, 1954); English trans. S. Kotb, *Social Justice in Islam* (New York, 1970).

M. Gilsenan, *Saint and Sufi in Modern Egypt* (Oxford, 1973).

Chapter 24 The Climax of Arabism (1950s and 1960s)

'Abd al-Nasir and Nasirism
P. Mansfield, *Nasser* (London, 1969).
R. Stephens, *Nasser* (London, 1971).
H. Heikal, *The Sphinx and the Commissar: the rise and fall of Soviet influence in the Middle East* (London, 1978).
H. Heikal, *Cutting the Lion's Tail: Suez through Egyptian eyes* (London, 1986).
M. Kerr, *The Arab Cold War 1958–1970*, 3rd edn (London, 1971).
E. O'Ballance, *The War in the Yemen* (London, 1971).
E. O'Ballance, *The Third Arab–Israeli War* (London, 1972).

Political ideas
J. 'Abd al-Nasir, *Falsafat al-thawra* (Cairo, 1955); English trans. *The Philosophy of the Revolution* (Cairo, 1955).
Egypt, Department of Information, *Mashru' al-Mithaq al-watani* (Cairo, 1962).
S. A. Hanna and G. H. Gardner (eds.), *Arab Socialism: a documentary survey* (London, 1969).
S. Botman, *The Rise of Egyptian Communism* (Syracuse, New York, 1988).
J. F. Devlin, *The Ba'th Party* (Stanford, California, 1966).
M. 'Aflaq, *Fi sabil al-ba'th* (Damascus, 1959).
M. 'Aflaq, *Ma'rakat al-masir al-washid* (Beirut, 1958).
M. A. al-'Alim and A. Anis, *Fi'l-thaqafa al-misriyya* (Beirut, 1955).
L. 'Awad, *Thaqafatuna fi muftaraq al-turuq* (Beirut, 1974).
A. Laroui, *La crise des intellectuels arabes* (Paris, 1974); English trans. *The Crisis of the Arab Intellectual* (Berkeley, 1974).
A Laroui, *L'idéologie arabe contemporaine*, revised edn (Paris, 1977).

Chapter 25 Arab Unity and Disunity (since 1967)

War and peace with Israel
E. O'Ballance, *No Victor, No Vanquished: the Yom Kippur war* (London, 1968).
W. B. Quandt, *Decade of Decision: American policy towards the Arab–Israeli conflict 1967–1976* (Berkeley, 1977).
W. B. Quandt, *Camp David: peacemaking and politics* (Washington, 1986).
H. Kissinger, *Years of Upheaval* (London, 1982).
J. Carter, *The Blood of Abraham* (Boston, 1985).
M. Riyad, *Mudhakkirat 1948–1975* (Beirut, 1985); English trans. M. Riad, *The Struggle for Peace in the Middle East* (London, 1981).
H. Heikal, *The Road to Ramadan* (London, 1975).
P. Seale, *Asad of Syria: the struggle for the Middle East* (London, 1988).

The infitah
J. Waterbury, *The Egypt of Nasser and Sadat* (Princeton, 1983).
R. Hinnebusch, *Egyptian Politics under Sadat* (Cambridge, 1985).
H. Heikal, *Kharif al-ghadab*, 2nd edn (Beirut, 1983); English trans. *Autumn of Fury* (London, 1983).
Y. Sayigh, *The Economies of the Arab World*, 2 vols. (London, 1975).
J. S. Birks and C. Sinclair, *Arab Manpower: the crisis of development* (London, 1980).
M. Bennoune, *The Making of Contemporary Algeria* (Cambridge, 1988).

Palestinians under occupation
H. Cobban, *The Palestinian Liberation Organization* (Cambridge, 1984).
M. Benvenisti and others, *The West Bank Handbook* (Jerusalem, 1986).
D. MacDowell, *Palestine and Israel* (London, 1989).

The Lebanese civil war
K. Salibi, *Cross-roads to Civil War* (London, 1976).
K. Salibi, *A House of Many Mansions* (London, 1988).
E. Picard, *Liban: état de discorde* (Paris, 1988).
Z. Schiff and E. Ya'ari, *Israel's Lebanon War* (London, 1985).
R. Khalidi, *Under Siege: P.L.O. decision-making during the 1982 war* (New York, 1986).

The war between Iraq and Iran
S. Chubin and C. Tripp, *Iran and Iraq at War* (London, 1988).

Chapter 26 A Disturbance of Spirits (since 1967)

Social divisions
S. Ibrahim, *The New Arab Social Order: a study of the social impact of oil wealth* (London, 1982).
R. Owen, *Migrant Workers in the Gulf* (London, 1985).
D. MacDowell, *The Kurds* (London, 1985).

Men and women
E. Fernea (ed.), *Women and the Family in the Middle East* (Austin, Texas, 1985).
L. Beck and N. Keddie (eds.), *Women in the Muslim World* (Cambridge, Massachusetts, 1978).
N. Hijab, *Womanpower: the Arab debate on women at work* (Cambridge, 1988).
F. Mernissi, *Beyond the Veil: male–female dynamics in a modern Muslim society*, revised edn (London, 1985).
N. Abu Zahra, 'Baraka, material power, honour and women in Tunisia', *Revue d'Histoire Maghrébine*, Nos. 10–11 (1978), pp. 5–24.

The movement of ideas
G. A. Amin, *Mihnat al-iqtisad wa'l-thaqafa fi Misr* (Cairo, 1982).
H. Hanafi, *al-Turath wa'l-tajdid* (Cairo, 1980).
S. J. al-'Azm, *Naqd al-fikr al-dini* (Beirut, 1969).
H. Djaït, *La personalité et le devoir arabo-islamique* (Paris, 1974).
M. A. al-Jabiri, *al-Khitab al-'arabi al-mu'asir* (Casablanca, 1982).
M. A. al-Jabiri, *Takwin al-'aql al-'arabi*, 2nd edn (Beirut, 1985).
F. Ajami, *The Arab Predicament* (Cambridge, 1981).

The reassertion of Islam
H. Enayat, *Modern Islamic Political Thought* (London, 1982).
R. Mottahedeh, *The Mantle of the Prophet* (London, 1985).
F. Rahman, *Islam and Modernity* (Chicago, 1982).
J. Piscatori (ed.), *Islam in the Political Process* (Cambridge, 1981).
J. Piscatori, *Islam in a World of Nation-States* (Cambridge, 1986).
J. R. Cole and N. Keddie (eds.), *Shi'ism and Social Protest* (New Haven, 1986).
G. Kepel, *Le prophète et Pharaon* (Paris, 1984); English trans. *The Prophet and Pharaoh* (London, 1985).
M. Gilsenan, *Recognizing Islam* (London, 1982).
S. 'Uways, *Rasa'il ila'l-imam al-Shafi'i* (Cairo, 1978).
S. Qutb, *Ma'alim fi'l-tariq* (Cairo, 1964).

Index of Terms

It is not always easy to decide whether a word which is common to Arabic and Turkish should be spelled according to the normal system of transliteration from Arabic, or in its modern Turkish form. In general, when words are used in an Ottoman context they are spelled in their Turkish form, otherwise in transliteration from the Arabic; but I have not been entirely consistent.

Page references indicate where the term is defined in the text.

Index

'Abbas, 32

'Abbasid dynasty, 5, 32–7, 83–4; creation of, 32–3, 142; cities and palaces, 33–4, 35–6, 56, 124–5, 130; bureaucracy, 34–5, 132; local dynasties, 38–40, 41; trade, 44; literature, 52; and Islam, 67; interest in Greek culture, 76–7; irrigation projects, 103; slaves, 116; poetry, 193; music, 197–8; medicine, 202; decline of, 85, 88, 189, 209, 212, 213

'Abbas I, Viceroy of Egypt, 275

'Abd al-'Aziz, King of Saudi Arabia, 280, 319, 334, 349, 365, 381, 410

'Abd al-Jabbar, 166

'Abd al-Latif, 165

'Abd al-Malik, Caliph, 27

'Abd al-Nasir, Jamal, 351, 362, 366–9, 393, 398, 405–7, 410, 411–12, 413, 416–17, 418, 423, 426, 428, 446, 448, 455, 456

'Abd al-Qadir (Algeria), 270, 312, 317

'Abd al-Qadir al-Jilani, 154, 157

'Abd al-Rahman, Sultan of Morocco, 274

'Abd al-Rahman III, Caliph, 43

'Adb al-Raziq, 'Ali, 346–7

'Abduh, Muhammad, 307–8, 312, 346–7

Abdülhamid II, Sultan, 281, 288, 309, 314

'Abdullah, King of Jordan, 318, 363

Abraham, 18–19, 28, 55, 150, 226

Abu Bakr, 22–3, 25, 153

Abu Dhabi, 269, 408, 421, 424

Abu Hanifa, 67, 69

Abu Midyan, 156

Abu Muslim, 32, 33

Abu Shadi, Zaki, 340

Abu Talib, 17

Abu'l-'Abbas, Caliph, 32, 33

Acre, 251, 296

Adam, 177

Aden, 269, 296, 319, 381, 408

Adunis (Ahmad Sa'id), 396, 397

al-Afghani, Jamal al-Din, 307

Afghanistan, 422

'Aflaq, Michel, 404–5

Africa: trade, 44, 45, 84, 90; spread of Islam into, 85; slaves, 117; pilgrimage to Mecca, 150, 222; see also Maghrib

Aghlabid dynasty, 38

agriculture, 45, 91–4, 100–3, 106, 210, 252, 287–8, 292–3, 334–5, 374, 376, 379–80, 437

Ahmad, Muhammad (*mahdi* in Sudan), 284, 313

Ahmad Bey, 274

al-Ahram, 304, 393

air travel, 425

'A'isha, 22, 25

Akhbaris, 241, 256

Akhtal, 49

'Alami family, 240, 246

'Alawis, 86, 185, 245–6, 253, 404, 436, 457

Albania, 321

alchemy, 76, 77, 204

Aleppo, 28, 91, 110, 111, 123–4, 176, 190, 226, 231, 234–5, 236, 237, 238, 242, 251, 254, 336

Alexander the Great, 9, 195

Alexandria, 7, 11, 75, 111, 124, 265, 268, 273, 283, 294, 296, 297, 303, 320, 354, 384

Algeria: Rustamids, 39; Almohad dynasty, 85; geography, 94, 99; climate, 98; shrines, 156; architecture, 191; agriculture, 252, 334; Tijaniyya, 257;